THE BIRTH
OF EUROPE

THE BIRTH OF EUROPE

ROBERT S. LOPEZ

Published by
M. EVANS AND COMPANY, INC., New York
and distributed in association with
J. B. LIPPINCOTT COMPANY, Philadelphia and New York

Published 1967 by M. Evans and Company Inc., New York
by arrangement with J.M. Dent & Sons Ltd.
Aldine House, Bedford Street. London
Library of Congress Catalog Card Number 66-23414

First paperback edition 1972

CONTENTS

LIST OF ILLUSTRATIONS

1. Two visions of the end of the world, Western and Byzantine. Detail from an illumination showing the resurrection of the dead in a manuscript belonging to the Emperor Henry II, now in the Bayerische Staatsbibliotek, Munich; Latin MS 4452, folio 201v. The Last Judgement, from a Byzantine ivory of the 11th century; by courtesy of the Victoria and Albert Museum, London.

2. Invading warriors seen as the gods of barbarian nations; equestrian portrait of the god Kuan Ti, who is a deification of the Chinese General Kuan Yu of the 3rd century; engraving taken from a plaque at Peilin, Si-ngan-fu, Chensi Province, quoted in *China, a short cultural history* by C. G. Fitzgerald, London and New York, 1942. Germanic horseman, probably the god Woden; carved stone now in Halle Museum: photo, Marburg Collection.

3. Two low reliefs of the 7th century. The Evangelists and Archangels from the Martyrium at Poitiers: photo by Desointre-Robuchon. The sun held by two angels, from Quintanilla de las Vinas near Burgos in Spain: photo, Mas, Barcelona.

4. Fresco from Santa Maria di Castelseprio in Lombardy, 8th century; the Nativity, showing the Virgin and the infant Jesus being washed by a midwife who doubts the virginity of Mary: photo by Alfieri. 10th century Byzantine miniature showing iconoclasts insulting images and acting out the offering of a sponge of vinegar to the crucified Christ; the Shludov Psalter, folio 67, now in the Museum of History, Moscow: photo, College des Hautes Etudes, Paris.

5. Byzantine mosaics. Detail of St Agnes, 7th century, from the church of St Agnes, Rome. 10th century detail of the Emperor Alexander, in the Sophia Mosque, Istanbul: photo, Byzantine Institute, Dumbarton Oaks.

6. Evolution of architecture. St Sabina, Rome, 5th century: photo by Anderson-Giraudon. Colonnade in the courtyard of the Umeyyad Mosque, Damascus, 8th century: photo, Roger-Viollet. S. Pietro, Tuscania, 8th to 12th centuries: photo, Alinari-Giraudon. Santa Maria la Blanca, formerly a synagogue at Toledo, 13th or 14th century: photo, Mas, Barcelona.

7. Watercolour copy of mosaic in the Lateran Church at Rome before its 18th century remodelling; this shows St Peter giving investiture to Pope Leo III and to Charlemagne; Vatican Library, Barbarini Latin MS 2062.

8. Two Carolingian Emperors. Louis the Pious (or Handsome) dressed partly in Germanic and partly in Byzantine clothing; from the National Library at Vienna, MS 652, folio 3v. Charles the Bald in Byzantine apparel receiving a copy of the Bible; miniature from the manuscript *Bible of Charles the Bald,* in the Bibliothèque Nationale, Paris.

ILLUSTRATIONS IN TEXT

Page

Page

FOREWORD

IN giving the title, *The Birth of Europe*, to a book on the Middle Ages of the West, I had no intention of committing a sin of pride. However important a part this small peninsula off Asia has played in history, we must not attribute the qualities of a Chosen People to the Europeans. The appearance of a European civilization, from which, much later, new overseas Europes were to spring up in America and the other continents, is not the only important event of the Middle Ages; but it is the only one which coincides exactly with their limits.

The term 'Middle Ages' is perhaps the most unfortunate of all the countless labels that we historians persist in attaching to arbitrary slices of the past. Every age might be said to be a 'middle age', a transition from past to future. The age we call medieval — the thousand years between the fourth and the fourteenth centuries — was really a transition only between the passing of the classical civilization of the Mediterranean and the coming of Modern European civilization.

It is no good trying to justify this chronological framework by this or that inner unity that later ages quite mistakenly saw in the 'Middle Ages'. We need hardly dwell now on the negative characteristics that seemed to the men of the Renaissance, the Reformation, the Age of Enlightenment, or the French Revolution, ample justification for wholesale condemnation of the Middle Ages, and thence for definition of them. Ignorance and localism, serfdom and feudalism (even if we admit that each of these phenomena was a step back from the 'golden age' of Greece and Rome) were not peculiar to the Middle Ages and did not monopolize them. The term adopted by romantics of the nineteenth century and our own day to rehabilitate this much maligned period — 'Age of Faith' or 'Age of Christianity' — is no more accurate. Faith is ageless: it belongs as much to the Egypt of the Pharaohs as to the England of the Puritans. Christianity is as old as Christ, which means that it was born in the reign of Augustus. In the eyes of believers who lived in 'mediaeval' times without knowing it, the age of transition stretched from the Fall to the Redemption, while their own times were the 'modern' period. Besides, though religion played a leading part in the Middle Ages, it was not their only motive power.

It was in the Middle Ages, on the other hand, that European civilization created its own peculiar unity. It would not have been enough that this civilization had a basis in the physical and human geography of the lands that were its birthplace. We are used to seeing on the map of the world a natural region stretching from Portugal to Russia and from the Arctic to the Mediterranean; the Ancients saw, just as distinctly, another natural region, centred on the Mediterranean and bounded by the Rhine and Danube to the north and the great deserts to the south. In both cases dissimilar peoples are linked by a common culture. The choice they made among the various possibilities afforded by geography is above all intellectual; it owes little — and certainly not every-thing — to the material conditions that went with it.

Yet it would be completely artificial, and so completely false, to attempt to portray an age without taking material conditions into account. What for the

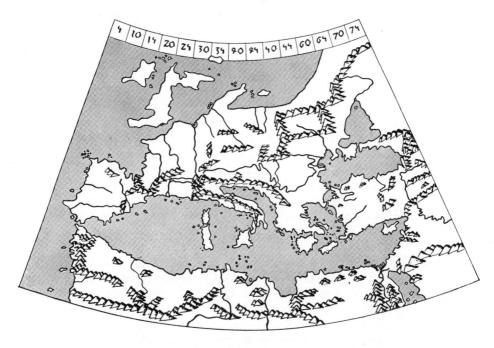

Map 1. Ptolemy's Mediterranean world, according to Renaissance geographers. From an incunabulum of 1490 (Yale University Library).

Middle Ages was a duel between spirit and flesh, soul and body, we see as the constantly renewed dialogue between intellectual and economic history. For-tunately the evolution of medieval economy has its own internal unity too. It covers a twofold movement of contraction and expansion — contraction from the third to the ninth century roughly, expansion from the tenth to the early fourteenth — after which we can detect the beginnings of a new cycle.

This economic ebb and flow, though it finds no place in the title of my book, is nevertheless one of its fundamental themes, in the same class, if not on the same level, as the formation of Europe. The peoples of Europe, at the lowest point of the declivity represented by the first five hundred years of the Middle Ages, were yet able to find the energy needed to build up a new society, more prosperous and less inequitable than that of the Ancient World: that is indeed a fact no less important than the creation of a new and lasting cultural unity.

Beyond this, side by side with these two themes, we shall exploit the other riches of 'mediaeval' history when ever they can be brought into our matter without overloading it. Our book will not, in fact, be the complete history of ten cen-

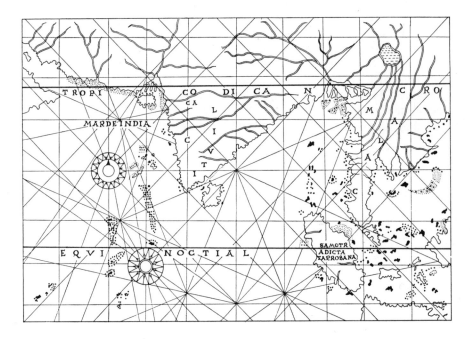

Map 2. Drawing of a late mediaeval Portolan map

turies. All that history could be recounted in four or five hundred pages — if that — only in a textbook, and I confess that this would be beyond me. What I offer the public is an *essay*, in the etymological sense of the word.

The general plan of the 'Destinies of the World' series, in which this work first appeared together with special volumes on the Byzantines, Slavs and Arabs, sets exact geographical limits to this essay: the Elbe, the Adriatic, the northern shores of the Mediterranean. Even Spain and Sicily pass outside these limits when they become provinces of Islam. I hope I may be forgiven, even within these limits, for lingering on the sunny shores of the Mediterranean, which are of such fundamental importance.

I was born in Genoa, and live and teach in the United States; if Christopher Columbus was no less a Genoese for having discovered America, his humble fellow-countryman can hardly be expected to preserve an indifferent neutrality. Copernicus notwithstanding, our vision is still centred on the earth, and each of us is to himself the centre of his earth.

Finally, I realize that in order to follow up what seems to me the clue running through this vast collective history I have sacrificed any study of individuals and battles, reduced complex evolutions to simple relationships of cause and effect, and ignored the sometimes widely diverging theories of my predecessors. Not without deep regret, for reality is endlessly made up of individuals and battles; human evolution is the product of countless incomplete causes and manifold consequences, direct and indirect; and I owe an immense debt to the historians of today and of the recent or remote past. From Tacitus and the two Plinys down to Fernand Braudel and my colleagues at Yale Medieval Studies. I thank them all. As I hand over these pages, possibly over-ambitious, I find comfort in a favourite metaphor of the Middle Ages: even a dwarf can see far, when he is hoisted on the shoulders of the giants who went before him.

BOOK 1

FROM THE COLLAPSE
TO THE REINCARNATION
OF THE EMPIRE

Chapter 1

TRACES OF THE ROMAN EXPERIMENT

I. THE MEDITERRANEAN COMMUNITY: ITS BOUNDARIES AND ITS NEIGHBOURS

'FIRST of all you must know that the Roman Empire everywhere contains the fury of the nations that howl round about it, and that perfidious barbarians, protected by the nature of their territory, on all sides covet our frontiers.' In these words an obscure writer of the fourth century, soon after Constantine's conversion to Christianity, describes the besieged fortress which the *Respublica Romana*, the great community of Graeco-Roman peoples, had now become.

The struggle had been much less bitter through the golden age of Augustus and the silver age of Trajan. In the iron age of Gallienus it had developed into a series of fights to the death, complicated by terrible internal convulsions. At last, by an almost superhuman effort, the Empire had rallied. The Emperor had recovered his authority over the troops, the troops once again contained the barbarians, and the *Respublica*, weak but convalescent, had gained a valuable reprieve. The constitution of the Empire, its laws, economy and art, might not be those of its youth — how could they have survived four centuries without change? — but its frontiers had scarcely altered (Map 3).

Civilized countries and the barbarian world

In its early years the power of Rome had reached to the limits of the civilized world, and even beyond them to annex the most fertile or the least backward of the barbarian lands. In maturity, it had taken up its stand in a long corridor, protected by the *limes* from the unco-ordinated onslaughts of the nomads or semi-nomads of north and south: barbarians of the grasslands and forests where the vine lacked sun to bear fruit, barbarians of the sandy and rocky deserts where the parched olive never came to flowering. Westward lay the abyss of the ocean, where only a madman would have ventured far. Eastward, Persia offered the spectacle of an empire less powerful and less refined than the Roman, but governed by principles not dissimilar, an empire to be tolerated for the time being since attempts to subjugate it had been vain. Further away still, almost unknown, China — *Serica*, the silk empire — reared other walls against other barbarians. These three proud states — Rome, Persia, China — formed an almost unbroken chain from the Atlantic to the Pacific, each taking over from the next, without fully realizing it, the function of organizing the civilized peoples and containing the savage.

It is true that 'savages' were not all equally so in the eyes of the Romans. Ethiopia had lost almost all contact with Egypt, after being first her vassal and then her overlord, but still enjoyed a certain reputation, chiefly as the source of gold, a variety of spices, and the Nile, which was more precious than gold. India too had dazzled the Greeks by her wealth, and still had commercial and cultural links with the eastern provinces of the Roman Empire. The Arabs were hardly noted for their wealth or power, but some of their tribes paid regular visits to Roman outposts in Syria and Mesopotamia, the last ports of call for the caravans before the 'waterless sea' of the desert, and had there picked up the rudiments of civilization. Even the Germans, in spite of the ferocity of their nature, were said to have their virtues. They provided authors with a model for the ideal portrait of the noble savage, the army with seasoned auxiliary troops, and merchants with easily pleased customers or, the gods willing, with blond slaves.

No doubt the gods had shown their anger in the third century, but those hard and testing times already belonged to the past. A series of great leaders, from Claudius II (268–70) to Diocletian (284–305) had built up again the Empire's army and administration, Licinius and Constantine (306–37) had reconciled her with the irresistible religion of Christ, and she could see as a passing crisis the tempest in which one emperor had been captured by the Persians and another killed by the Goths, while her best provinces defected. On the whole the Germans, and the still unconquered Berbers who in many ways resembled them, seemed less to be feared than the civilized state of Persia. At the time of the passage quoted at the beginning of this chapter, the Emperor Julian (360–3), the last champion of the old way of life, gave a striking illustration of this attitude of mind when he turned his back on the Germans, defeated but not crushed, to make yet another attempt to end victoriously the old duel with Persia.

Thus the frontiers of the Empire had hardly altered through the centuries. To the south there were the gorges of the Atlas Mountains, a Nile cataract, and everywhere else the desert: some forts had been abandoned without any sensible change in the situation. To the east, the desert again served as frontier in Palestine and Syria, and from there to the defiles of the Caucasus stretched mountainous country where Rome and Persia had fought each other stubbornly for a few shreds of territory without lasting result. To the north, the Danube and the Rhine, the long rivers which bisect what we call Europe, marked the limit between Roman and barbarian worlds. This limit extended, over the North Sea, to the mountains between England and Scotland. In Scotland, Swabia, Romania and (if only Marcus Aurelius had not died too soon, in 180) in Bohemia, the Empire had planned to protect her barrier with an outer glacis, but had had to abandon that ambition. In any case, even without the glacis the barrier still stood. It was a long frontier, certainly, but justified by the fact that it ran roughly parallel to the shores of the Mediterranean, so that it enclosed a ribbon of almost unvarying depth running the whole length of the sea.

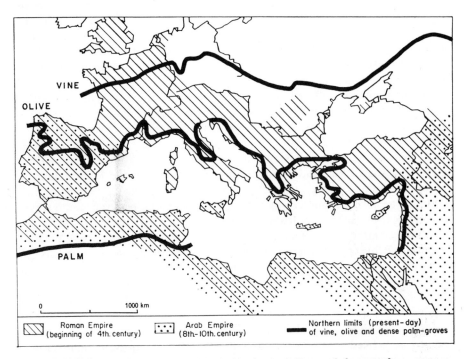

Map. 3. Northern limits (present-day) of vine, olive and dense palm-groves.

The Empire, the gift of the Mediterranean

It has been said that Egypt is the gift of the Nile. It could be claimed with almost as much truth that the Roman Empire was the gift of the Mediterranean. This physical and organic characteristic sets her apart from the other empires of the Ancient World, whose axes were valleys, and the great mediaeval kingdoms centred on a plain or plateau. So we might apply to the Graeco-Roman community the delightful metaphor that Plato used of his fellow-Greeks, huddled round the sea, near or far, 'like frogs round a pond'. The Mediterranean, in fact, held together the great *Respublica Romana*, guaranteeing it a relatively uniform climate and relatively easy communications. Rome herself, enthroned in the midst, sent out her orders and, by way of Ostia and the Tiber, received her supplies by boat.

No doubt the network of rivers and roads enabled the Romans to penetrate some way inland. The ingenuity and endurance of settlers succeeded in acclimatizing Mediterranean plants and methods some way from their place of origin (for example the vine, which they propagated towards the north). Nevertheless, the further the Romans left the warm and temperate sea behind them, the less they felt at home. Their 'logistic' and administrative problems became more complicated, their faculty of assimilating subject peoples weakened, their will to humble the arrogant wavered too. Though they liked to call their empire 'universal', they usually had the good sense to stop at the point where they found difficulty in renewing their strength by easy contact to their rear with the fostering Mediterranean.

A uniform climate and easy communications made possible that long miracle of the Ancient World: the transformation of an agglomeration of dissimilar peoples into a harmonious and homogeneous community. The emperor who celebrated the first millenary of the founding of Rome, in 248, was of Arab stock; he was suspected of having embraced the subversive and vulgar doctrine of the Christians. What did it matter? The inhabitants of the Empire had for centuries been accustomed to live together under the same government, and had come to have a common way of thought and action. A citizen could travel from York to Alexandria or from Trebizond to Cadiz without feeling any more out of his element than would a modern Englishman travelling from York to Plymouth, Belfast or Aberdeen. All free men were citizens, and if all citizens did not enjoy the same rights, still the inequalities were much the same from one end of the Empire to the other. Even the slaves had seen the philosopher-emperors set the first limits to the arbitrary power of their masters; and it had never been impossible for a slave to earn his freedom and become a full citizen. No man had identified himself with the glory that was Rome more closely than Horace, the son of a freed slave. Throughout the Empire, the army, administration, schools, theatres, drawing-rooms, were crucibles where resistances and local loyalties ran together in the heat of Roman patriotism.

True, no patriotism can entirely eliminate indifference or discontent, but in the absence of competition treason was almost impossible. Today, even the most ardent nationalist has to admit that his own nation is but one of a great family in which cultural differences do not go very deep; ancient Rome in the eyes of her citizens was the one and only human community, surrounded by Persian half-men and barbarian half-wolves. 'We, Romans, treat our slaves better than the King of the Huns treats his subjects', an imperial ambassador told a courtier of Attila. This was an attitude of mind that the universalism of a few Christian writers hardly succeeded in broadening.

Unity and diversity

There were of course local differences of speech, laws, institutions and rites, but they were attenuated, covered over by a uniform surface, glossy and firm. Two languages were almost universally understood, even if not spoken with equal facility: Latin for government and action, Greek for thought and elegance. A literature in two languages, but one in theme and spirit, preserved the primitive form of the two dominant languages, while a popular Latin and Greek gradually supplanted the local dialects. Arts and technics too spoke a uniform tongue, in spite of the variations arising from differences in talents and education, custom or climate. Elaborated by lawyers of genius and enriched by daily use, civil law gradually submerged particular customs. Gradually the countless local cults and gods blended in a uniform synthesis. At the same time, the formalistic 'religions' of the Western tradition lost ground to the mystic 'superstitions' of the East. Finally Christianity prevailed against the other universalist creeds of the East. The length and violence of the struggle cannot hide the mutual borrowings, or the profound similarities between mother-goddesses and trinities in all ages, or the affinities between Celsus and Origen, Augustine and Julian.

Of course, the layer of uniformity did not cover all classes or all provinces to the same depth. Within what we call Graeco-Roman civilization the stress fell on the word 'Roman' in the western part of the Empire, on 'Greek' in the eastern. For different reasons, England and Palestine were less profoundly 'Romanized' than Spain and Dalmatia. The Jews, proud of their illustrious past, refused to surrender their personality to a foreign culture; Britain had not been occupied long enough or colonized intensively enough to absorb thoroughly the higher culture of a more developed people. Similarly, the aristocracy of the cities found it easy enough to model themselves on the aristocracy of the City *par excellence*, but the peasants — as in all lands and all ages — still savoured more or less of the soil according to their distance from the towns, the sea, and routes of communication. At the beginning of the fifth century a bishop-magistrate of Cyrenaica ended his eulogy of country life in inland regions with these biting words: 'Of course we know that there is always an Emperor, for every year the tax-gatherers remind us of his existence; but who he is is not very clear. Some of us think our king is still Agamemnon, son of Atreus.' The fact remains that Agamemnon was part of the common heritage of Graeco-Roman culture, and the ignorance or discontent of country bumpkins only rarely produced organized revolt against the *Respublica Romana*.

II.   FORCES OF TRADITION

The long duration of the Roman Empire is more extraordinary than its eventual fall. Force and despotism, the usual ingredients of imperial rule, played an important part in building it up and keeping it together; but they were combined with an unusual tradition of responsibility and delegation of powers. Politically, the unity of the great Mediterranean community was based on collaboration more than on centralization; economically, it rested on the uniformity of its small agricultural components rather than on any commercial and industrial interdependence of its constituent provinces.

The Empire, still a republic

It is sometimes said that the Empire's greatest weakness was its failure to establish a firm principle for the succession to the throne: adoption by the living Emperor, designation by the Senate, proclamation by the army, inheritance from father to son, all of these means were alternatively tried and discarded. True, but the Empire never was called otherwise than *Respublica*, commonwealth; its leaders, no matter how authoritarian or wicked, held the *imperium* (that is, the power to command and coerce) by delegation of the people. The president of a republic cannot succeed automatically to a throne: he has to be chosen, supposedly because he is the most worthy or the most popular. Today we pretend to believe that the worthiest and best beloved man infallibly emerges through one or another combination of universal suffrage and representation; but representation did not exist in antiquity, and universal suffrage, while possible in small communities, would have been a sham if extended to an immense republic whose citizens had no means to obtain independent information on candidates and issues. None of the other means that were tried in ancient Rome was in itself preposterous, none was foolproof: adoption gave the *imperium* to Nero and to Marcus Aurelius, the army exalted Heliogabalus and Diocletian, the Senate chose Nerva and Gordian, inheritance fell on Julian and on Honorius. It may be hard for the people not to choose the president through free elections, but it is somewhat of a comfort to think that whoever is chosen is expected to govern a commonwealth, not merely to exploit a property of his own.

What really tempered the despotism of the emperors was the delegation of powers. The Empire strove to maintain all the bodies, organizations and guilds which could relieve it of one or other function of government. 'There is no peace without army, no army without pay, no pay without tribute; the rest is common to us all': these words, which Tacitus puts into the mouth of a Roman general addressing the Gauls, sums up the ideal, if not the realization, of imperial policy. Even the most despotic emperors of the first century, the Caligulas and Neros, usually spared the little senates of provincial towns the humiliations they were pleased to inflict upon the great Senate of Rome. Nevertheless, as the requirements of war and the burdens of administration increased, the central government gradually found itself compelled to increase its powers and multiply its offices. Thus a professional bureaucracy had to be created and grew relentlessly. In the last two centuries of the Empire, it became plethoric, encroaching, sometimes self-paralyzing, and too expensive for the services it did render.

Yet the emperors continued to the very end to support local government and sharing of responsibilities as best they could. Their reluctance to carry through a centralization that was not in accordance with the Roman tradition was shown in a series of measures that led to piecemeal division. The high command (that is the office of emperor, not the Empire which was and remained indivisible) was shared by two or even four men. Every one of the military and administrative posts in the provinces was directed to draw as far as possible on local resources. Municipal officers, presidents of trade guilds, great landowners, were given sufficient powers to pass on to their dependants the ever-increasing demands of the government.

The peasant army and the landowning administration

Paradoxically, the only state which has ever controlled the whole Mediterranean and made the sea its center of gravity did not use it to build up its commerce, but lived and died a nation of farmers. Everyone knows the edifying story of Cincinnatus going back to his plough after each of his victories. This always represented the supreme ideal of Rome, even though reality lagged ever farther behind it. When war had enriched some of the small independent landowners in Latium and ruined almost all of the others, the quest for a Cincinnatus spread further afield, to the rest of Italy, to Gaul, to the Balkans. New seeds of the peasant army were planted in every colony, the legions themselves provided nurseries in every garrison, and the tree, always threatened but still sending out fresh shoots, was protected by special laws. In the third century it was Illyrian farmers who saved the Empire; in the fourth, the army had to recruit barbarians but these, too, were given land and became peasants. In the general collapse of the fifth century, the last resistance against the invasions was to come from soldier-peasants settled on little free-holdings all along the frontiers. Elsewhere, the smallholders had long since surrendered their independence to the great landowners, whose large estates were better equipped to withstand the recurring scourge of invasion, the frequent catastrophes of bad harvests, above all the ever-increasing drain of taxation.

If the smallholders were the core of the army, it was the owners of medium-sized and large estates who provided the backbone of civil and military administration. During the troubles that preceded the end of the Republic, their hold on government had been threatened by the rise of the 'knights' (not feudal noblemen, but plebeians who had made their fortune as traders, money-lenders or contractors); had these won the day, Rome might perhaps have become more vigorous and enterprising, certainly less stable. But Augustus and his successors prudently relied on good landowning families, who could be expected to be moderate and conservative in outlook, and would not try to overthrow the government with the help of proletarian rabble.

Imperial Rome normally ignored the merchants as possible collaborators. They had to pay taxes and to give a hand in purveying food and supplies for the army and the bureaucracy; but they were not asked for financial advice or credit, even when credit would have been a better means than exorbitant taxation and inflation to face emergency needs. Rome never realized the possibilities of public debt. As long as the medium-sized property held its own beside the great estate, she was reasonably broad-based, above her peasant foundations. Her safety would be jeopardized, however, when inflation and taxation whittled down the middle class, and left only great landowners and starving peasants side by side.

A civilization built on cities

Though the Empire was rooted in the land, it was by no means countrified. Cities were the masterpiece of the Graeco-Roman world, the namesake of civilization; we still make the word 'brute' a synonym of 'uncivilized', that is, etymologically, 'not living in a city'. As a matter of fact, the *civitas* (city-state) was the fundamental cell of the imperial body politic. The members of the agrarian ruling class praised the country but went to town if they wanted to keep track of events. In each urban centre (*urbs*) they found a public square for political meetings and literary discussions, public bathhouses for the comfort of the body, and public theatres for the pleasures of the mind, to say nothing of public markets and shops. Yet that refined *civitas* was the product of a retarded development, the offshoot of the simplest type of organization that a nomadic society can create when it first becomes attached to the soil: a fortified nucleus, in the heart of a small agricultural district, where people can store food, meet on solemn occasions, and find shelter when needed.

At first the enclosure might contain only one building, for gods and chieftains, with a great empty space for assemblies. Gradually the houses multiplied, and often the village became a town, with a population of administrators, artisans, and merchants as well as landowners. But the landowners still dominated the political and social life of the town and at the same time ensured that it was linked materially and morally with the territory from which it sprang. The specific character of the urban nucleus was not due to the occupation of its inhabitants, but to the fact that they lived at close quarters while the other 'citizens' were normally widely scattered.

Almost inevitably, the city-state was only one stage on the road of empire or nation. Sooner or later a *civitas* more highly developed than the others, or an able military leader with effective backing, would impose his power on several city-states. Larger units began to take shape, often following the outline of natural regions; so in the Nile valley the independent 'nomes' died out under the domination of the god-kings who controlled the distribution of the life-giving floods.

But geography did not everywhere favour the integration of the town in an empire. In most of Greece and the Italian peninsula nature had built up mountain-ranges and dug moats round each city-state, leaving it a little strip of coast as its only outlet to the world. This often retarded the development of the monocellular state into a more complex organism. So the cells had time to bring to maturity the seeds of two qualities which withered away elsewhere, where they were prematurely merged in the unwieldy structure of an empire: a more obstinate individualism, and a closer collaboration. Their inhabitants knew one another better; each man contributed to the collective expression of common tastes and interests, while preserving his own initiative and personality. In Greece and Italy, when the independent city-state perished at last, it was too late to destroy local patriotism. Better to make use of it, and to transform the vanquished of yesterday into the fellow-workers of today.

Rome, born a *civitas*, constantly endeavoured to extend her rule not by destroying other city-states but by attracting them into her orbit and making them junior partners. Where no city-states existed, she founded them or encouraged the local population to set them up. Thus the Roman commonwealth grew as a confederation of urban cells, held together by a skeleton provincial administration, but fully autonomous in internal affairs. The map of the Empire, at any stage of its development, is a close stipple of city-states (five hundred in North Africa alone), with here and there an indistinct blur where tribes recently subdued or admitted as 'allies' are still serving their apprenticeship in the Roman, municipal way of life.

III. FRESH TENSIONS

To the majority of Roman citizens, who took for granted that 'the sun could not see anything greater than Rome', the decline and fall of the Empire was an unexpected, almost unbelievable nightmare. Orosius, St Augustine's disciple, pinned it to supernatural forces: the pagans 'charge that the present times are unusually beset with calamities because... idols are increasingly neglected', but the Christians know calamities are God's punishment for man's sins. All this is beyond the historian's province, but we may consider briefly some of the fresh tensions which did not break the Empire but forced it to find a new adjustment.

The crisis of the towns

It is undeniable that the fundamental cells of the Roman Empire came under ever growing strains. Even in the second century, when peace reigned and taxation was light, some cities lost their solvency by building greater theatres, bathhouses and monuments than they could afford. In the third century, they lost their security: the emperors hurried from one frontier to another in their attempts to make their presence felt and close up the breaches through which the barbarians were sweeping down on the *civitates*, already hit by extraordinary levies. In such conditions the towns inevitably suffered serious damage. But these disasters restored to the urban nuclei of city-states the original function they had lost in their heyday when, sheltered behind the continuous wall of inviolate and distant frontiers, they had no greater concern than beauty and the pursuit of happiness. Now every town got its garrison, and again shut itself up within its own walls, Rome like the others.

When peace and security were restored — for a while — urban life had lost some of its charm. The shrunken walls of most of the towns indicate that part of the population had left for good. The extraordinary levies had become regular contributions. Municipal self-government was subordinated to a plethora of employees, who held city officials responsible for the collection of taxes. Rich and poor did their best to escape into the country, where control was more difficult and food more easily available. Yet it would be inaccurate to say that towns lost their economic, political and cultural importance. On the whole, the last two centuries of the Empire were probably as hard on the country as on the cities; but citizens are more vocal and complained more loudly. Nevertheless, there was a limited economic revival in the larger centres of the east and even in some towns of northern Gaul, Britain, Africa and the plain of the Po; the Roman civilization, when the barbarians conquered it, was still based on cities.

It fell to the towns to bring to a successful conclusion the last great task that the Empire accomplished in its twilight years: the definition of orthodox Christianity and its propagation among the pagans (*pagani*: in good Latin, peasants). For the Church had modelled her organization on the structure of the Empire, choosing provincial capitals for her councils and *civitates* for her episcopal sees. Thence a well-disciplined clergy, exempt from taxation, directed the evangelization of the district. Moreover, Christianity had from its earliest years been an essentially urban movement. Its first adherents (proletarians), like its best propagandists (intellectuals), were mainly recruited from the largest centres, the most receptive of new trends. So, by reinforcing the urban nuclei at the moment when they were in a crisis, the Church acted as a stabilizing factor.

Human and divine law

To accuse Christianity of having hastened the dissolution of the Roman Empire is to confuse symptom with cause. No doubt the old order must have been seriously weakened for the new religion to assert itself in the face of the general hostility of the grand old families and of the keen intellectual and philosophical elite. Had there been a Marcus Aurelius in the fourth or fifth centuries, Christianity might not have been allowed to triumph; though Julian tried, and failed. But republican Rome had long since absorbed the equally uncongenial Greek ideas and mores without giving in to the nefarious effects feared by republican traditionalists; there was no reason why the Empire could not absorb Christianity without disaster, and as a matter of fact it did.

Actually the worship of one god may be a better prop of monarchical absolutism than a loose polytheism. The Sasanian monarchy found Zoroastrian monotheism helpful. Some Roman emperors of the third century tried sun-worship as a quasi-monotheistic solution. In the fourth century Christians were only a minority, but their spirit of discipline could be put to good use: in 314, shortly after the first edicts of toleration, the Council of Arles was already considering excommunicating those who refused military service.

Of course, when the emperors embraced Christianity they had to renounce the posthumous deification that paganism bestowed on them. But they compensated themselves by taking over direction of the Church. Better to live a reflection of the one light than to die a second-rate star in a dim firmament of gods. Moreover, through Christianity the Empire extended its frontiers from earth to heaven: its cause was no longer merely that of civilized peoples against barbarians — it was the cause of believers against infidels.

Christianity could hardly have been a unifying force if it had countenanced division in its own field. Every faith that claims a monopoly of truth contains the germ of intolerance: if persecutions do not smother it, they often make it more uncompromising. Less than a century was needed to transform Christianity from victim to persecutor. In 311, the Emperor Galerius had opened the narrow door of indulgence 'that the republic may enjoy perfect prosperity'; in 341, Constantius forbad pagan sacrifices except in temples outside the cities; in 392, Theodosius outlawed any manifestation of pagan cults, though the majority of the rural population remained attached to them.

Within the Church itself quarrels between rival sects had not waited for edicts of toleration before getting under way. They raged furiously as soon as the councils could count on the assistance of the State to execute their orders. But all these religious struggles only emphasized conflicts between aspirants to the Empire, and rivalries of the provinces. As long as the dissentients could hope to win the State over to their point of view, they attacked the governors rather than the government. 'As a matter of fact,' said Optatus, an African bishop of the fourth century, 'the Republic is not included in the Church, but the Church is included in the Republic, that is, in the Roman Empire; for above the Emperor there is no-one except God.'

Later, the uncompromising attitude of the 'orthodox' towards 'heretics' provided a new basis for patriotism. The Romans thought of the barbarian Arians as enemies as much of their faith as of their country. This is the feeling we find throbbing through the inscription carved out about 580 by a common Balkan soldier, in clumsy and touching Greek: 'Lord Christ, help and keep Romania!'

Because the Christian Church had more to offer than the pagan cults, she had none of their docility. Theodosius 'the Great', on whom St Ambrose of Milan is said to have inflicted penance after the massacre of the population of Salonika, became in 390 the first emperor who bought the salvation of his soul at the price of humiliation. But in everyday life the Church was by no means reluctant to come to terms with the State — the thousand years of Byzantine history afford proof enough of that. The Gospel had already separated Caesar's sphere from God's; in another connection, the contempt which such as Augustine affected for the Terrestrial City underlined the impossibility of governing it by the strict laws of the Celestial.

The pagan Empire, for its part, had never dabbled in theology. Its polytheism had been practical and concrete; abstract ideas and moral principles were the province rather of philosophy (for the select few) or law (for the people in general). Some differences were inevitable between Graeco-Roman philosophy and Judaeo-Christian religion, even though most thinkers found little difficulty in reconciling them. But there was no real antagonism between Christianity and the law which declared, through the mouth of Ulpian, 'The rules of law are to live honestly, to harm no man, and to give to each his due'.

None the less, if the priests had taken literally Jesus's admonition not to let one jot or tittle of the law of Moses pass away, or if the jurists had insisted over-much on their formula that 'jurisprudence is the knowledge of things divine and human', conflicts of authority, if not of doctrine, would have broken out at once. Fortunately, in the decisive years of the adoption of Christianity by the emperors, priests and jurists both showed themselves reasonable men. The collaboration of State and Church began on the basis of separation of powers.

We need hardly stress the importance of the spiritual message that the Law of Israel, as interpreted by Christianity, handed down to the Middle Ages. With the laws and philosophy of the Ancient World in eclipse, confronted with the worshippers of force and violence, its spokesmen were not always worthy of the message; yet the voice of goodness crying in the wilderness proclaimed the exaltation of the humble and meek and the peacemakers — a voice that could never now be silenced.

The responsibility of the emperors

Christianity being thus ruled out of court, can we accuse the growing absolutism of the emperors of destroying the citizens' feeling of participation and under-mining the Empire? Here again, we must not confuse cause and symptom. If absolutism was poison, it worked very slowly; if it became more stringent, it did so partly to fill up a vacuum created by existing disaffection.

In practice, political freedom had never flourished in the Empire except in the sphere of local self-government. Notwithstanding his eagerness to preserve republican forms, Augustus had transmitted to his successors unlimited powers. Even the 'good emperors' of the second century, who consistently asked the advice of the Senate, would not have accepted orders from it. Then the so-called military anarchy of the third century had destroyed the residual powers of the Senate, worn out the local self-governing bodies, and discredited the very authority of the Emperor.

To restore the imperial authority, Diocletian hallowed it. Henceforth the emperors robed themselves in purple, called their office a 'sacred Empire' and required their subjects to bend to the ground before them. The change was more formal than substantial; without being 'sacred', Nero had been more despotic than Diocletian and as blood-stained as Constantine. At any event, the Emperor could hardly help becoming a hallowed being once he took over the leadership of the Christian Church. By that time, senators and city magistrates were evading the responsibilities that weighed too heavy on them; an increasing number of intellectuals despaired of the City of Men and turned to God instead. In this broadening vacuum, even the most brutal or blundering emperors were the best upholders of what last remnants of liberty could be saved. They still acknowledged that the source of their powers was a 'perpetual delegation' from the people, and this was enough to put them on a different plane from that of the kings by right of conquest and the kings by divine investiture who were to succeed them after the Empire went down.

IV. THE EMPIRE WITH FEET OF CLAY

Still it must be admitted that the broadening vacuum was largely created by the excessive fiscal burden which the emperors of the fourth and fifth centuries imposed on the population. No doubt Diocletian had tried to make it more equitable by establishing a land tax proportional to the size, fertility and productivity of the soil. Some other dues were made easier to bear by being collected in kind: the merchants, who handled money, paid cash, but the farmers gave farm products and the labourers gave their labour. The rate of taxation may seem moderate in comparison with modern rates. But it was definitely too high for the Roman taxpayers' ability to pay. Had it been applied intermittently, it might have driven the people to meet emergencies with a supreme effort; enforced throughout two centuries, it proved disastrous whenever it was not ineffectual.

Merciless taxation

The economic policy of the late Roman Empire was seemingly based on the assumption that a government can and should impose its will upon the economic life of the nation. Debasement and counterfeiting of the coinage resulted in soaring prices: the law tried to peg them at a lower level, the same throughout the Empire. Some citizens were unable to pay their taxes or perform the services due from them: the law laid on their neighbours (citizens of the same town, peasants of the same village, members of the same guild) the obligation of paying or serving in their stead. The neighbours sought to escape this burden by changing house or profession: the law forbade them to leave their post, and fettered their children to it. At last the only choice remaining was whether to pay in money or in kind; nor was the choice always granted. In the long run, the powerful nevertheless found a way to evade orders, the weaker were crushed, and the poor disappeared from the list of solvent taxpayers.

The emperors, one might say, had no alternative: the war, almost incessant from the third century onwards, would not permit any rebate. This may be true, but the government never relaxed its grip, even when circumstances were favourable. Constantine 'the Great' overwhelmed his rivals, avoided foreign wars and seized the treasures of the pagan temples; but this did not prevent him from chaining fugitive smallholders as if they had been slaves, and imposing a tax on barter that his tax-collectors had to enforce with the whip. Such were the foundations on which Constantinople was built. The emperors did not merely fleece their flock: they skinned it.

Yet the fact that the Empire found it necessary to be merciless in order to meet any extraordinary expense, whether caused by war or by the building ambitions of a ruler, indicates that the foundations of Graeco-Roman economy had never been strong, balanced and elastic enough for the weight they had to bear and the blows they were subjected to. It is hard to realize: but the *Respublica* whose surviving monuments are a wonder to us, whose standard of living was in general higher than anything that had been known before or would be known for long after — the *Respublica* was nevertheless a colossus with feet of clay.

Agriculture witout surpluses

Agriculture was the pride of Rome, in many respects a well justified pride. With simple tools, but highly refined methods of soil and water conservation, a wide selection of plants, and tested principles of animal husbandry, the Romans employed manpower unsparingly to get from the minimum of soil the greatest possible yield. And yet, except in a few of the more fertile but over-populated provinces, like Egypt, the yield was modest, despite the remarkable skill and application of agronomists. In Italy, the corn harvest was on average no more than four times the sowing.

Nevertheless, the population had reached a level of density which was high for the period, because the peasants lived frugally on a predominantly vegetable diet. Livestock contributed little to food or to farm-work. More could not be expected unless a larger area of cultivable ground had been given over to them — and that would have been an unthinkable extravagance for the old city-states of the Mediterranean, crammed between mountains and sea. To extend their cultivated lands the peasants were reduced to terracing mountainsides, irrigating arid land, draining marshes. As regards livestock, they preferred to restrict themselves to small animals easily fed on what could not be used by men, and to wrest produce from the soil in the sweat of their brow. Their health did not suffer, because a light diet suits the Mediterranean climate; but they were never able to accumulate any surplus. Theirs was a subsistence economy, if a comfortable one.

Actually in the more recently conquered provinces, such as Great Britain or even Cisalpine Gaul, horizons were wider, livestock more plentiful, and the population more sparse. By substituting advanced Mediterranean techniques for the primitive methods of these lands the Romans could have built up a prosperous agriculture based on a happier balance between arable, pasture and preserves. They could have learnt from the north certain methods suited to the climate, the soil, the abundance of livestock, such as the harnessing of draught animals one behind another which Pliny tells us was used in Cisalpine Gaul. Unfortunately the conquerors, being accustomed to lack of space, did not fully appreciate certain advantages of the northern farming patterns, with their scattered settlements and vast stretches of grassland and forest. Such a disorder and waste of space seemed to them the product of a backward and untidy culture rather than of a bountiful nature. So the Romans clung to the traditional Mediterranean pattern of dividing the land into chequer-boards of tight rectangular plots, and cultivating the plots almost as kitchen-gardens. Thus their expansion contributed a good deal to population growth, by creating new farms, but little to economic growth. The smallholders still had barely enough surplus to set aside for a bad year, and not enough to re-invest it.

There were of course many great landowners, who could amass surpluses by the work of their slaves and dependent peasants. If they had invested their revenue in trade, industry or finance they could have set the whole economy moving, but this they did rarely and reluctantly, because it did not seem proper for a landed gentleman to become a business man. Some consumed as much as they could themselves and dispersed the rest in liberal gifts; others were only concerned to increase their possessions in property and slaves. Some went so far as to organize small industries to supply their estates without recourse to the urban markets, but none, or almost none, was prepared to tarnish his reputation by engaging in genuine manufacture for sale to the public.

Usury, though even more discreditable, attracted the aristocrats by its high rate of interest; but propriety required them to employ men of straw, and that prevented them from becoming bankers rather than lenders. The same was the case with trade. Besides, a fifth-century law, going back to the traditions and laws of the republican era, forbade nobles, rich men and high officials to engage in trade, 'so that plebeians and merchants may buy and sell more easily'.

Trade without prestige

All told, Roman society was too urbanized and complex to be hostile to the business man, but treated him with condescension. Landed gentlemen were fully aware of the services that merchants, shopkeepers and artisans living in the same town provided in supplying a variety of goods that no country estate could supply; but they agreed with Aristotle that 'the public square must not be dirtied by merchandise and should not be a thoroughfare for craftsmen and workmen. . . . The market place should be far from it and well distinguishable.' The government needed traders to obtain for its military and civil staff whatever was not made available by taxation in kind and by state manufactures; moreover, prosperous merchants would fatten the treasury, and discontented craftsmen might revolt. But this somewhat contemptuous benevolence was no basis for real understanding, much less for fruitful collaboration.

It is true, that the administration, and a good number of public-spirited citizens, endeavoured to promote the welfare of all citizens. But they built more theatres and aqueducts than breakwaters or mills. The superb military roads that furrowed the Empire were hardly designed with the interests of the commercial economy in view: they were narrow, steep, expensive to keep up. And though in principle the State did not interfere in private business, it had little hesitation in subordinating it to political interests. Craft guilds were tolerated or protected only for the sake of their functions of mutual aid and public service, but forbidden to act for the promotion of a higher standard of living. Foreign trade was suspected of opening a door to spies and smugglers, and hence closely controlled. As for domestic trade, the State edged the merchants out of some of its most profitable branches: salt and metals were governmental monopolies, corn was largely reserved for taxation in kind. The low purchasing power of the great majority of the population restricted opportunities for commercial gain still further.

Nevertheless, it was far from impossible for merchants to make money, especially in lending and in long-distance trade. In an empire so extensive and thickly populated, the refinement of Graeco-Roman civilization and the low level of internal customs duties encouraged financial and commercial activity. But most of those who made their fortune by these means followed the advice of Cicero, himself an intelligent parvenu: 'If the [long-distance] merchant, surfeited or rather satisfied with his profits, retires . . . to the country and an estate, he seems to me to deserve all praise. . .' As for money-lenders, it was almost inevitable that they should end their careers thus, taking over the lands they had seized from debt-ridden peasants. So the wealth won with so much difficulty and danger in trade or lending finally buried itself in the land, instead of fertilizing the business that had produced it.

Labour without equipment

It was practically impossible to make money as an artisan, an occupation which Cicero calls sordid and unworthy of a free man. Indeed, the meagre productivity of manual labour, which had only the simplest tools at its disposal, limited its profits, especially as the competition of a multitude of slaves prevented free craftsmen from raising their prices. No doubt Graeco-Roman technical knowledge was capable of inventing adequate tools, but workers were not wealthy enough to buy them and capitalists were not concerned to supply them.

To take only one example, the water-mill made its appearance in the eastern extremity of the Empire as early as the first century B.C. The relief it brought to the women who ground the corn had been celebrated in a Greek epigram, the first tribute of the Muse to industrial progress. But Rome did not adopt the mill until the fourth century; and outside Rome it was not generally used until the Middle Ages. Besides, what was to be done with the hands made redundant by the introduction of a machine? Only heartless contractors would have thought of growing fat on the hunger of the poor ... and in any case it was simpler to employ multitudes of slaves and underfed proletarians. It is said that the Emperor Vespasian, indifferent as he was to the smell of money, refused the offer of a machine that would erect columns inexpensively: 'Let me provide food for the common folk', he said. The common folk, often reduced to living on the alms of the rich, were the largest element of the population of the old metropolises, and with their wealthy protectors helped to make the towns parasites of the country rather than centres of industry and commerce.

The golden mean

The unobtrusive comfort of the first centuries of the Empire, the *aurea mediocritas* beloved of the ancient Mediterranean world, was thus the result of two vicious circles. These recur in almost all the great agrarian civilizations of antiquity, especially in China where they have survived down to modern times. At the bottom, the manual workers were poor because they lacked livestock and tools, and they lacked them because they were poor; at the top, insufficient capital was available to commerce and finance because they were despised, and they were despised because they had insufficient capital.

So there grew up an economy of saturation, without reserves and without possibility of progress; but it allowed the aristocracy to prosper and the people to increase as long as law and order were undisturbed. It could not be modified without being destroyed, or destroyed without inflicting much suffering generally. Workers had to be decimated before any effort was made to economize their strength or improve their remuneration. Merchandise and credit had to be almost impossible to find before merchants and lenders gained recognition. The urban centres had to be cut off from their territory before a new collaboration of town and country was established on more equitable foundations.

We shall shortly see that the first symptoms of this transformation were already making their painful appearance in the twilight years of the Empire. It is hardly surprising that the emperors did not understand the potentialities of a distant future, and clung desperately to the crumbling past, trying to bind every workman to his trade, every official to his employment, every soldier to his post, and even every price to its former level. Edicts and emperors were swept away by the current, but it was several centuries before the Middle Ages cleared away the ruins and built up an economy more elastic and better balanced — the economy which has been the basis of modern European civilization.

V. EPILOGUE

Though the organic disease of the Empire was economic, war was the apparent cause of death. The civil wars and barbarian invasions of the third century had strained its resources; the early fourth century had brought a reprieve, but only a long peace could bring a full economic recovery. There still were 'perfidious barbarians... howling' round the frontiers. The St Martin's summer ended too soon.

Before the end of the fourth century, Attila's Huns subjugated the Germans who had been their neighbours, and forced others to seek safety by a 'retreat forward' into the interior of Roman territory. A new series of invasions swept down on the Empire in the next hundred years. They were not more irresistible than the third-century invasions, but the Empire was no longer capable of sustained effort in all directions at once. The west lost one province after another, and the curtain rose on the last act in 476. Nevertheless the west had resisted long enough to secure a further delay for the east, which allowed Constantinople to follow its own path and survive not ingloriously for another thousand years.

The reader eager to reach the Middle Ages will not want to linger over the details of the Empire's death-throes. But if we are to be familiar with the materials which the Middle Ages were to use for their own building, we must broaden our perspective and consider the more serious and prolonged crisis in which the fall of the Roman Empire is no more than an episode: the decadence of all Eurasia in the first centuries of our times.

Chapter 2

PLUMBING THE DEPTHS

I. THE CRISIS OF A HEMISPHERE

'THE world has grown old and lost its former vigour. . . Winter no longer gives rain enough to swell the seed, nor summer sun enough to toast the harvest. . . the mountains are gutted and give less marble, the mines are exhausted and give less silver and gold. . . the fields lack farmers, the sea sailors, the encampments soldiers. . . there is no longer any justice in judgments, competence in trades, discipline in daily life. . . epidemics decimate mankind. . . the Day of Judgment is at hand.'

This list of misfortunes (which we have abridged) was drawn up about 250 by St Cyprian, as scientific proof that the prophecies, Christian and pagan alike, are inexorably coming true. The 'fatal sixth millenary after the Creation' is drawing to its end. The long struggle between God and the Devil is hastening towards its final explosion. It matters little that events gave the lie to St Cyprian's predictions. The feeling that the *dies irae* was at hand persisted for centuries, exasperated by every invasion, brought home with every famine, creating a psychosis of the anti-Christ who seemed to take human shape in every evil-doer. This fear was to vanish only gradually with the renaissance of the late Middle Ages, to become an object of ridicule only in the eighteenth century; it has been reborn in another form in our own days — the fear of racist madness and nuclear science. We find our comfort in the hope that reason will prevail in spite of everything, and progress continue on earth; St Cyprian's contemporaries took courage as they descried amid the signs of Death the promise of the Resurrection (Pl. 1).

The trump of Doom did not sound at the end of the 'sixth millenary', but the Ancient World died with it. It was not suddenly consumed in the flames of an Apocalypse; in 476, the deposition of the last Roman emperor in the West, which we usually consider the starting point of the Middle Ages, went almost unnoticed outside Italy. But the change was none the less radical for being unspectacular. If Plato or Alexander the Great had returned to earth seven or eight centuries after their death, in the days of Julian or even of the unhappy Romulus who lost his throne in 476, they would have had no difficulty in finding an admiring audience; five hundred years later, the contemporaries of Dagobert, Penda or Agilulf would have found them as strange and incomprehensible as people from another planet.

From Rome to China

The repercussions of the revolution reached far as well as deep. All the evidence is that the tremors were felt from end to end of Eurasia, wherever organized and civilized states confronted the barbarians. Unfortunately we do not know enough of the history of Persia to establish a useful parallel between its vicissitudes in the first centuries of our times and those of the declining Roman Empire. Besides, the differences between the political, economic and social structure of the two empires were so deep–rooted that close comparison is out of the question. The position is entirely different with China, whose past is better known to us, and whose fundamental structure was not too different from that of Rome, in spite of the gulf that separated them materially and culturally.

In China, as in the Mediterranean world, symptoms of disease had made their appearance in the second century A.D., and become alarming in the third. Civil wars, the division of the Empire, the short-lived restoration of unity, the conquest of the capital and half the Empire by barbarians from the north who had infiltrated long since — the drama was played out in the Far East in the same sequence and almost with the same timing as in the Far West, except that China's 'Byzantium' survived not in the eastern half of the Empire but in the southern. In China, as in the Mediterranean world, the political and military surface crisis concealed a deeper economic and religious one. The old Confucianism, withering away in the constant repetition of formulae, gave way to a Taoism native to China but transformed by Hindu influences, and most of all to Buddhism which was entirely foreign, mystical, ascetic and monastic. The population grew poorer and sparser, especially in the provinces over-run by the invaders, and citizens sought to escape oppressive taxes by emigrating or sheltering behind powerful protectors.

We need hardly stress that the resemblances between the two revolutions become less clear-cut when we come to study them in detail. Nevertheless the resemblances are so striking as to raise the question whether there was not a common cause behind such parallel developments. And this question brings with it another: did the political and military crises come before or after the economic and religious? This is perhaps the old problem of the hen and the egg; if civil war and invasion squandered material resources and turned men's minds to new beliefs, yet the weakening of the economy and world-weariness stirred up disorders and delivered the country into the hands of the invaders. So be it; but among the accompanying tensions that led to the final upsetting of the equilibrium, were there not degrees, if not a chronological progression?

No violent death

The hypothesis that the ancient civilizations died a violent death as the result of armed onslaughts cannot explain everything. We can pass over civil wars: the history of Rome and China is full of them from beginning to end. As for invasions, the Roman and Chinese Empires were not annihilated, since they retained a considerable part of their territory. Even in the occupied provinces the invaders did not formally overthrow the authority of the Empire or destroy it systematically (Pl. 2).

Fig. 1. Merovingian iron-work: inlaid buckle-plate, mid seventh century. Excavations in the cathedral of St Denis, 1953.

Besides, the victories of the barbarians can only be explained by flaws in the armour of Rome and China. Certainly from the second half of the second century the pressure of nomad and semi-nomad peoples increased along the whole length of the great walls. Soon some form of safety-valve had to be provided, and certain tribes were invited to join the defenders of the wall; but the pressure continued. Patient research in the fields bordering on history, such as archaeology and linguistics, will perhaps throw more light here: Mongol, Turk, Sarmatian or Germanic, the tribes of the steppes formed constantly changing confederations whose forward movement is the clue to the history of the invasions. Moreover, it seems possible to glimpse some material elements in the success of the barbarians: the progress of metallurgy outwards from its centre of diffusion in Central Asia provided them with swords stronger and more flexible than those of the Chinese and Romans (Fig. 1), and the development of the stirrup, the horseshoe and harness increased their mobility. Confronted with peoples who were better organized but immobilized behind their defences, a hard-hitting and swiftly-moving enemy held good cards. Although the barbarians rarely won pitched battles or took a town by storm, they were an erosive force which in the long run proved serious.

They were not, however, very powerful or very relentless enemies. Romans and Chinese recruited all the barbarians they wanted, and never found them any less loyal than national contingents — at least up to the moment when the national contingents had almost disappeared and the barbarians realized that they could take for themselves the provinces of which they were now the only defenders. Even then, they could often be restrained by presents, honours, the concession of naturalization, sometimes by their own conviction that they could not themselves shoulder the burden of government. Besides, they were divided into little groups hostile to one another, rent by implacable feuds between families, even between brothers. They have left no literature to show what they thought; but their legends, collected much later, agree with the descriptions given by Roman and Chinese historians and show that civilized peoples had no monopoly of vices, nor backward peoples a monopoly of virtues.

And the barbarians were few enough in number. Romantic historiography, which has pictured the invasions as an onslaught of human masses cramped for room even in the vast plains of the north, will not do when we read that the whole Ostrogoth people, led by Theodoric to the conquest of Italy, was able to shut itself up for some months behind the walls of Pavia, without even evicting the inhabitants. The Vandals apparently were no more than 80,000, including allies, wives and children. The picture is the same at the other side of the hemisphere: we are told that the T'o-pa, who ruled northern China for nearly two centuries, mustered no more than 50,000 fighting men; the whole population of Tatar stock in the region of their capital numbered 14,700 people (or families?), including the remnants of previous invasions. How could such puny assailants overwhelm two majestic Empires?

Fig. 2. Frisian art: gold buckle-plate, end of the seventh century. Frisian Museum, Leeuwarden (Holland).

St Cyprian's arguments

Let us turn back to St Cyprian's complaints. Among all the obvious exaggerations we can find the essential facts of the situation. On the one hand, the population of the empires had diminished; on the other, the leaders no longer had the energy needed to maintain the old balance or the flexibility essential if they were to adjust it to meet new needs. Corruption of manners, probably less serious and universal than a few preachers both then and now insist, must have been less telling than the resignation preached by Christianity and Buddhism. Excluded from effective power, crushed by taxation, and doomed to poverty, the masses were apathetic even when their life was in danger. The elite were not only demoralized, often to the point of coming to terms with the barbarians, but had even lost the faculty of original thought.

We shall come back later to this seeming loss of nerve. Did it really spring from the laxity of a society weakened by too much comfort, as some moralists claimed? Or was it connected with a physical decadence of which the decline in population was a direct indication?

There can be no doubt about this decline, in spite of many local exceptions and the difficulty of calculating its proportions exactly. A demographic deficiency is hardly surprising when we remember that the rate of increase in societies of the Ancient World was strictly limited by inadequate hygiene, deficient diet, hard work, frequent early marriages and exposure of new-born infants. A slight alteration in one or other of these factors was quite enough to produce a deficit. Wars killed many more by the misery they engendered than by battles. Sources which we cannot verify speak of an intensification of birth-control in lay society; monasticism too reduced the number of parents.

A possible cyclical explanation

But the most interesting factors are perhaps the cyclical ones. Although the medical history of mankind has not yet been written, we know that the great endemic and epidemic pestilences are subject to fluctuations of long duration, if only by reason of the ups and downs of collective immunization. It seems that the most terrible of contagious diseases, the plague, entered on a phase of extreme virulence with the great epidemic of A.D. 180, which killed Marcus Aurelius, the last of the 'good' Roman emperors, and sapped the power of the Han emperors to the profit of a miracle-worker. From then on, the scourge ravaged the world at frequent intervals until about the middle of the sixth century; after a recrudescence in the eighth century, it slipped into the background again until the Black Death of 1348. Similarly, in the last centuries of the Empire and the first of the Middle Ages, malaria (whose evolution has not been charted outside the West) made vast regions uninhabitable, which were re-peopled in the early Middle Ages and deserted again from the fourteenth century onwards. And since this disease is connected with water drainage, we find ourselves back again at what had seemed the most absurd of St Cyprian's claims: 'Winter no longer gives rain enough...'

Scientists are very rightly beginning to devote their attention to certain fluctuations of climate which seem to be periodical: variations of the southern limit of glaciers and floating ice, changes in the level of lakes, differences in the annual growth-rings of trees, advance and retreat of the boundaries of vine and corn growing regions. To these data from the objective book of nature should be added the often suspect information which the chroniclers give on floods, droughts and famines. None of this has yet been catalogued systematically or interpreted with the caution and subtlety it demands. But it may well be that the study of climate could help us to understand the apparent coincidence of the main long-term demographic and economic fluctuations throughout Eurasia.

The question would still remain, whether these phenomena of physical and moral decadence affected barbarian as well as civilized peoples; and this problem is well-nigh insoluble in the absence of any written evidence. Nevertheless a few archaeological and geological indications, the fact that climate and disease know no frontiers, and above all the behaviour of the barbarians after they came into the circle of the great settled civilizations, lead us to think that their condition was not essentially different.

Their turbulence must not be taken for vigour, nor their immaturity for youth. It is true that their loosely-knit and rudimentary organization was better suited to a world where men had become fewer and thought shallower. But their triumph did not bring in its train a new force of a kind to stimulate healthy reaction. It only accelerated the already pronounced decadence of the exhausted peoples of the empires.

II.   THE BARBARIAN STATES IN THE WEST

In the West, the dissolution of the Empire in the fifth century brought into being a number of barbarian states of moderate size, carved out haphazardly in the course of conquests or scuffles between neighbours, but often based on geographical units (as the Rhone valley for the Burgundians), economic assets (the rich cornlands for the Vandals), or administrative circumscriptions (the prefecture of Italy for the Ostrogoths). Some of these states, in particular that of the Franks, straddled the former Roman frontier. Others, still more primitive, came into being in the heart of Germany, which was to some extent brought closer to the Mediterranean world as this was Germanized. Similarly, the demarcation line disappeared between the independent Celts of Ireland and Scotland and their Romanized cousins, the Britons, who were gradually forced back by successive invasions into the strongholds of western Britain and Brittany. As for the Basques, they were not subjugated by the Germans, but lost in their isolated stronghold the Roman veneer they had acquired.

Barbarians and Romans: together, but not blended

The east amputated, part of the north brought in, multiplicity taking the place of the imperial unity: these were the first bars in the European symphony that was to follow the Graeco-Roman harmony. But the instrumentalists were far from ready.

Everywhere, except in Britain which the Anglo-Saxons wrested from its inhabitants in a prolonged and merciless struggle, the barbarians were perfectly willing for their Roman subjects to relieve them of the worries of an administration whose laws and machinery were too complex for their mentality. Everywhere, except in Italy where the Ostrogoths at once made some effort to assimilate the law and institutions of their subjects, the barbarians initially brought their own world with them, keeping their national customs and skimpy political

Map 4. Barbarian States at the beginning of the sixth century.

organization. Such contacts were not new; in the days of her power, Rome had admitted raw barbarian tribes to her territories, trusting that they would learn the rules and finally adopt the pattern of the city-state. But now the apprentices found themselves the masters, and it was beyond them to devise an organization that would allow the two societies thus thrown together to blend.

Harmony might have been attained without too much difficulty had the *rapprochement* been on the lowest level. The barbarians were soldiers by trade or inclination, but they were also peasants in the intervals of their migrations. They could have come to an understanding with the simple peasants of the Mediterranean world more quickly than with the nobles and intellectuals who served them for motives of self-interest or defeatism. The masses were ready to accept anyone who would lighten their oppression at the hand of tax-collectors and great landowners. But conquerors seldom choose to mingle with the humble. Moreover, class differences had always existed among the barbarians themselves, and became sharper after they settled down; for the steadily increasing importance of mounted troops depressed the status of ordinary peasants who marched and fought on foot.

Generally speaking, the *rapprochement* was attempted at the top. The old masters and the new ones had to assist each other if they were to preserve the fiscal organization and landholding system of which they shared the fruit. Their ways of life were not radically different: the Roman aristocracy had abandoned the ruined towns and lived in country estates, like the barbarian nobility; many of the barbarian conquerors had begun their career in the barbarized army of the waning Empire in the west and had relatives still fighting in the pay of the surviving Empire in the east. To be sure, a grand gentleman such as Sidonius Apollinaris, son-in-law of an emperor, sometime prefect of Rome and ultimately bishop of Clermont, would rather 'have braved destitution, fire, sword and pestilence' than submitted to the Visigoths. But when the Emperor surrendered southern Gaul without a fight, Sidonius resigned himself to rub shoulders with barbarians whose long hair reeked of rancid butter, only complaining that he could scarcely write good verses while everybody around him spoke German and wallowed in onions and garlic. The opening lines of an elegy by Maximian, a poet in Ostrogothic Italy, would seem to express a deeper grief: 'I am not what I was, the larger part of us perished, all that remains is languor and horror.' But if we read further, we discover that he merely mourned youth and love. Still, resignation does not mean friendship. There could be no blending until the slow upward progress of the barbarian elite met the swift decline of the Roman upper class.

Lights and shadows in the Gothic experiment

Ever since the beginning, the European symphony lacked a conductor. The two branches of Goths ('Brilliant', or Ostrogoths, and 'Wise', or Visigoths) were the most highly developed of the barbarians, the only ones who had a vague idea of empire. Cut to pieces in 269 by Emperor Claudius II, they had built up a great confederation under Ermanaric, and seen it crushed by the Huns in the fourth century. In the fifth, the king of the 'wise Goths', Athaulf, toyed for a time with the idea of 'transforming the Roman Empire into a Gothic Empire' (that is, if the historian who reports his intentions did not misunderstand them). Finally, the king of the 'brilliant Goths', Theodoric, lord of Italy and the surrounding provinces (493–526), tried to organize a league of barbarian kings under his auspices, stretching from Germany to Africa. But the kings showed little enthusiasm for this first pacific attempt at a concert of Europe, and the Goths, weakened by their old conflicts, were not firmly enough established in their own territories. Paradoxically, their conversion to Christianity (the first of all the Germans) served them ill, for they had accepted the new religion at the time when Arian doctrine had not yet lost its last battle in the Empire. The Goths inspired more aversion in their Catholic subjects as Arians and propagators of Arianism among their barbarian neighbours than they could have done as pagans.

Religious antagonism, and the mistrust between Romans and Germans, cut short the premature 'renaissance' which made its hesitant appearance in Italy under Theodoric. It was not enough that the Italian aristocracy had become accustomed to foreign domination under his predecessor Odoacer ('a well-intentioned man', as a chronicler records condescendingly), or that Theodoric was recognized in a kind of investiture conceded by the Emperor of Constantinople, or that he had rid himself of Odoacer by war and treason. Nor was it enough that Cassiodorus, the Roman minister of the Ostrogoth king, organized the administration and conducted official correspondence by all the rules of the dead Empire, that once more the people were given circus games, or that the king's victories over other barbarians shed over Italy some faint reflection of her former splendour. Theodoric would have had to become entirely Roman, without losing any of his ascendancy over the Ostrogoths — an impossibility, even had he wanted it.

What indeed did he want? The pompous letters of Cassiodorus, the history compiled by the Goth Jordanes, the Roman legend which paints Theodoric as a devil punished for his sins by being swallowed up by a volcano, the German legend that makes him out a hero without blemish — these give four very different pictures. All they have in common is their emphasis on his greatness. We are told that food was cheap in his reign, but we also hear of requisitions, famines and high taxation. His tomb, a stone reproduction of the nomad's tent, proclaims him a leader of nomads; yet his palace, as represented in a mosaic, confirms the judgment of a Byzantine historian: 'in name a usurper, in fact a true emperor'. Theodoric conferred the highest dignities upon Boethius, whose translations from the Greek were to be the main sources of musical and scientific knowledge during many centuries when virtually nobody in the west could read Greek. But Boethius wrote in prison his most inspiring work, *Consolation of Philosophy*, shortly before being executed on the charge of conspiring with the Emperor of Constantinople.

In spite of its tragedies and inconsistencies, the reign of Theodoric stands out as the last, blurred page of the old 'civility' (to use a word Cassiodorus loved to employ). The quarrels of his successors gave the eastern Roman Empire a pretext for intervention. Then the Ostrogoths found another talented leader, more generous and imaginative than Theodoric: Totila, who tried to parry the massive defection of the Italian aristocracy and clergy by setting free large numbers of slaves, distributing land to poor peasants and calling on them to join him. It was too late. The imperial generals finally overwhelmed the Goths, and one of the first acts of Justinian was to void the decrees of Totila (554).

The success of the Franks

Even before the failure of the Ostrogothic experiment to meet the Romans half-way, jungle law and the Catholic Church had together singled out for the leading role a hitherto undistinguished people: the Franks. In a rapid succession of bold strokes, many of which are wrapped in legend, Clovis (481–511) welded together the little kingdoms into which the Frankish tribes were grouped, defeated the Romans, Visigoths, Alamans, Thuringians and Burgundians who were in his way, occupied the greater part of Gaul and a portion of Germany, and established his capital in a small town with a great future: Paris. Originally a pagan, he converted to Catholicism. This was enough to make the Franks, in the eyes of the Gallo-Roman population, the champions of the orthodox faith against the Arian threat. There also is some reason to believe that, unlike the other barbarian conquerors, the Franks did not take for themselves a substantial portion of the land held by the native aristocracy. Though they were more unpolished than the Goths, they were able to enlist the collaboration of Gallo-Roman noblemen and clergy fairly easily.

The descendants of Clovis (Merovingians) found themselves the masters of the most extensive and fertile state in the west. They were too powerful and aggressive to leave their weaker neighbours in peace, war being their greatest amusement and source of booty. For a few years, it looked as though they might gradually bring under their thumb all of the European territory formerly dominated by the Roman Empire, with the addition of the western German lands. As early as the first half of the sixth century their ambitions were flaunted in the gold coins with the crowned head of Theodebert I (534–47), one of them giving the grandson of Clovis the imperial title of *Augustus*.

It was not for the Merovingians, however, to attain what Charlemagne would accomplish almost three centuries later. None of them was a man of imperial stature. Probably the best, according to their own chroniclers, was 'good king Guntramn', a jovial man who loved good food and coarse women, and 'when with his bishops conducted himself like one of them'. He shared with Pope Gregory I, his contemporary, the honour of being canonized, but he had a regrettable propensity for murder; among his many victims were two physicians who had failed to heal one of his queens, herself a most unlovable soul. On the other hand, two queens of the Franks were canonized with unimpeachable records; but one of them was born a Thuringian princess and the other a Saxon or Anglo-Saxon slave.

III. NEW SHAPES OF ROMAN GRANDEUR

Theodoric's mosaics and circus games; Theodebert's self-bestowed title of Augustus; the honorary titles bestowed by Byzantine Emperors on grateful western rulers; the attribute *Flavius* which some German kings wedded to their Teutonic first name; all that, and much else, expressed not so much the respect of the conquerors for the Roman civilization as their want of a political tradition that could make a state out of a conglomeration of tribes.

The Hunnic model and the Byzantine model

'Barbarian' originally meant 'babbler', then 'non-Roman'; it was merely a negative term. Almost all of the barbarians who settled on Roman territory spoke closely interrelated Germanic dialects and hence could understand one another; but they had hardly any consciousness of unity and were in fact of mixed race. Even the groups most proud of their ancestry had absorbed remnants of all the nomad and semi-nomad peoples of northern Eurasia who, at one time or another, had been swept into their wake: Balto-Slavs, Iranians, Turks, Mongols. Some of these remnants still kept their own identity at the time of the final onslaught, like the Alans (Iranians) who were the allies of the Vandals, or the Skires and Turcilingians (Hunno-Turks?) of Odoacer, the man who happened to depose the last Roman Emperor in the west. Intermarriage and initiation rites dissolved these minorities in the end, but the common fund of barbarian traditions was no more Germanic than central Asiatic.

Germanic and Scandinavian poems were to give pride of place to Attila, king of the Huns but married to a German (Ildico in history, Kriemhild in legend). For the migrating tribes, as a confederation of hordes controlled by strong warriors, the Huns offered to the Germans and the other barbarians an example of imperial organization which was not promptly forgotten. But the horde was suited for mobility and the steppe; it would not fit sedentary life in the forests and the cultivated plains. The Roman imperial order was the only alternative open to the barbarian kings once the migrations stopped.

As long as an emperor of the Romans reigned in Constantinople and proclaimed himself likewise sovereign of the West, with the full approval of the Catholic Church, the barbarian kings could not make the imperial idea their own absolute property. They accepted the pre-eminence of the Emperor willingly enough, since he did not ask them for troops or money or obedience. It was immaterial to them that their own coinage was ordinarily struck with the name and effigy of the emperors, or that their documents were dated by the terms of office of consuls appointed by Constantinople; the old names were useful to introduce the new ones, until such time as the barbarian king had prestige enough to stake his own independent claim.

The new image of the 'Roman' Empire

But Constantinople saw things in another light. She was the New Rome, temporarily unable to collect the heritage of Old Rome in the west, but well determined to make good her claims as soon as her forces would permit it. In 533 — half a century before the Chinese emperors of the south in their turn threw back the barbarians beyond the Great Wall — the armies of the Emperor Justinian swung into action. In less than a year Belisarius conquered the Vandal kingdom, but eighteen years of bitter fighting were needed to subdue the Ostrogoth kingdom. The eunuch Narses achieved it in 553, though isolated resistance continued until 563. Moreover, the 'Roman' troops (most of them, it is true, barbarian mercenaries) took Andalusia from the Visigoths and forced back over the Alps the Franks who in the confusion had possessed themselves of northern Italy. No doubt Italy had been thoroughly devastated, but the scars might have gradually disappeared, had a long peace succeeded the long war.

In a quarter of a century almost half the old West was rewon and almost all the Mediterranean became a Roman lake once more. At the same time, the rejuvenated Empire erected splendid buildings and codified the great body of Roman law. Perhaps this stunning turn of the tide led Justinian to think that in the end the barbarians could be totally obliterated. But although one of his laws expressed 'the hope that God will grant us the remainder of the empire that the Romans. . . lost through indolence', Justinian made no attempt to carry on the plan by following up the pursuit of Franks and Visigoths. The Empire was exhausted by the effort, and needed all the troops and money that still remained to it to contain the Persians, who coveted an outlet to the Black Sea through Byzantine territory, and a variety of barbarian people, both old and new, who were threatening the Balkans. Justinian's successors came safely through these trials, but never again found the peace needed to complete the conquests of the great Emperor.

It may be argued that these were precarious conquests: in 568, the Lombards invaded Italy; between 571 and 624, the Visigoths reconquered Andalusia; from 670 onwards, the Arabs battered at north Africa. True, but it was no mean fact to have re-occupied Africa and held it for a century and a half. As for Italy, the Byzantines disputed inch by inch every parcel of land which had not been lost in the early disasters. Ravenna was abandoned only in 751, Syracuse in 876, Bari in 1071. As for Venice, no one can say exactly when she cut free from Byzantium. At any rate, the Empire's return in arms to the very heart of the West had shown it to the barbarians in a very different light from that of its apparent waning in the fifth century. The new image of Constantinople may not have been as majestic as that of ancient Rome, but it was a powerful image, and because it had shed some of the classic refinement it was more attractive and suited for barbarian imitation.

Naturally her impact was most marked on the Lombards, whose territory was cut into or hemmed in for its entire length by Byzantine possessions. But the Visigoths too were deeply influenced, and even the Anglo-Saxons in their remote island from time to time borrowed from Byzantium rules of ceremonial, administrative methods, and elements of religious and artistic culture. As for the Franks, their imperial ambitions were set back for two centuries by the counter-offensive of the legitimate Empire. It is hardly surprising that they were hostile, in spite of several agreements for joint operations against the Lombards, agreements in which neither side showed good faith.

The Pope, a sovereign by default

While the new Rome of the Bosporus waxed strong and beautiful, the old Rome of the Tiber, dethroned by the barbarians, superseded by the Byzantines, deserted by most of her inhabitants, was threatened with the fate of Nineveh and Babylon. But unlike Babylon, Rome had the Pope, whose authority rose as she was slipping down the political ladder.

Yet at the beginning the political position of Rome had been the strongest asset of her Bishop. The other bishops could more easily challenge the theory of St Peter's apostolic succession than deny the special importance of the ecclesiastic administrator of the capital city, even if it was the capital of a pagan Empire. The emperors left Rome at the same time as they became Christian, but her capital rank was preserved: in 445 one of the last of the western emperors, Valentinian III, ordered the bishops of the western provinces to accept as binding 'all that is sanctioned by the authority of the Apostolic See'. Nevertheless the clergy of Africa and the East, at the instigation of the patriarchs of the greatest cities such as Constantinople and Alexandria, insisted on the fundamental equality of all bishops. Moreover, the Emperor, the first layman in the Church, still reserved for himself the right to convoke councils, to supervise their deliberations, to implement their decisions, and so to exercise unobtrusive but effective control over matters of discipline and faith.

These pressures weakened as soon as the West was wrested from the Empire by barbarians either indifferent because they were Arians, or deferential because they were new converts to Catholicism. The Pope had no serious competitors among the bishops of western Europe, and had now broken free from the political power of the Emperor. So in 494 Pope Gelasius I, repeating more boldly the theses put out by his predecessors and Ambrose of Milan, wrote to the Emperor at his seat of Constantinople that 'two powers chiefly share the empire of the world, the sacred authority of the pontiffs and the royal might; the responsibility of the priests is the more heavy because at the last judgment they must answer for the kings'. This was not yet the theory of the subordination

Fig. 3. Popular art: terra-cotta from Grésin (Puy-de-Dôme). Christ, dressed as a Roman general, triumphant over the asp and the basilisk. Musée des Antiquités Nationales, St Germain-en-Laye.

of Caesar to Peter but it was the prelude: in his capacity as head of the Church, the Pope was declaring his right to judge the Emperor in the tribunal of penance. An unrealistic programme, since the clergy was unmanageable, the king an Arian, and the emperor often heterodox! Gelasius' successor, arraigned by a section of the clergy, had to submit to the judgment of a council of Italian bishops convoked by Theodoric. After reconquering Italy, Justinian forced two popes to make concessions to the theological ideas of the Eastern clergy.

It was the Lombard invasion that freed the Papacy and enabled it to establish its supremacy finally over the whole of the West. For two centuries the invasion was halted at the gates of Rome, and the Roman territory thus became a frontier zone nominally Byzantine but forced to rely on its own resources. So the Bishop of Rome gradually became willy-nilly a temporal and independent sovereign.

It is not surprising that the Pope, absorbed by the immediate problems of this precarious balance, did not at once grasp all its long-term advantages. But we already find Gregory I mediating between Byzantines and Lombards, rallying the provinces which had no effective government, organizing the first of the great missions sent out from Rome to convert entire barbarian peoples both to Christianity and to the Roman obedience: the mission of the monk Augustine — St Augustine of Canterbury — to the Anglo-Saxons. The progress of conversion admittedly was slow and suffered many temporary setbacks before all of England was christianized, superficially at least, by the late seventh century. While tackling the pagans the missionaries of Roman obedience had also to face the co-belligerent, but not allied drive of Celtic missionaries, whose organization and observances had developed in virtual isolation and did not conform fully to the Roman norm. The rivalry sometimes was a contributing factor in the political game, culminating in an alliance of the heathen king of Mercia, Penda, with a Christian Welsh king, against the Roman-Christian king of Northumbria. The Roman observance, however, won the day at the Synod of Whitby (664), and England eventually became a most conformist daughter of Rome.

The organization of the English Church set a new example of Papal supremacy. Up till then, the churches which had been established in the barbarian kingdoms obeyed the Pope, but were autonomously organized within the framework of the different states. In Italy, moreover, the Archbishop of Milan had adopted an attitude of partial independence towards Rome. But the churches established by Gregory I and his successors — the Anglo-Saxon Church in 597, the Lombard and Frisian during the seventh century, and the German in the next century — submitted more strictly to the Pope's 'Catholic' (that is, 'universal' or supranational) discipline. Their example encouraged the older western churches to close their ranks about the Pope. Thus were laid the foundations of the union of Roman Catholics which, in the absence of any political unity, anticipated from the religious point of view the formation of a European community (Fig. 3).

IV.   THE APPEAL OF THE ECCLESIASTICAL LIFE

The steady progress of the Church, at a time when kingdoms and Empire were floundering in the mire, certainly cannot be explained by her material strength, which was paltry, or even by her temporal wealth, which was already considerable, but much less than she was to amass later on. She held, however, the keys of heaven. More than ever before, this hold overawed the great and touched the heart of the defeated, the unsatisfied, the desperate members of the secular community. Many of them found it less hard to forsake the world than to remain in it.

In ecclesiastical life all vocations could find their fulfilment, and humble birth was a stumbling block but not an unsurmountable obstacle to success. Some plunged into theological study, which was now the chief outlet for what intellectual activity still survived. Some devoted themselves to the day-to-day work of administration, made all the heavier by the feeble or trusting governments which delegated to the clergy some of the responsibilities for food-control, justice and even defence. Still others dedicated themselves to the conversion of heretics and pagans, knowing that often it would fall to them to teach their converts the elements of civilization too. And finally some, perhaps the most numerous, saw in the peace of the cloister the only answer for the individual to the problems which seemed insoluble in their corrupt and blood-stained society.

The monasteries: a great achievement

The monasteries were the greatest achievement of the early Middle Ages. What more stunning example could be given to the world than that of Cassiodorus, the Roman minister of four Ostrogoth kings, the writer versed in all the refinements of rhetoric and learning, who ended his life, his worldly dreams dissipated, by dictating the rule of the monastic order he had founded?

Yet it was not Cassiodorus, but a humbler man, Benedict of Nursia, who handed down to the generations to come the formula which distilled the long experience of Eastern monasticism for the service of Western ideals. Of recent years the originality of the rule that bears his name has been called in question, and it has been claimed that it is largely derived from an earlier model. Whatever the truth of this, it was St Benedict's text that asserted itself and ensured in Benedictine monasteries the triumph of good sense and a balance between the rigours of asceticism and the exigencies of mental and physical health.

'Hear, my son, the precepts of the master. Whoever thou art, renounce thy will, gird on the mighty and resplendent arms of obedience, and go to war under the true king, Christ the Lord'. Benedict's call rang out from Monte Cassino to Rome, England, Spain, Gaul, Germany. Gradually it supplanted the rules propagated by other saintly men such as Caesarius of Arles and Columba of

Ireland. The monastic communities, dedicated to manual and intellectual toil as well as to prayer, were for many years the only heirs of the Latin spirit of order and organization, the only centres capable of growing and multiplying amid dispersion and general confusion.

To some extent these communities took over the functions of cultural and economic centres which the urban nuclei were surrendering. In countries such as Ireland which had no towns as yet, they supplied the deficiency as far as their means permitted. But it was in Ireland that uncompromising individualism, the longing to withdraw completely from the life of men and converse alone with God, survived longest. In 891 the *Anglo-Saxon Chronicle* recounts the story of three monks 'who fled from Ireland in an oarless boat because they would be pilgrims for love of God'. With more profit for the salvation of their brethren, other monks in quest of isolation ventured among the pagans to win their souls. Still others lived cloistered in their cells, studying and transcribing the classical texts which a society relapsed into barbarism could no longer understand.

The Church: a power

There is nothing left to be said in praise of the early medieval Church; early medieval writers, nearly all of them churchmen, have shouldered the task. Without seeking to pick any quarrel with them, however, we may note that her great deeds were the proceeds of enormous investments in manpower and wealth. No trustworthy statistics exist, but we shall hardly be exaggerating if we reckon that at least one man out of twenty was of the clergy and that the proportion was higher still among men of talent and good will. The attention that such men devoted to the affairs of the world had to be subordinated to their duty to heaven (Fig. 4). They were forbidden to fight or to have children. They had to devote to the service of God a considerable part of the resources they accumulated by their own work and the work of the faithful. So at a time when productivity of labour and the excess of births over deaths were hardly more than the bare minimum needed for the survival of society, the Church borrowed from the lay world far more than its superfluity. Despite appearances, the barbarian states were too weak to stand up to her. Her hostility in the end broke up the Lombard kingdom, her embrace strangled the Visigothic kingdom, her prosperity weakened the Anglo-Saxon kingdoms, and all the prestige of the Carolingians was needed to re-establish any measure of balance for the benefit of the Franks (Pl. 7).

Generally speaking, and in spite of exceptions inevitable in a very large community, the Church of the early Middle Ages was more cultivated and more charitable than the average of the faithful. But this did not mean that she escaped the general lowering of standards.

It must not be forgotten that from the beginning the best representatives of classical civilization had seen Christianity as 'a foolish and excessive superstition' because it appealed to emotion and faith rather than to common sense and reason. However, before the eclipse of Graeco-Roman culture a pleiad of original thinkers had wedded the new religion with philosophy. The great heterodox writers of the early third century rationalized the mysteries of the Scriptures by interpreting them allegorically (Origen), or boldly extolled them in all their apparent absurdity (Tertullian). The councils of the fourth century and the first half of the fifth codified the profession of faith: not without struggle, for the triumph of the Western Christology produced revolt after revolt in the East — Arians, Nestorians, Monophysites.

Fig. 4. The ladder of salvation. Mural painting in Chaldon Church (Surrey), C. 1200.

Christian philosophy reached its heights with the Fathers who saw the death of Imperial Rome: Ambrose, Jerome, Augustine of Hippo. Then it suddenly slipped back.

Theological disputations had once achieved the subtle definition of a problem as fundamental as the position of Christ in the Trinity and his incarnation ('of one substance with the Father according to the Godhead, of one substance with us according to the Manhood... in two natures, without confusion, without change, without division, without separation' (Council of Chalcedon, 451)). Now, in the West, they revolved around questions as trivial as the form of tonsure or the date of Easter. Between the three doctors who came before 476 and the fourth, Gregory the Great, who traditionally ranks with them, stretches a gulf. Gregory condemns the study of classical literature, interprets the Scriptures as a collection of moral lessons veiled in allegory, and builds up a Christian mythology, as it were, by an assemblage of miracles where God and the devil, both humanized, confront each other. The wheel has turned full circle: reason and common sense have given way to emotion and faith.

But have we any right to be shocked by this? Gregory I, statesman, administrator and propagandist, speaks to the masses, leaving his more erudite predecessors to satisfy the few intelligences capable of understanding them. He advises missionaries to deal gently with the rites and feelings of the pagans and to lead them gradually to the truth; he is the first to call the Lombards 'unspeakable', and the first to welcome them to the fold; he submits to being called a fool by a talented emperor, and flatters his unworthy successor.   Always, and effortlessly, he stoops to the level of the simplest of his flock, for he is the heir of antiquity in his role as governor of a state, but a man of his time in everything that touches the teaching of the word of God. That is the secret of his immense success.

The humble style

The *sermo humilis* (plain or humble style) of Gregory the Great had some close antecedents, such as the *rusticus sermo* with which Martin, Bishop of Braga, endeavoured to persuade the peasants of the Portuguese region not to relapse into the worship of devils; if they must make incantations and magic signs, why not make the sign of the Cross and the 'sacred incantation' of the *Credo*? St Augustine himself, who knew every trick of classical rhetoric, had pointed out that the Holy Scripture was 'easily readable', and 'by adapting itself to babes did not shun any expression from which. . . our understanding may rise gradually to divine and sublime matters.' As time went on and education went down, the 'humble sermon' became not merely the preferable style, but the only one still accessible to such men as were able to write and desirous to be read.

This was not altogether an unfortunate development. Roman rhetoric of the latter days had become both turgid and stale. After the far-fetched erudition of a Cassiodorus, it is a great relief to read the simple prose of a Benedict of Nursia. Similarly, after the involute preambles of Justinian's decrees, one may find some pleasure in the pedestrian common sense of a Lombard law which forbids persecution of witches 'since it is not possible that a woman can swallow up a man alive.' Unfortunately, common sense is not very frequently met with in the legal or devotional writing of the barbarian age; simplicity is oversimplification, shallowness more often than conscious weeding of superfluous detail and verbiage. It does not really lead to 'divine and sublime matters.'

It is admittedly difficult for a man of the twentieth century to interpret the rare sources of the seventh and eighth centuries without superciliousness, yet without over-indulgence. All told, these centuries were not particularly warridden; the great migrations had ended, and there was hardly more than the ordinary amount of internal struggle, local outlawry, and border warfare. The savagery of most kings and superstition of the masses need not shock a generation that has known Hitler and his many followers. The discrepancy between the eagle's head on a French sarcophagus of the seventh century (Pl. 3) and the eagles of classical bas-reliefs is not greater than that between Henry Moore and Michelangelo.

Historians may have no calling to pass moral judgment and no authority to pronounce artistic judgment but they must assess the adequacy of means to their end. The religious literature of the seventh and eighth centuries was inadequate to convey the moral teaching of Christ; the laws did not go a long way towards ensuring peace and justice; agriculture fell short of feeding regularly the shrunken population; curiosity and invention, the basic instincts which had raised man from Neanderthal to Babylon, Jerusalem, Athens and Rome, were almost at a standstill. For two hundred years, we can detect virtually no progress and scarcely any motion. It is possible, though it cannot be proved, that something stirred deep under ground; on surface, however, we find only a dull combination of Roman senility and German immaturity.

V. GERMAN IMMATURITY

The barbarian state was a child of war. Its authority rested on the strength of small ruling circles, which were held together by the superior strength of a king. This means that, on the whole, it was congenitally inefficient and weak.

The shaky sovereign

Of the two basic tenets of the Roman idea of Empire — popular delegation and divine mandate — the second came more easily to the Germans. Some of their legends linked a royal family with gods or wizards; the Church preached the sacred mission of the monarchy; Byzantium set before them the example of an emperor crowned by the patriarch (after 457). But for all that, the religious colouring did not go very deep. When the chroniclers of the early Middle Ages give a king the nickname of 'Pious', it usually means that he is a fool or a weakling.

The king's prime duty was to lead the army to victory and to share out the spoils (Fig. 5). If he ceased to make conquests and to gather new riches that he might redistribute

Fig. 5. Merovingian art: royal sword, with gold hilt set with garnets, seventh century; from Paley (Seine-et-Marne). Coll. G. Lefèvre.

among his followers, his power dwindled. He then would have to dip into his own patrimony, or risk losing his crown. It is mainly in this sense, if at all, that one can speak of popular delegation. There were occasional consultations with assemblies of all able-bodied free men or smaller groups of retainers, but even these were geared to military affairs more than to ordinary administration.

Time and success usually tightened the grip of the king on the tribes that made up a barbarian folk, but they might also make the tribes feel that he was not really needed. After conquering the larger part of Italy, the Lombards did without a king for ten years. The Anglo-Saxons, though they recognized a high king (*Bretwalda*) from time to time, were content with kingdoms hardly larger than a Lombard duchy or a Frankish county, since their enemies, the Celts, were divided into still smaller units.

The underlying Roman tradition, however, suggested firm monarchical rule. This, and the extraordinary military successes of the first Merovingians, enabled Clovis to found a dynasty, and his descendants to share out the kingdom as though it were their private property. Then the quarrels and incompetence of the kings allowed the Frankish aristocracy to whittle away the royal domain. The mayors of the palace, who acted as chief stewards of the Crown, soon overshadowed the sovereigns; but it took a long time before they plucked courage enough to occupy the throne.

The Visigothic and Lombard aristocracy, on the other hand, withstood the efforts made by several energetic kings to establish their dynasties. In vain some of these tried to consolidate their power by borrowing from Byzantine ceremonial: only force commanded respect, and force was blunted by any form of refinement. None of the relatively civilized kings of late Lombard times equalled the prestige of the first conqueror, Alboin, who had crushed the Gepids in the region of the Danube, killed their king and married his daughter; then he had abandoned his transalpine kingdom to the Avars, but won a greater in Italy (568–72). He might perhaps have become another Clovis had he not made the mistake, in his cups, of offering wine to his wife in a goblet made of the skull of her father. She did not appreciate the joke, and had him assassinated. That is the story as it was told two hundred years later by Paul the Deacon, a pious but patriotic historian: without a word of blame for Alboin, he condemns the 'silly woman' who sacrificed the hero to a private spite.

Weakness of institutions

The solidity of the kingdom depended on the capabilities of the king, for its institutions were either disintegrating or rudimentary. It was not enough to have kept the Roman administrative system and personnel; they would have had to be completely reformed to halt the process of dissolution. Byzantium gave an example of moderate reform, but Byzantine influences came too late and were too superficial to take root strongly, except in a few fields of Lombard administration (the mint, police and customs) and, to a lesser degree, in other barbarian administrations.

As for Germanic institutions, designed for the movement of small groups and for war, they were weakened by the heavier burdens imposed by settlement over an extensive territory. The assembly of the people met more and more infrequently, and lost its political authority, except in Spain where it gained strength from its strange fusion with the councils of the Church. The bands of 'companions' and 'faithful' who surrounded their leaders in battles and feasts showed more determination at table than on the battlefield. The organizations of tribe, village and family lost their cohesion, and their links with the central government grew weaker.

Nevertheless, Germanic institutions survived better than the Roman, because they were better adapted to a shrinking state. Gradually the State gave up direct taxation, to the great relief of the people. It fell back upon the revenue of ever-diminishing public property, and set up countless tolls on roads almost deserted by traffic or ruined by lack of upkeep. On the other hand, the State no longer provided any services, not even those that might have brought in a profit. It no longer waged war, except intermittently, and at very irregular intervals meted out a form of justice based on fines.

Naturally this picture needs to be given light and shade. The Lombard kings were able to extend their domains, and the English kinglets to introduce strict cadastral surveys. In France, on the other hand (and nowhere else), bishops persuaded their kings to burn the registers of the Treasury for the salvation of their souls. Taxes that were not counterbalanced by services seemed to them pure extortion.

Traces of culture

The Germans had picked up from central Asia the most original motifs of their art: interlaced geometrical design, stylized animals, a taste for cloisonné work, glass beads, coloured gems. These tendencies which set little store by the observation of human and realistic themes influenced the art even of the more advanced Oriental peoples (Chinese, Persians, Byzantines) and was in harmony with Celtic art. It could achieve beauty, especially in jewellery, but lacked the infinite possibilities of renewal, elaboration and refinement afforded by

Fig. 6. Frankish tombstone, limestone, sixth century, from Niederdollendorf (Rhine/Westphalia). Bonn Museum.

more intellectualized styles (Figs. 1 and 2; pl. I). The few Germanic master-pieces are almost all of the first centuries; the rest are a repetition of a few for-mulae, which in the end become unrecognizable through excess of ornament or over-simplification. We will not linger over the rare attempts to represent the human figure (Figs. 3 and 6). Irish art was more creative, though its original vocabulary had been very limited; its native abstract and figurative themes continued to develop throughout the early Middle Ages, partly through the original re-interpretation of fresh Roman and Byzantine themes. That art, however, with its bizarre, dreamlike, haunting quality, does not belong to the Germanic world.

Irish architecture also has left a few impressive stone buildings, where one still recognizes the timeless stamp of megalithic art (Pl. 9). We are less fortunate with Germanic architecture. Brick and stone remained the speciality of the conquered Romans; whatever is known of constructions in less durable materials — wattle and daub egg-shaped houses, log cabins and wooden huts — can scarcely be described as a style. There is more talent in the wooden stave churches, some of which are still extant in Norway, but the known specimens do not belong to the early Middle Ages (Pls. 17 and 33).

We know for sure that epic poetry was cultivated throughout the early medieval barbarian world, but its quality cannot be assessed. Apart from legends preserved by Latin chroniclers, the only surviving sample of German epics before the tenth century is a short fragment (*Hildebrand*). It would be unkind to regard that modest performance as typical of the oral literature of a mostly illiterate civilization, but incautious to take for granted that such a literature was of the same standard as the extant poems of the later period. Only the Anglo-Saxons wrote down their legends before the end of the barbarian age. *Beowulf*'s verse grates on an ear accustomed to classical harmonies, and the pattern of alliteration recalls the interlaces of illuminated manuscripts. But the hero's struggle against the waves, monsters of the deep, and the cowardice of men, has a sombre grandeur. The poem ends on a note of despondent compassion which has led critics to see the hand of a cleric guiding the bard's. It is probably no accident that of this lone monument of early medieval epics only one copy has survived.

Elements of law

The barbarians were not 'noble savages'; they had anarchical tendencies but did not live in a paradise of total freedom. There is no liberty when everybody may disregard the rights of others; moreover, the family and the tribe limited in-dividual freedom to a considerable extent. The blood-feud (*faida*) was a wide-spread deterrent of antisocial behaviour; but the chain of retaliations, once started, could be terminated only when the wronged party, family or tribe, accepted a 'composition', that is to say, a material compensation as the price of blood. This could be done without any intervention of the state. The king, however, endeavoured to forestall the feud and transform the composition into a judicial fine, both to affirm his authority and to appropriate all or part of the fine. Thus, indirectly, the Crown came to be the guardian of order and peace.

A good number of barbarian law books have survived, most of them in Latin. Some bear traces of a systematic arrangement and of a real concern for the protection of the weak and the poor, others are hotch-potches of wildly pagan and scarcely Christian rules. One seldom finds any attempt at synthesis, any theoretical definition, any clear-cut distinction between the rights of the individual and the rights of the community or State. The law of contracts is, as it were, non-existent: one object is bartered for another or, if the exchange cannot be completed on the spot, the debtor gives the creditor a pledge, real or symbolic. Lawsuits are not judged on the facts or proofs adduced as evidence but according to the general trustworthiness of the accused and his kinsmen. Most penalties consist of fines fixed by a tariff — so much for breaking a tooth, so much for cutting off an arm — generally without regard to circumstances or the intention of the offender.

Law books were not the only legal sources. In the seventh century, a Frankish collection of ready-made models of deeds lists the following authorities: 'Roman law teaches, the custom of the village agrees, and royal power does not forbid' that a certain transaction be carried out. The councils of the Church, though irregularly held, also had some influence. This influence, like that of Roman law, contributed to bringing some order and moderation into the rudest customs, but it was not steady or growing. In the fifth century, the Goths and the Burgundians took over in their national codes a good amount of Roman law, but Justinian's legislation did not affect later developments; and while Lombard law became more humane as time went by, Visigoth law deteriorated. All things considered, German immaturity was less damaging at the time of conquest than during the long inactivity that followed it. Its fruits spoiled before they ripened.

VI.   ROMAN SENILITY

'Conquered Greece conquered her proud conqueror': the truth of the saying has often been proved, but not for the first centuries of the Middle Ages. Admittedly, the barbarians adopted the religion of the conquered Romans, just as the Romans had adopted a religion from Palestine after her subjugation. They habitually used Latin as their written language. They took over a number of Graeco-Roman ideas and institutions, not without passing on some of their own to the peoples they conquered; and though they did not give up butter in favour of olive oil, it did not take them long to appreciate the merits of wine. Nevertheless, the Romanization of Germanic culture was slow to come, until the conquering minorities had been physically absorbed into the mass of the Roman population and produced the first neo-Latin renaissance. It took at least four hundred years for the Franks to become French; later on, a hundred years were to be enough for the Normans, who were of no less Germanic stock. This would seem to indicate that the early Middle Ages suffered from a two-fold inertia: if the pupils were refractory, the masters were clogged with a dead past.

The extant monuments of the art, literature and ideas of the conquered Romans are numerous enough to warrant a general assessment, and this cannot be unrelated to the fluctuations of taste in our own days. Still it seems fairly safe to say that the ideas of the barbarian age, even among the 'Romans', lacked originality; that Latin literature, after producing some respectable, if not out-standing, works up to the middle of the sixth century, foundered for many years; that art, on the contrary, survived a great crisis and reached new heights, very different from the peaks of classical art, but of remarkable beauty, at least in those countries where Byzantine influence was felt. We call to mind names of authors whom only a few scholars read today, but whose fame lived long — Boethius, Fortunatus, Isidore. We remember the magic of the more familiar mosaics of Ravenna and Rome, the frescoes of Castelseprio, the jewels, minia-tures and enamels (Pls. 4 and 5, fig. 9) of a hundred collections. Without dwelling on details, let us note some essential data from monuments of art and literary works which can help us to understand the society which produced them.

A stiff and anonymous art

What strikes us first is the gradual disintegration of personality. The human figure is not eliminated, as it was in barbarian art, but attention is more and more turned away from it and focused on the clothing and insignia of power and profession. The individualized, realistic portrait becomes a stereotyped figure with wide eyes staring into nothingness, with simplified features and restrained gestures, always seen full-face. In literature similarly, biography is not neglected but is mostly concerned with standardized lives of saints, who are no more than miracle-working machines with none of the doubts, imperfections, and shades of character that distinguish every creature of flesh and blood.

Already in the fifth century history looked no further for an explanation of the defeats of the Roman Empire than the anger of the gods she had deserted or the displeasure of the new God. With Gregory of Tours it became a hotch-potch of common anecdotes, sins, divine interventions heralded by meteors, all thrown together with the same disregard for perspective as in the visual arts of the time. History sinks lower still in the collection of chronicles mistakenly attributed to 'Fredegarius', and even its compilers were conscious of its shortcomings. When one of them complains that 'the world grows old, the keen edge of wisdom is blunted, no one is the equal of the orators of the past and no one dares to claim equality', we can only agree with him.

No doubt this was an age of regression in culture and technique: as early as the fourth century, when Constantine 'the Great' wanted to adorn his triumphal arch with the subtle decoration of what seemed to him the best model of art, he had medallions torn from Hadrian's Arch, and for the rest must be content with a rougher decoration, which in fact we find just as pleasing. But even more incurable than the technical crisis (which could be solved by a change of formula) was the human crisis: the decay of the strength and dignity of individual man.

> How could human personality possibly have inspired in the artists of the early Middle Ages the interest and confidence it enjoyed in the old Roman cities? Citizens had been deprived of all initiative by the imperial power, and then, after its collapse, plunged into insecurity. The barbarians had trampled them underfoot, while Christianity exhorted them to humility and proclaimed that the Day of Judgment was at hand. They were consumed by poverty, decimated, by epidemics. To survive at all, their art had to become anonymous and collective.
>
> Its greatest triumph was the liturgical chant. This, like Christianity, had been imported to the West from the East well before the end of the Empire. But it was only in the dark years of the barbarian age that final form was given to the severe and solemn psalmody, the dialogue between narrator and choir, the alternation of choral groups answering one another in the antiphon, the hymns where the stress and rhythm of vernacular poetry took the place of the classical quantitative prosody. Tradition passes over the names of composers but extols two organizers: Ambrose, the friend and antagonist of Theodosius 'the Great' for the chant still to be heard in the churches of the diocese of Milan, and Gregory I 'the Great' for the chant that has prevailed in the rest of the Catholic world. Probably tradition exaggerated their merits and ignored those of countless collaborators and continuators, but essentially its judgment must be accepted.

Art wrapped up in symbolism

It would hardly be possible to exaggerate the suggestive power of music's abstract and direct language on the hearts of the simple: Arius, so his enemies said, enticed ingenuous souls into heresy by teaching them melodies borrowed from the songs of soldiers and sailors. But music was the only field of the abstract. In general, the barbarian age saw abstract ideas taking concrete form in material symbols, and theoretical explanations draping themselves in the veils of allegory.

Admittedly, this was nothing new. The orientalizing art of the late Empire was loaded with animal, vegetable and inanimate symbols; allegory had always been an important weapon in the arsenal of literature. But the barbarian period is outstanding in the extravagance of its allegory and in the intensity of its symbolism. It is not enough that the Hebrew prohibition of images gave way to anthropomorphic representations of the Godhead: the Son of Man must be shown as a peacock, fish, lamb or monogram. It is not enough that allegory

supported and supplemented rational interpretation: it became the ultimate
reality hidden behind the veil of apparent reality. To Gregory of Tours, the
falling of leaves in winter and their return in spring is significant only as a
symbol of Christ's death and resurrection.

> We can still find it amusing that a fifth century African, Marcianus Capel-
> la, should think up a *Marriage of Mercury and Philosophy* as the title and
> prelude to a treatise on the seven disciplines that were the basis of medieval
> teaching. We begin to get alarmed, however, when a seventh-century
> Frenchman, conferring on himself the name of 'Vergilius Maro', breaks
> up Latin into a series of hermetic languages and recommends writing it in
> the form of rebuses, to exclude the uninitiated. More generously, Isidore
> of Seville culls from the Christian and pagan authors furnishing the fifteen
> sections of his private library 'everything that must be known', and pre-
> sents it neatly to the general reader in a huge encyclopaedia. Etymology
> is the key to the understanding of each thing according to its essence:
> *formica* (ant) comes from *feret micas* (carrying crumbs); *nox* (night) from
> *nocendo* (harming), because it hurts the eyes. . . . What annoys a modern
> reader is not so much the absurdity of so many entries, which usually can
> be traced back to the blunders of Graeco-Roman sources, but the lack of
> organized thought and of interpretation in depth. Yet these shortcomings
> of Isidore's *Etymologies* were a major cause of his popularity, which
> persisted throughout the Middle Ages: his collection of unrelated anec-
> dotes was easy to read piecemeal and handy to quote.

Both 'Virgil' and Isidore belong to the seventh century, but their attitude is very
different. 'Virgil' clings to Latin as if to a title of nobility. He is one of those
cultivated Romans who display an equal contempt for the smelly, skin-clad
barbarians, and for the native country bumpkins wallowing in ignorance, superstition and slavery. With their outworn rhetoric, threadbare themes and archaic
language — a language that was becoming incomprehensible not only to the
German conquerors but also to most of the vanquished — these Romans were
the flotsam of the classical culture and doomed to disappear. In the same spirit,
in the sixth century, Procopius, the historian of the Byzantine reconquest, had
made a point of keeping the title of 'Italian' for the great landowners, and
ignoring the poorer natives and their Ostrogoth masters. It is easy to see why
Justinian's victories were not followed up in Italy.

Yet we must consider that Latin was the only international language still
understood by the educated throughout the West. Even Gregory I, who prided
himself on having 'despised the art of composition imposed by the rules of
worldly education', had to use Latin to make himself understood in ecclesiastical
circles. But he recommended that religion should speak to the illiterate in the
language of images — and this proves that he had small confidence in the Latin
teaching which, by order of the Councils, priests had to give the children of
their parishes.

Isidore and the beginnings of the new Spain

Isidore too (*c.* 560–637) wrote in Latin, the language of his ancestors, but he did not miss the opportunity of celebrating the surrender of the last Byzantine fortresses to his king: 'At last the valiant race of Goths . . . has wrested thee, O Spain, from the Romans . . . today the Roman soldier is the servant of the Goths'. How could he say more clearly that he was a Spaniard? His learning is sometimes as unreliable as 'Virgil's', but it is less irrelevant to life; often it has its roots in the dateless realm of folklore, the world of Aesop and the *Roman de Renart.*

The process of involution was drawing to its close: soon Roman decadence and German immaturity would meet. As ideas strayed further into the mists of allegory, as art became more and more fettered by symbol, as language became tainted with jargon and the clarity of Roman law was lost among the usages of customary law, better suited to barbarian customs, the day was approaching when victor and vanquished, rich and poor, would understand one another.

Some fifty years after the death of Isidore, Spain seemed to have travelled further than the other barbarian states along the road to this metamorphosis. Her artists had adjusted their formulae to meet the common taste of her mixed peoples. Her laws were now applicable equally to Visigoths and Romans. Her assembly of nobles and prelates functioned as a parliament in embryo. Her society seems to have been the cradle of certain feudal institutions. One of her kings, Wamba (672–680) even believed it possible to establish conscription — the touchstone of national unity — and to apply it even to churchmen and a part of the slaves. It is true that he did not succeed, and that the Visigoth state was about to collapse.

The weakness of the Iberian monarchy was as much the fundamental disagreement between king and nobles as their specific agreement on two points: the persecution of the Jews (that is, the core of the middle classes) and opposition to enfranchisement of slaves. When the Arabs invaded Spain in 711, a single battle brought the kingdom toppling down. Other kingdoms then took the lead, but there was no hope of building the new Europe until the foundations of society had been renewed and harmonized.

VII. THE UNKNOWN MASSES

It is always difficult for a historian to know what is going on beneath the upper strata of society and outside urban centres; for peasants are a slow, silent people. The furrow their plough drives deep and unregarded through the countryside alters it noticeably only in the course of centuries. The few writers of the barbarian age are not concerned with everyday life. The most they do is to tell us sometimes of the sudden calamities which transform the monotonous misery of the nameless masses into despair.

Here are three examples taken at random: 'When Chilperic died . . . the people of Orléans and those of Blois together fell on the people of Châteaudun and massacred them unawares; they burned houses, provisions, everything that they could not easily carry off; they seized flocks, and looted all they could take away. While they withdrew, the inhabitants of Châteaudun and Chartres . . . meted out to them the same treatment they had received.' (Gregory of Tours). 'Corsica is so oppressed by the tyranny of tax collectors and the burden of taxes that the inhabitants can barely meet them by selling their own children. That is why they are forced to leave the republic [the Byzantine Empire] and take refuge among the unspeakable Lombards. What more grim and more cruel fate could they fear from the Barbarians?' (Gregory I). After three years of drought, 'a terrible famine spread among the people and destroyed them. It is said that often forty or fifty people, exhausted by hunger, went together to a cliff top or to the sea and flung themselves over, holding hands.' (Bede)

A miserable living standard

No doubt it would be wrong to make up a picture of normal conditions of life from these catastrophes. Besides, local disorders reduced the possibility of general war. The magnitude of the sacrifice demanded by taxation resulted in regular flight to escape the heaviest burdens. The death-rate from famine eliminated surplus population and gave the survivors some degree of immunity. But if every disease brings its own remedy, this remedy in the barbarian age was always amputation.

Legal, archaeological and linguistic scraps of evidence — all we have to see a little way into the darkness of the period — indicates that even the great temporal and spiritual lords could keep no more than vestiges of the old luxury and that gradually the masses of the people were forced to surrender every material comfort. Lombard Italy must have been poor indeed for the theft of four bunches of grapes to have merited the attention of the legislator; the living standards of the Anglo-Saxons must have sunk low for the word *lord* (originally 'keeper of the loaf') to be the most frequently used of the thirty-six synonyms which in *Beowulf* express the idea of 'chief'; the purchasing power of the poor must have been considerably diminished for bronze coinage, the usual currency for small transactions under the Empire, to be no longer struck in the West. On the other hand, gold currency still circulated for international exchanges and was hoarded by the rich; it even penetrated regions where it had been unknown before the barbarian age, such as Scandinavia and Ireland. This is certainly proof of some progress in these regions, but also, and chiefly, of the gradual levelling-down of all Europe in an economy which made currency the repository of wealth rather than the day-to-day instrument of consumption.

A scanty population

With this economic regression there went, as we have seen, a far-reaching and prolonged demographic crisis. This did not destroy the contrast between the Mediterranean world on the one hand, settled and relatively compact, and the Nordic world on the other, with its scattered and floating population; but it made the contrast less clear-cut.

It is true that in vast stretches of northern and eastern Europe the emigration of the Germans and their allies intensified the demographic regression, but the gap they left was filled by new nomadic tribes: Slavs, Balts, Avars, Bulgars. . . It is possible that these were fewer and more primitive than the former inhabitants, but in any case their arrival could not much affect a landscape which men had never remodelled in their own image.

Finally it was the old Roman territory that underwent the deepest transformation, although its vicissitudes were scarcely more than the last stages of tendencies already pronounced long before the collapse of the Empire. For some time past the great landowners had been deserting the urban centres for their country seats (*villae*, the forerunners of the 'châteaux'). The peasants for their part were leaving their open villages for the shelter of the great properties. Forests, swamps and moors overran the land they had abandoned. This development, which tended to destroy the uniform pattern of intensive Mediterranean cultivation, was hastened by the influence of the barbarians' habits of rural, scattered settlement and the demographic regression. Almost everywhere, the network of towns frayed out, the chequer-board of cultivated fields broke up, and great unpopulated spaces stretched between the urban centres.

Roman traces in the geography of town and country

Nevertheless, the imprint of classical Rome was so deep that a very determined effort would have been needed to eradicate it entirely. No one had any wish to do this. No doubt the barbarians had little liking for the civilization of the towns: their bent for agriculture and hunting, their dislike of the limitations of gridiron streets and enclosed fields, are proof of this. But some acquired a taste for town life, especially among the Lombards. Others established fairly compact villages of smallholders, like those of the primitive north. Moreover, the inertia of agricultural traditions in the Mediterranean world slowed up the inevitable development of the great domains, and often prevented the peasants from taking advantage of the depopulation to round off their fields.

Even today, here and there, we can recognize the regular chequer-board, traced by Roman surveyors, marking the unchanged boundaries that have fenced in countless generations of peasants. It is more surprising to find, in the heart of many modern towns, that the Middle Ages alternately abandoned and rebuilt, the cramped chequer-board of the Roman town-planners (Figs. 7 and 8). Towns are always less conservative than the country and they were harder hit. But the Church could not stand aloof, for she had centred her episcopal dioceses on the cities. She did more: as in the case of Roman colonization through a network of new city-states, the propagation of the faith involved the foundation of new dioceses, and their sees became the stock from which towns grew up in regions till now townless. Trade too, although diminished, maintained many urban nuclei and sometimes created others. Thus, despite their physical and moral decay, towns in the barbarian age continued to play a part that was by no means negligible.

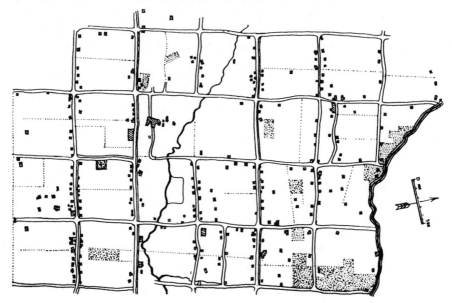

Fig. 7. Survival of the Roman centuriatio *in Italy: chequer-board pattern of fields near Padua. (After Meitzen.)*

A gradual revolution: the coming of serfdom

We must be careful not to under-estimate the importance of the survivals which passed on to mediaeval Europe some glimmer of the great light of classical civilization. But what counts in the barbarian age is more what it transformed than what it kept. Even if none of its transformations embellished the world, several prepared the ground for better days.

The transformation that most affected the greatest number, the development of serfdom, came about almost unnoticeably, through the failures or initiative of countless individuals, sanctioned from time to time by legislative measures. Like most of the revolutions of the early Middle Ages, it began long before the end of the Empire and was completed only in Carolingian times, but its progress, though the documentary sources hardly mention it, filled the history of the nameless masses of the barbarian age. Gradually the free men of the lower classes and most of the slaves mingled in a new class — the serfs.

If we have hardly mentioned the slaves of ancient Rome, that is because the historiographer is little concerned with domestic animals. The law and customs of the Ancient World rated slaves with livestock. The principle was not altered by the fact that some tender-hearted owners grew fond of a favourite 'beast', or some generous people exerted themselves to protect these talking animals from the cruelty of their masters. But nature offered slaves a way of escape that was

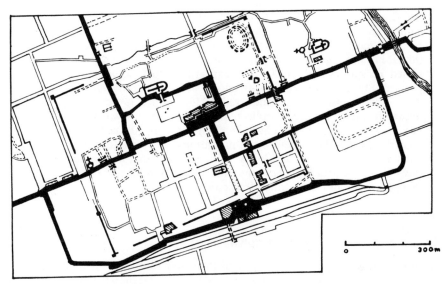

Fig. 8. Plan of present-day Aosta (Italy), laid out in chequer-board pattern.

not open to pet dogs or race-horses: they could be enfranchised and claim the rank of men and citizens, 'for by natural law all men are equal'. The civil law of the classical world, with its spirit of clarity, recognized no intermediate conditions between slavery and liberty, or degrees within these categories. But already the law of decadent Rome distinguished a number of sub-groups, such as 'powerful' and 'humble' among citizens, and 'fit for skilled work' or 'fit for agricultural work' among slaves. The law of the barbarians and the law of the Church multiplied these degrees. Only the highest of them conferred all privileges; the lowest involved complete subjection, and the others covered all imaginable stages of semi-liberty or semi-servitude. Finally, from all these limbos of legal thought emerged the serf, tied to the land or bound to his lord by obligations unworthy of a free man, but free (or very nearly so) in his relationship with a third party.

This legal development probably owed little to the mutations of religious and political thought which have often been credited with it. No doubt the Church embroidered on the assertions of the pagan philosophers about the natural equality of all men, but she had no more thought than they of overturning the imperfect institution which seemed a necessary condition of this imperfect world. On the one hand, she taught that slaves should not be ill-treated, and praised those of the faithful who were moved by exceptional charity or contempt for wealth to go to the length of en-franchising them. But on the other hand she often set her face against Utopian or spendthrift churchmen who threatened to compromise the economic stability of a religious house by emancipating its slaves. Indeed the Council of Orleans (541) decreed that illegally freed slaves of the Church should be claimed back without limitations of time. Nor could the religious tenet of human equality be more effective against slave-holding than it has been against modern racism, no matter how sincere and deter-mined its spokesmen. As for the barbarians, they sometimes found it profitable to allow a vague half-freedom, well suited to the lack of precise-ness in their customs, to conquered nations which it would have been impracticable to reduce to collective slavery; but this was certainly not because they respected the natural equality of men. All barbarian peoples possessed some slaves before the migrations. They continued to recruit them after the conquest and by the same methods that had served Rome: slave birth, war, trade, penal sentences, debts, purchase of children from their parents, and sometimes free consent.

Slaves go up, free men go down

However, the demographic crisis — and this is the fundamental explanation of the juridical development — hit the non-free even harder than the others. Human cattle, it has been said, is the most delicate of all livestock, and reproduces itself the least easily. As early as the first century of the Empire there were complaints of its inadequacy; in spite of some temporary recoveries, the decline in numbers of slaves became more and more serious during the decadence of Rome and the barbarian age. A dwindling herd demands special care. Slaves had perforce to be better treated, given a half-capacity in law, encouraged to set up a family by the provision of a cottage (casa) and a guarantee of possession in perpetuity of the plots they cultivated. In the case of craftsmen, their wages were fixed and they were granted well-defined legal protection. All these were no more than the expedients of stock-breeders who saw their property endangered, but the 'cattle' benefited, to the great advantage of what we call civilization.

But should the gains of the slaves lead us to believe that there was some progress in humanitarian feeling, we need only glance at the fate of free men to be undeceived. Except for the ruling class and a steadily decreasing middle class, free men gradually slipped down the scale to the point at which the ordinary peasant (colonus) was no better off than the slave who had a cottage (*servus casatus*), and where the craftsman no longer reaped any benefit from his free birth.

At the root of this decline, as of the slave's advance, lies the demographic crisis. We have seen how, when the Empire found itself forced to extort ever greater sacrifices in taxes and labour from a declining population, it applied the principle of collective responsibility to craft guilds, village communities and other groups. The present and financially solvent had to discharge the debt of the missing and insolvent. Work ceased to be a freely chosen profession and became an *officium*, an irrevocable public burden. Those who were unwilling to shoulder it could 'commend' themselves to a great man, that is, subordinate to him their freedom (full possession of their goods and the right to work for others besides him) in return for his taking over their responsibilities.

But was this really an alternative? The great man was himself hard pressed by taxation, and even more by the scarcity of manpower to cultivate his land and make objects for him. Hence he restored their property and initiative to his new subordinates only in return for obligations scarcely less heavy than those they sought to avoid.

The barbarian age carried this development further. Taxes diminished but the State became weaker, to the profit of no one but the powerful. Wealth was not enough to guarantee independence; it was essential to be well armed. Most of the free men who had not yet 'commended' themselves found that they were delivered up to the despotic whim of a lord. Gradually they lost even the memory of their former freedom, trade guilds and village communities became simply teams of serfs, and the laws punished as 'sedition' the few attempts of degraded free men to force the hand of the lords. Nevertheless, these half-free men, like the half-free slaves, found a measure of protection in the fact that the shortage of manpower obliged every lord who wanted to be a wise administrator to treat them with some sparingness.

Bankruptcy or promise?

Certainly the barbarian age was not entirely and everywhere an age of darkness. If we look at things from the point of view of Germany instead of concentrating our gaze on the Graeco-Roman world, we find the relationship between antiquity and the early Middle Ages reversed. For the Germans, the first centuries of the Middle Ages swept away the barriers which in the Ancient World had isolated them from the great centres of Mediterranean civilization and the Christian religion, and had slowed down their first advance towards a stable and organized political life. As for the Romans, they learnt only secondary skills from the Germans, such as the use of buttons and the making of felt. But they came into contact with a society which by living in a different climate at a different intellectual level had found different solutions to certain common problems. Some of these solutions contained seeds which could not come to much in the sterile Europe of the barbarian age, but were to bear fruit in the dawn of Europe during the later Middle Ages. We shall come back to them all in good time.

All in all, the invasions gave the *coup de grâce* to a culture which had come to a standstill after reaching its apogee, and seemed doomed to wither away. We are reminded of the cruel bombing in our own day which destroyed ramshackle old buildings and so made possible the reconstruction of towns on more modern lines. But if we remember that reconstruction after the barbarian onslaught had to wait for four or five centuries, we shall hesitate to give any credit for it to those responsible for the destruction.

Voltaire's Pangloss whispers in our ear that if ancient civilization had not been kicked out of its fine mansion, modern civilization could not have blossomed on that soil. What would have happened, in fact, if the mansion had not been abandoned? To find the answer we must look at the wing which suffered no change of tenant — the Byzantine Empire.

Chapter 3

THE EAST WITHDRAWS FROM THE WEST

I. 'IMPERATOR ROMANORUM, VASILEVS ROMEON'

'THE pope is a boor: he does not know that the holy Emperor Constantine transferred here [to Constantinople] the sceptre, the whole senate and the Roman militia, leaving only base serfs at Rome. . .' 'We are well aware that the Emperor Constantine came here; but as you have changed your tongue, your customs and dress, the most holy Pope felt that the title of Romans would displease you rather than not. . .'

This exchange of taunts between the Greek Emperor Nicephorus II and Liudprand of Cremona, the ambassador of the German Emperor Otto I, in 968, leaves us few illusions about the feelings the twin civilizations harboured for each other, five centuries after they emerged from the womb of the Graeco-Roman world. Another five centuries, and Constantinople would become Istanbul, with less regret, perhaps, than she would have felt had she become a 'satellite' of the Latins.

Prejudices ancient and modern

Beside the indisputable successes of which the western Middle Ages can rightly be proud, the gradual drifting apart of the peoples who had for so long shared the triple heritage of Athens, Rome and Jerusalem is a tragic failure, a failure not entirely without bearing on the antagonism between East and West which we suffer today. But no one likes to admit responsibility for lost opportunities, and some Western historians lay the blame on Byzantium, accusing her of debasing the culture of the Ancient World. Others excuse the separation by arguing that it was inevitable from the beginning, or claiming that it was necessary so that the West could turn to the north.

Both allegations are refuted by the history of the early Middle Ages. The Byzantine Empire spread its culture and religion northwards quite as successfully as did the Latins of the west. It created an orthodox Europe that ran the whole length of Catholic Europe from the Mediterranean to the Baltic; there was no insurmountable barrier between these two parallel extensions of the Graeco-Roman stock as long as the two centres of diffusion, Constantinople and Rome, were in agreement. True, their agreement was never very cordial, but the differences between Latins and Greeks were originally slighter than those between Latins and Germans or Greeks and Slavs.

The same ambassador who reports the dispute between the two capitals, a native of Italy and bishop of the Roman obedience, reserves his most severe criticisms for the citizens of his own metropolis: 'We Lombards, Saxons, Franks, Lotharingians, Bavarians, Swabians, Burgundians, have such scorn for the Romans that to insult our enemies we call them Romans ... for this title covers ... all vices that there are'. And for his part the Emperor Nicephorus, who treated the Pope so haughtily and flung at the Saxons an even more venomous epithet (*pellicei*, 'covered with skins', which to a Byzantine in his silks meant 'like wild beasts'), seized the opportunity of the first diplomatic quarrel with the Bulgars to call their Czar 'a prince clad in skins and reigning over filthy beggars'. But on the other hand the Germans thought Byzantine robes thoroughly effeminate!

The problem of language

We must be careful not to adopt these prejudices, this false patriotism, in our own fashion. If it is true that it is not the coat that makes the gentleman or skins the savage, it is just as true that Byzantium kept closer than the West to the traditions of classical culture. Certainly the West did in the end outshine Byzantium, after a long period of being her poor relation, but not through keeping more faithfully to the ways of the Ancient World; on the contrary, through a more fruitful debasement of them.

Of the three accusations that Otto I's ambassador levelled against the Roman legitimacy of the Byzantine Empire (the change of language, customs and dress), only one is worth dwelling on. After the time of Justinian, Latin was abandoned in favour of Greek as the official language of the Empire. From the time of Heraclius (610–641), even the title of the 'Emperor of the Romans' residing at Constantinople was translated into Greek: *Basileus Romaion* or, according to Byzantine pronunciation, *Vasilevs Romeon*. Later, in the ninth century, Emperor Michael III told Pope Nicholas I that Latin was a 'barbarous and Scythian tongue' — to which the Pope replied that 'an emperor who would be called Roman and does not understand the Roman tongue makes himself ridiculous'.

The total eclipse of Latin harmed the Empire still more than that of Greek damaged the western countries; for though Greek had been almost the second official language of the ancient Empire, Latin was far more widely known and continued to be the common medium for the western cultured people. It is true that knowledge of Greek enabled the Byzantine intellectuals to drink deep of the springs of classical thought; but since Byzantium at first made no attempt to impose that language on the liturgy of the Slav peoples she converted, Greek remained the property of her citizens only. The eastern community of nations, unlike the western one, had no common tongue that could ensure mutual understanding.

The religious problem

Nevertheless, beliefs and rites, which are more far-reaching and more charged with emotional force than any form of Esperanto, might perhaps have succeeded in holding the different Christian peoples together if only the spirit of the times had been as tolerant as it was religious. On the contrary, the bitterest quarrels of East and West were in the name of Christ.

We need not repeat all the old clichés: the theological subtlety of Byzantium, the indestructible paganism of the Latins, the blind fanaticism of the Middle Ages. Let us admit, rather, that in all ages and lands the delicate plant of tolerance does not flourish at the centre of our spiritual life; it grows precariously in fields which do not lie too close to our hearts. We have in our own times sinned too grievously by political and national intolerance to blame other ages for having rejected compromise or diversity in matters where eternal salvation seemed at stake.

From the beginning of the Middle Ages controversies over the nature of the Son and his position within the Trinity were an unfailing source of discord. The condemnation of Arius, who had denied the consubstantiality of Father and Son, almost succeeded in cutting off most of the Germans from the Christian republic, and with them, if their subject peoples had followed suit, almost the whole of the West. The struggle went on until the 'heresy' was extirpated. In the seventh century the efforts of the Byzantine emperors to find a formula on the two natures of the Son which would be acceptable to the Catholics of the West as well as to the Monophysites and Nestorians of Egypt and Syria, flung both these countries into the arms of the Persian and Arab conquerors. The Catholics were content with no less than the unconditional surrender of the emperors to their point of view. But then, in the eighth century, the measures which the emperors took against images inflamed the East and thrust the Catholic towards the king of the Franks. Once again, compromise and half-measures proved useless, and peace was restored only with the unconditional surrender of the emperors. Finally, did the Holy Ghost proceed from the Father alone, as in the formula of the primitive Creed, or from the Father and the Son, as the Catholics insisted? This problem started a schism which has never been ended.

These conflagrations were usually kindled, and in any case fanned into flame, in ecclesiastical circles; but they spread rapidly through all classes; not even the most remote localities escaped. It was not necessary to follow the arguments of the doctors to take a passionate interest in their consequences for a soul in quest of guidance, whether the problem was God's presence in the physical image or the equality of the incarnate Son with the Father in heaven. Almost always, when it came to a choice between two theories, the Western world cherished the one which brought God closer to men, while the East rejected any compromise that threatened to debase the spirituality of God. But other contrasts — the contrast between intellectuals and masses, between rationalists and mystics, who were to be found in the West as well as the East — were superimposed on the differences between the two Romes and made their opposition less clearcut.

In spite of these religious disputes, the political and cultural ties between Constantinople and Rome were for long proof against all strains. Justinian's reconquest, the Lombard invasion, the parallel progress of Greek and Latin influences on the Slavs, had thrown down the partition-wall, thin but easily visible, which had divided the Empires of East and West. The dividing-line now was shifting and discontinuous. Venice, Catholic but Byzantine; Moravia, converted by Byzantine missionaries but later won for Catholicism, are only two examples of the interdependence constantly recurring between two kindred civilizations.

Christian Europe or Catholic Europe?

All through the early Middle Ages Constantinople was the City of Light of Europe. One could condemn her doctrines, detest her customs, despise her armies, but it was almost impossible to escape her charm, or refuse the cultural and material gifts she offered her friends. True, her friends gradually fell away, until at last the West became the stronger and attacked Byzantium with all the insolence of youth. Even then, the opposite claims of the political and religious leaders of the eastern and western sides implicitly indicated that ultimately there was only one community of Christian people. Emperors of West and East, popes of Rome and 'oecumenical' patriarchs of Constantinople — they each claimed the whole heritage of Roman universality.

It is true that these ambitions condemned to failure all attempts to form a united Christian front against the Moslems. All the same, the attempts, which were constantly repeated until the end of the Middle Ages and after, show that the world of Byzantium and the Western world were worlds separated, no doubt, but no more strangers to each other than are Protestant and Catholic Europe nowadays.

If for all that our book gives only a side-glance at Orthodox Europe, that is not because we disown it. But an essay as clearly limited in geographical scope as ours can give only one projection: that of the West, since we write in the West. At least we can appease our historical conscience by adopting henceforth for this western world in gestation, which presumptuous usage calls 'Christian Europe', the more exact term of 'Catholic Europe'.

II. THE EAST'S TRUMP CARDS

There is no greater temptation than to explain the course of events by definite and inescapable causes. Since the Eastern Empire survived as best it could the storm which engulfed the Western Empire, historians have stressed the advantages, economic, strategic and intellectual, which they claim made it more robust or less vulnerable. Byzantium had more fertile land, more inhabitants,

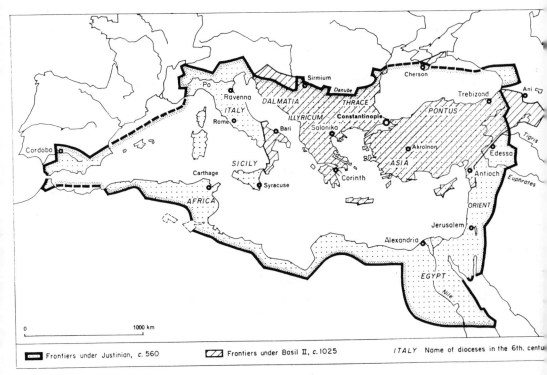

Map 5. The Byzantine Empire at the death of Basil II (1025).

more trade. Her frontier was shorter, and less exposed to Germanic attack, especially since the most warlike tribes had slaked their greed at the expense of the western countries; Constantinople especially, standing at the apex of a triangle of land, with the sea on two sides, was incomparably stronger than Rome, Ravenna, or any other of the western centres of resistance. Finally, the great cities of the Hellenistic East had never lost their superiority over the western towns as centres of culture and nodes of trade.

All that is true, but it is not the whole truth. The West too had its granaries and vineyards, and the East was not without its deserts and ravines. Though the Germans bore down harder on the West, the Slavs bore down harder on the East. Persian pressure fell on the eastern frontier alone, and the East was always the first, if not the sole, victim of attack from Asiatic nomads, Huns,

Avars, Bulgars, Hungarians, Petchenegs and Turks. These were redoubtable
neighbours indeed! Although the economic and intellectual development of the
eastern half of the Empire on the whole outshone that of the western half, it
would be a mistake to forget the industries of Milan or Cologne, and an injustice
to deny the cultural contribution of the Africa of St Augustine, the Gaul of
Ausonius, or the Italy of St Ambrose and later of Boethius.

The fact remains that the East had more winning cards, but not an overwhelming superiority: her fate was different essentially because the game did
not change hands. Graeco-Roman civilization, sick as it was, was not incurable
so long as the barbarians did not finish it off. In the East, where it escaped them
by a hair's-breadth, it recovered to live for another ten centuries, that is, all
through the 'Middle Ages' of the West (Map 5).

Byzantium survived by adapting herself

Naturally, Byzantine civilization survived only at the cost of many changes:
constant adjustment is the condition of life. Only a small part of these changes
represented a return to the pre-crisis régime. Gradually the pressure which
kept every worker, peasant or employee at his trade or his post slackened; some
of the heaviest taxes were abolished or lightened from the end of the fifth
century, which seems to have seen a modest economic recovery throughout the
Mediterranean world. In Italy and France historians give the credit for this
recovery to Theodoric, even to Clovis. It must not be forgotten that their
contemporary too, the Emperor Anastasius, improved the conditions of the
subjects of the new Rome, and left a well-filled treasury, with scarcely any
lowering of the standard that the Empire, even reduced to its eastern half,
owed to itself.

Justinian (527–65) had greater ambitions — to recapture dominion of the
world — and for these emptied the treasury and again overstepped the
limits that even a merciless financial system cannot ignore with impunity
if it has an eye to the future. His successors, between the end of the sixth
and the beginning of the tenth century, were forced on to the defensive,
and could count themselves fortunate if they regained one or other of the
provinces so recently wrested from them; but wars and natural calamities
prevented them from lightening the fiscal burden to any great extent.

Even without taking literally all the denunciations in Byzantine sources
of the rapacity of governments (has the tax-collector ever had a good
press?), we can be sure that taxes of all kinds were of far greater importance in Byzantium than in the barbarian states. But it is certain too that
the emperors never forgot the difference between public revenue and their
private income, and that the Byzantine government tried to match the
sacrifices it imposed on its subjects with real services. In any case the
sacrifices, though heavy, were bearable; the long survival of the Empire
proves it.

Mediaeval, but not barbarian

Most of the other changes during the course of the early Middle Ages were of the same nature as in the West, but slower, curbed by the resistance of the old institutions and traditions. Byzantium adapted herself without sudden changes of pace or direction. She too saw the gradual formation of a serf class: partially enfranchised slaves, and free men ensnared in the protection of the great. But she never saw either the slaves or the ordinary free men reduced to negligible quantities in economic, social and political life. It can even be claimed that at least until the mid tenth century the mass of free commoners counterbalanced the power of the privileged few. As in Catholic Europe, culture declined and tended to seek refuge in the churches and monasteries, but the secular upper class was not illiterate and held learning in high esteem. Classic Greek turned to vernacular, but the literary language was still used. The law lost its subtlety and precision, yet Justinian's corpus of Roman law was still read, translated, re-ordered and commented upon. Art became more and more symbolic and childish while producing a stream of masterpieces in a new style.

So many elements of greatness were mingled with the waning of the ancient world that we cannot call it simply decadence. There was no sudden collapse into an abyss, but a descent to a level which, though less impressive than that of antiquity, was not without original light. Byzantium was never without gifted theologians, chroniclers, architects, goldsmiths or merchants. The masses were well below that level, but their spiritual and material life was better maintained than in the West.

Whatever the inadequacy of 'popular' epics as a mirror of collective feelings, a comparison between Roland the Paladin and Digenis Akritas, his Byzantine counterpart, brings out the relation between Byzantium and the early medieval West most vividly. The real Digenis, who died in 788 (ten years after the real Roland) also was a frontier man, who spent his epic life fighting the Arabs for the sake of glory, God, and (to a lesser extent) his Emperor. Most of his legendary exploits would have suited Roland perfectly. But he was born on Hellenic soil, and the poets make him spend three years getting a literary education, and show him ever ready to succumb to the charms of spring fever and good-looking girls.

Byzantium, the melting-pot of nations

How far were these achievements the work of the people who gave to the Empire its admirable language, Greek? Some of the best Byzantine emperors were Armenians, the best lawyers were Syrians; the Slavs seem to have exerted considerable influence on agrarian economy and its institutions; Scandinavians and Italians apparently provided the models for shipbuilding; Iran and Egypt provided the most beautiful of the designs that Byzantine craftsmen wove with the thread of the silkworm, imported from China.

Whatever the case, the new Rome, like the old though to a lesser degree, was great because she was a melting-pot of nations, and original because she freely absorbed the ideas of others without losing self-awareness. While in the West 'barbarians' and 'Romans' took centuries to amalgamate — and then only by grouping themselves in separate nations — Byzantium made every effort to be the common motherland of all who were ready to accept her civil and religious laws and help her to mount guard against the 'barbarians' without. That, with the economic, strategic and intellectual advantages we have noted already, was her highest card.

III.   BYZANTINE CIVILIZATION OF THE EARLY MIDDLE AGES

To describe the original characteristics of Byzantine civilization in a few pages is a challenge we cannot take up. It needs a whole volume to itself. But we will at least sketch in two or three guiding lines as an indication of what the presence of Byzantium at her very gates meant to Catholic Europe in the early Middle Ages, that is, at the time when the West was most backward.

The only State worthy of the name

Probably what made most impression on the imagination of Byzantium's neighbours was the sight of a centralized state, with a standing army, an extensive and specialized bureaucracy, schools, state-aided hospitals — in short the only state worthy of the name that still remained in Christendom. Her sovereign was in principle required to respect his own laws and his predecessors', to consider the wishes of his people (expressed through different central and local organs), and to observe and enforce the commandments of the Church.

And yet, if these general rules were enough to distinguish him from the barbarian kings — leaders of the army and owners of kingdoms rather than sovereigns under public law — they limited only slightly the powers of an emperor who was soon calling himself *autokrator* and *isapostolos*, that is, the equal of the Apostles. The people had been brought to heel long before Justinian's time. They regained a certain influence in the course of the controversy over images, but usually their anger broke out only in rare revolts against some tyrant who seemed weaker than the others.

The Church was a more serious rival, but in the East she dared not contend with Caesar for what traditionally was his alone. The pope was too far from the Byzantine capital, and too often forced to displease the Greeks, to make himself the champion of the ideas of the Latins. The Patriarch of Constantinople, on the other hand, within striking distance of the Emperor and his army, needed their support to maintain an attitude of independence in his dealings with Rome.

Monks and iconoclasts

If a dangerous dualism existed, it was not between the accredited heads of the Church and the emperors, but between the emperors and the monks who swarmed in the monasteries, or perched on pillars in the town-centres whenever they were not leading a wandering and faintly picaresque life. Omnipresent, irrepressible, working miracles and prophesying calamities, the weapons they brandished were the countless relics and ikons that it was hardly possible for a believer to withstand.

> Reaction set in, however, just when their triumph seemed most certain. Some of the faithful still felt uneasy when they thought of the Biblical prohibition of the worship of images; even if they had forgotten it, there were the Jewish and Moslem polemists to remind them. The wealth the clergy had accumulated gave rise to criticism and envy. Widespread monasticism laid a still heavier burden on the laity, who, as a result of it, had to furnish the State with yet more recruits and workdays. Here were valuable allies for any Emperor who dared attack the only competitors for his power he need fear. Leo III, after his victory over the Arabs at the siege of Constantinople, felt strong enough to open hostilities on the home front, before continuing a campaign which would call for the mobilization of all the Empire's resources in materials and manpower. In 726 he destroyed the ikon of Christ over the gate of his palace. It was the beginning of the controversy which almost destroyed the Empire.

Iconoclasts and iconodules (that is, breakers and worshippers of images) fought each other by means fair and foul for more than a century. As in the Investiture Struggle which developed in the West much later, the Church won in the end on the question of principle: veneration of images, if not their worship, was finally re-established in 843 and the memory of the Iconoclasts anathematized (Pl. 4). But meanwhile the driving force of monasticism had been broken; even if the monks regained power, there was to be no theocracy in Byzantium.

Provinces and local autonomy

In the field of local autonomy the Emperor gained another half-victory. In the East as in the West the central government could not possibly have kept full power and personal direction of affairs through the whole extent of the Empire. Even after Germans, Slavs, Bulgars and Arabs had cut away its peripheral provinces, the Empire was unwieldily large.

The Emperor surrendered to his delegates (exarchs, dukes, *strategi* or, sometimes, municipal colleges) more and more of the responsibility for carrying on government and war, with the manpower they could find on the spot and without too much reliance on the instructions and reinforcements which the central government sent them when it could. Several of these delegated commands, surrounded by the enemy for years or centuries, ended by making themselves independent (as did Sardinia, Naples, the Dalmatian coast) or by letting themselves be swallowed up (like Carthage, Ravenna, Cherson). But others held out until a change of fortune restored them to the bosom of the Empire — for though the history of Byzantium, seen from a distance, may look like a long retreat, it was in fact an alternation of withdrawals and advances. Besides, the vital central regions of the Empire (western Asia Minor, Thrace, and the European coast of the Aegean) were not often seriously threatened, despite the extent of the powers of their *strategi* and the invasions which sometimes swept ruthlessly over them.

The Emperor took advantage of these flows and ebbs to replace the most intractable of his nobles and great landowners by others more loyal, or by communities of peasants transplanted from a distance and ready to shed their blood for their land in the Roman tradition of the soldier-farmer. Of course there were disloyal governors, incorrigible landowners, dissident communities. But the sovereign never became, as in the West, a 'roi fainéant' (sluggard king) or a marshal of the nobility or clergy. The law of the Empire did not have to bow to the will of individuals or to local custom. No one questioned the right of the Emperor to raise troops and taxes wherever he wished.

Sailors and farmers

The link between Constantinople and the provinces was not broken even at the beginning of the seventh century, when Persians and Avars almost succeeded in closing in on it in a pincer-movement, or later when Arabs and Bulgars again threatened its destruction. Without minimizing the Byzantine trump-cards we have noted, this recovery can only be explained by what a country gentleman of the eleventh century called 'the speciality of Romania' — her navy. It was not a question only of the Greek fire thrown *at longrange* from the 'siphons' of her ships, but far more of the feeling for the sea that never deserted the descendants of Ulysses. This ensured for Byzantium not only continued relations with foreign lands, but the essential minimum of internal communications, at a time when most of the world was splitting up into smaller and smaller watertight compartments.

The sea reached into the heart of the Empire and surrounded many of her provinces. The demographic crisis and economic distress might force Byzantium to let most of the roads that Rome maintained at vast expense fall into disrepair; trade and industry, the stimulants of city life, might decay, but enough remained to give Byzantine towns a life that few cities of the West enjoyed. Byzantium breathed through the sea.

We need not have a mental picture of crowds of merchants and mounds of merchandise. Nowadays a region as maritime and industrial as Brittany has 70 per cent of agriculturists, and we can well allow more than 90 per cent to Byzantium without bringing her into the same class as the nations which may have reckoned up to 99 per cent.

Unfortunately the non-agricultural classes were still too few to overcome the old prejudices which from antiquity had given agriculture the monopoly of social prestige and political authority. Byzantium, saved from defeat and rusticity by her seamen, let them govern themselves according to their own customs — the *Nomos Nautikos* is the only collection of private law which was honoured by inclusion in the ninth century in the great imperial code, the *Basilika* — but she dispensed her real favours to the great landowners or, at a pinch, to the peasants. We have already stressed how this impasse condemned the economy of the Ancient World to mediocrity.

The Byzantine economy of the early Middle Ages too, with its absence of any capitalist spirit and lack of mechanization, showed itself incapable of accumulating reserves against time of war or famine, or mobilizing its surpluses to make a good year the take-off for sustained economic growth. It never even equalled the successes of the Graeco-Roman economy of antiquity because its territorial bases were more restricted and it more rarely enjoyed the benefits of peace. The progress it did make in some fields — techniques of navigation and the silk industry, the use of serfs instead of slaves — was so slow that the West easily outstripped them in the later Middle Ages.

But there is little point in comparing the achievements of three different periods. In the general economic depression of the early Middle Ages, Byzantium reacted more vigorously than Catholic Europe: in the kingdom of the blind, the one-eyed man is king.

Literature and art

These considerations hold good too for the development of ideas. With the exception of a few writers of genius, becoming rarer and rarer, Byzantine literature of the early Middle Ages presents a rather depressing picture. Of course there are useful pieces of information in the chronicles; entertaining snapshots of everyday life find their way into the lives of saints. But in general those lives show the most naive credulity side by side with an unfortunate contempt for originality — for it can hardly be called originality when every narrator strives to go one better than his predecessor in his account of miracles and apparitions. The informed reader will console himself with the answer of the old superior in John Moschus' *Spiritual Meadow* to the young monk who was bored with convent life: 'You would not be bored if you thought about hell'. And it must be emphasized that the Byzantine people, like those of the West, expressed their emotions more successfully in liturgical chant and epic song, whose traces survive chiefly in works which incorporated them after the ninth century. Furthermore, the reaction which followed 843 created a great void in literary documentation by suppressing almost everything the Iconoclasts had written.

It made amends to posterity however, by ensuring the continuation of figurative art when it was threatened with extinction by the western peoples' lack of aptitude and the Moslems' religious scruples. The mosaics that are the

crowning glory of Byzantium did not go back to the realism of the Roman age
(besides the technical skill that would have been needed to reproduce it, the
taste for realism had vanished), but they passed through several phases of
abstraction, each one as striking as the next. Before the end of the seventh
century (Fig. 9) the theatrical compositions of the Justinian age, filled with
figures that were stylized but corporeal and heavily adorned, gave way to great
monochrome surfaces, against which one central image stood out, the sign of
the presence of God. At the same time allegorical representations of the Godhead disappeared, banned by the Council of 692 (which the West did not
recognize). Later, when the heat of the controversy over Images had died down,
this austere and aloof form of art mellowed. Without losing any of their dignity,
the madonnas and Christs were clothed in a beauty that was still a little stiff,
but profoundly human (Pl. 5).

*Fig. 9.   Parenzo (Yugoslavia): Bishop Euphrasius, founder of the basilica.
Mosaic in the apse, sixth century.*

Just as in her mosaics and paintings, so in the arts wrongly called 'minor',
Byzantium displayed that passion for rich colours and materials which seems
to become more marked in times when money and intellectual equipment are
scarce. No doubt the barbarians also covered their crosses, their crowns and
jewellery with glittering stones and multicoloured enamels. But Byzantium still
retained enough economic resources and artistic experience to outshine the
Frankish or Lombard goldsmith and engraver. Gold, silver, ivory, precious
stones, marbles, glass beads, cloisonné work, fabrics of silk and linen, everything

that shines or can take on irridescent colours, were used in a profusion that rivalled the masterpieces of the Arab or Chinese Empires, both infinitely vaster and more populous than Byzantium. Other civilizations have handed down to posterity the memory of power, poise or grace; it is the profusion of Constantinople that has made its mark on popular fantasy and the imagination of poets.

St Sophia, the masterpiece of Justinian's architects, and so many other churches of lesser size but glowing with colour and enhanced by a multiplicity of cupolas; the palaces traversed by processions of dignitaries clad in purple and brocades; the markets glutted with spices, scents, victuals; the gold coinage, especially the besant that holds all historical records for the unchanging survival of its name and weight through the centuries — these are the most striking symbols of the new Rome.

Economic policy

Yet Constantinople was not an Eldorado. Her walls, encircling an area scarcely greater than that of Aurelian Rome (one-third the size of Paris within the perimeter of her fortifications, or one-fifth of the Chinese capital, Ch'ang An, in the eighth century), sheltered plenty of the destitute. Several emperors tried to reduce their numbers by ordering the police to enrol all unemployed in the corporations of bakers and gardeners, where they would be set to arduous work. More charitably, Romanus II (959–63) partitioned off porticoes of the main streets to shelter from the icy winds from the Bosphorus the beggars who spent the night there. Even in the busiest and best paid trades, manual work was hard (Fig. 10); competition from slaves and serfs lowered the wages of free workmen. Distribution of bread to the populace, which ancient Rome bestowed on her proletariat at the expense of the provinces, did not survive the loss of Egypt in the seventh century. Though the government was anxious to pacify the crowds of the capital, it also wanted to spare the peasants of Asia Minor and Thrace, on whose prosperity depended the treasury and the army. But it did what it could, together with the city corporations, to prevent a minority getting rich at the expense of the community, and to ensure a cheap supply of bread, meat and fish. The result was the plethora of measures, sometimes contradictory, which every controlled economy brings in its train.

No other state of the early Middle Ages, or perhaps of antiquity, applied an economic policy so consistently, or with such awareness of its aims, as the Byzantine government. Unfortunately the aims were difficult to attain and hard to reconcile with one another. What Byzantium wanted was a magnificent Court, an overflowing treasury, and a satisfied people.

It was not altogether her fault that she so rarely achieved the third item of this programme; even if she had been able to force the rich to share their superfluity with the poor, she would not have got enough to satisfy all needs at all times. It is remarkable enough that she was concerned with the problem at all, in an age when the rich were so indifferent to the welfare of the people.

To fill the treasury without adding overmuch to the already dangerously heavy burden of taxation, Byzantium tried almost all the means that were later to be used with more coherence and strictness by the experts of the age of mercantilism, they ranged from measures designed to increase agricultural and industrial production, to restrictions on export of precious metals, strategic materials and essential foodstuffs. After a brief interval of liberal euphoria our governments have come back to a policy of the same kind, though they have not managed to eliminate its disadvantages or guarantee its success.

Byzantium succeeded better over her magnificent Court. Before we deplore the undeniable fact that it was extremely expensive, we should emphasize that its pomp impressed foreigners and pleased the citizens. It survives in works of art that delight us even today.

IV. ENTER THE ARABS

We have noted (p. 35) that Justinian's 'reconquest' came shortly before the Chinese Empire took the offensive again; but China was completely successful, while Byzantium was halted half way. Without carrying a comparison between two such different empires too far, we should note that the Chinese were fighting only barbarians, while Byzantium had to wage war simultaneously against barbarian enemies and civilized ones: first Persia, then Islam.

Rightly or wrongly, the Romans had almost always considered a war against their inferiors less pressing than one against their equals. The barbarians, it was believed, only half completed their conquests, and sooner or later relaxed their grip. Also they could be held in check by fortified towns, egged on to fight among themselves, sometimes even made into good citizens. Faithful to this tradition, the first successors of Justinian temporized with the Lombards and Visigoths, Slavs and Avars, the better to contain the Persians. Then the sudden overwhelming victories of the 'King of Kings', Chosroes II, came within an ace of winning the duel finally for Persia; but they were followed almost at once by a dramatic reversal of fortune which allowed the Emperor Heraclius, between 614 and 630, to bring Persia to bay. Egypt was rewon, Jerusalem recovered in an expedition which aroused religious fervour foreshadowing the crusades; Chosroes was deposed by his son, who accepted a humiliating peace. The dream that had been vainly pursued by Crassus, Caesar, Antony, Trajan, the Severi and Julian seemed about to become reality.

Unfortunately at that very moment a people till then obscure, little less backward than the Germans and far less numerous, changed the dream into a nightmare. How could the Vasilevs of Constantinople or the King of Kings of Ctesiphon, locked in their epic struggle, be expected to take any notice when in 622 a herdsman and trader, inspired with the spirit of prophecy, fled with a handful of followers from Mecca to Medina? The episode seemed even more insignificant than the crucifixion of a poor wretch at Golgotha, in the reign of Tiberius! But ten years later, when Mohammed died, the latest of the great religions of the world was fully formed, and its believers ready for the holy war which in less than a century carved out for Islam an empire greater than the Roman Empire at its height.

As early as 638 the Arabs had swallowed up all Persia and seized from Byzantium Palestine and Syria; they had taken Egypt in 642; well before 732 they had won central Asia as far as the Roof of the World, northern Africa to the fringes of the tropics, the Iberian peninsula up to the gorges and passes of

Fig. 10. Builders erecting a column. After a Byzantine miniature, Bibliothèque Nationale, Paris.

the Pyrenees. Their vanguard had even passed, or would soon pass, beyond those limits, in a series of offensives against Chinese, Hindus, Byzantines and Franks, which, taken as a whole, could be called the first 'hemispheric' (or even 'world') war that earth has known.

Originality of the Arab synthesis

Despite some characteristics which they shared at first with other barbarians, and which time and success never wholly effaced — a leaning to nomadic life and adventure, impatience with any form of government outside the framework of family or tribe — the Arabs from the very first gave evidence of qualities as assimilators and organizers that no barbarian people had shown before them. They combined the fruit of experience with the flexibility of a fresh start. Quicker than the Germans to make use of what was still viable in the surviving Graeco-Roman tradition, with more freedom than the Byzantines to choose between that tradition and the almost equally rich heritage of Persia, closer to the language and atmosphere of the Old Testment than any other of the peoples who found inspiration in Jewish thought, the Arabs forged a powerful and original synthesis. Because they had no hesitation in borrowing whatever they lacked, they could develop and propagate their adolescent culture in their own fashion without surrendering any of its essential characteristics.

These characteristics went back in part to the pre-Islamic age (their poetry, for instance, had flowered before Mohammed), but the new religion entirely remoulded them. Islam not only established the foundations on which rested the spiritual conscience and the aggressive patriotism of the Arabs, but also their system of government, canons of law and even linguistic standards, for the Koran, read and learnt by heart in every Moslem community, has remained to our own day the unalterable standard of Arab literature. The Old Testament had done as much for the Jews, but the Jews had remained a very small nation. The Gospel had conquered the Roman Empire, but had given to Caesar his due. No doubt it had influenced the language, law and political theories of the peoples who accepted it, but it had not swamped their pre-existing traditions.

The new religion confronts the old

The impact of Islam had revolutionary consequences in most of the territories conquered by the Arabs: the structure of government and administration, the legal institutions, the very spirit of the law and even the language and writing of the country, gave way and adapted themselves to the teaching of the Prophet, as found either in the Koran or in a more or less authentic oral tradition. This was a triumph of religion, not of theocracy, for Islam had neither consecrated clergy nor any spiritual head of the Church. Her caliphs were the successors of the Prophet only in the temporal government. Among the regions where this triumph was most complete must be counted Palestine, Syria, Egypt and north Africa — a good third of the old *Republica Romana* and, it may be noted, the third which had received the Gospel first.

> What was the attraction of the Moslem religion? It is not a historian's business to pronounce on questions of faith, but he may be allowed to point out that Islam, the child of the early Middle Ages, was as well suited to its times as Christianity had been to the declining years of the Ancient World into which it was born. It was a straightforward religion for a destitute age. Its fundamental principles were abstract enough to satisfy the intellectuals, its promises concrete enough to attract the masses. Its uncompromising monotheism eliminated all those problems that divided Christians, the mysteries of the Trinity or the value of images. Jesus was honoured as the greatest of the prophets after Abraham and before Mohammed, but was no more than a man; Allah, like the Elohim of the Old Testament whose attributes he shared, was out of reach of the humanizing effect of images. On the other hand, the paradise which lay open to those who lived or died for the faith had all the human characteristics that the austerity of the creed withheld from the Creator: it was full of material, palpable pleasures. (Westerners have never forgiven Mohammed his *houris*, the eternal virgins who awaited the blessed; but except for *houris*, the paradises which early medieval Christian writers naively described to the faithful were hardly more idealized.) To these attractions must be added the prestige which naturally attaches to the religion of a conquering people, and the material advantages which conversion to Islam brought to their subjects. Indeed, though Moslems treated Christians, Jews and Zoroastrians with a tolerance extraordinary at that time, they began by imposing a special tax on them which did not apply to believers, whether of long standing or recent converts.

It can be questioned whether the Byzantines understood the revolutionary importance of the Moslem religion: their theologians obstinately refused to consider it as anything but a Christian heresy invented by a madman or an impostor, and Catholic theologians followed suit (Fig. 11). Yet the fact that the Arabs were not ordinary 'barbarians' certainly did not escape the Byzantines. The place once occupied by Persia, the traditional counterpoise of the Graeco-Roman community, reverted by right to the conquerors of Persia. Certainly, the imperial chancellery never renounced its claim to the West; certainly, the emperors were often forced to divert troops from the main 'front' to meet the pressure of some enemy invading the Balkans or another of the Empire's European possessions; but henceforward the attention of the Byzantine state and people was concentrated on the Arabs. The chief Greek historian of the time, Theophanes, may confuse one pope with another, but he is perfectly sound on the succession of caliphs. At the beginning of the tenth century the Patriarch of Constantinople writes to the Emir of Crete in these terms: 'The two powers of the universe, Saracens and Romans, shine out like the two great

Fig. 11. Caricature of Mohammed, in the margin of a Latin translation of the Koran. Manuscript in the Bibliothèque de l'Arsenal, Paris, 1162.

luminaries of the firmament. So we must live together as brothers, although we differ in custom, manners and religion.'

Obviously these diplomatic compliments were dictated by mutual fear rather than cordiality. Each of the 'two powers' was watching its chance to expand at the expense of the other; each was taught by its faith to expect the damnation or conversion of all the other's nationals, sooner or later before the Last Judgment. But the fact remains that from the middle of the eighth century onwards the two rivals were resigned to co-existence on equal terms, until such time as the 'iron curtain' between them should be thrown down by the triumph of Truth.

The 'hemispheric war' and the new equilibrium

This equilibrium was the outcome of a bitter struggle, in which the 'hemispheric war' was the last phase. The Arab tide ebbed, after four battles, two at the centre and two at the opposite ends of the vast deployment of Islam. Our textbooks, which take their bearings from the Greenwich meridian, mention only one, the defeat which Charles Martel inflicted in 732 or 733, between Poitiers and Tours, on a Moslem advance-guard swelled by contingents from Aquitaine. But the fame of this battle in the Christian West was infinitely greater than its military importance; in fact, the Arabs had no longer enough impetus to support them for long in a region so far from their starting point.

This conclusion is inescapable if we compare the results of Poitiers with those of another battle which the Arabs, with Turkish reinforcements, won over the Chinese on the banks of the Talas, in Turkestan, in 751. There they crushed the best general of the T'ang Empire and led back thousands of captives. Chinese expansion in central Asia was shattered, to the delight of poets like Li T'ai-Po, who had accused it of provoking endless and useless slaughter. But the Arabs advanced no further; in the Far East, as in the Far West of their empire, their impetus could no longer carry them. India, too, lay open after the Arabs conquered Sind (712); but it took a long time before they could make further inroads.

It was in the centre of their state, before their successive capitals of Damascus and Baghdad, that the Arabs could show the full measure of their power. But what they had to deal with there was the Byzantine Empire, indomitable even in disaster. Several times thrown back from the very gates of Constantinople, they suffered a serious defeat at the hands of the Emperor Leo III — the enemy of images — at Akroinos in Asia Minor (739). In 747 the Byzantines again triumphed, in a sea battle. The frontier between Islam and Christendom then became fixed, to all intents and purposes, half-way between the Byzantine and Arab capitals. The Arabs kept three-quarters of the territory they had seized from Byzantium, but Byzantium had been the bulwark of an area large enough to be the cradle of Europe (Map 6).

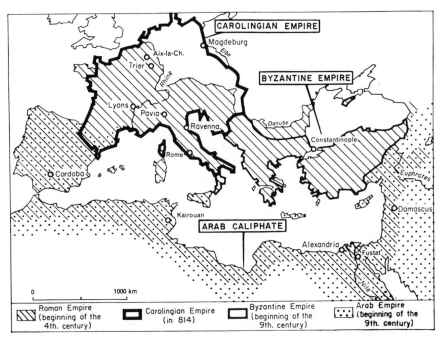

Map 6. Roman, Arab, Carolingian and Byzantine Empires (fourth to ninth centuries)

V. THE ARABS AND EUROPE

If the Germans made the birth of Europe possible, the Arabs made it inevitable. But for Mohammed, Byzantium now freed from the Persian peril would probably have resumed Justinian's plans for reconquest of the West. Even without political reunification, a spiritual and economic community, spreading towards the north but still centred on the Mediterranean, might have blossomed on the old stem of the *Respublica Romana*. This ceased to be a possibility when Byzantium had to entrench herself, militarily and commercially, within what remained of her Empire, and when the African and Asiatic shores of the Mediterranean were bound by religion, language, law, institutions and way of life to a different cultural group: the Islamic community.

Left to herself, western Europe was disoriented. The prestige of the apostolic see, memories of imperial might, the material resources of the strips of Mediterranean coast still remaining in Catholic hands — Languedoc, Provence, Italy as far as the outskirts of Naples and Bari — still pulled her towards the south. But a new Mediterranean, comprising the North Sea and the Baltic, and surrounded by Germanic and Slav lands, had emerged from the mists of prehistory to counterbalance the old Mediterranean, now exhausted and dislocated. Midway between these two seas, in the rural interior of the continent, were to be found the most seasoned warriors and the most fertile lands. It was there that medieval Europe, after some groping, was to find her new centre of gravity: Aix-la-Chapelle under the Carolingians, Goslar under the Salic emperors, and finally — for good and all — Paris.

Three levels, three cultures

Nevertheless we must be careful not to give the Arab conquests the character of a sudden upheaval that we have already refused to see in the Germanic conquests. Old ties are not cut; they loosen slowly, through the centuries. Besides, Europe was at first too poor (and later too exuberant) to constitute a world in itself, like the Graeco-Roman world. Even when international trade was reduced to a minimum by the economic decay of the west, it still bound the shores of the Mediterranean together and linked them with the seas of the north. Rome, the religious capital, absorbed Nordic contributions while ensuring the predominance of the Latin and southern tradition throughout western Christianity. Byzantium withdrew only gradually; her power in the tenth century, her weakness in the twelfth, her fall in the fifteenth, were all occasions that brought the two Empires together, even if not in reconciliation. It is one of the paradoxes of history that it was Islam which after 1000 provided western Europe with important Greek texts that the Roman tradition and the Carolingian renaissance had failed to preserve for her.

At first the contrast between the worlds of Christendom and Islam was not manifested in the same way at all their points of contact. Byzantium clothed her civilization in the same garments as the Catholic West, but in richer materials. In some respects it was easier for her to come to an understanding with Baghdad (which wore clothes of different cut, but the same material) than with her poor country cousins. When we read the accounts of the many Byzantine and Arab travellers who went through the 'iron curtain', we find no doubt plenty of signs of misunderstanding and disapproval on both sides, but also the clear admission of absolute parity in most fields: political institutions, social structures, urban life, intellectual and commercial development.

On the other hand, a vast distance separated Moslem Spain and Catholic France. To get any idea of it, necessarily inaccurate since we have no well-founded figures or general description, we must think of the disparity that existed a hundred years ago between a European nation and its colonies. In the

early Middle Ages writing was a very rare accomplishment north of the Pyrenees; in the south it was almost universal in the upper classes and widespread
in urban populations, if not in the country. France exported practically nothing
but raw materials, Spain the finished products.

The civilization of Moslem Spain (*al-Andalus*) is essentially part of Islamic history, and we will not try to make a place for it in a book on
European history. We need only recall that after a difficult start, under
governors sent out by a caliphate too far away, a period of recovery and
reconstruction began in 750 with the constitution of an independent Moslem state, with its capital at Cordoba. The newcomers, Arabs, Berbers,
slaves and freedmen of all nations, and the old inhabitants, Ibero-
Romans, Jews and Germans, worked together in a climate of toleration.
Each group could keep its own faith and customs, and even close relations with co-religionists living abroad. But the prestige of Islam made
many converts, and Arabic became the chief, if not the only, language.
Al-Andalus shone like a star of the first magnitude in the constellation of
the states which, though developing their own local characteristics, found
their common inspiration in the Koran. In the tenth century, at her
zenith, she would almost equal the political power, the economic wealth
and the intellectual splendour of the Byzantine Empire, which shone
over Europe from the other end of the Mediterranean.

The day was not far off when Catholic Europe, once again struggling to
her feet by her own efforts, would be in a position to benefit from relations
with her Moslem neighbours. But in the early Middle Ages she was
doubly far from this. Both the model of their civilization and its fabrics
were foreign to her; it was beyond her power to imitate them. Even the
little Christian states which sprang to life south of the Pyrenees, born of
a Visigothic nucleus imprudently overlooked by the conquerors in the
mountains of Asturias, generally found inspiration more easily in Carolingian and Capetian France than in the Caliphate of Cordoba. In the
eleventh and twelfth centuries Italy was in many ways a better conductor
of Islamic influences than the 'five kingdoms' (the Asturias and Leon,
Castile, Navarre, Aragon and Portugal) of Catholic Iberia.

Moats and foot-bridges

It is true that wars were an obstacle to communications between Christendom
and Islam. The struggle for the *Reconquista* of the Iberian peninsula, although
interrupted by long truces, went on throughout the Spanish Middle Ages. From
time to time Byzantium imposed very effective blockades on Islam, by land and
sea. But there is no reason to believe that these wars dug deeper moats between
them than did the conflicts between peoples of the same religion. Besides, the
Moslems found allies, whether professed or secret, in several parts of Catholic
Europe; they themselves ceased to form a common front as soon as the Caliphate began to break up, in 750. Half a century later, Charlemagne and

Harun-al-Rashid formed an alliance against the united forces of Byzantium and Cordoba. A hundred years later, Pope John VIII (872–82) tried in vain to detach the bishop-duke of Naples from his Moslem alliance. Let us note in passing that the papyrus on which the pontiff wrote his official letters was made in Egypt, and was headed by an Arabic inscription in honour of Allah — an inscription which as far as the Pope was concerned might just as well have been double Dutch!

Even in the field of religion there were fewer conflicts between Moslems and Christians than between 'orthodox' and 'heretics' within each religion. The doctors on either side were too sure that they had the monopoly of truth to fear the propaganda of the other seriously; at most, they advised their co-religionists who were unskilled in theology not to engage with a doctor of the other faith in arguments in which they might well find themselves inferior. Further, there were many conventions providing for the upkeep of churches in Islamic territory and of mosques in Christian territory, for the use of racial minorities and foreign merchants. In the case of lay sciences, such as medicine, mathematics or astrology, no one was really concerned about the beliefs of their few adepts. Although some suspicion of sorcery attached to a man who was too well versed in these arts, it was thought safer to secure his services than to risk his enmity. Gerbert of Aurillac's erudition in the field of astronomy and Arabic mathematics, meagre enough in all conscience, did not stop his becoming Pope at the end of the tenth century; it signifies little that legend later made him out to be a heretical magician.

All in all, different religions were less harmful to the exchange of ideas than different languages. Latin and Arabic, canon law and Sunnite law, images and arabesques, had too little in common to make intelligent discussion possible. It was only in the eleventh century that enough interpreters could be found not only to read the Arabic originals but to retranslate from Arabic the Greek originals that had been forgotten or lost. The Arabs for their part hardly bothered to translate the western mediaeval texts. Their contempt was understandable at first, but was to prove damaging later on.

Commercial exchanges

Similarly, in the matter of commercial exchanges, the new obstacle was not so much the difference in religion as the extent of Arab conquests. The Moslem religion was characterized from the first by the favour it showed to merchants, Foreign merchants in particular found the Caliphate more accommodating than the Byzantine Empire. But inevitably the formation of one political unit and customs system, which stretched from the Bay of Biscay to the delta of the Indus, developed internal economic currents at the expense of relations with the Christian shores of the Mediterranean.

It is true that a territorial whole as vast as the Moslem world could export a much greater variety of merchandise to Christian Europe than Roman Africa and Asia had ever sent to Roman Europe, and that consequently it could also have imported more. It even seems possible that the purchases of Moslem merchants in Catholic Europe may have provided her with the minted gold and silver she needed for her own purchases in the Byzantine Empire, and left her a credit balance that could be used for the subsequent development of her trade.

But we must be careful not to imagine an extensive trade in the course of the early Middle Ages. The merchandise which the Islamic world required of Europe for the most part came into the category of goods that no government willingly sends to eventual enemies: strategic materials, arms, boats, slaves. Business is business: the slave trade might be banned by all governments and anathematized by the spokesmen of all religions, but nevertheless it became one of the most important branches of international commerce in the early Middle Ages. As the supply of prisoners of war was not sufficient to maintain it, children were stolen, or, more often, bought from parents made callous by poverty or greed. This traffic went on everywhere, in England, Lorraine, Tuscany, Bulgaria, Syria, Egypt. . .

The demographic crisis continues

The fact that men were one of the most sought after 'commodities' is indication that the demographic crisis, so devastating at the time when the empires of antiquity were crumbling away, was far from being resolved at the moment when the Arab Empire was coming to full flower. Perhaps the capital 'hemispherical' event of the eighth century was not the war of the four battles, but the plague of 742–43, which spread outwards from the heart of China to the middle of Europe and ravaged the homes of Moslems and Christians without distinction. Unfortunately the demographic and economic history of Asia in the early Middle Ages has not yet been thoroughly explored. In the case of Europe, it is a tangle of insoluble problems, for no statistical exactitude is possible on the basis of the rare and indefinite sources of the time. We know enough, however, to be convinced that even if periodic fluctuations produced an alternation of moderate recovery and deeper depression, the fundamental tendency was everywhere and always the same: insufficiency of men and means, contraction of production, difficulties of distribution, low level of consumption.

One can get used to anything: these bleak conditions did not prevent the rise of empires which had their hour of glory, but did limit their scope and duration. One after another, the China of the T'ang dynasty, the Byzantine Rome of Justinian and Heraclius, the Caliphate of the Omayyads, even the Carolingian Empire, lived through times of renaissance, military and cultural, more or less pronounced. Yet each was a sickly giant, condemned to premature death by the weakness of its material foundations and its biological nature. It is not our task to trace the vicissitudes of the empires of the East, but to consider the fate of the Western Empire as restored by Charlemagne.

Chapter 4

THE CAROLINGIAN EMPIRE,
A FRAIL GIANT

I. FROM MAYOR OF THE PALACE TO MASTER OF EUROPE

'CHARLES, wise and modest . . . master of the world, beloved of the people . . . summit of Europe . . . hero, august . . . pious . . . is tracing out the walls of the Rome of the future.'

Thus an unknown poet describes Charlemagne and his capital (Aix-la-Chapelle, not Rome) some months before the Christmas of 800 when the Pope placed the imperial crown on the head of the monarch (in Rome, not at Aix-la-Chapelle).

In 801, as soon as the effects of shock produced by the coronation had been absorbed, Charlemagne — or his chancellery — adopted another string of titles, half Germanic, half Roman: 'Most serene Augustus, crowned by God, great emperor and peacemaker, governing the Roman Empire and, likewise by the mercy of God, king of the Franks and Lombards'. His scholars bestowed still more titles on him: 'King David', which well became the Anointed of the Lord, or 'the shepherd Palaemon', which on the other hand was ill-suited to the tastes of this mighty hunter. History does not record whether he was given other names by the wife he repudiated, the nephews he dispossessed, or the Saxons he had hunted down, massacred, forcibly baptised, or deported if they were 'treacherous' enough to revolt. The empire he established by force of arms was already beginning to disintegrate before his death, but the imperial idea which it had nurtured was to dominate Europe until the end of the Middle Ages and beyond.

The image of Charlemagne

The image of Charlemagne, embellished in the biography of Eginhard, who had known him, but still human, was transfigured by legend. An eleventh-century monk was told by an eye-witness that in the year 1000, when Otto III opened the tomb of the founder of the Empire, he found Charlemagne 'seated on a throne as if he still lived. . . none of his members was corrupted'. The epic, as we all know, attributed to him, with embellishments, the exploits of his whole dynasty, a life-time of two hundred years, and the flowing white beard that it seems he never wore (Pl. 7). In 1165 the Church bowed to tradition (and to the wishes of Frederick Barbarossa) and admitted Charlemagne to the number of her saints. That was enough to drown the discordant voices of certain poets who represented him as a greedy old dotard.

It is not easy to analyse a man who was the embodiment of so many ideals throughout the ages. We know that he was energetic, active and courageous; that he had a firm belief in Christianity according to the Roman formula and in his own mission to uphold and propagate it, by sword and book; that he accepted and sought the collaboration of warriors and learned men of all nations, but held himself to be of Frankish race (which does not mean either German or French) at the most important occasions and public appearances of his life. His other characteristics elude us. The sources, which are fairly full for a time which does not over-indulge us, lend themselves to different interpretations.

But whatever the part played by his personality, his successes and failures are best explained by the fact that he came on the scene at the moment when the elite of the West was impatient for restoration of the Empire, but when the political and economic instruments needed to maintain such an Empire were certainly not up to it.

Frankish trump-cards

The Frankish army was almost ready. From the time of Clovis, as we have seen, the Frankish people seemed marked out for the hegemony of the West. They controlled a larger territory and a more numerous population that the other barbarian kingdoms. They had promptly solved the problems of their relations with the Catholic Church and the Gallo-Roman masses, and yet controlled enough Germanic lands not to lose their cohesion among the Roman crowds, or the autonomous character of their clergy. Justinian had halted Frankish expansion, it is true, but nothing could have stopped their taking the offensive again after his death if their monarchy had been able to keep its authority over the nobility.

This had not been the case. The Merovingian aristocracy, anarchistic, greedy for pleasure, indifferent to ideas, profited by dissension or the incompetence of the sovereigns, then by the rivalry of the Mayors of the Palace, to grow powerful at the expense of the State, the Church and the people. At least it kept in good training for war, thanks to internal struggles between Austrasians, Neustrians, Burgundians and Aquitainians, and though it suffered some defeats at the hands of the Avars, Slavs, Lombards or Bretons, it never allowed any incursion into what was, strictly speaking, Frankish territory.

Moreover, the fundamental unity of the Frankish nation took definite shape in the world of ideas at the very moment when in fact it was falling to pieces; it was the seventh century that shaped the legend of a Trojan origin for the Franks, as for the Romans and Macedonians. A little later, the prologue to the Salic law was a hymn to the *gens Francorum inclita*, valiant in war, unshakable in peace, uncontaminated by heresy. No doubt patriotic expressions of the same kind are to be found at the same date among the Anglo-Saxons, Lombards and Visigoths. But of these only the Visigoths were of stature to rival the Franks, and they fell before the Arabs. As for the Anglo-Saxons and Lombards, they had not even achieved the conquest of the regions where they had settled, Great Britain and Italy, and they were too few to aim higher. The horizons of the other barbarian nations were even more limited.

The rise of the Carolingians

So to become masters of the West the Franks needed only to find a leader and learn how to obey him. At the beginning of the seventh century, while the members of the royal line were busy devouring one another in the famous quarrel between Fredegund and Brunhild, an Austrasian family of great landowners put forward its claim: the Arnulfings, ancestors of the Carolingians and perhaps prototypes of the Nibelungen of the epic where they appear in company with Attila, Theodoric, and other heroes of still more remote times. In 656, Grimoald, son of Pepin the Old and all-powerful Mayor of the Palace under king Sigebert, had the audacity to install his own son on the Austrasian throne, having first had him adopted by the king. The time was not yet ripe; father and son were put to death, but the Arnulfingian family soon recovered itself, producing more Mayors of the Palace. Pepin II was victorious over his Neustrian enemies, raised Frankish prestige in Germany, and sent missionaries to complete the work of his soldiers.

There was another set-back at the death of Pepin II, another advance under his illegitimate son Charles Martel. Defeating the Moslem Arabs and their Christian allies north of the Pyrenees, conquering the Frisians, Saxons and other still pagan Germans, Charles managed to grab Church possessions to reward his knights, without forfeiting the favour of the missionary clergy, who had need of his support. The Pope himself offered his alliance to the Mayor of the Palace in return for help against the Lombard King Liutprand; but Charles Martel gave preference to Liutprand, who was his ally against the Arabs and became godfather to his son (Pepin 'the Short') in a Germanic ceremony which 'grafted' the young man on to the royal stock of Lombardy. The Franks themselves were without a king at this moment, the Merovingian pretender having died in 737. The vacant throne was only one short step away.

This step was taken by Pepin the Short, in a way that radically transformed the Frankish kingship by covering its military and Germanic foundations with a sacerdotal and Roman veneer. Other barbarian kingdoms had already gone the same way; the Visigoths had even adopted the Hebrew rite of consecrating the king with holy oil, though they did not surrender their right to depose him. In England, the mystical fervour of some of the kings was not always popular; it is said that Sigeberht of Essex was killed 'because he was accustomed to spare his enemies and forgive them the wrongs they had done him'. All the same, increasing emphasis on a religious symbolism seemed to be the only corrective for political ferocity.

A symbolism of this kind seemed needed to take the place of the ghost of the Merovingian king, '*fainéant*' but legitimate and quasi-sacred. When Pepin the Short ventured on the usurpation that so many others had achieved in neighbouring kingdoms, he was anxious to purify it by the most unassailable form of consecration possible. First, he made the Pope declare that the royal title ought to fall to the man who held the real power. Then, after being elected king by the assembly of nobles, he had himself anointed by St Boniface, the most famous of the missionaries, in the presence of the Frankish bishops. Finally, in 754, he knelt before the Pope who had come to France, led the Pope's horse by the bridle, and promised him armed protection. In return he obtained a new consecration by the head of the Catholic Church in person, and in addition the title of 'patrician of the Romans' which he had probably not asked for.

Henceforth the path of the Carolingians lay clear before them; their triumphal progress in the second half of the eighth century, as well as their difficulties in the ninth, bound them closely with the papacy. Patricians, conquerors of Italy and Germany, emperors or competitors for the Empire, they poured the profits of their arms and their administration into the common funds of a company in which the Pope was first a junior partner, then an equal, and finally a claimant for the over-all directorship.

II.   FROM THE ADMINISTRATION OF ROME TO THE TUTELAGE OF THE WEST

In fact, the protection Pepin the Short had promised to Pope Stephen II, in 754 implied acceptance of the principles contained in a document which the pontifical experts had, it seems, just drawn up to meet the needs of the cause: the *Donation of Constantine*. This put into the mouth of the first Christian Emperor, the founder of Constantinople, these surprising words: 'We deem it proper to move our Empire . . . for in the place where the sacerdotal principality and the capital of the Christian religion have been installed by the Emperor of Heaven, it is not right that the terrestrial emperor should exercise his power . . . We concede and abandon [to the Pope] . . . the town of Rome, together with all the provinces, localities and cities of Italy and the western regions, to be held by him and his successors in their power and tutelage.'

We must resist the temptation to treat this 'donation' as a forgery; its very language, which is certainly anachronistic, betrays the uncouthness of Roman culture in the eighth century, yet its authenticity was not seriously questioned before the Renaissance. Forgery presupposes an intention to deceive; but the clerks who drew up the *Donation* to fill what they felt was a lacuna in the archives were no doubt convinced that the facts had been much as they described

*Map 7. Italy at the
beginning of the seventh
century.*

them. Since God had willed that the Pope should have the West in his tutelage
and Pepin the Frankish monarchy in his power, it was an act of faith to provide
an incontestable legal basis for them. But the mutual guarantee which the two
protagonists exchanged, against any claim by a third party, made a long-
standing but distant friendship into real complicity, first against the Lombards,
then against the Byzantine Empire.

The 'donation' transformed the political destiny of the papacy as radically
as that of the Frankish state which the papacy was prepared to wed in order to
secure Rome and Ravenna as dowry and the West as joint estate. A hasty marriage, all things considered, and fraught with consequences that the popes had
probably not clearly foreseen or desired: irreparable separation from the East
and the final partition of Italy (Map 7).

The Popes between Romans and Lombards

Long before the compact with the Franks Gregory I was, in fact, already the
administrator of Rome. This involved no conflict with the Emperor, since a law
of Justinian conferred on all bishops extensive powers over the civil authorities.
If the papacy subsequently looked more and more to the barbarian West, yet

the spiritual unity of the two Romes had for long been ensured by the recruit-ment of popes. Between 606 and 752 there were thirteen popes born in the East or in Byzantine Italy. Gregory III, the enemy of the iconoclast emperors, was a Syrian.

Nevertheless the political unity of the two Romes was difficult to maintain. The elder Rome was too far from Constantinople, too close to the Lombard border; inevitably, Byzantine Italy and barbarian Italy attracted each other.

In the course of the seventh century the increasing difficulties of the Em-pire in the East left its delegates in Italy almost entirely to their own resources. Exarchs of Ravenna, dukes of Venice and Naples, archons of Sardinia, 'masters of soldiers' and 'tribunes' of the different districts — some sent from Constantinople, others elected from the local aristocracy with the express or tacit consent of the Emperor — relied more and more on the native population, in a disorder not very different from the anarchy of the Merovingian kingdom. The Pope, who had fewer mili-tary forces than they but was consecrated by his ecclesiastical office and possessed of vast estates throughout Italy, consolidated his Roman do-main and extended his influence through the rest of the *pars romana* or *Respublica Romanorum* (Byzantine Italy), of which he gradually be-came, as it were, president. His frequent clashes with the Emperors, over religious or practical matters, were no doubt often serious embar-rassments to him, but his own perseverance and the solidarity of the Italians always enabled him to emerge victorious. At the beginning of the eighth century even Ravenna, the seat of the chief lieutenant of Byzantium and of a bishop whose autonomy Byzantium had established by decree, sought the protection of the Pope against Greek officials and against the Lombards who were closing in on her. In their turn, a few Lombard dukes appealed to the Pope for help against their kings' policy of centralization. These were all excellent chances to develop the func-tion of mediator between 'Romans' and 'Lombards' which Gregory I had so successfully inaugurated.

Despite the quarrels and confusion which prevailed on the surface, there were signs of a reconciliation between the peoples of Italy. The Lombards, who dominated most of it, were originally one of the most backward Germanic peoples. The mark they left on the country was in brutal contrast with what survived of traditional Italian culture, but was all the more susceptible to the influence of the civilization round about them. Between the end of the sixth and the beginning of the seventh century, the Lombards in fact abandoned their Arian beliefs, their Teutonic tongue, their way of dressing. Their law put up a stronger resistance, but mingled with the other legal currents in Italy, Roman law, canon law, customs born of day-to-day experience. King Liutprand felt it necessary to state categorically that Lombard procedure was just as valid as Roman. To forbid the marriage of a widow with the cousin of her dead husband, he invoked the authority of the Pope 'venerated through the whole world as head of the Church'.

That does not mean that the Lombards were no longer conscious of their individuality, but that the *pars Langobarda* was now identifying itself with the entire kingdom, in which all inhabitants were grouped according to their social rank rather than their ethnical origins. Even rank would not weigh with king Aistulf, the son of a duke and a peasantwoman, who in 750 mobilized land-owners and merchants side by side, according to wealth and not to birth.

The downfall of the Lombards

Across the Italian peninsula, a strange indented frontier marked the place where the Lombard conquest had been halted on the death of the last Arian king, in 652. This frontier was not an effective barrier against penetration, whether economic, cultural or religious. On the one hand, Ravenna diluted its Byzantine colouring and became almost barbarian. On the other hand Pavia, the Lombard capital, increasingly welcomed Byzantine influence. In 725–6, when the *pars romana* revolted, first against a tax for the war against the Arabs and then against the iconoclast measures of Leo III, the Lombards, who were on the side of the images, had a chance to present themselves to the rebels as the lesser of two evils.

At that point Liutprand invaded the territories of Ravenna and Rome; but he was undecided, ill supported by his dukes, intimidated by the popes, who had designs on the whole region and used all possible weapons to stop him before he reached his goal. The opportunity was lost and never recurred. When later Aistulf took Ravenna at one fell swoop and claimed that his sovereignty be recognized by Rome (no doubt without prejudice to the rights the Pope had acquired), the agreement of 754 unleashed against him the superior might of the Franks. Once the Lombards were crushed, Pepin the Short gave Pope Stephen II Ravenna, which, together with Rome, was to be the first nucleus of the pontifical State.

Twenty years later, King Didier lost his crown in an attempt to carry out Aistulf's plans; Charlemagne, King of the Franks, became also King of the Lombards by conquest, and patrician of the Romans by papal nomination (774). For though the popes wanted no sovereign at as close quarters as Didier would have been, they needed a sovereign at a distance, more respectful, capable of defending them against the lordlings who swarmed among the ruins of the Lombard state and the fragments of Byzantine Italy. So they heaped favours on Charlemagne, in a crescendo that led to the 'imperial restoration' of Christmas 800.

The coronation of Charlemagne: several wills coincide

The last act was played in the best Byzantine tradition: coronation by the metropolitan bishop (in Rome, the Pope), acclamation by the people, adoration of the Emperor by all present. It might be objected that these were not really the proper actors or the proper theatre, but at that moment Constantinople had only an empress, who, though she showed due respect for images, had acceded to the throne of Constantine by deposing and blinding her own son. To get rid of her, it was said, Charlemagne had a choice of three methods: to depose her, marry her, or persuade her to recognize him as a colleague (in fact, she was overthrown by her own people before the choice was made; and it took a war to extract provisional acceptance of the third alternative from one of her successors).

Though the official acts were all accomplished by popes, none of them apparently of outstanding intellectual or moral stature, the restoration was the result of several wills coinciding. First of all there were the builders of the Empire, Charlemagne and his noblemen, who were perhaps not bent on the coronation taking the exact form it did, but who no doubt welcomed any formula that might express the superiority of the victorious monarch over all other kings, past or present. Lombards, Bavarians, Saxons, Frisians, all the old enemies of the Franks at last subdued; the Avars of the Danubian plain, only a short time ago a force to be feared even though weakened by their struggle with Byzantium, now reduced to unconditional surrender together with their Slav subjects; the Arabs, in spite of Roncevaux, thrown back south of the Pyrenees and beyond the glacis of the Spanish marches — these were the tangible titles that made Charlemagne worthy of a special title.

But in the eyes of the Nordic clergy his piety was a still more important merit. By the protection he accorded to the Church in the land of his ancestors, in the provinces won from the pagans, and even in Jerusalem under infidel rule, Charlemagne gave reality to the ideal of St. Augustine, the 'Christian Empire' in which the City of Men prefigured the City of God.

Finally, all who were not resigned to the death of the Roman Empire or its exile in the East, all who idealized ancient Rome as the model of justice or peace, might or intellect, saw in this German 'clad in the skins of beasts' the man destined to give flesh and blood once more to the ghost of the Empire. A ghost indeed, for history never retraces its steps, nor was Rome ever so beautiful as she appeared in dreams; but an all-conquering ghost, who accomplished the miracle of its own resurrection.

III. PRELUDE TO EUROPE, OR A FALSE START?

What strikes us most, after so many dormant years, is not the confusion and conflict of intentions behind the momentous decision of Christmas 800, but the re-emergence of a will to experiment and build. The Carolingian restoration is like an early thaw which spends its heat before all the snow has melted: most plants are dead or barren, but some have buds, and there are ephemeral flowers to announce the hardier blossoming of the spring to come. Universalism, Europeanism, feudalism, nationalism: all of these trends found a first expression, more or less rudimentary, in the ninth century. On the almost blank book they had inherited from the earlier age, the Carolingians wrote down many

PICTS
SCOTS
KINGDOM OF
NORTHUMBRIA
IRELAND
WALES
ANGLO—SAXON
KINGDOMS
KINGDOM OF
MERCIA
KINGDOM OF
WESSEX
BRITTANY
Paris
Poitiers
AQUITAINE
Toulouse
KINGDOM
OF THE
ASTURIAS
Burgos
Ebre
SEPTIMANIA
SPANISH
MARCH
Barcelona
EMIRATE OF CORDOBA
Cordoba
ARAB EMPIRE

JUTES
DANES
Elbe
Oder
SAXONY
Magdeburg
SORBS
Herstal
Aix-la-Ch.
Worms
ALAMANNIA
BAVARIA
CARINTHIA
MORAVIANS
Danube
MARCH
OF
PANNONIA
AVARS
LOMBARD
Pavia
Venice
KINGDOM
Ravenna
CROATS
PROVENCE
CHURCH
STATES
DUCHY OF
SPOLETO
Rome
DUCHY OF
BENEVENTO
Naples
Palermo
BYZANTINE
EMPIRE

0   500 km

Carolingian Kingdom in 768   Occupied countries,   Territories conquered
                                  not pacified in 768   between 768 and 814
Carolingian Empire in 814   Tributary territories in 814   Zone of Carolingian influence, 814

Map 8. The Carolingian Empire in 814.

important questions; satisfactory answers were found only at a later period, when the problems themselves had substantially changed.

The European framework

From a geographical point of view, it is not unwarranted to regard the Carolingian Empire as prelude to Europe. Even if it did not exercise effective power over all Catholic Europe (not to mention Byzantium), it came nearer to doing so than any state in later years, except perhaps Napoleon's Empire (Map 8). It is true that Catholic Europe, in the time of Charlemagne, did not yet include the Scandinavian countries or the Iberian peninsula (except the Spanish March and the little Visigothic kingdom of the Asturias, whose sovereign recognized the Frankish monarch as his superior). The Slavs, too, were represented only by a few Slovene tribes, precariously attached to the Carolingian possessions of Bavaria and Italy. Nevertheless Charlemagne made so deep an impression on the Southern Slavs that his name (Charles, *kral*) became the title of royalty in their tongue, as Caesar's name was in many others.

The family of Catholic nations, such as it was at the time, had thus come almost entirely under the direct or indirect authority of Charlemagne. England was the most important exception; even there, a king of Northumbria recovered his throne through diplomatic pressure by the Emperor and the Pope, but the powerful King of Mercia claimed an equal footing with Charlemagne. Certainly Mercia was puny as compared with the Carolingian Empire, but King Offa had no map, and was entitled to be proud of the great earthwork he had built along the Welsh border. Ireland, further away, was left to anarchy, scarcely mitigated by the presidency of her *Ard-rí* (high king) over her two hundred kinglets. She did, however, contribute stars of the first magnitude to the intellectual firmament which was the glory of the Carolingian court, and which included a fair number of English and Spaniards, besides subjects of the many provinces of the Empire.

Though the European framework of the Empire was never acknowledged in the Carolingian official vocabulary, it did not pass wholly unnoticed in the literature of the time. The name of Europe, known in antiquity but seldom mentioned in the barbarian period, dramatically reappears in one of the earliest accounts of the battle of Poitiers, described by a Spanish chronicler as a triumph of the *Europeenses* over the Arabs. In the ninth and tenth centuries, literary references to 'Europe' grew more numerous, then faded away. The mutual distrust of Rome and Byzantium, both aspiring to universal predominance, made it impossible for that notion to prevail over the rivalry between West and East. All this has a familiar ring.

Return to universality

Had Charlemagne entertained no greater ambition than that of being the 'summit of Europe', something like an *ard-rí* or *bretwalda* of the Catholic West, he would have encountered no obstacles: he was an eminently successful warrior, whose frequent expeditions brought fresh conquests and booty for distribution to the largest army in the continent. To be 'Emperor of the Romans', however, meant much more. It entailed an all-embracing responsibility to ensure the moral and material order of the City of Men and a claim to universal rule, if not over the entire world (for neither the Roman Empire nor the Roman Church ever were literally universal), at least over the civilized commonwealth.

On the first score, Charlemagne performed remarkably well, especially if we consider how little most of his predecessors had cared for the responsibility of kingship. Within the limits and forms of his own culture, he was as well aware of his public duties as the most conscientious of the Byzantine emperors. He did his best to order and improve everything, from the morals of the clergy to the alloy of the coinage, from collections of legal texts to popular epics. But he did not perceive as clearly the universal significance of the imperial crown. He tended to the day of his death to govern his state as a simple 'extension of the kingdom', or rather a collection of territories and tribes which his personal talent had brought together and his personal whim could re-distribute among his relatives according to Frankish custom. A few household officials helped the Emperor to take care of general affairs: the 'master of the chamber', a weakened substitute of the Merovingian mayor of the palace; the 'seneschal', a chief steward; the 'count of the stable'; the 'butler', and other officials whose titles remind one of the barbarian notion of the state as a private property. But each of the kingdoms included in the Empire maintained its own administration, institutions and laws.

The Empire would have been partitioned at Charlemagne's death, but for the fact that only one of his sons happened to survive him: Louis 'the Pious'. He had been indoctrinated by the imperial-minded clergy enough to discard at once the titles of King of the Franks and King of the Lombards and style himself Emperor, *tout court*. In 817, Louis proclaimed that any division of the Empire would be contrary to the will of God and the unity of the Church. One of his bishops, applying St Paul's words to a new context, added that the entire population of the Empire must be 'one body in Christ'. A body with an imperial head: in 824, Louis ordered that no pope should be consecrated before taking an oath of fidelity to the Emperor. Meanwhile, growing Italian and Byzantine influences blew faint whiffs of Roman air into the Germanic atmosphere of the Carolingian court and administration. Charles 'the Bald', one of Louis' sons, was even to shock his Frankish retinue by dressing like a Byzantine Emperor (Pl. 8).

It was, however, either too early or too late. Louis may have been more far-sighted than Charlemagne, but lacked his iron will and overwhelming prestige. The anarchical tendencies of the Franks broke the spell cast by the first Emperor; Louis' sons and grandsons tore the Empire to pieces, before the imperial theory could fully mature. Yet it had developed far enough to survive, independently of the Frankish hegemony, the person of the Emperor and the integrity of the Empire, as the dominant political symbol of the Catholic world.

The Christian republic in the West

Not quite ready when it might have been strong enough, not strong enough when it might have been almost ready, the Carolingian Empire may appear to a modern eye as a most ineffectual body politic, wrapped in mystical haze. But the men of the ninth century saw a *Respublica Christiana* embracing most of Europe and functioning with unprecedented harmony. State and Church were merged within it to the point at which the intiative could come from one or the other, according to the needs of the moment or the talents and energy of their respective heads, without causing conflict or serious divergencies.

Collaboration was particularly fruitful in the lands recently won from the pagans. Here the clergy formed a sort of army of occupation and administration, larger and better organized than the soldiers and lay officials. Just as the appearance of a stipple of towns formerly showed that Rome had tamed some barbarian nation, so the network of parishes and monasteries indicated that some new subjects of the Carolingian Empire had served their apprenticeship in the civilization of the old provinces. Certain usages condemned by Christianity, such as human sacrifices and polygamy, were forbidden; the elementary methods of Frankish or Lombard agriculture were imported, by means of direct colonization or instruction of the natives: native ecclesiastical cadres were formed, reading and speaking Latin after a fashion and teaching as best they could a 'Christian' way of life. Because the Carolingian culture was simpler than Roman culture of the classical age, it was more easily assimilated. Several centuries were needed before provincials proved themselves capable of governing the *Respublica Romana;* a century and a half was enough for the newly converted Saxons to take the helm of the *Respublica Christiana* after the Franks let it slip from their grasp.

State and Church collaborated too in the old provinces, but their work there was done with less enthusiasm and produced no radical changes. The susceptibilities of the two capitals, Rome and Aix-la-Chapelle, had to be reckoned with, and their traditions and aims did not always provide a meeting point. Besides this divergence, there was provincial opposition, ranging from the turbulence of Aquitaine to the rebellions in Brittany and the Lombard principality of Benevento, which had escaped the fate of the Lombard kingdom; incidentally, Benevento and Brittany recovered their independence in the end, and the main body of Lombard Italy had to be granted a large degree of autonomy.

The main enemies were demoralization and ignorance, shared by most of the clergy and nearly all the flocks. But it was possible to believe without understanding every dogma or keeping every commandment. Heresies seem to have found few adherents among the people, though the problem of predestination was a source of quarrels among the learned. Pagan superstitions were more widespread, but superstition does not exclude faith.

The whole population of Carolingian Europe, the humble and obscure as well as the powerful and illustrious, rested on a uniform religious basis. This, and the fundamental similarity of customs, made possible the gradual development of a rudimentary commonwealth. Its memory has long haunted the imagination of historians and politicians; it was evoked recently by Napoleon's courtiers and ultimately by European federalists in our days. Yet it would be improper to carry the comparison too far and call 'the first Europe' what actually should be defined, in the light of the present, a false start. For the word 'Europe' today implies not so much a single body of beliefs or a universal state as the sum of political institutions, secular learning, artistic and literary traditions, economic and social interests, created by many independent nations. From this point of view the Carolingian Empire must seem to us a remarkable effort but, when all is said and done, an irrelevant one.

IV.   BEGINNINGS OF FEUDALISM, GLEAMS OF NATIONALITY

For the discharge of the heavy tasks that fell to him as head of the *Respublica Christiana* the Carolingian sovereign had at his disposal, first and last, the political framework which had served the Merovingians so ill: collective organs, local agents, personal assistants and servants. Collective organs of a 'democratic' kind (that is, assemblies formed by the adult males of the ruling nation) could hardly be used for functions outside local justice. At any rate, the general assembly of free men had been transformed into a council of military and religious notables, who alone still enjoyed complete liberty. As for the local agents, such as counts and their subordinates, they would have found their task hard if they had attempted to carry it out with any measure of zeal. But they almost all had become independent property-owners, ungovernable and irremovable, for in the absence of regular taxes the royal domain of their district was their salary and the price of their loyalty. If loyalty wavered, how could the salary be retracted?

So the main weight of the task fell on the king's intimates and personal servants, who made up a floating group, of differing ranks and with ill-defined functions. A good servant was not content to be 'kept' in the king's palace. He wanted to be bought by the gift of lands where he could live as master rather than servant. Gradually the Merovingians stripped themselves of a vast patrimony of estates, ruining themselves in the vain hope of governing.

The problems of government

Of course the first Carolingians were in a much better position than their immediate predecessors. They were the acknowledged leaders of a competent and loyal clergy, and their military successes and their unequalled energy compelled recognition by laymen. They had at their disposal a fresh supply of estates, lands acquired in the service of the Merovingians, Church property seized by

Charles Martel, conquests of Pepin the Short and Charlemagne. Propelled by their vigour, the old wheels of government began to turn again, though they still creaked: the assembly deliberated, counts (and later dukes and marquises) carried out orders, the household servants of the palace exerted themselves in all directions. Then the wheels were greased: everything possible was done to instruct the staff, to explain their duties clearly (in writing, if the recipient could read), and to prepare lodging for them if they had to travel. But in spite of all this feverish and well-directed activity, there was no question of making one ill-conditioned jade do the work of several well trained horses.

To govern as the Byzantine emperors did, the emperors of the West would have had to re-establish the Roman system of taxation and use the proceeds to pay in money a large staff of civil employees whose salary could be withdrawn at the first sign of insubordination. They did not even consider it. A revolution of this kind, even if the economic conditions of the Carolingian Empire had allowed it — and that is doubtful — would have been repugnant to a society which met most of its needs without recourse to money and respected only the land-owning military class. There was no alternative to granting land in order to reward service. Like the Merovingians, the Carolingians would have to squander the royal estates in order to rule.

No doubt; but steps could be taken to prevent the disloyalty of the grantees. While distributing land, the Carolingians endeavoured to tighten the bonds of loyalty. The simplest means, widely used by the Merovingians and other barbarian rulers, was to require an oath of fidelity that would stress the personal bond between sovereign and dependant, and call God as a witness and avenger of broken pledges. Experience, however, had abundantly proved that no promise will create loyalty where loyalty is not present from the start; the path which led the Merovingians to their doom was paved with faithless oaths.

Nonetheless, Charlemagne demanded oaths from all free men, and closer oaths from his closer retainers ('vassals'), with an insistence bordering on obsession; he also encouraged his vassals to demand oaths from their own dependants. At the same time, he groped for devices that could compel obedience. He and his successors endeavoured to preserve loyalty by retaining ownership of lands conceded to dependants, to hallow it by strengthening the religious symbolism of the oath, to stabilize it by playing it off against rival loyalties, and to control it by periodical inspections. Their methods were neither entirely new nor always consistent, but they formed the first nucleus of what was later to be called feudalism.

The dawn of feudalism

For the moment we shall do no more than indicate the chief characteristics which emerged thus before the mid ninth century. Unconditional gifts of freehold lands were replaced by the concession of 'benefices' in simple possession. The grant implied perpetual obligations of obedience and service. These duties had to be acknowledged by a promise of 'fidelity', impressively staged and including the taking of an oath on relics. Clergymen serving the government received privileges which enabled them, in spite of their military inferiority, to act as counterbalance to the lay vassals, Itinerant officials of high rank, the *missi dominici*, armed with full powers, checked the performance of the vassals at frequent intervals.

These practices, like the imperial theory, needed time to be tested and imp-roved upon. They could not at once make up for the lack of public spirit; their observance still depended upon the personal qualities of the sovereign and the assistance of his family. However, the heirs of Louis the Pious began to quarrel among themselves and attack him even during his lifetime. With the Empire rent by these internal wars, new waves of barbarians broke over it and hastened the collapse of central authority. This resulted in an accelerated development of feudalism, but in a direction which Charlemagne had not foreseen. At first, the holders of benefices sold their loyalty to the highest bidder among the claimants to the throne, and demanded larger grants in return for smaller ser-vices. Then, as the paralysis of the central government progressed, they stepped into the vacuum, took over more fully the defence and administration of their land, and governed it with little if any reference to the paramount interests of the sovereign.

Thus, after a first stage during which the sovereign had emphasized the duties of the vassals, there was a second stage during which the vassals affirmed their rights. The third and final stage, that of balanced reciprocal obligations, was still a long way off. But even the chaotic second stage was not entirely negative. It placed an increased responsibility on the shoulders of the vassals and almost forced them to reconstitute to their own profit those local cells of government that had disappeared with the downfall of the Roman network of city-states. We shall see shortly that the revival of local government and initiative was an essential factor in changing the false start made under the Carolingians into a real beginning of Europe.

Nation comes from 'nasci', to be born

Modern Europe, however, does not rest directly on local governments but on nationalities. Ancient Rome had melted primitive nationalisms into a universal patriotism; nationalities were a product of Middle Ages, and the Carolingian period made some contribution, although unconsciously and unwillingly.

There is a great difference between the solidarity of tribe and folk, such as the barbarians undoubtedly had always known, and nationalism based upon the relation of a people to a home land. This feeling had obscurely grown with the long stay of the Lombards in Lombardy, the Bavarians in Bavaria, the Neust-rians in Neustria, and, in each region, with the gradual fusion of barbarians and natives. The vague universalism of the Carolingian Empire, however, was not favourable to the development of nations as distinguished from kinship groups.

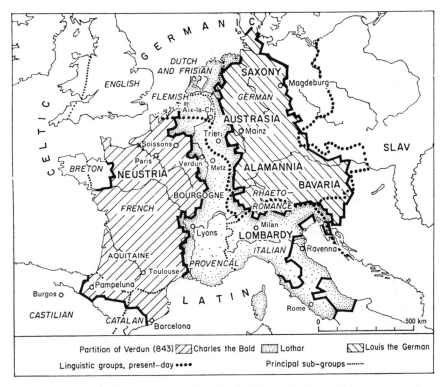

Map 9. The Partition of Verdun in 843, and linguistic groups.

The emperors allowed their subjects to practise the tribal customs of his ancestors. Under their rule a great number of curious formulae appeared in legal
documents, in which each of the interested parties declared that he 'lived according to the Frankish law' — or Lombard, Alamanic, Visigothic or Roman, as
the case might be — 'by virtue of his birth' (*ex natione*). But *nation* in these texts
had a meaning quite different from the one we give it; it ignored geographical
context, by-passed administrative divisions, and recognized only ties of blood.

But even this criterion allowed of exceptions. We find individuals who professed a different law from their fathers'. Automatically entry into the Church
implied adoption of 'Roman' law, which indicates the extent to which the
Catholic Church disapproved of any manifestation of nationalism within her
bosom. Her insistence on the Latin of the liturgy, in contrast with the more
accommodating attitude of the Orthodox Church, is further proof of this.
Without going as far towards universalism as the Popes, the first Carolingian
Emperors took some steps in the same direction. They promulgated capitularies
that were valid throughout the Empire, and though they codified the 'national'
laws they left them to decay for lack of fresh ordinances. It is said that Louis

the Pious considered imposing Salic 'national' law as the general law of Europe, but never put his plan into execution.

From the Council of Tours to the Partition of Verdun: the separation of languages

Several more centuries were to pass before true nationalism was born, but the preliminary conditions that were to transform Europe into a pattern of natio- nal states made an early appearance, as a result of struggles for the succession. The repeated partitions of the Carolingian state under the heirs of Louis the Pious were based on lines familiar to us on the maps of modern nationalities, with a persistence that it is difficult to attribute to mere chance. At any rate, they corresponded roughly with the linguistic frontiers for which the Carolingian age provides our first reliable evidence. In 813 the Council of Tours recommen- ded the clergy to translate sermons into the Romance or Teutonic tongue, so that the people might understand them. Twenty-nine years later, the two younger sons of Louis the Pious and their armies took an oath of mutual aid against the elder son, the Emperor Lothar: the soldiers of Charles the Bald took the oath in Romance, those of Louis the German in Teutonic. The Treaty of Verdun in the next year almost translated the Strasburg oaths into a political partition: the entirely French provinces went to Charles the Bald, those entirely German to Louis the German. Lothar kept for himself, besides the Italian and Provençal provinces with particularly marked Romance characteristics, a long strip of intermediate lands, in which even in our own days the languages interlock: the Low Countries, Dutch and Walloon, Lorraine and Alsace which are still bones of contention, and polyglot Switzerland (Map 9).

Nevertheless it is certain that criteria of nationality played no *conscious* part in the Partition of Verdun, which was brought about by transient and accidental causes. The problem was to make three shares, roughly equivalent from the point of view of their economic and military resources, adding to the regions already under the control of each brother the bordering districts needed to make the parts equal. The younger brothers, the real winners, kept the more compact slices for themselves, though they left to their elder brother the two capitals, Rome and Aix-la-Chapelle, which fell to him with the imperial title. Further, the officials who counted the abbeys and counties assigned to the three brothers were little concerned with linguistics, and as they had no atlas were not even in a position to form a clear mental picture of the mass of states they were carving up.

The fact remains that two of the kingdoms of 843 stood firm against all the currents of the future and provided the framework of modern France and Germany. The third, on the other hand, bisected by the Alps and peopled by races who could not understand each other's speech, disintegrated almost at once. Gradually France and Germany absorbed its northern provinces. The transalpine section, for which the name of 'Italy' was again beginning to be more common than that of 'Lombard kingdom', might still have occupied an honourable place in the triad if it had succeeded in extending its territory south of Rome, where the Lombard and Carolingian conquests had been halted. But the Emperor Louis II, Lothar's successor, failed completely in his military and diplomatic efforts to rally under his authority that other 'Italy' (Lombard Benevento, Byzantine possessions, towns that were autonomous but threatened by the Arabs). Too small without its southern part, the 'garden of the Empire' (to borrow Dante's expression) was for the pleasure of others; indeed, a hundred years after the Partitions of Verdun it became a dependency of Germany in a lame Empire which did not include France. From the ninth century onwards the inequality of the Italian partner compromised the second political solution open to the Carolingians: failing European unity, a balance of three national kingdoms.

V. THE BALANCE-SHEET OF CAROLINGIAN CIVILIZATION

Carolingian culture, a transitional culture, found its lasting formula in the restricted fields of handwriting, Latin grammar, and the indispensable classical texts.

The reform of handwriting was its most important success. Formed in the *scriptoria* (copying-centres) of France, the 'Caroline' minuscule ousted, one by one, the 'national' hands: Visigothic, Merovingian, Lombard, Irish, Anglo-Saxon, all of them developed from decadent non-epigraphic Roman scripts (uncial, semi-uncial, cursive). It triumphed in the end, long after the extinction of the Carolingians, as far afield as Spain, England and the Italian south. The Caroline minuscule had not perhaps all the virtues that its success has attributed to it: the national hands were more imaginative, the capitals of classical inscriptions and expensive manuscripts were more harmonious and could have been just as economical of space if their size had been reduced. But the Caroline minuscule is clear and does not tire the eyes; we can speak of it in the present tense, for this book is printed in Caroline minuscules that have hardly been modified, with the addition of capitals that the humanists were to rediscover in the inscriptions of Roman monuments (Figs. 12–19). It is one of the first in the series of standards that simplify international life: the Gregorian calendar, the metric system, a universal postal union.

Literary renaissance: its limitations

In the same order of ideas comes the work of official Carolingian circles in establishing the elementary rules of classical Latin and the models of language and style as contained in the great books of Christian or pagan literature. There was no time to lose: national languages were already thrusting up through the clumsy jargon of Continental writers, though they had not yet, as in England,

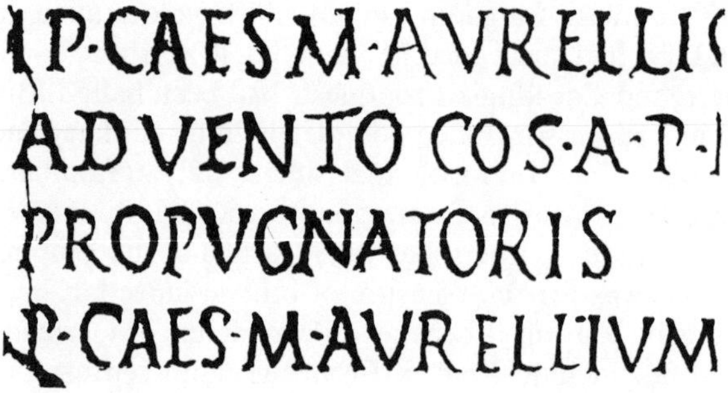

Fig. 12. Roman capitals, third century.

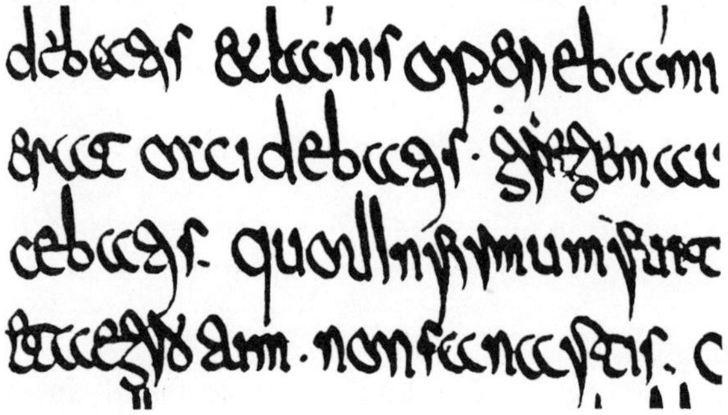

Fig. 13. Merovingian hand, seventh century.

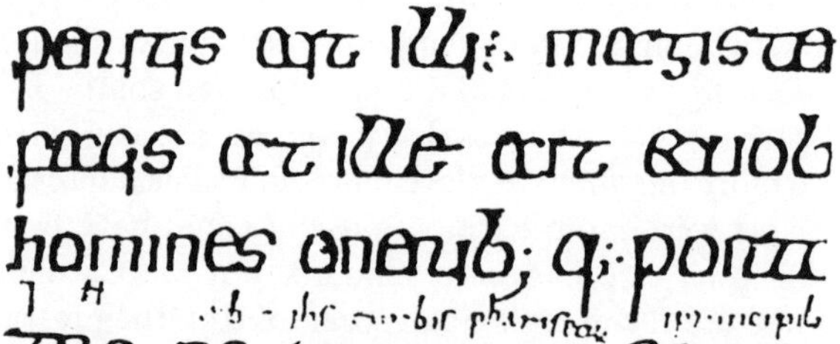

Fig. 14. So-called insular semi-uncial (Anglo-Saxon), eighth century.

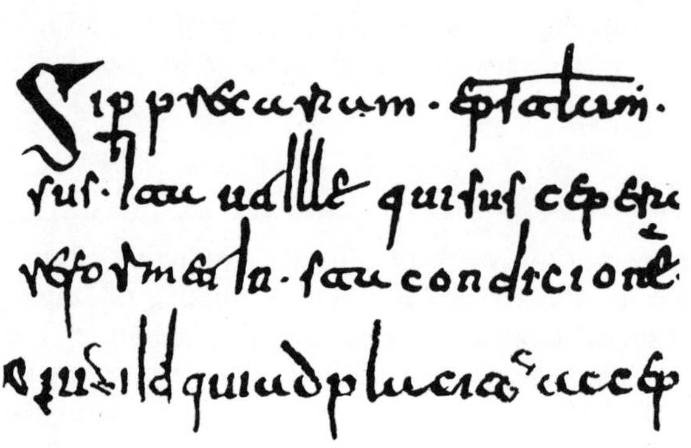

Fig. 15. Visigothic hand, ninth century.

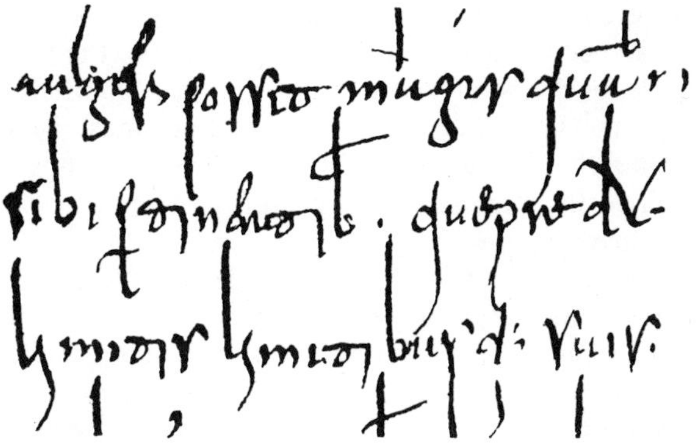

Fig. 16. Lombard hand, tenth century.

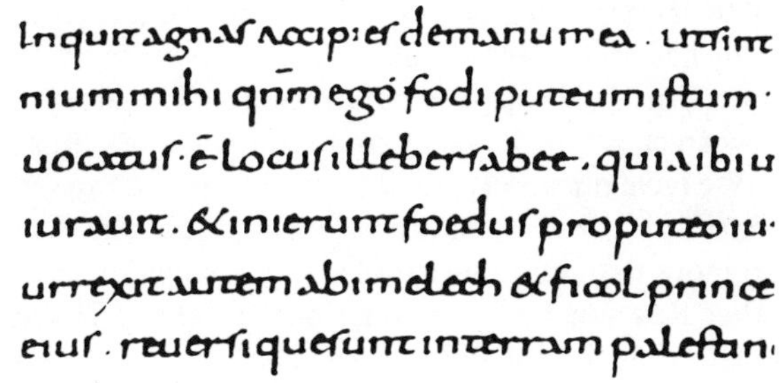

Fig. 17. Caroline minuscule, ninth century.

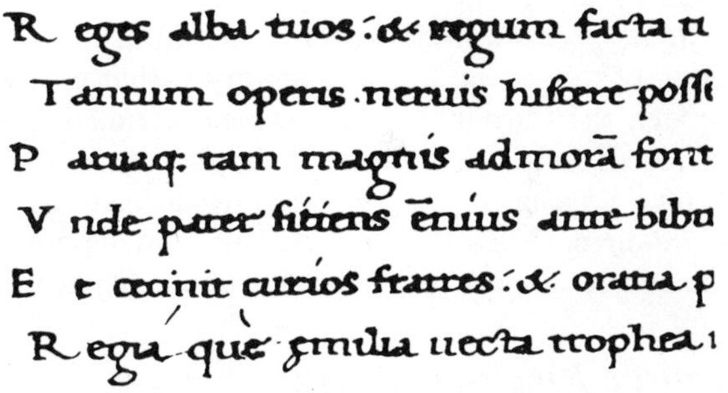

Fig. 18. Humanistic hand of the fifteenth century, derived from the Caroline minuscule (above) and the Roman capital.

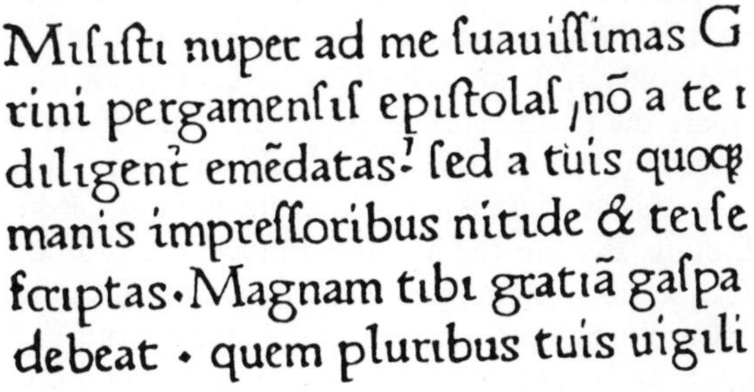

Fig. 19. Printed characters (1470), derived form the humanist hand (above).

achieved the status of literary languages. True Latin was dead, and must be embalmed to serve for the understanding of the Scriptures, the conversation of the learned, and official acts applying to a community speaking different idioms. Also the less futile of profane authors must be preserved before their last manuscripts were lost, or effaced by some industrious monk eager to cover their costly parchment with one of the holy texts of which there could never be too many copies.

We can measure both our great debt to the 'Carolingian renaissance' and the limits of its culture if we draw up a list of the Latin classics which have come down to us (almost invariably, the manuscript tradition goes back to a Carolingian archetype), and compare it with the mass of lost works. A revealing symptom of the spirit of this age is that the pagan poets found favour more often than men of science, in spite of the difficulty of neutralizing the poison of their sensuality or worldliness by allegorical interpretations. Truth, it was said, had not been revealed to the Ancients, but they possessed the secret of style. This style was successfully imitated: there was a sudden outburst of poetry in correct classical meters, and Eginhard took Suetonius as a model.

We have purposely used the word 'renaissance', which some would like to see restricted to the humanist age. No doubt the Carolingian renaissance lighted no more than an altar candle, which shone in surrounding darkness, while the other Renaissance took some of the light of heaven to give it to man. But the intellectual elite of the two ages had in common a feeling of the discontinuity of the past, and the desire to suppress the most recent phases and revive the ideal of an earlier age.

Some poems and drawings of the ninth century are like pages torn from a book of the second or third century — but a book of very modest worth, for though the Carolingian renaissance recruited a number of men of talent, it produced only one thinker of the first rank, the Irish philosopher Johannes Scotus Erigena. It is true that Erigena knew Greek well. As a result, he had more direct access than most of his contemporaries to Byzantine civilization, the source of classical, hellenistic and oriental inspiration.

Artistic Renaissance: its complexity

As for the arts, which needed no translator, Byzantium freely furnished the Carolingian renaissance with craftsmen, motifs and techniques. We must not think only of Rome, which lay hardly outside the political orbit of the East and where the ninth century produced some of her most beautiful mosaics, or of Ravenna, though her San Vitale supplied the main inspiration for Charlemagne's church at Aix-la-Chapelle, but also of the Asiatic core of the Byzantine Empire. Even in the heart of France, the church of Theodulf at Germigny-les-Pres seems to stem from an Armenian model, the cathedral of Echmiadzin.

Carolingian art was more original and fruitful than literature. It absorbed all kinds of foreign influences, made use of all native themes available in the vast

Empire (from Nordic interlace to the palmetto of the Mediterranean), and occasionally recovered aspects of the classic naturalistic tradition at its best. The human figure again became a centre of interest — and that is the first step on the long road of humanism. Some of the Carolingian themes in turn nourished later artistic revivals — the Ottonian and Anglo-Saxon 'renaissances' of the tenth and eleventh centuries — and some had an influence on Romanesque art. But in its own time, the art of the Carolingians had little impact beyond a few centres (Pls. 8, 9, 10 and fig. 20).

One feature is common to all the manifestations of the Carolingian renaissance: they were hot-house plants, cultivated by a handful of intellectuals who, in their turn, relied on the encouragement and support of a handful of patrons: the sovereigns, the Court, a very small number of ecclesiastical institutions. Even the reform of handwriting at first concerned a few thousand people at most; the others could not write.

Commerce: of small value, but influential

How many people were affected by the other stimulant of local life, international trade? In the absence of statistical data we may guess at some tens of thousand customers: those who were refined enough to want ornaments, arms, medicines, seasonings, and above all rich enough to buy them; that is to say, a part of the nobility and high ecclesiastics. As for the suppliers, they could not have been more than a few thousand, even if we take into account those who trafficked in slaves, in wood, metals and other products of the West (raw materials for the most part) that could command a sale in Byzantine and Arab markets. It is impossible to estimate the number of merchants engaged in domestic trade, if only because a considerable proportion of this trade was in the hands of people normally employed in other professions: landowners, farmers, moneylenders, fishermen.

Not only in Catholic Europe, but from one end of the Old World to the other, the greatest merchants were Jews. We recall in particular those of whom the ninth-century Arab sources say that they spoke seven languages and operated a shuttle-service between Spain and China over three parallel routes, of which one ran through the whole length of the Carolingian Empire. Purveyors to the Merovingian and then the Carolingian kings, organizers of the slave trade, wholesale dealers in wine and salt, the Jews owed their success chiefly to their intellectual equipment: widespread education, exchange of ideas and techniques between communities in all countries, respect for commercial activities, at a time when the West had little esteem for any but the soldier and the priest. But they were also served by the exceptional treatment which, in so many other respects, was their misfortune: because they had no full citizen's rights in any state, they escaped the restrictions that every country placed on the movement of aliens, especially in time of war (Pl. 10).

Less important than the Jews, but destined for a more brilliant career in the centuries to come, the citizens of the autonomous Byzantine ports of Italy — Venice, Amalfi, Naples, Gaeta and yet others — were beginning to enjoy similar advantages without suffering the same inconvenience. Their ambiguous political status allowed them to arrive at all frontiers as friends rather than aliens; their relations with the Byzantine and Arab world opened windows on cultures more advanced than that of Catholic Europe, whose outer wall they skirted. In its turn, the Carolingian Empire possessed a culture more advanced than that of its neighbours to the north, all along a semicircle running from Ireland to Bohemia. The profitable but intermittent trade carried on in these areas swelled the meagre income the Frisians drew from the agriculture practised in their swampy country. Finally, the Scandinavians often deigned to buy products they could quite as well have taken by force, or sell products which they had stolen in one or other of their raids.

Certainly we must not measure economic currents by their volume, and use the scale of our own days to plot them. The few thousand people selling little groups of slaves or thin rolls of material (or, over shorter distances, enough salt to fill a barge or two) did valuable work in keeping open a ventilator in the dark cellar where, but for them, the Carolingian economy would have been locked up. Similarly, the few native traders who still lived in the decayed towns of the interior and drew their resources as much from their landed estates as from local trade and money-lending were not a negligible quantity. Socially, they were the shadow of a middle class inserted between the great and the poor (Fig. 21), both fettered to the land. Economically, they prevented money from going out of circulation altogether, and each village from becoming an island abandoned to its own resources. In the northern provinces of the Empire, where urban life had altogether ceased or had never existed, the merchants joined the missionaries and the soldiers in conjuring up small towns, such as Quentovic and Dorestad, which blossomed brightly before disappearing totally in the turmoil of the following centuries. In all probability these merchants, whether foreigners or natives, of whom we know next to nothing (for they had no pretensions to literature, and no commercial document of the ninth century has come down to us), played a part as important as any Erigena or Eginhard. Like them, they ensured for the life of their day the survival of marginal activities, and possibilities for the immediate future.

The true scope of the Carolingian revival

Marginal: that is the word that comes to mind as soon as we move away from the three pillars of Carolingian civilization: religion, war, agriculture. Even in these three fields the orders and advice of the active minorities were stifled by the inertia of the majority.

On a clergy lacking zeal and a people lacking fervour, the religious learning of Alcuin or the holiness of Benedict of Aniane had little hold. The severest punishments and the most extravagant rewards were hardly enough to mobilize recalcitrant and greedy vassals against the most dangerous enemies. It should have been easier to organize agricultural work: serfs could hardly refuse to co-operate, and in any case man must plough if he would eat. But hands were few, the little properties lovingly tended by independent peasants had almost all disappeared, and the great estates were only oases in the midst of a deserted countryside. To make any profit at all, the lord's agents had to exercise un-wearying vigilance. These estates tried to produce everything so as not to have to buy anything; because there was no need to buy, there was no incentive to produce surpluses for resale. It was hardly possible to accumulate enough reserves to avoid the famines of lean years. Even Charlemagne, when he had not the windfall of a profitable war, went back to supervising his kitchen-gardens, his hen-runs, the weaving of wool by his maid-servants. In an empire of farmers he was a model farmer.

Meanwhile under his orders new land was cleared all along the frontiers, in the same spirit that led Rome and her heir, Byzantium, to provide the districts exposed to attack with soldier-farmers. But the progress of Carolingian agriculture all too often resembled the movements of nomadic tribes: behind the ploughmen who opened up a clearing, the forest closed in again on the fields they had just left. Similarly, the roads that the Carolingians strove to repair, just as they restored the Latin grammar, were soon obliterated again; not enough people passed to trample the weeds down and keep them open. To maintain the cohesion of the Empire, to stir up a bureaucracy barely sufficient to govern it, ceaseless journeys on horseback were needed.

This was, in fact, the beginning of the age of the mounted knight; but if knights may sometimes conquer vast areas at lightning speed, they cannot hold them long without the help of the humble farm cart. The new Europe was almost in sight. It was to be built from the bottom rather than the top, thanks to better farm carts rather than to more fiery horses. In the ninth century the Carolingian Empire, that frail giant, was sinking to its premature grave; in the tenth century structures that were more

Fig. 20. A carpenter. From a miniature in the Ebbo Gospels, ninth century. Epernay Library.

viable because smaller and better provided with manpower would rise in its place, and usher in a thousand years of almost unbroken economic and intellectual growth.

BOOK 2

REBUILDING FROM
THE BOTTOM UP

Chapter 1

THE DAWN OF EUROPE

I. IN THE TENTH CENTURY: 'DARKNESS IS LIFTING'

'L'ALBA part umet mar atra sol — Poy pasa bigil, mira clar tenebras' (Dawn on the sombre sea brings on the sun — Then passes the hill: look, darkness is lifting). This verse, written in the tenth century in a language which is no longer Latin and could not yet be identified as one of the modern romance languages, is not among the most harmonious of poems inspired by the advent of morning. But the historian of the origins of Europe finds it as moving as the first cry of a new-born baby. To the relentless prophets of woe, to those charters which append to the date of the current year the formula 'as the end of the world is impending', these poor lines seem to reply that a new age has just been born. Theirs is not the only voice; a thousand others proclaim the good news, but they are scarcely audible amid the cries of pain accompanying the birth of Europe.

In fact between the middle of the ninth century and middle of the tenth, Christendom was ravaged throughout by the most brutal enemies it had ever met with since the fall of the Roman Empire in the West (Map 10). The suffering was the more cruel since the new invaders had neither the means nor even the intention of undertaking the thorough conquest of Europe and thus at least, through servitude, of restoring peace.

Europe torn to pieces

On the islands of the Aegean, at the gates of Rome, even on the Côte d'Azur, Mohammedans set up their numerous robber strongholds and pirate lairs. From the Côte d'Azur they pressed forward as far as the passes of the Swiss Alps, killing or holding to ransom, plundering and destroying everything that fell into their hands. They were indeed the dregs of Arab society, miserable representatives of the great Muslim civilization. As a matter of fact, the central Caliphate of Baghdad had been partitioned at the same time as the Empire of Charlemagne and successor states were racked with quarrels among themselves and internal problems. The only believers left to carry on Islam's Holy War against the Infidels were greedy adventurers, 'evil-doers, rebels, rabble of many nations, panders, contemptible men', to use the obviously biased comments of a learned Baghdadi.

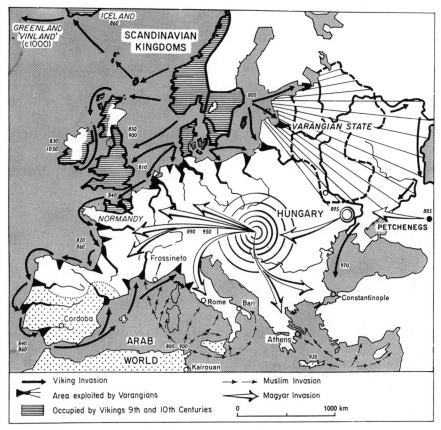

Map 10. Ninth and tenth century invasions

The Scandinavians plundered their way down the Atlantic coast and into the Mediterranean, penetrating into the heart of France both by land and water and landing on the coast of Tuscany to sack the town of Luni, which they mistook for Rome. By way of the Russian rivers they reached the Black Sea and the outskirts of Constantinople. Ever since the Bronze Age they had built up a material civilization of some splendour and originality but they had scarcely improved upon it in the following centuries. Despite their frequent contact with more advanced peoples both east and west of them, they retained some prehistoric customs. They did not show respect for their chiefs, or for their parents. Sometimes they would offer human sacrifices to Odin, their highest god, but again sometimes they refused all worship because like those two founding fathers of the Icelandic community mentioned in *Landnámabók* 'they believed only in their own strength.' One might add that this strength consisted almost as much of guile as of physical force.

As for the Hungarians whom the Eastern Roman emperors had called up from the steppes to make life harder for their Bulgarian neighbours, they turned on the Danubian plain, but recently evacuated by the Avars, like an embodiment of the horsemen of the Apocalypse (Figs 22 and 47). From there they raided as far as Aquitaine and the outskirts of Rome. They may have been less wild than other non-Indo-European peoples who before them had forced their way into Europe, such as the Huns, the Avars and the Bulgarians. Nevertheless, it was their name that became a word to frighten children: 'Ogres'.

Swallowed by the Ogres, young and promising Moravia, the first organized state of the Western Slavs, disappeared. Farther north, Slavic tribes of various strains broke through the weak defences of the *Respublica Christiana*, into the lands of the Bavarians and the Saxons. Other Slavs, strengthened perhaps by Scandinavian elements, raided the Adriatic shores.

All of these pressures, added to family strife and personal inadequacy, made the burden of the Carolingians impossible to bear. Though there continued to be claimants to the imperial title, after 887 no descendant of Charlemagne was able to bring together, through talent or luck, the dismembered fragments of the empire. Ironically, the Roman Empire, prepared by mythical Romulus and inaugurated by Augustus, had ended five centuries of rule in the West with the deposition of the child emperor Romulus Augustus. No less ironically, the Carolingian Empire, started by Charles 'the Great', went down with the deposition of Charles 'the Fat.'

Fig. 21. Human head, in carved wood, from Novgorod, twelfth century.

Resistance on the local scale

The network of communications and command being so slack throughout Europe, resistance was but slowly organized. It was only at the eastern end in the Byzantine Empire and at the western end in the Caliphate of Cordova that regular fleets, standing armies and frontiers garrisoned or at least patrolled by professional troops existed. The border marches established by the Carolingians and their successors to act as buffers were too weakly held to absorb the initial shock. Inland vassals showed no undue haste in leaving their fief in answer to the call of the sovereign to whom they owed military service. In Britain and in northern Italy, there was not even a recognized ruler of the whole country who might have co-ordinated defensive efforts.

But if it was impossible to stop the invaders — and buying their withdrawal served only to invite further extortion — the prudent course was to conceal one's most precious possessions, seek shelter, and watch for an opportunity to fall upon columns weighed down by their booty. Towns and monasteries which had at first been taken unawares and sacked, began to build strong fortifications. Castles rose up on every hilltop and on the banks of every river. Kings, popes, leagues of nobles or townspeople organized a local resistance which gradually stiffened and ultimately brought victory. Occasionally there was a pitched battle, the most notable being the severe defeat which Otto 'the Great', duke of Saxony and king of the Germans, inflicted on the Hungarians in 955.

Fig. 22. Drinking vessel, with bovine head, proto-Bulgarian art, ninth century; from the Treasure of Nagyszentmiklos, Kunsthistorisches Museum, Vienna.

Still it was above all thanks to her lack of centralization and the poverty of her land that the spineless Europe of the tenth century withstood the invasions better than the Roman Empire of the fifth century had done. Nowhere was there a vital centre, main road or economic node whose loss could cause the downfall of a whole province, but self-supporting villages and almost self-supporting towns were countless. To destroy one by one those minute cells would have required a plan of action and a steadfastness of purpose which the aggressors by no means possessed.

Europe enlarged

Worn out by their very effort, thrown back here and there, softened, moreover, by their contacts with settled people, the invaders finally became attached to the soil in the territories they had wrested from the old states of Catholic Europe and even in their native lands. This made them more accessible to the influence of their neighbours, whose warlike nobility and poverty-stricken peasantry differed from theirs in degree of development more than in kind. After a while, most of them embraced the political and religious institutions of the older nations and set up a Christian church and state of their own. In this way the area of the Christian community known to Charlemagne was almost doubled, and the family of European peoples that we know today was nearly completed (Map 11).

Assimilation was fairly easy for the Scandinavians, both in the many bridge-heads they established in the British Isles and Normandy and in their home countries, soon to be consolidated as the three Catholic kingdoms of Denmark, Norway and Sweden. It was harder for the Hungarians, the only people not of Indo-European stock that took root in the heart of medieval Europe without losing their language and identity. Yet even before they became a Catholic kingdom, a Latin poem, *Waltharius,* made room for them in its expanded European horizon: 'A third of the earth, called Europe, is home for diverse races, differing in customs, languages, culture, name and faith. One of these races, whom we call the Huns, live in the Pannonian plain. . .'

Similarly, the evangelization and political education of the Slavs, which had already produced results in the Balkans and in Moravia in the ninth century, were almost completed in the course of the tenth under the influence of rival religious and diplomatic missions sent from Byzantium and the West. All along the frontier between Orthodox and Catholic Europe certain groups of Slav tribes formed kingdoms: Poland, Russia, Bohemia, Croatia, to which must be added their elder sister Bulgaria, founded by Hunnic tribes but deeply influenced by the Slavs in the course of the centuries. After much hesitation Bulgaria and Russia joined the political and religious family of Byzantium. The other Slavic states ended by choosing the West, as did Hurgary and the Scandinavian states, but tried to emphasize their obedience to the Roman pope in order to escape the heavy overlordship of the German kings.

Unlike the other invaders, the Moslems could not be attracted by the religion and culture of Catholic Europe; but the abatement of their raids led to intensified exchanges of wares and ideas. Long settled in the Iberian peninsula, the Mohammedans retained nothing of their later European conquests except Sicily. This island, which had been taken from the Byzantine Empire in the ninth century by the regular armies of the African emirs, was soon turned into a brilliant independent emirate. Byzantium fully compensated for this in the tenth century by pushing back the Asian frontier of Islam as far as the approaches to Palestine.

Europe shielded: the triumph of localism

The emergence of fairly orderly Christian states in the northern and eastern periphery of Catholic Europe, at the very moment when a general recovery was at long last possible, is an event of capital importance. In the tenth century for the first time in history, the older core of Europe was protected by an outer

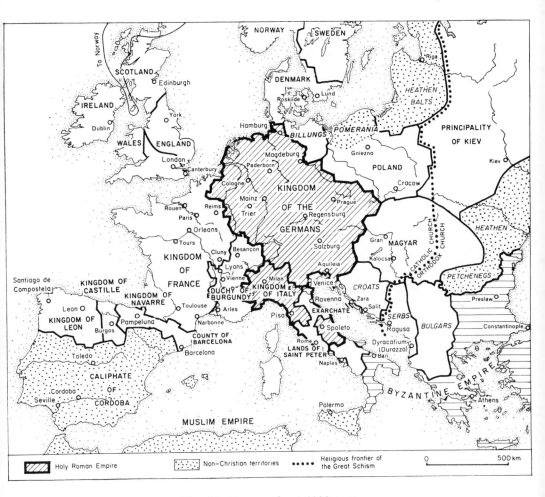

Map 11. Europe about 1000 A. D.

bulwark against which the invasions of successive centuries wore themselves out.

It had not been improper to describe the *Respublica Romana* as an immense fortress besieged by barbarians howling at its walls; the *Respublica Christiana* of the Catholic faith, shielded in the south by the unfriendly but civilized power of Islam, sheltered in the south-east by the inconvenient but familiar presence of the Byzantine Empire, cushioned in the north and north-east by the very peoples who had up to then been a constant threat, no longer had any direct contact with untamed 'barbarians'. More fortunate than Asia, Africa or even Orthodox Europe, which continued to be exposed to the attacks of nomadic people, Catholic Europe has for the last thousand years developed her civilization without intrusion of unpredictable assailants.

Had the decisive turning point arrived a hundred years earlier, it might have given a new lease of life to the Carolingian Empire and started new-born Europe on a uniform basis. Whatever its shortcomings, the central government in the ninth century was a more active driving force than the local units. But in the tenth century the material strength of the empire had melted away, while the beginning demographic and economic revival aroused each cell of the European tissue from its torpor. Localism became the dominant factor in the history of Europe.

Men need ideals, but they must solve daily problems. While local forces with a short radius of action tackled the problems, the dream of the *Respublica Christiana* survived. It was not to recede into the background until the time came for the national state to take over its heritage. Then, but not till then, did Europe grow up in the form that we know and love: not indeed a uniform civilization bearing the heavy stamp of authoritarian government but a pattern of independent and allied cultures, joined together only by affinities of intellect and spirit.

II.   KINGDOMS AND EMPIRES

Before passing on to examine the phenomena which brought about the profound revolution of the tenth century — demographic and economic recovery, localism and individualism — let us glance rapidly at the official historical powers: empire, papacy and kingdoms.

Their impotence was a distressing spectacle for anyone still faithful to the Carolingian dream. Indeed it might seem scarcely possible to rebuild a harmonious union of State and Church out of rugged castles, isolated monasteries, ruined towns, brutal noblemen, narrow materialistic clergy, ignorant wretched peasants, over which the central government had so little control.

Iron popes for an iron age

It is true that during the second half of the ninth century two courageous and intelligent popes, Nicholas, and John VIII, had endeavoured with their limited forces to take over from the collapsing Empire the political direction of the *Respublica Christiana*. At the same time they strove to increase the authority of the Holy See over the episcopacy and to take a stand against the demands of the Byzantine church. A day was to come when their claims would be cited as important precedents in the growth of the pontifical power, but their immediate effect was scarcely visible amid the disasters which shattered Catholic Europe and reduced Rome to the state of a beleaguered city. Ever since the regular succession of the Carolingian dynasty was broken, the pope became the only authority that could step into the breach and confer the imperial title. The vacuum nevertheless persisted: an imperial crown did not convey to the papal choice the power or even the earnest desire to rescue the sovereign pontiff from the Hungarian or the Moslem threat, leaving the Holy See at the dangerous mercy of local lay lords.

There followed then a series of iron pastors for an iron age, often raised to the pontifical office and ejected from it against a background of violence and crime. Some were remarkable men like John X (915–928), whose relations with Theodora, the Roman patrician, were denounced by slanderous gossip, but who fought in person against the Moslems, brought about a temporary reconciliation with Byzantium, upheld the use of Latin among the Slavonic clergy, and died smothered in prison after fourteen years of struggle. Though they were not always above reproach, the popes of this epoch remained for a long time the sole spokesmen for the theoretical unity of that Catholic Europe which, despite its defeats and its moral crises, continued to acquire new provinces.

At the sign of imitation: the Empire's second renewal

Shortly after the middle of the tenth century Otto I, 'the Great', succeeded in carrying out a second 'renovation of the Roman Empire'. Others before him had tried in vain, but he alone among the kings who divided the ruins of the Carolingian state had the trump cards needed for success. Duke of Saxony by birth, he could count on the ancestral loyalty of this folk inured to war and newly opened to civilization. Elected King of the 'Eastern Franks' (soon they were to be called Germans) because his father had reigned over them with a measure of success, he increased the prestige of the crown by resounding victories against the Hungarians and the Slavs. The King of the 'Western Franks' (the future French) had to surrender Lorraine to him. In Italy the great princes of Church and State were ever ready to accept a new sovereign, the better to disobey the old. Thus Otto was able to annex the Italian kingdom without difficulty. In 962 he had himself crowned emperor by an unprincipled pope, and later finding him unreliable, did not hesitate to nominate another (a mere layman the day before) whom his supporters immediately proclaimed to be the better.

The Empire thus refurbished conformed as much as possible to the Carolingian model. No tribute to Charlemagne could have been more eloquent: Otto I took over his political plans, religious organization, administrative institutions, educational projects, architectural style, methods of colonization and even his capitals, Aix-la-Chapelle and Rome, rarely visited, however, by an emperor who was always on the move.

The imitation was altogether inferior to the model. The shrunken territorial basis of the Ottonian Empire — Germany and Italy, without France — made the disproportion between the universal ideal and the limited reality more obvious. The clash between the Saxon emperor and a pope elected by the Romans underlined the old contrast between the theory of harmonious collabo- ration of Church with State and the reality of mutual misunderstanding, now gliding into a conflict of local loyalties, if not yet of nationalisms. Nevertheless, Otto's empire was destined to last, if only because there was no acceptable alternative. It was by far the largest mould for the political dream which helped the people of Europe to bear an unpleasant state of things.

Farther west: diminishing greatness, increasing solidity

Another dream of unity, less ambitious in scope but even more ineffectual, sustained the monarchy in France. Here the power and prestige of the sovereign had become almost negligible well before the end of the tenth century. A hund- red years of rivalry between the descendants of Charlemagne and the heads of the most powerful aristocratic family — the marquises or dukes of 'France' (the region around Paris) — ended in 987 with the election of Hugh Capet, one of the latter. Hugh, son of Duke Hugh 'the Great' (never was this epithet used more frequently that in that century, so unpropitious to greatness), controlled the old Neustrian capitals of Paris, Soissons and Laon and somebody at any event had to have the title of King. But his direct domain, whittled down by a long competition with the Carolingians in purchasing loyalties, was hardly more extensive than those of several great vassals.

Let us pass over the kings of Burgundy or Arles, whose rule was even more ineffectual than that of the first Capets. The modest extent of this fragment of the Carolingian Empire, covering what is today south-eastern France and western Switzerland, might have made the task of central government easier. Local forces, however, took advantage of it the better to free themselves from a ruler of whom nobody was afraid.

The only Western states in which the monarchy maintained its grip, Wessex and the Asturias, were two very small outlying kingdoms which had never been part of the Carolingian Empire. In the Asturias, Alphonso III 'the Great' (866– 910) boldly attacked the mighty state that cornered him in the mountains, the Emirate of Cordova. Victory and defeat alternated under his successors, but the Asturian monarchs kept control of their sinewy strip of land where free men were numerous and influences from abroad did not affect deeply the rustic atmosphere. In England, Alfred 'the Great' of Wessex, a contemporary of Alphonso III, was in the first place obliged to put up with the unchallenged occupation of most of the Anglo-Saxon territory by the Danish invaders. In return he gained a respite for the regions of the south-west, where henceforth the cause of Wessex became that of the Anglo-Saxons. He took advantage of it to promote a religious and cultural renaissance comparable, on a smaller scale, to that which the early Carolingians had fostered in continental Europe. His successors returned to the attack and gradually managed to extend the rule of Wessex to the other kingdoms that the Danes had overrun.

The idea of empire still haunts people's minds

The triumph of localism did not in any way diminish the spell of the imperial idea. Such was its prestige that even in the small western kingdoms intellectuals claimed imperial dignity for their masters: Spanish and English sovereigns were sometimes decked out in the title of *imperator* or *basileus* or *Bretwalda* in this or that charter or chronicle. It is true that claims of this kind were often linked to plenitude of power or superiority over the sovereign's immediate neighbours rather than to Roman universalism.

> The fashion spread as far as Bulgaria. The last representatives of a dynasty which had reached power and glory without paying attention to mere labels, wanted the proud *vasilevs romaion*, the Byzantine emperor, to recognize their self-promotion to the rank of *basileus*. This was an unpardonable insult to Byzantium: she bided her time, but before the end of the tenth century she had embarked upon a struggle without quarter which was to end in the destruction of Bulgarian independence.
>
> In an age when local forces alone were capable of taking the lead, the pursuit of these dreams was as dangerous as it seemed attractive. Most states over-reached themselves at the very time when safety lay in contraction. The Fatimite caliphate of western Africa, the strongest state born of the dismemberment of the caliphate of Baghdad, lost its impetus as soon as it moved its centre to Egypt to claim the whole of the heritage of Islam. The Umayyad emirate of Cordova, self-promoted to caliphate in the tenth century, likewise wore itself out in vain attempts to wipe out the gains made by the Christians in the preceding century.

The oldest and most legitimate carriers of the imperial title, the Byzantine emperors, in the tenth and the early eleventh centuries achieved their greatest triumphs since the age of Justinian and embellished them with a brilliant intellectual and artistic renaissance. Even Byzantium, however, eventually paid dearly for its conquests in Asia and Europe. Increased taxes weakened the mass of peasants and free sailors who had supported the Empire during the terrible ordeals of the three preceding centuries. The emperors spared no effort to protect them, but in vain. The small landowners became dependent upon the military aristocracy, the small shipowners and merchants succumbed to the competition of foreign merchants, and this double downfall gradually dragged the government, and the nation, into ruin.

The heavy burdens of the Ottonian Empire

As for the Ottonian Empire, its ambitious designs doubtless offered the German nobility more rewarding war aims than the petty quarrels of the French nobility. Adventure abroad indirectly favoured the cause of order inside Germany. The resumption of the eastward drive against the Slavs and the Hungarians removed the threat of invasion at home. But when undertaking the exhausting task of subduing Italy and keeping it under control, the Ottonian Empire ran into endless trouble.

Otto I, at least, had stopped at Rome and avoided involvement in the Byzantine and Muslim south and the French west. His successor, Otto II, (973–983), plunged into battles in France and Calabria, without achieving his goal of enlarging a state already too extended for its inner resources. Along the eastern frontier, Slavs and Hungarians had been obliged to recognize a vague German overlordship, but learnt much from their defeats. At the first signs of slackening of the imperial supervision they were ready to turn their incipient organization and their improved armies against the Empire.

Finally, when a young Saxon Emperor (Otto III, 983–1002) and an old Aquitainian Pope (Sylvester II, the great Gerbert of Aurillac) tried to interpret literally the 'renovation' of the Roman Empire and make Rome the true centre of a government which would prevail less by its armies than by its moral authority, they were unsuccessful. Yet Otto was not without energy nor Sylvester without finesse. The former had had useful advice from his mother, a Byzantine princess, and Gerbert had acquired in Spain, France and Italy a culture unusual for his times. But their plans did not allow for the pressing realities of life. The Germans would not take to the strange climate and habits of Rome, the Romans could not barter their local lords for great foreign chieftains; as for the Slavs, they only waited for the first opportunity to shake off the unwelcome domination of an alien emperor. Revolts broke out on all sides. It was only by a return to brutality that Otto III, was able to regain a footing just when events were about to submerge him.

III.   THE TURN OF THE DEMOGRAPHIC TIDE

The truth of the matter is that the most significant events of the tenth century are not to be found in the chronicles and scarcely involve the famous men. To observe the dawn of Europe now beginning to gleam we must leave the lofty spheres of political and intellectual history and descend to the very springs of life.

There is every reason for believing that the general demographic decline of the early Middle Ages was halted soon after that 'world plague' of 742–3 whose ravages we have pointed out. Indeed it is possible that a very modest revival may have shown itself as early as the ninth century: the Carolingian attempts at colonization, the beginnings of social organization amongst the Slavs, the progress of Byzantine and Arab trade, the advance of Indo-China and Japan, and perhaps the revival of the T'ang Empire after the disasters which had struck it in the eighth century could support such a hypothesis. But the indications at that time are too slight, above all too ill-documented and little studied, to allow us to draw definite conclusions. And even if there was a change, the first effects of demographic growth would be limited by the fact that the starting point was a population reduced to a minimum.

In the tenth century there is no more room for doubt: in Spain as well as in China, in Sweden as well as in Egypt, the population began rapidly to grow. Men are the basic material of history; this increase, which went on without wavering to the second half of the thirteenth century and only ceased completely in the mid fourteenth, is the prime mover of all the events of the late Middle Ages. That does not necessarily mean that it was the most important event; universities and cathedrals, parliaments and cities may be far more significant than the number of births and deaths, but the upsurge in population was definitely the constant drive that made all accelerations possible.

Causes of the recovery

The demographic revival can be explained more easily than the decline which preceded it. The natural tendency of every species is to increase, if external causes do not impede it, to the very limits set by the resources of food it can obtain.

Between the tenth and the thirteenth century none of the great scourges of humanity, except perhaps leprosy, seems to have raged at full force. In particular, there is no further talk of grave outbreaks of plague. Malaria, it seems, assumed a less malignant form. There was no abnormal biological check to population growth.

War, that other obstacle, played only a negligible part in the demographic history of the late Middle Ages. In spite of its reputation, the age of feudalism used only very small armies, and if it delighted in innumerable skirmishes, it fought very few pitched battles. The prestige of the knights was based on the fact that they were not anonymous fighters lost in the armed crowd, but an elite of warriors who knew how to sustain hard blows without being killed.

Some thousands of combatants, some hundreds of dead: these are the terms for evaluating the most bloody contests, those described in the most dramatic tones by the chroniclers. There were often more victims among the non-combatants: for instance when Jerusalem was captured by Godefroy de Bouillon, the Crusaders 'rode in blood up to the horsemen's knees'. Not a single Jew escaped, we are told. Yet a letter recently discovered in Egypt asks for help on behalf of the Jewish 'survivors' of the massacre of Jerusalem. Again, it is unquestionable that even in wars against fellow-Christians, feudal armies would remorselessly burn harvests and peasants' cottages in order to starve the hostile lord. All the same, they were not sufficiently numerous, did not campaign long enough, and were too ill equipped to produce the destruction which war creates in our time.

As for available resources, it is certain that at the beginning of the tenth century untilled territories exceeded considerably the total area of cultivated lands. Not only were there wide empty spaces between one village or cluster of villages and another, but unused land could be found even in the most densely populated districts: was there not a marsh at the gates of Paris, another outside the Moorgate of London and a wood in Milan?

In addition, the possibilities for agriculture were gradually enlarged by a slow improvement in the climate. Of this we have such indications as the retreat of polar ice in the sea and of glaciers in the mountains, the extension of vine-growing to countries like England, where it is no longer practicable today, and the plentiful supply of water in some regions of the Sahara later reclaimed by the desert.

Lastly, a series of technical improvements enabled farmers to extract, with less expenditure of effort than before, more frequent and more plentiful harvests from the soil, and to transport them more easily to distant markets. An increasing population would not be exposed to a shortage of food.

Europe's good fortune

Even as the demographic crisis of the age of transition between antiquity and Middle Ages engulfed many countries besides Europe, so did the demographic growth of the transition between early and late Middle Ages. It would be interesting to compare its effects in each of the countries which experienced it. It seems that in China it brought an economic, intellectual and political revival under the Sung dynasty, without, however, modifying radically the agrarian, almost static nature of its civilization. In Moslem Africa it apparently promoted a rapid, exuberant flowering, soon followed by a profound decline. But we will restrict ourselves to observing as best we can what happened in Catholic Europe.

Here the demographic upsurge of the tenth century was the beginning of a chain reaction which has not yet ended after a thousand years. Gradually, as the demographic revolution became an agricultural revolution and that in turn became a commercial revolution, Catholic Europe passed from the rear to the lead in world economic development. Then, during the fourteenth and fifteenth centuries, she went through the new crisis which seemingly affected the whole world. Her progress was hindered for a while, but the solid foundations laid by the commercial revolution of the Middle Ages proved firm enough to endure and support the huge impetus of the industrial revolution from the eighteenth century onward.

What enabled Europe to emerge finally on top? Obviously, her initial gains, no greater perhaps than those of other continents in the tenth century, cannot alone be responsible for her later career; nor can her progress be expressed solely in terms of economic growth. We have just pointed out an essentially political and military factor that was Catholic Europe's great fortune: the absence of great invasions for a thousand years. To appreciate just how privileged the West was, it is sufficient to consider how disastrous were the Turkish invasions for the Byzantine territory, the inroads of the Bedouin for North Africa, and the Mongolian conquest for most of Asia and for Russia itself.

> Intellectual factors also must have played a part, but it is difficult to assess them in an objective way. Whatever may have been the favourable influence of certain original traits of European culture, it seems better to pass it over in silence than to indulge in chauvinism or allow full play to subjective judgments of value.
>
> Even if we consider only the economic causes, as soon as we focus our instruments on a particular spot or a precise moment they reveal a myriad of conflicting drives and prove the inaccuracy of any general explanation. But there can be no synthesis without some sacrifice of exactitude. Therefore it seems proper to suggest tentatively a few original trends which may have provided Catholic Europe, from the tenth century onwards, with reasons for success not granted to the other great regions of the world.

Mainsprings of the economic growth of Europe

Four new trends, first noticeable in the tenth century, characterize the economic expansion of Europe in the late Middle Ages. They are not exclusively European, but nowhere else do they appear to have played such a dominant role. Let us summarize them in simplified statements before analysing them one by one in a general survey of European economic growth:

a redistribution of agricultural man power tends to offset the opposite but equally harmful effects of under-population and over-population;

a more equitable valuation of the social status of merchants enables them to make the most of economic opportunities;

the importance and usefulness of machines and techniques obtain some recognition in practice if not in theory;

the extreme fragmentation of political organization and the weakness of governments favour local initiative and private associations.

IV.   THE GROWTH OF AGRICULTURE

If one considers only the number of persons employed and the total volume of production, agriculture, along with herding, and with such indispensable village crafts as rural forges, is the only economic activity that really matters in the tenth century. The privileged classes depend on it to the same extent as the masses, for nobles and clergy alike derive most of their revenue from the land. Without agricultural growth no other advances would have been possible.

Unfortunately for the historian, the problems and development of agriculture are the most difficult to grasp. Sources are scanty, changes slow and gradual, and the story of each village too individual to allow for any generalization regarding the neighbouring one. In the tenth century, as always, the agrarian scene, so uniform and colourless at a glance directed on it from afar, subdivides into a number of different, changing units. Nevertheless, it seems that a new trend is gaining ground from the tenth century onwards. It is the fortunate confluence of two unfortunate currents which thus gradually correct each other.

Auspicious blending of two opposing systems

On the one hand there had been a regression of classical agriculture, whose parsimonious, intensive methods, in spite of the faults which we pointed out in the first chapter, had been sufficient in its finest days to feed a dense population and support the development of a majestic civilization. As the number of labourers and artisans dwindled, and as liberty and security, those great incentives for the farmer to devote to his land the maximum effort for the maximum return, disappeared, the compact Greco-Roman rural settlements withered away and the area under cultivation shrank.

On the other hand, barbarian agriculture, with its wasteful, rudimentary methods, gained ground. This pattern of agriculture, only one step removed from nomadism, knew scarcely any other remedy for soil exhaustion than to shift from one plot to another and let a large part of the arable land lie fallow. Because it could not produce enough cereals it needed large herds, providers of milk and meat (and also mounts for hunting and war); and because it devoted so much space to herds, it did not manage to produce enough cereals. Yet barbarian agriculture, whose shortcomings have been purposely over-emphasized in order to bring out its difference from classical agriculture, had certain advantages over the more advanced and sophisticated patterns. It spared a good deal of land for successive increases of population, and it made more anima's available to the peasant, to help him in his work, to break the monotony of a diet too rigidly vegetarian and to leave dung on the fallow.

During the early Middle Ages the two patterns were drawing closer to each other. From the tenth century onwards they blended in a happy medium between waste and saturation.

This does not mean, of course, that there was everywhere a successful compromise. Shortages of man power and over-population often persisted side by side. What we call 'happy medium' is all too frequently an ideal mean between villages that are still isolated in the midst of forests haunted by wolves and robbers, and other villages that have encroached upon even the small woods which provide indispensable timber for heating and building and fodder for pigs and sheep.

In an age of rapid demographic growth, over-population is a constant threat in settlements of long standing. Thus in the Ile-de-France, in Lombardy, and in other regions which had always been relatively densely populated, it does not take long before two or more families are crowded together upon one single 'manor' (the elementary unit of agricultural settlement, originally the portion of land cultivated by one family of peasants). In spite of new techniques for increasing the yield of the land, it is certain that the parcelling of estates and holdings is sometimes excessive and that emigration does not always suffice to re-establish a balance.

Under-population eventually tends to be cured by demographic growth and immigration, but the lack of security, of communications, or of initiative may slow down the process considerably. In the periphery of Europe, peoples accustomed to vast horizons sometimes seek new empty lands before filling completely those where they believe themselves cramped. The Norwegians provide the most impressive example of this.

The amazing expansion of the Scandinavians

Not content with spreading over the virgin territories still plentiful in their native land and with carving enclaves for themselves by force of arms on all the north-western coasts of Europe, the Norwegians successfully carried out one of the most extensive peaceful emigrations recorded in history. Between 874 and 930 they founded a republic of farmers and fishermen in Iceland, the country until then known as 'the Desert in the Ocean'; half a century later they had established almost three hundred farms in Greenland, a country where no farming is attempted today; about the year 1000, they set foot somewhere in America. It was a stunning achievement for a people whose technological equipment and political organization were so modest, and it produced remarkable literary fruits also. But the dispersal of effort, undertaken in forbidding climates and often on unrewarding land, restricted the returns. Norway was to play but a modest part in the late Middle Ages, and America had to be rediscovered much later.

Sweden profited even less from the brilliant exploits of her warriors and merchants (the Varangians) who in the ninth and tenth centuries set themselves at the head of the primitive Russian state, spreading from the Baltic to the Black Sea. There were hardly any farmers amongst these Varangians and the Scandinavian cadres were soon absorbed by the Slav majority. Commercial and diplomatic contacts were maintained only with difficulty into the eleventh century between a Sweden still half-barbarian and a Russia refined by contact with Byzantium, Islam, and the peculiar Judeo-Khazar state.

Mass migration through the moving frontier

Apart from this extreme case, the progress of European peasants and farmers was fairly smooth and regular. At first they intensified the exploitation of their native countries. They brought under cultivation part of the waste lands which surrounded each village, opened up clearings in the forests, drained marshes, irrigated heathlands. Then, as soon as the pressure became excessive, they migrated farther and farther into neighbouring provinces towards a frontier which advanced with them.

This mass migration, anonymous but powerful, begins slowly towards the middle of the tenth century, quickens and snowballs up to the end of the twelfth, keeps up during the thirteenth, and stops abruptly in the fourteenth, simultaneously with the growth in population. Peasants take part in the move in all possible forms and ways: individually, in small groups or in a mass; by cautious encroachment and squatting or by armed invasion of the lands which great lords had reserved for their flocks or their hunting; or again attracted by the protection and privileges offered by monasteries and princes anxious to increase their revenues and to gain defenders for their outlying possessions. We shall not attempt to summarize in a few lines a story composed of innumerable details or to cut up into a series of stills an expansion whose most striking characteristic was continuous motion. In order to appreciate its magnitude, it is best to look ahead and gain a general view of the final results.

The advance of the Germans beyond the Elbe and the Oder by means of axe and sword into the forests and heathlands thinly occupied by Slav and Baltic tribes was the most massive. At the floodtide it had swallowed up more provinces than existed in the original nucleus of the Germany of Otto I. The most distant ones were lost at a later time, but an area as large as England was durably Germanized. This extension partly consisted, it is true, in a reoccupation, for the Germans had ruled over some of these regions before being drained off into the Roman Empire. But it was not until the tenth century that they learnt how to take root by means of agricultural colonization, using on a foreign soil that collaboration of soldiers, missionaries and peasants which the Carolingians had deployed to break their own resistance in Saxony and Frisia. By the thirteenth century the development of the great belt east of Germany had become almost routine business, usually entrusted by the princes to specialized *entrepreneurs* (*locatores*).

> The *entrepreneur* advertised the opportunities in the new open land, reccruited the peasants, escorted them to their place of destination, prepared temporary shelter in enclosed camps, and finally became the local administrator and governor under the suzerainty of the prince. Slav and Hungarian princes also employed *locatores*, often on land where a native settlement already existed and was growing but could gain by the addition of foreign techniques and manpower. 'Immigrants from different countries', proclaimed Stephen, the first Christian king of Hungary, 'bring in different languages, customs, tools and weapons. This diversity is an ornament for the realm, a decoration for the court, and an object of fear for our enemies.'

Likewise in the Iberian peninsula, the slow progress of the Christian *Reconquista* was accompanied and consolidated by a blossoming of new centres of peasant colonization, most frequently founded by the kings themselves The bulk of the colonists were of Iberian stock, but French knights and farmers also were welcome. This immigration gave new life to areas devastated by the war and by the flight of some of the Moslem inhabitants; little by little it restored a Western look to the countryside. On a smaller scale there was also some Anglo-Saxon colonization towards the Celtic and Scandinavian frontiers of Wales, Scotland and Ireland.

Internal development and saturation of the land

Although the expansions which accompanied conquest strike us first of all because they are marked by changes of frontiers, it is clear that internal colonization achieved much more. It multiplied farms and villages in Europe without leaving wild empty spaces like those of tropical Africa, or creating stifling agglomerations as in China (Figs. 23 and 24).

From this point of view France offers the most remarkable example. Even though her inhabitants willingly emigrated from one province to another and provided recruits and leaders for many colonizing enterprises in other countries, from Spain to Syria, they nevertheless did not 'Frenchify' any territory outside their frontiers. By way of compensation, however, they filled with homesteads and activities all the wide gaps in which collective efforts and far-sighted initiatives had up to then petered out. Political history, which takes account only of conscious drives, praises the kings, the knights, sometimes the townsmen for having transformed France from a powerless collection of poorly linked fiefs into the greatest nation state of medieval Europe. Yet the peasants unwittingly contributed much more to this achievement by eliminating the empty

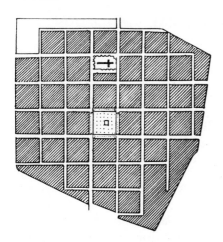

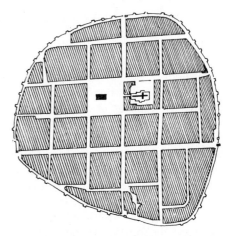

Fig. 23. Chessboard plan of Mirande, (Gers), a town founded in 1285 (P. Lavedan, Histoire de l'Urbanisme)

Fig. 24. Plan of Soldin (Mark Brandenburg), a town built between 1262 and 1280 (P. Lavedan, op. cit.)

spaces which divided a country whose geography was so well suited to unification. What is more, they assured to a very dense agricultural population (as
dense as today in one of the few measurable instances, that of a rural district in
Normandy) a modest but substantial and widespread prosperity.

Over a smaller surface the development of agricultural England was similar
to that of France, except that the nobility took a more direct interest in organizing the exploitation of the land. The population spiralled: in 1086, it seems,
there were about 1,100,000 inhabitants; in 1340, 3,700,000. The standard of
living rose. Apart from grazing reserves and royal forests (the latter often
resented by the subjects as blatant manifestations of tyranny), the soil was
everywhere fertile and well cultivated.

Germany and the Iberian peninsula included a few thickly settled regions,
such as the Rhine and Ebro valleys. The proximity of fluid frontiers, however,
generally maintained a much slacker structure of internal population.

On the other hand, the remoteness of open frontiers soon forced the people
of northern and central Italy and of what is now Belgium with the surrounding
provinces to exploit all usable land down to the last acre. Thus the Flemings,
after having drained the swamps along a coast fortunately stretched by the
gradual receding of the North Sea, brought under cultivation even the pastures
which supplied wool for their nascent industries. Likewise the Tuscans, after
having almost doubled the area under cultivation by drying up marshes which
had defied the Etruscans and the Romans, stripped their hills of woods that
prevented erosion. Italy and Belgium emerged then as the most densely populated countries in Europe. But they escaped poverty by developing another
frontier: trade.

V. THE BEGINNING OF THE COMMERCIAL REVOLUTION

Although commerce never directly occupied more than a tiny minority of the
mediaeval European population, its enormous development in the course of the
late Middle Ages had consequences even more revolutionary than the growth
of agriculture. It was not so much a quantitative change as a transformation
in kind, the addition of a new element at the helm of society.

It is true that at the beginning of the tenth century Catholic Europe was not
without merchants, but she looked to them to provide for her extravagances
and emergencies much more than for her ordinary needs. Commerce did bring
spices to the rich table of the archbishop and salt into the coarse sack of the
shepherd. However, both table and sack hardly ever came from a shop and
rarely from a market stall, for every man normally tried to be self-sufficient
either through his own handiwork or that of his dependants. But between the
tenth and the fourteenth centuries commerce passed from the fringe to the very
centre of everyday life. It became the driving force of economic progress and
in the end affected every aspect of human activity almost as decisively as the
Industrial Revolution changed the modern world.

By analogy, we can therefore speak with justification of a 'commercial revolution' in the late Middle Ages. Similarly it would be suitable to adopt the neologism 'commercialization' to indicate the slow but radical change which was the medieval equivalent of modern 'industrialization.'

A newcomer to society: the gentleman merchant

The commercial revolution is closely linked with the growth of towns, to which a later chapter is devoted. Let us pause only for an analysis of the early successes, those which allowed the European merchants to take over the direction of urban life. It was a phenomenon without precedent in ancient Europe and without parallel in the medieval history of other continents. Still it must be pointed out that the status gains of the merchants were generally much slower and more limited than their material profits. For a long time, their wealth was not so highly esteemed as that of the landowners. The smell of the herring in the cask seemed more difficult to get rid of than that of the dunghill near the castle; so much so that a number of merchants, obsessed by their feelings of inferiority, tried to overcome them by buying land (which was, after all, good ballast for a man engulfed in the risks of business).

> While winning less respect than land property, the merchants' possessions excluded them from such theoretical sympathy as religion would extend to the humble and the poor against the great ones of the earth. Thus in the tenth century, Rathier of Liège, the irascible Bishop of Verona, did not for a moment doubt that the merchant was 'a slave of vice. . . a lover of money'. And even Aelfric, the gentle Abbot of Eynsham, while pointing out that the merchant was entitled to profit from his activities 'useful to the King, the magistrates, the rich and the whole people', awarded highest honour, among secular occupations, to 'agriculture, because it feeds us all'. These attitudes were modified little by little, but were not dispelled until the end of the Middle Ages and well beyond. The clergy always criticized the merchants for usury and hard bargaining; the great nobles objected to their humble origin, more so when it was wrapped in pride. The merchants took their revenge as best they could, railing against the stupid or seedy noble and the ignorant or hypocritical clergyman. Their views, however, won complete acceptance only in the larger cities.

Nevertheless, the entry of merchants into the society of wholly honourable men, whether by the front door or the side entrance, was a most significant change on the European scene. The merchants at last escaped from the vicious circle described in the first chapter: insufficient capital because they were despised, contempt because their capital was insufficient. In this vicious circle the brilliant opportunities offered by Greek genius and Roman peace had been wasted. A first improvement appeared in Islamic society, which displayed from the beginning a certain congeniality with traders, the sympathy of the nomad for the traveller. Yet Islam, too, eventually had delivered to landed noblemen the commanding positions in government and status. Thus it was the mediaeval West which did most for the rehabilitation of the merchants. Paradoxically, the decisive turn occurred amid most unfavourable circumstances, in a Europe originally more countrified, poor and devastated than the ancient Greco-Roman community or the Oriental communities of the tenth century. This requires some explanation.

As in the case of agriculture, we shall find clues in a series of handicaps gradually turned into advantages. The disappearance of its lower layers thinned out the merchant class, but it also lightened its burdens. In the early Middle Ages its best-known representatives were not shopkeepers or small traders but the specialists in large-scale international commerce, purveyors to the Court like Abraham of Saragossa, the protégé of Louis the Pious, or like the 'opulent' Luitfred of Mainz, the ambassador of Otto I to Constantinople. The decay of towns deprived the merchants of their normal place in the lower strata of urban society, but gave them a chance to return in more favourable conditions, as strangers endowed with autonomous status. Because they were alien bodies within an agricultural, military and feudal environment, they adapted their customs more easily to those of the nobility: they bought lands, girded on the sword, organized themselves into caravans and armed associations. Some of the nobles were in turn attracted to commerce because it was henceforth an adventure, an opportunity for fighting. The appearance of the gentleman merchant prepared the way for the merchant gentleman.

In Italy: revival of maritime commerce

We cannot watch the take-off of commerce in every country of Europe. Documents are relatively numerous only in the case of Italy, and fortunately Italy is the outstanding country in this respect. At the beginning of the commercial revolution of the late Middle Ages she in fact played as leading a part as did England at the outset of the modern Industrial Revolution. Moreover, she retained and increased her lead for several centuries.

Venice, Amalfi, Naples and other Italo-Byzantine ports separated from their agricultural hinterland by the Lombard invasion were the first homes of the new merchant class. Their inhabitants were gradually driven to rely upon trade for the means of subsistence they could no longer obtain from their lost rural districts. Cautiously, by manoeuvring between their distant Byzantine sovereigns and their close neighbours the Lombard, Frank and Saxon kings of Italy, and, a little later, the rulers of Moslem strongholds on Italian soil — they attained full political autonomy. At the same time they made sure of the role of commercial intermediary between these rival powers. Doubtless they were not the only ones: we have seen that the Jews fulfilled the same function. But the Italo-Byzantines had other trump cards: being Christian, they met with religious obstacles only in Moslem territory, where such obstacles were less forbidding than elsewhere; and being their own masters at home, they placed their military power at the service of their private interests.

Since each man was usually a fighter as well as trader, class distinctions were soon founded on wealth rather than birth. As early as 829 landed property and liquid assets invested in maritime trade are mentioned side by side in the will of Justinian Partecipazio, the Doge of Venice. At the beginning of the eleventh century a Lombard writer pointed out the amazing fact that the Venetians 'do not till the soil, do not sow, do not gather vintage' and consequently depend on the market of Pavia for their grain and wine. In exchange they hand over oriental products and their sole crop: salt from their lagoons. Indeed Venice was the first state to live exclusively by trade. Ancient Athens and Carthage owed to merchants much of their splendour, but a good number of their citizens, including the governing class, were landowners and farmers.

Obviously the case of Venice is exceptional, for in the eleventh century there was still sowing and tilling of the soil even inside the most advanced cities (in the more backward it continued to the end of the Middle Ages). Commercial activities, however, soon set the tone for economic and social life, not only in the Italo-Byzantine ports but also in the Lombard ports of Pisa and Genoa. The Pisans and Genoese found their vocation during the tenth century, after the Muslim raids had laid waste their fields and forced them to equip their fishing boats and traders for war. They passed to the counter-offensive in the Italian mainland, the islands of Corsica and Sardinia and lastly the Iberian and African shores. By pillage they obtained capital; on landing on foreign coasts they learnt what could be exported from them; as conquerors they demanded custom exemptions from their former enemies so as to invest both capital and experience in trade. Nobles and commoners had shared the dangers of the undertaking. They also shared the profits and joined hands in setting up the autonomous government of their towns while regional and central authorities were losing their power.

Commercialization spreads inland

Commerce was certainly not new to the Mediterranean shores, but even in its Greco-Roman heyday it tended to lose impetus as it moved west and inland. Granted that Italy may be a natural bridge between the Levant and the core of Europe, she had not fully exploited her vocation in antiquity and the early centuries of the Middle Ages, when Greeks, Syrians and other Orientals were foremost in trade. What made her predominant in the later Middle Ages and transformed the superficial commercialization of the seaboard into a commercial revolution engulfing all of Catholic Europe was the awakening of inland cities between the Alps and Rome.

The first tokens were visible even before the tenth century. In the Lombard period, and in the Carolingian era, a few Italian inland towns had retained a

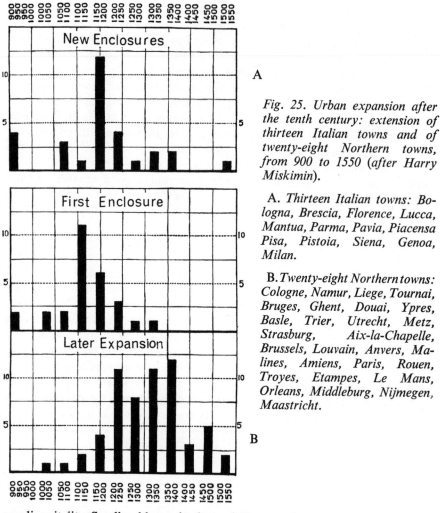

Fig. 25. Urban expansion after
the tenth century: extension of
thirteen Italian towns and of
twenty-eight Northern towns,
from 900 to 1550 (after Harry
Miskimin).

A. Thirteen Italian towns: Bo-
logna, Brescia, Florence, Lucca,
Mantua, Parma, Pavia, Piacensa
Pisa, Pistoia, Siena, Genoa,
Milan.

B. Twenty-eight Northern towns:
Cologne, Namur, Liege, Tournai,
Bruges, Ghent, Douai, Ypres,
Basle, Trier, Utrecht, Metz,
Strasburg, Aix-la-Chapelle,
Brussels, Louvain, Anvers, Ma-
lines, Amiens, Paris, Rouen,
Troyes, Etampes, Le Mans,
Orleans, Middleburg, Nijmegen,
Maastricht.

peculiar vitality. Small nobles and substantial bourgeois lived side by side within
their walls, sat on the same tribunals, and sometimes intermarried. Men, money
and goods circulated more freely than elsewhere; literacy was relatively widespread; even the military ability of the merchants (negotiatores) was considered
equal to that of land-owning horsemen as early as 750.

When the great demographic expansion of the late Middle Ages came, urban
growth in upper and central Italy took on a particular intensity (Fig. 25). The
country had never been depopulated to the same extent as the rest of Europe,
and emigration was restricted by the natural barriers of the Alps and the sea.
A study of family names in the twelfth and thirteenth centuries indicates a
peasant origin for two thirds of the inhabitants of certain Italian towns. Noble-

men, especially children of large families whose estates had been split into minimal parcels, also sought in urban trade the opportunities they could scarcely find in the country.

> As early as the tenth century Italian towns had become far larger than those of the other countries of Catholic Europe, although much inferior to those of the East. While the walls of Constantinople enclose a surface of about five and a half square miles (3,520 acres, of which only a part, however, was built upon), Paris measures twenty acres and Tournai thirty. Between these extremes, Milan is beginning to burst the boundaries which had enclosed her when she was the capital of the Western Empire: 283 acres. Land, much dearer than in the country, increases rapidly in price; the town already possesses paved streets, public baths, a hospital for foundling children. The story goes that a Milanese butcher at that period has refused ennoblement because he does not want to become a vassal of the archbishop. By 1035 the noblemen living in Milan lead the bourgeois militia against that archbishop and the emperor himself, in order to win self-government for the town by force of arms.

While agricultural colonization lags, most of the usable land being fully occupied, commercial emigration and colonization begins. And there again Italo-Byzantine cities are in the van: in 996, according to an eastern chronicler, more than a hundred merchants from Amalfi are victims of a pogrom in Old Cairo. This setback, of course, does not prevent Amalfi and Venice from establishing permanent colonies in Constantinople, Antioch, Jerusalem and perhaps in some African seaports before the end of the eleventh century. The Italians from the interior move on later, and in smaller groups, mostly towards north-western Europe. But their activities are important enough to make Pope Gregory VII, in 1076, demand from the King of France the restitution of 'infinite sums' extorted from the Italian merchants who visited his fairs.

Growing trade and towns in other countries

The progress of towns and trade in other European countries was more modest and circumscribed, but numerous traces of it are to be found in scattered documents of the tenth and early eleventh centuries. Here are a few random examples: shops multiply in several Castilian towns; usurers become prominent at Arras; the merchants (*negotiatores*) of Hamburg, Bremen and Magdeburg gain imperial privileges; Scandinavian kings organize fairs and commercial expeditions; urban crowds conspire against the Bishop of Cambrai, set up a revolutionary commune at Le Mans. . . . We hear from Arab travellers that Prague is an important commercial centre and that 'Britain is the market of the Romans and the Spaniards'. In turn, an Anglo-Saxon legal memorandum of the early eleventh century notes: 'If a merchant so thrived, that he crossed three times the open sea at his own charge, then was he thenceforth entitled to the status of a thegn'.

Yet it was not by rising to the ranks of the old nobility that the merchant bourgeoisie was to affirm itself, but by breaking loose from its lords and claiming the right to self-government. For the town, like the castle and the fief, was a child of localism. In the tenth century it was the weakest child, and hence it had to lean on such lesser nobles as would lead the townspeople's struggle for better economic and political conditions. But unlike the Greco-Roman city, open to the great landowners and dominated by them, the medieval town was to grow as a community of traders, therefore as the deadly enemy of the great landed nobility.

Half way between the famous knights and clergymen who were the pride of the feudal society, and the obscure peasants who supplied the effort of the agricultural expansion, the commercial revolution inserted a growing number of people who through their own exertions would make a name for themselves. In the closed order of the Middle Ages it opened the door to infinite possibilities and experiments.

VI.   THE NEW TECHNIQUES

The Middle ages were less steeped in routine or immersed in contemplation than is commonly thought. Although the material and intellectual poverty of the early Middle Ages was hardly favourable to technological progress, 'necessity', as the saying goes, 'is the mother of invention'. The barbarians themselves brought with them a fair number of small practical novelties from the button to beer and from certain types of soap to certain kinds of swords. And while the more sophisticated Greco-Roman techniques lost their appeal and died out, a few simple innovations which had met with moderate success in antiquity found their usefulness in the straitened circumstances of the early Middle Ages. The awakening of the later Middle Ages did not bring about a full technological revolution, but was the cause (and to some extent the consequence) of very significant technological improvements.

Demographic change and practical inventiveness

Some of the most important advances in medieval technology have been directly related to the impact on man-power of the major turns of the demographic tide.

The first turn, demographic decline, need not have upset the balance of man-power if the number of producers and that of consumers diminished simultaneously. Production, however, was especially weakened by the decline of those workers who consumed the least and carried the heaviest burdens: the slaves. This phenomenon was not exclusively European, but Catholic Europe experienced it in its most intense form because her population fell more sharply and because more of her slaves were transformed into serfs. Moreover, Moslems and Byzantines drew from her, by way of war or commerce, as many slaves as they could obtain for their richer, more demanding economy.

When the second turn came and the rapidly growing population of Europe called for increased productivity, the supply of slaves was almost exhausted. Serfs and free labourers worked hard, but could not be mercilessly overworked and underfed. Means of saving labour had to be found by making a better use of animals and machines. Some of these means were new, others had been contrived before or during the age of demographic contraction. It may also be argued, if not proved, that the latter were instrumental in making demographic expansion possible; but this is the problem of the chicken and the egg. In turn, demographic expansion by replenishing the ranks of the labourers might have diminished the need for labour-saving devices; but since the growth continued, each innovation inevitably brought others, for every acceleration in one section produces a shifting of balance, and this again has to be corrected by another acceleration.

Fig. 26. 'Ancient' type of harness, eleventh century; Bibliothèque Nationale.

Fig. 27. 'Modern' type of harness, first half of tenth century; Bibliothèque Nationale.

A mere list of the new processes and tools adopted in Europe during the late Middle Ages would fill too many pages. Let us restrict ourselves to a few examples preceded by a generalization: nearly all the innovations were the product of manual and mental ingenuity rather than of the conscious application of scientific principles (Figs. 26 and 27). Hence their virtue but also their limitation. Each was perfectly adapted to specific needs, but none opened up those wider horizons which only pure thought can perceive.

In the Middle Ages there is virtually no applied science to link pure science to technology; philosophers and engineers are unaware of each other. This lack of collaboration, whose effects we shall see further on in education and culture, prevented the Middle Ages from breaking one of the vicious circles of the Greco-Roman economy which we pointed out in the first chapter: the manual workers were poor because they were ill-equipped with animals and machines, and they were ill-equipped because they were poor. Still it does not seem fair to blame the commercial revolution for not having solved a problem which the industrial revolution, liberalism and socialism were to tackle in their turn without completely eliminating it.

Agricultural techniques

In agriculture, progress in the late Middle Ages was most notable in the utilization of animals. It matters little that most of the changes were not original contributions of Catholic Europe but felicitous adaptations of something that classical antiquity, the nomads of Asia or the great civilizations of the Near East had already discovered without exploiting it to the full. Better feeding and judicious cross-breeding produced stronger horses, cheaper mules, sheep with longer wool, possibly better milch cows. The substitution of iron for wood, and the improvement of models created more efficient ploughs, supplemented by stronger harrows, hoes, and pitch-forks. The rigid horse collar, iron horseshoes, tandem harnessing, axled wheels and other improvements brought about the greatest changes in traction that occurred between the age of Babylonian chariots and the age of steam. At the same time there was an increase in the number of animals in use.

In order to feed both more animals and more men, it was necessary to increase the yield of the land. This was achieved partly by methods already well known to classical agriculture — manuring, irrigation, repeated ploughing — and partly by acclimatizing several varieties of cereals, beans and other plants with a high food value.

The transformation of the cycles of cultivation was slower but more revolutionary. Not only did the primitive method of itinerant cultivation disappear almost everywhere, but also an effort was made to replace the two-field system (whereby each field was allowed to lie fallow on alternate years in order to recover its fertility) by the three-field system: spring harvest, autumn harvest, fallow. The first information about this accelerated rotation, which drew a crop from the same land two years out of three, comes to us from northern Gaul in the ninth century, but it took a long time for the new methods to win the day even in the regions most suited to them. The rainy climate of the north, its denser and heavier soil, and also the absence of a strong Roman tradition which might have resisted them, made it easier for the triennial rotation of crops, the iron ploughshare, and the use of the horse for cultivation to spread through northern Europe. The south on the whole remained faithful to biennial rotation, the wooden ploughshare, and the use of oxen for draught. Some historians maintain that this contrast, which became more marked as the three-field system and the other innovations gained ground, is one of the chief reasons for the gradual removal to the north of the material and spiritual centre of gravity of Europe in the late Middle Ages. It is an oversimplified and exaggerated conclusion, to be sure, but one which nonetheless contains a grain of truth.

Fig. 28. Viking art: fantastic animal's head in carved wood, decorating a sledge found in the boat of Oseberg, Norway (fig. 29).

Maritime techniques

Other ingenious but equally oversimplified theories explain the shifting fortunes of Atlantic and Mediterranean peoples in commerce and navigation as byproducts of the types of ships they used. Here is a bird's-eye view of the main developments in maritime techniques.

Already in the tenth century the equipment of the two leading seafaring peoples in the West, the Italians and the Scandinavians, bears the marks of two radically different traditions.

The Scandinavian shipwrights started from a prehistoric prototype used by a large number of barbarian nations (including the Balkan Slavs who employed it in the Mediterranean): the 'monoxylon' or hollowed treetrunk. In its simplest form this boat was well adapted to pass from the sea to the shallowest rivers or to be carried if necessary. These were valuable qualities in an age when, through lack of good roads, waterways were exploited to the full. Through the addition, of planked gunwales the boat became roomier without losing its ease of movement, thanks to the sharp angle formed by the planks superimposed upon the trunk (which then acted as a keel). But it was impossible to enlarge it too much without weakening it. Hence it was better suited to carry the quality products of early commerce than the bulkier wares of the later stages of the commercial revolution. In spite of their daring — they would venture in the ocean in these frail boats, without any navigational instruments — the Scandinavians soon lost the lead which their first exploits had won for them (Figs. 29 and 30).

The Italian shipwrights, on the other hand, built within the framework of the Greco-Roman tradition, modified at Byzantium. This tradition preferred larger and more complex ships but, generally speaking, slower ones. Nevertheless, certain enormous ships with superimposed decks, of which the lower ones lacked air and light, disappeared with slavery. The galley (*galaia*, swordfish, as it was called because of its slender shape and of the long ram on its prow), first mentioned in the tenth century, had a single deck and was manned by free oarsmen; a streamlined descendant of the classical trireme, it was the swiftest unit of the Byzantine fleet before the Italians adapted it for trade. It was far stronger and better balanced

than the smaller monoxylon, yet almost as pliable, though it could not
navigate shallow rivers. Its size could be enlarged without danger, but it
used the oar more than the sail, which made it too expensive for the transportation of heavy, cheap goods. Fortunately the lateen sail (a Greek or
Syrian invention, in spite of its name) made it possible to navigate with
relative ease even the broader sailing ships, notwithstanding their unwieldy rounded keel (Pl. 24). Finally, the adoption of improved astro-
labes in the eleventh century and of the compass somewhat later consolidated the pre-eminence of the Italian and other Mediterranean mariners over the Atlantic ones, who took longer to get used to them (Fig. 32).

However, the last word had not been said. By improving their ship
design the Atlantic mariners — Hanseatic, Dutch, English, Portuguese —
finally succeeded in making the most of the potential advantages afforded
by the northern shipbuilding tradition. The end of the Middle Ages was to
witness the triumph of Nordic cogs and Portuguese caravels, the first to
replace the oar-like lateral rudders with a central rudder fixed to the stern-
post of the keel. It is often claimed, though not finally proved, that the
combination of the new rudder with other characteristics of the Atlantic
ships was the decisive advantage that inaugurated a new era of sailing on
the wide open seas.

The faltering progress of industrial equipment

Once again, as in the case of agricultural expansion, it has been necessary to look
ahead and pick out the general trends rather than the early stages of a development which continued through the late Middle Ages. On the whole, the story

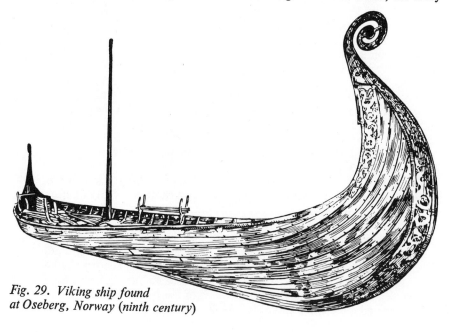

*Fig. 29. Viking ship found
at Oseberg, Norway (ninth century)*

of medieval techniques is rather uneventful: there are no great discoveries made by certain scientists at certain dates and celebrated in books, but just a succession of unheralded new contrivances which spread like a heath fire and are reported casually, very often long after they have been first used.

Fig. 30. Mediterranean galley of the twelfth century
(after a miniature by Pietro
da Eboli, Liber ad honorem
Augusti, Bibliothèque de la
Bourgeoisie, Berne.

In fact, which is the date to remember? The moment when an innovation is conceived, or when it is adopted in a progressive environment? When its basic principles win general acceptance? When its applications have been worked out and put to use? Any two of these moments may be centuries and continents apart. The silk worm, China's first direct contribution to the industrial equipment of Europe, was imported into the Byzantine Empire at the time of Justinian; it first appears in northern Italy in the tenth century, becomes a typical Italian product during the Renaissance, but does not cross the Alps until the modern era. Paper, another Chinese product, is said to have been imported into the eastern provinces of the Caliphate by prisoners captured in the battle of Talas (751), but Moslem Spain is not known to have produced paper until the twelfth century, only a short time before Italy.

Apart from those rare inventions of whose origins, progress and results we have some knowledge, how many others there are about which nothing or hardly anything is known! Take, for example, a simple but essential labour-saving device of the largest medieval industry: the pedal loom. When was it invented and by whom? By a cabinet-maker, perhaps. Applying a pedal to the old hand loom required no major outlay of capital or effort of imagination, but the ancients had not thought of it, probably because the time and the fatigue of weavers were matters of hardly any consequence. In the late Middle Ages, a weaver became something more than a cipher, and the pedal loom appeared; when, exactly, we cannot tell, but by the twelfth century it suddenly was mentioned in places as far apart as Flanders and the Byzantine Empire. In turn, the quickened tempo of weaving called for an acceleration in the production of yarn. This was made possible by another simple invention, occurring at about the same time as the pedal loom: the spinning wheel. Thus the progress of the woollen industry in the late Middle Ages resembled on a minor scale the develop-

138

Fig. 31. Scandinavian boat, fourteenth century fresco in the church at Skamstrup (Denmark), about 1375; National Historiske Museum, Frederiksberg.

ment of the cotton industry in the early stage of the Industrial Revolution, when spinning improvements proceeded simultaneously with improvement in looms.

We are a little better informed about the vicissitudes of the water mill, a Hellenistic invention which the ancients had not fully exploited, no doubt because they found it cheaper to put slaves or animals to the grind. To make the installation of a water mill profitable, it was necessary on the one hand that the price of slaves should rise, and on the other hand that the investor should be assured of a plentiful and continuous supply of grist. Both conditions were fulfilled when the slaves were converted into serfs and the lord of a manor was able to compel his dependants to send their corn to his mill. In 1086 almost five thousand mills, almost all of them water mills, were counted in England alone — one for every four hundred inhabitants. As early as the Stone age, fire had been subdued and put to work on behalf of mankind; in the Middle Ages, water became the second great natural source of energy exploited for the industrial needs of the masses (Fig. 33).

Gradually, as 'commercialization' stimulated new branches of industry, so the principle of the water mill found new applications. By the beginning of the fourteenth century it was used in the fulling of cloth, the preparation of paper, and the grinding of the ingredients for dyeing and tanning. It also operated trip hammers and bellows in forges, mechanized saws, and silk-winding devices. In its original function of grinding cereals, it had been not displaced but bolstered by another engine which harnessed a third natural source of energy wherever water was unavailable or insufficient: the windmill.

Would it have been possible to use water power for the mechanization of looms, which would have given to the largest medieval industry an impetus comparable to that given by steam to nineteenth-century industries? Perhaps. But even after the disappearance of slavery, the time and fatigue of a weaver were not worth more, in the calculations of the merchants who controlled his industry, than the purchase of a plain pedal loom. Thus the commercial revolution had to stop short of the industrial revolution.

VII.   PRIVATE INITIATIVE AND ASSOCIATIONS

Machines do not deserve the scorn poured upon them, even in our own mechanized age, by certain intellectuals; for is not a machine a creation of human intelligence, much as a work of art? Yet neither should their importance be over-estimated. No machine on its own can be the beginning of an economic revolution; rather, we believe, it is the revolution which produces the machine or endows it with usefulness. The tool has value only through the hand which uses it and the brain which directs it.

Still if one turns to intellectual equipment and initiative, one feels once again that the tenth century and the years immediately following mark a new dawn. There is a reaction against that inertia of spirit and will which for five or six centuries had pinned down Europe to poverty and ignorance. Not that the inertia had ever been total; even in the most discouraging periods there had been talented individuals, lively religious communities, sometimes enterprising laymen grouped around an ambitious ruler such as Charlemagne or Alfred 'the Great', Their efforts, however, had failed to stir deeply a sluggish, uncommunicative environment.

*Fig. 32. Venetian galley, fifteenth century;
from a bas-relief on the Contarini tomb, Padua.*

Fig. 33. Fortified mill at Barbaste (Lot-et-Garonne) fourteenth century.

Self-help in late mediaeval Europe

The great challenge to private initiative in late medieval Europe came from the fact that local and individual energies were stimulated by the demographic and economic growth while central governments and public authorities were still unready to channel them and indeed inadequate to maintain order and peace. A few individuals felt strong enough to do without any assistance and made their own laws. The others clung together as best they could, by contract or oath, through bonds of parentage or neighbourhood, or according to interests and ambitions held in common. Thus between the tenth and the twelfth centuries two apparently opposite tendencies came simultaneously to the fore: on the one hand, anarchic individualism; on the other, fraternities and voluntary private associations.

Individualism, the spirit of association, absence of governmental restrictions: these, until the era of contemporary state planning, are characteristics we invariably meet in all rapidly expanding economies. Separately, we find one or other of these characteristics in the Moslem states as well as in the Byzantine and Chinese Empires. But in these Empires, at the decisive turn of late medieval economic growth, individualism and the spirit of association found themselves hamstrung by governments suspicious of independent initiative and bent on insuring stability at the cost of flexibility. In the Islamic world, uncompromising individualism tended to paralyse the spirit of association, and the lack of organized collaboration finally left for the government no middle ground between despotism and total anarchy. It is only in Europe that the three characteristics were united, once at the beginning of the commercial revolution of the

Middle Ages, and a second time at the start of the Industrial Revolution of the modern age. And in both cases this combination seems to have helped Europe to get ahead of the rest of the world.

Commercial Contracts

In the medieval contracts of maritime trade individualism makes to the spirit of association only the indispensable minimum of concessions necessary for the temporary pooling of capital and spreading of risks. The most typical agreement is the *commenda*, unknown to classical antiquity, sparsely outlined in the Moslem and Byzantine Near East by the seventh century, mentioned for the first time in the West in a Venetian document of the tenth century but universally used in the Mediterranean seaports, both Christian and Moslem, in the twelfth and thirteenth centuries. This contract binds, for one single commercial venture — an outward and return voyage — a non-travelling investor and a travelling manager. The investor bears any loss on the capital and takes the larger part of the profit (usually, three-quarters) in case of success. The manager risks his labour for a quarter of the possible profit. The sharing of risks and profits introduces a social element into an agreement which is otherwise indistinguishable from ordinary loans, the investor bearing no liability beyond the capital he has entrusted to the other party and taking no direct part in the management of the affair.

> Commercial 'venture', we said; in fact, in the oldest contracts, the voyage is called *taxedion* (from the Greek: 'military expedition'), the activity of the manager *procertari* (from the Latin: 'to engage in a struggle'), and the action of investing capital is *iactare* (to 'throw' it, as in casting dice). But risks are, generally speaking, well calculated. We know a case in the twelfth century where a Genoese capitalist trebled his first investment in two years, thanks to three successive *commenda* contracts, while the traveller amassed a sum almost equal to that which the capitalist had entrusted to him at the start. In this particular case the investor was a rich man whereas the manager was a youth whose only assets were initiative and intelligence. But the roles were often reversed; the humblest people offered their mite in *commenda* to a rich traveller in the hope of being thus linked with his fortune. Also two merchants of similar status often took turns in the roles of investor and manager.
>
> In a more rudimentary form, contracts similar to the Mediterranean *commenda* are found in the commerce of the North Sea and the Baltic from the thirteenth century onwards. Is this a derivation or a chance similarity? Since no documents of the earlier period have come down to us, we can only make a few guesses. It is possible that the northern version of the *commenda* goes back to the even more informal contracts mentioned in the Scandinavian sagas, and thence to the Byzantine maritime customs of the tenth century. The influence of Jewish and Italian law can also be invoked. But all things considered, it seems more probable that the parallel demands of maritime trade independently suggested to the

men of the north solutions comparable to those which the sailors of the south had found. England, it is worth noting, was closer to the Mediterranean but never used the *commenda* contract or its northern parallel.

In overland trade the contract which played the most prominent part — the fraternal society or company (literally, 'sharing of bread') — was founded on the principles which governed the joint administration of undivided inheritances. It often happened that the rightful claimants to the succession of a fief, an estate or a fiscal revenue left their shares in joint ownership in order to keep the property intact. Similarly the original members of a *compagnia* were brothers, cousins, sometimes brothers-in-law who agreed to pool their capital and their labour for a certain number of years; their best employees might later be promoted to membership and, at the same time, marry the daughter of one of the partners. All members of the company shared risks and profits in proportion to their contribution to the common capital and assumed joint and unlimited liability for all obligations contracted by any of the partners.

The *compagnia* was as tight and rigid as the *commenda* was loose and flexible. It was better suited to long-term projects, to patient and powerful planning. But it was more vulnerable than the *commenda:* the mistake of a single partner could undo the gains of several years and involve the other partners in a common ruin. Even among brothers, it required extraordinary trust.

Professional guilds

While a great variety of commercial contracts between individuals and families met specific business needs, professional associations and guilds promoted basic aspirations of broader groups.

What is the origin of these associations which blossomed suddenly in the tenth century in several cities of Europe, and soon became an essential part of urban life? Some of them were probably descended from the professional corporations of the Romans and Byzantines, or from the teams of serf workers of the early Middle Ages. Others may have stemmed from religious brotherhoods or from Germanic fraternities whose members met to drink and, in case of need, to help one another. But even where no precedents existed, trade associations emerged wherever a group of workers wished to protect their collective interests. Nor was this phenomenon restricted to Catholic Europe; from the tenth century onwards, trade guilds sprang up in China, in the Islamic world and at Byzantium, but nowhere did they enjoy as much freedom of action as in Catholic Europe.

In the early stage of the commercial revolution the same association, guild, hansa or corporation might include the greater merchants and capitalists as well as the humbler townspeople, retailers, shopkeepers, pedlars, crafsmen and apprentices. A common front was often helpful in the struggle for municipal self-government, in the organization of outgoing caravans and convoys, or in dealing with foreign merchants and governments. But even where a single association had originally existed, it soon split into a growing number of specialized tradesmen's and craftsmen's guilds. The guilds of the wealthier traders tended to become political pressure groups rather than economic bodies. On the other hand, the guild or corporation remained in general the typical economic organization of the smaller merchants and, still more, of the craftsmen and skilled manual workers.

Its aims have often been misunderstood by historians who were haunted by problems of their own age. Some have taken too literally the moral precepts which embellish most corporate statutes. Whatever he may claim, the main object of a trader could not be to serve God and mankind, but to sell his goods at a profit. The measures taken to guarantee quality and limit price sprang less from a regard for honesty than from the fear of antagonizing difficult customers; for in the Middle Ages, even at the height of the commercial revolution, the customer (as we say nowadays) is always right. On the other hand, the modern critics of medieval guilds think chiefly of the restrictions adopted after the fourteenth century, in an atmosphere of depression which transformed open associations into exclusive clubs. During the commercial revolution as a rule the guilds welcomed into their ranks as many new recruits as economic growth allowed them to absorb. Apprentices were of course in a subordinate position, but not on an unequal footing, each of them being destined to become master in his turn.

In order to appreciate fully the role of the guilds, it must not be forgotten that while a merchant could increase indefinitely the volume of his business, the artisan was limited by the moderate return of manual work. He could not increase his return either by exploiting cheaper manual labour which since the disappearance of slavery no longer existed, or by relying upon machinery which was still at an embryonic stage. Even in a fully expanding economy, therefore, a craftsman soon reached the ceiling of his productivity and ran the risk of being exploited by capitalist merchants who could hire the services and finance the workshops of many artisans at once. If the demand lagged, he might be undercut by fellow craftsmen who worked faster or used inferior materials. The guild strove to protect him by bringing the entire profession under unified rules, standards and leadership while preserving the autonomy of his workshop. It only partly succeeded, at the price of restrictions, some of which may have hindered initiative and growth. But in as far as it succeeded, it prevented the commercial revolution from inflicting on the workers the sufferings which were to accompany the beginning of the Industrial Revolution.

As the representative of a trade, the guild had an important part to play. In the political and economic councils of the town it spoke with an authority which none of its individual members could have wielded. It sometimes carried out important negotiations with foreign governments and acted as a cartel in buying raw materials and selling products. By standardizing the production it facilitated international distribution. A workshop of Ypres would be known only in the town, but 'Ypres cloth' of regulation size and quality guaranteed by the seal of the guild was known and sought after from Novgorod to Alexandria.

Unfortunately the success of Ypres cloth brought about the decline of guild ideals. Any industry which asserted itself in the international markets was bound sooner or later to outgrow the resources of craftsmen, attract outside investments, and fall into the power of the great merchants. Thus, in Ypres, the *entrepreneurs* who bought the wool in England and sold the cloth to the international clientèle of the Champagne fairs determined by the amount of goods they ordered the prosperity or the failure of master craftsmen and apprentices. Capitalism could rise in industry, but it was commercial capitalism.

Even the sensational discovery in the tenth century of deposits of copper, lead and silver in the Rammelsberg in Central Germany did not transform the miners into industrial capitalists. The 'silver rush' it occasioned, and later rushes caused by discoveries in other parts of the region, established for the whole of the Middle Ages the supremacy of German mines and miners. Europe was hungry for metals to feed her mints, improve her tools and accelerate her progress. But non-precious metals were sparingly used in her modest industrial equipment. Gold and silver are not in themselves wealth and, besides, the commercial revolution was based above all on credit. It was not the manufacturers of silver but the traders in silver who amassed the fortunes. As for the miners, they formed companies in which masters and workmen fairly equitably divided a modest income and were content to earn their living without being anyone's serfs. Theirs was no doubt an uneventful life with a restricted outlook, but it was certainly much better than that of the slaves and convicts who had worked in the mines of Athens and Rome.

Slavery and serfdom

It seems fitting to end our brief survey of the revival of initiative in the late Middle Ages with those who had no right to show any: the slaves. In the tenth century a linguistic innovation — the gradual adoption of the term *sclavus* in the place of *servus* to describe the man without rights — marks for us the end of the long journey which partially redeems, in our eyes, the discouraged muddling of the early Middle Ages. Slavery finally became an abnormal status for a native of Catholic Europe, serfdom becoming thenceforth the minimum condition of life. It was no longer acceptable that a Christian of established stock should be reduced to the state of cattle, but only a Slav (*sclavus*) or other infidel. (On the other hand, a *sclavus* was not automatically enfranchised after he had been baptized, and as late as the mid eleventh century the Bishop of Chur saw nothing wrong in colecting twopence per head for slaves sold in his market).

Another linguistic fact, the disappearance of the term *colonus* (originally 'farmer' or 'peasant') from the vocabulary of the tenth century emphasizes the other mass change which had been completed at the same time as the limited emancipation of the slaves: henceforth the small tenants, who were formerly free but degraded, could scarcely be distinguished from slaves who had been upgraded but not totally freed. Both were in fact serfs, that is legally free in relation to everybody but their lord; both were attached to their lord and through him to the soil which they cultivated. They owed to him in perpetuity various services and payments whose nature often depended not on the personal status of the man, but on the kind of tenure by which the land was held (freehold or holding in villeinage, 'servile' or 'ingenuile' parcel of land). These bonds, more elastic but more tenacious than the slaves' chains — for it is more difficult to modify the routine of a property than to free a man — had been formed in an age of stagnation. Mobility, the characteristic of the age of expansion, could not abolish them immediately, but it loosened them in some cases and broke them in others.

Towards the end of the tenth century, in fact, disobedience becomes almost general and the struggle dramatic. Otto III legislates against 'the serfs aspiring to liberty' who deny their lords; the duke and nobles of Normandy suppress with bloodshed a raging revolt of their peasants. (Incidentally, this is also the era of the Kharidjite and Qarmate peasant revolts in the Moslem world, and of the unsuccessful attempts of Byzantine emperors in defence of small farmers oppressed by the 'powerful'. The results are different, but the general demographic upsurge causes high tides everywhere.)

Then the conflict between serfs and lords, between numbers and strength, breaks down into a thousand separate clashes, among which are interspersed as many cases of peaceful and fruitful collaboration. Towns, those strongholds of free initiative, also intervene. All this will be part of the background of the following chapters.

There is no liberty without danger, no growth without conflict. The tenth century tore Catholic Europe from the wretched security she had found some hundred years earlier. In exchange it gave her opportunity. Only a minority were able to seize their chance; a minority which included men of all classes, from Hugh Capet, probably a descendant of a Saxon adventurer of the ninth century, who picked up a crown, to the obscure French slave who obtained from a Spanish ruler personal liberty and a plot of land freshly wrested from the still threatening Moslems. Social groups, too, competed doggedly for their chance. Even after the first fifty years of the tenth century, the harshest, this struggle still too often resembles that of wild beasts for us to overlook the distress of the losers. Yet the essential fact is that Europe is on the march and that a new society, more robust and more enlightened, is taking shape amidst the storm.

Chapter 2

THE TRIPARTITE SOCIETY

I. THE HARDENING OF THE SOCIAL HIERARCHY

'IN order to escape the evils which they saw coming, the people divided themselves into three parts. One was to pray God; for trading and ploughing the
second; and later, to guard these two parts from wrongs and injuries, knights
were created.' This is how Philip of Vitry, the secretary of Philip VI, described
in 1335 the formation of the harmonious trinitarian society of which France
was the finest example, the fleur-de-lys with three points the most appropriate
symbol. In forms less tinged by patriotism these ideas were generally accepted
in the whole of Catholic Europe, at least from the twelfth century onwards.
They met the general desire to see the concordance between human society and
the celestial order sealed, as it were, with the stamp of the Trinity. And all
things considered, they corresponded well enough to the actual hierarchy of
classes (or *orders*, as classes were then called) in the chief Western monarchies.

Of course, there were variations on the theme. For example, most writers
pretended not to see the profound difference between uppish merchants and
lowly peasants within the third order, or glossed over the belated appearance
of the knights. Others preferred to compare the social body to the human body,
with the feet representing the peasants. Still others saw not so much three
classes of men as a trinity of institutions: the Church, the Monarchy, the
University. There even were bourgeois writers who would not recognize the
superiority of the noble order, but they respected the ecclesiastic order though
not always individual clergymen.

Is it necessary to point out that the ideal of tripartite, hierarchical society was
to continue to inspire many philosophers, statesmen and privileged groups until
the era of the great Declarations of Rights? In the eyes of many people, moreover, such an ideal is still inseparably associated with the Middle Ages, as the
idea of empire is associated with ancient Rome.

Initial fluidity of classes, institutions and laws

The Roman Empire, however, constituted only the last phase of a civilization
which was previously republican. Similarly the tripartite society was but the
final hardening of an initially fluid social structure. In the tenth and eleventh
centuries the three orders were not unheard of, but their boundaries were ill-
defined. Church and state, priestly class and military class overlapped without

any precise ruling to specify their respective spheres. Again, the test of nobility and that of serfdom were so unclear that it was possible to speak officially of 'serf knights' in Germany and of 'peasant knights' in Castile, without offending anyone's sense of logic. None of the classes was closed as a caste; members entered and left an order by a voluntary act or by a stroke of fortune rather than by right (or default) of birth. The tenth century in particular witnessed sweeping changes in the ranks of the nobility: the noble lineages of old standing perished in the struggle or died out without heirs, and their place was taken by new-comers who did not care to remember their ancestors. In our day there is no family possessing an authentic genealogical tree which goes back, in the male line, further than the last years of the ninth century.

This fluidity was engendered by the social mobility and governmental disorder of the period and reflected the haze of political and legal notions. Only one political theory was available, that of the Carolingian *Respublica Christiana*, with its interlocking priestly monarchy and monarchical priesthood. In the realm of symbols, its validity is proved by its extraordinary duration; in practice it looked towards the past more than towards the future and hardly took account of the impelling realities of its own present. It is true that during their short rule the Carolingians had been great promoters of new legislation and collectors both of barbarian customs and of canon law; but law 'is born old', that is, at best it gives recognition to established principles and needs constant revision. After the Carolingian Empire broke down, there elapsed a long period of time during which the kings of France scarcely drew up a single regulation (nor would the regulation have been enforceable beyond their immediate domains, if it had been issued), while the German king-emperors made do with a few laws of restricted application. Only England, which had not been part of the Carolingian Empire, continued to produce collections of royal legislation from time to time. These were small, sketchy codes devoted largely to element-ary rules of administration and of penal law. Even this limited activity was regarded as aimed at declaring existing norms of legal behaviour, not at influencing the behaviour itself. In the twelfth century Glanvill, the author of the first general treatise on English law, stated that 'the lord king neither wishes nor dares' to go against ancient and just customs.

While the theorists and the lawgivers rested, things changed too fast for the humbler clerks and administrators who had to take practical decisions. Nobody was there to remove the misgivings of a monk of Chartres who towards the end of the eleventh century was setting in order the charters of his monastery and found that none of the legal forms and definitions used in the charters of the tenth century seemed to fit his own time.

The development of customary law

In the absence of an official written law, society organized itself as it pleased according to its own customs. This was not altogether a new direction: barbarian customs and customary interpretations of Roman and Church law had been the main sources of the early mediaeval legal tradition. The tradition, however, usually presupposed a central enforcing authority and a standard text, be it the Theodosian Code, the Decretals, the Salic Law or the Edict of Rothari; no matter whether or not the text was actually available to the judge. It is only in the tenth century that the central authority steps aside, and local precedent triumphs over formal legislation.

Henceforward, the decisive argument for the legality of an institution, an action, a property right or a bond of dependence is the simple finding that the practice has existed for a long time and goes back to time immemorial. And as men's memory is short and influenced by self-interest, anyone who has taken possession of another man's rights — whether by force, cunning or perseverance — has a fair chance of not being disturbed by him. But on the other hand, if a person wishes to defend an ancient right against the claims of a newcomer it is absolutely necessary for him to see that the memory of it be not lost. Hence the tendency to multiply written documents that will prove usage from time immemorial; and if proof is lacking, to produce a forged document with a false date.

Thus the halt in state legislative activity coincided with a renewal of private legal industry. This at first took the modest form of private deeds and of inquests to ascertain precedents according to the testimony of the oldest members of a community. Later it gave rise to ever more searching studies which in the twelfth century led to an exuberant renaissance of the law and hence to a sharper definition of the three orders: noblemen, clergymen and peasants.

The three pillars of society and the missing fourth

At this point, the three pillars of society had actually become four. Townsmen no longer were a negligible quantity. But the symbolic City of Men made no special provision for the crude reality of city people. Western kings sometimes thought of grafting a town collectively into the feudal order, by calling it a 'vassal'; at the eastern end of Europe, a city called itself 'my Lord Novgorod the Great'. On the whole, political theorists ignored the fourth pillar, and for the time being we can do the same.

We shall now endeavour to describe the three orders, not at the moment when they have finally hardened but during the period of formation, between the late tenth century and the late twelfth. Occasionally, the thirteenth century will also supply details which earlier sources do not disclose. A really detailed image of society during two hundred years which were full of change is of course more than can be provided. We shall succeed at most in sketching a few impressions.

II.   UBIQUITY OF THE CHURCH

Whether or not the eleventh and twelfth centuries really deserve to be called 'the Age of Faith' *par excellence*, this much is certain: the ecclesiastical order held a higher place at that period than it has ever occupied since then. Materially, to begin with: small villages built as many as ten churches; towns with five to ten thousand inhabitants possessed several dozens; monasteries such as Saint-Riquier or Saint-Gall were far larger in area and population than many an urban centre; monastic orders such as the Benedictines and the Cistercians had more subordinates than certain kingdoms. Politically, too: apart from the indirect control over temporal affairs and individual consciences that stemmed from their religious functions, members of the clergy constituted, until the twelfth century, an absolute majority of the administration in most of the great states; at the head of perhaps a quarter of the local governments, they did not even refrain from leading personally their armies when it seemed necessary. Lastly and above all, culturally: although the identification of the cultured man with the member of the clergy (which has left its linguistic mark in the word 'clerk') gradually lost its validity, nevertheless the ecclesiastics continued until the thirteenth century to outnumber the laymen at all levels of the intellectual world.

> It is true that in the eleventh century a German chronicler remarked that 'in Italy all the children go to school' and it is not thought 'useless or unseemly to educate a child not destined for an ecclesiastical career'. But that was one of the many extravagances of a country contaminated by the Byzantines. In France Abelard's father, a knight who dabbled in literature and wanted his children to do the same, no doubt seemed quite as eccentric as his famous son was to appear at the beginning of the twelfth century. Afterwards the education of laymen made rapid progress, especially in practical fields such as administration, law and medicine, but did not prevent the clergy from dominating the arts: theatre, music, architecture, painting. They yielded courtly love to the laity, though it was a royal chaplain, André, who wrote the standard handbook on the subject; but their hand can be seen in secular or even anticlerical works such as the epics and the Goliardic songs. Moreover, clergymen were almost the only historians (until the twelfth century in Italy, in France until the thirteenth), thus making it more difficult for us to arrive at a just appreciation of the part played by the laity.

Clergy and laity: a world full of God

Is it not an anachronism, at any rate, to discriminate between 'lay' and 'ecclesiastical' in an epoch when this distinction had become so elusive? Although popes and emperors, bishops and princes fought innumerable battles for precedence and jurisdiction, although their disputes over specific portions of land or sources of revenue were relentless, not one of them (with the possible exception of Pope Paschal II, at a desperate dead-lock of the Investiture Struggle) ever considered untying the knots they so often had to cut. In their eyes, separating Church from State, establishing one compartment for religion and another for secular life, would have meant divorcing heaven and earth, an act not only impious but in fact impossible. Whereas sectarian minorities saw the devil's claw in all human institutions, the vast majority of men were certain that the whole world was a hierarchy of churches and God was present in all of them. Above, the Church triumphant of the blessed; on its fringe, the Church suffering of the souls in purgatory; here below, the Church militant of all the faithful, equally compelled to serve and glorify the Lord according to their different abilities. As Dante was to put it: 'The glory of Him who moves everything — Penetrates through the universe and shines — More here (in Paradise) and less elsewhere.'

What Dante sets forth was present in every mind. It was thought natural that laymen should ever be ready to assure the smooth working of ecclesiastical life with the help of their arms and the support of their advice, and just as natural that clergymen should have their say in all the functions of secular life. Of course there was discussion over the details, the extent and the form of the assistance which one branch of the Church militant owed to the other. But the clergy could not refuse their services to any of the faithful, excommunication being in principle only a temporary punishment, and the laymen had no objection if the specialists in prayer, the experts in theology, the channels of grace, levied tithes from them and judged them before granting absolution.

Unbelief is impossible

This ideal is not exclusively mediaeval: a section of the contemporary Church militant still longs for it. But it was in the Middle Ages, between the tenth and the thirteenth centuries, that it came nearest to being universally accepted in Europe and that it was most faithfully reflected in social life.

God was called to witness in every agreement; a blessing was asked on every enterprise; a pious pretext was sought for every amusement; time was measured in canonical hours. There was an exorcism for every illness, a formula to excommunicate the insects which devoured the harvest. God was invoked to establish the truth in legal proceedings, by means of the duel for the nobles, and by the ordeal of red-hot iron, fire or water for the commoners; or if these methods were discarded so as 'not to tempt the Lord', by the sacred oath of the interested parties on the Gospels or on a relic.

Faith did not take the same forms at all times or for all kinds of people, but the general outlook was alike. About the year 1000 the instinctive animism, taste for the miraculous and fondness for magic ritual of the uncultured masses came half-way to meet the mysticism of the intellectuals, their leaning to the supernatural, their love of the liturgy. Both of them saw in the scrupulous observance of rites, indeed in the repetition and multiplication of religious observances, an indispensable means of propitiating, on all occasions of life both trivial and solemn, a divinity still more feared than loved.

Some two hundred years later, the masses had gained some polish and the intellectuals had become more numerous and refined, but they still met halfway. It is no longer a question of appeasing God but of returning His love. Learned men ascribe to divine love the immutable laws of nature and the changing events of their own life; popular sentiment demands of divine love the granting of specific desires and hopes by prayers to influence the natural course of events.

Perhaps the most striking characteristic of the late mediaeval religious atmosphere is the fact that unbelief did not exist, or if it existed at all it was so rare, so well concealed that it has left no trace in the sources. We meet the last atheists in the pagan literature of Scandinavia. Later, Europe knew infidels (Jews, Moslems) and heretics of all shades, including those who denied the immortality of the individual soul, but she does not seem to have known either agnostics or atheists. The fact is that the whole Europe had advanced well beyond primitivism, which does not trouble to explain the hidden causes of things, but had not yet acquired sufficient scientific knowledge from which to draw explanations capable of offering an alternative to those which religious learning was always able to supply. A thousand years ago, God's wrath was the most clearly identifiable cause of a disaster, and divine assistance the surest remedy. It was possible not to be content with these and to seek temporal causes and cures, but it would have been recklessness to trust only in the latter.

Should we pity the men of the Middle Ages for their inadequate science which made them so vulnerable to disaster and disease? Should we envy their limited vision, which enabled them to rest in the physical centre of a universe moved by divine love? These are fascinating though insoluble questions which will occupy us again in another chapter.

A devil lurks everywhere

A huge cloud, however, darkened the spiritual horizon of our ancestors: for if it was possible to temper the wrath and deserve the love of God, it was impossible to steer clear of all the snares of the Devil. Banished for ever from heaven, the Enemy pursued the faithful on earth as shadow follows the light. He was the ubiquitous source of Evil, opposed to the source of Good, in this world where science and popular opinion were scarcely aware of indifferent or blind causes and effects. The antagonism was sharp enough to give the Demon a prestige which he no longer possesses today.

A frankly dualist current runs right through the Middle Ages. Manichaeans of Zoroastrian origin or Western inspiration, Byzantine Paulicians, Bulgarian Bogomils ('Bougres'), Western Neo-Manichaeans and Cathars (the 'pure' or 'good' men), and still others, isolated or grouped in dissident sects and churches, carry defeatism almost to the end. Ultimately God will triumph, of course, but here and now the Devil is on the point of prevailing; one must refuse and deny one self almost everything in this life if one wishes to win with God in the life to come. The earth is evil, the flesh is evil, procreation is wicked, meat and eggs are foul, the organized Church is corrupt. During the barbarian centuries dualism seems to have weakened as have all intellectual activities in the West. But it reappears for a moment in the sources of the Carolingian age, and shares in the general awakening of the following centuries. Immediately after the year 1000 it bursts out in a multiplicity of centres in France, Italy and Germany. Though mercilessly repressed by the official Church which sometimes likes to call these radical servants of God, 'worshippers of the Devil' dualism nevertheless continues to gain support.

The moderates differed from the dualists only in degree; after all, the Devil has his place in the Gospels and the Lord's Prayer. King of Hell and consequently associated with the Lord in the supreme administration of justice, Satan was conspicuous in all written, painted and sculptural representations of the Last Judgment (Fig. 34). Shortly before the Day of Wrath, which might be not too far away, he would be allowed to come very close to victory under the attractive garb of the Antichrist. In daily life he seduced men and women, sometimes begot children on the latter: even Thomas Aquinas believed it.

Nevertheless, let us point out that in the Middle Ages proper, the trials for witchcraft were far removed from the paroxysms they were to reach during the Renaissance and the first centuries of the modern age. Even the early medieval Lombards were sceptical enough to forbid witchcraft charges as contrary to common sense; it would take an alliance of obdurate superstition with inadequate science for common sense to fall into abeyance. The Devil repelled any would-be worshipper by his ugliness and grossness: unimpeachable witnesses saw him covering with excrement a holy nun from the Rhineland who resisted him. This episode took place, however, in the thirteenth century, when Satan had lost a little of the sinister dignity which still surrounded him in the pious legends of the tenth and eleventh centuries. As fearless as an epic hero, he then dared to face the saints in combat in order to turn them from their vocation or to prevent them

Fig. 34. The claws of the Devil; tympanum of the cathedral of Autun (Saone-et-Loire), twelfth century.

from saving a penitent sinner, consecrating some place or curing someone possessed. With the aid of myriads of demons who could change form and place at will, the Devil remained everywhere on the lurk. Caesarius of Heisterbach, a widely read writer and monk who died about 1240, detected his presence in thunder, hail, floods, illnesses, sudden noises, the howling of the wind and the rustling of leaves.

Intercessors are always at hand

Fortunately there were as many angels to support the faithful as there were devils to make them stumble. Often the fate of a soul was decided at the hour of death by a duel or a debate between these immortal creatures who were equally eager to gain new subjects for their celestial or infernal patron (Fig. 35) Every man, of course, was entitled to his own guardian angel.

Then there was a legion of saints. The piety of the people continually enlarged it, with the support of religious institutions which benefitted from it. Until 933 A.D. the canonization of a new candidate did not have to be authorized by a pontifical decree. The relics of the saints extended, in a tangible manner, their sojourn on earth and performed miracles which a faithful might think unobtainable from their intangible spirit.

Fig. 35. The Weighing of Souls; detail from an altar-screen by the Master of Soriguerola, Romanesque period. Barcelona Museum.

The role of the Virgin, still restricted in the theology and devotion of the early Middle Ages, was very rapidly enlarged during the eleventh and twelfth centuries. It is true that theology lagged behind popular piety: Thomas Aquinas, for instance, did not pronounce himself clearly on the doctrine of the immaculate conception, which was to be dogmatically defined by the Roman Church only in 1854. The faithful, however, increasingly relied upon the Virgin as the intercessor par excellence. On the altars, her countenance shed the stiff majesty of early medieval mosaics and ivories: she fondled her child, smiled at the gazing worshippers. To the harsh and basically anti-feminist religion of a violent age, she brought the ineffable sweetness of maternal and feminine love.

Christ, too, though still somewhat remote in the iconography and feeling of the tenth century, was to draw nearer to men in proportion as religion emphasized His human nature rather than His divine, transcendent quality. He still was crowned by the glory of Heaven, but, on the cross, he was represented realistically as a suffering man. From the twelfth century on, even the Holy Spirit, up to then regarded by Western religion as too abstract for personal devotion, began to raise the hopes of a large number of men, who impatiently awaited the fulfillment of the triumph of justice announced by the Son. Only the Father remained inaccessible; His reign seemed to have ended with the coming of the Son, and prayers were addressed to Him largely through Christ. For Jesus was both advocate and judge; His sacrifice was renewed constantly at the Eucharist, with the Church as intermediary, and even the humblest layman could strive to imitate Him and reach Him directly.

The stream of mysticism had never dried up from the beginnings of Christianity, and it was to be swollen in the course of the late Middle Ages. Nevertheless, almost all the faithful counted on the assistance of the clergy, who were the first link in the chain of intercessors with God. In spite of doubts raised in some quarters on the validity of sacraments administered by unworthy priests or on the actual presence of Christ in the bread and wine, orthodox doctrine removed people's anxiety. It was not absolutely necessary that the clergy should all be models of virtue or paragons of science, so long as ordination qualified them to celebrate the rites and dispense the sacraments which led to eternal salvation.

III.   THE PROBLEMS OF THE ECCLESIASTICAL ORDER

The denunciations of the great reformers of the age of Gregory VII still ring in the ears of church historians. In keeping with them, the period between the dissolution of the Carolingian Empire and the beginning of the Investiture Struggle may be described as a monstrous moral decline, explainable only by the abnormal interference of the laity in the administration of the Church. Dominated and contaminated by the base passions of the secular nobility, the clergy are said to have lost their ideals and yielded to the temptations of luxury and avarice. The healthy minority, long powerless to restore a corrupt majority to the path of righteousness, had to break the power of the laity and to defy the emperor in order to assert itself. Such is the picture given in most text-books.

That picture ought to be qualified. Granted that lay interference was excessive in the tenth and eleventh centuries, it could not be called abnormal; even Charlemagne, that dutiful son of the Church, had tightened the reins over ecclesiastics in need of discipline. And though clergy and nobility alike shared the coarse habits of a coarse society, they did not on that account cease to produce saints and men of virtue. When the need to clean up the ecclesiastical order became evident enough to a sufficient number of clergy, the laity supplied considerable support to the reform movement.

Saints and sinners

In essence the religious ideal never changed. Although there are a great many curses, excommunications and formulae of pride and violence in the sources of the tenth and eleventh centuries, one also finds in them the language of the Sermon of the Mount, the Fathers of the Church, and the Benedictine Rule. Plain goodness never attracts the attention of chroniclers, but there must have been men and women of goodwill beside the celebrated Saints of the period.

A sermon, an illness, a prodigy temporarily recalled to duty the most hardened sinners. Let us only consider three lay members of a family of illustrious cut-throats, the Counts of Anjou: Fulk II, who, it is said, put on a clerk's habit to sing the offices; Fulk III, who had himself dragged with a rope round his neck before the Holy Sepulchre in Jerusalem by two serving men who cried as they beat him, 'Lord, have mercy on this traitor and perjuror!'; Geoffrey Martel, who, on seeing a meteor fall ominously in his garden, hastened to build an abbey there at his own expense. No doubt a virtuous life would have been more commendable than these theatrical demonstrations but they show, nevertheless, that the great were convinced that the narrow gate of heaven is opened only to those who humble themselves.

When applied to religious life, this principle could lead very far. Nilus, born about 910 into a great family in Byzantine Calabria, became a monk without much enthusiasm, until an illness converted him to the most rigorous asceticism. His fasts were broken only by scanty vegetarian meals; for clothing he used only a goatskin which was covered with vermin, for he changed it but once a year. Still he loved singing, calligraphy, reading and taking strolls. Otto III came in person to pay homage to him and wished to take him to Rome, whence his light could have spread more easily. Nilus refused: like the unicorn, he was 'an animal who lives free and independent'. At most he would be willing to visit nearby Monte Cassino, but he turned back in horror on learning that the abbot and his monks had taken a bath and on hearing the sound of a guitar coming from the refectory. Yet Monte Cassino had just been reformed under the direct inspiration of the saintly Abbot of Cluny, Odo. Far from being shocked by music, Odo was the author of the first manual systematically using seven letters for pitches. One of his favourite sayings was: 'If I am to be damned, I prefer that it should be because of my mercy rather than my severity'.

Nilus' inflexible virtue and remarkable learning inspired a small number of imitators, but the Cluniac order attracted a far larger following thanks to its spirit of compromise, which was so close to the moderation of Benedict of Norcia. To the scholars who reproached the Cluniac rule for its tendency to multiply prayers to the detriment of intellectual and manual work, the Abbots of Cluny could have replied that the essential thing was to lead the monks back to God by the road they understood and liked best.

Nicolaism and simony

Although Catholicism has always praised continence, clerical celibacy did not become an obligation until the fourth century. The Eastern churches still admit exceptions; in the West the observance varied. In the eleventh century almost all the priests were 'Nicolaites', that is to say, married or concubinary. Many of them justified themselves by explaining that their slender incomes would have been insufficient without the help of a housewife. The Gregorian reform was to forbid this practice, though with only partial success. For a long time popular literature continued to speak of 'priestesses' more in jest than indignation. The numerous loves of certain bishops, the promiscuity in certain monasteries, the sexual perversions (the prevalence of which has probably been exaggerated by Saint Peter Damian and other zealous reformers) must have shocked public opinion more, though opinion was not easily stirred up at that time.

On the other hand, no objective historian can adopt without qualification the statement that all married clergy put the interests of their family above those of the Church. There were honourable dynasties of bishops at Quimper, Nantes and elsewhere. Pope John XI (931–936) according to the best informed, official sources was the son of Pope Sergius III and, in political matters, the tool first of his mother, then of his brother. But his name is joined to the decisive pontifical privilege which put Cluny in a position to pursue the good work of moderate reform without interference from lay or ecclesiastic powers, at a time when 'almost all the monasteries' (in the words of the Pope) 'have been turned from their objectives'.

Simony, that is to say the sale and purchase of ecclesiastical offices, and of the acts a clergymen could perform, set a much more serious problem than Nicolaism. In its broadest sense it included any fee demanded for any religious service. In 1301, for instance, Boniface VIII — whom Dante nevertheless placed in the circle of Hell where simoniacs are punished — forbade the Breton clergy, on pain of excommunication, to charge for funerals 'anything at all, except what might be given them out of mere generosity'. (Sometimes, he said, they demanded up to a third of the deceased's mobile goods.) But the charges for specific, legitimate services, which it has never been possible to eliminate completely, are not such serious matters as the sale and purchase of an office in the Church.

It is true that those who indulged in these practices pointed to the distinction between ordination and consecration on the one hand (conferred by God through his ministers) and appointment to a specific position. Since the holder of the office of archbishop, priest or abbot possessed certain endowments and revenues, it seemed normal that a new nomination should give rise to such payments as any transfer of goods would ordinarily entail. Most of the faithful saw abuse in it only when the greed or favouritism of the contracting parties allowed the sacred office to fall into the hands of an incompetent or unworthy man. A viscount of Narbonne recounts without the slightest embarrassment the sale of the archbishopric of Narbonne (vacated by the death of his uncle) to his wife's uncle, and the fact that the latter in turn had given the office to his son, a boy of ten. 'I am not complaining of that', he continues, 'but of his conduct after he became archbishop'. On the other hand, in 1045, when a most virtuous priest bought, in exchange for a pension, the resignation of a deplorable pope, and was elected in his place under the name of Gregory VI, the opponents of simony hastened to congratulate him. It is true that the following year the Emperor Henry III, who was annoyed by an irregularity he had not personally sanctioned, had Gregory deposed, and imposed his own equally virtuous candidate. The latter was acclaimed in his turn, generally by the same people who had placed their hopes in Gregory VI.

Spurred on by laymen, the reformers get under way

By punishing a well-meaning act of simony, was Henry III exercising a time-honoured right of imperial intervention, or was he infringing the principle that God alone could judge a sovereign pontiff, as Wazon, the fearless Bishop of Liege, wrote to him in so many words? This was an administrative problem, not a theological one. Had a doctrine been involved, the emperors would have promptly yielded, for, unlike their Byzantine counterparts, they felt too unlearned to express a theological opinion of their own.

The interference of the temporal power was limited to the recruitment and discipline of the ecclesiastical staff. It was founded on three well established legal principles: the responsibility of the State for the maintenance of order and the functioning of the public services, of which public worship was unquestionably the most important; the role of the State as mouthpiece of the laity, whose co-operation was indispensable in ecclesiastical elections; finally, the right of the State to choose its officials, a right which could be invoked whenever a cleric exercised temporal powers.

The first of these justifications went back to Roman law and the Empire of Constantine. The Carolingian restoration had revived and consecrated it. It could not have been rejected without condemning all Charlemagne's work.

The second justification was pegged to the tenacious, yet vague and inconsistent customs of canon electoral law. The primitive church required the participation of the laity as well as that of the clergy in every election, but the choice of the spokesmen for the laity and their actual powers varied according to the period, the country and the office. By the tenth century, since political assemblies of free men were reduced to councils of nobles, and the councils were seldom consulted, it is not surprising that the main body of lay faithful at most was invited to ratify elections by acclamation. Usually, however, what were called 'the principal elements' of the people took a more active part in the election; or else the lay voice could be concentrated in the person of the sovereign or of the descendant of the founder-owner of a church or monastery, who indicated his candidate directly to the representatives of the clergy. In their turn, the ecclesiastical electors varied from one place to another. It was only gradually that the tendency prevailed of having bishops (including the Pope, Bishop of Rome) nominated by the principal clergy of their diocese ('cardinals', 'canons'), and lower ranks of clergy nominated by their bishops.

As for the third justification (the fact that most clergy exercised functions of government), it brought the clergyman-vassal under feudal law: in return for investiture on the part of the suzerain, he had to do homage and swear fidelity to his lord. In principle, fidelity to a suzerain and obedience to an ecclesiastical superior were in no way incompatible. Wazon, that jealous defender of the independence of the Pope, had no qualms about writing to Henry III: 'We are responsible to you for our secular administration and to him in all that concerns divine service.'

Thus, when the movement to restore order and good behaviour among the members of the clergy got under way, there was no deep conflict between Church and State. Clear-sighted princes and conscientious prelates alike showed a desire to rebuild a clergy worthy of confidence, as much for the government of men as for the service of God. The princes were able to act first because they had might on their side and also because it was easier for them to cauterize an infection which was not their own.

The first moves were of necessity on a limited, local scale. When Duke William I of Aquitaine founded the Abbey of Cluny in response to the exhortation of the blessed Bernon (910), he described his aims in the usual, rather self-centred way: 'I trust and hope that even though I myself am unable to despise all things, nevertheless by taking charge of despisers of the world whom I regard as righteous men, I may receive the reward of the righteous'. Less usual was the fact that he isolated the abbey from contaminating surroundings, and that the abbots could place themselves under the direct jurisdiction of the Pope. Other centres of reform arose in Lorraine, in England and in Italy, and their example spread from monastery to monastery during the following 150 years.

Finally, from 1045 onwards, Emperor Henry III transplanted the headquarters of reform to Rome itself, by selecting a series of popes sprung from the clergy of Germany and Lorraine, where discipline had been best maintained. The work of religious regeneration, which had meanwhile grown from a mere purging of glaring abuses to a deeper understanding of the tasks of the Church, was now entrusted primarily to the Pope, who was assisted by a small army of hermits, preachers, and monks recognizing no other superior than him.

The Popes take over the reins

At this point the struggle began to change its nature and to be inserted into the general counter-offensive of monarchs against localism. The papacy wished to reaffirm its absolute primacy over the ecclesiastical order and free it from all dependence in relation to the lay, feudal order. France, with its turbulent feudalism and its discredited simoniacal king (Henry I, 1031–1060), seemed to be a more accessible area than the Empire. In fact Pope Leo IX (1048–1054) had no difficulty in convicting dozens of bishops of simony and in excommunicating several. The partial submission of France soon led to that of England, where Norman influence, already pronounced under Edward the Confessor, was to end in the Norman conquest in 1066. (The Norman kings, however, were readier to reform the Church than to share power with the Pope; an agreement was reached only in 1106, with Rome gaining a good deal on principle but not much on practical grounds.)

On the other hand, the uncompromising attitudes of both the papal legates and the Patriarch of Constantinople, the former determined to impose outright the supreme authority of Rome and the latter to reject it outright, broke in 1054 the last threads attaching the Byzantine Church to the West. It has been argued that the break was the inevitable conclusion of several centuries of mounting tension. Perhaps it was, but the schism was a great defeat for Catholicism, all the more serious because at the time it occurred the parties did not realize how final it was.

In the Western Empire the popes had to wait until the minority of Henry IV created a favourable opportunity. In 1059 Nicholas II cut the knot of papal subordination by decreeing that the popes would henceforward be elected by the Roman cardinals (and then acclaimed by the clergy and the people of the diocese), without any pressure from the laity or from the clergy outside the region. At the same time he forbade all priests to accept investiture of a sacred office from a layman. The first decree was imposed quite rapidly; it still governs papal elections in modern times. By contrast the other was only partially carried out until Henry IV, now of age, opposed it openly. This opposition started the Investiture Struggle, whose ups and downs, direct and indirect consequences were to shake the entire structure of Europe.

IV. FEUDALISM, A SYSTEM OF GOVERNMENT AND A WAY OF LIFE

In popular opinion the feudal system comes near to being placed beside simony among the great sins of the Middle Ages. The very expression was born under an unlucky star, in the decree of the National Assembly which on 11 August 1789 'completely destroyed the feudal system' in France. Later the 'feudal system' was to share with the 'capitalist system' the scorn of the Marxists. Finally, the adjective 'feudal', which does go back to the Middle Ages and describes definite legal relationships, is most commonly associated in our textbooks with the noun 'anarchy'.

Actually feudalism was not anarchical except when it failed. It was a form of government, like liberal democracy or socialism, to both of which it bequeathed many ruins to clear away, but also some useful material to be salvaged. Today it is as easy to criticize it as to prove that the telephone is better than the carrier pigeon. The fact remains that before electricity was tamed the pigeon was helpful.

Comparisons, antecedents, genesis

If we dispense with a strict definition, we can say that the feudalism of mediaeval Europe belongs to a large and cosmopolitan family. Sociologists have found parallels ranging from Egypt five thousand years ago to Ethiopia thirty years ago, and passing by way of Confucius' China and Zarist Russia. Such parallels are always instructive: they correct the specialist's tendency to see merely the imprint of unique local traditions and circumstances where general causes should be invoked. Nevertheless, we must emphasize that the feudalism of Catholic Europe bears less resemblance to the other so-called feudalisms than the British Empire does to the Roman Empire, or the democracy of 1789 to Athenian democracy. Moreover, modern democracies and empires are fond of comparing themselves with their ancestors; medieval feudalism did not even suspect that it had any. At most the tales of chivalry disguised Alexander and Caesar as medieval knights.

> Legal historians, who have a greater concern with exactitude, have found more direct antecedents to feudal institutions among the primitive Germans, the Romans of the decadence, the Celts and even the Moslems of Spain. Even without going that far, we cannot deny that the constituent parts of feudalism — vassalage, benefice, immunity — existed in germ throughout barbarian Europe. Perhaps they would have ripened in the Visigoth kingdom if the Arabs had not shortened its life. Still, the essential fact is that they did not.
>
> The Carolingians were the first to transform their dependants systematically into vassals, and tenth century France was the first to adopt feudalism as the only satisfactory form of government. Germany followed suit after some delay; the Roman territory resisted feudalism to the end. Therefore it seems pointless to ascribe the rise of feudalism to the Teutonic mind or the Latin tradition. If a native soil must be found for it, it can only be in France.

The child of experience rather than of abstract principles (like most medieval inventions) feudalism rebuilt the state on the foundation of voluntary private solidarity. It was high time. Even the most capable sovereigns could not communicate their will and enforce their command throughout their kingdom; political institutions were inadequate to the most elementary administrative tasks and ceased to function at the first crisis; loyalties did not carry beyond the local scene. A ruler could only count on a few faithful men whom he knew personally.

Originally this retinue included destitute people, serfs, adventurers, as well as rich, powerful and high-born ones. This motley group of 'faithful' had 'recommended' themselves to the master, had promised him their 'loyalty' and had pronounced themselves his 'vassals' (from the Celtic gwas, man). For his part, the master had promised them his protection and his support: they were to share with him the spoils of war, eat at his table and sleep under his roof, or receive a property supplied with the tools, animals and persons necessary to draw a living from it ('benefice', or later, 'fief'). Until then, vassalage and benefice had been quite separate; both were essentially private contractual relationships. They became a system of government when they interlocked, the vassal gradually was charged or charged himself with the administration and defence of the fief, while his superior ('suzerain' or 'lord') took less and less responsibility for it. Every layer of function of government that passed from the lord to the vassal (such as low and high justice, minting, collection of tolls) was an 'immunity'; the transition was completed when the immunity was total.

At first the powers of the vassal on his fief were not radically different from those which any government would delegate to its paid officials. He performed public services and collected the proceeds as a representative of the lord; the lord could dispatch to the fief other representatives to control or supplement the work of the vassal and could order the vassal to serve outside the fief. The accumulation of immunities, however, caused the vassal to take over virtually the entire administration of the fief, keep back nearly all the proceeds, permit no other representative of the suzerain to trespass on his ground, and limit his outside services to a minimum. This, too, in a time of difficult communications and frequent emergencies, might be regarded as the most practical solution for both the vassal and the lord. And if localism was to win the day, even the loosest bond of vassalage was the only alternative to the complete disintegration of the state.

The success of feudal government depended largely on the balance of immunities. If they were not ample enough, the vassal felt restricted in his functions and insufficiently compensated for his services; his pledge of loyalty would not restrain his inclination to revolt. If immunities were too ample, the fief became an independent entity and the suzerain gained nothing from it except an abstract recognition of his paramount dignity.

The second danger has particularly struck the modern critics of feudalism; it is what leads them to speak of 'feudal anarchy'. But feudalism, by its very nature, was no more adapted to anarchy than it was to tyranny. It was based on a theoretical equipoise of reciprocal obligations, a balance always upset, to be sure, by the weight of the stronger. The vassal was the stronger in tenth-century France and thirteenth-century Germany; but in twelfth-century England and fourteenth-century France the stronger was the king.

An aristocracy of specialists

At the end of this evolution, which we have had to reduce to its salient features, the feudal order had become an aristocracy of specialists. The vassal was by definition a nobleman and hence only concerned himself with noble occupations: war, religion, justice, administration. The 'benefice' was almost always identified with land, the most convenient and valued source of revenue in an epoch when agriculture was the queen of the economy. Amply assured of his maintenance, the lay vassal improved his equipment and military training. His horse, sword, armour and skill at arms made him invincible to non-professional armies. His castle protected him from surprise attacks. Some lay vassals acquired a taste for law and administration, especially in England, but the great majority were content to know just enough about them to govern their fief.

Their intellectual shortcomings were made good by the opposite leanings of the ecclesiastic vassals, who for their part were rarely great fighters but developed their administrative and legal skills. Wealth was a temptation: it nurtured simony and engulfed the holders of fiefs into secular affairs. But it could also be a tool: it supported the building of churches, the study of theology and the struggle against simony. And so the most conscientious prelates were often the most zealous collectors of fiefs: such were the abbots of Cluny. They also tended to be punctilious administrators, less capricious than most lay vassals but more inexorable in exacting all that was due to them.

We know too little about the conditions of the masses during the barbarian era to determine whether feudalism as a whole represented an improvement or a change for the worse as far as they were concerned. But certainly the feudal aristocracy fought, prayed and governed more competently than the barbarian nobility it replaced.

The feudal style

Feudalism was more than a method of government. Like democracy and socialism it became a way of living, an attitude of mind whose stamp marked all social intercourse. It affected the relationship of man to God, husband to wife, student to teacher, apprentice to master, friend to friend. It still marks certain of our relationships today. To give a superficial but familiar example, socialism expects us to call the woman who works with us 'comrade'; democracy teaches us to treat her as an equal; but it is because of feudal traditions that we call her 'madam' and that we have her walk on our right in case we might have to defend her 'with our sword'.

It would be naive to deduce from this, as has sometimes been done, that the feudal age changed into sceptres every kitchen broom, but unfair to forget that it was less coarse than the barbarian age and gained refinement as it advanced. To be sure, the nobles of the late Middle Ages often had all the faults we tend to attribute to them. They were warlike, fratricidal, dissolute, selfish, ignorant, hypocritical, capricious; and if they washed less rarely than most people think, they sometimes requested young girls to 'scratch' them, according to a tale of chivalry. But the shortcomings of individuals should not be taken as evidence of the attitude of a whole society. Not unlike democracy and socialism, feudalism cannot be fully understood without reference to its political and religious ideals.

It is true that the rules of conduct of feudalism were formulated and codified long after its birth, practice having preceded theory by a long way. But the seeds existed from the beginning, in the very conception of vassalage and in the religious colouring which the Carolingians imposed on it. The relationship between lord and vassal was essentially that between a father and an adopted son. It usually started with the 'mingling of hands', an ancient ceremony which must have symbolized the mixing of bloods before it represented the entrusting of one man to another: the vassal knelt down and placed his hands in the hands of the lord, the lord clasped the vassal's hands between his own and kissed him on the mouth. After this dramatization of the ambivalent position of the vassal — he bent his knees like an inferior, then was kissed as an equal — there was the specific pledge. The vassal took an oath of fidelity: as a typical formula of 1034 puts it, he undertook to be 'as faithful as a man must be to his elder (*senior*, whence *segneir, sir*)'. In turn, the lord 'invested' the vassal with a fief, by handing over to him a symbolic object; for customary law required concrete tokens of every transfer of possession. Had the vassal been a Byzantine or Moslem official, he might have been more literally 'invested' by receiving a vest or robe of office; in feudal Europe he had to be content with a piece of turf, a standard or a pastoral staff, or else he received the lord's sceptre or ring but had to return it at the end of the ceremony.

The nature of the bond: family or contract?

In theory, the vassal assumed far broader obligations than a simple employee or an ordinary subject. He became 'the man of' the lord to whom he had paid 'homage', that is to say, he devoted his whole existence to him. In practice, of course, specific terms had to be defined. Soon custom outlined certain negative duties (not to harm the lord, not to betray him) and positive duties (obedience, respect, help and advice). Later the obligations were spelled out more and more precisely: so many days of military service, so many dues in kind or in cash, so many appearances at the lord's court of law, such a present when the lord's eldest son became a knight or his eldest daughter married, or such a contribution to his ransom should he be taken prisoner.

For his part, the lord had a greater stake in the welfare of the vassal than that of a mere employer. Practically he might limit his contribution to conferring upon the vassal a specific fief; the fief, it was soon recognized, was a sufficient cause and compensation for the fidelity of the man who held it. Theoretically, however, the lord owed the vassal constant care and, if necessary, prompt help and advice. If the vassal died, the lord assumed the guardianship of his widow and minor children, unless he provided the widow with a new husband. But although the lord in certain respects held almost a father's role, he usually did not live close enough to his vassals to make them feel like members of his family, as did the courtiers of the *Ancien Régime*.

Family ties are by definition indissoluble, but a feudal bond, no matter how formally contracted and consecrated, remained basically a voluntary, personal and revocable act. Thus, it is because it was applied to feudal tenure that the word 'precarious' (granted in response to a prayer) acquired the modern meaning of 'unstable'. Any serious violation on the part of the vassal gave the lord the right to take back his fief; on his side the vassal was released from his pledge if the suzerain failed to keep his promises. Likewise, the death of one of the parties released the other from the contract. It is true that the pressure of public opinion, more sensitive to family ties than to contractual engagements, and still more the interest of the contracting parties in perpetuating conditions that had proved advantageous, caused both homage and investiture to become in practice hereditary. This is the meaning of a picturesque French legal saying, 'le mort saisit le vif', the dead man puts the survivor in possession. But even after this custom won general acceptance and was ratified by laws, the personal character of the bond was preserved in the obligation to renew the promises formally each time there was a change of either lord or vassal (Pl. 13, *left*).

The ceremony could be carried out by a presumptive heir in his father's lifetime, or be postponed to a time when the parties could meet without too much inconvenience, or even be replaced by recognizances of lordship or vassalage by proxy or by letter. And yet for all that the absolute and automatic right of inheritance was never admitted. The *de facto* dynasties which were established on the thrones of Europe were built up by kings elected one by one by their vassals, often as a result of explicit new pledges. Similarly, the children of a deceased vassal could be certain of being invested with his fief only if they were capable of carrying out the obligations involved. The lord who dismissed them because he considered them inadequate might be regarded as ungenerous, but did not commit a breach of contract.

Chivalry comes of age

As for the religious underpinning of feudalism, its chief virtue at first was that it supported family and contractual obligations by threatening divine punishment for anyone who evaded them. But in proportion as the religious attitude developed from fear of a God of vengeance to imitation of a God of love, it added to the traditional ideals of all fighting men — courage, strength, straight-forwardness, liberality, loyalty — the virtues of chivalry.

The new trend was scarcely noticeable in the tenth century but made rapid progress in the eleventh and twelfth centuries. Soon it will no longer suffice for a member of the feudal family, whether king or merely knight, to have his arms blessed at the outset of his career, a normal precaution for any warrior wishing to reinforce the temper of his sword by supernatural means. Little by little, the vassal's specific obligations towards his lord will become only the hard core of his duties towards society as a whole. He will even refuse to carry out his feudal obligations if they are to serve an unjust cause. Finally, caught up in the mobility of the age, he will become, if occasion demands, the itinerant protector of the widow, the orphan and the disinherited.

Remarkably, this evolution was not limited to Christian countries: the Islamic world in particular knew institutions as close to chivalry as they could be in a society where feudalism had never developed. It is no chance that chivalry, born in Celtic and Romance France, found its last champions in the Iberian penin-sula, the meeting place of Christianity and Islam: King Sebastian of Portugal and — why not? — Don Quixote.

On the other hand, if some knights became soldiers of fortune and highway robbers, if they chose to protect such widows as were beautiful and wealthy, if they slipped from the defence of feminine weakness into adultery, this was hardly unnatural. When have the professional champions of the weak ever been totally disinterested? The essential point is that public opinion imposed upon those who wielded power the responsibility of using it for the good of others. Greek philosophy, Roman law, Christian religion had done much to shape the conscience of Europe. Feudalism likewise made an important contribution by stressing that bonds of dependence are woven from mutual obligations, and that each right must bring with it a responsibility.

V.   THE PROBLEMS OF THE FEUDAL ORDER

It is often stated that feudalism was the child of the natural economy. Money did not circulate easily, and it was necessary to recompense dependants by distributing land to them. These grants were not entirely unlike a salary, because the vassal who proved unfaithful or incompetent ran the risk of losing his land, just as the salaried worker who does not satisfy his patron can lose his appoint-ment. If on the other hand the vassal deserved promotion, he could hope for an extension of his fief or for wider immunities in the estates he already possess-ed. Nevertheless, the system lacked adaptability, for it is not as easy to evict the owner of lands as it is to suppress payment of a salaried worker. In addition, as the amount of available land was limited, how were extra workers to be hired for occasional service at certain times of crisis? The only solution then was to appeal to the goodwill of established vassals and hope that they would rise to the occasion and make a greater effort.

From a land economy to a money economy

Feudalism, it is also stated, lost its attraction as soon as the economy became more fluid. Anyone who had money income at his disposal, whether he were prince, prelate or bourgeois, hastened to recruit his dependants by means of a salary. In the commercial towns feudalism disappeared completely. It survived in the larger states, where agriculture maintained its economic and moral supremacy, but commoners took over most of its administrative functions.

> These statements no doubt correspond on the whole with the truth, but an unqualified truth which may mislead us over the real nature of feudalism and its problems. Certainly there are many links between the political institutions of feudal society and the stagnant economy in which they developed, but it would be an exaggeration to speak of a direct relationship of cause and effect. There never was a time when the ruling classes were completely without money or indifferent to opportunities of acquiring it. Even in the period when its circulation was most restricted, minted or unminted gold and silver were used to attire jewelry, robes, homes and graves, to obtain spices for a banquet and grain against a famine, to buy land and slaves. It would therefore not have been impossible to hire dependants. If generally speaking it was preferred to install them in a benefice, it was not only because economic conditions made this solution easier, but also because feudalism was congenial with the spirit of the times.

At any rate, there was a significant lag between economic and political evolution. The lowest point in the monetary economy was reached in the late seventh century, that is to say, at the embryonic stage of feudal institutions. On the other hand, the first signs of an economic recovery in the tenth century coincided with the most complete triumph of feudalism in France. Later, in Italy, the growth of the commercial cities in the twelfth and thirteenth centuries was to sound the knell of the feudal system; but would the result have been the same if the emperor had succeeded in bending the middle classes and their monetary wealth to his will? We observe that in England, at the same period, the king granted charters to cities in exchange for an annual payment, and demanded from his vassals contributions in cash which he used to recruit non-feudal auxiliaries; nonetheless it was in England that feudal government reached its most perfect form.

It seems proper to conclude that feudalism was indeed suitable to the agrarian economy which prevailed at the time of its formation, but could adjust to the progress of the monetary economy so long as political power did not change hands. Nothing prevented a lord from engaging vassals in return for a salary. Thus, towards the end of the Middle Ages the words *fee* (fief) and *honorarium* (honour, benefice) passed gradually from the vocabulary of the land to that of money.

Conflicting obligations

When feudalism was in its prime, its most serious problems did not spring from changes in economic conditions, but from shifts of the balance of reciprocal obligations.

Conflicts between lords and vassals were inevitable, since they were concerned with the interpretation of a contract often unstated, rarely written, and still more rarely defined in all its details. Even when both parties wished in good faith to respect the contract (which was the exception rather than the rule), each was inclined to show himself inflexible in the defence of his rights and negligent in the performance of his duties. And since the age of feudalism is also the age when custom took the place of law, the fact that a clause had not been observed for several years was often sufficient ground for invoking a new custom against the old one, which was nonetheless still valid in theory. Sometimes the difference was submitted to inquiries or the judgment of arbitrators, but most frequently the right of the strongest prevailed.

Later the situation improved, it is true: customs were codified, the authority of the king or the resistance of the vassals enforced them. But even in England, and at the end of the thirteenth century — that is to say, in the most settled and mature of feudal monarchies — when King Edward I sent his commissioners to check the warrant by virtue of which the Earl of Warenne exercised a certain jurisdiction, the latter drew his sword and replied: 'Here is my warrant. My ancestors conquered their lands by the sword and by the sword I shall defend them against all usurpers'. And the commissioners bowed.

The other congenital problem of feudalism was the tangle of obligations. Homage was in principle a promise of total unlimited devotion to one lord, but almost all vassals were in practice the 'men' of several lords. As a matter of fact, a vassal who had any ambition would not be content with one single fief but collected several, often acquiring in the process just as many suzerains. To this series of parallel obligations were added almost as many vertical series as there were fiefs; for, except for benefices coming directly from the king, every benefice was a parcel of a larger one, and the immediate lord of that parcel was in his turn the vassal of some other lord. Finally, the chain of lay loyalties was matched by a chain of ecclesiastical loyalties and these chains were independent of each other, even when applied to the same fief (Pl. 13, *right*).

The vassal wishing to perform punctually all his duties towards all his lords found himself in the position of a man trying to reconcile his duties to his wife, his parents, his brothers and a most numerous family. This is always a difficult task; it is absolutely impossible if all those who have a claim do not live in complete harmony, which was normally the case in the feudal family. In practice the vassal most frequently allied himself with the strongest, the nearest or the most assertive of his lords, when he did not take advantage of the multiplicity of bonds to evade them all. In this limited sense we may use the term 'feudal anarchy'; yet we ought to remember that illwill needs no pretexts to have recourse to disobedience and that goodwill often finds a way of satisfying, at least partially, all obligations at the same time.

The unstable feudal pyramid

Jurists soon set about finding a solution for conflicting obligations. At first they thought they had disentangled the knot by means of the 'liege homage', a vow of absolute loyalty which when paid by a vassal to one of his lords took precedence over simple homage paid to the others. But each lord demanded liege homage, which brought the problem back to its starting point. Yet the notion of 'ligesse' or liegeancy was of some help when the kings of England and France imposed on their vassals that every feudal contract should carry a reservation of paramount allegiance to them.

The theory by which the feudal system as a whole consisted of one single hierarchy, a pyramid of dignities rising step by step from the simple knight or clerk through the emperor or the pope to Almighty God, had a greater influence. It developed slowly, almost spontaneously, as a reaction against rampant localism.

> Many strains went to form the theory of the feudal pyramid: notably the memory of the vaster units which had preceded the disintegration of kingdoms; common interests, sometimes leading to assemblies of notables and leagues (for example of fiefs lying in the same valley, or threatened by the same enemy); the growing desire for peace and order amidst the general confusion and violence; the ambitions of the most powerful lords, trying to gather the mob of minor vassals under their orders. But the theory could not be applied without encountering serious difficulties. Thus, how were the two pyramids, lay and ecclesiastical, to be brought into one? How could the principle of the universal Roman empire be reconciled with the existence of independent pyramids in each of the great kingdoms? What was the place of the person who was the vassal of one man in one fief but the lord of the same man in another fief, a paradoxical but not exceptional case? The feudal era is full of diatribes on these problems which had no valid solution.

The feudal pyramid had no power of its own. Yet it occupies an honourable position in the long series of attempts to reach a compromise between localism and unity, of which the League of Nations, the United Nations and the Council of Europe are the most recent examples in a larger setting.

In the tenth and eleventh centuries the attempt was almost desperate. The bubbling energy of the fiefs, already stimulated by the upsurge of countless nodes of population, contrasted with the feebleness of kingdoms, still cut up by the great empty spaces between one node and another. At that time the strongest monarchies were not those which had advanced furthest into feudalism, like

France and the kingdom of Arles, but those in which a sparser, more archaic society had preserved around the king the close ties of the tribe and the armed retinue: Germany, Hungary, Poland. Nevertheless, in the long run the feudal monarchies were to show greater strength because the king could be more efficiently assisted by men accustomed to rule their own domains and to face, when dealing with their own vassals, the same problems as the king had to face when dealing with them.

By sitting on top of the feudal pyramid, the king added moral prestige to the material resources which he drew, like his vassals, primarily from his direct domain. For the Capets were in the first place dukes of France, that is to say, of the Paris region; the kings of Germany were dukes of Saxony, Franconia or Swabia; the kings of England were the direct lords of several baronies scattered all over the island. Similarly, each duke was the lord of a number of counts but in part of his territory he exercised in person the powers of a count. And if 'it is true that the king is sovereign above all', it is equally true that 'each baron is sovereign in his barony'. This contradiction, which Beaumanoir, the bailiff of two kings of France, noticed in 1283 without being shocked by it, was completely resolved only in places where the king was also his own baron.

Rome, a city-state, had constructed her empire in the form of a confederation of city-states; the feudal kings of the Middle Ages rebuilt their kingdoms in the form of a pyramid of fiefs. Without forgetting the part played by the cities, let us emphasize that it was the most thoroughly feudalized monarchies which gave Europe its first major national states: England and France. Let us add, however that neither of them succeeded in stabilizing their pyramid until the direct domain of their kings was sufficiently extensive.

VI. LIBERTY AND LIBERTIES

If in the tenth and eleventh centuries the powers of a king and a feudal lord are ill-defined and weak outside his direct domain, they are most extensive within the domain. The essence of the age of localism lies in this contrast which is valid for the emperor as for any vassal. The lord finds in each of his castles and fortified towns, and in the fields visible from the top of the towers, an oasis of security and almost absolute control in the midst of a world in which every expedition is a veritable adventure. In his domain the lord must, to be sure, take account of custom, public opinion, and the competing rights of other lords. But these restrictions hamper him much less than the present-day separation of powers restricts the authority of any head of a modern democratic government. Roman and barbarian traditions combine to confer on the lord such a mass of unquestionable rights as few dictators would dare to claim today. Like a Roman emperor the smallest lord may demand heavy forced labour from the inhabitants of his domain; like a German or Slav conqueror, he behaves as much like the owner as the governor of the territory under his direct control. Against such a fullness of power, any appeal to other authorities has scarcely a chance of success. Whether they were originally free, half-free or slaves, his subjects become in the eyes of their lord a mere mass of bowed heads.

Eclipse and break-up of unconditional liberty

Liberty is not dead, but it has lost the godlike, inflexible quality it had in the Greco-Roman ideal. The church now exalts submission to the divine will and calls its supreme pontiff by the title of Servant of the servants of God. The state, in turn, is conceived as a chain of dependencies, of which not even the summit can claim unconditional liberty since he governs as direct vassal of the Lord. Vassalage and serfdom were at first scarcely differentiated: the English word 'knight', though originally meaning simply 'young man', comes from the same root as the German *Knecht*, 'serf'. Although from the dawn of the tenth century onwards the boldest men found some hope of improving their lot, for the great majority the goal to be attained was not progress but equilibrium, the assurance of enjoying in perpetuity the rights attached to a definite status.

Therefore, the sources rarely speak of liberty, in the singular, and stress specific 'liberties' instead. These are not natural rights but privileges, immunities, exceptions to the rule. An individual or a community is exempt from a certain tax, labour service or military obligation. The more liberties one has, the higher one is on the social scale. But nobody dreams of absolute liberty, which is not possible in this world, and the difference between a free man and a serf is not a sharp contrast between light and darkness. It is a series of gradations and shades framing a vast zone of dim light, of quasi-liberties and quasi-servitudes.

It would be wrong to suggest premature legal classifications while the reality is hazy. Even in the towns of the tenth century it is difficult to distinguish between free labourers who are still required to supply some work and finished products to a lord, and serf labourers who owe to the lord an unlimited amount of labour but accept all the same the orders of other people. Again, it is not always clear where to place those *negotiatores* or traders who appear to engage in commerce on their own account but who seem to act as administrators and men of straw for the monasteries and the lay nobles.

In the country, where money, that great maker of class distinctions, plays a restricted part, the confusion is still greater and lasts longer. Usually a peasant listed as a serf has to perform more days of work on his lord's land than his free neighbour, but they are both liable for *corvées* (unpaid labour service) and neither of them is really *corvéable à merci* (liable for labour service at the lord's discretion), whatever a slogan of the *Ancien Régime* may say. The charters continually show us people of all ranks who symbolically commit their persons and their lands to a religious institution or a great layman, to receive them back again on payment of a rent. Did they become less unfree because they gave up their independence, or more free because they acquired protection? Perhaps they would not have known the answer any more than we do.

In the tenth and eleventh centuries unconditional liberty, total liberty as we conceive it today, was sometimes, as in Italy and some other regions near the Mediterranean shores, a token of persisting classical traditions: Gerbert of Aurillac had to face it when his Italian tenants opposed to his requests the written proof of their freedom from the normal servile dues. More often, unconditional liberty was a sign of anarchy or a manifestation of political inferiority. It is found, for example, among the Jews and other international merchants because they are not recognized citizens of any state; among exiles, beggars, wandering monks, because no social class offers them a shelter. We come across it here and there in the mountains, swamps and forests; among the rude Saxons, the fierce Frisians, the wild Scandinavians; in the strips of frontier land newly torn from Moslems or pagans.

Castille provides a striking example of what could be called the maturing of an underdeveloped equalitarian society into a hierarchic and well-differentiated nation. About the year 1000, its nobles and its commoners, its small bourgeoisie and its larger free peasantry all seemed to live together cheek by jowl. Two hundred years later all ranks from the highest vassals to the lowest serfs will be clearly set apart from one another.

The air of the town

As a general rule, however, the march of social history during the late Middle Ages does not go from primitive liberty to servitude but from serfdom to enlarged liberties. The towns usually lead the way; more than the peasants, the townspeople feel the need to move about, to expand, to exchange goods and services without hindrance. They have money to buy their liberties when they can neither win them by force of arms nor obtain them as a reward for armed support. At no time had their population been entirely unfree; from the tenth century onwards, one town after another pursues the goal of collective 'liberties' for the entire citizen body, including new settlers and run-away serfs. Self-government will be the next step: as early as 897 the 'citizens' of Turin oust the bishop from their town, in 958 there is an unsuccessful 'conspiracy' against the episcopal government in Cambrai, in 998 the people of Cremona have set up a town hall, and by that time there are assemblies of citizens in a good many urban centres from England to Spain. Full autonomy is still a long way off in the eleventh century, except in Italy; but the progress of liberties is revealed in a decline of serfdom, first within the town walls, then in an ever wider circle round the urban centre.

Often enfranchisement is achieved by stages, the actual liberties preceding or replacing the legal recognition of liberty. Thus in several towns extending from Arras to Worms the privileged serfs of certain churches begin to act as urban aristocracies well before severing their bonds of dependence. At Huy the charter of 1066 in which the Bishop of Liège recognizes the autonomy of the citizen body, still assumes that the serfs dwelling inside the walls will remain in the service of their lords. Sooner or later the custom is nevertheless established that a person who has lived in a town for a year and a day must be considered a free citizen. 'The air of the town makes one free', says a well-known mediaeval proverb. Its effects spread beyond the walls. To persuade the peasants to stay on the land, many lords grant them some of the liberties they might otherwise seek in the towns. Wherever the town encroaches upon feudal territory, it brings to the peasants a taste of freedom.

The progress of urban liberties varies from town to town. In the large Italian cities the triumph of the middle class breaks down entirely the old social framework and dissolves the feudal bonds of dependence. Well before the end of the twelfth century prosperity in business matters more than noble birth, serfdom is disappearing throughout the wide area under urban rule, and 'liberties' in the plural are fading as the unconditional liberty of the Greco-Roman city state revives.

At the opposite pole of urban development, a large number of English, French, German and Slavonic towns must be content with liberties subordinated to the monarchic and feudal paramount authority. The influence of urban law on the country is neither deep nor broad.

Between these two poles are other towns which outgrow the old social structures without eliminating them completely. The merchant cities of Provence and Languedoc, of Flanders and the Moselle region, of the Rhineland and of Catalonia belong to this middle group.

The vicissitudes of relative liberty

However, until the end of the twelfth century and beyond, the influence of the castle and the manor continues to outweigh that of the town over most of Catholic Europe.

Here, without the stimulus of urban growth, the progress of liberties is slower and often crossed by currents tending in the opposite direction. The same causes seem to produce different effects in different places. We have seen that the increased mobility of the population, a direct consequence of demographic expansion, gave birth to many communities of free peasants, especially along the moving frontiers of Catholic Europe. But it also uprooted many children of large families and forced them to accept new bonds of serfdom in order to obtain a parcel of overcrowded land. Again, the increasing use of money payments enabled a good number of serfs to redeem their obligations and eliminate heavy labour services. But money payments personally rendered by individual free men (capitation, *chevage*) often came to be regarded as proofs of serf status. In spite of endless efforts to define the rights and duties of lords and tenants by litigation, inquest and court order, the world of the peasants remains the most illiterate part of a scarcely literate culture. It is, therefore, ill equipped for defense against arbitrary action or collaboration in view of a distant goal. Every crisis of government makes it easier for the stronger party to grab privileges not belonging to it, and any protracted abuse is transformed into legitimate use by the force of custom. In this ebb-and-flow struggle between aggressive lords and acquisitive peasants, erosion works both ways.

Without forgetting the infinite variety of local solutions, it seems possible to single out predominant trends in the main countries of Europe. In several French provinces the elaborate distinctions between free, semi-free and unfree peasants gradually lost their sharpness, all tenants in a manor being regarded as belonging practically to the same class. But this fusion resulted sometimes in an upgrading of serfs to a status close to liberty, and sometimes in a downgrading of the higher sub-classes of the semi-free (villains, 'culverts', 'coloni'). Contrariwise, English jurists worked out ever more precise distinctions between different types of tenants. Each sub-class was more assured of the rights or 'liberties' belonging to it, but the freezing of legal definitions tended to inhibit osmoses and collective progress. In Germany the persistent fluidity of classes led to total inversions of status. While a large number of *servi ministeriales* who were entrusted with confidential missions by their lords finally rose from serfdom to the lower ranks of the nobility, most of the *censuales*, whom the charters of the eleventh century called 'eternally free', slipped down into serfdom in the course of the following century. Changes of this kind were particularly sharp in the outer regions of German colonization. The word *Diener*, servant, became *tiun* or *tiwun* in Russian and Lithuanian and designated a high official; the word 'Christian', first applied to the civilized élite, eventually described in Russian the mass of normally unfree peasants!.

Legal categories, at any rate, do not tell the whole story. By the end of the twelfth century, liberty had become the normal status of the peasants only in the more urbanized regions of Italy. Yet personal freedom alone, without ownership of land, was not an unmixed blessing. The bourgeois landowner was often more demanding than the feudal lord had been and had the same contempt for his rustic tenants. Besides, if greater liberties offered the peasant fresh opportunity to strive for personal profit, serfdom diminished his responsibility in case of loss. And all in all, the kind of tenure mattered less than the quantity and quality of land under cultivation. *Primum vivere:* in the Middle Ages as today, a good tenure was the one which enabled the peasant and his family to have their fill.

VII. THE PROBLEMS OF PEASANT SOCIETY

In the tenth century the population of Catholic Europe found it hard to feed itself. Normally every village endeavoured to produce, with a scanty labour force and mediocre techniques, all it needed for its own subsistence. The church took a tenth of all animal and vegetable products, often merely to hand it back to a lord who had taken possession of ecclesiastical revenue. The military class was not too fastidious as regards lodging and clothing, but had a formidable appetite, celebrated in the medieval epic poems. No doubt they had a supplementary source of food: hunting, which was at the same time their favourite amusement, their training for war, and their best means to break the monotony of their diet. Their preserves, however, took from the peasants land which could have been cultivated. Finally, the lord levied for his table the few head of cattle which could be spared from work in the fields and stockbreeding. If he happened to be an important man with a large retinue, his passage was enough to consume in a few weeks the reserve of food accumulated over a year; after which he had to move on and exploit another village. Indeed the constant journeys of kings were the most practical way of collecting taxes — by eating them.

What was left to feed the peasants? Most of the fields which biennial or triennial rotation of crops left available for cultivation were devoted to corn. But the harvest, which varied greatly according to the nature of the soil and the techniques employed, was not, on poor ground, more than three or four times greater than the sowing. Hence it was necessary to set aside up to one third for the following year's sowing. In the north, where the vines would not grow, the peasants had to set aside some corn for the production of beer, for they had a mistrust of water which was only too justified by sanitary conditions. And if the south was favoured by the resources of its vineyards and olive groves, it was handicapped by its less fertile soil and by the inadequacy of its rainfall, which made necessary a rotation of crops at greater intervals. What meagre surpluses might be gathered in the better years were scarcely enough to prevent starvation in years of famine. As for meat, it was rare for the peasants to treat themselves to beef, except at Martinmas, when, by tradition, they slaughtered the animals which could not be fed during the winter. Pork was more easily available; the plump outline of the pig never fails to appear, as one of the great blessings of life, in three or four of the dozen 'labours of the month' represented in the bas-reliefs and manuscript calendars of the period.

The pattern of manorial agriculture

Without lingering over the details of a diet which in any case varied according to the place and the means of the peasant, let us glance at the essential characteristics of what could be called the typical agricultural pattern of the medieval manor; typical, that is to say, as Rheims cathedral or the Divine Comedy or the Plenary Parliament are models of their kind. What we are looking for is not the most common but the most successful and best balanced form of agricultural organization. Some of its elements were borrowed from the *villa* of the late Roman Empire and the large estate of the barbarian age, but its mature expression differs from them as the Gothic cathedral differs from both the classic basilica and the early medieval chapel.

What strikes us at the outset is the division of the land under cultivation into two unequal parts, one of which — usually the smaller — is farmed directly by the lord, while the other is divided among the tenants. Although this arrangement is dictated primarily by economic considerations, it is much like the political division of kingdoms into duchies and counties, one or two of which are governed directly by the king, while the remainder is entrusted to vassals. Taking in hand the whole manor, having it cultivated by men selected and remunerated expressly for that purpose: what a headache, what a labour for a noble lord, even if he passes it on to his agents! It is much more convenient for him to retain only a limited demesne and to keep in his immediate service, in addition to the indispensable stewards and butlers, only a skeleton team of peasants who will ensure continuity of work. Over the rest of the manor each tenant has the run of his land, on condition, of course, that he pay dues in money or kind, and that he take turns on a certain number of days in the week or year in helping the resident staff on the lord's demesne.

Actually 'the run of his land' is not the correct term for any of the inhabitants of the manor. The real master is the village community as a whole, harnessed ever since its prehistoric beginnings to the basic and essential tasks of feeding all its men as well as possible, sparing a modest surplus for the managers, and building up some provisions for the inevitable famine to come. The lord is of course the most powerful member and principal manager of the community, but he has to respect its immemorial customs if he does not want to jeopardize the economic balance of the village on which he depends no less than the villeins. It is up to him to supply the protection of his sword, the technical and legal experience of his agents, and the more costly permanent installations: mill, wine-press, barns. In turn the peasants supply their labour, their beasts, their carts, their tools.

No doubt it would have been difficult for the peasants to stint their services, to overdo their rights of pasture or to poach in the manorial forest. But it was equally unwise for the lord to demand exorbitant dues, encroach upon the common pasture, or challenge the peasants' right of access to the woodlands from which they collected dead wood for their hearths and green wood for their tools. All this did not prevent disputes and usurpations on both sides; nevertheless, a watchful collective conscience assigned to each member of the village community his land, his tasks, and his customary rights. It restricted individual liberty, but ensured to all, on a low level to be sure, what we should today call 'full employment'.

North and south: the solidarity of the village

Over a large part of northern Europe and in some southern regions, the solidarity of the village was strengthened by the allotment of the land (Fig. 38). Neither the demesne nor the parcels of individual tenants formed compact blocks but usually consisted of a large number of narrow strips scattered all over the manor. These ribbons of land were not separated from the adjoining strips by any permanent enclosure. Such patterns, traces of which survive here and there (especially in England but also in France and central Europe), seem strange to us today; in the Middle Ages, it is claimed, they were the most rational system for the agriculture of the time. The strips were open so that cattle could go onto them after each harvest, eat whatever they could find, and enrich the soil with their manure. They were scattered so that each member of the community should have an equal share of good and poor land. They were long and narrow so that the heavy plough, indispensable on a heavy soil, should not have to turn too frequently. This plough did its job rapidly, but needed as many as eight draught horses; it was therefore normal for ploughing to be done communally, by harnessing together the horses of several tenants.

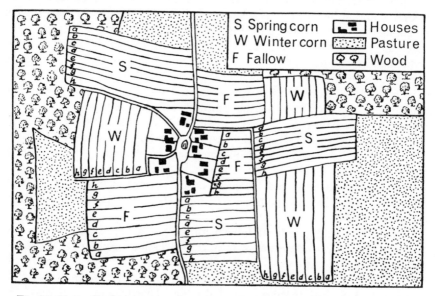

Fig. 36. Typical cultivation of a mediaeval manor; plan of a village surrounded by open fields; the letters a, b, c, d, etc. indicate the owners having a strip in each of the fields; according to Gordon East; compare with Fig. 7.

Whether designed on purpose or brought about by unconscious tradition, this arrangement had the advantages which modern historians ascribe to it. Unfortunately the absence of hedges and the dismemberment of tenures discouraged efforts to improve, changes of routine, and individual initiative. Nevertheless, if an innovation managed to overcome collective inertia, the stragglers were quickly compelled to fall into step with the group.

All of these traits were by no means restricted to northern agriculture; in a more or less modified form, they can be found even in the vicinity of the largest towns of Italy. Nevertheless, individual initiatives and resistances, as a rule, manifested themselves more freely wherever the tenures were more compact and the soil lighter or more pebbly. This was the case in some regions of the north such as Wales and more generally over most of southern Europe.

Here, in the environment which had produced the classical Mediterranean agriculture, the soil and the climate demanded a larger input of human labour and ploughing had to be done repeatedly but with a lighter plough. It was possible to a certain extent for each peasant to specialize and shut himself up in his own enclosed tenure. Village solidarity was above all political and fiscal: often the whole community was responsible to the lord for the dues of each peasant, and negotiated collectively with the lord for the total amount. A certain economic solidarity was also expressed in common undertakings: the peasants had to help each other and to assist the lord during the harvest and vintage seasons as well as with the maintenance of irrigation works and the sharing of water supplies. In all these respects — and in spite of substantial changes in the political organization, patterns of settlement, crops and techniques, the peasant villages of Europe south of the Garonne and the Alps were normally closer to the traditions of Greco-Roman antiquity than to those of the manorial communities of the mediaeval north.

The force of tradition

Agricultural traditions based on soil and climate are slow to die. An almost invisible but continuous line connects the latest Italian Bonifiche (settlements on reclaimed marshes) to the classic Greco-Roman village. Another line links the Soviet Kolkhoz to the northern mediaeval village.

That is why we have chosen to describe the 'typical manor' not before but after the demographic and economic development which was to bring about its decline. Whether great lords or poor labourers, countrymen are almost always conservative. Equilibrium, self-sufficiency and the full employment which we have just stressed gave them a feeling of security which any change, even for the better, appeared to disturb. Every time they found themselves obliged to change their habits, they did all they could to establish a similar equilibrium at a higher level. We see lords of the twelfth century, and even merchants of the thirteenth, recreating demesnes broken up one or two hundred years earlier by parcelling out among the several heirs of an estate, or by the reckless expenditure of a bad administrator. Similarly, peasants left to their own resources in lands newly opened to settlers often formed co-operative villages around a lord, as soon as they were established in a virgin, unfamiliar environment. Agricultural methods could become more rational, contracts and wages could replace bonds of dependence and payments in kind, landowners and labourers could change their rapports. This would not necessarily cause the organization of the work to alter its characteristics, which were imbedded in nature, regardless of the passing of time.

From subsistence economy to economy of exchange

Nevertheless, a conservative disposition does not mean immovable stagnation. After pointing out the demographic, technological and legal factors of change in the peasant society down to the end of the twelfth century, let us now stress the progress made with regard to the basic problem of food production.

Much of this progress cannot be measured but must be postulated on the basis of indirect evidence: the population keeps growing, the average span of life lengthens, famines become less frequent, nobles and middle class sourly note that the rustics look well fed and adequately clothed. Their subsistence being normally assured, the peasants are in a position to sell the surplus; thus agriculture decidedly turns from self-sufficiency as a goal to an economy of exchange.

By the end of the twelfth century, the increased yield of the earth and of labour has removed the economic necessity for dividing villages into demesnes and tenures, both of which were mainly destined to satisfy the different appetites of their occupants. 'Commercialization' has spread from the towns to the country: farmers who are aware of the market begin to specialize, choosing for their holding such plants as are best suited to the soil and most easily salable. While such regions as Sicily and Germany beyond the Elbe provide corn for regions with a shortage and Gascony does likewise for wine, parts of England and Castille are devoted to the production of wool, and a few Italian and Catalan valleys concentrate solely on the cultivation of plants for medicines and dyes. Market gardens and orchards thrive in the vicinity of every town.

It is true that the Greco-Roman agriculture already had attained similar results; but its progress had largely rested on the merciless exploitation of slaves and the endless toil of poor farmers, mostly for the benefit of a small élite. The late Middle Ages reduced the toil through improved techniques and spread its profits a little more equitably among all classes. It did not solve the problem of subsistence for the poorer peasants, but it created enough leisure to enable the other members of the society to refine their way of living and thinking.

Chapter 3

THE SOARING OF THOUGHT

I. TRUTH PROVED BY REASON

'There is no other authority than truth proved by reason...'; 'Nowadays an illiterate priest is like a noble unfit for war....' The new directions of thought in twelfth-century Europe are illuminated by these sallies from Honorius of Autun and Gerald the Welshman: the former German or English, the latter Celtic, but both belonging to the cosmopolitan intellectual *milieu* of the Parisian region.

Common opinion, of course, did not go as far as these avant-garde writers. The supreme authority of the Revelation was invulnerable to attacks from reason; illiterate priests kept jobs more easily than unfit nobles. Besides there was no shortage of learned clergymen, like St Bernard of Clairvaux (1091–1153), who would rather cling to the formula of St Augustine, repeated in the eleventh century by St Anselm of Aosta: 'I believe in order to understand'. Too much subtlety is a sin of pride; not flinching from the use of unfair arguments, Bernard temporarily managed to bring about the condemnation of the most conceited of the new scholars, Abelard.

Abelard the presumptuous and the development of dialectics

Nevertheless Abelard triumphed after his death (1142). He had made Paris the philosophical centre of Christendom, at a time when it was not yet the political centre of gravity of France. It matters little if this attractive and unbearable man was not the most profound thinker of his epoch; he was a superb teacher and knew how to reach a wide audience. Each of his books, enriched by the progress made in two revolutionary centuries of thought, was a stepping stone for future intellectual advances.

In *Know Thyself*, Abelard, by insisting on the intention of the sinner rather than on the nature of the sin, shifts the emphasis from repression to spiritual therapy. Penitents must not be subjected to a series of punishments, a ready-reckoner as rigid as the tariffs of penalties in barbarian codes and penance books, but they must be submitted to an examination of conscience designed to rouse contrition.

In *Logic for Beginners* he directs towards a compromise solution the sharp debate between 'nominalists' and 'realists', which threatened to become a stumbling-block for any research at its very beginning: the 'universals', that is to say concepts or ideas, are inherent in the objects we see and the notions we conceive. Whether they are in fact mere names invented by our ability to abstract and generalize (as Aristotle and the medieval nominalists would have it), or on the contrary pale reflections of a real, perfect model in Heaven (as Plato, the neo-Platonists and the realists would have it), there is only one way to understanding and knowledge. One must observe the objects and notions carefully, and apply thought to them.

In *Yes and No*, Abelard points out the apparent disagreement of the greatest authorities, such as the Scriptures and the Church Fathers, even on essential problems of faith, by placing side by side their conflicting statements on 158 selected points. The aim is not, of course, to invite scepticism, but to sharpen the tool of doubt; 'for by doubting we are led to questions, by questioning we arrive at the truth'. A challenging but dangerous method, so long as the last step is not taken: restoring harmony by reconciling the discrepant statements.

This step will be taken for the first time, not in Paris and in the lofty sphere of theology, but at Bologna in the practical field of canon law. Shortly before or after the death of Abelard, the monk Gratian will, in his *Concordance of Discordant Canons*, supply both a list of authorities on the two sides of every question and a solution of the conflict. Soon after, in Paris, Peter the Lombard will in turn solve theological arguments by the same method. Mediaeval thought will thus have perfected the dialectic, destined henceforth to dominate the schools.

Discussion is the best tool of the mediaeval scholar. By challenging not the authority itself but its interpretation, he sharpens his logic; he collects and tests citations as eagerly as the modern scholar will collect and test experimental facts. Towards 1170 Peter Comestor (the 'devourer' of books) compiles an *Ecclesiastical History,* a veritable encyclopaedia of the Bible for the use of students; other arsenals of knowledge will appear in growing numbers and supply fresh ammunition to the debate. Before the end of the century an abbot of Paris will state with undisguised horror: 'People dispute publicly, in violation of sacred decrees, about divine mysteries. . . . The indivisible Trinity is cut and pulled to pieces in the squares. There are as many errors as doctors; as many scandals as audiences; as many blasphemies as public places'. This denunciation is strangely reminiscent of the complaints of Gregory of Nyssa on the subject of the public debates in fourth-century Constantinople: 'This city is full of me-chanics and slaves who are all learned theologians preaching in the shops and the streets. . . . If you ask the price of a loaf, they reply that the Son is lower than the Father. . . .' Had Paris awakened a Byzantine city, after eight hundred years of slumber? Not really, but she needed her mental gymnastic to be able once again to develop her thoughts (Pl. 14).

The diffusion of knowledge and the formation of a public

The intellectual growth of the West between the tenth and the twelfth centuries has its inner reasons and independent drives, which belong to the realm of the history of ideas and cannot be linked directly to the demographic, economic and social expansion of the age. But in so far as the development of thought is revealed in the form of a greater diffusion of knowledge, it has its place in that expansion, as a brief description of its successive stages will show.

In the tenth century and during part of the eleventh, we come across only a small number of enlightened monasteries such as St Gall and Monte Cassino, a few intellectual 'families' such as the pupils of Gerbert and their pupils, and a few centres of secular studies, medicine in the region of Salerno, law and administration in the centres of Ravenna, Pavia and perhaps in Provence. These centres were much like oases in a desert of letters. Scholars at that time were closely linked to one another because they scarcely had an audience, encyclopaedic because they had access only to very limited information, and wanderers (in spite of the difficulties of travel) because manuscripts and scholars existed only in a handful of famous localities. The journey from Rheims to Chartres is certainly not long, but Richer, who made it in 991 in order to increase his medical knowledge, has left us an anguished account of the difficulties of the trip. Yet his master, Gerbert, had not hesitated to travel all over the Catholic west, including Catalonia on the threshold of the Moslem world where he had gained the most unusual (and, according to rumour, dangerous) parts of his knowledge. Richer and Gerbert were both kings' councillors and Gerbert became pope, but it is far from certain that their remarkable learning helped them in the government of an almost illiterate society.

In the course of the eleventh century wandering scholars become legion, cultural centres multiply, communications improve, society is less inaccessible to the influence of intellectuals. The twelfth century, then, will be the golden age of the Goliards and their songs, the age of the sudden but fleeting vogue of this or that school made brilliant by a teacher more eloquent or more subtle than the rest, until Paris will eclipse all other centres by the number and quality of its masters. It will bring about a second wave of humanism, more original and spirited than Carolingian humanism, and almost as fruitful as Humanism *par excellence*, that of the Renaissance. So much so that modern scholars often speak of a 'Renaissance of the twelfth century'; somewhat improperly, to be sure, because the thinkers and artists of the twelfth century offered no apologies for any mediaeval decline, never forgetting that being Christian was a greater achievement than being Olympian. Nevertheless, there was an impressive return to ancient models, whose distinguishing feature is the careful, but not slavish, imitation of the best Latin classics, and whose decisive turning-point is the rediscovery of Aristotle and Ptolemy.

New texts, including Greek works retranslated from Arabic into Latin, are added to the remnants of Greco-Roman culture salvaged by the Carolingian scholars. Translations of original Arabic and Judeo-Arabic works also bring new knowledge, especially in the fields of medicine and the mathematical and natural sciences, where the Arabs have gone farther than the Greeks. Italy, where localized conflicts with the Moslems have never prevented commercial and cultural exchanges, has centres for translation as early as the middle of the eleventh century. Spain, where contacts with Moslems are even closer but too often warlike, also plays a very important part. On the other hand, the Holy Land, where relations between the two cultures will always be strained, will give hardly anything.

However, the essential point is not the importance or the sheer amount of the material which Catholic Europe received at that time, but the very fact that once again she is desirous and capable of learning and assimilating. Authorities are quoted on every subject, they are pillaged unscrupulously, but there is a conviction that the possession of the Revealed Truth gives the humblest Christian an advantage over genius who has never known it. To outstrip him, it is only necessary to set to work. The production of books surpasses in quantity and quality all that has been written in Catholic Europe since the crumbling of Greco-Roman culture. Theological works once more take precedence over mere lives of saints; law, political science and natural science vie with religious studies for first place, or rather are regarded as indispensable assets for an intelligent Christian; the number of manuscript copies remaining to us of the most frequently read books bears witness to the increasing number of readers.

In fact, a reading and listening public is now growing fast. The clergy are no longer the only significant audience, but merely the most sophisticated one. The bourgeoisie make up the mass and the nobility are occasional customers, often distracted but capable of passionate interest if the subjects intrigue them. From the mid eleventh century onwards public opinion comes to life; emotional appeals easily sway it, of course, but rational argument is not lost upon it. The Investiture Struggle produces not a series of miracles but a host of pamphlets, in which the opposing sides display their historical, philosophical, literary and legal erudition. If most of the population cannot read (except in certain Italian towns and in ecclesiastical communities) those who can are asked to explain the issue to those who would like to know. And since to do this they will have to translate Latin texts into the 'vulgar' or popular tongue there is a double reason for speaking of 'vulgarization' or popularization in this connection.

> Let us not under estimate the revolutionary power of popularized culture. Today the promises of communism may seem more attractive to those who have not read Karl Marx than to those who have studied him. Similarly, at the end of the eleventh century papal propaganda, translated to the people by travelling monks and lay market-place orators, led crowds of townsmen and villagers to expel simoniacal bishops and priests. The popes then needed supporters too badly to worry about less than orthodox interpretations which fanned the flame: some preachers denied the efficacy of sacraments administered by unworthy priests, others demanded that the Church should return to evangelical poverty, still others inclined towards dualism. Before the end of the twelfth century, however, the popes triumphed and were able to tighten the reins. In this way the name

Patarin (rag-seller, beggar), originally designating adherents of the papacy in the Lombard towns, came to be applied to the partisans of a condemned heresy.

The struggle for souls: conservatives, heretics, scholars

Unquestionably, the spread of culture added popular support and intellectual depth to the orthodox drive for the uplifting of the Church, which had begun more modestly as a minority reaction against gross improprieties. Large sections of the clergy greeted it with enthusiasm, but the conservative elements, including prominent members of the new religious orders founded around 1100 (Augustinians, Premonstratensians, Carthusians, Cistercians) received it with mixed feelings. Hasty learning and hasty popularization favoured criticism, and criticism increased the number of non-conformists. Easier communications enabled hitherto isolated groups of heretics to get together and build up organizations which looked like a serious threat to the Roman Church.

The most important of these organizations, the Cathar ('pure') church, almost overcame Catholicism in some cities of northern Italy and in several centres of southern France. In spite of the extreme severity of its dualistic tenets, it continued to gain ground until 1209, when the 'Crusade against the Albigensians' was unleashed to suppress it with bloodshed in the place where it was most strongly established. It survived in Italy, but had almost everywhere to go underground.

A gentler heresy, that of the 'Poor Men of Lyons' won a large following on both sides of the Alps. It had abandoned its obedience to Rome only reluctantly, the Pope having refused its founder, the merchant Peter Waldo or Valdez, permission to preach in the vernacular language without the authorization of the bishops (1179). His original programme, based on strict adherence to the Bible, did not depart radically from the principles which were to be adopted by the Cistercians and other reformed monastic orders aspiring to restore the primitive strictness of the Benedictine rule. Rejection, however, drove the Waldensians or Poor Men farther astray.

Like the orthodox reformers, the heretics recruited a large number of their followers from among the humble, who were less stirred up by theological controversy than by denunciations of greed and corruption in the privileged classes. Yet their leaders usually came from the upper classes, and always included a few idealist intellectuals.

If the Catholic Church held its ground against popular non-conformism, she owed it in part to those schools and that education which the traditionalists feared so greatly. For through the discussions of the schools her theologians learned to reply to the objections of unauthorized interpreters, to fill the gaps of doctrine where orthodoxy lost its way, and to detect unwitting errors or covert heresy.

In the second half of the twelfth century schools of all kinds sprang into vigorous life, and the town replaced the monastery as the principal seat of studies. The *studium* or university of Paris reigned supreme. Its first college, in which eighteen students were lodged at the expense of the chapter, was founded in 1180; the corporation of masters received its first privileges from the Pope in 1194; in 1200 King Philip Augustus exempted the students from lay jurisdiction. And if it was still thought necessary, shortly after, to entrust to soldiers the suppression of the 'Albigensian' Cathars, the schools had their revenge in 1229, after the Albigensian Crusade was ended. In that year, the Pope founded the second oldest French university at Toulouse, in the centre of the re-conquered land, so that it might help doubting people by questioning to arrive at the truth (Pl. IV).

II. THE LOVE OF LAW

The philosophical 'renaissance' was paralleled by a legal 'renaissance' which went through roughly the same stages with the same enthusiasm. Notwithstanding their proclivity to break specific laws, medieval people normally bore for the Law the greatest veneration and love (Fig. 37).

'Take care not to subvert in any way the law of our most holy predecessor Justinian', says a formula for investing Roman judges with their office, which may have been used by Otto III towards the year 1000. The candidates were expected to reply: 'If I do, may I be struck by eternal curse!' Conversely, the Lord would bless those who endeavoured to restore Justinian's rules: it is reported that the famous thirteenth-century jurist Jacopo di Baldovino, being unable to reconcile an apparent conflict between two passages of the *Digest*, prayed all night. At dawn he received the solution by divine inspiration.

Throughout the Middle ages, public opinion and religious teachings agreed in reminding kings and princes that the administration of justice was the most important and noblest of their duties, God himself being the supreme Judge. If their courts offered them less amusement than war, they provided a more continuous occupation and, thanks to the fines, a profitable one. That is why all those who had any authority strove hard to establish their courts of justice and to extend their sphere, even when this meant encroaching upon the jurisdiction of others.

From Roman law to 'Romance' law

In the tenth century what hindered justice was not only the collapse of central authority but also the overlapping of legal traditions. Barbarian and Roman laws, ecclesiastical and secular jurisdictions, royal decrees and local customs were intertwined beyond the discriminating ability and power of what judges could be found. The Carolingians had endeavoured to bring some order to legal matters, but had been far less successful in this field than in giving laws to handwriting and Latin grammar. On the one hand, they had collected and codified various barbarian laws; on the other hand, they had proclaimed their respect for 'Roman law' where it survived ('nothing has been enacted, either by us or our predecessors, against that law', said a capitulary of Charles the Bald); they also had permitted the growth of canonical legislation, enriched at their time by a number of spurious documents (notably the so-called Pseudo-Isidorian Decretals). Ultimately, they had allowed everybody to manage his affairs according to the law of his choice. As for their own legislation, it could scarcely maintain its force after their power crumbled.

To find some direction in the maze, the successive generations had to choose between two basic conceptions: feudal, Germanic and localist, or civil and canon, Roman and universalist. Local courts and judges in their practical decisions would be naturally attracted to the matter-of-fact quality of the former conception. The greater refinement and abstraction of civil and canon law, however, would have a stronger appeal on cultured minds, the more so as the intellectual and economic level of society rose. Though feudal and Germanic customs had their internal consistency, only Roman law offered a systematic frame in which individual cases could be fitted. No doubt an act of faith was needed to test contemporary lawsuits by a system that was six to nine centuries old; but had not faith already driven people to restore the Roman Empire for Charlemagne and his successors?

It was inevitable that the desire to renew the Roman imperial dream should spread from the realm of government to that of law. 'By the law of the Romans, it has been ordained for the whole world. . .', states a French charter of 903. Yet the actual content of that law was so ill known that

a Dalmatian charter of the same period quoted as *romana lex* a chapter of the edict of the Lombard King Rothari! In fact most people knew no more than the local customs as handed down by oral tradition. Therefore it was necessary to set to work upon the books. First of all the students of law applied themselves to the surviving parts of the *Corpus Juris* and of the compilations of Roman law before Justinian. They also took up again the texts of canon law, in which Roman influence permeated ecclesiastical sources. The principal centres for the study of these latter were in Lotharingia (Lorraine) between the Rhine and the Meuse and in northern France. Lay sources were consulted more frequently in southern France and in Italy.

Fig. 37. Justice: column from Strzelno (Poland), twelfth century.

Then, between the end of the eleventh century and the early years of the twelfth, just at the time when Aristotle was being rediscovered, the gradual rediscovery of the *Digest* and of the complete text of the *Novels* opened a new era of legal speculation. In this field as in the sphere of philosophy, the recovered master-pieces provided Catholic Europe with general ideas and with the logical method of which the new society stood in need (Pl. 16).

While admiring the genius of the ancients, the mediaeval students of law did not lose sight of the realities of the present. They abandoned neither the con-quests of Christian morality nor the innovations of commercial law, nor even a considerable part of the barbarian and feudal customs. It was easier for them to adapt the Latin *Digest* to their still Latin-speaking, Rome-centred world than it was for religious people to harmonize Greek philosophy with Judeo-Christian theology. It was not a question of translating a strange language, but only of understanding older forms of a still familiar legal language. That is why the renewal of Roman law, especially in territories where the legal traditions of antiquity had faded but not completely died out, has been properly compared to the dawn of the Romance languages and of Romanesque art.

Among these territories, Romagna proclaimed by its very name its tenacious adherence to the Roman and Byzantine heritage. Ravenna, its ancient capital, was one of the centres in which the formal teaching of law had continued. Towards the end of the eleventh century a great master, Irnerius, did for another of its cities, Bologna, what Abelard was to do for Paris a little later: he founded a school there which eclipsed all the others. In 1158 when Emperor Frederick Barbarossa granted their first privileges to the students and masters of the city, Bologna's international fame was already established. Her Glossators ('inter-preters') were recognized as Europe's best experts in civil law; Gratian's work was the cornerstone of canon law.

Before the end of the twelfth century, the Bolognese school was sending 'missionaries' abroad. Placentinus introduced the methods of the Glossators to Montpellier, where the second great faculty of law developed. At Oxford Vacarius wrote a summary of Justinian's Code and Digest 'for the sake of poor students', so that they could buy it cheaply and learn it quickly. Germany, Spain and northern France, where there were as yet no universities, sent their students to Bologna and to other Italian centres. Thus Roman law re-interpreted for the needs of the Middle Ages — Romance law, as we might call it — supplied a theoretic background for local laws and began to be named 'common law of all men'.

The diffusion of Roman law: attraction and resistances

The wave of popularity of 'Romance' law cannot be explained only by its great virtues of clarity, flexibility and sagacity but also by the fact that the juridical encyclopaedia of Justinian offered arguments for all causes. The supporters of Gregory VII and of ecclesiastical reform found in it justification for papal universalism. More properly, the adherents of the Empire saw in it the consecration of the absolutism of the emperor, 'living law on earth', by perpetual popular mandate. In their turn the citizens of free communes placed the stress not on the delegate but on those who had originally appointed him, that is to say, on the principle of popular sovereignty. Lords and vassals sought in this same law means of transforming their feudal tenures into unconditional properties; men of business drew from it a sophisticated and flexible theory of obligations and contracts; moralists, an emphasis on the supreme validity of natural law and great ethical principles; cynics, a very nice distinction between what is honest and what is lawful.

Moreover, in Italy, where there was no native dynasty that could serve as a rallying focus, Justinian and his law became patriotic, almost national, symbols. Thus in the twelfth century the unknown author of a little book on the 'Subtleties of the Law' gave vent to his resentment against the 'transalpine kings' who had allowed barbarian laws to be used and reopened in this way 'the wound of ancient sorrow'. The descendants of the Romans wanted Roman law.

For similar reasons 'Romance' law met the first opposition towards the end of the twelfth century, not on the part of Italian students of Germanic law (who consented to handle Lombard laws, feudal customs and municipal statutes as mere complements to the Roman 'common law'), but on the part of foreign rulers, wherever an energetic dynasty strove to impose its own laws upon the whole of the kingdom.

> King Philip Augustus, fearing that the reception of Roman law might lend support to the pretensions to universal suzerainty of his enemy the Emperor, forbade the teaching of it at the University of Paris in 1219. Nevertheless the schools of Roman law continued to flourish not only in southern France, which was still autonomous, but even in the royal city of Orleans. This city, formerly a prominent centre of twelfth-century humanism, now received permission to offer courses in Roman law, which had been refused to Paris. In Spain the conflict was less sharp. Although the sovereigns always insisted on the precedence of royal ordinances over all other legal texts, they generally allowed jurists to quote Roman law above all, in support of their opinions.

England reacted with special violence. By order of King Stephen, Vacarius was 'reduced to silence', books of canon and civil law were confiscated and the teaching of the subject was forbidden. The storm did not last, but resistance continued. If the English jurists wished to create a doctrine valid for the whole kingdom, they were to base it not on imported generalizations but on local precedents, feudal customs, court decisions and royal statutes. Though the royal judges of the thirteenth century were not insensitive to the influence of Roman principles and definitions, the legal system that began to emerge under Edward I sprang from native roots. In this way, the expression 'common law', contrived on the continent to designate Roman as opposed to national law, came to mean in England (and still does in all English-speaking countries) national as opposed to Roman law.

Even where it met opposition, however, the work of the Glossators gave a new impetus to legal studies. In order to withstand the competition of 'Romance' law all feudal and national customs had to be tidied up. They had to be put in writing, systematized according to the logic of civil and canon law, and fitted for the expression of abstract notions. When Ranulf de Glanvill (or perhaps his nephew and secretary) composed the first general 'Treatise on the Laws and Customs of the Kingdom of England', about 1189, he used his knowledge of Roman law to give it a structure. In the thirteenth century manuals and collections of local and national law multiplied all over Europe. Whatever they contained, their framework almost always revealed the influence of the Roman organizing mind.

*Fig. 38. King Magnus IV, Legislator of Norway;
Carving in Stavanger cathedral, Norway.*

The other legal traditions

The content of the laws developed more slowly than their form. Except in some cities, twelfth-century society was too different from Roman society to adapt the latter's fundamental rules for its own needs. The ancient conception of absolute, exclusive and perpetual ownership was incompatible with the feudal organization of domains broken down into a number of layers entrusted to several overlapping, temporary tenants. The ancient categories of free men and slaves were not applicable to the mediaeval serfs. The power of action given by the ancients to the free woman contrasted with the regime of perpetual minority to which the early Middle Ages subjected her. In these sectors, and in many others, 'Romance' law could at most supply a Roman wrapping to Germanic customs.

Is it proper, however, to oppose 'Germanic customs' to Roman or 'Romance' law? Family feuds, judicial duels, compurgation (that is to say, proving one's innocence by the oath of next of kin), law of shipwreck (seizing the goods and often the persons of shipwrecked sailors): of these and other institution, which usually are linked to the Germans, we find no mention in the Visigoth codes of Spain. Yet they appear in the Christian states of Spain after the Arab invasion. One wonders whether they are typically Germanic or merely uncivilized.

Throughout Europe the progress achieved during the late Middle Ages was bound to make the roughest customs intolerable. The readiest model for reforming them was Roman law; sooner or later most countries borrowed from it massively. England, however, took over only a few clarifying elements (for instance, neater distinctions between contracts and torts, and between tenure and ownership). On the whole, she succeeded in bringing her customs up to date by modifying them radically without casting them off: compurgation, for example, was gradually transformed into trial by jury. The English experience proves that no legal tradition has the monopoly of a sense of justice, and that it was possible to construct a valid legal system without depending heavily on 'Romance' material.

Nevertheless, the honour of having produced the first national code of the late Middle Ages belongs not to England (she still does not possess one!) but to Norway. Here, by initiative of King Magnus 'the Mender of the Law' (1263–80), the laws issued by provincial assemblies and towns were brought up to date and codified. As for Germany, the judge Eike von Repgow compiled, between 1221 and 1224, a private collection of customs (*Sachsenspiegel*, 'Mirror of the Saxons') which seemed destined to stabilize native legal tradition more satisfactorily than the imperial code of Frederick II, promulgated in Sicily at the same period and imbued with Roman law. One might have thought that the disintegration of the 'Roman Empire of the Teutonic nation' after the death of Frederick II would favour local customs; on the contrary, Roman law and canon law were to influence more profoundly another private collection dating from 1274 (*Schwabenspiegel*, 'Mirror of the Swabians'). By the end of the Middle Ages the law of Rome had become practically the national law of Germany. Thus, a thousand years after his death, Justinian won his finest victory.

III. THE PASSION FOR BUILDING

Much as we may admire today the harmonious and learned structures built by twelfth-century philosophers and jurists, we do not love them as much as we love the works of the architects, their contemporaries. The fact is that learning feeds progress and thereby is condemned to be outstripped. Art remains, and finds fresh youth through the interpretations which successive ages place upon it.

Among modern interpretations of the Romanesque and Gothic styles, the most popular one sees in them a contrast of religious attitudes. The massive horizontality of Romanesque architecture would seem to express the submission to God of a society barely emerging from a long slumber; the light verticality of Gothic architecture would reflect the soaring flight towards God of a society more sure of itself. And yet this contrast between 'architecture of humility' and 'architecture of impetus' was completely unknown to the writers of the time. What they usually praised can be summarized in three words: grandeur, harmony, magnificence. But these intuitive values belong to the aesthetics of all times. They are not exclusively religious.

The role of symbolism

It is true that churches were the glory and the supreme endeavour of the mediaeval builders. An enormous endeavour, which raised much criticism: a Raoul
Glaber in the tenth century, a Bernard of Clairvaux in the twelfth, a Rutebeuf in
the thirteenth, were shocked that ever larger and more richly adorned churches
should be built when there were old ones in good condition, and so many people
in need of help. But Suger, abbot and royal minister (c. 1081–1151), did not
hesitate to cover the altar of Saint Denis with gold. 'The holy matyrs themselves', he explains, 'tell us with their own lips: "We want the very best that can
be had".' Could pomp and beauty be justified by clothing them in symbols?

Very many people believed so. The greatness of a church provided a foretaste
of the immensity of the heavens. The harmony of its proportions was measured
in numbers consecrated by the celestial hierarchy (the three of the Trinity, the
twelve of the Apostles and so forth) and distributed on intervals suggested by
that echo of the harmony of the spheres which is man-made music (1/2, 2/3, 3/4,
etc.). Its magnificence imitated the splendour of Nature, the daughter of God,
and of the Creator himself, by the liveliness of colours and the profusion of light.

The inner and outer decoration of a church, its ground plan, its location in
the urban street pattern, all served to announce and dramatize the divine
message. Gigantic bell towers, rising up suddenly behind the corner of narrow
lanes, proclaimed to the tiny houses around them the power of the Lord. Cruci-
form plans with three naves transformed basilicas into allegorical structures.
Mosaics, paintings and stained glass windows turned to gold, purple or sparkling sapphire the pale and variable azure of the real sky. Sculpture, that Bible
of the illiterate, served as a popular commentary and historical illustration of
the theological abstractions built into the architectural frame. On this ground,
it could be forgiven for the almost idolatrous devotion it inspired in the simpler
souls, and for the worldly pleasure it gave to eyes too easily attracted by beauty.

Nevertheless, theology and symbolism explain only certain aspects of religious
art and do not fully illuminate the evolution of styles. They could not exert any
direct influence on military and civil architecture or on ordinary houses. When
a tenth-century Roman noble and a twelfth-century Flemish vassal constructed
towers which were called 'skyscrapers' (inter coelos, coelo contigua) their aim
was not to draw nearer to God but to be able to pour boiling oil and throw
stones on any assailant from a vantage position. More castles were built than
cathedrals: between 1135 and 1154, according to a source, the English barons
are said to have built 1,115 'unauthorized castles' in a kingdom already bristling
with authorized ones. This figure is probably exaggerated — a modern scholar
estimates that there were never more than five hundred castles in the whole of
England — but one must also count the towers of the bourgeoisie, fortified
houses and town walls.

Civil or domestic architecture played a significant part. Sooner or later all
cities and a number of small towns wanted their town halls and hospitals, their

fountains and bridges. Lastly, let us consider the mass of private dwellings, both urban and rural. The poorest were barely shelters but there were increasing numbers inspired by artistic ideas. These no doubt influenced the evolution of styles.

Fig. 39. Pre-Romanesque architecture; basilica of St Agnes-without-the-walls, Rome; transverse section; seventh century.

The role of materials

All in all, the contrast between Romanesque and Gothic seems less old and less important than that of materials: on the one hand architecture in stone or bricks; on the other, architecture in wood, thatch, *pisé* and later in glass.

Originally this contrast springs from the conditions of soil and climate. It tends to divide Europe into two zones, roughly set apart by a line running from the estuary of the Loire to the delta of the Danube. To the south of this line there is an abundance of stone or clay. Walls are built thick as a protection against the heat of the sun. In the north there is plenty of wood to be found for building, heating and if necessary, for glass-making; but lighting is difficult in the mists and rains of winter. There are of course enclaves: wood is abundant in the belt of Alpine forests; Belgium can use her stone quarries and her brick-clay; all this is not without effect on local architecture. But in the main, the mutual suitability of materials and climate sustains two different traditions, northern and southern. Then, as tradition moulds artistic taste and style, people carry it along in their migrations even where surroundings no longer justify it.

It is thus not without reason that a Lombard text of the seventh century or of the early eighth calls the two types of building *opus romanense* and *opus gallicum*. The first of these terms reminds us that stone and brick had constituted the technical and aesthetic postulate of Roman architecture and maintained their prestige in the two Romes of the early middle ages (the eastern Rome of the Byzantines and the western Rome of the popes). Stone and brick were to prevail in the course of the artistic renaissance that modern historians likewise call Romanesque. The term *opus gallicum* underlines the fact that Gauls and Franks were for a long time attached to wood, *pisé* and other light materials. They took to stone, but their ultimate reaction produced that architecture in glass framed by a minimum of stone that the Germans were to import, in the thirteenth century, under the name of *opus francigenum*. We erroneously call it Gothic.

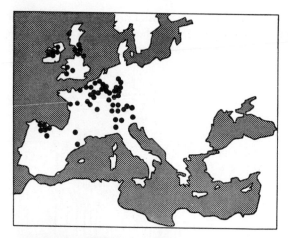

Map 12. The expansion of
art in Catholic Europe from
the seventh to the thirteenth
centuries

PRE–ROMANESQUE ART

7th to 9th centuries

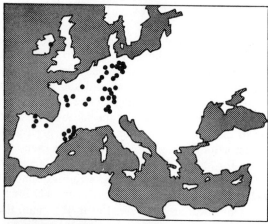

10th century

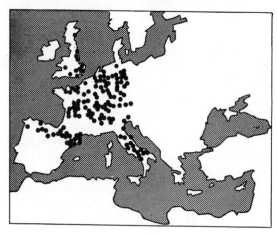

ROMANESQUE ART

11th century

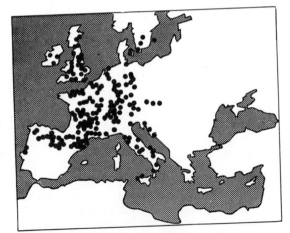

12th century

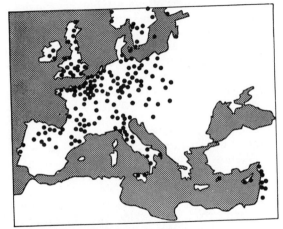

GOTHIC ART
13th century

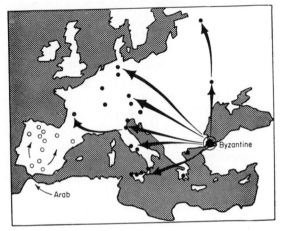

Oriental influences from
7th to 13th centuries

Techniques and materials, too, do not explain everything, but, unlike symbolism, they affect all buildings both public and private. In religious architecture they raise the problem upon which the development of Romanesque and Gothic styles so largely depended: spanning wide open spaces with heavy solid structures. The problem became harder as churches increased their proportions and stone replaced timber not only in lateral walls but also in ceilings. To reach ever bolder solutions the builders of Catholic Europe embarked upon a series of experiments; they learned a good deal from the example of their eastern neighbours and their western ancestors, but the final results were utterly original (Figs 39, 40, 41).

The key technical problem was that of absorbing lateral thrusts; for large openings can be bridged only by arches, and arches under weight will tend to open up. Architects went to work on four basic elements: the vault, the buttress, the system of interlocking counterthrusts and the arch itself. (Domes also were often used, but they did not become an essential feature of western architecture until the Renaissance). Barrel vaults were replaced by cross vaults, whose entire thrust was conveyed to the four corners; then the cross vaults were built on a skeleton of arches or ribs. Buttresses propped up the arches and most particularly the four corners of the cross vaults; they were steadied by pinnacles, topped by flying buttresses propping up the upper wall or flanked by flying buttresses propping the buttress itself. The system of counterthrusts was perfected by multiplying the rows of mutually supporting arches and cross-vaulted sections. The rounded arch was gradually replaced by a pointed arch, whose lateral thrust was slighter and partly absorbed by the pointed top.

Almost all these devices appeared in the course of the Romanesque period, if not earlier. When they were systematically co-ordinated and fully exploited, Gothic art blossomed out. Technically, then, Gothic art was not a reaction against Romanesque, but rather a further stretch of the same road. Artistically, it can be called either the glorious fulfilment or the exaggeration of Romanesque art, according to our personal taste.

Development and diffusion of Romanesque architecture

The transition from wooden beams to stone for the roofing of churches is usually regarded as the initial move of the new architecture; hence the interest taken by art historians in the rare testimonies in stone or brick earlier than the revival of the tenth century. In the ninth century the King of the Asturias built in stone the great hall of his palace at Oviedo (Pl. 17). Converted into a church, it escaped the destruction which fell upon the Carolingian palaces and other civil buildings. France, Germany and Italy have handed down a few documents, plans, and more rarely, whole churches, The Roman and Byzantine tradition generally plays the chief part in them, but one may also trace some fresh oriental influences. What is more, some local innovations in the ground plans and in the arrangement of the towers seem to herald the awakening of the passion for building.

In the tenth century and the early eleventh, the movement gathers speed. There is good reason to believe that a building revival occurred at the same time as the philosophical and legal awakening, often in the same centres and with the same patrons. Such centres were no doubt relatively few and scattered over regions where architecture was not yet an art but merely a handicraft. The patrons, however, were generally great lords, monastic communities, prelates whose fame and influence shone far afield, and who often went so far as to draw plans for the buildings.

The masons and sometimes the materials came from afar and were moved at the bidding of clients. Old foundations, columns and fragments were re-used whenever they came to hand; Greek and Italian specialist builders, patterns and ornaments were employed whenever they could be paid for. Nevertheless, local stones and local artists predominated, especially for buildings on a modest scale which were in a majority. The largest churches, and perhaps the most beautiful, were erected in imperial Germany, which at that time extended as far as the Moselle region and the vassal states of Poland and Bohemia. Yet this 'Ottonian art', which carried on, not without originality, the Carolingian tradition, lost its creativity towards the end of the eleventh century. The beginnings of Romanesque architecture proper must be sought for in the south and west of Europe. Even there, very few monuments remain which can be definitely attributed to this dawn of a new art, for successive generations were rich enough to rebuild the churches and warlike enough to reconstruct the castles according to more 'modern' standards. As for the ordinary houses of that period, we know nothing of them (Pl. 9).

Though Raoul Glaber, the French chronicler, already noted that 'soon after the year 1000. . . the world was shaking itself and throwing off its old rags to reclothe itself in a white robe of churches', the movement gained full speed somewhat later, between the mid eleventh and the mid twelfth centuries. The same energy which created villages in the midst of clearings and transformed villages into towns, also filled the spaces but lately empty with monumental buildings. Thus the progress of the vineyards in the Bordeaux region followed the same curve as the foundation of Romanesque rural churches. There initially were several distinct artistic provinces — Catalonia, Lombardy, Tuscany, Provence, Poitou, Auvergne, the Moselle region and the Rhineland, and so forth — but the differences gradually faded and common trends prevailed. Fresh classical and oriental influences enriched them without altering their nature. Here and there we can detect the personal stamp of an architect, not always anonymous, or the suggestions of travellers returning home: pilgrims from Rome or Compostella, Italian merchants, crusading knights. In buildings as in books, monks gave the first impulse, but they gradually were surrounded by an articulate public opinion.

Buildings became larger and larger, whether to shelter the crowds brought together by increasing population and easier communications, or to fulfil the urge for grandeur, harmony and magnificence. The balance between these two

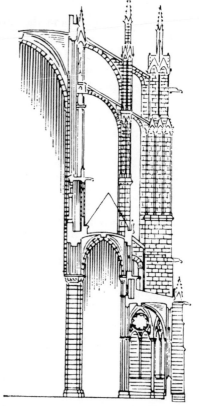

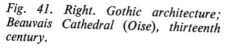

Fig. 40. Romanesque architecture; section of Saint-Austremoine d'Issoire (Puy-de-Dome); beginning of twelfth century.

Fig. 41. Right. Gothic architecture; Beauvais Cathedral (Oise), thirteenth century.

motives (practical and aesthetic) was expressed in a simultaneous expansion on all planes. 'Width, length and height go hand in hand', proclaims a writer of the twelfth century. At its zenith the Romanesque church is more powerful and bolder than the early medieval basilica while preserving its calm, solemn rhythm. Military and civil buildings such as the imperial palace at Goslar, the castle of the Flemish counts at Ghent or the house of Crescenzio in Rome, are almost squat.

The triumph of Gothic: rationalism or decoration?

Finally the tendency towards height won the day. In 1144, exactly fifty years after the rudimentary Gothic of Durham cathedral, the choir of Saint-Denis, the first masterpiece of fully developed Gothic, was consecrated. Half a century: this is less than the architecture which we call 'rational' or 'modern' has taken to eliminate the conventional styles of neo-Romanesque and neo-Gothic.

In recent years the victory of the Gothic style has been interpreted as a triumph of medieval rationalism. From one deduction to the next (it has been said), the first cross vaults on pointed arches had to lead to the cathedrals of Chartres and Reims as inevitably as the first syllogisms led to the synthesis of Aquinas. And it has been emphasized that in the Gothic age the architect-engineer begins to supersede the patron as protagonist. The bishops and princes spoil him, the chroniclers go into raptures over his talents, the whole population of a village or a diocese offers him money and occasionally (though more rarely than has been claimed) manual help. It matters little if the architect is often mistaken over the effectiveness of his devices, if ribs (like the transverse arches which preceded them) are of dubious functional value, if a certain pointed arch does not actually give support, or if a certain buttress is a mere decoration. The essential thing is that the builder believes in his logic as the theologian believes in his dialectic, and that there is perfect agreement between them. 'God is light', states the theologian, and the architect transforms the blind wall into a transparent surface, the heap of stones into a cage of glass. Nor is it chance that the initiative in architecture, which originated in the south like 'Romance' law, ended in the north like the philosophy of Paris (Pl. 17).

True, but it is necessary to recall once more that mediaeval architects did not restrict themselves to building cathedrals. Castles and fortifications have nothing to do with symbolism: they need solid walls. These the Romanesque style had already provided. Gothic, however, had certain practical advantages to recommend it: height of towers, resistance to shock, economy in materials. Fashion, which makes its way into the most uninviting precincts, helped to win acceptance for the new style, not of course in its most revolutionary form of wide openings shut by fragile glass, but as a moderate change of proportions.

For ordinary houses the change does not mean much more than the introduction of the pointed arch, more for its aesthetic value than for its functional merits, and of some decorative elements. The most important innovation in domestic architecture is the substitution of stone, brick or *pisé* for wood. This is actually the first stage of the Romanesque renaissance penetrating to the lowest level, but extremely slowly; most American houses are still made of wood. Art historians have paid but little attention to the architecture of the common man. This is a great pity. Just as bishops and counts are not the only people to occupy the political scene, so cathedrals and castles are but a part of the architectural landscape.

IV. THE PLEASURES OF WRITING

Let us tear ourselves away from the dazzling spectacle of the art of the first three centuries of the late Middle Ages — only specialized books can do it justice — to turn for a moment to the riches of literature. We do not find here the guiding line provided for architecture by the development of Romanesque and Gothic. Nevertheless, underneath the variety of style, subject and language we can perceive the persistence of certain *leit-motifs*.

History and hagiography

It would be ungrateful for a historian not to begin his tour with his fellow-historians. They were among the first to recover. If the early Middle Ages produced only one historian worthy of the name, Bede; the ninth century already had two, Eginhard and Nithard. In the tenth century there were several, most unequal in talent and temperament, but all endowed with some gifts. In the two succeeding centuries there is a vast selection of distinguished writers: philosopher-historians like Otto of Freising, municipal annalists like Caffaro of Genoa, learned monks like Orderic Vitalis, pugnacious prelates like Guibert of Nogent, budding nationalists like Ugo Falcando, reporters of noblemen's life like the chronicler of the counts of Guines, and so many others.

Nevertheless we have to admit that none of these witnesses of the mediaeval scene, to whom we owe the best part of our knowledge, was a great historian. Certain of them had artistic quality though they were hampered by the fact that they generally translated their vernacular thoughts into Latin. Several of them were reliable and penetrating, many had lively and original minds. But they all lacked the urge for ultimate synthesis which is the mark of the truly superior historian. Between Tacitus and Machiavelli, the only historian of genius we come across is Ibn Khaldun, born at Tunis in 1332.

On the other hand, the taste for history finds striking expressions in literature proper, much of which is devoted to the praise of true or legendary deeds of the heroic past. In the early Middle Ages its written products had been most profuse in hagiography: 26,000 lives of saints, composed between the sixth and the tenth centuries, are collected in the Latin volumes of the Bollandist Fathers. Between the late ninth century and the mid eleventh, the first known pages of French literature still belong to this genre: *Sequence of Saint Eulalia*, *Vie de Saint Léger*, *Vie de Saint Alexis*.... This last begins with a nostalgic description of the past: 'Good was the world in the time of the ancients — for there was faith and justice and love.... — It is all changed, it has lost its colour!'

As a matter of fact, hagiography was on the decline. It maintained a certain vitality only when it rose to the standard of poetic hymns or when it descended to the level of popular theatre. There is some liveliness in the religious plays which the nun Hrotswitha, Otto I's niece, wrote in Latin, after the style of Terence; but they had no influence outside the convent for which they were composed. On the other hand, the sketchy dramatizations of the Easter liturgy, attempted by the clergy and within the church in the same period, were to lead to the staging of complete dramas, in the churchyard or the street and with participation of the laity. But the greatest attraction of the earliest dramatic masterpiece— the *Jeu d'Adam*, in French — was the very secular scene where the serpent flatters Eve with the timeless language of seducers and almost seems to foreshadow the adulterous triangle of the modern middle-class comedy.

The epic superman

Was the miracle-working saint really the supreme literary hero of the early Middle Ages, as the almost exclusively ecclesiastical documentation of that time would have us believe, or did the warrior play a still greater part, through largely unrecorded oral literature? In any case, at the beginning of the later Middle Ages, it is the warrior who has pride of place. He was called Hildebrand in a German poem of the late eighth century, and Walter of Aquitaine in a Latin poem of the tenth; he will be called Sigurd or Siegfried, Roland, the Cid Campeador, Cuchulainn in the sagas and heroic songs of the Scandinavians, Germans, French, Spanish and Irish in the following era.

Unfortunately it is often impossible to discover to what extent any particular literary reincarnation of the ideal long before presented by Gilgamesh, Samson and Achilles is derived from an earlier oral tradition, to what extent it has been christianized and polished by clergymen, and to what extent it is based on actual historical facts. Literary stratigraphy is a hard, highly controversial science and it does not belong here. The real masterpieces — *Chanson de Roland, Cantar del Cid, Nibelungenlied* — are stamped with the personality of their authors, though they spring from many sources and from different periods.

In the crudest epic versions the hero is a warrior endowed with supernatural powers. His body is invulnerable, his sword is invincible, and his exorcisms get the better of any spell. His stature, his strength, even his appetite are fabulous. Such a superman ought to make short work of all his adversaries, but to break the monotony which a succession of predictable victories would create he is made the victim of treachery. His personal drama is usually framed in a collective historical drama, equally uncouth. Thus Roland illustrates not Charlemagne's many victories but his one defeat at Roncevaux; Siegfried does not commemorate the German conquest of the Roman Empire, but the fleeting triumph of the Huns over the Germans; the Cid exemplifies not the methodical progress of the Spanish *Reconquista*, but the struggles between kings and vassals that marred it.

In turn, historical circumstances cast a vaguely religious, patriotic, monarchic or feudal light over the hero. Even if sentiments of this kind do not go far beyond the surface, they temper the brutality of the primitive heroic image; Superman will have not only muscles, but a heart and a brain as well. No western champion will equal the literary culture of Byzantium's Digenis, but Roland the valiant will have his double in Oliver the wise and the Cid will blend guile with daring. Raoul of Cambrai, insulted by his lord as the Cid was by his king, will kill the lord but feel remorseful for the rest of his life. Thus the clash of swords is succeeded by spiritual conflict: the epic glides towards lyric poetry and the novel.

The lady on a pedestal

Henceforth the heroine will vie with the hero for the centre of the stage. The ideal woman, equal or superior to the ideal man, will be the great innovation in European literature of the late Middle Ages. While Roman law had respected the personality of women, classical literature had celebrated them especially as the instruments of pleasure and physical love. Between the ninth and the twelfth centuries the lyrical poets of the Latin renaissance took up once again this erotic theme. As for the hagiographers and epic poets, they did not conceal their contempt for a sex which proved weaker in every battle, whether spiritual or military. At most they excused a few asexual women, ascetic virgins or muscular valkyries. What, then, is the origin of the poetic revolution which in vernacular lyrics placed a few selected ladies on a pedestal? We cannot really tell.

> Some people assign a decisive role to the increased devotion to the Virgin in the later Middle Ages; but the filial cult of Mary bears little resemblance to the type of love, sensual even when it was platonic, which inspired the early Provencal poets. Some others stress the Spanish-Arabic and Celtic contributions to Provençal poetry and to the romances of the Breton cycle; rightly so, but women do not appear to have enjoyed a high status among the Arabs or the Celts. More recently, psychology and psychoanalysis have been invoked to explore the subconscious sources of courtly love; someone still ought to tell us why the subconscious should suddenly have awakened precisely in the eleventh century, between the Loire and the Pyrenees. Perhaps the most plausible explanation is that from the eleventh century onwards a feminine public came into being in regions where serious men were not in the habit of reading. Troubadours and romance writers composed their works for this public, often accompanying themselves on the stringed instruments which at that time were becoming widely used in noble and elegant society.

The heroine of courtly literature, as everyone knows, was noble, rich, beautiful, good and almost always married. Poets praised her piety, her wisdom and the very disdainfulness which they proposed to bring to terms. Her moral and physical portrait was so vague and impersonal that it soon lost contact with reality. The conventional image created by the first poets in *langue d'oc* (or, less properly, Provençal) passed, simultaneously with the metres of their poems, into the other vernacular literatures. There was no need to characterize more closely a woman whose principal function was to serve as a mirror for the feelings of men. The best poems vibrate with masculine emotions; a lady cannot respond.

While the ideal woman hardly changed, the love of which she was the object developed according to the times and the artists (Fig. 42). Amid the contradictions which this sentiment is bound to inspire, in art as in real life, one tendency affirmed itself: love became ethereal. The earliest Provençal poets, in spite of their declarations of platonic feelings, had often let slip some expressions of a desire as sensual as that of pagan writers. Not so their successors, in Provence and elsewhere. Their heroine's pedestal became a throne — nay, an altar; so much so that ultimately a poet could compare his lady to the Virgin without fear of blasphemy.

As the end became inaccessible, the poets turned their attention towards the means: they discussed the rules of the almost feudal service and the almost

PLATE 1. *Two visions of the end of the world, Western and Byzantine.*
The Resurrection of the Dead (detail); early eleventh century, Book of Pe-
ricopes *of Henry II; Munich Library.*

The Last Judgment; Byzantine ivory eleventh century; Victoria and Albert
Museum, London.

PLATE 2. *Warriors of the invasions, in the form of gods. The god Kuan Ti (Kuan Yü, the Chinese general, deified); third century. Print from a stele of Pei-lin, Si-ngan fu, Chensi province.*

The god Woden as a Germanic horseman, seventh century; Halle Museum.

PLATE 3. *Two bas-reliefs of barbarian times (seventh century).*
The Evangelists and Archangels, sarcophagus lid: Poitiers, Hypogeum Martyrium.
The Sun supported by two Angels, Quintanilla de las Viñas, near Burgos (Spain).

PLATE 4. *Fresco from Santa Maria di Castelseprio (Lombardy), eighth century: the Nativity. Iconoclasts profaning images, and simulating the offer of vinegar to Christ, as before his death. Shludov Psalter, Moscow.*

PLATE 5. *Byzantine mosaics: St Agnes (detail), seventh century, Church of St Agnes, Rome. The Emperor Alexander (detail), tenth century, recent discovery at St Sophia, Istanbul.*

PLATE 6. *Development of the arcade. Left to right: St Sabina, Rome, fifth century; Great Mosque of the Omeyyads, Damascus (Syria), eighth century; San Pietro, Tuscania (Italy), eighth century interior; Santa Maria la Blanca, formerly a synagogue, Toledo, thirteenth century.*

PLATE 7. *Watercolour by Grimaldi representing the mosaic of the Lateran, Rome, before reconstruction in the eighteenth century: the investiture of Pope Leo III and Charlemagne by St Peter; Vatican Library.*

PLATE 8. *Two Carolingian Emperors*
Louis the Pious, in half-Germanic, half-Byzantine dress. Vienna (Austria), National Library.

Charles the Bald, in Byzantine costume, receiving the Bible. Paris, Bibliothèque Nationale.

PLATE 9. *Palatine chapel at Valkhof, Nijmegen, in the Netherlands, tenth century. Bronze keys (at left) of the Carolingian era and Byzantine design, eight-tenth century. Le Secq Museum, Rouen. Group of stone beehive cells in the sixth century; Irish island monastery of Skellig Michael.*

PLATE 10. *Saint Ambrose being fed by the bees; bas-relief of an altar in gold repoussé, basilica of Saint Ambrose, Milan, ninth century.*

Slaves and slave-sellers presented by St Adalbert to King Boleslas 'The Valiant'; detail of bronze door of the cathedral of Gniezno, Poland, twelfth century.

PLATE 11. *Marble statuette of a monk, probably from southern Italy, twelfth century; Detroit Institute of Arts, Detroit.*

PLATE 12. *Christ carved on a runic stone at Jelling (Denmark). eighth-ninth century, cast in the National Museum of Copenhagen; Viking warrior in wood, decorating the wagon found in the ship at Oseberg (Norway), eighth-ninth century.*

PLATE 13. *Feudal homage paid by the nobles of Perpignan to Alfonso the Chaste, King of the Asturias;* Liber Feudorum Maior, Archives of the Crown of Aragon, Barcelona.

Ecclesiastical feudalism; standart of St Kilian used at the battle of Mühlberg (1266); Mainfränkisches Museum, Wurzburg.

PLATE 14. *Prophets in discussion; bas-relief in Bamberg Cathedral, 1237; University of Paris, Faculty of Arts. Seals of the four nations, 1398; left to right: Normandy, England, France, Picardy; National Archives, Department of Seals.*

PLATE 15. *The Labours of the Months; fresco decorating an arcade in the church at Pritz (Mayenne), thirteenth century. Bottom to top left and top to bottom right: March, April, May, June, July, August, September, October. Museum of French Monuments, Paris.*

PLATE 16. *The Law: the oldest manuscript, full of corrections and notes, of the municipal laws of Pisa (Constitutum Usus), twelfth century; Coll. Thomas E. Marston, Yale University. Left: two capitals in the cathedral of Modena: 'Man Oppressed' by injustice, and the 'Upright Judge' showing the text of the Digest, twelfth century.*

PLATE 17. *Left to right* (*top*): *Famagusta Cathedral* (*Cyprus*), *later mosque, fourteenth century; Wooden church, Heddal* (*Norway*), *thirteenth century.* (*Below*) *The Church of Santa Maria de Naranco, Oviedo* (*Spain*), *former hall of the Royal Palace of the Asturias, ninth century; Romanesque houses at Tournai* (*Belgium*), *twelfth century.*

PLATE 18. *Martyrdom of Saint Thomas à Becket, from the cloister of Seligen-stadt; Bavarian Museum, Munich. Return of the Milanese after their victory over Frederick Barbarossa at Legnano; Museum of the Castello Sforzesco, Milan.*

PLATE 19. *Christ on horseback; fresco in the cathedral crypt, Auxerre (Yonne), end of eleventh or beginning of twelfth century.*

PLATE 20. *Cathedrals and towers in the mediaeval city, Beauvais (Oise) dominated by its Cathedral, thirteenth century. Lucca (Italy), fourteenth century, towers of private buildings dominating the city; Archivio Capitolare, Lucca.*

PLATE 21. *Towns of South and North. Todi (Italy); La Piazza del Popolo, town hall and houses of twelfth and thirteenth centuries. Lübeck (Germany) Hansa town; seventeenth century warehouses in the traditional style of the Middle Ages.*

PLATE 22. *New nobility of the town and feudal nobility. Alderman and Captain Guillaume Wenemaer, funeral plaque, Musée de la Biloque, Ghent, fourteenth century. Knight-at-arms originating from the abbey church of Notre-Dame-de-la-Règle at Limoges, twelfth century; Musée Municipal, Limoges.*

PLATE 23. *Tapestry, church of Skog (Helsingborg) Sweden; the faithful, meeting in a 'stave church', ringing the bells, about 1100; State History Museum, Stockholm.*

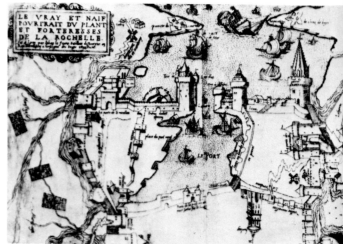

PLATE 24. *(Top) Port of Pisa in the thirteenth century: Lapidary Museum of St Augustine, Genoa. (Center left) Seal of La Rochelle 1308; Archives Nationales. (Center right) Port of La Rochelle, two entrance towers and pond from fourteenth century; Orbigny Museum, La Rochelle. (Below) Loading baggage for a crusade 1352; Bibliothèque Nationale, Paris.*

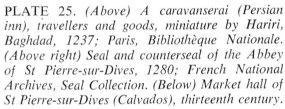

PLATE 25. *(Above) A caravanserai (Persian inn), travellers and goods, miniature by Hariri, Baghdad, 1237; Paris, Bibliothèque Nationale. (Above right) Seal and counterseal of the Abbey of St Pierre-sur-Dives, 1280; French National Archives, Seal Collection. (Below) Market hall of St Pierre-sur-Dives (Calvados), thirteenth century.*

PLATE 26. *(Above) Urban public services; Arab baths, in Palma, Majorca. Aqueduct at Salerno (Italy) thirteenth century. Fortified bridge at Monmouth, thirteenth century. (Below) Fortified bridge at Orthes (Lower Pyrenees) thirteenth century.*

PLATE 27. *Iron gate, Lisbon Cathedral thirteenth century. Cathedral of Coimbra (Portugal) mid-twelfth century. Casket of the Five Moroccan Martyrs' fifteenth century; Machado da Castro Museum, Coimbra.*

PLATE 28. *Jews at prayer in a synagogue, in Spain, fourteenth century; British Museum. Winchester, Great Hall of the King's Palace, on the far wall a table, said to be that of King Arthur and his Knights, arranged for twenty-five places. English thirteenth century gates; Victoria and Albert Museum.*

PLATE 29. *Stained glass from St James's Church at Flums (Switzerland), twelfth century; Schweizerische Landesmuseum, Zurich. The Masons; detail from reliquary of St Culmin, at Mozac (Puy-de-Dome), Limoges twelfth century enamel.*

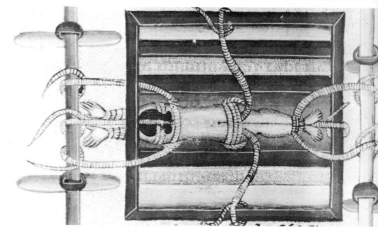

PLATE 30. *Medicine: incision of a tumour; medicinal herbs; feeling the pulse; blood-letting; reduction of fracture of the spine; urine analysis; purging of a pregnant woman; medicinal precious stones;* Codex Paneth, *Medical Library, Yale University.*

PLATE 31. *The Black Death (1346–1350), inhabitants of Tournai burying their dead; Bibliothèque Royale Brussels,* Annales de Gilles le Muisis.

The battle of Crécy 1346, Chroniques de Froissart, *Bibliothèques de l'Arsenal, Paris.*

PLATE 32. *The Fool, sculpture in wood from a stall in Cologne Cathedral, fourteenth century. Balcony of Angel Musicians, (fragment), Exeter cathedral, fourteenth century.*

religious cult to which their amorous devotion subjected them. They no longer wrote for their idol, but for the initiated, and often in a secret jargon of their own (*cantar clos*). Their art was degenerating into an irrelevant exercise when the Albigensian Crusade scattered the initiated. A number of them were thus brought into contact with a different environment, that of the Italian towns. Here, lyric poetry was to come out of the blind alley it had reached and eventually to win back its public through a 'sweet new style'.

Fig. 42. Eve picking the forbidden fruit. Romanesque basrelief in Saint Lazarus Cathedral, Autun (Saone-et-Loire), twelfth century; Rolin Museum, Autun.

The romantic hero and the shepherdess

The sublimation of courtly love left a gap which was partly filled by a new genre, the 'romance' or vernacular novel, and by a very old genre, pastoral poetry. Without lowering the heroine, the romance sets ever more perilous steps by which the aspirant can raise himself to her level. This formula had its greatest success after the middle of the twelfth century, in the *Tale of the Cart* by Chrétien de Troyes. After having gone through extraordinary adventures which leave the reader breathless, for love of Queen Gwinevere, Lancelot is worthy of reaping the fullest reward for his devotion. It is dangerous stuff: more than a hundred years after the composition of this skilful blend of suspense, sex and chivalresque doctrine, Dante will accuse 'the book and its author' of having pushed Francesca da Rimini into adultery. Yet it is doubtful whether the good fortune of Lancelot entranced people as much as the tragic end of Tristan and his beloved Iseult, carried away by a fate stronger than their will. Their story, like that of Perceval (or Gawain) and the Holy Grail, may have its origins in the remotest prehistorical past; but it fitted the emotions of the late mediaeval society perfectly, and it comes down to us through innumerable literary and pictorial interpretations.

> The theme of innocent love, which triumphs over all ordeals and even over differences of class, develops a little later. At the beginning of the thirteenth century the unknown author of the tale of *Aucassin* (Al-Kasim) *and Nicolette* mingles Hellenistic and Moslem erotic themes with the pathetic romance of lawless feudalism, and sets the stage for a scandalous free union between a nobleman of Languedoc and a Saracen slave-girl. Incidentally, he takes snapshots of the ugly life of the poor, throws out some irreverent quips about Paradise and describes a battle waged with pieces of cheese. All ends well when it is discovered that the Moslem slave-girl is in reality an African princess baptised in infancy.
>
> The half-sentimental, half-roguish tone of French Aucassin is in sharp contrast with the sinister undertones of *Poor Henry*, the German romance of Hartmann von Aue. A physician, or rather a magician of Salerno, promises to cure of leprosy the knight Henry if a maiden will consent to give her heart-blood to him. Henry, whom the author describes as a paragon of virtue and generosity, nevertheless prepares to accept the sacrifice of his tenant-farmer's daughter, who is desperately in love with him. At the last moment he is overcome by remorse and divine grace saves them both.

Pastoral poetry did not need so many emotions and stratagems. A shepherdess could hardly expect the consideration due to a well-born woman. If she had not the good sense to prefer a lover of her own class to the knight who asked for her favours, she became a legitimate prey for the latter. And since poets no more stooped down to her soul than knights, the portrait of this daughter of the people was from the beginning even more conventional than that of the lady on a pedestal.

An attractive description of the landscape could have redeemed the pastoral story, but Arcadia is far removed from real nature; nor was nature of much interest for medieval poets before Dante and Petrarch. Nevertheless, dawn, spring, flowers and sometimes moonlight formed part of the compulsory background to invitations to love. And even Roland's companions cast a glance at the grim mountains as they march towards Roncevaux; but what they see is a sketchy, barren landscape like that of contemporary mosaics and paintings.

Realism and 'anti-epic'

Mediaeval realism is said to reveal itself mainly in the 'fabliaux', short stories in French verse derived both from observation of daily life and from Greco-Roman, oriental or popular traditions. Indeed these fables aim at realism, but up to the fourteenth century the characters are usually sketchy, the action is clumsy, and the caricature is heavy. Cheated husbands, avaricious wives, hypocritical priests, dull sly peasants: such are the protagonists of most of the 'fabliaux'. Granted that in real life one meets more clowns than heroes, most people are just ordinary men and women. It is easier to come across them in occasional close-ups of Latin chronicles, in certain Goliardic drinking songs or even in a few naive, sentimental folk songs. The great era of the realistic tale will come later, when the genius of Boccaccio, Chaucer and Rabelais will give new life to the humble material of the 'fabliaux'.

Fig. 43. English caricature: fox disguised as a bishop and preaching to geese, from the Luttrell Psalter; after G. M. Trevelyan

In the realm of parody, however, we must give a special place to what we should like to call the mediaeval anti-epic: the tale of Reynard the Fox and Ysengrin the Wolf. It has come down to us through a mediocre Latin tenth-century fragment, *Ecbasis captivi*, and several later amplifications, alterations and improvements of the original story in French, Flemish and English, to say nothing of oral transmission and of representations in the figurative arts (Fig. 43). The old themes of Aesop's fables are taken up again and enriched so as to provide an ironic and bitter commentary of the whole of mediaeval society. Violence, hatred and fraud reign on earth. In order to survive, if one is not strong, rich and noble, one has to flatter fools, coax the powerful, deceive the ill-intentioned. That is the way of life of the hero, or rather anti-hero, Reynard the Fox, who emerges triumphant from all ordeals by doing deliberately the opposite of what a Roland or a Lancelot would have done.

There could be no better proof of the extraordinary success of his story than the fact that the Old French name of the fox, *goupil*, has been superseded in modern French by the proper name *renard*. Paladins and Knights of the Round Table also gained a popularity which has resisted the irony of Ariosto and Cervantes; in our own days the Sicilian carts, fishing boats and marionette theatre still borrow some of their decoration and scenes from the Carolingian and Arthurian cycles. The metres, the conventions and to some extent the sentiments of our lyric poetry are derived more or less directly from the poetic works of the Provençal school and of the imitators it inspired all over Europe. Although the writers belong to a restricted circle of clergy, nobility and wealthy bourgeoisie, the literature of the late Middle Ages cannot be considered solely as the pleasure of a small minority.

However, no society is entirely revealed through its literature. To reach the very root of mass consciousness, the best means probably is to consider the direct creation of the whole people: language.

V. THE TOWER OF BABEL

A social historian finds the vicissitudes of certain words peculiarly fascinating. An Irish word, *cisel*, may contain in a nutshell the whole mass of narrative, legal, economic and archaeological evidence at our disposal as to the fiscal distress of the Roman Empire in its agony. This word means the Devil and is derived, it seems, from the Latin *censalis*, collector of taxes. Two Romance words light up the horror southern gourmets felt at the manners of northern 'barbarians': the French *boire* and the Italian *bere* come from the Latin *bibere*, but if it is a question of immoderate or vulgar drinking, recourse is had to the Germanic *drinken*, which gives respectively *trinquer* and *trincare*. And what commentary on the intellectual depression and social isolation of the early Middle Ages may be more eloquent than the disappearance of the Latin word *loqui*, meaning to talk? It would be tempting to assume that conversation in French and Italian was only by means of allegory (*parler, parlare*, from the Greek *parabole*, comparison or allegory), and in Castillian and Portuguese, conversation was only for telling fables (*hablar, falar*, from the Latin *fabulare*).

It would indeed be very rash to accept blindly the etymological evidence of isolated words. We are on firmer ground, however, when a group of borrowed words reflects large-scale borrowing from cultural and social life. In all the languages of Catholic Europe, both Romance and Germanic, the ecclesiastical vocabulary is Latin, except for certain older Greek and Hebrew words. On the other hand, Arab, Greek and, later Italian have moulded to a considerable extent the international vocabulary of commerce and navigation. These are two cases in which history and linguistics support each other.

Germanic penetration and resistance of the Latin foundations

Language is especially telling when the variety of origins indicates a crossing of influences. Walter Scott justly remarked that in English the names of the chief domestic animals are Anglo-Saxon (ox, swine, lamb) but become French (beef, pork, mutton) as soon as the animal passes from the stable of the native serf to the table of the Norman lord. Again, Germanic languages have given to the Romance languages most of the basic military terms; Latin, however, has continued to provide officers' titles and French has supplied the neologisms of chivalry and tourneys.

To be sure, the marks of the Germanic conquest in Romance linguistic territory are not limited to the military sphere. They comprise words as essential as many elementary colours (in French: *brun, blond, gris, blanc;* but the latter's opposite, *noir,* comes from Latin) and other terms in daily use (*riche, échine, salle, balcon,* in spite of the fact that balconies are mainly Mediterranean). Some of these borrowings go back, it seems, to the period before the conquest; the Roman Empire opened its doors to the Germans before they broke them in. Other imports are relatively late. As a whole they would prove, if no other testimony existed, that the relationship between the handful of conquerors and the mass of the conquered was close at all levels.

What is most striking, however, is not the penetration of the German language on Roman soil but the resistance of the Latin foundations. The Arabs were not more numerous than the Germans, yet they drove Romance languages out of Africa. The Slavs were not more cultured but they ousted Greek from three-quarters of Byzantine Europe. As for the Germans, they only rolled back Latin from a relatively narrow strip to the west and south of the Roman frontier of the Rhine and the Danube: the Netherlands, the Rhineland, northern Switzerland, southern Bavaria and Austria. They won the day only in England and by radical means, not by transmitting their language to the natives but by driving them bodily out. Still it must be noted that ecclesiastical Latin and above all French, imported later to the island by two foreign dynasties, was to bring back a substantial portion of the Romance word treasury. This explains why, although the grammar of modern English rightly places it in the Germanic family of languages, its vocabulary yet presents a strange admixture. Almost all essential words come from the Anglo-Saxon, but by and large Latin derivations are more numerous than the Germanic ones. (Map 9).

The English example has no counterpart in the Romance family of languages. The three Iberian languages have taken a very large number of words from Arabic but less than 150 from Visigothic. Italian has borrowed about 350 from Ostrogothic and Lombardic. French has been more exposed to infiltrations since it was originally localized in a linguistic peninsula surrounded by the Germanic currents of Germany, the Netherlands and England; nevertheless, it has received hardly more than 500 words from Frankish. It is true that one of these words is France (while Italy and Spain have maintained their Roman names). On the other hand, it is possible that the German pronunciation of Latin, which drowns unaccented syllables in the sonorities of the principal tonic accent, may have driven to the limit certain French contractions (*oculum, oeil; asinus, âne*). Contractions, however, had been frequent in popular Latin and its Romance developments; they would have occurred even without German pressure. As for morphology and syntax (inflexion of words, turn of sentences), in French as in the other Romance languages there is no trace of Germanic influence.

The vitality of literary Latin

Since the failure of German in Latin countries cannot be explained solely by the material and cultural weakness of the invaders, another cause must be sought which would not have held good for the Slavs and the Arabs. This cause, we believe, lies in the support given to the Romance dialects by the survival and prestige of Latin as the language of religion, administration and literature. How astonishing that Latin culture should have wielded so much power at the very epoch when it was least widespread! Without the evidence of language, who would think that some half-understood prayers and legal formulae, some official announcements of dubious effectiveness, perhaps a few pious or fictional literary texts explained orally to crowds of illiterate people by a wandering scholar, could have opposed an impenetrable barrier to the infiltration of Germanic languages among the lower classes?

Even after its final separation from popular Latin and the proto-Romance dialects, after its immobilization by Charlemagne's grammarians, the literary Latin of the Church, of the State and of the schools kept its vitality. One might call it an artificial language, because it no longer was anybody's mother tongue; a conventional language, because its best models belonged to a society long vanished; but not a petrified one. No doubt there were erudite men, especially in the early Middle Ages, who treated it like a fossil: they would extract whole sentences from Virgil or Saint Augustine and re-arrange them into unoriginal mosaics of their own. But a talented writer or a bright administrator would bend the classical examples to his own needs, enrich the vocabulary with all the useful neologisms and make the solemn old language hop to the vigorous rhythms of mediaeval prose and poetry.

The position of literary Latin in the late Middle Ages is somewhat similar to that of modern Italian in regions where the inhabitants speak only the local dialect, or that of French and German in former times where the language of Languedoc or Low German prevailed: only the select few could use it with great ease, but there was scarcely anyone so dull as not to understand at least a few words. Latin was common property because it did not belong to any nation in particular. Later on, when international snobbery tried to replace it by one or other of the contemporary languages and when patriotic zeal drove even the men of learning to use only the national language, a void was created which we have never been able to fill.

All who love Europe bless mediaeval Latin! Since it was accepted not only by Romance peoples but also by Germans, Hungarians and most of the western Slavs, it has become the most efficient instrument of the European community. Not without great loss to themselves did the Byzantines and eastern Slavs turn their backs to it. Whereas in medieval Catholic Europe some people could refuse obedience to an emperor and others to a pope, literary Latin drew together educated men of all parties and all countries.

Simplicity and flexibility: the parallel evolution of vernacular languages

While literary Latin developed but slowly, the Romance languages, unhampered by learned models, changed much faster in the directions indicated by popular Latin of the Roman Empire. Many formal words were replaced by homely ones: terms of affection such as *beau* or *bello* (from *bellus*, pretty) for *formosus*, beautiful; terms of mockery such as *tete* or *testa* (from *testa*, earthen pot) for *caput*, head; terms from cookery such as *foie* or *fegato* (from *ficatum*, stuffed with figs) for *iecur*, liver. More and more, phonetics reflected the mispronunciation of the lower classes. Morphology and syntax moved from synthesis towards analysis, from the abstract to the concrete, in keeping with the trends we have encountered in law, philosophy and literature of the early Middle Ages.

Not all of these changes, which are clearly visible in the Romance languages (and to some extent in Byzantine Greek as well), can be traced in the scantier documentation of the Germanic languages. We do not know what differences there may have been between the pronunciation of the early Germanic upper classes and that of the unpolished masses, or indeed whether any distinction existed. Moreover, Germanic had no written classics and no learned grammarians that could parallel the restraining influence of a Virgil or even a Boethius. Nevertheless, whenever it is possible to compare Germanic and Romance linguistic drifts, we find them going in the same direction if not necessarily with the same speed.

> The first change, which every schoolboy knows: the declensions disappear in Romance languages, are reduced to the optional Saxon genitive in English, and are simplified and standardized in German. They are replaced by prepositions, which are much more adaptable and varied in meaning. Singular and plural survive, but the 'dual number', already dead in classical Latin, dies out in the Germanic family also.
>
> The second change: the conjugations shed many of their 'simple' forms (in reality, harder) obtained by inflexion, and create in their place 'compound' forms (easier to learn) by using auxiliary verbs. This phenomenon is perhaps even more striking in the Germanic than in the Romance languages. Let us take the future, a really new tense since *Urgermanisch*, the hypothetical original language of all Germanic peoples, was content with the present and knew no future. For a long time, in Old English and Old German, there is a choice between several auxiliaries meaning 'to become', 'to have to', 'to be able to', 'to want to'. Finally German opted for *werden*, to become, Danish for 'shall', while English still hovers between 'will' and 'shall', not to mention roundabout expressions such as 'I am going to' or 'I am to'. Much the same evolution occurs in the Romance languages, although classic Latin had a 'simple' form of the future. On the edge of the Romance area — Rhaeto-Romanic Switzerland and Rumania — we find both 'to come' and 'will', the latter used also in modern Greek. In the centre, the auxiliary 'to have' wins the day. When

placed before the participle of another verb, this obliging auxiliary indicates a form of the past; after the infinitive of the same verb, it denotes the future: *amare habeo*, corresponding to the English 'I have to love'. This is, however, only a transitional phase. Soon the contracted auxiliary will unite with the main verb and a new 'simple' form will arise in place of the old one: in French, *j'aimerai*, instead of classical Latin *amabo*.

Third change: in both the Romance and Germanic families the definite and indefinite articles, derived respectively from the demonstrative 'that one' and from the cardinal number 'one', entrench themselves before the noun. They serve to make it more graphic, to emphasize what distinguishes it from countless homonyms. Literally, 'the woman' means 'that woman yonder'; 'a woman' means 'one woman only' or 'a certain woman'.

Fourth change: the hierarchy of main and subordinate clauses weakens. It is no longer necessary to prepare in advance a subordinate clause so that it may be properly inserted into the main one: the narrative tends to be loosened up into a series of co-ordinated clauses and thus largely freed from syntactical restraints.

While waiting for the day when linguistics will shift its emphasis from abstraction to the history of language as a human artifact, we may venture the following plain conclusions: In the early Middle Ages languages reflected the general depression through their impoverished grammar and homely speech. Yet they found, at the bottom of the pit, fresh colour and agility. The searing thought of the late Middle Ages had thus at its service not only the disciplined, lofty style of an ancient language, but a great variety of new expressions that were incomparably spontaneous and free.

From chaos to plurality

Liberty has a price. Released from the authority of a unitary school, the spoken languages of Europe multiply and diverge more and more. Verbal localism accompanies and outstrips political and economic localism. At the end of the thirteenth century Dante will point out that in Italy not only are there as many linguistic variations as there are regions and towns, but, he says, in Bologna the residents of the St Felix district do not speak in the same way as those in the High Street. Without literary Latin, this 'Grammar' *par excellence* which is made the compulsory foundation of teaching in all good schools, how would the children of Europe understand each other if they go even a short distance away from their native province?

Medieval Europe is a Tower of Babel. This gives special significance to the numerous drawings and texts which describe and deplore the consequence of Nimrod's foolish act of pride. The decline of Hebrew, the universal language before Babylon, seems to presage the fall of Latin in the Babylon of the Middle Ages.

Still it will be possible to bring a little order into this chaos by checking not plurality but excessive localism. The dialects of adjacent districts are alike; sometimes one of them is more widespread than the others. This will be the starting-point of a new literary language, more down-to-earth than Latin, easier to learn, let us say more democratic. National pride will be flattered by its growth; in its turn the national language will feed on this pride. Alas! The newcomer will then have to be subjected to rules, be taught in the schools, protected, like Latin, from over-rapid transformation by the local dialects.

Once more let us listen to Dante: 'The vernacular tongue. . . which we learn without rules by imitating our nurses' is more natural, hence more noble than 'the artificial grammar' of school Latin. And where should one find good 'verna-cular Latin' if not in Italy? But it is no use looking for it in the dialect of a particular town — not even in Dante's Florence — for only the 'illustrious vernacular', spoken everywhere by the administrative and literary *élites* of the whole of Italy, is capable of expressing the most elevated conceptions of philo-sophy and art. It must be protected from 'rustic words and faulty constructions'.

Language and nation

National language, national feelings: these are kindred streams no doubt, but sometimes divergent, in the Middle Ages as today. The possible sources are always the same: common beliefs and loyalties, easy economic and intellectual contacts, uniformity of the geographic background, historical and literary memories, or merely a common goal to be reached, an enemy to be feared or scorned.... But what people specifically draw from the sources depends on their choice.

The claim that national languages invariably represented a reaction against Latin is utterly unwarranted. In the ninth century at the court of Alfred 'the Great', Anglo-Saxon and Latin studies were seen to flourish anew side by side. In the twelfth century the Latin renaissance stimulated literary production in French, often by the same authors. It was not until the thirteenth century that the exuberant growth of the vernacular literatures threatened to stifle their elder sister. Even so, are we to forget that Dante wrote in Latin that pamphlet in praise of the 'vulgar (vernacular) eloquence' which we have just quoted?

The diffusion of culture in lay circles, whether noble or bourgeois, does not necessarily favour the national language, as it did in France. In Italy the very ease with which educated knights and merchants used Latin put back the development of a national literature by two or three centuries; it was only in the thirteenth century, after the foreign languages of the troubadours and *trouvéres* had both been tried, that the step was taken of writing in Italian. For a German, Latin is very difficult; nevertheless there were merchants on the Baltic who as late as the fifteenth century used the language of Augustus to keep their account books.

It has been pointed out that the fortunes of literary Latin were mainly linked

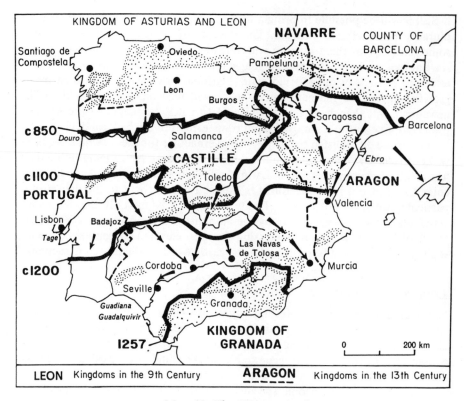

Map 13. The 'Reconquista'

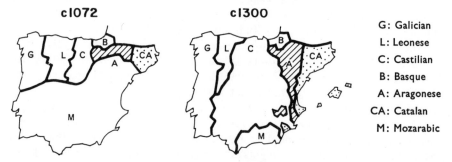

*Map 13a. The expansion of the Iberian language about 1072 and about 1300;
after F. Yndurain*

to those of the Church, the State and the schools. The first of these supports
was denied to the national languages: 'vulgarized' preaching in the vernacular
was suspected of indiscipline or even of heresy. The Latin church did not begin
to relax until the thirteenth century; in the liturgy, Latin preserved still later

its strongholds. The schools — certain schools, at least — proved less intractable. The merchants especially were not so particular: the study of professional techniques, of foreign languages too, were more rewarding than the *Aeneid* learnt by heart. Still, Latin was indispensable for commercial and civil law.

Only the State had much to gain by favouring a national language, but it was not always aware of it. The kings of England, usually so quick to seize upon anything that would strengthen their hold over the kingdom, oppose the already advanced development of English by adding to it not only Latin but also French. Castilian spreads from one end of Spain to the other, to the gallop of knights driving back the Arabs (Map 13), but in the middle of the thirteenth century Alfonso X, the King of Castile, writes his poems in Galician. (All the same he will strive to purify the 'correct Castilian' of his capital, Toledo.) As for Parisian French, it must have been King Arthur and the Paladin Roland who prepared its path, for it embarked on the conquest of France long before Philip Augustus. On the other hand, Italian takes its first literary steps with the support of Frederic II but reaches its climax at the period when the last hopes of monarchical unification are fading. Finally Provençal, promoted to literary fame by poet-princes, is caught up in the eddies of the political disaster of southern France.

Writers are the real kings and builders of language and literature. Crowned kings also have given occasional help, but their contribution to the building of Europe lies principally in other spheres: war, diplomacy, administration. This is where they must be watched at work.

Chapter 4

THE TRANSFORMATIONS OF KINGDOMS

I. SPLENDOUR AND INADEQUACY OF THE GERMANIC EMPIRE

'What fruits are produced by the transformations and annihilations of kingdoms is a problem which must be left to God, from whom nothing useless can proceed. Nevertheless, there is no lack of people to maintain that God wished to humble the Kingdom in order to exalt the Church. In fact, nobody doubts that the Church, exalted and enriched by the strength of the Kingdom and the beneficence of the kings. . . has been able to humiliate the Kingdom to such a point. . . that it is destroyed not only by the spiritual sword but by its own material sword.' Such were the melancholy reflections, towards the middle of the twelfth century, of the author of a chronicle of the 'Two Cities', the city of Men and the city of God inextricably entangled.

The writer, Otto, was a Cistercian monk, the future Bishop of Freising, but he also was the half-brother of Emperor Conrad III, and consequently affected by the sorrows of the Empire. In fact a little later the initial successes in the reign of his nephew Frederick Barbarossa were to inspire him to pages full of hope: the great struggle which had begun a hundred years earlier was not yet ended, and the Empire still had days of glory before it. Nevertheless, Otto of Freising's first diagnosis was well founded. Of all the obstacles which frustrated the emperors in their endeavours to control their states and establish their hegemony over Catholic Europe, the resistance of the popes was the strongest.

On the surface: greatness and peace

However, between the event which contemporaries called 'the handing over of the Roman Empire to the Teutons' (the imperial coronation of Otto I in 962) and the threatening letter from Gregory VII to Henry IV which began the Struggle of the Investitures in 1075, there was an interval of more than a century, to which we must first give our attention. It was the age of localism, and we have already noted its disintegrating effect on all monarchies, including the papacy. The emperors defended themselves against it somewhat better than most other kings, because they gave without stint the little that was demanded of a monarch in the tenth century and the first half of the eleventh: essentially, fair judgments at home and military victories abroad.

The second goal was more easily reached than the first, for the imperial army was indisputably the most powerful in Catholic Europe, and the emperors almost always proved to be competent generals. But the imperial administrative staff was scarcely more adequate than that of the Carolingians; the burden of government rested primarily on the shoulders of the Emperor. He did earn the loyalty and affection of his vassals by enlarging the frontiers of the Empire, repressing over-flagrant violations of human and divine laws, and occasionally weeding out discredited or inefficient popes and prelates and choosing 'better' ones. On the other hand, the fact that the Emperor was not scrupulously obeyed when he was not on the spot surprised nobody and did little harm to his prestige. It could even be maintained that the irregularity of his interventions made them more effective: the vassals most jealous of their privileges were resigned to bowing the head provided that the Emperor did not ask them to do it too often.

In the long run, however, the states which maintained their position were not those with the largest armies, but the ones which created a well balanced and vigilant administration. In this respect the Empire was at a disadvantage. It was almost as extensive as the Carolingian Empire and included peoples and civilizations just as dissimilar (Map 14). It was extremely difficult to make them collaborate harmoniously, and the Emperor had to keep on the move to make his personal influence effective at all points. The problem is graphically described by Otto of Freising: 'The emperor crossed the Alps: his presence restored peace to the Germans, his absence took it from the Italians'.

Italy was the weakest link of the chain. It was internally divided by the most tenacious localism and separated from Germany by her higher level of culture and economy. The Emperor had no more permanent support than that of one of its factions, and this in turn relied upon the descents of the imperial army to defeat the rival faction. All too infrequent descents: it has been calculated that between the coronation of Otto I and the end of the twelfth century the Emperor appeared in Italy on average only one year in five, with a maximum absence of twenty-six years between one descent and the next.

As soon as the German army, weakened by the Italian climate and recalled by domestic problems, crossed the Alps again, insurrections broke out in Italy and spread from region to region. The Emperor's reprisals each time he returned embittered the struggle without ending it. We have seen that Rome, proud even in her poverty and incurably Byzantine in spite of her long rivalry with Constantinople, was the centre of opposition under the three Ottos. But the opposition moved and gained strength as northern Italy developed. On the death of Otto III the lay nobles of Lombardy gave themselves an independent king, Arduino, for several years; but for the hostility of ecclesiastical vassals, he might have won the day. In 1024 the population of Pavia, the administrative capital of Italy, burned down the emperor's palace. A little later the Milanese rose against Conrad II and his ally the Archbishop of the town. Well before the Investiture Struggle, certain Italian towns behaved as independent states, taking no more notice of the Emperor than the great French vassals did of their king.

Thus we should not be misled by the extent of the territory theoretically

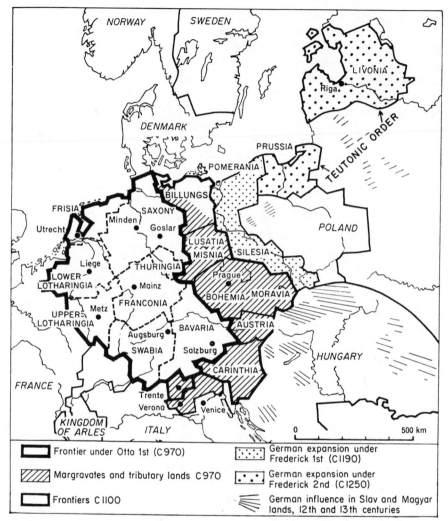

Map 14. The German Empire from the tenth to the thirteenth century

subject to the emperors. Even when partially obedient, Italy was only a pleasure-garden for them, maintained for reasons of prestige at the price of a great dissipation of energy. Burgundy, the former kingdom of Arles, which was bequeathed to the Emperor in 1032 by its last King, was a nest of feudal disorder. Its lord drew no real profit from it and was satisfied if it caused him no trouble. Lotharingia (Lorraine and the surrounding portions of Belgian and Rhineland territory) was an inadequately controlled outpost. It is true that the emperors drew from its agricultural, commercial and industrial wealth, inferior only to those of Italy, and that its enlightened clergy provided the Empire with some of its best administrators. But local interests and international connections brought imperial Lorraine close to Flanders, a French fief which was gradually to join it in a new cultural and economic unit.

The German core and the eastward thrust

Originally the imperial power rested mainly on the support of the four duchies which corresponded to the four principal sub-divisions of the dominant people: Saxons, Franconians, Swabians and Bavarians. In this German reduit, society and institutions developed more slowly than elsewhere. A happy combination of barbarian customs, Carolingian traditions and cautious innovations allowed the monarch to obtain obedience respectively as head of the army, moderator of the Church and direct lord of a very extensive domain. Ducal Germany provided the Ottos with the few thousand knights necessary to ensure their superiority at a period when the massacre of 1,500 knights at Firenzuola (923) had just made a gap in the ranks of the Italian armies which, it was said, could not be filled in half a century. She did not refuse to the Henrys and Conrads the slightly larger contingents made indispensable by the demographic recovery.

Even in the German reduit, however, localism was a growing threat. It would have been impossible for the emperors to break every resistance; more and more, they resorted to the subtler policy of pitting one vassal against another and reconstructing on top the unity which had been destroyed in the lower ranks. So long as a system of checks and balances worked, the weakness of his subordinates would compensate for the monarch's insufficient strength.

There was no preconceived plan but a succession of measures designed to repress each feudal layer as it rose too high. In order to weaken unruly dukes, the emperors increased the number and power of the counts; but the counts in turn became threateningly strong. To hold the counts in check, the emperors took from them the administration of the county's capital city and placed it under the full authority of the bishop; a bishop could not hand on the power to his descendants, and usually his successor was chosen by the Emperor. Then, in order to reduce the power of the great hereditary nobility still further, Conrad II made minor fiefs hereditary, forbade great vassals to deprive minor vassals of their fiefs without the consent of their peers, and submitted contested cases to the imperial courts (1037). Again, Conrad II employed some of his serfs (*ministeriales*) to carry out functions previously reserved for nobles; these serfs would assist him in holding the feudal class in check without hoping to join it.

While it was often difficult to bring together the German forces in the defence of common interests at home and in the Italian expeditions, the struggle against the Slavs and other Eastern peoples provided a more popular rallying point. It yielded greater dividends for a smaller effort. The emperors were the natural leaders of the thrust to the East, this *Drang nach Osten* which missionaries, nobles and peasants had been pursuing ever since the time of the Carolingians, with the methods and the contrasts one so often finds in the history of colonization. The sources bear witness to selfless preaching of a more humanitarian faith, sincere efforts to improve the standard of life of the natives, admirable energy in clearing and cultivating virgin lands. But they also reveal excesses of greed, violence and cruelty which often provoke mass insurrections.

Moreover, the progress of colonization clashed henceforward with the rise of the first Christian Slav states. Their resistance hardened wherever mountains, marshes or other natural barriers broke the onslaught of the feudal cavalry. Eventually the Wendish and Obodrite kingdoms (in present-day East Germany) were crushed and absorbed into the new marches which were the offshoots of the German duchies. Poland and Bohemia, however, successfully defended their political and cultural identity, if not their absolute independence.

Fig. 44. Baptismal font from Canossa (Italy), eleventh century, Canossa Museum.

Imperial Germany at its zenith

Shortly before the Investiture Struggle, Emperor Henry III (1039–56) was undoubtedly the most powerful monarch in the Christian world. The death in 1035 of Canute 'the Great', King of England and Denmark and lord of other lands, had hastened the dissolution of the only Catholic state capable of counterbalancing the Empire. Ten years earlier the death of Basil II 'the Bulgar-slayer' had ended the series of warrior emperors under whom Byzantium, 'this old woman' (to borrow the image of a chronicler) 'resembled a young girl adorned with gold and precious stones'. The only Christian monarch whose stature could in some way be compared to that of Henry III lived at the far end of Europe: Yaroslav, grand prince of Kiev (d. 1054). Poland, Bohemia and Hungary acknowledged Henry's overlordship.

For the first time since Charlemagne and Louis the Pious, the Emperor had given himself a capital of his own. This was a significant testimony of the economic and institutional recovery, which allowed the sovereign to await in an appointed place the payment of his revenues and the return of his armies. Moreover, the capital was Goslar, near the Rammelsberg mines, the importance of which for the mints and foundries of the period has already been stressed. We have seen that Henry III imposed a series of reforming popes upon his other capital, Rome. There was as yet no better support for a monarch so overburdened with work than priests of sterling character.

His heir, Henry IV, was only a child in 1056 and could not prevent an outbreak of feudal disorder; but as soon as he came of age he spurred the Empire on to more rapid progress. In place of the castle at Goslar there rose up a palace surrounded by rural manors from which his serf-knights (*ministeriales*) set forth to give orders to the nobles. The young Emperor claimed all the rights which had fallen into disuse during his minority or even earlier: monopoly of higher justice, patronage of abbeys, forests and domains recently lost or recently conquered, dues which nobody had paid for a long time. Incensed by this despot from the south (Henry was a Franconian), the peasants and nobles of Saxony, the northernmost duchy, rebelled in a body. He subdued them.

This brilliant success, however, did not eliminate the chronic frustrations of personal government: when the Emperor was a minor, fell sick or turned his back, all his work was undone. An alternative was at long last close at hand: building up a larger administration. Though the French kings at that time could not even manage the government of their direct domain, William the Conqueror was beginning the reorganization of his Anglo-Norman state. What was Henry IV planning to do? Would he increase the number and powers of his serf-knights? Was he going for the first time to demand staff from the bourgeois classes of Italy and Lorraine, although these regions were seething with unrest? We shall never know, for the Investiture Struggle broke out in 1075. Suddenly Henry IV found himself abandoned even by the lay and ecclesiastical vassals who had supported his father twenty years earlier.

The great battle is joined

The dramatic ups and downs of the Investiture Struggle cannot be summarized in a few lines. The contest began with a limited but delicate conflict between feudal law and canon law: whose right was it to confer investiture upon clergymen whose spiritual office entailed the rule of a fief? But long before the question was settled with a compromise (the Concordat of Worms in 1122), the struggle had become a rivalry for universal political supremacy. In the process, Catholic Europe was thoroughly shaken: religion and law, upper and lower classes, country and town, everything felt the impact, and it is not unwarranted to describe the Investiture Struggle as the prime impulse which sent off the crusades and started self-government in the towns.

At first the duel seemed unequal. The Empire was powerful, rich, obeyed by laymen and clergy alike; the Papacy was unarmed, relatively poor, and criticized by many prelates who feared papal dictates more than lay interference. Again and again, the cause of reform seemed doomed. Yet by 1122 Rome had brought the ecclesiastical order largely under its control and weakened the hold of the Empire on the feudal order. Only the upsurge of religious feeling seems to explain the resilience of the weaker contestant: no defeat was final because persecutions reinforce faith, none was total because the kingdom of Saint Peter was partly of another world, the world which laymen entered upon their knees.

Yet if we try to single out the precise contribution of religious feeling we are perplexed. Most people saw no further than narrow, concrete issues: they would deplore the fact that in a certain church the alms for the poor were used to feed a lord's dog without concluding that the Church should not recognize *any* lord. At any rate, the feudal bond of the vassal to his suzerain was not less sacred than the obedience of the priest to his ecclesiastical superior. We now perceive that the fairest solution would have been for the clergy to surrender their fiefs, thus removing all grounds for lay investiture; but Pope Paschal II, who suggested it in 1111, met with almost universal disapproval. The clergy needed land to live on and feel secure; the lay rulers needed the clergy to assist in the administration of land.

On the other hand, the spiritual authority of the Pope was a double-edged weapon. It empowered him to excommunicate the sinner but commanded him to forgive the penitent. This was made clear in 1077 at Canossa: by a single act of contrition, dramatic but transitory, Henry IV recovered nearly all he had lost till then in his struggle against Gregory VII (Figs. 44, 45, 46). A Christian king could humble himself before the Lord without losing his prestige: a hundred years later, Henry II of England was to submit to an equally dramatic penance and overcome the impact of Becket's murder (Pl. 18).

It is not sufficient for a cause to be good: it must also be well pleaded. Although there were outstanding advocates on both sides, Gregory VII (1073–85) surpassed them all by his eloquence, activity and energy. Blunt and inflexible on questions of principle, but pliant and tactful where his deepest convictions were not involved, he is in our view the greatest Pope of the Middle Ages, great in his mistakes as much as in his virtues. Beside him we dimly perceive a feminine figure, inadequately illuminated by the sources but perhaps just as remarkable in her culture and talent as a leader: Countess Matilda of Tuscany.

The popes found the most effective strategy in turning against the Empire the emperors' own methods of government, dividing in order to rule. Even as the emperors had directed and continued to direct the clergy to depose 'unworthy' popes and appoint anti-popes, so the popes spurred the vassals to desert 'unworthy' emperors and rally to anti-emperors. Vassals against monarchs, sub-vassals against vassals, lay lords against pro-imperial ecclesiastical lords, townspeople against their government, serfs against their masters: all those who had a grudge and wanted to revolt could merge their cause in that of the Roman Church. The emperors tried to reciprocate, by inviting disobedience in the papal

ranks, but could not harm their
adversaries as deeply. To stem the
flow of desertions, they had to
distribute favours on all sides; to
pursue the fight in Italy, they had to
abandon the only undertaking that
produced lasting benefit, war on the
eastern front. The crisis of leadership
taught German lords and Italian
towns to make war and peace their
own private affair.

*Fig. 45. The Emperor Henry IV and
the Countess Matilda; after a manuscript in the Vatican Library.*

The Empire up for auction

The Concordat of Worms, like all compromises, satisfied neither of the adversaries but gave both a chance to dress their wounds. Unfortunately the Emperor
who had signed it, Henry V, died three years later without direct heirs. The
crown then became the object of an auction, maintained by two factions of the
nobility (the 'Guelfs' and 'Ghibellines') and fed by the papacy. The latter
profited by it to pursue its claims. Germany, it is true, does not seem to have
suffered from it. The standard of living continued to rise, the richest peasants
crept into the nobility and the nobility, free to enjoy their leisure or to spread
beyond the Elbe, thought emperor Lothar II a model sovereign in spite of, or
rather because of, his mediocrity. Lothar was the candidate of the Guelfs; his
successor Conrad III was that of the Ghibellines.

   In 1152 the factions temporarily agreed over the choice of Frederick I
('Barbarossa', as the Italians unadmiringly called him), allied to the Ghibellines
by his father and the Guelfs by his mother. It so happened that this young man
had the making of a great king: he was religious and unscrupulous, energetic
and flexible, ambitious and realistic. But his assets in Germany were only a
remnant of the old imperial estate: his direct domain was smaller than that of
his cousin, Henry the Lion, and his financial revenue was inadequate. Moreover,
having been elected by lords often as powerful as himself, he could scarcely
count on their obedience. Therefore he sought new foundations of power by restoring the rights, long neglected but imprescriptible, of the imperial crown in Italy.

   In order to have his hands free, Frederick demanded only moderate feudal
service from his vassals and allowed Henry the Lion to carry out functions

*Fig. 46. The expulsion of Pope Gregory VII; left, the emperor Henry IV
and the anti-pope Guibert; after a miniature on a manuscript of Otto of
Freising, preserved at Jena (detail).*

corresponding roughly to those of a lieutenant-general in the old German
duchies and the marches of the East. Under this leader, whose direct domains
covered a large area of central Germany, expansion into Slav territory made
great strides. Frederick himself, with the help of such vassals as were more
tempted by a southern than by an eastern adventure, plunged into a new fight
with the powers which had established themselves in Italy and did not want a
foreign ruler at any price.

The first step led to others: in three generations the emperors were to change
from Germans to Italians and transfer their capital from Goslar to Palermo,
while Germany became a confederation of almost independent fiefs and towns.

II.   STRENGTH AND WEAKNESS OF THE ITALIAN PAPACY

Could the popes have replaced the emperors in the double role of monarchs
building a feudal and national state and of moderators of the international
community of Catholic states?

The first reply that comes to mind is that the popes were better equipped than
the emperors to play an international role. The jurisdiction of the Church did
not stop at any political frontier and proceeded from the only Lord before
whom every earthly lord was not ashamed to bow down. On the other hand, the
popes did not seem well suited for a feudal and national role. Dynastic continuity, military prestige, ethnical solidarity: none of these props of patriotic
and national loyalty could be used by them. Yet the history of the popes in the
eleventh and twelfth centuries shows, on the one hand, more brilliant than
lasting victories in the international sphere, and on the other hand, modest but
consistent progress in the construction of a papal state in Italy. As always,
reality is too hazy to be contained in a summary definition. For a closer analysis,
we shall have to go back and examine briefly the chief trump cards of the papacy.

The trump cards of the Roman Church

Supremacy over the ecclesiastical order was the popes' master-card. 'Only the Pope deserves to be called universal; his legate in a council is superior to the bishops; no synod qualifies as general without his order; he alone gives law to the Church. . .; he may depose and absolve bishops; he may transfer them. . .; he can be judged by no one. . .; no one may amend his pronouncements.' These statements from the *Dictatus Papae* of Gregory VII could obviously not be enforced without wavering or without exceptions. On the one hand there had to be compromise with the autonomism of national and local churches. On the other hand, it was necessary to come to terms with lay powers. By the concordats of the twelfth century, kings and emperors recognized what no pope could have surrendered: the right to confer formal religious investiture on high prelates. The Pope for his part granted to the sovereigns what no sovereign would have been prepared to surrender to him: a right of intervention, varying according to country and circumstances, in the nominations of high prelates. As far as the choice of lower clergy was concerned, papal influence was generally insignificant.

Fig. 47. Crown, eleventh and twelfth centuries, said to belong to St Stephen; treasure of the Royal Palace, Budapest.

If the papacy had been able to monopolize the services of the clergy for its political ends it would probably have dominated Europe. Actually it had under its direct orders only the small number of clergymen employed at the Roman curia and in the papal state. Thanks to them the papal administration became one of the most efficient in the Western world. The other clergy, however, even if they submitted to the spiritual discipline of Rome, kept their initiative in temporal affairs: Suger and Lanfranc of Pavia (or of Bec) were the servants respectively of the Kings of France and England, not of the Pope.

Nevertheless, the very close links between religion and secular affairs on the one hand, and the special statute of the clergy on the other, offered the Pope many opportunities of reaffirming his influence and of obtaining some income in certain sectors of public and private life. Ecclesiastical courts, immunity of the clergy, jurisdiction over marriages and divorce provided so much common ground where the Pope and the ecclesiastical order were often united against the civil powers. This interference and other privileges of the clergy impeded the kings seriously in limited spheres, but did not attack their political independence.

> The theory of the subordination of the temporal sword to the spiritual sword, that is to say, of papal supremacy over all secular monarchies, played an important part in the realm of ideas but was of little practical effect. It provided a justification for the Pope's allies against the Emperor, but it is doubtful whether it won support or resources which the Pope would not have obtained without it. Neither did the imperial cause win many champions through the opposite theory, which subordinated the spiritual sword to the temporal. The discussion was so abstract that it was possible to argue passionately about it in Paris and London without a thought of having to yield one inch of the sovereignty of the kings of France or England.

> Nevertheless, the right to legitimize and consecrate sovereigns, claimed since Pippin the Short, was used more than once by the papacy to establish closer political ties. About 1000 Sylvester II had sent a crown to the Hungarian leader, the future Saint Stephen, who had just had his people baptised (Fig. 47). Since then, Hungary had shown an unfailing devotion to the Holy See, but did not feel by that token obliged to rush to the help of the Pope against his enemies. Much the same can be said about Poland, whose king Mieszko I had accepted a vague papal overlordship. Papal suzerainty, however, became more meaningful when applied to territories closer to Rome. In 1059, the very year of Nicholas II's reforming decrees, Robert Guiscard, captain of the Norman bands which had just created a new state in southern Italy at the expense of the former occupants (Byzantine governors and Lombard princes), received from the Pope the investiture of his conquests. Thus the papacy established a claim in that part of Italy which the Western emperors had never succeeded in subduing. The claim remained valid for eight centuries, almost to the end of the Kingdom of the Two Sicilies; it had only nominal effect when the king was strong but was an excuse for papal intervention when he was weak or hostile.

The popes direct the holy war

Up to the eleventh century the popes had played no direct part in the defence and propagation of the faith by armed forces; this was the task of lay powers, and only the immediate threat of Arab raids into Rome had moved John VIII and John X to take a hand in local military action. The investiture given to Robert Guiscard in 1059 opened a new alley. It is true that his conquests in continental southern Italy represented gains for the faith only to the extent that they favoured the Latin rite in territory but lately Byzantine. But when Roger, brother of Robert Guiscard, wrested Sicily from the Moslems, the alliance between throne and altar against the Infidels became more evident. It also grew in Spain: hard pressed by a Moslem attack, the King of Aragon in 1086 gave his states in fief 'to God and Saint Peter' and in return won the support of the Holy See in recruiting reinforcements in France and Italy. Other Iberian kings were to follow his example.

There was much less of an alliance when sailors of Pisa, Genoa and Amalfi stormed Mahdiyah, the capital of an African state (1088). The winners massacred the 'priests of Mahomet', sacked the city and withdrew only after obtaining commercial privileges. Pope Victor III, deeply involved in the Investiture Struggle, restricted his co-operation to blessing the expedition. It was no more than a piratical raid, but it portended greater things. The idea of the Crusade was in the air. Gregory VII had already announced plans for an operation against the Seljuk Turks, who had broken through the Asian frontier of Christianity so long defended by the Byzantine Empire. Finally, in 1095 Urban II judged the moment timely for realizing this plan on a more ambitious scale, and gave the signal for the First Crusade. From then on, and for two centuries, the papacy was at the head of an international military enterprise, the only one in which the whole of medieval Europe, Catholic and Byzantine, participated (Pl. 19). Even if only by proxy, the Pope thus took a distinguished place among the military powers.

No doubt the direct conduct of the war was not within his province; the papal legates could scarcely give orders to lay chieftains, some of whom were princes, kings or emperors. The crusades proper, however, were brief conflagrations; during the long intervals which separated them it was the task of the Holy See to maintain contacts, prepare help and organize future campaigns. Rome distributed indulgences, centralized money contributions and wielded a vague authority over the Christian states of the Holy Land, to which was added, in 1204, the Latin Empire of Constantinople. Meanwhile, the political influence of the popes spread. Sometimes out of self-interest, sometimes out of devotion, other European governments sought investiture or at least the moral patronage of the Holy See. Little by little Rome built up a constellation of states which sent her money (or as the case might be, demanded subsidies), submitted certain problems for her decision and behaved towards her somewhat as vassals towards an undemanding lord.

The papacy, an Italian power

Nevertheless, in the feudal age the power of a lord depended less upon the number of his vassals than upon the extent of his direct domain. The domain of the emperors was centred upon the German duchies; that of the popes could only be centred on Rome and Italy.

In fact the forged 'Donation of Constantine' assigned to the popes most of
the peninsula and the islands; the less generous but more authentic dona-
tions of Pippin and Charlemagne gave them merely a part of central Italy.
Even thus reduced, this territory had proved still too vast for the grip of
the popes. In the tenth century they had had to win the good graces of the
emperors and of the petty vassals of Latium in order to maintain just a
precarious hold over Rome. In the mid eleventh century three popes,
strangers to Italy and ill-disposed towards the Romans, seemed to prepare an age when the Bishop of Rome would break off all relations with
his diocese and preserve only a foothold in the Vatican and its surroundings. The last of these popes, Leo IX, threatened in Rome by the Normans, spent a long time traveling in France and Germany.

Then, in 1059, the wind changed. By the law which reserved to the
Roman cardinals the right to elect popes, the papacy once again cast its
lot with that of the local clergy. By the investiture of Robert Guiscard it
safeguarded the southern limits of its domain. A little later, the support
it received from the Lombard towns and from Countess Matilda of Tuscany tightened its bonds with the north and centre of Italy, which became
henceforward the nursery of most of the popes and of the majority of
their political and financial assistants.

The Concordat of Worms in 1122 underlined the Italian orientation of the
papacy. From the point of view of investiture, it divided the imperial territory
into three zones: Germany, where the choice of bishops was practically surrendered to the Emperor; Italy and Burgundy, where it was left to the chapter and
the Pope; the direct papal domain, where all investitures, whether ecclesiastical
or lay, were conferred by the Pope. This domain was consolidated and extended: Rome and the 'Patrimony of Saint Peter' in Latium were recovered
first, other territories in the nearby regions were added, and Countess Matilda
bequeathed to the popes her vast possessions on both sides of the Apennines.
It is true that the emperors contested this legacy, but the other domains gave
the popes a solid base in central Italy. It would have been unthinkable for them
to make a reality of the 'Donation of Constantine' by outright conquest; but
could not Rome become the centre of a network of alliances bringing the
whole of Italy within the sphere of influence of the papacy?

Towards the middle of the twelfth century such an undertaking appeared
difficult but not impossible. In the south, Roger II had welded all the Norman
possessions into a single kingdom and was looking for further expansion. It
would have been foolhardy to insist on his status as a vassal. But his enemies —
German emperors, Byzantine emperors, Moslem powers in Africa — were also
the enemies of the papacy, for which the kingdom of Sicily became by that very
fact a natural ally.

In the north, the so-called kingdom of Italy had practically disintegrated: in
its place there was a mosaic of city-states, the communes. As a matter of fact
the simoniac bishop-counts whom the emperors had entrusted with the government of most cities had been driven out by the people, at the instigation of the

reforming popes; their successors, and other bishops who saw the coming tide, surrendered effective power to the laity. Then the townspeople had turned against the great vassals and imperial representatives who held the countryside and had driven them back to a few rural castles or the high valleys of the Alps and Apennines. But the sweeping triumph of the communes had brought no peace. In every city, families, factions, social classes and pressure groups opposed one another relentlessly. Each commune, in turn, tried to win space at the expense of its neighbours. Milan in particular had become the terror of the smaller Lombard cities: she had destroyed Lodi and was threatening Como and Cremona. This state of affairs gave the clergy and the Pope himself numerous opportunities of offering their good offices as peacemakers and umpires.

A mission of this kind would require infinite patience and tact, but the Pope had good cards and the stakes were high. By the mid twelfth century the commercial and industrial development of northern Italy, its small but fertile territory and the very abundance of its man power made it the richest prize in Catholic Europe.

Test and triumph of the fighting townspeople

Unfortunately for the popes, Frederick Barbarossa upset the game when it had scarcely begun. A member of the feudal society by his education and preference, he was the first European sovereign to realize fully the newly acquired importance of the cities and to think of exploiting it (Fig. 48). In Germany the financial support he obtained from the cities of the Rhine partially compensated for the concessions he had to make to the great vassals in order to involve them in his Italian campaigns. In Italy, on the other hand, he rallied beneath his banner the remains of the feudal class, who wanted their revenge on the townspeople, so as to force the cities to render to the Empire the tributes and obedience which they had not been paying for a century. But he also posed as the champion of the smaller Lombard towns against Milan and invited the scholars of Bologna to present arguments from Roman law in support of his imperial authority. To win over the Pope, he burned Arnaldo of Brescia, a heretic who had led a communal revolt in Rome. Some of the towns came to terms; Milan, twice

Fig. 48. Frederick I (Barbarossa); bas-relief from a portal of Freising Cathedral, Germany.

compelled to capitulate (1158, 1162) — the second time after a memorable siege — was joyfully destroyed by the inhabitants of enemy communes.

Then Frederick showed his hand: like Henry IV before Canossa, but with the thoroughness made possible by a richer, more cultivated and more complex society, he tried to impose his personal rule over the entire country. All the Italian communes, including Frederick's allies, had to receive and obey his representatives. These agents, surrounded by German knights, extracted from the citizens tributes which at that time looked enormous. Frederick also took over the domains which Matilda had bequeathed to the Pope. All resistance was mercilessly crushed. The Empire had never seemed so powerful.

Yet Frederick's triumph was deceptive because it was not accompanied by moderation. Most of the Lombard cities, shocked by the excesses of the con-querors, formed a coalition against the Emperor, rebuilt Milan and founded a new fortified city to bar Frederick's way. They named it Alessandria, in homage to the new Pope, Alexander III, who had become their ally. Venice, long independent, and the Normans of Sicily also joined the league. Frederick was powerless against so many enemies and against the plague which was decimating his troops. He returned to Germany and devoted six years to the unending task of patching up the imperial domain, restoring harmony and discipline among his vassals, and reaffirming the German protectorate over the Slavs along the eastern frontier. When he felt ready to descend upon Italy again, it was too late. Alessandria victoriously withstood a long siege. Finally in 1176 the unheard-of, incredible event took place: the forces of the Lombard League met Frederick's imperial host at Legnano and inflicted upon him a terrible defeat (Pl. 18). For the first time since the decline and fall of ancient Rome, a non-professional army drawing most of its strength from massed foot soldiers had overcome the best professional cavalry that could be mustered.

Legnano was not only the test of strength of the free communes but, in a way, also the first page of Italian history, for the victors loudly pronounced the words 'liberty and honour of Italy'. Though the coalition developed cracks immediate-ly after the battle, Frederick saw the writing on the wall. In 1183, by the Peace of Constance, the independence of the Lombard cities was recognized, with a few reservations which never had any practical effect.

Moreover, Legnano indirectly caused the destruction of the only conglom-erate of fiefs large enough to form the nucleus of a new German state capable of taking the place of the Germanic Empire. Henry the Lion having refused to help his cousin in the ill-fated expedition against the Lombard League, Frede-rick punished him by confiscating most of his possessions. This brought no direct gain to the Emperor, for German customs forced him to redistribute the spoils to the other vassals who had helped him against the rebel. Never-theless, Frederick again was able to get together enough nobles and serf-knights to make other Mediterranean forays in central Italy, in the Kingdom of Arles and lastly in the Levant, where he was to die at the outset of a crusade (1190).

Always victorious in battle (except at Legnano), ever called elsewhere, the Emperor with the red beard had won much prestige but little real power. All in all, the most lasting success of this tireless fighter was a diplomatic victory, the marriage of his son (the future Henry VI) to the heiress of the Norman kingdom of Sicily. But this marriage was to make the Empire both weaker and more threatening: weaker because it increased the problems of governing an over-extended, motley, spineless body; more threatening because it incorporated what had been the best ally of the Pope and of the Lombards and placed them between the German hammer and the Sicilian anvil.

After Legnano: the conflict reaches deadlock

Henry VI inherited from his father a crushing commitment. The extraordinary fact is that he came near to keeping it. By fighting without pause and without mercy, he moved his German vassals to help him to conquer Sicily, suppressed a mass rising of the Sicilians, forced the Pope to recognize the *fait accompli*, reconstructed an imperial party in Lombardy and obliged the supporters of Henry the Lion, who had raised their heads, to submit. As if such dispersion of energies were not enough, he tried to be a universal Emperor in the full meaning of the term. The King of England who had been arrested, in defiance of the law and of public opinion, on his return from a crusade, had to render homage to the Emperor and pay an enormous ransom. The Byzantine Emperor was summoned to yield his European domains or face a war. France, Spain and Africa were next on the list of Henry VI's future claims.

This grand plan of expansion, more ambitious that those of Charlemagne and Otto III, reflected the progress of Europe: in the twelfth century a king had resources unknown in the eighth and tenth centuries and could reach out further. What strengthened Henry VI, however, also favoured his opponents, although they were initially stunned. At 32, in 1197, Henry was more powerful than his father, but also more feared and hated. Death carried him away before his enemies had time to recover and combine to attack him.

Then a great Pope, Innocent III, in his turn used the accumulated resources of the Church to pursue the most ambitious policy the Church had ever conceived: direct rule over central Italy, protectorate in Sicily, control of the Empire, effective suzerainty over other Christian states all the way from Bulgaria to England. Like Henry VI, Innocent III seemed close to his goal; like him, he died before seeing the inevitable collapse of his castle of cards.

Although the struggle continued after his death, the essential facts had been settled since Legnano. While the two protagonists held each other in check, a third force, born of the old localism, had emerged. In the larger part of Germany this force was in the hands of feudal princes and aimed at a chain of regional states. In the Italian communes it had assumed a new dignity and pointed to a new direction. Many people called it liberty.

Both Italy and Germany thus lost all chances of forming national states.

Many historians have compared their restless life with the triumphs of France and England during the first centuries of the modern era, and succumbed to the temptation of deploring on the one hand the megalomania of popes and emperors, and on the other the shortsightedness of the Italian cities and the German nobles. But this is an unhistorical interpretation. The ideals of the Middle Ages were not ours: both Italians and Germans then were aiming less at unity than at peace, and a national monarchy is not necessarily a guarantee of peace. Moreover, mediaeval universalism and autonomies, driven to the very limit in Italy and Germany, have bequeathed to European civilization precious antidotes for the narrowness and tyranny of integral nationalism.

III.   SPONTANEOUS REGENERATION OF FRANCE

If the Empire provides an example of a state which was originally powerful and grew weaker in the course of the centuries, France illustrates the opposite case (Map. 15). In the tenth century the material and spiritual revival of society had benefited only local centres of energy. Castles sprouted everywhere, as brushwood in a garden without a gardener. Good fortune and personal talents enabled certain vassals to carve themselves larger counties and duchies than others. As for the Capetian monarchy, it owed its survival to its original mediocrity: without overshadowing anybody, it formed the indispensable summit of what was later called the feudal pyramid.

Indeed it was almost by chance that France was not swallowed up in the Empire of Otto I. The Neustrian nobility, like the Lombard nobility, was fickle enough to desert its kings; nor could it have collected an army as powerful as Otto's. But the latter found it expedient merely to favour the dynasty of the dukes of France who were illegitimate and consequently not dangerous, in preference to the kings of the Carolingian line who could have become his rivals. Unlike Pavia, Paris did not bar the road to Rome and the imperial crown; so it was not urgent for Otto to establish himself there as master. The problems of the Empire later proved sufficiently absorbing to prevent Otto's successors from making a detour to the west, and France lived because she had been permitted to be born.

The south, almost another nation

It also was almost by chance that the dukes of France, now kings of France, maintained their nominal overlordship over Aquitaine. This province had resisted the Carolingians so strongly that even Charlemagne had deemed it prudent to make it into an autonomous kingdom for one of his sons, and his successors had followed his example. In the tenth century it could have been expected that the autonomy would become complete independence but no such thing happened. Perhaps it seemed useless to quarrel over titles with no practical value; thus the counts of Barcelona, who ruled the former march of Spain snatched from the Arabs by Charlemagne, broke all the bonds which attached them to the French crown but did not care for a royal title. Likewise, the members of the new dynasty which established itself in Aquitaine resumed the pre-Carolingian title of dukes and did not dispute the theoretical pre-eminence of the Parisian kings, which barely inconvenienced them.

Nevertheless, Aquitaine remained as far removed from Neustrian France by climate, culture and way of life as she was close to Provence, an imperial territory attached to Germany by even looser bonds. In its turn Provence felt the double attraction of Liguria and Catalonia. These two regions were separated from Provence by mountains but linked by the sea, by similar dialects and by legal customs closely related to Provence's so-called 'written law'.

Shortly after the year 1000, when King Robert 'the Pious' brought to Paris a Provencal wife who surrounded herself with followers from Aquitaine and Auvergne, it was as if foreigners had invaded the capital. 'Men of utmost frivolity of mind, perverted in morals and dress, disorderly in arms and the harness of horses, the top of their skull bare, their beards shaved off like actors, unsuitable shoes and leggings, inconsistent in regard to oaths of fidelity and peace': this is how Raoul Glaber, a chronicler who detected the Devil in anything unfamiliar, describes the new arrivals. Actually, in his times, the heavily Romance south was not an anomaly in the French nation. It was another nation.

One thinks of the fine kingdom that Provence and Aquitaine might have formed if there had been a conqueror to unify them as the Normans unified the more scattered fragments of the Italian south. The opportunity seemed to arise more than once in the course of the twelfth century, but under a slightly different form: that of a Pyrenean kingdom excluding western Aquitaine and including, in addition to Provence and the county of Toulouse (eastern Aquitaine), Catalonia and Aragon. It all came to nothing. The military and literary prowess of the dukes of Aquitaine or Poitiers and of the counts of Toulouse, their greatest vassals, increased their prestige but scarcely enlarged their possessions. The last duchess of independent Aquitaine, Alienor (whom we often misname Eleanor), remains one of the most discussed and most attractive figures in history. Her true glory shines where nobody can attack her, in the realm of poetry.

The French south split into fiefs of different sizes and autonomous towns which for a long time gravitated alternatively towards Spain, Italy and England before falling once again into the orbit of royal France. Many of its knights, jurists, merchants and artists played important roles abroad. Some of them helped the kings of Castile, Navarre, Aragon, Sicily and Jerusalem to consolidate their states. But they were less zealous when it was a question of collaborating with their own lords. At the most they supported the associations for the Peace of God and the Truce of God which endeavoured to restrict the consequences of the disorder which reigned in their sun-drenched land. The sombre

Cathar religion was the only movement of more than local significance that won adherents ready to sacrifice everything for it. Unfortunately it was not a constructive movement, since it attacked the existing society, property, hierarchy and institutions but offered no system of government that could replace them in this world.

The great fiefs of the north, virtually independent states

To the north of the Loire, on the other hand, duchies and counties embracing whole regions were formed early. Their extent, although very variable, was in some cases as large as that of the German duchies, but often the lack of ethnic unity and well-defined geographic boundaries revealed a recent and artificial construction. Brittany alone had a language and history of its own which brought it closer to the Britain beyond the channel, while estranging it from France. It became French but very slowly, under the influence of its expansion into the French-speaking territories of Rennes and Nantes. Flanders, although geographically well defined, was linguistically split into Germanic and Romance territories. Champagne was an irregularly shaped shred of Neustria. Normandy was another fragment, which the Parisian king had tendered to Scandinavian raiders as a ransom for the rest of his states. Anjou, Maine, the county of Blois, in spite of their compact appearance, were only conglomerations of towns and castles subdued by violence or constructed for violence. The duchy of Burgundy was a remnant of the kingdom of the same name; the remainder had fallen into the orbit of the Empire, like the French-speaking provinces of Lorraine.

For two centuries at least — until the middle of the twelfth century or even later — each of these feudal states, and the smaller fiefs which bordered on them or formed enclaves, grappled with their own administrative problems and scarcely paid attention to the king of France. The two states which managed their affairs in the best way were Normandy and Anjou, both destined to have a prolonged political association with England. Flanders, though smaller, also advanced with vigorous strides.

> The counts of Anjou, who were remarkable warriors descended from a mere knight, forged their state piece by piece with the persistence which gained for one of them the surname 'Martel' (hammer). More devoted to God than to his commandments, they were the terror of their subjects before earning their gratitude for the order they established in the county.
>
> The dukes of Normandy had begun no better, but they became refined a little more rapidly. They soon lost touch with their Scandinavian home-land but did not lose their fighting mettle. They secured the assistance of a competent and in some cases very cultured clergy. They set up in every canton viscounts and other lay subordinates who firmly administered justice in the duke's name. Vassals had to pay their dues punctually; merchants were submitted to tolls; a peasants' rebellion in 997 was merci-lessly suppressed. Yet this revolt does not prove that they were more

maltreated here than anywhere else; indeed it seems to indicate that their condition had been improving. There are seldom rebellions where there are no hopes.

The counts of Flanders, aided by 'chatelains' (district governors based on a castle), ruled their fief almost as efficiently as the dukes of Normandy. They built dikes to keep the tide off low coastal regions. They created new urban centres. Soon the growth of the towns, which here showed a particular vigour, brought them great fiscal revenue. It also caused them serious problems; townspeople are less submissive than peasants.

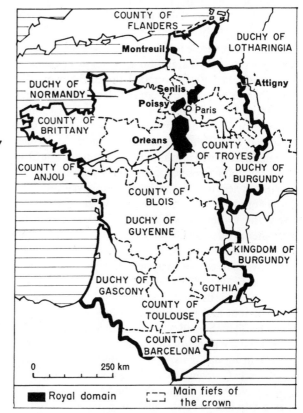

Map 15. France in 987

The other major vassals were not as successful. The dukes of Burgundy, like those of Aquitaine, never managed to control all their sub-vassals. Similarly, the achievements of the counts of Blois and Champagne were not on a level with their inordinate ambitions. It would be tedious to survey all the other fiefs.

Altogether, good government was not unknown, but it was only a tedious necessity for large numbers of the French feudal class. Their ideals, as reflected in the mediaeval epic poems, found better outlets in adventures, crusades, and war conceived as a work of art and an end in itself.

What the French kings could do

In their direct domain kings faced the same problems as their great vassals. The royal domain was neither very large nor particularly rich. But it was called *Francia,* was in the centre of Neustria and bestrode France's largest rivers, the Seine and the Loire, in the middle of their course. The land was fertile and offered to merchants good road and river communications. It is perhaps no accident that the first information on certain technical innovations (triennial rotation of crops, modern methods of harnessing) comes to us from the Parisian region. The fair of Saint Denis was the oldest and for a long time the most important in France.

Inside his restricted domain the King had a hard time keeping in check his petty vassals, but in relation to foreign enemies he was as protected as in a cocoon. Great fiefs surrounded the domain on all sides and interposed themselves between it and the external frontiers. This guarded the monarch against the temptation to launch out in rash enterprises (like certain of his vassals) or to waste efforts on distant conquests (like his German colleagues). Nothing prevented him from concentrating upon the immediate task of tidying up the domain, a task which was not accomplished until Louis VI (1108–37) knocked down the petty vassals, almost one by one.

Without leaving his backyard the sovereign could easily have extended his moral influence over the whole kingdom. Paris, the old Merovingian capital where the Capetians settled down long before the emperors tried to have a permanent residence at Goslar, was an excellent starting point. It is true that the King was not strong enough to enforce his orders at a distance, but he could offer advice, intervene in an undecided contest and play the part of champion of impartial justice. Heir to the almost priestly dignity of Charlemagne, endowed with a mysterious fluid that enabled him to cure certain illnesses by his touch, he had latent and inalienable powers somewhat resembling those of the Pope. Many clergymen in all parts of France acknowledged him as their only temporal head. Like the popes of the same period, the King was asked to confer privileges on certain monasteries, which called him their defender though they knew he could scarcely defend them. Had he been at all willing to take the initiative, he would have found the whole Church and a good many vassals ready to collaborate with him in re-establishing peace and order. In a kingdom swarming with great and small tyrants, the oppressed were not all weak. They were the elements of a large army — in search of a leader.

These advantages worked for the early Capetians almost without their knowledge, certainly without their initiative. It is impossible to discern in one or other of their actions, arbitrarily selected from an inconsistent policy, a plan for methodical reconstruction, patriotic aims, or a real awareness of the royal mission. In fact, until the accession of Philip Augustus, the kings attacked indiscriminately neighbouring barons, great vassals, or foreign sovereigns. They did not wait till they had reorganized their domain before picking a quarrel with the powerful emperor Henry III on the old question of Lorraine, with Henry I of England (upheld by the Emperor Henry V) on the question of Flanders, or with Henry Plantagenet for the French fiefs within his reach. If Louis VI, with his jerky but unrelenting activity, made a better showing, it was largely because Suger was at his side.

Although the early Capetians were generally very pious they were only faintly interested in the great problems and aspirations of the Church: associations for the Peace of God, Cluniac and Gregorian reform, crusades. Their piety did not prevent them from quarreling frequently with the Church over their stormy married life. Perhaps the only unruffled marriage was that of Henry I with a daughter of Grand Prince Yaroslav of Kiev (1051), but this marriage was an act of megalomania on the part of a King with such a precarious throne. Nevertheless, we have to remark that the wives of the Capetians gave their husbands children who came of age before being called upon to rule. This accidental fact spared French royalty the troubles of succession which were so harmful to other dynasties both feudal and royal. It also allowed the French kings to profit by the successional troubles of the others.

Development of the French nation

Thus it was not the dynasty which brought about the regeneration of France; rather France regenerated itself. During the two centuries which followed the reign of Hugh Capet there had been great progress in every direction. The 'sweet France' of the *Song of Roland*, the nation of the great cathedrals and the famous schools could not be for ever satisfied with political fragmentation. The most populated and best cultivated part of Europe, the home of so many skilled craftsmen and traders could not indefinitely accept economic localism. Who could polarize this quest for wider horizons better than the King?

By the end of the eleventh century the texture of French society had already tightened up enough to support efficient government on a broad scale. But the King was not ready; hence the great vassals were the first gainers. The duke of Normandy had a stronger army, the count of Flanders a larger income, the count of Champagne attracted more poets; and if the King witnessed the rise of the first university in his own capital, the merit was Abelard's, not his. The consolidation of the major fiefs was beneficial for their inhabitants, but hemmed the King more tightly in his domain; he could not hope to divide and conquer the feudal class, as the emperors did.

Yet another loophole was provided by the growth of towns. The French cities were weaker than the Lombard cities and had not the Pope on their side. Those which were governed by a bishop usually found him as unyielding as the Italian bishops, by choice or necessity, were pliant. Lay rulers were often more amenable to concessions, either through foresight or through carelessness; but the increasing demands of the urban class were bound sooner or later to provoke a conflict. The King could be their best ally and, by supporting the weaker contestant (the towns), he had a chance to rise above the stronger one (the vassal). To do so, however, would have meant favouring gangs of revolutionary commoners against the established feudal and ecclesiastical orders. This required more elasticity than the early Capetians had shown.

> As late as the thirteenth century Jacques de Vitry, a learned prelate who had seen the free Italian communes at work, inveighed against the 'violent and pestilential' communes of France. In this conservative surrounding it is easy to understand why, in the early twelfth century, Louis VI of France and his neighbour and rival, Henry I of Normandy and England, did not support the bids for self-government of their towns except in a few isolated cases. Even when Louis VI endeavoured to mobilize 'all France' against the 'Teutonic' emperor who was threatening Rheims, his ecclesiastical capital, he addressed himself chiefly to the nobility and did not think of the towns. Somewhat later, Louis VII of France and Henry II of Anjou, Normandy and England were mildly interested in the growing French communes but still uncertain whether to throw in their lot with the townspeople. At that time, Frederick Barbarossa was waging and losing his decisive battle against the Lombard League; it was good chance for the French kings that their towns were not yet strong enough to fight on their own and throw off both the feudal and the royal control.

Philip Augustus

Philip Augustus (1180–1223) seized all the opportunities which his predecessors had failed to exploit. His surname, 'Augustus' not because he resembled the Roman emperor but because he 'augmented' his possessions, indicates that his contemporaries admired above all his territorial acquisitions. To be sure, he wisely avoided the risky adventure he might have run by intervening in the Albigensian crisis, in that distant, rebellious south where his father had tried in vain to establish a foothold. But he surrounded his ancestral lands with a chain of rich, well administered provinces which he acquired by conquest or marriage: Normandy, Anjou, Maine, Touraine, Artois. He thus fulfilled the first condition for all future expansion: the domain directly governed by the King was henceforward more extensive than that of any one of his vassals.

In our eyes, probably the greatest achievement of Philip Augustus is that he systematically established with the towns the understanding which his predecessors had scarcely begun, and which his successors were to maintain loyally if not enthusiastically. Had he sensed the economic importance of the bourgeois revolution? Had he envisaged the young communes merely as 'collective vassals' whose military support could be valuable? Be that as it may, he consistently granted new charters or confirmed old ones for all towns that would offer him their money and their militia in return. It was the eleventh hour: the Count of Flanders by favouring the towns of his domain had won their support against the claims of the King. But other cities made very significant monetary contributions to the royal cause; and though they could not have won a battle by their single-handed efforts, they helped the King to tip the scale. As early as 1188, the defence of Mantes by her militia saved Paris. No French army was a match for Richard Coeur-de-Lion, but against John Lackland, a weaker enemy, the towns had a better chance. Finally, in 1214, the transport and the contingents supplied by the towns were instrumental in winning at Bouvines, against the combined forces of the King of England, the Emperor and the Count of Flanders, the first great victory of the French monarchy.

Nevertheless Philip Augustus was not consistently the champion of autonomy but, on the contrary, the first of a long line of centralizing monarchs. During his reign both the central and the local administration of the kingdom came out of the paternalistic, ecclesiastical rule which Suger had maintained under Louis VI and Louis VII. In Paris the formless royal council or king's court (*curia regis*), which was substantially a weakened continuation of the Merovingian and Carolingian assemblies of lay and ecclesiastical notables, became more competent and more specialized. Within its main body a number of technical councils (the future ministries) began slowly to take shape. In the provinces bailiffs, appointed and paid by the King and liable to recall at his will, helped him to exploit the enlarged domain and to give a taste of royal authority over the whole of the kingdom. In all these respects, however, Philip Augustus was an innovator only by comparison with his Capetian predecessors. Before him the two French dynasties reigning in succession in England had laid the foundations on which the earliest of all the national states of Europe was to be built.

IV. ENGLAND, OLDEST OF THE NATIONAL MONARCHIES

Only one of the many states founded by the barbarians on the ruins of the Roman Empire was still in existence in the tenth century: the kingdom of Wessex, soon renamed kingdom 'of all Britain'. As a matter of fact, Alfred's son and grandson, Edward the Elder and Aethelstan, subdued the Danes and imposed their paramount authority over the Welsh and Scottish 'sub-kings' (*subreguli*). It is true that Aethelstan's power outside England proper remained questionable, even after his signal victory over Constantine of Scotland and the latter's Welsh and Scandinavian allies at Brunanburh (937); but England was firmly in his hands.

The kingdom was archaic in more than one way. At the outset the Anglo-Saxons, unlike other Germans, had driven off the Romanized natives and largely rejected Roman culture; they had mellowed at a later time, but still showed their fidelity to their Germanic origins by using their own language in written literature and laws. A fresh barbaric strain was added by the Danes who remained in England under Anglo-Saxon rule. And since the Anglo-Saxons lived on an island, the frontiers of the known world, their only neighbours were peoples more primitive than themselves: anarchic pastoral Celts in Wales, Scotland and Ireland, Scandinavian pagans still holding Dublin, the Isle of Man and the

Orkneys. This explains the persistence or reappearance of certain traits closer to the Homeric world and the Germany of Tacitus than to the pattern of Catholic Europe in the tenth century.

Anglo-Saxons and Danes

The structure of the enlarged kingdom was not unlike that of the early German and Scandinavian states. Like the Viking chiefs, Aethelstan was celebrated as a 'bestower of bracelets' to the brave men who helped him at Brunanburh: the bracelets, some of which have come down to us, had notches which permitted the owner to cut them into standard sizes whenever he wanted to convert the jewel into ready cash. An assembly of notables (*Witan*) without precisely defined functions helped the King in the government and the framing of laws. Local assemblies composed of all free men (who were still the majority of the population) saw to the observance of those laws in the administrative and tribal divisions of the kingdom. In each district or shire, a shire-reeve or sheriff appointed by the King collected the royal revenues and presided over the people's courts of justice. Reeves of a lower rank did the same in smaller districts and in the fortified towns, most of which were no more than large villages. Kings and noblemen alike maintained bands of warriors and possessed large estates. The power of the King depended not on feudal obligations but on his personal prestige and on the size of his armed following and landed property, all of which had grown in the Danish wars.

Nevertheless, the influence of the Roman Church, contacts with the continent, and perhaps some memories of ancient Roman institutions had left their trace. Aethelstan, like Otto I and Hugh Capet, his brothers-in-law, was the secular head of the clergy and enjoyed a vaguely religious authority. His clerks knew Latin and insisted on calling him emperor and *basileus*. His minters, subjected to a discipline which no longer existed on the continent, coined good money which circulated more easily than broken bracelets. Anglo-Saxon merchants, diplomats and clergy crossed the channel often enough to bring back valuable wares and ideas. England tantalized the Scandinavians with what looked to them like an ancient culture and a storehouse of wealth. They had been beaten, but were ready for another try if a weaker Anglo-Saxon king offered them an opportunity.

The opportunity came: Aethelred II, being no warrior, tendered to the Scandinavians blackmail money, the *Danegeld*, which he collected repeatedly from his subjects through a general levy. To no use: Svein 'Forkbeard', the Danish King, undertook the conquest of the island and Canute, his son, completed it and appropriated the *Danegeld* to create a permanent army and navy. There had been no general tax and no standing armed forces anywhere in Catholic Europe since the fall of the Roman Empire, and it is somewhat paradoxical that these two pillars of orderly government should have been first raised by an incapable Anglo-Saxon and a rude Dane in the extreme European frontier. It is true that the tax was not very regularly collected and that as late as 1027 Canute wrote from Rome to his English subjects that he would come back only when he 'could gather a fleet'.

'You were quite young when blazing houses marked your advance': this had been Canute, the Danish raider, in the recollections of a poet; but the same Canute, King of England (1016–35), married Aethelred II's widow, settled down as a member of the respectable family of kings, and channelled his wanderlust into a pilgrimage to Rome. His ambition was to make England the main body of a federal empire for which the Scandinavian territories, stretching on both sides of the Baltic to the threshold of Finland and Poland, would have formed the wings. He would have thus given a political frame to the loose economic unity of the 'Northern Mediterranean' which was maintained by ships ploughing the North Sea and the Baltic. The plan fell through: Canute died at the age of forty, and his children, who in any case would not have had the same ability, soon followed him to the tomb.

Thus it came about that in 1042 England took back as king the son of his widow and of Aethelred II, Edward the Confessor who returned from exile in Normandy. Pious and insignificant, he reigned by granting all their wishes to the clergy, the nobles, the Normans of his entourage and any taxpayer who resented the Danegeld. Meanwhile large estates grew larger, private bands and courts became more unruly, and localism broke out in the island, as it had on the continent somewhat earlier. Another lag also tended slowly to disappear: both the slaves and the poorer free men were merging into a single class of serfs.

The parting of the ways at Hastings

When Edward died childless in 1066 three claimants to the succession endeavoured to draw England into three divergent routes. Harold, son of Godwin, the greatest noble of the realm, would have ushered in some sort of feudalism, similar to that of France but with an even narrower horizon; Harold Hardrada, the Norwegian King who in his early years had married a daughter of Grand Prince Yaroslav of Kiev and served in the Byzantine army against the Sicilian Moslems, promised a return to the maritime vistas of Canute, perhaps extending as far as the Mediterranean; and finally William, Duke of Normandy, would renew the ties with the continent that had been broken ever since the fall of the Roman Empire. Everything was decided in two months by the chance of two battles. Harold Godwinson defeated and killed the Norwegian king at Stamford Bridge. Then he rushed south and succumbed at Hastings.

Thus England was welded to France, as Italy had been to Germany a century earlier. Although the centre of gravity was bound eventually to move from the conqueror's duchy to the conquered kingdom, the ruling class was nonetheless French. This characteristic was to be emphasized in 1154, when Henry II added to the Anglo-Norman state a new series of fiefs in France and spent most of his time on the continent. Until the beginning of the thirteenth century the Anglo-

Angevin Kingdom and the Romano-Germanic Empire, two artificial unions of peoples whom geography, language and historical traditions tended to separate, covered half Catholic Europe. One could hardly have forecast that the future belonged to national states!

Whereas the Empire was to collapse and leave Germany and Italy hopelessly dislocated, the Anglo-Angevin state, though it was neither as extensive nor as long-lived as the Empire, left to its heirs a tidier estate. France took from it a solid group of rich and well administered provinces. England became the first national, centralized government in Europe.

To explain the contrast between Anglo-Angevin achievements and imperial frustrations, it is not enough to point out the disrupting influence of the Investiture Struggle, for the Empire was only involved in it after a century of religious peace. The essential difference goes back to the start. Otto I never subjugated Italy completely, nor was he able to place his own men in all of the key Italian positions; moreover, he found the archaic institutions of his Saxon home ill-suited for the government of a more advanced land. William of Normandy, on the contrary, conquered England almost with one single stroke, saturated it with his own personnel, and adjusted skilfully the advanced institutions of his duchy to the more primitive but solid framework of the Anglo-Saxon state. He thus fitted together the best materials of his age: on the one hand, the unshaken traditions of a still vigorous patriarchal monarchy, and on the other, the dynamism of a fully developed and orderly feudal system.

The progress of government and administration

The warriors from all parts of France who had answered the call of William 'the Conqueror' (no more than a few thousands between feudal levies and volunteers) received their full reward. They were given fiefs in every part of the strange and still hostile British island. The King encouraged them to build castles and fortify themselves against any revolt of the natives or return of the Scandinavian raiders. But he demanded from each of them liege homage and the contribution of a number of knights for the royal army: about five thousand in all. To make sure that no compact fief could defy his authority as his own fief had defied the royal authority in France, William set apart in each shire a direct domain larger than that of any vassal. In the considered judgment of the main chronicle of his time, he was 'a very wise and great man', but 'severe beyond measure to those who opposed his will'. We are also told that he loved the stags 'as if he were their father', but the love of a hunter is not of the same kind as that of a shepherd.

After him, William II (1087–1100) and Henry I (1100–35) ruled the country with the same inflexible energy, though perhaps not always with the same wisdom, making the most of the rights to which a feudal monarch was entitled over his subjects, whether noblemen, commoners or serfs. The solidarity of king and vassals against the common people tamed the Anglo-Saxon population. In turn, the King found it possible to lean more and more on the Anglo-Saxon population, when necessary, to hold in check recalcitrant vassals.

The struggles over the succession in the time of King Stephen (1135–54) began a period of disorder, but seventy years of firm rule had caused the feudal class to forget how to make good use of independence. Henry II was able to take over the reins fairly easily, and in spite of his prolonged absences, in spite of those of Richard Coeur de Lion, the collaboration between monarchy and nobility made new progress. Gradually, between 1066 and the end of the twelfth century, the King was transformed from gang leader to chief administrator, and the vassals from companions in arms to associates in the management and exploitation of the commonwealth.

William the Conqueror and, still more, Henry I secured the collaboration of the clergy on the basis of a concordat with Rome guaranteeing great influence to the King. The agreement was endangered by a number of jurisdictional conflicts but survived all of them. In 1171 the authoritarian measures of Henry II and the assassination of Thomas à Becket, Archbishop of Canterbury, by over-zealous vassals, provoked a more serious crisis. In spite of appearances, however, Henry emerged from it stronger than ever. Without being exemplary, the morals of the English clergy were not on the whole so bad as to shock public opinion. The movements for monastic and religious reform which kept the continent in almost continuous turmoil reached the island with some delay, their main impetus already spent, and spread without causing great upheavals.

At all levels of administration the monarchy strengthened its authority and improved its methods by degrees. It did not have to rely upon upstarts like the German serf-knights or upon middle-class commoners like the French bureaucrats of a later period, but it recruited its best servants in its own *milieu*, by paying and training selected members of the feudal nobility.

Local government in the age of localism was everywhere more efficient than regional and central government. In England, it rested on sound Anglo-Saxon traditions and could be built up on strength. The talent for evolution without revolution which was to become a distinguishing feature of English public life first manifested itself in this sphere. The main elements, of course, were less original than some modern historians seem to think: courts of justice, communities, autonomous bodies of all descriptions were as much European as insular phenomena, and legal culture was on the whole more advanced in southern Europe than in England. But English courts and moots were outstanding in certain respects. They were very numerous and evenly distributed throughout the land, met frequently, functioned rather smoothly and enjoyed a fair amount of authority.

Local moots of vill, hundred and shire, baronial and ecclesiastical courts became schools of practical administration and meeting grounds where the differences between Normans and Anglo-Saxons, privileged orders and lower classes very slowly levelled out. There could be no question of absolute equality, to be sure, but the right of every person to be judged by his peers was sometimes recognized, the testimony of the poor was often received, and even serfs were heard in certain cases. King's judges and royal courts gradually asserted themselves, even on the local level, at the expense of other jurisdictions; but this was not only the result of the sovereign's unilateral will. It also stemmed from the fact that these judges were more competent and consistent than feudal judges.

Regional administration usually was the weakest link of feudal government, but in England it worked with a remarkable degree of success. William the Conqueror's sheriffs had been great nobles without any specialized administrative experience; those of Henry I were small nobles more amenable to direction: Henry II's were fairly competent men, controlled by more competent travelling inspectors.

Central administration had to be carried out personally by the King with what assistance was readily available to him. While in Germany and France the general assemblies of notables did not meet regularly and had little business to transact, in England the general council or king's court (*curia regis*), whose origins could be traced to the Anglo-Saxon general assembly, was still consulted in cases of exceptional importance. For day-to-day affairs a more restricted council, proceeding from the wider one and bearing the same name, functioned regularly and was gradually divided into committees of specialized experts. The earliest of these committees was concerned with finance; it was called the 'Exchequer' after the rudimentary instrument used in keeping its accounts (*échiquier*, chessboard).

England's good fortune

In this steady, harmonious development geography must be taken into account. The kingdom was large enough to form the basis of a respectable state, yet small enough to be traversed from end to end in two or three weeks by the King and his agents. This is what made it possible for William the Conqueror to undertake in 1086 what no other King in the West could have achieved before the thirteenth century: an inventory of the assets of his kingdom as detailed as if it had been a private estate. In each community the priest, the reeve and four free peasants testified: 'it is a shame to report it, though he felt no shame in doing it, there was not a single ox, cow or pig which was not recorded in the inventory', remarked an indignant chronicler. This document (the Domesday Book), part of which still exists, records the results of an inquiry which was the first of a long series. In this way the Conqueror's successors were able to know exactly the resources of their kingdom — and consequently to tax them.

Taxes increased with the growth of the population and production of England. From the first they included money dues, a heritage of the *Danegeld:* this money made it possible for the King to pay soldiers and civil officials without depending entirely upon feudal service. In the time of Henry II (1154–89) the fiscal revenue was swollen by the fines levied by ubiquitous royal courts and the fines paid by the growing towns in exchange for limited autonomy. Although the English towns were even smaller and fewer than the French communes and the whole kingdom hardly richer than Lombardy, the King of England was the best endowed monarch in Catholic Europe.

Finally — and this is perhaps the most important factor — England was the only European monarchy not to have dangerous enemies on its territory for a century and a half. The Scandinavian raids ceased; the Welsh, Scots and Irish were too weak to be a serious threat; the kings of France restricted themselves to occasional attacks on the continental possessions of their formidable neighbours, and none of them before Philip Augustus was a formidable adversary. Besides, the kings of England were strong enough in their island to stand a few reverses on the continent without essential damage. In the eleventh century the counts of Anjou were their most dangerous competitors on the continent. After fighting them for a long period, Henry I thought he had solved all his problems by marrying his daughter and heiress to Geoffrey Plantagenet, the heir to Anjou. The English barons thought otherwise. On the death of Henry I his succession was contested and Stephen of Blois, grandson of the Conqueror, was chosen in opposition to the Angevins. Finally the death of both Geoffrey and Stephen left the English throne to Henry II, son of Geoffrey, grandson of Henry I, and second husband of Eleanor of Aquitaine.

From triumph to disaster, from disaster to equilibrium

The success of Henry II is in striking contrast with the failures of his great contemporary, Frederick Barbarossa. The latter let Germany go to pieces while vainly trying to affirm his power in Italy; Henry tightened the administration of England while devoting most of his time to his possessions in France. By paternal descent, maternal descent and marriage, he was in effect the lord of half France (Map 21). His domains extended without a break from the Channel to the Pyrenees and covered a larger and more densely populated area than his island kingdom. Unfortunately, however, each one of his French fiefs raised special problems and aroused additional enemies. Though Henry was not able to fulfil an old dream of the dukes of Aquitaine — turning the Count of Toulouse into an obedient vassal — he kept to the end almost all that he had possessed in France at the beginning of his reign. He would have finished this reign more happily if his sons had not revolted against him.

A tireless soldier and administrator, Henry even found time to stake out English claims over the rest of the British Isles. The King of Scotland was beaten and forced to pay homage. Several petty kings in Ireland did the same, while some of Henry II's vassals actually occupied the region of Dublin and established the first English bridge-head on Irish soil.

Henry II's son, Richard Coeur-de-Lion, lived the ten years of his reign as a knight-errant in search of adventure. In arrogance and cruelty he was a worthy antagonist of Emperor Henry VI. Less persevering than the latter or than Philip

Augustus, he cut his way out of the difficulties repeatedly caused by his own recklessness, thanks to his swordsmanship, which had no equal in the entire feudal age. The troubadours celebrated in him a prince who resembled them and wrote good poetry (or instructed others to write under his name). Modern historians are more impressed by the sums he was able to raise, thanks to new taxes, during his long absence from England. But this fiscal exploit was not attributable to Richard in person; it rather was the test of the robust structure of English administration built by many generations of Anglo-Saxon and Anglo-Norman kings and brought to unprecedented efficiency by Henry II. The kingdom was strong and united enough to function even without a king.

English unity withstood the even more oppressive fiscal policy of John 'Lackland' (or 'Soft-sword', as he was also called because of his military ineptitude) but it turned against him. Most of his predecessors had on many occasions violated the feudal contracts binding them to their English vassals and to their French suzerain; but they had made up for it by their outstanding performance as fighters and administrators. They also had been fortunate in meeting no opponents of great stature, with the possible exception of Thomas à Becket; nor did the opposition have a clear vision of the issues in dispute.

In his capacity as vassal of Philip Augustus for his French fiefs, John exposed himself to conviction for felony. Others had done the same, but it was John who lost Normandy and Anjou almost at one stroke and could not prevent the French King from annexing the 'escheated' fiefs to the royal domain. In his capacity as King of England, John did not keep the oath he had sworn at his coronation. It is true that this oath, still used today, was originally only a very vague verbal undertaking to maintain peace and justice, an undertaking barely reinforced since the time of Henry I by an equally vague written pledge. However, as the King's justice had grown more pervasive and strict, so the vassals had become anxious to limit it in terms defined by law. The storm which had long been threatening broke after John's quarrels with the Church — a Church headed by Innocent III and presided over in England by Stephen Langton, both of them remarkable men — and became uncontrollable after John's defeat at Bouvines. Almost fifty English barons, a good number of prelates, the citizens of London and Prince Llewelyn 'the Great' of North Wales joined forces against the King. In June 1215 he was forced to affix his seal to the 'great charter of liberties', the *Magna Carta* (or, in the learned spelling, *Magna Charta*). He promptly broke the engagement, but his death less than two years later made it possible for the barons to have the charter confirmed by his minor son, Henry III.

An unwary modern reader may be surprised that this feudal document, where over-general clauses alternate without apparent order with over-detailed clauses, should have served as the cornerstone for the most venerable of representative systems. In fact, Magna Carta was great chiefly because of what was to be built upon it later. It is similar to other promises extracted from other kings by other vassals at about the same period. A close examination does, however, reveal nuances not found elsewhere. The vassals undertake both to uphold the justice of a just king and repress the injustice of a king who has not kept his own laws. The ecclesiastical order and the bourgeoisie are directly protected only by very vague clauses, but some indirect protection is assured for the whole population: the king cannot increase feudal dues or levy certain extra-ordinary taxes without the consent of those who would be affected. These are only outlines of great constitutional principles, but they already reveal the spirit of compromise which will lead the subject to collaborate with the sovereign on condition that he does not abuse his power.

What a contrast between the return of Philip Augustus and that of John Lack-land after Bouvines! In France peasants strew the road with flowers and branches and the students of Paris make merry for a week. Without any long administrative or judicial preparation, and in a territory as yet restricted, national unity is outlined. It is compatible with the liberties of the communes and the vassals who have helped the King, but the latter may see in his triumph a dangerous temptation to absolutism. In England, on the other hand, the vigorous forces of a kingdom already united and well organized complete the humiliation of the King. But they stop in time, and lay the foundations of a new and more flexible union that will be capable of withstanding all adversities.

V.   THE SMALLER POWERS

If we leave aside for the time being the independent cities whose problems were different from those of the territorial states, it remains only for us to consider a few smaller powers: the Scandinavian kingdoms, the Iberian kingdoms, and the Sicilian kingdom. All of these, the still smaller Celtic states and the European countries to the east of the Empire (outside the framework of our study) played at this period a less important political part than that of the four powers whose evolution we have just outlined. Nevertheless, they enriched European civiliza-tion by their original contributions, and it is not without regret that we shall restrict ourselves to the barest account of their history.

Two common handicaps explain in part (but only in part) their relatively minor role: firstly their remoteness from the physical centre of Catholic Europe; secondly the fact that their population was smaller than that of France, Italy north of the Tiber, Germany and England. Still it must be noted that England itself would not have counted amongst the great powers but for the extraordi-nary efficiency of her government. The English kingdom was in fact not much larger or more populous than the Kingdom of Sicily; and if Sicily was peripheric in relation to Paris, so was England in relation to Rome.

The Kingdom of Sicily

The Normans of Sicily have been often compared with the Normans of England, and Robert 'Guiscard' (the Astute) with William the Conqueror, his contemporary. Actually the resemblance was superficial. Before crossing a narrow channel to become King of England, William was Duke of Normandy; when he departed, Robert was but one of a dozen children of a petty squire, an adventurer among other adventurers seeking fortune far from their native land. Between the papal investiture of 1059 which legalized his first conquests, and that of 1139 which marked the final triumph of his nephew Roger II, eighty years elapsed: eighty years of battles, insurrections and repression, but also of wise compromises and intelligent toleration. Far from being superimposed on an already established political and cultural unity like Anglo-Saxon England, the Kingdom of Sicily was a patchwork of detached fragments of other states (especially the Byzantine Empire), independent principalities (the Lombard states of Benevento, Salerno and Capua, the Moslem emirates of Sicily, and so forth) and semi-independent cities, all of which had hated one another for a long time.

Christians against Moslems and Jews, Greeks against Lombards and Normans, Arabs against Berbers, townspeople against countrymen, feudal nobility against free peasant villages — the Norman kings needed as much tact as energy to smooth out all these conflicts and harmonize so many divergent interests. Externally they had to defend themselves against their powerful enemies, the German emperors, and their meddlesome suzerains, the popes. As if this were not enough, their own ambition and aggressiveness led them to attack the Byzantine Empire in its inner provinces of the Balkans, the Moslem states in their African homes, and both the Islamic and the Christian powers in the Holy Land. This restless activity subjected the new, budding state to an excessive strain.

All the same, the ethnic and cultural diversity of the kingdom was a source of riches and its unbounded ambitions were tokens of greatness. No doubt the praise lavished by Idrisi, the distinguished Arab geographer, on his Norman employers was magnified by the spirit of flattery and coloured by love of exaggeration. But it is none the less certain that at the beginning of the twelfth century the Norman state was unusually prosperous and Palermo, its capital, surpassed all other Catholic cities in population, area and magnificence. Nowhere else could one have found an administration as complex and polyglot yet so capable of unifying the motley components of the population under its control.

Even as Sicilian art of the Norman period brings together Byzantine mosaics, Moslem decoration, Lombard and French architectural structures, so does the royal administration. For example, the office corresponding to the English Exchequer is called *dohana*, from Arabic *diwan*: its two sub-sections, *a secretis* and *baronum*, recall respectively the Byzantine fiscal system and the Anglo-Norman feudal finances. Indeed the King of Sicily took his wealth wherever he could find it. Like an oriental monarch he lived ostentatiously and paid his debts in *aurum tarenorum*, the only gold coinage struck in Italy before 1252. He had conquered the land like a barbarian raider, demanded obedience like a Roman emperor and expected loyalty like a feudal monarch. By the late twelfth century there even were kings — William II 'the Good' and Tancred — who won the affection of their subjects. Too late to prevent the conquest of the kingdom by Henry VI and his 'barbarians' (as an impassioned chronicler calls them), but in time to convert Frederick II, the son of the German conqueror and of a Sicilian queen, to the idea of bringing the centre of the 'Roman' Empire back to the heart of the Mediterranean.

The Scandinavian kingdoms

In the ancestral home of the Normans at the other end of Europe the states which today form the Scandinavian triad were slowly and painstakingly organized. Like primitive Germany, pagan Scandinavia had found military leaders in the prominent families who claimed descent from gods or sorcerers. From this milieu came the three dynasties which kept the crown until they became extinct; in the case of Denmark and Norway, they lasted until the fourteenth century.

Originally the sovereign drew his power from his extensive private domains, whose revenue enabled him to maintain a larger band of warriors than that of his strongest subjects. But he could scarcely issue orders without the consent of local and regional popular assemblies (*thing*). In Iceland and Greenland a general assembly (*althing*) did without a king until the thirteenth century; and even this form of government, but one step removed from total anarchy, seemed an inevitable hindrance to the descendants of the rugged individualists who had sought limitless independence amidst arctic glaciers and erupting geysers and volcanoes.

In Denmark, Norway and Sweden, as the growth of the population tightened the bonds of society, the King little by little imposed himself, transforming his armed guard into a quasi-feudal army and relying on the Church for support (Pl. 12 and Pl. 23). The Church itself made very slow progress. In Sweden the great pagan sanctuary of Uppsala, long famous for its human sacrifices, was not destroyed until the end of the eleventh century. In Denmark the Gregorian reform was not established until a little before the middle of the twelfth century, thanks to the efforts of an archbishop who was married and had children.

One might have thought that the Nordic people, whose scattered scions had grafted themselves so brilliantly in England, Sicily and Russia, would give their best on their native soil once they were gathered under the guidance of kings. There was nothing of the kind. Economically Scandinavia remained above all a land of poor peasants: the afflux of precious metals and valuable wares dwindled after the age of the Vikings, peaceful commerce scarcely developed and towns were small and few. Politically Denmark and Sweden strove with some success to expand towards the eastern Baltic, and Norway retained a nominal suzerainty over some of the western Scandinavian colonies (Iceland, Greenland, Orkneys, Hebrides, Isle of Man), but the age of lightning successes was gone. Art lost its rough but powerful originality as it fitted into the periphery of the Romanesque style (and, later, of Gothic). The themes of Provençal poetry, first noticed by Rögnvald (Ronald), the Scandinavian earl of the Orkneys in the mid twelfth century, made their way to the three kingdoms, but the finest literature was produced in kingless Iceland, mostly on early mediaeval themes.

Should we conclude that the genius of the Scandinavians could not bear the control of a central authority? Let us rather say that the population was and remained sparse. Consequently the monarchs were more successful in suppressing personal initiatives than in channelling them towards their own ends. Moreover, Scandinavia's few writers and artists, no matter how distinguished, could scarcely steer an independent course once they entered the mainstream of European culture.

The history of Iberia: an enigma?

It is much harder to explain the limited progress of the Iberian states, which a modern Spanish scholar calls an enigma of history. Certainly in the tenth century Iberia seemed destined for the most brilliant future. It is true that the Caliphate of Cordova, master of four-fifths of the peninsula and a worthy rival of the Caliphate of Baghdad and the Byzantine Empire, at that time outshone the small states of the Christian north. But its tolerant attitude to the other 'peoples of the Book' (Christians and Jews) guaranteed to them a fair share of the economic and intellectual prosperity of a state which was far ahead of its Catholic neighbours.

As for the Asturian-Leonese Kingdom, it had inherited the most vigorous traits of the Visigothic Kingdom while shedding its worst liabilities. In the austere surroundings of the Cantabrian and Pyrenean mountains the political interference of the clergy, the indiscipline of the nobility and the discrimination against the Jews had diminished, the decadence of the towns had come to an end, and the condition of the peasants had improved. The King exercised a kind of protectorate over the other Christian states which were springing up all along the northern frontier of the Caliphate. Though he had fewer subjects than certain French dukes, he was pleased to be called 'emperor by divine will', and there were prophets who told him that he would rule 'soon over the whole of Spain'.

In the principal as well as in the satellite kingdoms, the struggle against the Moslems had restored to the King his role of general and of manager of conquered lands. Each patch of ground recovered from the Infidels had to be resettled, restored to cultivation and defended by an army of pioneers ready for any emergency. The common danger diminished social distinctions and made collaboration indispensable. About the end of the ninth century, when the Count of Barcelona wanted to attract colonists to his castle of Cardona, he offered freedom to all slaves, adulterers or criminals who might wish to come. In the seesaw progress of the Christian counter-offensive (*Reconquista*), which began almost as soon as the first Arab wave of invasion stopped, what mattered was not sweeping through enemy land but holding it through permanent settlement; and it was to be no small glory for Sancho I, the Portuguese King, to be nicknamed *Poplador*, 'founder of populated centres' (1185–1211).

A good start, a loss of impetus

Castile and Catalonia both originally meant 'land of castles', but the Iberian castle was less like the feudal manor than the small agricultural town, with its municipal pride, its free landlords, its modest group of merchants and artisans. Royal authority limited the autonomy of each town but protected it from the envy of its rivals and the covetousness of the nobility.

The nobility included 'rich men' (*ricoshombres*) and mere 'children of well known fathers' (*hidalgos*). As a whole it was too poor to be a serious counterpoise to the King. Its ranks were often decimated by war but were refilled by the admission of courageous peasants and French adventurous knights. The most illustrious of the latter, Henry of Burgundy, married the daughter of the Castilian King and founded the Portuguese state at the end of the eleventh century.

At this period the disintegration of the Caliphate of Cordova hastened the advance of the *Reconquista*. But this progress, while increasing the resources of the Christian states, had the curious result of weakening royal power: distances, in a chronically underpopulated country, made the transmission and enforcement of orders more difficult. In this way, little by little, the patriarchal monarchy was changed into a feudal monarchy. No doubt the example of France, Iberia's only Christian neighbour, was a strong influence. In Spain, however, resistance to the central power found original expression in the Cortes, where the representatives of the autonomous towns sat side by side with nobles and bishops. This rudimentary constitutional organism grew out of the assembly of notables before the end of the twelfth century (by 1188 in the Kingdom of Leon), thus preceding by a hundred years the beginnings of the English Parliament.

In spite of these assets, to which must be added a cultural development of the highest order, the Iberian states by the dawn of the thirteenth century hopelessly lagged behind the principal Catholic countries in many respects. Economically they had been outstripped by Italy, France and England. Their towns were growing slowly, their great domains gave a poor yield, their commerce and industry were of modest proportions. Politically the 'five kingdoms' of Castile, Leon-Asturias, Portugal, Navarre and Aragon had ceased to recognize the superiority of a 'king-emperor'. Though the five dynasties continuously intermarried, each one sought allies wherever it could, even on the Moslem side.

The reconquest, which had seemed so near achievement a century earlier, had been twice halted by Islamic counter-offensives. First the Almoravides, then the Almohades had brought fresh and fanatical forces from Africa to bolster their coreligionists in Spain, who were more civilized but more resigned to defeat. It is true that in 1212 three Christian kings in coalition were to win a decisive battle at Las Navas de Tolosa and to smash the remaining Moslem defences, but theirs was a triumph too long deferred.

The never-ending war

A triumph too long deferred: could that be a key to the 'historical enigma' of Spain? Even for the victor, war is a profitable operation only if it ends swiftly. At its outset it does not seem to have hindered the revival of the Iberian peoples; but, prolonged for centuries, it absorbed too large a share of the energies which other peoples at the same time were applying to productive tasks. The *Reconquista*, by becoming the most important and durable enterprise of the entire nation, accustomed too many men — to quote an expression from the *Cantar del Cid* — to 'obtain their bread by taking it from others'. What is more, this unending war did not lead to the fusion of the conquerors and conquered, but opened deep rifts where originally there was no unsurmountable cleavage.

> Under Islam a fusion of all the peoples in the peninsula might perhaps not have been impossible in the tenth century. Under Christianity it appeared obtainable shortly after the middle of the eleventh, when Alfonso VI took the title of 'emperor of the two religions', maintained the most cordial relations with the Emir of Seville and showed unusual tolerance to the Jews. Then both Catholics and Moslems were caught in the international currents of the crusades and of *jihad* (the Islamic anti-crusade) which revived their mutual hatred. The favourable moment was past. To be sure, until the end of the Middle Ages there still were enlightened or cynically greedy princes who surrounded themselves with intellectuals and financiers of different faiths, or private individuals who stretched out their hands to their human brothers across the fences, or religious minorities which survived in relative security in spite of ever stricter coercive measures. Nonetheless, the epilogue was always the same. Sooner or later, Jews and Moslems had to take flight or were expelled from Christian land.

Although the Iberian peoples cannot be especially blamed for sharing the common error of most Europeans in the Middle Ages, it is certain that intolerance harmed them more than the others. Both by their numbers and by their culture, the non-conformists occupied a most considerable place in Spain and Portugal. Reconstruction without them was an overwhelming burden. It was no doubt eased by the more or less spontaneous conversion of some of the Infidels and by the immigration of some non-Iberian Christians. Nevertheless, when the 'five kingdoms' hampered the activities of religious minorities they weakened a collaboration they could ill dispense with. When they drove these minorities from their soil, they opened in their own ranks gaps which they were never able to fill.

VI.   THE CLASH OF WEST AND EAST

The incompatibility of religions had more disastrous effects on the eastern frontier than on the western end of Catholic Europe. During two centuries of crusades men of all classes expended treasures of devotion, courage, blood and money, usually in the conviction that they were performing a pious deed and labouring for the propagation of the True Faith. Alas, the lasting results of their efforts were the overthrow of Byzantine Christianity, the stiffening of Moslem orthodoxy, and the recrudescence of anti-Semitism in Europe.

This verdict on the most famous enterprise of the Middle Ages may seem too severe. Has it not been generally agreed that the crusades renewed the economic and cultural exchanges between East and West, and fostered chivalrous and evangelical ideals in a stagnating Europe?

The avoidable but not avoided hatred

Certainly there was substantial progress in these directions during the crusades, but the crusades were consequences rather than causes of that progress. Artistic and literary borrowings, philosophical and scientific translations, commercial exchanges antedate Godefroy de Bouillon; so does the awakening of Christian ideals. The launching of the first crusade was an episode in the Gregorian reform movement. Without the previous experience of the Italians in commerce and naval warfare, without the demographic growth and political exuberance of the French, without the overflowing vigour of Europe as a whole, the crusades would have been inconceivable. They hastened and strengthened the contacts with the Oriental world and gave the Western peoples invaluable experience of a field in which they were to assert themselves in the modern period: overseas colonization. Europe learnt a great deal, but it was a school where masters and students hated one another.

Would this hatred have been so violent if the crusades had not embittered it? We do not believe so. Wars against Greeks and Moslems and persecutions of the Jews were by no means unknown before the crusades, but they had not acquired the character of a permanent and sacred enterprise, utterly different from the internal struggles and slaughters which ravaged the Catholic community. 'We worship the same God, albeit in a different form', wrote Gregory VII to the Emir of Bougie. 'We should be profoundly distressed by the misfortunes of this great [Byzantine] Empire', he stressed when urging the faithful to help the Greeks, not of course in Jerusalem which did not belong to them but in their own territories of Asia Minor overrun by the Turks. Newly converted Jewish financiers, the Pierleoni, were close friends of Gregory VII; Alexander II, his predecessor, had taken the side of unconverted Jews in Narbonne and Benevento against their persecutors.

Such was the attitude of the reforming popes on the eve of the First Crusade. It was in accordance with the anti-militarist tradition of the primitive Church, and it agreed with the belief that the Jews would voluntarily accept baptism shortly before the Last Judgment. To say that this state of mind was universal would be a manifest exaggeration. It existed nevertheless, even in unimpeachable circles, and it found independent support among those who had something to gain from the peaceful development of cultural or commercial exchanges.

What transformed into merciless wars those crusades, which their contemporaries never called anything but 'voyages to Jerusalem' or 'journeys to the Holy Land' that is to say, 'pilgrimages' ? The problem, if it is a problem, hardly warrants the debates it has provoked among historians. It seems pointless to distinguish religious motives from economic or political motives. Most of the crusaders could not have said which factor had been foremost in their mind: indeed it was the combination of faith and interest that launched the crusades and made them popular. Moreover, it is a tale a hundred times repeated that a fight begun in the name of an ideal develops in a direction opposite to its avowed aims, and that practical gains, after supporting sentiment, end by stifling it. The campaigns of the Germans against the pagans east of the Elbe are particularly like the crusades by virtue of their religious colouring and surpass the crusades in greed and violence. What distinguishes the crusades is not the inevitable disparity between promises and fulfilment, but their extraordinary size and impetus. They recruited fighters from all Catholic nations and were described as more divine than human fights: *gesta Dei per Francos,* God's deeds by the hands of Franks, as a chronicler called them.

Certain modern historians have taken over this myth to the extent of failing to distinguish between normal phenomena of an age different from ours and pathological phenomena of collective hysteria or criminal fringe. They have thus closed their ears not only to any voice not proceeding from the Catholic West but also to expressions of common sense among the Western nations. Their heroes are the 'small people', that is to say, those fanatical crowds who confused non-conformist Christians with the Infidels, mere spectators with enemy fighters, rash improvisation with courage and faith. According to them, this popular crusade was led astray by the 'crusade of the barons', the only one authorized and conducted by the papal legate. The efforts of the leaders to keep to a relatively concrete and realizable plan are described as egotistical ambition and thirst for gain. As for the seamen of the merchant towns, those ancient defenders of the Christian frontiers who wished to make a Christian Holy Land a bridge to the outer world, they become the sordid profiteers of mediaeval war.

The absurdity of such an interpretation is evident as soon as one looks at the authentic sources. Let us stress the word *authentic:* the letter said to have been written by the Byzantine Emperor to seek the assistance of the Western world is a forgery. As for the rumours then current (and still current in certain primers) about maltreatment inflicted on pilgrims by the Moslems, these are echoes of incidents which took place a century before the First Crusade.

The failure of the 'small folk' and the exploits of the barons

What actually happened after the convocation of the First Crusade in 1095 by Pope Urban II? A few visionaries got together crowds of adventurers, beggars and simple peasants, who set out in spring 1096 without waiting for the Pope's signal. Similar elements had performed remarkable deeds in the agricultural colonization of the European frontier, but could not possibly have carried out on their own the conquest of the Holy Land. They relied on heaven rather than on their efforts, their leaders lacked authority and experience, their goal was a promised land on a frontier which none of them knew.

Some of these crusaders paused in the Rhineland to fight an easy and profitable holy war next to their homes: they massacred the Jews and shared the spoils with the local petty lords. Other crusaders proceeded with pillage and murder as far as Hungary, where the furious inhabitants in turn put them to death. A minority reached Constantinople. Emperor Alexis, who had not called for them, transferred them to Asia Minor, bidding them not to precipitate a conflict. At that time the Byzantine Empire had partially recovered from the 'misfortunes' mentioned by Gregory VII: Alexis had defeated his enemies in the Balkans, halted the Turks and assembled sufficient forces to attempt a counter-offensive, with the support of regular Western troops whose arrival was expected. But could he hope that the 'small folk' would be more patient with the Infidels than they had been with the Hungarian Christians? The remains of the unauthorized crusaders returned to their pillaging and were easily exterminated by the Turks.

A little later, four regular armies — mostly knights from Provence, Lotharingia, northern France and Norman Italy — converged on Constantinople from four different directions. In return for feudal homage in the Western manner and for the promise to restore to Byzantium the provinces which would be won back from the Turks, the 'barons' obtained from Alexis (who did expect them, but had not bargained for such a large number) unenthusiastic military aid and indispensable revictualling. For the first time in the feudal age an expeditionary force was able to operate without interruption for three years, until the fall of Jerusalem (15th July 1099).

This 'Iliad of the Barons' cannot be told in a few lines. Let us not spoil the picture engraved by legend and poetry on our childhood memories. Even if the crusaders were helped by the quarrels between the Turks of Asia Minor and the Arabs of Egypt, even if they were violent and quarrelsome, they nevertheless gave extraordinary proofs of courage and endurance. When they had passed the frontiers of the Byzantine Empire and exhausted the patience of that reluctant ally, the supplies and armed assistance of the Italian seamen, freshly arrived by sea, saved them from disaster. When they finally reached their goal, they tarnished their victory by massacres, the importance of which, however, has been exaggerated by sadistic reporters. War is never a beautiful sight, but its horrors are quickly forgotten if the victors know how to reconstruct and pacify.

Outremer: a brave new world

Reconstruct and pacify: was that really a suitable role for an assemblage of wild, intractable warriors encamped in the outskirts of a hostile world and surrounded by subjects who were more cultivated than they but spoke and behaved in a variety of incomprehensible ways? The crusaders mistrusted all the natives, including non-conformist Christians — not without reason — and did not trouble to convert them. Yet only one road was open to them, that of tolerance. After some hesitation, they took it. Immigrants joined them and helped to establish in the Kingdom of Jerusalem and its dependencies the first overseas European nation, a sort of America before its time.

Scarcely twenty years after the conquest, Foucher of Chartres, a citizen of this brave new world, described it enthusiastically as follows: 'We have already forgotten our birthplaces... some of us possess house and servants... others have already taken as wife a Syrian woman, an Armenian, sometimes even a baptized Saracen.... Confidence reconciles the most strange races.... A man with only a few pence finds himself here in possession of a fortune. A man who in Europe owned not even a village becomes lord of a whole city in the East'. More tinged with Oriental fantasy than he suspected, Foucher had acquired the habit of magnifying. In reality, the riches of colonial Palestine were not worth the resources of many European areas of colonization, and had not attracted enough settlers to exploit them adequately.

Nevertheless, thanks to its exotic plantations, its function as commercial intermediary for East and West and its large-scale exploitation of pilgrim-tourists, the Kingdom of Jerusalem with its dependencies had solid economic foundations. Its institutions, based on a freely imitated model from southern France, reflected the ideals of feudalism. Not those of 'feudal anarchy': for though the vassals enjoyed a very broad autonomy and the right to give the King counsel which he could not neglect without risk, the King was entitled to call the vassals to arms for an unlimited period, down to the lowliest knight.

Even geographically, the kingdom was not as vulnerable as is often claimed. In the west it bordered on the Mediterranean which was controlled by Italian fleets. In the north it was sheltered by the small Armenian state of Cilicia, recently founded by refugees from Greater Armenia which had been overrun by the Turks; and above all it could use the backing of that Byzantine Empire which had kept the Moslems in check for centuries. To the east and the south, the mountains of the Lebanon and the desert protected the frontiers.

Defeat in Jerusalem, success in Cyprus

Europe overseas could have survived indefinitely, had it overcome the aggressive spirit that had produced it. A large number of the 'Poulains' (as the Syrian-born descendants of Europeans were called) adapted themselves to the customs and climate of the country. While keeping their faith they did not mind establishing good-neighbourly relations with both the Byzantines and the Moslems. Byzantium proved by its example that it was possible to fight from time to time for limited aims without destroying all chances of co-existence of two religions, each of which was too strong to be annihilated by the other.

Battle without quarter and implacable hatred, however, had numerous supporters in the kingdom. The military orders founded by crusaders (Knights Templars, Knights Hospitallers, Teutonic Knights) were committed to bellicosity by their peculiar status, which combined religious vows and the chivalrous vocation. These monk-soldiers were often lax in the performance of their ecclesiastical duties, but they knew how to fight and conceived war as an end in itself. Moreover, hardly a year passed without the arrival of newcomers from the old continent, who brought with them their zeal, their prejudices, their impatience to wash away their sins in the blood of the Infidels before re-embarking as soon as they decently could. Other elements of the same kind who had remained in Europe — fanatical believers or devout criminals — kept the fire of anti-Semitism burning and from time to time, in spite of papal vetoes, unleashed a massacre of Jews. Sometimes, however, they were content with seizing the Jews' possessions.

In 1147, news of a reverse suffered by the 'Poulains' in an outlying section of the Holy Land set in motion the Second Crusade. Bernard of Clairvaux spared no effort to revive the former enthusiasm. There were fewer beggars, fewer adventurers, and the Kings of France and Germany (Louis VII and Conrad III) headed the crusaders. With the help of Manuel, the Byzantine Emperor, and the support of the 'Poulains', such an expedition could have accomplished much more than the First Crusade, had it been well led. It was not, and ended in complete failure: the Kings quarrelled with Manuel, spread alarm in the Moslem world, and returned without having won anything for their cause. In spite of this, the Kingdom of Jerusalem had a forty-year spell of relative prosperity. It is true that a new Moslem power was being formed where the first crusaders had found only small rival states, but as yet it did not constitute a threat to a vigorous Christian state which kept good watch while avoiding useless provocation.

Suddenly, in 1187, the irresponsible attacks of an unruly Frank vassal and of the Templars reopened the conflict. A great Moslem ruler, Saladin, vainly tried to obtain satisfaction by diplomatic means; then he attacked, and crushed the Kingdom's host at Hattin. There was scarcely any reserve force to close the gap. The Moslems retook Jerusalem and drove the Christians back towards the sea.

This time a new crusade was indispensable to re-establish the situation. Three kings led it: Frederick Barbarossa died *en route*, but Philip Augustus and Richard Coeur de Lion, valiantly supported by the Italian mariners, ensured the preservation of a long coastal belt before returning homewards. As Jerusalem remained in Saladin's hands, St John of Acre became the capital of a narrow but still viable kingdom.

At the same time the Byzantine island of Cyprus, seized in passing by Richard Coeur de Lion, sold by him to the Knights Templars and by them to the former King of Jerusalem (the loser at Hattin), became an independent Frankish kingdom. Knights and merchants, while still holding to the fortified bridge-heads of Palestine, gradually moved their centre of gravity towards this natural keep, for which the Mediterranean, guarded by the Italians, served as a moat. In this relative security the Franks successfully took up again the plans for colonization which enemy pressure and their own mistakes had doomed to failure on the continent.

Cyprus, with its famed vineyards, indigo fields and sugar plantations, with its markets and ports, its Gothic churches (Pl. 17) and oriental houses, its French-speaking nobility and Greek-speaking peasantry, its cultural refinement and its warlike spirit, was the finest success of the Crusades. It proved the most enduring: it was to hold out for several centuries after the final collapse of the Kingdom of Jerusalem.

The onslaught upon the 'Sick Man'

The Third Crusade had stopped short of its final objective; a Fourth Crusade composed of barons and mariners began to move in 1204. It was destined to get no farther than Constantinople, where it achieved what the earlier crusades had already presaged: the city was taken and sacked, as if it had been a Moslem lair, and the victors divided the spoils of the Byzantine Empire. While the remains of the Greek forces organized 'governments in exile' in various provincial towns, a weak 'Latin Empire' was installed at Constantinople. Frankish baronies and principalities sprouted throughout the conquered territory, and the Venetians reserved for themselves most of the commercially important positions including the island of Crete.

Is it necessary to linger over the long-debated question of the responsibility for the 'diversion' of an expedition officially intended to deliver Jerusalem? No doubt the Venetians, who had already provided some of the ships at their expense and were unable to obtain repayment of other expenses, asked the crusaders to make a first diversion and capture Zara in lieu of a financial settlement. But the second 'diversion', to Constantinople, had been secretly planned from the beginning by the barons leading the crusade; and the fact that Constantinople could serve as a base of operations towards the Holy Land was an extenuating circumstance. The

Pope, who knew their plan, did not warn the Byzantines of the danger, and while denouncing the 'diversion' accepted its dividends: he installed obedient clergy in the capital that had defied him for so long. The knights and the small fry, too, were delighted to fulfil their vows by dispossessing 'bad Christians' who were rich and badly armed.

Perhaps the chief responsibility for the 'diversion' of the Fourth Crusade falls upon the Byzantines. Is it not a mistake to be rich and badly armed? After its triumphs of the tenth century, the old Empire had declined more and more. Not that its peasants had lost their endurance, or its merchants and craftsmen their skills; but they were overwhelmed by taxes, exploited by the nobles, and victimized by Turkish and Slav invasions. What is more, the Byzantine Empire was ill served by that spirit of conservatism which had so long ensured its prosperity. Amidst a rapidly advancing society, whoever slows down is bound to be overtaken. On the eve of the crusades Byzantium was already a 'sick man' and did not realize it. Attacked simultaneously by the Turks in Asia Minor and by the Normans in Europe, the patient was even more seriously threatened by his allies. It would be impossible to decide which of the latter offered the most formidable danger. The knights despised Byzantium's customs and laughed at its armies. As for the mariners, they overcame its navy and attacked the Empire at the very source of its greatness: commerce.

Venice, eldest daughter of Byzantium, dealt it the death-blow: a shocking sight! Yet there was a certain justice in that the heritage of the last representative of the old civilization passed to the earliest independent city: for the future lay with cities opening on to vast horizons.

BOOK 3

MEDIAEVAL EUROPE
AT ITS ZENITH

Chapter 1

OPEN HORIZONS

I. THE REIGN OF PLENTY

'THE population increases every day, and the city spreads out with new build-ings.... The fertility of territory and the abundance of all goods useful for human consumption are evident... Any man here, if he is healthy and not a good-for-nothing, can earn his living with the decorum appropriate to his station... On festive days, when one looks at the merry crowds of dignified men, both of the nobility and of the people, also at the bustling throngs of children incessantly scurrying here and there, and at the comely gatherings, the comely groups of ladies and girls walking back and forth or standing on their doorsteps, as dignified as if they were the daughters of kings, who would say that he has ever met such a wonderful show of people on either side of the sea?'

These words, written in 1288 by Fra Buonvicino della Riva in eulogy of his beloved Milan, are not at all extraordinary in themselves. About a hundred years before, William Fitz-Stephen had extolled with just as much zeal a London which, at the time, numbered about 20,000 inhabitants; and he stressed that founded as it had been by Brutus of Troy, it was 'considerably more ancient than Rome.'

What does make these words of Buonvicino extraordinary is, rather, the fact that they are based on statistics which can be verified from official sources and are, on the whole, worthy of credence — statistics which indicate some 200,000 inhabitants, more than 40,000 citizens capable of bearing arms, 12,500 houses with one or more suites of rooms, more than 1,000 shops, not counting open-air stalls, 120 doctors of Law, almost 200 doctors or surgeons, 25 hospitals through-out town and suburbs, 300 bakeries used by the public and registered at the town hall, approximately 8,800 hectolitres of salt passing through toll each year, 1750 hectolitres of grain ground and taxed daily.... here we may add a graphic, though unstatistical comment: 'In Milan, the animals alone consume as much bread as the entire population in many a large Italian town; in our city, it is a wonderful life for those who have money enough.'

Some comparisons of size

At the end of the 13th century, we see Milan as probably the most populous town in Catholic Europe, but Venice, Florence and Genoa too must assuredly have populations exceeding 100,000 (Fig. 49). Many other Italian towns can count more than 20,000 heads. Today these figures do not make much of an impression on us, but if we consider that around the year 1000 there was perhaps no town in Catholic Europe which could number its population at 10,000, the urban growth of the late Middle Ages becomes comparable with that of the United States during the course of the last two centuries.

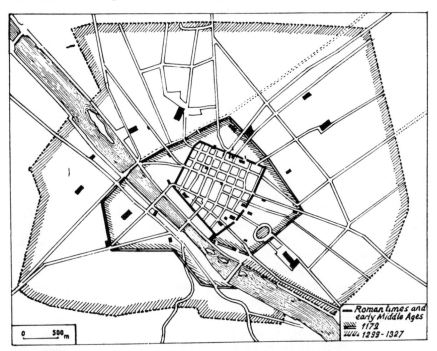

Fig. 49. Plan of Florence at beginning of fourteenth century; Roman boundary, 1172 boundary, and boundary between 1299 and 1327

Outside Italy, we may observe the same phenomenon, albeit in less spectacular proportions. There are but few towns which have not seen expansion of their suburbs and had to extend their boundaries more than once. However, only Paris (with some 80,000 inhabitants?) comes anywhere near the Italian growth-rate.

Let us point out, moreover, that in 1292 it is an Italian, the manager of a branch of a Piacenza bank, who heads the list of Parisian ratepayers, with a taxable income of 5625 pounds. Second to him is another Italian, then comes Pierre Marcel, undoubtedly an ancestor of the famous Etienne Marcel of the 1365 revolution (2900 pounds), and then four more Italians are listed. It is true that the nobility is exempt from tax, whereas foreigners are unmercifully taxed.

Paris, capital of the largest kingdom in Europe and seat of the biggest University, was obviously a special case — a centre consuming goods rather than a centre of production or distribution. Only in the extreme north of the kingdom do we find large towns living exclusively on commerce and industry. Ghent, the most densely populated of all, will have had about 50,000 inhabitants; Arras 20,000. A number of commercial towns with sizeable populations can also be found in the far south, especially in Provence, but in referring to these we have wandered outside the kingdom proper.

In Germany and in England, the populations of centres proudly describing themselves as towns remain below 10,000 and no centre equals the population figure of Ghent. In Catalonia, Barcelona 'is forced into continual expansion as a result of the ships crowding its port' but in the towns on the Christian frontier, as it moves southward, rulers are hard put to it to fill quarters evacuated by Moslems. It is the same in other areas of colonisation, where the optimism of those who start new market towns is often misplaced.

The pulsating life of the large cities

More significant than the number of inhabitants in towns is their dynamic spirit and way of life. The city of the late Middle Ages stands out in sharp relief against the drowsy countryside around it in a way unknown even with Graeco-Roman towns (Pl. 21,).

What, then, are the characteristics of the town? They are abundance, mobility and speed. Scanning the notaries' registers, where the Genoese have all their private commitments recorded, the historian stands amazed. Men and women alike, lonely widows, or children in the care of guardians, clergy, nobles, the ordinary man, all invest their money or their labour in trade, near and far, oversea and overland, or in the crafts, in the bank, in naval construction, in building work; or they speculate in the money exchange and in the shares of the national debt. No article is too mean, or too precious, to be sold in bulk; we have only to turn a few pages to read of a hardware merchant buying 100 chamber pots and of a jeweller selling 111 rings, 169 sapphires and topazes. 348 hard stones, 59 pearls and 132 cameos, one of which contains a fragment of the Holy Cross. Servant lends to master and master to servant. Even with the widest possible distribution of investment, risks remain, but there is practically nobody who does not have a stake in the commercial economy, be it a matter of many thousand pounds, of a few pence, or days and days of work.

The time factor is of crucial importance hence agreements bear not only the day's date, but also the exact time of day. So precious is time that great merchants summon a notary to write contracts on board a ship already to set sail again for distant parts, or they make him work after curfew, far into the night. At this speed, tens of thousands of contracts are signed annually and each year business turnover increases. In 1293 the farmers of the tax on maritime trade anticipated that the value of taxable goods would reach a minimum figure of 3,822,000 pounds for the year, four times the amount for 1275 and, by and large, a figure which represents three and a half times the annual receipts of the French royal treasury for the four previous years (1289–1292).

In Florence, slightly later, evidence from different sources reveals a very similar outlook. Anything may be forgiven here except inertia, and Dante sets apart the most ignominious place in the hereafter for the inactive — 'those who lived without blame and without praise.' Paolo di Messer Pace, that author of a curious work *Book of Good Usages,* gives the following advice to his fellow-citizens: 'If you have money, do not stand still nor keep it at home dead, for it is better unprofitably to act than unprofitably to stand by; because if you act and gain nothing else, you do not lose your trade contacts. And so long as you lose nothing of the capital and maintain your trade contacts, you gain enough.'

In workshop, shop and at the loom, be one rich or poor, work begun in adolescence is continued until death. Even before adolescence, one must have been to school, for the man who cannot 'write his accounts clearly without making mistakes' is not fitted to enter the ranks of the merchants. In Florence, around the year 1336, with an annual birthrate of 5,500–6,000 live births (approximately 5 per 1,000), it is calculated that there are between 8,000 and 10,000 school boys learning to read, more than 1,000 studying mathematics and 550 to 600 grappling with literature and philosophy.

The busy life of lesser centres

Let us stress that the four great Italian towns — Milan, Venice, Genoa and Florence — represent mediaeval urbanism in the same way that New York and London represent contemporary urbanism. They undoubtedly reflect general basic trends, but are by way of being phenomenal cases going well beyond the average, even in Europe's most urbanized country.

Outside Northern and Central Italy, most of the towns, although quietly gathering wealth, are still rural. The periodic market, rather than the permanent shop, is the hub of trading activity. There, no distinction is drawn between banker and pawnbroker, and the lower middle class rubs shoulders with the aristocracy without consorting with it; and when the harvest is ripe, townsmen go out to lend a hand to the country-man. It is true that centres like Cologne, Bruges,

Fig. 50. Clocktower, from the Villard de Honnecourt sketchbook, Bibliothèque Nationale, Paris.

Southampton, Toulouse and Seville are already aware of both the advantages and the problems of metropolitan life, but the tempo of life there is scarcely any faster than it is in numerous Italian towns of secondary proportions, such as Siena, Pisa, Piacenza, Verona.

In fact, there were many factors which seemed to mark Italy out for an avant-garde position in this multifarious commercial revolution of the late Middle Ages — such as the survival of urban tradition during the barbarian age, the fluidity of social classes, the early appearance of municipal autonomies, easy contact with developed societies, Byzantine and Moslem, together with a peculiar shortage of agricultural resources which very early on forced enterprising men to look further afield. No one of these advantages by itself, however, could guarantee pre-eminence lasting for centuries. Southern Italy, which had been first to forge ahead, was also first in allowing itself to be overtaken by Northern Italy. In the North itself, towns such as Pavia and Ravenna, former capital cities of the *pars longobarda* and *pars romana* before the time of Charles the Great, were caught up with and overtaken by a rival which, so to speak, had no history — Florence. And whereas Venice and Genoa were almost obliged, by reason of their natural barriers, to seek outlets by sea, Milan might well have been satisfied with the exploitation of her own territory, one of the most fertile in the world. The constant urge for more, on the part of Milan, was due to what was sometimes called 'the innate industrious spirit' of its inhabitants.

Economy and architecture

Actually this spirit of industry was by no means lacking in other countries, but in them it was spread over too many fields. In Paris it nurtured Philosophy, Literature, Art, public administration and Court life; it is not surprising that trade and industry were sacrificed amid so many enthusiasms.

Let us pause a while at Beauvais, where we have a significant, but simpler, example. The chief town in a very rich agricultural district, Beauvais in the 12th century was engaged in the manufacture of woollen cloths famous throughout Europe. New fulling mills were set up there in large numbers at the end of the century. At the beginning of the 13th century it became necessary to set the walls of the town wider and, to judge by its finances, Beauvais was then and remained for more than fifty years, the second richest city in the Royal domain, after Paris. In 1259–1260 the town paid to Louis IX, in two instalments, a poll-tax of 3,500 pounds (Amiens, its immediate follower, paid 1,237 pounds) and at the same time Beauvais was preparing to redeem a national debt of 6,129 pounds, a sum modest in itself, but higher than that for other French communes. Then, suddenly, a spring snapped. True, the fulling mills did not come to a halt, and the surrounding countryside still enjoyed that good order which Beaumanoir idealized in his *Coutumes du Beauvaisis*, that monument to French feudal and administrative law, composed by a man who was acquainted with both Roman and canonical jurisprudence. But the population remained stationary. Industry did not continue to develop, as it did in Flanders. The Commune kept going by means of expedients, barely avoiding bankruptcy.

Clearly, then, this is the problem: why, after such a promising beginning, did Beauvais not profit from the atmosphere of general prosperity, unlike most other towns, who went forging ahead during the second half of the 13th century?

An answer may perhaps be sought in its splendid cathedral. Although incomplete, it still overshadows the modest private houses around it as if to crowd them out of a place in the sun (Pl. 20). Beauvais was well provided with imposing churches already existing when the Bishop and Chapter decided to construct another, surpassing in height all other cathedrals of the time. Work was begun in 1247, but suffered an interruption in 1284 when the main arches, too boldly constructed, crumbled. It immediately began again, and the cost, in a mere fifteen years, amounted to 80,000 pounds. Admittedly, it was not the citizens who footed the bill—they could not have afforded it. Nonetheless, the capital which the bishops and clergy were tying up in stone came from their taxes and from local revenue. Serfs and wage-earners alike dedicated to the ambitious cathedral hours, days, weeks and years of toil, which could have been invested in industrial and commercial production.

Italy, although much richer, has no parallel example. The wealthy town of Venice begrudged nothing in the way of gold or marble for St Mark's, but the actual building was spread over centuries and some of the priceless decorations were prizes from Constantinople. In the 13th century, the inhabitants of Milan built a new town hall; the idea of building a new cathedral did not occur to them. In Genoa, the bishop made do with a modest cathedral, leaving his tithes to reap their harvest in trade. At San Gimignano, a town about equal in importance to Beauvais, church towers were dwarfed by proud and privately-owned turrets, and it was the same at Lucca. (Pl. 20).

Nevertheless, the case of Beauvais was not unique in Europe. The passion for building ever higher, ever larger, spread from country to country. Hundreds of medium-sized or small urban centres sought to out-do each other, constructing enormous piles and covering them with sculpture and decorating them with stained glass. Similarly, a thousand years before, hundreds of Roman municipalities had vied with one another in the building of baths and theatres, which were out of all proportion to their needs and resources. Even then, it was the middle classes who paid the bill, not with money but with lost opportunities, and many a municipality ended by becoming insolvent.

It is true to say that 'Art has no price.' Let us give due admiration to Roman theatres and Gothic cathdrals; let us acknowledge the humanism that built the theatres and the faith which inspired the cathedrals, for nothing could be more just, but let us not forget, all the same, the enormous sacrifices thus imposed on economies as yet incapable of producing a sizable surplus. Economically speaking, it would have been wiser to wait for a surplus before investing so heavily in the realms of art. Not everyone will be convinced by the cold logic of such a conclusion. It seems paltry to haggle where beauty or faith are concerned. One would fain reject the views of the materialists by proving to them that this art, so dear to us, produced nonetheless its own not inconsiderable revenue. Alas, however, there is no argument which will hold good.

Religious buildings, we are told, gave work to masons and architects, encouraged pilgrimages and fostered tourism, then as now. Indeed, there is no paid work — even if economically unproductive — which is not of benefit to someone or other. Productive labour, however, has the added advantage that it in turn creates new opportunities for work. A permanent market hall, a market square, a bridge — such as were built everywhere to some extent in the 13th century, but especially in Italy and Belgium — can very well combine the useful with the aesthetic (Pl. 25 and 26).

As far as pilgrimages are concerned, they are more bound up with relics themselves than with the jewelled caskets in which these repose. Stripped of the venerable remains of St James, or the miraculous picture of the Blessed Virgin, the artistic splendours of the cathedrals at Compostela and Le Puy would not have attracted one single pilgrim.

In the Middle Ages, tourism was no more than a feeble movement and, even in modern times, the hotel industry is not enough to guarantee Venice that economic pre-eminence of which she was assured of old by a port bursting with ships and by the unceasing labours of her weavers.

Rome, for centuries a centre of tourism, of pilgrimage and art, is not and never was a centre of commerce or industry of any importance.

> But, someone will say, did the great buildings of the 13th century not appease the hunger and thirst of men for God? Of course they did; but faith did not call for such extravagance. The very humble church of St Francis of Assisi was adequate in the sight of God. Granted, there were some of the faithful who desired to express their gratitude to the Creator in loftier spires and colours yet more brilliant, but the moral worth of the offering was dependent only on the intention which prompted it. Besides, gifts were not always disinterested, nor were they always spontaneous. When parishioners of Andres, near Boulogne, were proving somewhat reluctant in the payment of 100 marks they had promised for a new abbey church, the Abbot ordered saucepans and cooking pots to be seized from every household. At Beauvais, work on the cathedral was punctuated by revolts against the bishop; in 1305, his chapel became the object of special attention and the rebels looted and desecrated, defiling and despoiling anything they could not carry off.

Townspeople versus lords

In order to exploit to the full a favourable situation it was not enough to put all available resources to profitable economic use; it was just as necessary to eliminate the dead weight accumulated by a feudal and rural society on top of that somewhat negligible quantity which formerly was the urban society.

Yearning as they are for wider horizons, the bourgeois classes in Europe are bound to come into conflict with established authorities at every level: bishops, abbots, counts, marquesses, kings, emperors and popes. On the whole, they do not rebel against the authorities as such; conflict arises because they jib at payment of taxes which profit them nothing, at obeying laws which completely disregard their interests, at fighting wars which paralyse their trade and lay waste their lands solely for the benefit of the lord — if of anybody. It matters little to them that the gain, if any, takes on the shape of a new cathedral or castle or that one province more is added to the royal domain.

They are demanding, both for themselves and for others, freedom of movement; they want their goods to circulate without being subject to tariffs and other forms of tax which are too numerous and too heavy. They desire that merchants shall come and go without stop or hindrance, and that those who wish to emigrate to a town and enrich it with capital, intelligence and skill shall be able to do so without being immediately held back by the enforcement of old bonds of servitude or vassalship.

In the beginning demands put forward were of a practical moderate kind; but appetite grows with what it feeds on and it was because these claims were too long disregarded that they passed from a purely practical plane into the realms of ideology.

Every town has had its own particular story in these constant disturbances. Incidents and the demands which provoke them vary as between town and town, as do the authorities who have to be fought and the length of the struggle — or the precise scope of the ultimate victory. The victory in turn will be exploited by each town more or less fruitfully according to whatever opportunities present themselves by reason of its geography or the energies of its inhabitants — and these also vary from place to place. Still, without a minimum of self-government, there is little room for manoeuvre. Absolute liberty represents the ideal condition for a strong and harmonious community, but where a commune is weak and divided against itself, it has its dangers.

In this very varied picture a few predominant trends emerge, nevertheless, in each country. In the greater part of Western Europe the bourgeois classes are seeking to wrest a certain degree of self-government from their immediate overlords at the price of increased subjection to the person of the king — a remote person and, therefore, a less exacting one. The Communes tend to insinuate themselves into the feudal pyramid by means of freedom charters putting a seal on a compromise rather than a decisive victory. Each article of the charter defines, on the one hand, a right already acquired, but on the other, a limit which is not to be overstepped. The least free of all, perhaps, are those towns in England who are often content to redeem, for a fixed annual sum (*firma burgi*), local taxes and basic costs of administration and justice. On the other hand, even if less free, they are peaceful; the English king is capable of exacting obedience from all.

In Germany, by contrast, the disintegration of the monarchy, while giving freedom to the towns, leaves them at the mercy of the feudal lords, often more powerful than they. There they are, like oases in the midst of hostile territory, trying with varying degrees of success to support each other by the formation of regional leagues. This struggle will continue well into the 14th century. And victory will not necessarily go to the largest cities, but to those leagues best protected by natural obstacles (such as the rural and urban cantons in Switzerland) or to those who will join forces with one lord or another in a joint expansion programme (like the Hansa towns).

In Flanders and in Provence, conflict between the local lords and those in distant parts creates specially favourable conditions which allow the Communes to wax strong without, however, acquiring total independence. Even the spectacular victory of the bourgeois foot soldiers at the Battle of the Golden Spurs at Courtrai in 1302 will not prove decisive enough to sever all the bonds by which the Flemish communes are attached to their overlords.

Only in Italy, between the Alps and the Tiber, do the towns become absolute masters of their fate. They need no charters of freedom; they had made sure of their independence as early as 1176 at Legnano. The feudal nobility has no choice but to bow before the laws of the communes or disappear. The whole territory (apart from a few valleys lost high in the mountains) belongs to the communes and from now on, they have nought to fear except their own appetite, which can cause weak towns to fall into the power of strong ones or impel those strong cities to devour each other.

Political emancipation and economic expansion go hand in hand along parallel roads. Those communes enjoying the greatest freedom are nearly always also the largest and the most prosperous. All urban Europe is astir, with Italy in the forefront: and as we cannot dwell at length on all the variations in the different regions, it is, therefore, to Italy that we shall give the major part of our attention.

II.   THE STATE AS A BUSINESS ENTERPRISE

The Renaissance princes, we are told in a famous work, ruled their states 'like works of art'. It would be equally proper to say that the mediaeval townsmen ruled their states 'like business enterprises.' Their politics were steered for economic goals.

This trend is visible ever since the early stages of urban revival around the year 1000 and becomes evident when self-government is organized, usually under the name of community or 'commune.' It is not the result of any conscious political doctrine as much as the outcome of practical considerations. Nearly always in Italy, and frequently in other countries, urban communes begin their career as voluntary private associations. Their political powers sprout from illegitimate origins even when they are not contrary to law.

From temporary private association to permanent body politic

The birth date of the earliest communes is usually unknown: before we come across a document with the technical name of 'commune', a self-governing community has existed for some time and has survived its critical early days. There may be no birth date at all: a group of influential citizens who have been accustomed to advising and helping the local ruler gradually take over the reins, and a commune emerges quietly. More often, however, a commune is the child of riot and revolution: a number of citizens combine their efforts to forward their private interests through political action, take an oath to support each other, obey the leaders they have chosen and sworn in, and conform to certain rules of their own doing. In these cases, such terms as *coniuratio,* conspiracy, or commune may appear as early as the tenth century; but the conspiracy is crushed, dissolved or absorbed into a larger one. To become a full-fledged commune, the conspiracy had to outgrow the parent clique, obtain an oath of allegiance from all the inhabitants of the town and the surrounding district, and fulfill the ordinary tasks of government; this, even in the earliest and strongest cities of Northern and Central Italy, does not happen before the late 11th century (Map 16).

Naturally the positions of command are initially given to the highest-born, the richest or the most powerful among the 'conspirators.' So long as commerce is not yet in full swing, it is primarily a case of members of the lesser feudal nobility who owned suburban land, invested in trade and lived in town. In this sense, but only in this sense, can one refer to the communes as having an aristocratic origin. Moreover, a distinction is often made between mounted and foot soldiers, or between 'the better, the middle ones and the smaller'; but these inequalities of status are not insuperable. One is a member of the community by contributing what he can, in whatever way he can; his niche in the organization does not depend on birth, but on the importance of the contribution.

As time goes by, the fact that a town must be entitled to some kind of self-government will be taken for granted, even outside Italy. Kings and vassals will include a communal charter among the conveniences offered to settlers on newly founded villages, usually a copy of a standard pattern (law of Lorris in France, law of Magdeburg beyond the Elbe); but these liberties fell short of the hard-won freedom of communes born through conspiracies. Even these never lost some of the characteristics of voluntary and private associations. The Commune can face up to bishops, counts and kings; it can gain total independence, but it does not deny the theoretical paramountcy of pre-existing authorities. These are responsible for the highest duties assigned to Church and State by the political doctrine of the age; Justice, Peace and Religion are the province of the Pope and the Emperor (or king). The municipal administration does not feel obliged to cope with the higher problems of justice, peace or religion except in so far as it has to protect the interests of the community. A law promulgated as late as 1369 expresses in the frankest terms the indestructible nature of the difference between the State, a moral entity, and the urban state, an economic reality.... 'Against these who claim that exchange and insurance agreements are usurious according to Scripture and who appeal to Church courts to get them rejected...... whereas if such agreements were not honoured then citizens and merchants of Genoa would suffer great loss.... let whosoever invokes this kind of plea be sentenced in all justice to pay one half of one pound [as a fine] for each pound that he shall have refused to pay.'

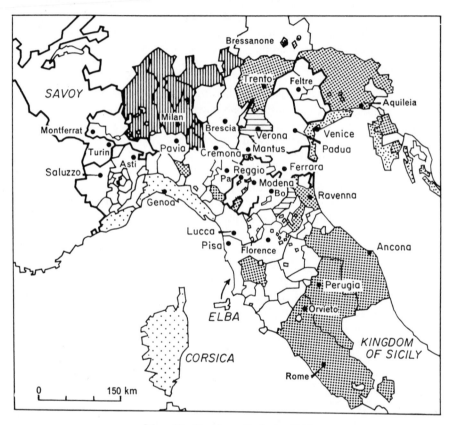

Map 16. Northern Italy in 1300

Communal institutions: how far democratic?

The urban commune is equipped with the same means of government as the sovereign state; assembly, councils and executive body. The plenary assembly of all free citizens takes place on the main square, with more informality than a royal assembly. It votes by acclamation on matters concerning war, peace or laws of vital importance. It is true that as the commune grows, so does the size of such a gathering increase, and in consequence plenary assemblies will become less frequent and less effective all the time.

Their decline coincides with an increase in the power of more limited bodies, the greater and smaller councils. Like lesser Senates, they sit periodically, make their deliberations under the arches of the town hall or in a closed room. They recruit their members by every conceivable means: from the most important families; from legal experts, through the intermediary of electors delegated by the plenary assembly; by direct nomination entrusted to the chief magistrates; by indirect election under the patronage of ecclesiastics of irreproachable character; by drawing lots, on recommendation from wards or town gilds. Inevitably, the plenary assembly is open to tumults and threats. The councils, by contrast, are protected from this by reason of the fact that their meetings are secluded. Before long, they will vote by secret ballot, using beans or balls of different colours.

As for the supreme executive power, it is usually vested in a body of colleagues at least in the early stages. Later, outside Italy, the majority of these colleges will have a president or a 'major' (mayor, maire, burgmeister), usually drawn from the ranks of their own particular social class. Some Italian towns of Byzantine origin also have presidents, but these come from a different stem: that of former officials of the Imperial government who have lost their earlier authority when their offices became elective. A familiar instance of this is that of the Duke, or Doge, of Venice. Here, self-government begins earlier than in Lombardy, but democracy comes slowly.

In the Lombard cities no one presides over the college of Consuls. Their title evokes grand old memories of Rome, but in reality derives its origin from the word' Counsellor.' The consuls, whose number varies from two to more than twenty, are generally elected for one year and are not eligible for immediate re-election. The supreme civil and military powers are equally shared between them, as also are financial and judicial responsibilities. This aspect of the office, at the same time temporary and pluralist, is designed both to prevent the magistrate from becoming a despot, and to preclude as far as possible the danger that the management of public affairs might provide him with unlimited opportunities to forward his own private affairs. There will be other precautions too before much time has passed. As soon as they lay down their seals of office, Consuls will be required to give public account of their administration.

Generally speaking, municipal governments did not constitute either the golden age imagined by nostalgic writers of succeeding centuries (including the 19th), nor yet the tyrannical and oppresive regime which historians closer to our day have described. By comparison with any other political structure, prior to the American and French Revolutions, the government of the communes was the one which offered to the greatest number of people the opportunity of airing their views in matters of public affairs. Compared with the monarchies of the period, it deserves to be singled out — let us express it in these terms — as an effort to establish a progressive democracy. True, the public square, meeting place of the plenary assembly, was not an ideal setting for the expression of public opinion, but it did offer a rostrum for anyone who had the breath and the courage to speak; royal assemblies even when they were summoned were only for those who were invited. Counsellors and chief magistrates, although not elected by universal suffrage, were more representative of the mass of citizens than were the elected members of parliament in England and France during the twilight of the Middle Ages. In those parliaments, moreover, the 'elected' members only constituted a minority.

Obviously, communal democracy was not, and had no desire to be, egalitarian and total. Any claim to absolute equality would have seemed a revolt against the very order of things laid down by God himself, author of man's inequality. On this point, the opinion of the common man differed but little from that of the aristocrat. In communes, as in kingdoms, it was not absolute majority that was sought after, but rather, according to the definition given at the beginning of the 14th century by Marsil of Padua, the great political writer, 'the general agreement of the worthiest part.' In the communes, however, worth was not dependent on circumstances of birth and was not limited to a narrow minority. It was a goal to be won, and not a barrier which one had to climb over. The poor could reach this goal by becoming rich, the weak by taking up arms, the inhabitants of rural areas could achieve it by emigrating to the city and living there for some length of time. While none of these conditions was simple to fulfill, none of them was impossible either, at a period when the economy was expanding, when communal armed forces needed considerable numbers of infantrymen, when the constant cry of the towns was for manpower.

Political instability

This hope of promotion in the social scale, and even more the lack of well-defined rules for the election of magistrates or for the calculation of valid majorities, condemned these urban democracies to a restless and most unstable existence.

In a state governed by businessmen and used by them to further the prosperity of their own interests, the deepest roots of all social and political strife could be none other than economic. Public office was tempting; whosoever held one manipulated wars and treaties, levied and distributed taxes, contracted for supplies and loans, sat in judgement on trade issues, regulated pay and conditions of labour, without forgetting for one instant the interests of his own family or his own advantage. On surface, however, the alleged causes of strife originated from differing ideologies, from social rivalry, and from personal antagonism. Hypocrisy? Yes and no. It was at that time, as it is in these days, impossible to distinguish between conflict of interests and conflict of passions. The reasons which induced a citizen to embrace one party rather than another frequently remained mysterious — even in his own mind.

Fig. 51. Genoa: battle on three levels between the occupants of the two towers, 1194, from a miniature from the Annales Januenses, *Bibliothèque Nationale, Paris.*

No single-tracked explanation will account for the intricacies of the political alignment inside a commune. For it would be naive, for example, to accept at face value the tradition of chroniclers who attribute to a broken engagement and the ensuing blood feud the origin of parties in Florence, yet equally naive to believe that an insult of this kind was a mere cover for a premeditated political manoeuvre. Again, the fact that one party embraced the Guelf cause and the other the Ghibelline one certainly cannot be ascribed to selfless love of some for the Pope and others for the Emperor, but even if it could be proved that expediency alone dictated the choice of partners, a marriage of political convenience may produce a sincere devotion to a cause. Beneath such labels as Guelf and Ghibelline in Italy, Catholic and Cathar in Languedoc, royalist and partisan of the Count of Flanders in Belgium, one may notice the preferences of specific economic, social or professional classes, but no one class identifies itself wholly and constantly with a party as such.

In short, whatever the motives or pretexts, almost every town was rocked by conflict and disturbance, which spread rapidly from one town to another, creating a network of regional alliances and counter-alliances. Most particularly, Italy north of the Tiber was a veritable chessboard, where Guelf communes and Ghibelline communes alternated regularly, and each city fought its neighbours with the assistance of its neighbours' neighbours. All this, however, was no worse than feudal wars, where commoners would have been mere pawns.

Peace is better than war, but conflict is a proof of vitality. Inside every commune, citizens were at last awake to political problems. By dividing themselves into parties, they started a debate which was exasperating, yet indispensable for democratic expression. Unruly as it was, the debate foreshadowed that endless two-party contest between Conservatives and Liberals (or Socialists), or between Republicans and Democrats, which is so characteristic of modern parliamentary life. Even on the international plane, the appearance of two rival blocs, each intent on its own advancement, did not preclude peaceful co-existence, a striving for balance of power or efforts to triumph over each other by means other than war.

Unfortunately, the Italian communes were not sufficiently experienced to maintain internal and external equilibrium in this political balancing game, 'Every house has a tower', writes Rabbi Benjamin of Tudela concerning Genoa in 1172, 'and when war breaks out among them, the terraces on the towers' tops become battlefields.' (Fig. 51).

In vain the heads of communes try to deter such battles by ordering that the fortified house of some rebellious citizen be razed to the ground as a prelude to sending him into exile. It is just as futile for bishops and monks to exhort the whole population to lay down their fratricidal arms and exchange the kiss and oath of peace with their enemies; it is to no avail that the temporarily victorious side tries to conciliate the vanquished by a generous armistice, or, more often, endeavours to annihilate them completely by excluding them from public office and sentencing their leaders to very heavy penalties, usually in their absence.

Whether it be under old names or new labels, no longer Guelph or Ghibelline, but Black or White, Capulets or Montagues, dissensions still arise. There is always another town (a neighbour, hence an enemy) only too pleased to welcome refugees and to plot with them for revenge for the latest battle fought and lost for control of a road, or a mine, or a trading post. Moreover, since trade and industrial rivalries go even deeper than partisan feelings, it is not unusual for a top-level change of side in a commune to spark off a change in the opposite direction in neighbouring communes; if Bologna become Guelph, Modena will become Ghibelline. What matters is that the fight shall go on, usually with little bloodshed, but with the maximum damage to the economy of the enemy commune.

> Amid such chaos, the largest cities prevail over those with smaller populations, and within each city there are new men pushing their way to the forefront. The situation would be tragic were it not for the fact that for the vanquished also there are some compensations in economic expansion. In spite of the humiliation of seeing themselves beaten by upstarts or recent immigrants, members of ancient families fallen from power can recoup their fortunes in their own town, or, if it holds memories too bitter to be borne, in a nearby commune. The conquered towns, even if irrevocably surpassed by a richer and more powerful competitor, find a way of increasing their own wealth, albeit more slowly, by exploiting those branches of industry and trade of which the dominant town does not hold a monopoly.

Even the conquest of one commune by another does not occasion any great constitutional changes. Like ancient Rome, the Italian city-state of the Middle

Ages does not aim at the suppression of local autonomy in subject towns. At most, it reserves the right to appoint or confirm the appointment of their chief magistrates. The dominant town takes over the direction of external policy and defence, and also reserves for its own citizens a particularly coveted sector of the economy, such as long-distance voyages in particular areas, import and export of certain specific commoditites, or the manufacture of a particular type of cloth. In other respects, satellite cities, treated as allies, plainly benefit from inclusion in a larger and more diversified territory.

Thus at the beginning of the 14th century, Genoa controls almost all of Liguria, and Milan a large part of Lombardy; Florence commands half the Arno valley, Venice a chain of ports and islands, and Pisa a piece of the Tuscan coast. Fifteen centuries before, confederations of similar scope had paved the way for the much greater federal union over which Rome would preside; but in the late Middle Ages there were too many cities aiming at control and these were roughly equal in importance. Their rivalries resulted in no more than a precarious balance between the strongest of them.

New experiments, new disappointments

In every town, the advent to power of the lower classes was characterised by great upheaval and change. The most singular of these changes was, in Italy and in Provence, the creation of the office of Podesta. The Podesta, a salaried administrator, took the place of the consuls or was appointed above them, initially in exceptional years and later every year. His duties vaguely resembled those of the *city manager* appointed nowadays in many American towns. One appealed to the Podesta as to an impartial judge, who was above party strife, unaffected by preconceived ideas, and free to administer and to pass judgement in a town where he himself had no ties. As a further guarantee, it was obligatory for him to linger in town after the expiration of his term of office until such time as he had rendered an account of his administration.

Some Podestas had the honour of seeing their portraits, painted at the expense of the town council, adorning the walls of the town hall. Others, rightly or wrongly, had the hard luck of suffering fines or imprisonment, or were forced to flee as a result of bodily threats. Despite the hopes which impelled commune after commune, between the middle of the 12th century and the middle of the 13th, to try a system of Podestas, it was finally borne in on them that a stranger, often ill-informed and generally inadequately supported, could not be asked to perform the double miracle of establishing peace in the city and ensuring a fair deal for all. Actually the confusion grew worse: as towns became larger and richer, the number of complainants and the variety of complaints increased, and both the rivalries between dominant families and the restlessness of those who failed to be admitted to the governing circle were embittered.

About 1250 (and as early as 1198 in the case of more advanced Milan), many disgruntled citizens lost confidence in the habitual and continual new growth

which swept into public office the more conspicuous of the nouveaux-riches,
alongside old families of grandees or 'magnates'. Instead of setting their sights
squarely on communal government, they organised a government of their own
closely resembling it. This state within the state was based generally on corporations of craftsmen already in existence and endowed with assemblies,
councils and magistrates, much like those of the commune. People called it the
'Lesser Commune' or 'People's Commune.' It was sometimes led by a college
of Gild Priors (similar to consuls) or, more frequently, by a People's Captain,
drawn from outside (similar to the Podesta). By degrees, this para-government
assumed the functions of the real government or even completely replaced it,
sometimes as the result of a series of peaceable reforms, seldom without the
backing of some popular revolution.

Fig. 52. The Podesta of Genoa
ordering the demolition of the
luxurious house of a rebellious
citizen; from Annales Januenses,
Bibliothèque Nationale, Paris.

Notwithstanding its name, the People's Government did not hoist into the
saddle the poverty-stricken lower class — the 'lean ones', as Florence
picturesquely described them — who had taken their part in the revolutions, but rather the upper-middle class 'fat ones' who had been their
leaders. By income and inclinations, these people were associated more
with the magnates than the proletariat. Yet the well-fed, triumphant
bourgeois rendered manifold services to the whole community: they suppressed the gravest abuses in the administration of justice and in the
distribution of taxation, and they adapted to urban government those
efficient practices which they had brought to perfection in the administration of their own businesses.

Although more alive to problems of the lower classes and more flexible
than the magnates, the 'fat ones' were also more stingy — and while they
did not wish the poor to go hungry, they were fearful lest the 'lean ones'
should 'fatten up' enough to carry as much weight as their employers. So
they tightened up the control which professional capitalists had over the
manual trades. At the same time, however, they set in motion accelerated
programmes of public works and assistance for the needy. Unemploy-
ment and poverty were breeding grounds for new revolts. Similarly, with
a view to forestalling counter-revolutions, they barred the magnates from
public office. This was an important symbolic gesture, like the abolition
of titles in some modern democracies, but it had only a limited value in

practice. The magnates, in fact, could circumvent the restrictions by becoming members, like everyone else, of a gild of 'men of the people.' Despite these precautions, the People's Commune, threatened from above and below, was tossed like a shuttlecock between those who had already reached the top and those who were striving to get there — or to return where they had been.

Ultimately, in some towns, impatience and lack of confidence on the part of the citizens suggested a solution similar to the calling in of a People's Captain, but a solution of despair: the acclamation of a dictator (*Signore*) who would put discipline into constitutional institutions without destroying them. In most cases, however, these 13th century dictators did not establish roots; as long as economic expansion went on, any form of government was prone to fresh about-turns on the part of the ever waxing people. Personal rule still was acceptable only as a temporary expedient in time of crisis.

Let us mention, however, one instance, at the end of the 13th century, of the success of the authoritarian principle; the transformation of the Venetian oligarchy (comprising old 'magnates' and nouveaux-riches) into a permanent collective dictatorship — a success due, let it be clearly stated, to an extraordinarily high degree of self-discipline and moderation. The men in the government devoted their energies to maintenance of good order and the prosperity of the community as a whole, mercilessly suppressing attempts among members of their own group to further personal ambition and abandoning with good grace to the lower strata of society those offices which although lucrative were devoid of political importance, and inviting, as it were, each and every citizen to the banquet table.

Throughout Europe 'life' signifies 'strife'

Outside Italy, a fair number of oligarchies entrenched themselves in the government of towns. Let us not however compare these wizened fruits to the lush Venetian oligarchy — the fruit of a political sagacity which foresees and eliminates discontent. More often than not, the nerveless calm which exists in many communes is a symptom of slow economic and social development. Self-government is beyond repair; there is not even the hope that a local dictator may restrain the abuses of the ruling clique, the lower classes may only rely on the levelling justice of the king or a feudal lord. 'We have seen many a dispute, in fine towns...... poor against rich or even the rich against each other;' says Beaumanoir, 'neither the poor nor those in the middle have any part in the administration of the town.... they do not really know how to pursue their rights.' Consequently, 'good towns.... and the common people must be under [royal] guardianship.'

Let us repeat: to say 'life' is to say 'strife.' In certain urban centres, across Europe, the first oligarchic leaders are at each other's throats, teeth bared, and are soon caught and supplanted by new oligarchies, who are themselves swept away by new revolutions. The more a town prospers, the more do its troubles remind us of those of the Italian towns, though they seldom equal the intense and dramatic political life of those towns.

How could we possibly make reference to all the hundreds of constitutions and revolutions? Even for a description of trends prevailing in the main regions of Europe, we should need an entire volume. Each town is a world on its own, reflecting in its own way the greater world outside. Each community is small enough to allow all its members to know one another, large enough to include every degree in the social hierarchy, imaginative enough to seek its own formula for overall liberty ensuring, *in theory*, that individual liberties shall rot be trodden underfoot.

III.   FREEDOM FOR THE POOR

The most difficult of all liberties to achieve and to maintain is that of the lowly — the lowliest of all being the peasants. In most cases, their fate is not directly bound up with that of the commune of the city, whose control barely extends beyond the outskirts of the town. Italy north of the Tiber is the only European region where the commune dominates almost all the countryside around.

There the commune administers the land, in the interests of trading efficiency, without unreasonable harshness, yet with scant tenderness towards the peasants. Serfdom has no place in urban law, though it may be tolerated whenever and wherever it has a purpose to serve. Serfs entering the city become automatically free, and emancipation for them is regarded with favour throughout the territory. Freedom, however, has a price: they shall pay taxes, produce food and raw materials without feudal interference, and provide cheap manpower, of which the urban economy has an insatiable need. Similarly, the commune does not permit mass immigration of peasants, for the country also needs labourers; nor must they set up rural industries in competition with those of the town, or sell their grain outside the commune unless its shops have been stocked up first at a predetermined price. Protests are useless; workers on the land have no more opportunity of expressing their opinions under the bourgeoisie than they had under the aristocracy.

In Italy: increased mobility and well-being

However, freedom of contracts and of movement which allows the more enterprising peasants to choose both their lands and their employers, or to seek their fortune in town, constitutes in itself a decided advantage. In Italy north of the Tiber, this freedom gains strength from the individualistic traditions of Mediterranean agriculture and from Roman law; it finds employment through the demand of the towns (there is an insatiable hunger for men and materials from the rural areas) and it is enhanced by the open opportunities and open-mindedness of the urban society. 'He was a mighty lord; his dogs loved him much:' thus does an ingenuous bard extolling the chivalrous life in France imagine his hero, master of countless serfs. But the glossator of Bologna, Azzo, a contemporary of this poet, looks around him with eyes that see and expresses thus his compassion: 'In this our day the peasants are in a state more pitiable than I can describe; they are worn out and starving.'

> From this point of view, one may say that the decrees of collective en-franchisement published by many Italian communes during the 13th century were well-meant, even if not entirely innocent of ulterior motive. The first of those decrees is the 'Concord' solemnly sworn in 1210 in the public square at Assisi, possibly in the presence of St. Francis, and certainly with his approval. Grouped together in the great brotherhood of a peace pact, 'greater' and 'lesser' citizens abolish serfdom and all feudal rights in the territory of the commune. Former masters, however, receive compensation and retain ownership of land. In 1257, the 'Memorial' of Bologna, 'which must in all justice be said to be inspired by Paradise', goes one step further. Just as in Paradise, before original sin, Man was born free, so has every inhabitant of the state of Bologna a natural right to liberty. The commune 'which has always fought for liberty' will pay to former masters a compensation of 10 pounds per adult and 8 pounds for minors of less than 14 years; after which the freedmen will be registered on the list of taxpayers. A Paradise indeed — but with taxes.

With or without decrees, serfdom by the end of the 13th century has virtually disappeared from the entire region between the Alps and the Tiber, and the standard of living of the peasants has gone up considerably. Under the influence of the cities, literacy, payments in cash and specialized agriculture penetrate one village after another, domestic industry makes its appearance, rural gilds of the simpler crafts and rural stores are being organized. The townspeople build roads, canals, bridges, mills, admittedly for their own purposes, but not without benefit for the country people, be they independent farmers, free tenants, sharecroppers or hired hands. Much land is now owned and rationally exploited by the bourgeoisie; around 1305 a Bolognese judge and landowner, Pietro de Crescenzi, writes a remarkable manual of agriculture indicating both the survival of the best Roman practices and the introduction of new techniques. The diet of the farmer has improved. More important still, all peasants are getting into the habit of wearing a shirt — a most common item of clothing today, a new luxury at that time. . . and one that can be washed.

Towns and peasants in the rest of Europe

Outside Italy, the influence of urban communities has been more limited, for better or for worse. Here and there, competition from rural craftsmen has however provoked some conflict with the town gilds. In Belgium, the cities themselves organise armed expeditions into the villages, to destroy or carry off looms and fulling apparatus; in England, where towns are less powerful, appeals are made to the king, asking him to forbid weaving in country areas.

The task of supplying food for the town is less acute than in Italy: those peasants who live within the town walls and till the suburban fields are often enough to solve the problem. But the standard of living of the rural classes also rises more slowly than in Italy, and the emancipation of serfs is not always complete, though the territory of the communes is smaller.

Beyond the tiny urban State stretch the estates of the aristocracy, the clergy and the king, and here the fate of the peasants lies at the mercy of the masters. Even when they are represented in the assemblies of a kingdom, the towns do not intervene between serf and master. In 1281 the Barcelona parliament ratified a royal decree forbidding the peasants to leave their lands without first paying an indemnity. Thus it is that right into the 14th century we still find great numbers of serfs at the gates of the largest Catalonian commune.

In heavily urbanized Flanders, on the other hand, rural serfdom is already on the way out by the end of the 13th century. What is more, Flemish peasants transport freedom with them into the colonisation areas beyond the Elbe. But, in these cases, it is difficult to say if the atmosphere of liberty derives from the example of the towns or from a necessity to give preferential treatment to the pioneers of cultivation in the swamps of Flanders and the virgin territories of the East.

Growth and problems of the woollen industry

Even if the bourgeoisie did not do for the peasants all that it might have done, it would be unfair to blame it for a poverty which was not of its creating.

True — but what shall we say concerning that other poverty, for which the upper classes are directly responsible — the misery of the urban proletariat? The trade revolution of the late Middle Ages, in such small measure as it also constituted an industrial revolution, faced the same problems as the modern Industrial Revolution. Let us see how it solved them — or left them unsolved.

Let us take the most typical case, or perhaps the most aggravating — that of the woollen industry (Maps 17 and 18). By reason of the manpower it employs, the complexity of its operation, the volume of its products, it is the only mediaeval industry which may be compared — from a distance, it is true — to the great industries of modern times. In Florence at the outset of the 14th century, production will be more than 100,000 pieces of cloth a year, coming from some 300 workshops. Thirty years later, the number of workshops is reduced to 200 and that of the pieces to about 75,000, but these are of better quality, with the result that the woollen industry, with a turnover of a million florins, is providing a livelihood, we are told, for a quarter of the urban population. The Lombardy towns concentrate on more ordinary cloth or a mixture of wool and cotton. The quantity they produce is probably greater, but its market value is lower.

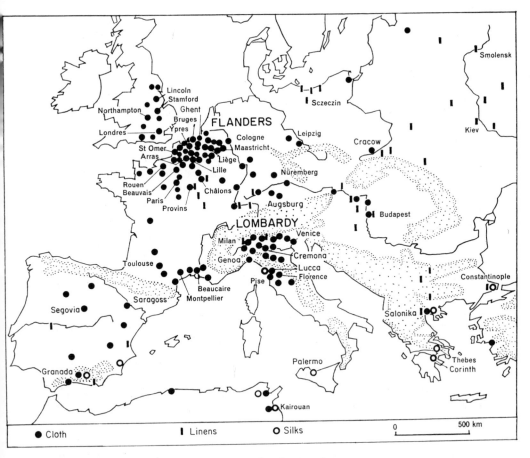

Map 17. Textile centres in Europe in the thirteenth century

The English towns, on the other hand, manufacture expensive cloth, in limited quantities. However, it is in Flanders and the neighbouring regions of Belgium and Northern France that we find the most old-established and most impressive industrial concentrations (in the town of Ypres alone 92,000 pieces were stamped for export in 1313). It is there also in the 13th century that we find the most complex hierarchy and the most marked economic and social differences.

In these Franco-Belgian regions, a powerful inter-urban cartel, the 'Hanse des Dix-sept Villes' (during the 13th century the number of federated cities will rise to more than 20), co-ordinates as best it can the export of the famous 'francigene' materials to the market fairs of Champagne and beyond that to the rest of the world.

In every city, the industry is dominated by a few capitalist entrepreneurs, who are traders rather than industrialists and who in any case do not soil their hands with manual work, but exercise control over its first and last stages; purchase of raw materials, sale of finished goods. They are the strategists of production and they decide to a large extent what the output and prices shall be in the light of foreseeable demand in an international market which is competitive and hence may dramatically expand or contract. The government of the town is in their hands or in those of their friends.

Behind them, there is a much larger mass — the swarm of masters, apprentices and journeymen who take care of the more remunerative phases of the work: dyeing, fulling, and shearing. Although the capitalists look down on them, nicknaming them 'blue nails', they are more middle-class than proletariat. For have they not their own professional organisation, a special apprenticeship, costly tools such as dyeing vessels, fulling mills, long shearing scissors? Thanks to these tools, their skills can earn speedily a good return. Thus they can handle large quantities of cloths, accept orders from several entrepreneurs, turn down the less advantageous bids. Inside the gilds, only the masters have the right to vote, but apprentices and journeymen expect sooner or later to become masters one day. The discipline of the gild is strict, but fair, and, all in all, profitable.

Weavers, carders, combers are at the lowest point in the middle classes, on the border line of the proletariat. They do have their own special technique and a few tools. The weavers also have their own gild. In a flight of fancy, a 12th century writer compares them to 'cavalrymen on foot who, leaning on their stirrups [the pedals of the loom] ceaselessly urge on their sober steeds'. It is as well that their steeds are sober; for the work of the weaver, essentially manual, progresses but slowly and pays very little. The slightest illness or the smallest industrial crisis, even temporary, forces them to run into debt or sell or pawn their tools, thus mortgaging their future at the hands of the entrepreneur or of the moneylender, who are often the same person. When faced with such circumstances, those with most spirit try to emigrate; already in the first half of the 13th century we see numbers of weavers of Flemish origin arriving in Italy. Weavers from Lombardy in turn move southwards when there is a crisis in their home town.

Finally, at the bottom of the social scale, come the true proletarians: working men and women with no special skill who are concerned with the threshing and washing of the wool, with warping, with spinning and who are often employed in the entrepreneur's house, helping him as domestic servants as well. This army of poor people is recruited mainly from the rural areas (many, moreover, are those who do similar work without leaving their villages) and lives in a fashion more wretched, perhaps, even than that of the rural serfs. Still the city has its attractions and diversions — and the lure of a possible fortune. Although this hope is seldom realised, the excitement of town life seems preferable to the monotony of a duller life with more security.

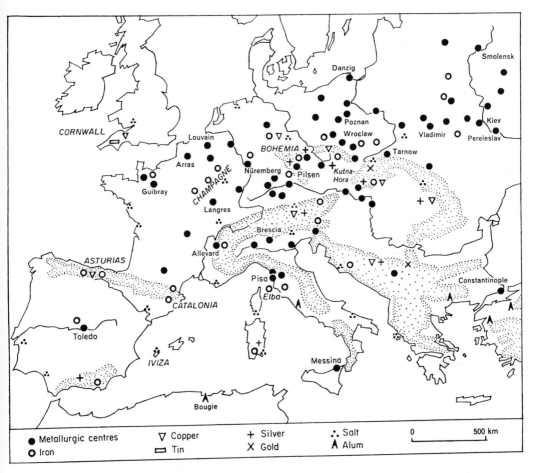

Map 18. Metallurgy and Mines in Europe, thirteenth century

Exploitation of the workers

There are revolts but what kind of people are those who rebel? At the head of
many a riot against the capitalist entrepreneurs, one finds, in general, not the
unskilled workers, but craftsmen in the higher categories. As early as 1225, at
Valenciennes, weavers and fullers launch an attack on the houses of the rich.
At the end of the 13th century, revolt flares up almost simultaneously at Douai,
Tournai, Ypres and Bruges. After a bloody struggle (which includes the famous
battle of the Golden Spurs at Courtrai to which we referred earlier) the insur-
gents finally obtain some measure of participation in government for a few
representatives from the craft gilds. Is this unrest a symptom of unbearable
sufferings, or is it rather a positive result of that economic and social progress

which ever since the communes were set up has been constantly opening the doors of government to new men? There must be two sides to the answer to this question.

The distribution and organisation of work, dictated by tradition and by the exigencies of an insufficiently mechanised industry, are not in themselves in-human. Hours of work, it is true, are long (from 8 to 13 daily) but there are very many feast days. Wages are low, strikes forbidden, but lawful forms of collective bargaining are not unknown. At Douai in 1229, a decree states that carders, after consultation with the town inspectors, may request the chief executive body of the city (the *échevins*) to order an increase in their wages, provided that this is compatible with the cost of living and market trends. Every reduction in wages must likewise be approved by the *échevins*. It is true that these latter are none else than the capitalist entrepreneurs; but who can better judge whether the state of industry allows of changes that will affect production costs? Is it not in their own interests to ensure that all their dependants receive reasonable wages (in proportion to their individual competence and productivity), since this will keep the workers contented and industrious?

Unfortunately, no such illusion can be entertained when we read an investiga-tion made, about 1287, by the executors of the will of Jean Boinebroke, of Douai, entrepreneur, owner of houses and land, usurer, and nine times *échevin* (notably in 1280, when a strike of weavers was mercilessly suppressed).

What we read is a never-ending list of complaints by former employees. They assert that while their master was still living, they dared not speak out, but now they demand compensation for wrongs of which, in actual fact, they furnish no written proof of any kind, nor, often, any reliable witness. The complaints are probably exaggerated; the executors will not be obliged to pay out their own money, and the dead man can make no cross-examination. But the mere half of the evil deeds attributed to Boine-broke would be sufficient to darken his memory. Not content merely to pay starvation wages, he paid them late, often in kind rather than in cash. By contrast, no-one was more punctual than he in collecting the exorbitant rents paid to him by his workmen for the hovels they dwelt in; or in exact-ing crippling interest rates and appropriating wages whenever some un-fortunate worker got into debt. He supplied his workers with inferior and short-weight materials, but expected a heavier weight of fine quality finished goods. If his underlings appealed to his charity, he made fun of them; if they showed signs of rebellion, he appealed for help to the muni-cipal police, which of course had to obey the *échevin*.

One would like to hope that not all employers were so harsh. However, docu-ments from other towns and other areas, including Italy, indicate that there was exploitation, barely concealed under a veil of hypocrisy and carried far beyond what was required by the technical or marketing condition of the woollen in-dustry. In an age of expansion, thorough mastery of the craft might achieve promotion through all grades into the higher ranks, but did not lead to affluence unless one arrived at the very top and passed from the great mass of the exploited into the select group of exploiters. This was expressed quite plainly in the statutes of numerous English villages; a weaver or a fuller, who had grown rich and wished to gain admittance to the ranks of the 'merchants' or bourgeois had first and foremost to abandon the tools of his trade.

Those who vegetate; those who rise

Economic and social differences are less marked wherever capitalist undertakings are lacking or just beginning. In such cases, the general way of life is more modest, and if a balance is maintained, it is at the price of missed chances. It is a world of small shops, petty craftsmen, little retailers, existing for a limited market in the town or neighbourhood. Here corporative rules are observed in all their wisdom but in all their straitness also. Masters follow in their fathers' footsteps, apprentices strive to become masters, with no ambition beyond that of preserving good traditional methods. In this atmosphere of golden mediocrity, knavery itself tends to assume a reasonable almost good-natured form. One comes across forged weights and measures, damaged goods, or tricks such as the slit an English baker made in his counter, with an apprentice hidden beneath to catch a portion of the dough which customers brought for baking. What is there by way of amusement? — A few processions, a few religious feasts, promotion banquets given by new masters, a Sunday visit to the tavern, a game of dice for the more daring; altogether not many events which might add a little colour to a monotonous existence.

This drab background is somewhat relieved by a few trades and a few individuals who stand out. Bakers, butchers, fishmongers can become well-to-do in many towns where the law sets limits to the number of ovens or stalls, while population is increasing and individual consumption is going up. Making their way up also are masons, minters, travelling tradesmen, who move from town to town, snapping up with alacrity the best-paid work and the most important customers. In the shipyards, where there is a certain concentration of manpower and capital, the best of the carpenters are carving out their careers. Tanners, furriers, and tailors, execute delicate work on costly raw materials; the most energetic and the most skilled among them are comfortably off and respected. An expert swordmaker can be sure of a good market for his blades and may enjoy an international reputation. Jewellers, by reason of the high price of the raw materials they use and the artistic nature of their profession, are almost always brought into the upper bourgeoisie. Painters, who do not work with precious materials, rise out of the ordinary class only if they have exceptional talent — Giotto, born poor, but enriched by his paintbrush, for instance. These riches, let it be said, he lent to a weaver, against the security of his loom, at an interest of 120 per cent, proof that not all artists have their heads in the clouds!

In reality, each and every road may lead to success; the late medieval town is a world of opportunity. Among the richest members of the bourgeoisie we find lawyers, notaries, physicians, owners of buildings or lands, moneylenders, town officials, men-at-arms, craftsmen and traders of all kinds. In a moderately successful town, such as Lille, the typical climb to the top may take a long time: first, immigration into the town from a rural area, then two or three generations in trade or craft practice, followed by entry into municipal office, and, lastly, the acquisition of land, both as a conservative investment and as a status symbol. In the more dynamic cities, however, it is not uncommon for a man to go from rags to riches in his lifetime, and owning land, apart from one's own house, is almost irrelevant to status.

Actually the diversity of professions and careers is so great that we cannot carry precise classification any further. In Florence, notwithstanding the preponderance of industrial and commercial activities, a few landed aristocrats of ancient lineage, like the Firidolfi, contrive to stay in the forefront; without any change of occupation, they are merely adapting the administration of their estates to fit in with the new economy. In Venice, when the hoary oligarchy freezes its membership and makes it almost impossible for new families to join it, the 'new houses' whose wealth is of recent origin quietly slip into step beside the 'old houses' of noblemen; and even there among the 'old houses' one finds families like the Malipiero, descended from a 10th century craftsman 'mastro Piero' or the descendants of Debramir, a Dalmatian slave.

One road to success, as we have said, is as good as another, but in general the best road is still the longest leading furthest afield. In the vanguard of the middle classes, it is nearly always the great international merchants who advance, never resting from their travels and galvanizing their towns each time they return home. Let us take to the road with them, on horseback or on a mule. Let us go aboard their ships, which, as some contracts say, are to sail 'wherever God shall guide us in the divers parts of the world' *per diversas mundi partes.*

IV.   TO THE FOUR CORNERS OF THE WORLD

The sea is the true kingdom of liberty. Sailors aboard their ships are free, despite an indispensable minimum of discipline; the ship herself is free, the moment she has left port, leaving behind her the taxes and other obstacles which states multiply along all land routes. The merchant too is free, having at his disposal both his own capital and that of others, usually within the elastic limits of a *commenda* agreement, and knowing that on his return he can take to sea again with whom he wishes, bound for whatever ports he wishes.

When there is a choice in the matter, sea transport is preferred to carriage by land, for it is less expensive — twenty-five times cheaper, in one extreme case! — and better suited to the varied nature of the cargoes. For 'minute' (light) luxury

*Fig. 53. Lighthouse of Aigues-Mortes (Gard),
    on the Constance tower, thirteenth century.*

goods there are slender boats, propelled by oars,
with a powerful armed escort; for 'gross' bulky
goods, slow sailing boats with rounded sides.
Even in this latter case, cargoes are of modest
weight, especially in Northern seas: a few tens
of tons, or at the most a few hundreds per boat.
The number of boats, however, is increasing and
in the Mediterranean and the Black Sea at least,
the season for voyaging is getting longer. After the middle of the 13th century,
navigation will hardly know the meaning of the term 'close season' even in the
dangerous depths of winter. With the progress of map making, and the perfec-
tioning of course-finding apparatus and naval construction, storms no longer
hold the same terrors. There remains the hazard of hostile peoples — not the
Moslems, for they were already contained in the 10th century and were decisively conquered in the 11th, but the Christians, for inter-town wars give still fewer
respites at sea than on land. So one defends oneself as best one can, relying
on the speed of boats, or by sailing in convoy. For single ships, simple forms
of maritime insurance are gradually coming into being. (Pl. 24).

'Gross' and 'minute' commodities

Though luxury articles, which can bear high transportation costs, made up a
larger part of trade than in modern times, the majority of cargoes consisted of
ordinary foodstuffs and raw materials, such as salt, wine, grain, fish, cheese,
butter, oil, cotton, flax, wool, common dyes, non-precious metals and timber.
Products of this kind are found almost everywhere, but regions having surpluses
export them to the nearest regions where there are deficiencies. A famine, a war,
a change in tariffs may make it worth while to transport these very goods over
longer distances. Some deficiencies are critical enough for a country to import

a 'gross' commodity at any cost. Egypt needs timber and iron from Europe, Italy needs Syrian cotton; no rise in prices, no embargo, no war can stop that trade. Without English wool (a 'gross' good, but the best of its kind), the Flemish industry cannot survive. Without wine from Gascony, the English nobility and middle class would have nothing to drink but beer — and their palate is not ready for that.

Increasing population, improving standards of living, sharpened interest in foreign products cause all forms of commercial traffic to soar throughout the 13th century. There is reason to believe that by the beginning of the 14th century it reached a peak which was not only higher than anything experienced before, but also as high or higher than European trade at any later time up to the 18th century. Overall figures, however, are hard to come by. The accuracy of the figure of 750,000 hectolitres of wine which Gascony is said to have exported to England in a single year has been challenged. It is certain, however, that the total exports from England often rose to as high as one quarter of a million pounds sterling; a figure all the more remarkable by reason of the fact those exports did not include one single rare commodity, and only two kinds of goods commanding a relatively high price — raw wool and a few thousand lengths of cloth.

Yet even if the higher value of the pound sterling is taken into account, this figure is well below the four million — or nearly — Genoese pounds of Genoa's sea trade; it is not even as great as the volume of sea business effected by the Genoese colony of Pera (Constantinople), which for 1334 was 1,648,000 pounds. This difference may be partially attributed to the fact that this trade is mostly transit trade, and partially to the higher standard of living of the Italian population and its concentration in the towns, more avid consumers of foodstuffs and heavy raw materials. It cannot be denied, however, that the inclusion in the cargoes of a greater number of spices and other 'minute' items has considerable influence on the total value of the merchandise.

Spices are to sea trade what fine quality cloths are to industry; not its most bulky products, but its most significant. They do in fact call for the greatest concentration of capital, they give a means of livelihood, indirectly, to the greatest number of people, and conduce to the development of a select professional group in the trade. The two aristocracies work together; on Italian ships, woollens from the West (and, to a lesser extent, Swiss and French linen, and Italian silks) are the counterpart of spices imported from the East. Venice, more distantly situated than Genoa from the great centres of the textile industry feels obliged however to add to the cloth her own glassware, as well as metals, both precious and non-precious, from German sources. Genoa itself carries some gold from Senegal in order to settle her accounts. Another Western contribution of paramount importance is the Lombardy steelworks.

Let us not imagine, however, that all 'spices' are Eastern, aromatic or precious. In his manual on trade practice, compiled during the first half of the 14th century, Francesco di Balduccio Pegolotti of Florence listed 288 'spices,' including not only condiments, drugs and colourings from the Middle and Far East, but also inexpensive goods from various places, such as glue from Florence and Bologna, paper from Fabriano, copper from central Europe, wax from Spain, Poland and Riga. This list does not include the twenty-three qualities of raw silk which Pegolotti quotes a little earlier, nor the one luxury article coming from Northern Europe — furs. There are, then, spices *and* spices.

Odyssey of the merchants, Iliad of the barons

At the beginning of the Commercial Revolution, there was intensive sea traffic in each of the four seas surrounding Europe — the Mediterranean, the Black Sea, the North Atlantic and the Baltic — but communication between one sea and another was almost exclusively effected by land routes. By their gradual opening of a direct maritime route linking these seas, Italians, Scandinavians and Germans became the authors of one of the most important pages in the annals of European unification.

On this same page are inscribed the successes and reverses of Christian expansion. There is no reason why the story should not begin as it usually does, with the First Crusade, but not without due emphasis on the fact that what some historians call the 'Iliad of the Barons' was preceded, accompanied and surpassed by the Odyssey of the Merchants. All things considered, the dramatic struggle of the 12th and 13th centuries was less decisive than the erosion begun by Italian communities during the two previous centuries. During those two centuries of adolescence, they clung to empires which were richer and more civilised than themselves, and yet, because of these very riches and civilization, were less eager for novelty, profit and progress. Smuggling, piracy and, above all, lower prices, and freer initiatives, constituted the weapons of the Italian traders at this early stage.

Byzantium had herself opened her gates to the Italians whom she regarded as vassals or poor relations. She saw no danger in inviting them to serve in her navy and to use her *mitata,* those markets with lodgings available where foreigners were permitted to stay for a maximum of three months. The splendour of the Empire in the 10th century seemed to confirm the wisdom of this traditional policy. Who could have foreseen that in less than a hundred years Italian help would be indispensable in saving the Empire from economic and military bankruptcy? Yet in 1082, faced with the problem of the Seljuk Turks unleashed in Asia Minor and the Normans in the process of bursting out over the Balkan peninsula, Emperor Alexis I had an exhausted treasury, a demoralised army and an inadequate navy. He bought help from the Venetians by giving them access to all the Byzantine ports of the Mediterranean, with no restrictions as to residence and with total exemption from customs duties — a tragic decision for the future of Greek merchants who, not being exempted, were thus placed at a disadvantage in their own country.

Their situation deteriorated still further when Pisa, Genoa and, later, other Western towns obtained similar exemptions and set up permanent colonies in the ports of the Empire.

In similar fashion, the Italians managed to make themselves indispensable to the Moslem states of the Levant, Africa and Spain, by importing into them raw materials essential to industry both in peace and war — timber, iron, copper and pitch. Popes and kings, preaching a united Christian front, thundered in vain against a trade so profitable to both sides. The Moslems, for their part, failed to unite, in spite of many ominous signs: the Pisan and Genoese victories in Corsica and Sardinia, the Norman conquest of Sicily, the surprise attack by Italian sea towns on an African capital, Mahdiya (1081). Whether by force or by diplomatic means, the Italians secured customs privileges, warehouses, and sometimes extra-territorial sections of the town in Moslem ports in the Mediterranean, even in regions untouched by the crusades or the Iberian *reconquista*.

In the states of the Crusaders, many Italian, Provençal and Catalan towns received still more generous privileges and quarters, particularly after Saladin's victories reduced the 'Kingdom of Jerusalem' to a strip of coast which depended entirely on relief by sea. Despite these advantages and their profits from transports and supplies, the merchants did not find the Holy Land an El Dorado. Wars made it difficult to develop in the Holy Land centres of production for exotic commodities, and detracted from the usefulness of the colonies as bridgeheads of trade. But this does not mean, of course, that the Holy Land was a mere liability. 'Soldiers are busy with their wars, peoples trade in peace, and the world belongs to whoever grabs it' — writes an Arab traveller in his Palestine diary.

The west knocks at the gates of Africa and Asia

Even under the most favourable circumstances, the riches of Asia and Africa reached the Mediterranean coasts at inflated prices via innumerable middlemen. To eliminate them, it would have been necessary to pry open the gates of the Mediterranean — to push on through the Black Sea towards Central Asia and China, through the Red Sea to India and Indonesia, through the Atlantic towards the mysterious gold mines of Senegal. Now the keys to all this were still in possession of Byzantium, who controlled the Dardanelles, Egypt who dominated the Suez peninsula, and Spanish-Morroccan Islam, who held the Southern side of the Gibraltar Straits and was encroaching on Andalusia; and these keepers of the golden keys were either Infidels or 'bad Christians.'

Hopes conceived in the 12th century were partly realized and partly disappointed in the 13th century. With the Fourth Crusade, the Venetians won the keys to the Black Sea and numerous sections of the Byzantine Empire. Some of them were fertile, Crete, for example, where Venice, that city of sailors, attempted agricultural colonization with some measure of success. Others were ports which enriched the network of her trading colonies. In Constantinople and in the Black Sea, the Venetians permitted settlement by other Western merchants, but kept the lion's share for themselves.

However, the Byzantine Empire was not dead. Banished to Nicaea in Asia Minor, it was patiently preparing its revenge. In 1261, Emperor Michael Paleologue made his entry into the former capital and rewarded the Genoese, his allies, by allowing them to demolish the palace of the Venetian Podesta of Constantinople, to the lively sound of trumpet and drum. It was too late to restore the political and commercial importance of the Greeks; the Genoese, now uppermost in the restored Byzantine Empire, shared its legacies with Venice. They extended their possessions in Greece, in Asia Minor, in the Crimea, in the Caucasus, and spread their economic penetration into the interior.

Two Crusades against Egypt (1219 and 1248) ended in failure, although both enjoyed the same initial success — the capture of Damietta. In consequence, any hope of forcing an inlet into the Red Sea faded away.

Between the first expedition, carried out by Italian sailors under the leadership of a Papal Legate, and the second, commanded by Louis IX, came the strangest of all the Crusades. Frederick II, excommunicated emperor and king of Sicily, temporarily re-captured Jerusalem, not by force of arms, but by means of a treaty with the Sultan of Egypt (1229). A commonsense solution, no doubt, but ahead of its time in its liberality. This compromise which might have brought a peaceful end to the Crusades and paved the way for mutual tolerance between the two monotheistic religions, gave scandal to devout Christian and Moslem alike. It soon was broken and the Moslems recaptured Jerusalem. And since experience had proved that the Christians could neither conquer Egypt, nor consolidate their positions in Palestine with a hostile Egypt at their gates, the 'Kingdom of Jerusalem' was abandoned to its fate in spite of the crocodile tears of all Europe. Little by little, Egypt restored it to Islam Its agony, prolonged by the unexpected intervention of the Mongols against Egypt, lasted right into the year 1291 (the date of the fall of Saint-Jean-d'Acre).

From Peking to London: peak of the Italian commercial empire

Meanwhile the conquests of Gengis Khan and his successors had changed the face of at least a quarter of the inhabited world and opened up immense horizons for Italian trade. (Map 19). It is true that in the beginning Catholic Europe could see in the Mongols nothing but a fearful threat — not without cause, for the drive, the ambition and the ferocity of these disciplined horsemen far exceeded anything the world had so far encountered.

They had overrun Russia, crushed Hungary, smashed to pieces a German army hastily assembled when one of their flanks came momentarily into contact with a corner of the Empire. Fortunately for Europe, their impetus wore out on the threshold of a Western world which was not yet prepared either to fight them or to collaborate with them. And while over boundless expanses the *pax mongolica* was succeeding the horrors of the Mongolian war, the conquerors began to seek help in exploiting and administering provinces which were terror-struck but still unreconciled to their rule. Western merchants and missionaries were welcomed, and for about a hundred years, up to the middle of the 14th century, the Italian colonies in the Near East became bridgeheads for the penetration of the Farther East.

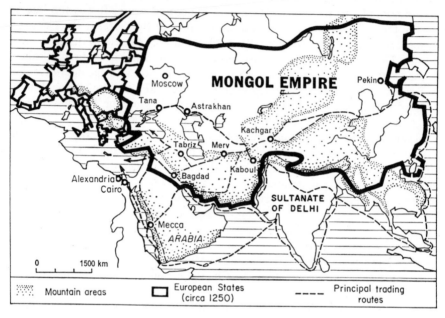

Map 19. The Mongolian Empire about 1250

Three routes, each allowing for many detours, linked these colonies with China. The northernmost one started from the Crimea, crossed Russia and Turkestan, and took about nine months to its terminus in Peking; it was, according to Pegolotti, 'perfectly safe by day and night'. The second, shorter but more arduous, left from Trebizond and continued via Persia and Afghanistan. The third, longer but cheaper because it went mostly by water, began in Cyprus or at Ayas on the opposite coast of Asia Minor, continued by way of Iraq, and then, by sea, coasted round India and Indochina; it took somewhat under two years.

Naturally, most Westerners did not go all the way to Peking. Tabriz and Astrakhan became for the Italians places of residence as familiar as Constantinople and Alexandria had previously been. The Genoese sailed the Caspian Sea and the Persian Gulf in ships which they built on the spot. Farther in Central Asia, Urgench (the 'Organdy' which gave its name to the cloth) and

Almaligh became transit stops and markets for Venetian caravans. An Italian colony sprang up in Peking, and another at Ts'iuan-tcheu (Zayton), opposite Formosa, where Franciscan monks built an inn for transient European merchants. Other traders and missionaries crossed the border into India and settled down there. Whole families fell in love with the Far East: in 1338, when only just back from China, Giovanni Loredan of Venice set off again for Delhi with his brother Paolo; shortly after, Francesco Loredan in his turn left for China, armed with a letter of recommendation from Pietro, his uncle. The letter read in part: 'If his journey ends well, I shall live comfortably for the rest of my days; if not, I must sell all I have got.'

> Italian merchants also made progress on the shorter distances of the West. It is true that in Africa the 'crusades' of European kings constituted more of an embarrassment than a help. That of Louis IX against Tunis came to grief in 1270 leaving a wake of ill-feeling behind it. Ten years earlier, a crusade of Alphonso X of Castille against Morrocco captured Saleh on the Atlantic but had to evacuate it almost at once. Nevertheless, Genoese merchants kept their connections there and in Safi, farther South. At the beginning of the 14th century, they pushed on as far as the Canaries and the Azores. They did not succeed, however, in achieving their final ambition, finding and capturing the gold-producing region of Senegal. The Negro king of Mali, who controlled the source of gold, kept competitors in the dark.

The reconquest of Andalusia by Castille during the first half of the 13th century attracted increasing numbers of ships from the Mediterranean towards the coasts of the Atlantic, first to Cadiz and Sevilla, then farther north to La Rochelle, Southampton and London, Sluys (the port for Bruges) and other ports of the North Sea. By the year 1277, the galleys of the Genoese Benedetto Zaccaria, admiral, merchant and industrialist famous throughout the Levant, were heading for England; in 1281, a galley from Majorca dropped anchor there. In 1291, this same Zaccaria, now in the service of the King of Castille, was sweeping away the last traces of the Moslem barrier at the Pillars of Hercules, crushing the Moroccan fleet in the Straits of Gibraltar in the process. At the beginning of the 14th century, the communes of Genoa and Venice, who were organising a network of convoys destined to sail the Mediterranean and the Black Sea, with pre-determined ports of call and regular timetables, included in their arrangements a line which would serve Flanders and England as well; and it was there that the western end of a commercial empire stretching from London and Bruges to Ts'iuan-tcheou and Peking became embedded.

Birth of the German commercial empire

While the Italians controlled all aspects of trade on the Mediterranean and the Black Sea, despite the presence of rivals who had to be reckoned with (the

Fig. 54. The oldest known Western example of a hinged axial rudder; German ship of the thirteenth century; Commentary on the Apocalypse, *1242.*

Catalonians, and to a lesser extent, the Provençals), they confined their activities beyond Gibraltar to the transportation of goods sufficiently valuable to justify the use of rapid, but costly galleys. French and Portuguese salt and wine, for instance, made the journey by local sailing ships. For areas beyond Flanders, the bulk of the cargoes consisted of dried cod, herring, salt, butter, timber, and, later, grain. The sea voyage took four or five times longer than overland routes linking the Mediterranean to Northern Europe. Here the Italian commercial empire ended and a new one was emerging, much more restricted — but none the less vigorous — that of the Germans, extending from Bruges and London to Bergen, Visby and Novgorod (Fig. 54).

This empire too was the achievement of free towns, assisted by concomitant expeditions by princes and crusaders, but nevertheless bearing above all else the mark of bourgeois initiative and ideals. It was a young empire. As a matter of fact, in the early Middle Ages, when Venice and Amalfi were taking their first steps, the most active seamen in the North were the Frisians. They were soon overtaken by the Scandinavians, who were more daring, more enterprising. But their ships were small, their contracts and gilds were primitive, their merchants, for the most part, were peasants engaging in commerce only as a sideline, and their towns were hardly more than villages. In the 12th century, when German expansion got into its stride along the Baltic, the Scandinavian economy, if not static, was to say the least out of step with the more dynamic parts of Europe.

Just as the Byzantine empire and the Moslem states had voluntarily opened their gates to Italian traders, so the Scandinavian kings and Slav princes were often the first to invite the Germans to buy from them fish, timber and furs; in return, the Germans brought in goods and techniques from the more advanced countries. Only the Danish kings occasionally endeavoured to assert themselves over these foreigners and compete with them for political and commercial domination the Baltic. But the defeat inflicted on Valdemar II at Bornhöved (1227) marked the end of the Danish offensive and once again opened the way for German expansion, reinforced by peaceful immigration. In 1378, a fifth of the population of the capital, Copenhagen, was of German stock.

In Norway, in 1278, King Magnus VI made concessions to German 'guests' who visited his country, but he limited his hospitality to the summer season. In 1294, his son, Eric II, victim of a disastrous blockade, was forced to give the Germans permission to stay for as long as they wished. He kept for himself only the trade carried on to the north of Bergen and towards Iceland and Greenland, which became a royal monopoly.

Sweden, for her part, had exempted the traders of Lübeck from customs duties as early as the end of the 12th century. These merchants took advantage of this to settle in the new town of Visby on the island of Gotland, which had constituted a crossroads of commercial traffic since the end of the Roman era, but had no urban centres up to the beginning of the 12th century. The 'Community of German visitors to Gotland' established in Visby before 1225 soon overshadowed the old 'brotherhood' of the Danish merchants on the island, and was the first nucleus of the future Hansa League which would one day comprise some 70 towns.

The Hansa League was not formally constituted until 1369, a time when it took in Cologne, that old and active metropolis of German trade, as well as other Rhine river ports. By then, however Cologne had been overtaken by Lübeck (Pl. 21) which dominated the outlet into the Baltic of the short land route across the neck of Jutland to the North Sea, The other German towns in the Baltic were already in the habit of ordering their political and diplomatic activities as directed by Lübeck.

Cologne prided itself on its Roman origin, whereas the Baltic towns were founded only in the 12th and 13th centuries, often in places where there existed already small agglomerations of Slavs, Balts or Scandinavians. Lübeck, the oldest of them, was first founded at the beginning of the 12th century with the consent of the Slav king of the region. After its destruction by a German lord, it was re-founded by Henry the Lion. Other ports, like Rostock and Wismar, were developed within the orbit of religious, military and agricultural colonisation between the Elbe and the Oder. Here the long struggle against the native population, which belonged to the Western branch of the Slav races, had ended towards the end of the 12th century with the victory of the German colonists.

Beyond the Oder, however, the Poles who were Christian and definitely of a mind to resist, constituted an obstacle which proved too difficult to eliminate. But still further on, at the eastern end of the Baltic, there dwelt a whole world of pagans, a promised land for whoever would hunt souls or slaves, or fields to cultivate, or produce to export and retail.

Riga, established as a town in 1201 by the Knights of the Sword and their leader, the inflexible Bishop Albert, was the first German bridgehead in Latvia. To curb its activities, the Danes founded Reval (Talinn) in Estonia, but it was not long before the town became Germanized. In 1274, the townsmen of Reval addressed those of Lübeck as follows: 'Our towns are joined like the arms of the Crucifix.' Finally, the Teutonic Knights of Hermann von Salza, returning defeated from the first of the crusades against Egypt, sought to get even by launching a crusade against the Prussians (a pagan population, related to the Lithuanians, and living in what today is called Prussia). They also entrenched themselves in the territory of the Polish Duke of Masovia, who imprudently had spurred them on to this expedition. The towns which they founded or stirred to new life joined the Hansa League. So did the Teutonic Knights, now merged into a single Order with the Knights of the Sword; but in the role of 'protectors', not as ordinary members.

Finland, long disputed between the Germans, the Russians and the Swedes, had lately been evangelized and conquered by the Swedes. At the end of the 13th century, only Lithuania remained pagan and independent.

Urban civilization in the Baltic

Despite their diversity of origin, the Hansa towns were dominated by interrelated families descended from those who had first organised colonisation. The majority of these adventurers came from Westphalia, itself a former frontier and an area of colonisation. Flanders and Holland also had supplied free agricultural settlers. The basis of the population was Slav and Balt. Alongside this urban efflorescence, dominated by the Germans, there sprang up another budding crop of towns in the territories under the domination of Slav kings and princes. But this development is outside the scope of this present volume.

German emigrants, welded in a close political and commercial solidarity, brought to the depths of these forlorn forests and swamps the most recent techniques from Western Europe and the choicest products of the Mediterranean and Asia. The liveliness of their culture, the spirit of economic adventure, flexibility in contracts and social intercourse, impatience with feudal bonds, even the very titles of the chief magistrates (consuls): all these constitute so many similarities between the Hansa towns and Italian towns, although the latter were larger and more sophisticated. But there was no parallel in Italy, except perhaps in Venice, to the restrictions imposed by the Hansa on the trade of foreign merchants, or the strict dividing line between great merchants and retailers, or the aristocratic nature of the communal councils, on which no one who worked with his hands might sit.

Behind the brilliant commercial and bourgeois façade of the Baltic towns, there nevertheless showed through the influence of an agricultural, manorial, feudal hinterland. The cities had grown and multiplied within the framework of German territorial colonisation. This colonisation, governed as it was by principles of military discipline, of fear of and contempt for the 'native' populations, was altogether much harsher and sterner than the Italian expansion in the Levant. It is true, however, that the 'natives' of the Mediterranean Levant possessed a culture which could not be disregarded as easily as that of the Balts and Slavs.

The difference was less marked in those places where the Hansa merchants were unable to create independent towns, but had to be satisfied with autonomous colonies within foreign towns, as was the case in Novgorod, Bergen, London and Bruges. There, as in the Italian settlements of the Levant, the population of the colonies initially consisted, for the most part, of young men who were eager to make a quick fortune and then leave the colony for home. Subsequently, the colonists began to take root overseas, marrying women from the area, or sending for them from the mother country. Although they were still willing to travel when necessity demanded, they began to deal with part of their business by correspondence. This development resulted in the formation of new communities, attached to their town of origin, but more motley, more cosmopolitan than they, and more liberal.

Words written by an obscure Genoese poet of the end of the 13th century can be applied to all the 'colonials', whether Italian or German: 'So many are the Genoese — so scattered world wide — that they build other Genoas — wherever they reside.'

V. INLAND TRADE

Hampered by the high cost of transport, by innumerable customs and tariffs, by restrictions imposed by princes and communes, inland trade gathers substance more slowly than sea trade. Its heroes are inconspicuous men, such as those agents of the great Florentine companies who make the round of the remotest villages of Apulia in search for cheese, or that notary and clothier who in the space of a single month, in 1331, contrives the credit-sale of 36 cuts of ordinary cloth in the little town of Forcalquier in Upper Provence. Its gains are sometimes so unspectacular that we hardly find reference to them in the documents, but their cumulative effect is of prime importance. The gradual shrinkage of the isolated areas, where there are no shops, barter is the main form of exchange, and even the travelling merchants are seldom if ever seen; the multiplication of small periodical markets, where household goods and inexpensive cloth manufactured in town are exchanged for foodstuffs and cattle; the co-operation of abbots and barons with local and foreign traders in organizing crops and pastures with an eye to commercial demand; the quiet work of confraternities and communities who mend roads and build hump-backed bridges in the more lonely regions — all this, and much else, transmitted a faint repercussion of the Commercial Revolution to the rural foundations of Europe. On these broadening foundations it was possible for the urban, commercial and industrial superstructure to gain balance and weight.

The mass of small merchants and the financial giants

Inland trade, especially when carried out on a local scale, tends to present both smaller risks and smaller profits than sea trade. It does not require large amounts of capital. Hence it offers an outlet to a greater number of people, mostly of modest standing.

Within the limits prescribed by professional and municipal rules, any craftsman may retail goods in his own shop, without having recourse to wholesalers. For his part, the wholesaler does not despise deals in small lots or in articles outside his range when the occasion warrants.

Lack of specialization and slow growth are mainly the consequence of the fact that regular customers are relatively few except in the larger cities or in food shops and shops selling essential items. Outside Italy, local trade depends almost entirely upon the wishes and tastes of the upper classes — nobles, churchmen, top bourgeoisie. The standstill of business in the interval between one weekly market and the next disappears only in big Italian towns of the interior, as it also does in Paris, Bruges and a few other centres sufficiently populous to ensure a daily demand; 'With us, it is market day every day' proudly proclaims a Florentine writer.

And yet, even in Florence, selling on good terms counts for more than selling in great quantity. Hence there is care over quality and durability of products; the chronicler Giovanni Villani is no wit perturbed by the fact that the number of pieces of cloth sold has decreased by 25 per cent in 30 years, since the selling price by the piece is double. On the other hand, any form of advertising in aid of sales promotion is forbidden; in this respect rules and customs run parallel throughout Europe. Moreover, laws governing expenditure aim at reducing 'extravagant' spending by the middle classes. It is true that nobody observes them literally.

In general, the unspectacular nature both of risks and profits and the lack of specialization conduce to small-scale business and a narrowness of outlook, but is so happens that it enables a few modest family firms to grow into gigantic undertakings. In the 'company' operating on land, indeed, it is neither necessary nor possible as is the case with maritime *commenda*, to envisage every operation as a single adventure, hectic but short-lived, over and done with at the end of every voyage. The partners in the company invest a fixed capital of their own for a certain number of years; they increase this capital by means of deposits from outside, attracted by the prospect of an interest rate which, if not high (from 8 to 10 per cent usually) is relatively safe. In this way, they can provide simultaneous finance for all manner of commercial transactions, take on staff and multiply their representatives and branches abroad (in 1336 the Peruzzi company of Florence has 88 agents distributed over 17 branches). However, as a result of this desire for increased profits — be it only in order to pay regular interest on deposits — the partners yield to the temptation of transferring from ordinary trading to money lending and financial operations an ever-increasing portion of both their own capital and that of other people. Is not buying and selling on credit the very essence of commerce? Money lent to a king — what a weapon for extorting trading privileges since an inland merchant cannot, like sea traders, use powerful galleys as a mouthpiece! But it is a two-edged sword.

Debtors who wear crowns are frequently more treacherous than the waves, greedier than pirates. Even a land company can founder in shipwreck.

A few figures

Although the company is probably as old and as widespread as the maritime *commenda*, it is not until the middle of the 13th century that it develops fully, and it reaches its highest potential only in a few Italian towns; Asti, Cremona, Piacenza, Pistoia, Lucca, Siena, Florence.

A few figures will suffice to give some idea of size. In 1260, Salimbene Salimbeni, a member of one of the largest Siena companies, donates a sum of 118,000 Sienese pounds to his city to help with the expense of the war against Florence, and commits himself to pay once again as much in the future. In 1318, the Bardi company of Florence balances annual accounts to the tune of some 875,000 florins. Twenty-five years later, it will be bankrupt, with books showing 900,000 florins outstanding in respect of the King of England and more than 100,000 for the King of Sicily. Rather than attempting to compare values and figures of different periods let us state that in 1348 Pope Clement VI paid 80,000 florins to the queen of Naples for the purchase of Avignon, his future capital, and that the following year, the King of France bought Montpellier for 120,000 crowns (133,000 florins) — in other words, less than one-sixth of the Bardi annual turnover paid for the most important Mediterranean town between Marseilles and Barcelona. Consider also that in 1360 France could only raise 400,000 crowns (450,000 florins) for the ransom of her king, captured by the English at the Battle of Poitiers; and the total ransom was never paid.

Let us also seek a few comparisons from the world of sea trade. The sum spent by Salimbeni in 1260 is equal to at least three times the estimated value of the personal property and estates of Riniero Zeno, Doge of Venice, at the time of his death in 1268 (50,000 Venetian pounds at least). But it is certainly lower, and considerably so, than the patrimony of Benedetto Zaccaria, the Genoese merchant to whom we have already referred (and who died in 1307 or 1308) — a complex patrimony of galleys and other ships, of alum mines and mastic plantations, of all manner of merchandise, public debt securities, properties, salaries and pensions, and still other sources of income. Its total value cannot be accurately assessed, but the alum mines of Phocaea in Asia Minor alone produced 13,000 *cantari* (750 tons) annually, with a value of at least 50,000 Genoese pounds.

These Rockefellers and Rothschilds of 13th-century Italy have no parallel in other countries, and even in Italy they are the exception. Although some of Zaccaria's employees share in the profits and receive, for a single voyage, more than 100 pounds in wages, many people more humbly employed who died in his service in Phocaea leave behind them estates worth less than 10 pounds. Agents of the Florentine companies earn a few tens of florins per annum; the increases which they receive from time to time are hardly enough to offset the continual rise in the cost of living. (In the absence of adequate studies on prices in Italy, let us observe that in England the cost of living has by and large quadrupled between 1150 and 1325).

In the case of the very lowest bourgeoisie and the proletarians, the situation is worse. For them life passes as if gold coins had never been heard of — these gold genovins first struck in Genoa, or the gold florins struck almost immediately afterwards in Florence in 1253. Small copper coins, with a small addition of silver barely increasing their value ('deniers'), are enough for them, or, at best, the heavier coins of real silver ('groats'). Plagued as they are by usurers, it matters little to them that the average rate of interest in business investment has fallen during the 13th century from 20–26 percent to 8–12 per cent, proof of the extraordinary availability of money and credit in Italy. In Bruges, where credit is so widespread that at the end of the 14th century one person in forty will have his own bank account, the normal interest is, however, maintained above 40 percent — and no gold coins are being minted. At Nuremberg, the most flourishing centre in South Germany, the legal rate is 43 per cent, but the Holzschuher company charges 94 per cent for loans to Jews.

However, the urban proletariat is not quite at rockbottom. Recipients of public relief in Florence are used to having white bread; when, during the course of a lean year in 1346, the Commune distributes less than two pounds of that bread a day, they protest, Yet this is not so bad when compared with the peasants of surrounding areas who have to make do with black bread!

What benefits does the Commercial Revolution offer for the underprivileged peasant? One only, perhaps, but an important one: the almost complete disappearance of the spectre of famine. Not only in affluent Italy and in fertile France and England, but also in the Low Countries and Germany, chroniclers mention fewer than ten years of general famine during the 12th century, and two or three only in the 13th. This is due primarily to the peasants themselves, to their harvests; but also to the fact that when the harvest fails, grain may be obtained from distant countries. In 1276, for instance, the Commune of Genoa appeals to Manuel Zaccaria, Benedetto's brother, to import grain from the Balkans as a matter of urgency, and is thereby enabled to 'open its hands in charity' and feed a host of refugees who have come from as far as France. Genoa, however, can make use of the sea; where water ways are lacking, transportation of bulky goods is costlier and slower.

On the roads: merchandise and ideas

The progress of communications over land in the late Middle Ages is measured by the number of roads rather than by their quality (Map 20). There is nothing which compares to Roman military highways, built regardless of expense by a State controlling massive armies, myriad slaves and peasants liable for forced

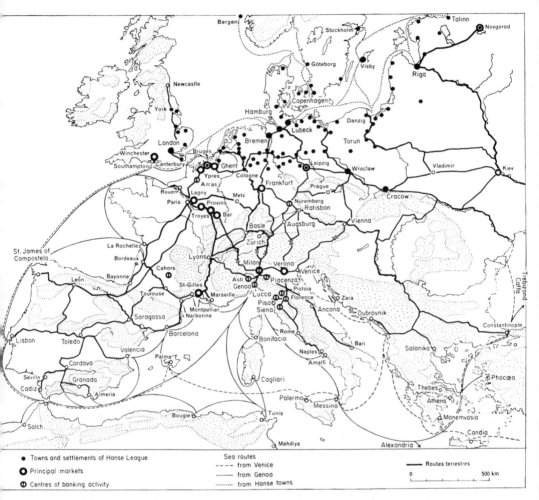

Map 20. Land and Sea routes in the eleventh to thirteenth centuries.

labour. On the other hand, no medieval village, no church, no market is without an access road – simple dirt roads or tracks reinforced with pebbles and planks. Between one centre and another there is a choice of numerous roads. This compact, elastic network began to take shape in the age of particularism, and it continues to develop thanks to the initiative of local authorities, religious brotherhoods, merchant associations; seldom under the patronage of the central government. Mediaeval knights have no need of paved roads, on the contrary. Pilgrims are easily satisfied. The merchants, of course, would like something better; but they prefer mediocre roads to expensive causeways, however excellent.

The most famous route? Undoubtedly, that leading from France to the shrine of St James at Compostela. Yet despite its importance for the spread of religious, artistic and literary ideas (at least at the beginning of the 13th century), its usefulness in the economic sphere remains modest. Small market towns are increasing in number along it, but they stay small. The countryside through which it passes remains poor and sparsely populated. There is grandeur of spirit, but a dearth of people and buildings. Again, in 14th-century England the route followed by pilgrims to the shrine of St Thomas à Becket ran through a fertile region — and yet were not Chaucer's Canterbury tales the most precious harvest reaped along this route?

The highroads crossing the Alps constitute the most concentrated, and on the whole, the most profitable system as regards trade. Special attention is lavished on them during the whole of the 13th century. Companies of waggoners and muleteers shuttle from one side to the other of the mountains, vying with each other for customers, improving their means of transport and lowering prices. At the beginning of the century, the construction of a boldly-contrived bridge opens a short cut through the St Gothard pass to beasts of burden; a century later, the Septimer pass, close by the St Gothard, will be made practicable for the passage of carts. Further north, the town of Schaffhausen will carry out costly excavations in the rock in order to reduce the gradient of the road to Coblenz and the lower valley of the Rhine.

Let us recall that through these roads there passes something more than material goods. The liberty of the masses, born in the Lombard plain, is being transported along them too, towards the mountains in which it will find its staunchest defenders. The Swiss are the only people who today still think of themselves as citizens of a Commune, rather than a national State.

The most important road junction, at the north of the Alps, is not in Switzerland but in the open plains of Champagne. Here, along the axis joining the two most economically advanced regions of Europe (Italy and Belgium) are the terminals of roads coming from the Rhone and Rhine valleys. Here too flows the Seine with its main tributaries. The cathedral at Rheims serves as a setting for the coronation of the kings of France. The Court of Troyes stands out behind the poets, grouped first around Countess Marie of Champagne, daughter of Alienor of Aquitaine, then around the extravagant, congenial Thibaut IV, himself a poet. There is a galaxy of smaller centres producing famous wools and linens. But much more famous still are the market fairs which meet six times a year in the four neighbouring towns of Provins, Troyes, Lagny, Bar-sur-Aube; in practice, they last almost throughout the whole year. In the 12th century they take over from other markets which had enjoyed more modest prosperity in this same region during Roman and Carolingian times. For a long time to come, they will constitute the vital hinge for exchanges between Southern and Northern Europe for almost all the 13th century up to the time when the decisive triumph of all-sea routes from the Mediterranean to the North Sea condemn them to decay and disappearance.

The market-fair: oasis of peace and field of experiment

There is a complete world, humming with activity, at which we have barely the time to cast even a glance: the world of the international fairs of Champagne, the fair at St Denis, those of Berg-op-Zoom, Cologne and Salonica; the regional markets organised in certain urban centres (Fig. 55); annual meetings of pedlars, pilgrims, peasants and layabouts held in thousands of villages on the occasion of some Saint's day. The role played by this world of market and fair (the two terms are practically interchangeable), of paramount importance while there hardly were merchant towns in the real sense of the term, is diminishing as time goes by and the commercial economy expands, but it remains nonetheless relatively important.

> In the barbarian age and at the beginning of the feudal period, the main attraction of these gatherings during times of difficulty for trade and traders was undoubtedly the 'peace of the market.' To those who came visiting his market, the local lord would promise protection against external robbery and aggression, spare them in addition his own particular 'annoyances.' Foremost among these inconveniences were the 'aubaine' (confiscation of a merchant's goods if he happened to die abroad) and the 'reprisal' (seizure of effects and often imprisonment of fellow-citizens of those who defaulted in their obligations). The lord usually offered also favourable customs regulations; he made houses and warehouses available, had money specially minted, and allowed traders to avail themselves of special speedy courts. England, expressing a certain degree of contempt for those who used them, called these 'courts

Fig. 55. Market Hall of Evron (Mayenne); completely wooden, 1350.

302

*Fig. 56. Cross in Trier Market Place, 958, the oldest
monument of a mediaeval market still standing.*

for those with dusty feet' — a fitting enough description for itinerant
merchants, but less apt for great traders such as the Italians, who were in
the habit of demanding public baths in all their colonies. This 'peace of
the market' was sometimes highlighted and dramatised by translation
into concrete symbols, like the cross erected around a thousand years
ago which still stands in the market square at Trier (Fig. 56), or the stone
laid in 1111 beneath the portico of Lucca cathedral bearing witness
down to our own day to the promise of moneylenders and spice-sellers
that they would never commit 'theft, fraud or falsification in the market
of St Martin'.

By the 13th century, commerce in distant parts was no longer regarded as a
somewhat abnormal activity, which needed to be kept apart and protected in a
sphere limited by time and space. Nevertheless, certain obstacles persisted in
several countries. They are partly to be explained by survivals of feudal mentality, but more often by the jealous attitude of the new class of local merchants.
In their view, any inhabitant of any other town, even one of the same kingdom,
was a foreigner. For example, in England, a special permit was required for a
stay of more than 40 days and a deed of naturalisation was necessary to break
down the barriers of municipal protectionism and royal fiscal laws. In many
German towns, a 'foreigner' could not participate in retail trading, and he had
to confine his activities to buildings under the supervision of the authorities.
Even in important centres like Paris and Barcelona, there was no lack of
impediment. The monarchs, although not economically informed enough to
formulate any precocious 'protectionist' or 'mercantilist' doctrine, knew quite
enough about these matters to use import and export permits or prohibitions
for their own ends. England had its own policy for wool, Norway for timber
and Sicily for grain.

It was only in the Italian, 'Belgian' and Provençal Communes that an instinctive economic liberalism coincided with political and social liberty. In these
countries, practically everything that might hamper trade had disappeared in
almost every town. Legislation, made by merchants and for merchants, was
speedy; the 'aubaine' or escheatage law was rejected as a feudal or barbarian
custom; and cases of 'reprisals' were usually settled through legal channels.

Foreign merchants were not regarded as dangerous competitors and enjoyed almost unlimited freedom both in the scope of transactions and the length of time they might stay. There were numerous inns, with accommodation available at a moment's notice. When markets were held, it was with one object only — to take advantage of especially favourable dates and places — for example, the arrival of convoys from the Levant in Venice, or arrival of convoys for Flanders from Bruges. To attract buyers from the advanced countries, it was not enough to offer the 'peace of the market'; what was needed was an efficient organization and special opportunities for trade.

Probably the best organized fairs were those of Champagne. A modern traveller, looking at the tiny market square of St Ayoul in Provins, would hardly believe that products from all over Europe and more distant places could ever be piled up in such a limited space. Actually, for most of the merchandise, it sufficed to exhibit a sample, since the best grades of cloth came in pieces of standard size and quality, guaranteed by the seals of famous cities, and the finest spices were identified according to origin and quality according to their smell, colour and consistency. The bulk of the merchandise was at hand in warehouses or would be shipped against firm order. From the fairs of Champagne, the agents of a Siena company remitted to the home office weekly lists of current prices, a survey of political and commercial news, and a statement of their own transactions. These were usually effected without any outlay of cash, by entering records of sale in the registers of the fair and balancing periodically the entries by compensation. What debit or credit remained at closure would be carried over to the next session by means of a written document (letter of fair). Exchange contracts made it possible for credit to be extended in all countries where a merchant had correspondents, and often enabled the merchant to undertake bold speculations on the course of currencies.

VI.   THE FLESH AND THE SPIRIT

The fairs of Champagne (or the permanent markets of Bruges and London when the fairs declined) and the main Italian business centres served as financial headquarters of Europe and contributed to the diffusion of a comparatively uniform economic technique, based on the use of correspondence, accountancy and credit. But the varying degree of skill and sophistication among those who met there maintained and increased the gap between old-fashioned and progressive merchants.

The new methods enabled the Italians to take a lead in a field where prior to the 13th century they had been undistinguished: the field of lending, exchange and banking. It was a vast, diversified world, including alike the sordid pawnbroker and the most respectable exchange dealer, and it embraced petty deposit banks as well as the great companies of international merchant bankers. The specialists in lending and banking also were drawn from many sources. There were the ubiquitous Jews, ever ready to hasten wherever there was a prospect for commerce in money. There were exchange dealers from Montpellier and Majorca, rich 'usurers' from Arras and Cahors, English business men like the De la Poles. The Italians, however, possessed a special trump card, the support of the Pope. The Holy See made use of them to collect contributions in all Catholic countries from the Holy Land to Greenland, and to deliver goods and letters to the four corners of the earth. Thus the Italian bankers constituted a kind of subsidiary bureaucracy, such as was indispensable to a universal Church. They did not ask for much by way of commission but were certain of the backing of the Pope — at times, even through the dread weapon of excommunication — when other means of getting a debt repaid were exhausted or when a king threatened them with some exorbitant duty or a decree of expulsion.

The haunting problem of interest

In spite of this, Popes were the first to condemn lending for interest, and this condemnation provided a good excuse to the debtors of the Italians for refusal to pay, for extortion, for expulsion. Money does not deteriorate with use, nor can it yield fruit; it must be freely lent for love of God to a brother who asks you for it; usurers therefore are acting against nature and sinning against Charity — all ideas which Catholic morality had inherited from Greek philosophy and Jewish ethics, both of which were generated in an environment unfavourable to traders and preoccupied above all with what we still call usury— the lending of money at exorbitant rates to the poor and to the thriftless. At the time of economic awakening the Church had still not succeeded in freeing herself from her own doctrine by drawing a distinction between usury and commercial interest. Therefore, those lenders who feared the Judgement of God and that of men were forced to resort to all manner of compromise.

> We must leave the task of describing these compromises one by one to specialized works. The most satisfactory solutions were contracts in which the loan was tied up with elements of partnership or risk-sharing, as was the case with the very ancient *foenus nauticum* (sea loan) or less ancient *cambium trajecticium* (long-range exchange contract); but such contracts were not always applicable, nor could they always be justified. The most ingenious solutions, but too obvious not to be incriminated both before the courts and in the very consciences of those who resorted to them, were those which involved the use of formulae under which a sum acknowledged as a 'free loan' embodied a hidden interest in some shape or form. The ultimate remedy, for this as for other sins, was deathbed repentance and restitution to debtors, to the poor, or to the Church — a restitution normally limited to a token offering.
>
> The Church, for her part, was wilfully blind, applying to usurers the same criterion as she applied to sins of the flesh; that is, she did not go hounding down fornication committed in private, but only its public manifestation — prostitution; she did not prosecute interest as such, but

only the operation of a usurer's establishment, openly advertised as such. The theory lives on, but practice, that is to say life, contrives numerous more or less legitimate compromises which are only attacked when it is absolutely impossible to overlook them, and which do not bother the faithful overmuch until death is upon them.

When drafting his will, Vita Rastic, a merchant from Ragusa (Dubrovnik), set aside a sum of 35 pounds 'for goods wrongfully acquired; for it seems to me, having been a merchant, impossible that I should not have acquired something by wrong means.' The Bardi company of Florence maintained in its ledgers a personal account headed 'Mr God,' and was most meticulous in crediting thereto a share of its interest profits; a dividend which came back to the poor.

There are similar instances which illustrate the depth and sincerity of the faith of the mediaeval trader, yet at the same time reveal his firm resolve not to let religion escape with more than its fair share of the profits. For the business-man, faith was a cherished and indispensable companion, but it was not his master.

Absolute religion or compromise religion

Nevertheless, there existed businessmen for whom a religion so compartment-alized did not suffice, and who gave all their belongings to the poor — as a means of investing them in Heaven. This is what the Lyonnais merchant Pierre Waldo did about the year 1170; the Waldensians, named after him, spread out into the trading towns of the plain before persecution forced them to seek refuge in the mountains of Piedmont. Not much later, there was the similar case of the son of the merchant Pietro Bernardone of Assisi, the future St Francis. The three orders he founded were not enclosed in remote monasteries, as had been so many monastic orders of the early Middle Ages, nor did they work for land improvement or agricultural colonisation, like the Cistercians and other reli-gious orders founded at the beginning of the late Middle Ages. The Francis-cans, in fact, entered wholeheartedly into urban life. The Dominican order, also, was essentially urban, despite the fact that its founder was neither mer-chant nor son of a merchant. This trend in thirteenth century monastic life indicates not only that towns were beginning to count for more than rural areas, but that the mysterious mills of God were finding grain, and good grain, among the bourgeoisie. Just as noble families had done, the great bourgeois families were to give to the Church their quota of ascetics, priests, popes and saints.

There is no more reason to equate urban society with lack of faith than to identify baronial circles with piety. Those who preferred flirtation with Riches to marriage with Poverty were not necessarily irreligious. Dante, bourgeois and layman as he was, has left us the most striking conception of Hell and Heaven. In his well warranted fear of Hell, Baude Crespin, notorious usurer of Arras, in whose debt were all the great Flemish communes, wished to be buried in a Benedictine habit. In his epitaph he commended his soul to the prayers of 'humble wage-earners and workmen'. A tardy contrition, it is true. But what shall one say of Benedetto Zaccaria, that sharp business man always on the look-out for gain, who broke off the blockade of Sluys and Bruges, from which both in his capacity of admiral and that of trader he might hope for great benefits, to organize a crusade which had as its goal the reconquest of the Holy Land? The expedition is said to have included among its participants many ladies of the merchant aristocracy of Genoa, who were to don armour and fight. But Pope Boniface VIII forbade the would-be Crusaders to reap even the smallest personal advantage from any victories they might win; the expedition faded out, evidence of the fact that even the most sincere faith could not be divorced from practical considerations.

The arts, the sciences and public utilities

A practical, utilitarian purpose very often is wrapped in the gifts which merchants made with the hope of commending their souls to God and their memory to posterity. They donated churches, chapels or stained glass, like the noblemen, but their real preference was for good works which were of direct benefit to the poor and the community at large. There is virtually no Genoese will which omits a legacy to be used for construction work on the light tower and docks. In Venice, as early as 977, Pietro Orseolo, doge and merchant, had founded a hospice. In Ghent, in 1200, the Uten Hove family founded a hospital with a great central hall which still today forms the centre of the town's largest hospital. Arras, the town of the 'usurers', at the beginning of the 14th century possessed at least twenty-three hospitals, leper houses, and homes for the needy — capable of taking in altogether some 1.000 souls — all founded by the bourgeois. The entire population of the town, at that time, could not have exceeded 20,000. In these buildings, as well as in bridges, aqueducts, fountains and other public works, the majestic lines of Romanesque architecture and the bold lines of Gothic architecture found new applications. Many of these works are still in use (Pl. 26). Painters and sculptors embellish these buildings with such appropriate subjects as allegories of good government, municipal prosperity and peace.

A robust realism, responsive to ideals but not submerged in them, is the trade mark of urban society. Mindful of the divine 'Scales in which we all shall be weighed', the merchants adjust their own scales, work out flawless accounts and eventually write up their ledgers in accordance with a new technique which we still use in our rationalistic age: double-entry book-keeping. To make the most of opportunities in markets and goods, they study arithmetic, geography, map-making, astronomy and the natural sciences.

This accumulation of knowledge represents so many victories for European culture. In the dissertations of Leonardo Fibonacci of Pisa, merchant and son of a merchant, we find the beginnings of modern mathematical science. Marco Polo, a 'universal man' if ever there was one, brought back from his journeys cultural riches which were much more precious than the most beautiful silks that China could offer. His book of true adventures, prophetically dedicated to 'emperors, kings, dukes and everyone else', was destined to displace the imaginary adventures of Chretien de Troyes and to become the most widely read secular work in the whole of Europe.

The Renaissance around the corner?

All this is not yet the Renaissance, but in a thousand ways its imminence can be sensed. There is no question, it is true, of art for art's sake, or of pagan Augustus being preferred to Christian Justinian. Yet there is a gust of classicism sweeping through Italian towns, chasing away some of the clouds. St Francis is wide awake to the beauty of this world below, 'the various fruits, multicoloured flowers and grass.' Bourgeois poetry brings the ordinary man into the picture for the first time, endowing him with unordinary qualities of soul. In fact, Love, with a capital letter, which Provençal poets and their imitators had kept exclusively for those of noble birth becomes an attribute of the 'noble mind' in the *Dolce Stil Nuovo* poetry of Bologna and Florence. Now the noble mind is not passed on from father to son; it is fashioned by a progressive refinement of sensibility and urban good manners. As if to underline this point of view, a Spanish poet who had been initiated into the life of chivalry in France and Germany, declares that he wishes to perfect himself therein in 'Lombardy', that is, in the Italy of the towns.

Admittedly, the military might of these cities does not match that of ancient Rome, nor does their population equal that of the Chinese cities which Marco Polo describes with amazement. But they do surpass China in their spirit of independence and initiative, Athens and Rome in the freedom of a society without slaves. They are richer, too, though not so much in hard cash as in flexible credit. Private business is based on drafts and promises to pay. Public finance is based on the funded debt. Had this invention of the thirteenth-century Communes been known in the mighty Roman Empire, perhaps the barbarians would have been held in check.

Puffed up by their power and culture, the gentlemen-merchants look down upon the world of barons and country squires. To all appearances they have every reason to do so. At the end of the 13th century, and at the beginning of the 14th, the Empire is broken, the Papacy is about to leave for exile, and France, the greatest monarchy in Europe, hires Italian admirals to command her fleet, Genoese bowmen to protect her knights, and Florentine financiers to administer her treasury.

Yet the bourgeoisie, dynamic though it is, is too small in numbers to lift up and carry along the great agricultural masses. Europe's political future at the turn of the Middle Ages will not be decided in the free towns, but in the feudal monarchies and at the expense of urban freedom.

Chapter 2

THE ADOLESCENT NATIONS

I. TOUR OF EUROPE: KINGS, LANGUAGES, NATIONS

'OH flowers, flowers of the green pine tree. — If you can tell where my friend may be, — Oh God, where is he? — Oh flowers, flowers of the branches green, — If you can tell where my love has been, — Oh God, where is he?' Thus, with a sigh, Denis 'the Farm Labourer', king of Portugal (1279–1325), begins the most winsome of the lyrical poems (a hundred or more) which he composed. In the fashion of true noblemen, Denis was well schooled in the 'Provençal style' but his poems were above all inspired by popular themes and were sung to traditional tunes stemming from both Arab and Gregorian music. Nor was he content with being merely a poet; he directed the adaptation and translation into Portuguese of all manner of works, historical, theological, juridical and didactic, written in other Romance languages, in Latin, in Arabic and in Hebrew. He ordered that Portuguese should become his country's official language.

King Denis is not an exception. In the springtime of vernacular literatures, the great family of thirteenth-century monarchs was hard at work. Alfonso X of Castille, Denis's grandfather, had left behind him a voluminous output (a good proportion of which, however, was not actually written by him but merely commissioned): in Galician, a cycle of canticles on the miracles of the Blessed Virgin and a number of secular poems; in Castilian, some love poetry, a series of chronicles, books of astronomy and natural science, and a massive juridical encyclopaedia (*Las siete partidas*) which was later translated into Portuguese by Denis. Frederick II, Emperor and King of Sicily (Alfonso's second cousin), had written a good deal in Latin and Italian; notably a Latin essay on falconry, a subject he knew from personal experience, and a few Italian poems on the sorrows of unrequited love, a subject about which he must have known far less. Three of his illegitimate sons — Enzo, king of Sardinia; Manfred, king of Sicily; and Frederick of Antioch — wrote Italian love poems in a similar vein; so did Pier delle Vigne, his chancellor, and other members of that extraordinary court. Love poems of the same kind, but in German, were written (or at least signed) by Frederick II's grim father, Emperor Henry VI, and by Frederick's romantic grandson, Conradin. Leaving aside many other members of the family of crowned poets, let us note that even sovereigns with little inclination to waste their time in literary frolics, like James I of Aragon (Alfonso of

Castille's father-in-law) and Louis IX of France (Blanche of Castille's son), dictated didactic works: James, a chronicle of his own reign, in Catalan; Louis, a manual of moral 'Instructions' for his son, in French.

In Portugal

In actual fact, even when the theme was frivolous, this royal literature was not merely a pastime. It enabled the sovereigns to identify themselves with their own nation, to engage in conversation with those of their subjects whom they could reach. Denis distinguished himself the most among the kings; he was, in his own country, the greatest poet of his time. His cultural efforts ranged from short songs which were well within the scope of the people, to the foundation of the first Portuguese University.

> The activities of the 'Farm Labourer' were not confined to the literary field. Even though he never once engaged in battle, his peaceful achievements nevertheless made him the third founder of the Portuguese nation, after the first Count and the first King. The broad lines of his programme were not new, but they were put into execution with new energy; it championed the State's authority vis-a-vis the Church, forced the nobility and bourgeoisie to take their share of government responsibilities, nurtured agriculture and industry.
>
> Denis built castles and villages by the score, granted liberally the right of holding markets, confiscated a number of large estates and redistributed them to whoever would undertake to cultivate them. To counter the bias of a nobility which tended to respect the military profession alone, he declared that one might equally devote oneself to agriculture with no loss of dignity. To make sure that naval yards had the materials essential to the building of ships, he planted in the Leiria region the pine forest which can still be seen there today, perhaps the very forest to which the sad maid in the song confides her anguish.

Unified as it was within frontiers almost identical with those of today, Portugal could only expand through the sea. As yet its role in international trade was still modest, but it could grow. Denis summoned from Genoa Admiral Manuel Pessagno; under his direction, the Portuguese navy began to set course for a brilliant future (Pl. 27).

Aragon and Catalonia

On another Iberian coast, the Aragonese kings, James I (1213–1276) and Peter III (1276–1285) achieved speedier and more spectacular successes, though less durable ones. Their kingdom brought together two regions which differed sharply in cultural and economic characteristics and levels — Catalonia, with a language of its own, related to Provençal, and Aragon, where a dialect resembling Castilian was spoken.

Aragon gave its name to the kingdom but, like the small neighbouring kingdom of Navarre, it was backward; it had a turbulent aristocracy, while the mass of the people were rugged mountaineers and poor peasants. To the west and south, the obvious expansion routes for Aragon were blocked by Castille; in the north, Aragon's hopes in Languedoc had just crumbled to dust at the battle of Muret.

Along the Catalan sea coast, on the other hand, towns were numerous and the horizon stretched far into the distance. James I put his stake on the adventurous spirit of the lesser aristocracy and the emerging middle-class of Catalonia and it paid dividends. The Balearics, Valencia and other coastal provinces, wrenched from the Moslem and colonised by James I's subjects, increased the area of his kingdom by a half. Peter III, in turn, made himself master of Sicily, which was in revolt against Charles of Anjou; then he put to flight the French king who had invaded Catalonia with a view to avenging Charles, his uncle. This definitely established the kingdom of Aragon as a great power.

The death of Peter III did not halt its great surge forward. James II occupied a great part of Sardinia and, less successfully, tried to conquer Corsica. A band of Catalan soldiers of fortune founded an independent state in Greece and placed it under the protection of the kings of Aragon. Meanwhile, in Barcelona and in other Catalan ports literary culture was becoming more refined, commercial methods were coming close to those of Italy. It seemed, for a few years, as if Barcelona would eclipse Genoa and Venice. These two, being free towns, had to carve their way by themselves; the Catalonian towns, by contrast, enjoyed the armed support of the landed nobility as well as the goodwill of the king, who was quite prepared to issue protectionist decrees and to place his diplomatic representatives at the service of merchants.

Yet independence is not without its advantages. The Catalan towns slowed down because they caught the germ of inertia as it were, from the kingdom which encased them. The kingdom was made up almost entirely of rural provinces where an unproductive aristocracy ruled over a mass of serfs. Its ports were but the gilt façade, so to speak, of a building of clay.

In Bohemia

Another bilingual kingdom of the 13th century, Bohemia, leapt to the rank of a great power in one single bound, under the impetus of an ambitious and intelligent sovereign. It distinguished itself from other Slav states in that it became a member of the conglomeration of fiefs forming the Germanic Empire while preserving its Czech identity and autonomy. (Fig. 57).

These two factors, which were contradictory but not incompatible, were determined at two different times; first, Duke Vladislas II of Bohemia was raised to royal dignity by Frederick Barbarossa, as a reward for faithful aid against the Lombardy towns (1158); and then his son obtained from Frederick II a 'Golden Bull' reducing his obligations to the Empire to a minimum, without however reducing his rights within it (1212).

Although as early as the 9th century it had been responsible for the first Slav urban civilisation, the Czech society kept for a long time an essentially agrarian character. The reigning dynasty boasted of its descent from the legendary 'Przemysl the Labourer'. The Commercial Revolution was slow to reach Bohemia, as was also the case with other Slav countries and a great part of Germany, but it was sustained by the exploitation of the rich silver mines. German miners and other immigrants, either invited by the king or attracted by the upsurge of the towns, built up the Germanic element in Bohemia. The Czech aristocracy, however, held fast to its traditions. Both cultures found their expression, the one in the lyricism of the Bohemian Minnesinger (German poets of the Provençal school), the other in epics and historical poems in Czech. Latin, the language of officialdom and literature, served as a bridge between the two peoples. It was in Latin that the most important documents were written — such as the Bohemian national chronicle by Cosmas (12th century) and the influential mining laws of 1249 and 1300.

Fig. 57. Four just men of Bohemia in the city of God, about 1200; Detail from an illumination, Prague, Library of the Chapter of St Guy.

On these foundations, King Przemysl Ottokar II — whose very name was half Czech, half German — endeavoured to build hastily a great State. He had military skill, diplomatic talent, and financial resources. To the hereditary lands of the Bohemian Crown, he added Austria, Styria, Carinthia, driving on as far south as the Adriatic. In 1256, when his vote on the choice of a new Emperor was canvassed, he manoeuvred things so as to leave two rival contestants grappling with each other, in the hope that he himself would eventually gather in the votes.

Had his scheme succeeded, a Slav-Germanic Empire might have arisen, in the place of the almost bankrupt Romano-Germanic Empire. It failed. The German princes wanted a weak emperor. After a long interregnum, the throne went to a country squire from the hills of Switzerland and Alsace who alarmed no-one, Rudolf of Hapsburg. This very obscurity enabled Rudolf to align against Przemysl the numerous German princes who feared the Bohemian king's enterprises, and coveted one or other of his lands. The King of Hungary joined the coalition. The Czech king appealed, too late, to Slav solidarity, in terms which have a strangely modern ring: 'Among all the nations of the earth, the Polish race is most like unto our own. We are bound by language, by origins, by blood and proximity. If we fall, insatiable German beaks will open yet wider and their greedy and destructive appetites will strike at your country too.' Trapped between Germans and Hungarians, Przemysl was overcome and slain in 1278. The Austrian lands went to Rudolf of Hapsburg, and thus, almost accidentally, the Hapsburg family began to be identified with Austrian destinies.

With all hope of aggrandizement in the West lost, the first successors to Przemysl turned their eyes towards Poland and Hungary, both outside the scope of this present volume. Later, it is true, Bohemia and the Empire were to be again reconciled politically under one sovereign, but cultural integration, barely begun when it was interrupted in the 13th century, was not achieved. Inside the kingdom of Bohemia, Slav majority and German minorities were to confront each other with growing mistrust, and to fight, each side intent on the destruction of the other. In our time, the Gordian knot has been cut by the expulsion of the minorities.

In the Celtic countries

At the other end of Catholic Europe the admixture of an exotic culture helped Scotland to find its national identity. To understand this paradox, we must remember that the ethnic basis of the population included both Celtic groups and elements of a yet earlier people, the Picts. Further, the Celts were divided into a Brythonic language group, almost indistinguishable from that of Wales and Northern England, and a Gaelic language group, the Scots proper, who began to immigrate from Ulster about the year 500 A.D. All these societies were non-urban and unaccustomed to a firm, centralized rule. In order to carry on government, the Celtic kings were obliged to borrow manpower and institutions from across the frontiers. The Continent was too far away, while Scandinavia was hostile and scarcely more civilized than Scotland itself. There remained England, which was not constantly hostile, despite the chronic irritation of frontier disputes that had persisted since Roman times. From the days of Emperor Claudius down to 1603 the 'debatable land' remained debatable by force of arms, yet the wars into which the debate often turned were usually wars of limited objective, never of annihilation.

The kingdom of Scotland had barely completed the gathering of its people under one rule when Macbeth, the sinister hero of Shakespeare's tragedy, emerged in the uncertain light of a history scarcely known to the author, and still imperfectly known to us. Macbeth was really the last champion of the North, and of a North more closed to Anglo-Saxon influence, but accessible to Scandinavian sympathies. After the accession of Malcolm III, the son of Duncan, whom he avenged on Macbeth (1053–1093), the cultural influence of England (strengthened after 1066 by the immigration of Anglo-Saxon aristocratic and ecclesiastical refugees as well as Norman knights) began to be felt in the lowlands of the South, to spread gradually towards the rugged north.

By the 13th century, the superficial Anglicization of the country was an accomplished fact. Canon law, Roman law, feudal institutions, and some legislation borrowed from the enactments of the English Crown, had almost entirely supplanted the customary law of the Celtic tribes. North and west of a well-defined linguistic frontier the people still spoke Gaelic, but Norman French had become about as current in the upper circle as it was in England, and the rest of the aristocracy and the middle classes, as well as the mass of the people in the Lowlands, spoke what they called 'Inglis.' This language, the Middle Scots of modern philologists, would scarcely have been recognised as English in Southern England, but it was probably intelligible to most Englishmen born north of the Trent, and it became the vehicle for a considerable literature, both popular and courtly.

It was in 'Inglis' that an unknown poet composed the eulogy of the last Celtic king, Alexander III, who died in 1286. The peace, order and prosperity he brought to his kingdom, and in particular his treaty with the King of Norway (1263), whereby the latter yielded the Western Isles and the Isle of Man to Scotland, keeping only the Orkney and Shetland Islands under Norwegian control, would be enough to ensure Alexander a niche in the gallery of great kings of the 13th century. But once he was dead, the English kings again brought forward their claim to sovereignty over the whole of Great Britain. In the long war that followed, the bravery of Wallace, of the Bruces, and of their adherents, preserved the independence of the Kingdom of Scotland. Alone among Celtic nations, Scotland showed herself capable of resisting an enemy more powerful than she, with whom she partly shared a common language, but whose roots were profoundly different. Yet the very names of these two Scottish national heroes bear witness to more than one strain. Wallace means literally 'the Welshman:' the family must have come from Wales, or from the Welsh political enclaves further north, unless it derived from the older 'Brythonic' population of Scotland. The Bruces were a family of almost unmixed Norman descent, whose representatives had come over during the reign of William the Conqueror if not actually present at Hastings, and had long maintained their estates in Yorkshire. Like most Normans of any distinction, they also boasted Norwegian blood.

The example of Scotland remained without parallel. Although certain Celtic literary motifs were current throughout Christendom, and although the fine flower of Celtic prose and poetry (both the early mediaeval heritage and more recent works) had at last been collected in Irish and Welsh manuscripts, the political independence of the Celts was on its deathbed. Cornwall, traditionally King Arthur's country, had been incorporated in the Kingdom of Wessex as far back as the beginning of the 9th century. The last speaker of the Cornish language was still alive in the lifetime of Napoleon, but Cornwall was no longer a special national unit in 1337, when it was made into a Duchy vested in the heir to the English throne.

Wales was now the last refuge of the traditional Brythonic society and language. By fits and starts the star of the princes of Gwynedd burned brightly, as under Hywel 'the Good' in the early 10th century, Llewelyn ap Eorwerth 'the Great' (1194–1240), and Llewelyn ap Griffydd (1246–1282). But these moments of splendour did not last, because they depended mostly on the internal crises and difficulties of the English kings, such as the insurrection that led to *Magna Carta*. At last Edward I overthrew

Fig. 58. Portrait of St Louis, from a miniature executed about 1320; French National Archives, History Museum of France.

the Celtic principality and transformed it into an apanage for the heir apparent to the English throne. The Welsh tribes counted themselves lucky in being able to preserve a certain local autonomy including the use of their language and the greater part of the traditional laws attributed to Hywel 'the Good.'

Ireland, being larger, afforded more room for manoeuvre. In this theatre, the Celts ought to have been better able to organise military resistance. They had thrown back the Norsemen, after a struggle lasting more than two centuries and culminating in the dramatic victory of Brian, the Irish *ard-ri* (high king), at Clontarf (1014). The English, however, were better armed and organised, and Irish co-operation did not survive Brian. Nevertheless, it seemed between the years 1315 and 1318 that the island might achieve its political unity, under the leadership indeed of a foreigner but not of an Englishman. This was Edward, brother of King Robert Bruce of Scotland, the victor of Bannockburn. But Edward Bruce was defeated and killed, and the Irish chieftains relapsed again into their perpetual clan feuds. The English (or rather, their army, consisting largely of Norman officers and Welsh mercenaries) resumed their advance, which was often difficult, but in the long run proved irresistible.

From Iceland to Finland

Another island, proud of its own literature, but desperately poor and rent asunder by internal strife — Iceland — had been obliged, from 1262, to surrender its independence in favour of the King of Norway. The Swedes had asserted themselves in Finland some years previously. Further south there stretched a whole graveyard of nations suffocated by German conquest before they had been able to make themselves heard — Estonians, Letts, Slavs from Pomerania, Prussians....

The Prussians disappeared, leaving no souvenir apart from their barbarity and their name to a province; Letts, Estonians and Finns retained their identities in popular traditions, such as the enthralling Finnish epics which have been gathered together in modern times under the title of *Kalevala*.

One wonders what contribution these people might have made to the civilization of the late Middle Ages had they not been reduced to silence. But in the 13th century there was no longer room for leaderless peoples, disorganised societies or backward cultures and economies. The nations which disappeared were destroyed less by the arms of their conquerors than by the Commercial Revolution and the intellectual Renaissance of the West. They were the victims of progress, which often has its own cruelties.

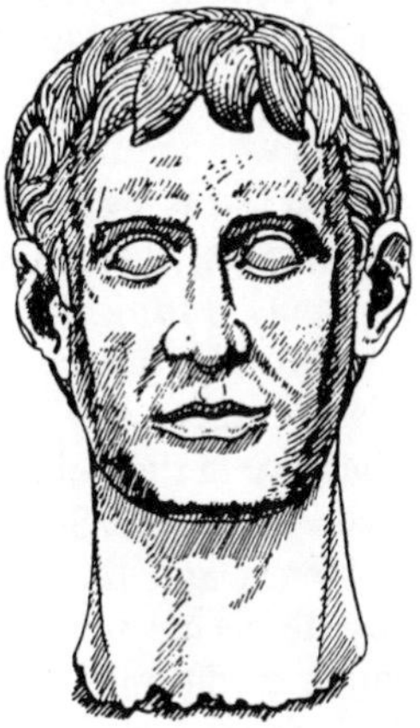

Fig. 59. Frederick II, king of Sicily and Emperor, thirteenth century; from a bust of the German Archaeological Institute, Rome.

Two great kings: the sceptic and the angelic

Progress, on the other hand, strengthened the forces of those nations who welcomed it, and brought to the fore sovereigns of great energy, even in second-rate states; Haakon IV and Magnus VI in Norway (Fig. 38) Valdemar II and Eric Menved in Denmark, Ladislas 'the Short' in Poland, Bela IV in Hungary, Manfred and Charles of Anjou in Sicily, Count Floris V in Holland, Regent Birger in Sweden, ... The more powerful countries of Castille, England and France had more famous leaders; Popes who were full of energy governed the Church. Two monarchs in particular stand out from among the rest. They made both on their contemporaries and on posterity a profound impression, the one by reason of his angelic virtues, the other by his devilish skill; Louis IX of France, 'Saint Louis' (1226–1270) (Fig. 58) and Frederick II, Emperor and King of Sicily, the 'wonder of the world.' (1197–1250) (Fig. 59)

Because of his urge to resemble Caesar rather than Charlemagne, his universal curiosity, his calculating realism, Frederick might seem a harbinger of the Renaissance. No matter whether politics, or legislation, or art is involved, he goes to great lengths to repel the barbarian heritage and feudal tradition, in order to draw closer to classic Roman antiquity. He is interested in all the sciences, and all foreign cultures attract him. Even though his name is linked to no discovery of an original nature, he burns with a desire to learn, to observe and to experiment. By studying philosophy, by practicing diplomacy, by keeping many contacts with non-conforming Christians and with Jews, his naturally violent and authoritarian character acquired the habit of doubting sometimes, and, what is more, of toleration.

Louis, by contrast, models himself on the traditional picture, sketched in the time of Charlemagne, and embroidered by succeeding generations; the picture of a king who is at once father and shepherd of his people, the enemy of sin, the defender of justice and peace. Staunchly upholding the established order, he favours a trinitarian society, customary law, and Gothic art. He cultivates the virtues of feudal chivalry to the highest possible degree — strength, courage, loyalty, generosity. His piety is genuine, but more akin to the plain asceticism of Cluny than the bold scholasticism of Paris; his respect for the Church never goes as far as sacrificing the authority of the State, and his simple goodness entertains no indulgence where heretics or infidels are concerned. If Frederick II was led astray by his own cleverness, which bewildered his friends and shocked his enemies, then St Louis was led into error by his unmovable ignorance, especially during the two Crusades which he led without ever consenting to listen to the advice of experts.

Yet is there any century where one cannot find two such opposites? The difference in their characters, moreover, was not the only thing which separated Frederick II and St Louis. The problems they had to face were not the same problems, and the view from Paris could not resemble that from Palermo. Despite his cosmopolitan attitude and his German origin, Frederick respected Italian traditions, tastes and prejudices. Notwithstanding his insistence that all Christian kings were one family (all, in fact, were more or less related to him), Louis thought and acted like a Frenchman.

Viewed from yet another angle, the two sovereigns were far more attached to the opinions and passions of their times than might seem to be the case. Frederick the Sceptic sent many a heretic to the stake, Louis the Angelic jealously defended class privilege. Frederick was not an enthusiastic Crusader, but he restored Jerusalem to Christendom; Louis, despite his fervour, diverted the second Crusade to Tunis where there was something to gain for his brother, Charles of Anjou. Thus with opposing principles, and by methods different as their starting points, the two monarchs envisaged the same ultimate goal—the use of the new resources offered by the economic and intellectual progress of their century to mould the State into an instrument which would be tractable in the hands of the monarch.

II. THE DRAMA OF THE UNIVERSAL MONARCHIES

These new resources constituted a two-edged weapon. The king could use them either to make his kingdom prosperous and peaceful, or to satisfy his appetite for conquest. Vassals and autonomous towns might exploit them either to collaborate more efficiently with the king, or to resist him with renewed vigour. Hence the most solid States were not ipso facto the largest, but those where there existed a happy balance, a mutual support between central government and local government; in other words, regional states, or at most, national, not universal.

The Empire and the Papacy, universal States by definition, were the only ones to become weaker during the 13th century. They had the greatest number of vassals and collaborators, but they also faced the greatest degree of opposition, inside as well as from outside. Their sovereigns were kept occupied with the defence and multiplication of their distant interests and were embroiled in the old duel between Church and State, and they hardly had time to apply themselves to the pressing problems of their own domains.

The Pope, triumphant everywhere except at home

Obviously if we look only at the extension of territory under indirect control, the 13th century would seem to pinpoint the peak of the Papacy. Men of singular talent, schooled in philosophy, law, economics and diplomacy, succeeded one another to the chair of St Peter and carried off brilliant victories in the international sphere. Innocent III (1198–1216) has a hand in the affairs of practically every European State, imposing his will on famous kings; — Gregory IX (1227–1241) sets up the Inquisition and introduces it into several countries: Innocent IV (1243–1254) enters Naples as a conqueror, Gregory X (1271–1276) through the intermediary of Byzantine delegates, receives the submission of the Greek Church....

As regards the clergy, the Holy See fulfills its most daring ambitions. Its power to discipline, its authority in cases of disputed or deferred elections, its right to gather in taxes on the revenue of ecclesiastical prebends and monasteries, are acknowledged throughout the Catholic world. At the same time, new collections of Pontifical Decrees are taking their place in schools and tribunals alongside the Justinian Code; they represent a kind of other 'common law' to be observed in all domains where the Church's law complements local laws or replaces them. The Church has full jurisdiction, not only in matters concerning ecclesiastics, crusaders, widows and orphans, but also in matters of heresy, sorcery, annulments of marriage and usury.

On the other side of the scale, however, we must put the failure of the Papacy in its own temporal domains. The expression 'States of the Church' covers, in reality, a miscellany of semi-independent urban Communes (and, around Rome, semi-feudal baronies) which frequently refuse to their suzerain even the most elementary gestures of homage. The Commune of Rome itself is usually dominated by the Ghibelline party, notwithstanding the advantages which the occasional presence of the Sovereign Pontiff procures for it.

The thirteenth-century Popes, almost all Italians, fairly often Romans and noble, strove in vain to re-introduce some semblance of order at home. Conferences, exhortations, money and first-class administration wherever they succeeded in installing their representatives and officials, all were to no avail. The weapon of excommunication, brought into use against the most stubborn of their enemies, has lost its edge by reason of too frequent use and it no longer serves much of a purpose. The Popes end by falling back on crusades, first against heretics, then against Frederick II (classed as a heretic), and finally against any political opponent who appears to constitute a danger. This weapon also, being used indiscriminately, is losing its effectiveness. In 1297, Boniface VIII launches a crusade to drive out of Palestrina, in the neighbourhood of Rome, a great family rivalling his own. Palestrina capitulates, is destroyed; but in 1303, the Pope's rivals, supported by an emissary of the French king, take their revenge by arresting Boniface at nearby Anagni. It is true that the shocked population of the town sets him free a few days later, but the episode brings to the forefront in dramatic fashion the chronic impotence of the Pontifical monarchy in its own Italian base. This weakness had already cast a shadow over the international successes of Innocent III and Gregory X; it was to render irreparable the defeats of Boniface VIII at the hands of the French and English monarchies.

Decline of the Empire in a shattered Germany

The German home of the Imperial monarchy had crumbled even earlier — by the early 13th century. On the death of Henry VI (1197), his son, Frederick II, still a child, inherited only the Kingdom of Sicily, while in Germany two claimants to the Empire rekindled the old war between Guelphs and Ghibellines. When Frederick entered the lists in his turn, and inherited what was left of the Empire, he did not try to rebuild all the ruins, as his predecessors had done again and again. The title of Emperor was no doubt attractive and bestowed an air of legality on all future ambitions. But it was impossible to govern Germany from Palermo or Naples, and Frederick would not leave these bases for long. At the most, one might require the German princes, in exchange for liberal concessions, to help in the restoration of the imperial power in Northern Italy.

Two decrees, dating from 1220 and 1231, gave official blessing to the liquidation of Imperial control over the great German vassals, both ecclesiastical or lay. The former obtained from Frederick almost all sovereign rights, while the lay princes were proclaimed 'lords of the land' and confederated under the presidency of Frederick, rather than under his command. This presidency itself was to be delegated to two of the Emperor's sons successively.

In 1256, after the death of Frederick II, the death of Conrad IV, his son ,and the death of Count William of Holland who had in feeble measure assumed the direction of the Guelph party, the Empire became a confederation with no president. It had by then become customary that in the absence of a direct heir, the choice of a successor to the throne would be entrusted to seven lay and ecclesiastical princes, representing the mass of the German vassals. Two foreigners who aspired to the Imperial Crown, king Alphonse X of Castille and Richard of Cornwall, brother of Henry III of England, spent fortunes to buy support, but could not substantiate their claims by means of armed force. The German princes (one of whom, we have seen, was the King of Bohemia) kept this greasy pole in operation for eighteen years. Even the free German towns, which had long and vainly hoped for imperial protection against the princes, adapted themselves to the situation and provided for their own defence by means of regional leagues.

The interregnum might have lasted indefinitely and the Empire passed away in its sleep, had not Pope Gregory X, in 1273, brought pressure to bear on the princes in behalf of a new candidate, Rudolf of Hapsburg. As a matter of fact, the Pope desired a weak Empire, but not an Empire without an emperor; he wanted the secular arm to put into effect the mandates of the ecclesiastical arm. Though there was no love lost between the two powers, they needed one another.

Rudolf, however, had no universal ambitions. This is precisely what enabled him to rescue, in as far as it could be rescued, an almost desperate cause. Having acquired at the expense of Przemysl Ottokar II a direct domain sufficient to enable him to cut a dash without alarming his neighbours, Rudolf was content to be chief among his peers, the German president of a German confederation. The degree to which he opted out of Italian and universalist politics is emphasized by the fact that his chancellory abandoned Latin in favour of German.

His successors did not completely manage to cut loose from the fascination of the Imperial title, or of the riches that might be culled in Italy, but their practical achievements were generally in proportion to the attention they gave their own domain to the north of the Alps. Certainly, there still existed in Germany a Supreme Court, the Council of the Seven Prince Electors and the General Diet of the Empire. But all these institutions were thin veils, even more transparent than that of the phantom monarchies of the 10th century. The task of re-organising and perfecting the system of government from then on devolved upon the various autonomous German States. Most of these progressed no further than feudalism, but feudalism did not have to be disorganized; the free towns developed efficient administrations; the Teutonic Knights edified a robust State, governed with military discipline, but exploited with flexible economic methods. Altogether, it does not seem that Germany was much the worse for the disappearance of a strong central power.

The mirage of an Italian empire

The decline of the Empire in Germany was strictly connected with its failure in Italy. Let us go back in time, then, to Italy in the years of Frederick II's concessions to the German princes. Those very years — 1220 and 1231 — also mark the beginning and the completion of the collection of laws promulgated in the kingdom of Sicily by the same Frederick, with utterly different ends in view. While biding his time in Germany, in Italy he brought into being the first Imperial Code since that of Justinian, drawing its material from the authoritarian legislation of his Norman predecessors and the absolutist interpretation of Roman Law.

In this code (*Liber Augustalis*) and in Frederick's government in Italy, some modern historians have seen the prototype of the modern State. But this is an exaggeration which can only be justified if one equates 'modern' with 'centralizing' and considers the purpose rather than the results. The purpose was to uproot all forms of localism in order to pave the way for a paternalistic, absolute, bureaucratic monarchy. The results lagged far behind the goal. It would have been impossible to erase centuries of feudal and ecclesiastical fragmentation at a single stroke.

The Emperor, 'the earthly embodiment of the law', sends out his officials into the provinces, builds palaces and fortresses, founds schools of law and medicine, develops the road system, protects trade, agriculture and stock-breeding, encourages immigration. 'The wealth of his subjects is the glory and well-being of the sovereign.' There we have a maxim worthy of Colbert; but Frederick II (like Louis XIV in Colbert's time) takes back with one hand what he has given with the other, stripping from the young tree fruit which is not yet ripe. If he has deferred the assertion of his power in Germany (the third stage of his imperial programme), it is in order to complete at all speed the first stage — putting to a test his new methods in the little kingdom of Sicily — and proceed with the second stage: the extension of his firm rule to the whole of Italy.

Re-organizing North Italy as well as Sicily into regional governments, placing rural areas under vicars and the Communes under Podestas appointed by him, making the Church serve the State and the State direct the consciences and private life of the citizens; these are the ultimate goals of Frederick, as far as can be discerned amid the innumerable deviations inflicted on him en route by political resistance and military strife. Sicily, bled-white, gives money, Germany gives soldiers, exiles and adventurers from Northern and Central Italy help to fill military and administrative posts. In every town of Tuscany and Lombardy, there is a Ghibelline party anxious to crush its own foes with the Emperor's help, even at the price of the independence of the Commune. As for the Pope, Frederick's most stubborn enemy, it would not be impossible to come to terms with him and ask for reasonable concession in exchange for full co-operation both in crusades and in other spheres. But Frederick is impatient, he is incapable of compromise; he wins every battle, then loses every war. He is to die in 1250, leaving behind an exhausted Sicily and an Italy north of the Tiber still unsubdued.

And yet his career holds such a fascination for those who watch it that his successors on the throne of Sicily, in their turn, will endeavour to gain mastery of the whole of Italy; first Manfred, his son, supported by the Ghibelline party; then Charles of Anjou, raised to royal status by the Pope, and supported by the Guelph party. Manfred will be impetuous and chivalrous, Charles obstinate and calculating. Both of them will have ability, but neither will have the genius which Frederick possessed or the prestige of the imperial crown. Both will experience the hour of triumph, followed by the hour of catastrophe. Manfred will lose both his kingdom and his life in a single battle in 1266. Charles, victor of the day, will lose only one half of his kingdom (in 1282) but this half is Sicily from which the state takes its name. And he will lose it in the most humiliating fashion — as a result of a popular revolution prepared by the local nobility (the 'Sicilian Vespers' of Palermo) and the intervention of the King of a small state, Peter III of Aragon.

The mists of the Castilian empire

Of those who suffered defeat in the 13th century, the most pathetic was Alfonso X 'the Wise', King of Castille (1252–1281) (Fig. 60). Scientist and man of letters, warrior, king, and candidate for the Imperial throne, Alfonso was perhaps an even more complex personality than Frederick II. This latter, however, saw the Empire as his vocation, science as his hobby, while Alfonso X took science seriously and the Empire as a dilettante.

Yet his career had begun under the most favourable auspices. As Crown Prince he had helped his father, Ferdinand III, to break down Islam's last barrier in Andalusia and to plant on the southern coast of Spain the standard which the first Count of Castille had unfurled two hundred years before in the mountains of the far north. Having become king, he had conquered Cadiz and Niebla, but had allowed a Moslem vassal, the Emir of Granada, to entrench himself in the most southerly mountains. He saw no greater danger in this isolated pocket than in the other Jewish and Moslem communities enclosed within his kingdom; these Infidels might be of help to the king when Christian nobles, churchmen or merchants joined forces to resist his will.

Fig. 60. Alfonso X of Castille 'The Wise', king of Castille-León. From a miniature of the Cartulary A 1255, Archives of the Cathedral of St James at Compostela.

The dangerous Infidels were not the meek and refined ones of Spain, but those of Morocco. Here was a reserve of fanatical and hungry warrior tribes who, twice already, first under the leadership of the Almoravides, then under that of the Almohades, had crossed into Spain and upset the time-table of the Christian *Reconquista*. Against the new masters of Morocco, the Merinids, Alfonso attempted a naval expedition in 1260 (the 'crusade' of Saleh) and was preparing another in 1264. His attention, however, was distracted by so many other ambitions at the same time, that he could not concentrate on any. Midway between a poem and a horoscope, he put forward incongruous claims to Portuguese Algarve, Gascony, Sicily, Lombardy, Swabia, the imperial crown, and especially in the vain pursuit of the Empire he wasted a great deal of money. At the same time, he proclaimed loudly that 'a king holds power as great as that of the Emperor' and, further, 'is entitled to transmit this power to his heirs, whereas the Emperor may not do so.'

While the king-astronomer was star-gazing, the earth was giving way beneath his feet. His last twenty years were as harrowing as a Greek tragedy. A massive Moslem revolt in newly conquered territories was only quelled, at great cost, with the co-operation of James I of Aragon. Then the rebellions of the Castilian nobles burst upon him. Following this the Emir of Morocco, at the instigation of his counterpart in Granada, subjected southern Castille to an ordeal of blood and fire. Sancho, second son of Alfonso and claimant to the throne, had the ineffectual and wasteful king deposed by the Cortes (1282). In this extremity, Alfonso appealed simultaneously to the Pope and the Emir of Morocco, this 'Commander of the Believers.' The Pope excommunicated Sancho, and authorised the old king to spend ecclesiastical tithes to quash the rebellion. The Emir arrived with an army and even wrote to the French king to urge him to re-establish order in the family of kings. With the help of the Moroccans and troops which remained loyal to him, Alfonso was in process of recovering the lost ground when suddenly, says tradition, the news (false as it happened) of the death of his ungrateful son broke his heart.

III.   FRENCH PRIMACY IN EUROPE

The disappointments of certain rash monarchs should not blind us to the continuous progress of monarchical institutions during the 13th century. Throughout the disasters and changes of dynasty, even the Sicilian government attracted more than one undisciplined and adventurous noble into its service, inured many town magistrates to act as officers of a central administration, propagated uniform, if not identical currencies and standards, tightened its control on trade and the export of grain, emphasized the predominance of the royal tribunals over the ecclesiastical courts.

Other governments asserted themselves generally with more discretion, making detours around obstacles which it behove them best not to confront squarely. They were unable to put an end to all local conflicts and private quarrels, but they did succeed in limiting them and moderating their violence. They did not dispute the validity of local laws, or of feudal, ecclesiastical or municipal justice, but promulgated decrees and collections of laws applicable to the whole State, and encouraged appeals to royal justice. They did not deny the feudal axiom that ordinarily 'the king must live on his own possessions', that is from the revenue of his private property, but they increased the number of 'extraordinary' taxes raised for specific purposes and strove to make them almost a regular feature.

If the king asked for more, he also gave more, except when he was involved in external wars which were too consuming. In order to win a following, he no longer needed to be a great soldier or to distribute lavish gifts as in the barbarian period; it was enough if he administered the State wisely. 'Be so upright that you never refuse to adopt a strictly righteous course because of anything that may happen.' 'Be careful to protect within your land men of every station.' 'Give freely of power to men of good will who know how to use it properly.' 'Beware of foolish outlay and poor income.' Such are the 'Instructions' which St Louis gives to his son. If a sovereign pays but the least attention to these precepts, his success is assured. Gradually, the sound forces of the kingdom — nobility, clergy, traders and intellectuals — will close their ranks about him, sustaining him against his more turbulent subjects, upholding him against foreign powers and, when appointed to official duties, show themselves often more royalist than the king.

Paris, the 'Athens of Europe'

It would be a lengthy and tedious process to trace the course in each European State of an evolution composed of small changes, small victories for central government, with no sensational upheavals. Let us confine ourselves to tracing its lines of development in that State which, during the 13th century, moved out of its inconspicuous position to the foremost place in Europe — the kingdom of France.

This leap into prominence, for all that it was stupendous, was none the less inevitable. Only Germany was larger than France, and only Italy was richer. On the whole, France was their superior, because her resources in men and food were more abundant, and were more happily spread among the various classes and provinces.

As the 12th century drew to a close, France already was setting the tone for Europe in all matters of art and culture. Her religious architecture and related manifestations — stained glass, enamels (Pl. 29), jewellery and sculpture — were fountainheads of new ideas, which French artists exported far and wide. Her epic literature, her lyrical poetry in both of her main tongues

(*langue d'oc* or Provençal south of the Loire, *langue d'oïl* or French proper
north of the Loire), her novels ('romances', as they were called because they
were in Romance language), her theatre, her sacred and secular music — all
were imposing their themes, their metres, their symbols, and even their two
languages which in the 13th century were competing with Latin as international
vehicles of thought. Her philosophy, her theology vied with those of Rome: it
required a long struggle to persuade the University of Paris to accept unreserved-
ly into its teaching body Dominican and Franciscan friars, who were too
closely bound to their Orders and in consequence to the Pope. After Cluny,
Cîteaux and Clairvaux (all of them originating in France), had been the most
important nuclei of monastic reform in the 12th century: in the 13th century,
in competition with the new mendicant Orders from Italy and Spain, they
nevertheless continued to exercise their influence far and wide. French feudalism
and the French code of chivalry provided a model for the aristocracy of all
countries and gave champions and recruits for every venture against either
Infidel or Christian.

There was a strong reverse current operating as a counterpart to the emigration of French talent — the drift of intellectuals towards Paris. 'Just as the
town of Athens in olden times was the mother of the liberal arts and of letters,
the nurse of philosophers and all manner of science, such is Paris in our day,
not merely for France, but for all Europe' says Bartholomew 'the English',
monk and encyclopaedist of the first half of the 13th century. 'In her role as
mother of Wisdom, Paris welcomes all comers from every country in the world,
and helps them in all their needs and governs them in peace.' Every country
in the world is somewhat of an exaggeration; all Catholic countries, yes, that
does due justice to the international role which the French capital is beginning
to play. The fact that Albert the Great was born in Swabia, Thomas Aquinas
near Naples, Siger of Brabant in Belgium and Boethius 'the Danish' in Sweden
makes them no less Parisian as teachers.

The kings of France assemble their kingdom

As long as the central government remained weak, the brilliance of France and
her capital could avail it nothing. When, however, the monarchy was galvan-
ised by Philip Augustus (1180–1223) it suddenly found that it had no serious
rivals: Emperors and Popes were locked in a fight to the death, England was
passing from the tottering government of John 'Lackland' to the still more
inept government of Henry III (1216–1272). For the kings of France many
prospects were opening; they could choose adventure and claim the heritage of
Charlemagne, frittered away by the Germans; or they could seek a return
match with England and cross that Channel which their Anglo-Norman and
Anglo-Angevin foes had crossed so often in the other direction; finally, they
could carry on the work of Philip Augustus and make themselves undisputed
masters of their own kingdom. It was the latter course which they chose to take

— the most prudent one — and along the route they also found greatness, which they had not sought (Maps 21 and 22).

Was this choice a matter of mature and calculated wisdom, or simply of lack of imagination and ambition? Probably it was a combination of the two. It is true that Philip Augustus' son (the future Louis VIII) tried to grab the English throne; it is also true that Philip II yearned for the imperial crown, and that Philip IV claimed it for his son. But these were transitory whims, not deep-rooted passions. At the first check, the kings reverted to a policy in accordance as much with the scruples of St Louis ('Beware, so far as it depends on you, of making war on Christians') as with the greed and administrative pedantry of Philip le Bel and his advisers. It was a strictly home-based policy based on insistence, if not on planning. Cautiously, without occasioning alarm or revolts, the sovereigns swallowed up one fief after another, one town after another. A hundred years after the death of Philip Augustus, an official enquiry conducted in 1328 reveals that more than three quarters of the territory of the kingdom was then a part of the direct domain of the king (Map 21). The immediate master of these vast territories, almost all of them fertile, was well entitled to call himself 'Emperor in his kingdom'.

> Those who endorsed most enthusiastically this formula were the jurists of Languedoc, the farthest of the annexed provinces, proof, if need be, of the solidity of the royal acquisitions. The journey from Paris to Toulouse, on horseback, took a dozen or so days, and on arrival one was in a completely different world: law, customs, climate and language, all were different. But these were not insuperable obstacles. Provençal and French belong to the same family. Roman Law, as taught in the schools of Languedoc, proclaimed that the people had irrevocably delegated plenary powers to the sovereign. The horrors of the Albigensian Crusade, the rigours of the Inquisition that was its aftermath had destroyed completely whatever urge there might have been towards independence either in politics or religion. The most turbulent of the nobles were either dead, or in exile. In the south there remained only two considerable vassals — the kings of Aragon and England; but even they had had to agree, as a result of treaties with St Louis, to renounce the greater part of their claims. In return for this, the English king retained what was left of the Duchy of Aquitaine, that of Aragon a few strips of land along the Mediterranean.

Two regions only, those where non-Romance languages were spoken, resisted absorption: Flanders and Brittany. The Duke of Brittany gave homage to the king, but sent back with scant ceremony any official from the central government whom he had not invited. As for the Count of Flanders, the king could not place much reliance on him; for had he not cut off from his country its rich southern districts? The Flemish nobility, bourgeoisie, lower classes, all would fight one against the other, but they would unite as soon as any heavy-handed authority appeared on the scene. Royal France had its partisans there, it is true, but England, a producer of wool, had its clients.

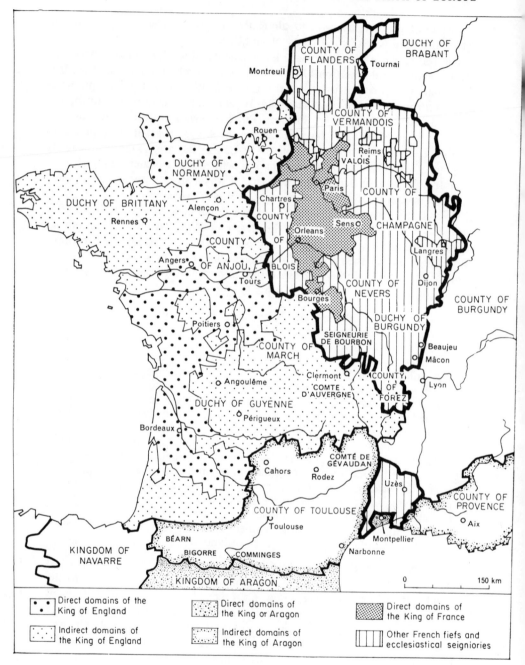

COUNTY OF FLANDERS
DUCHY OF BRABANT
Montreuil
Tournai
COUNTY OF VERMANDOIS
Reims
VALOIS
Rouen
DUCHY OF NORMANDY
Paris
COUNTY OF
DUCHY OF BRITTANY
Chartres
COUNTY
CHAMPAGNE
Alençon
Rennes
OF
Sens
Orleans
Langres
COUNTY
OF ANJOU,
BLOIS
Angers
Dijon
Tours
COUNTY OF
NEVERS
COUNTY OF
BURGUNDY
Bourges
Poitiers
DUCHY OF
BURGUNDY
SEIGNEURIE
DE BOURBON
Beaujeu
Mâcon
COUNTY OF
MARCH
Clermont
COUNTY
OF
FOREZ
Lyon
Angoulême
COMTE
D'AUVERGNE
DUCHY OF GUYENNE
Périgueux
Bordeaux
COMTÉ DE
GÉVAUDAN
Cahors
Rodez
Uzès
COUNTY OF
PROVENCE
COUNTY OF TOULOUSE
Aix
Toulouse
Montpellier
KINGDOM OF
NAVARRE
BÉARN
BIGORRE
COMMINGES
Narbonne
KINGDOM OF ARAGON

0   150 km

Direct domains of the King of England
Direct domains of the King or Aragon
Direct domains of the King of France
Indirect domains of the King of England
Indirect domains of the King of Aragon
Other French fiefs and ecclesiastical seigniories

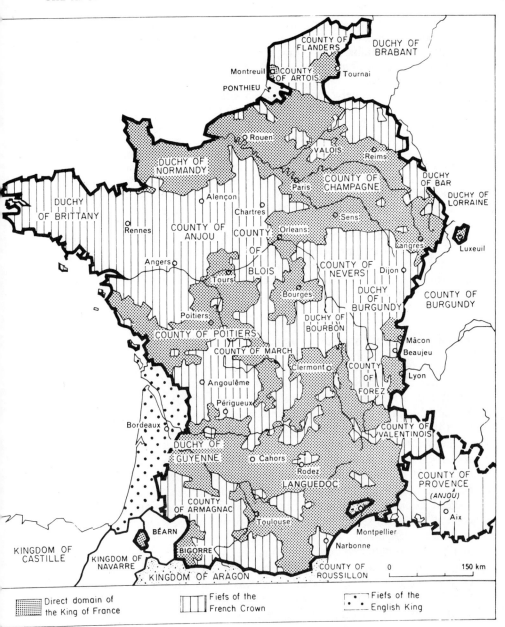

DUCHY OF
BRABANT

COUNTY OF
FLANDERS

Montreuil
PONTHIEU
COUNTY
OF ARTOIS
Tournai

DUCHY
OF BAR

DUCHY OF
LORRAINE

Rouen

VALOIS
Reims

DUCHY OF
NORMANDY

COUNTY OF
CHAMPAGNE

Paris

Alençon

Chartres
Sens

DUCHY
OF BRITTANY

COUNTY OF
ANJOU
COUNTY
OF

Orleans

Luxeuil

Rennes

Langres

Angers
BLOIS

COUNTY OF
NEVERS
Dijon

COUNTY OF
BURGUNDY

Tours
Bourges

DUCHY
OF
BURGUNDY

Poitiers
DUCHY OF
BOURBON

COUNTY OF POITIERS
Mâcon

COUNTY OF MARCH
Beaujeu

Clermont
COUNTY
OF
FOREZ
Lyon

Angoulême

Périgueux

Bordeaux
COUNTY OF
VALENTINOIS

DUCHY OF
GUYENNE
Cahors

Rodez

COUNTY OF
PROVENCE
(ANJOU)

LANGUEDOC

Aix

KINGDOM OF
CASTILLE

BÉARN

COUNTY
OF ARMAGNAC

Toulouse

BIGORRE

Montpellier
Narbonne

KINGDOM OF
NAVARRE

KINGDOM OF ARAGON
COUNTY OF
ROUSSILLON

0   150 km

Direct domain of
the King of France

Fiefs of the
French Crown

Fiefs of the
English King

Map 21 (left). France in 1180, at the accession of Philip Augustus
Map 22 (above). France in 1328, at the accession of Philip VI

Outside these areas, lords and communes were sufficiently pliable to constitute a support, rather than a hindrance, to the central government. Like ancient Rome, royal France had everything to gain from the existence of these local organisations, which relieved her of some of the administrative duties.

Rightly or wrongly, the king also hoped that his near relatives would be trustworthy collaborators; therefore he freely ceded fiefs as 'apanages' to members of his family, as was the custom at that time throughout Europe. The most enterprising of these vassals of the blood royal, Charles of Anjou, extended his possessions well beyond the borders of the French kingdom, carrying French influence as far as Sicily. Sicily, of course, was too far away to become a French province, but Provence under Charles' successors gradually freed itself from its nominal subjection to the Empire and drew ever closer to France. Philip 'the Fair' in turn won the allegiance of the imperial city of Lyon and obtained a footing in the small Franco-Spanish kingdom of Navarre by marrying its crown princess. The myth of 'natural boundaries' (the Rhine, the Alps, the Pyrenees), which was to play such an important role from the French Revolution on, had not yet been created, but already royal France was reaching for land that had never been included in the Capetian heritage.

From plume and sword to pen and ink-well

The organisation of administration proceeded at the same pace as territorial expansion. The France of Philip 'the Fair' could not be content with portable archives or a movable treasury like those which Philip Augustus, defeated by Richard Lionheart, abandoned on the battlefield in 1194. At the beginning of the 14th century, the central treasury of the Louvre and the central archives of the Sainte-Chapelle were the chief permanent depots of State assets and securities; nor were they the only ones. The King could no longer deal with his business at haphazard through the two amorphous and unspecialized councils—the *Curia regis* (King's Court) and the *hospicium* (Household) that had sufficed to the early Capetians. Little by little special committees within these councils had been set up by the King; a supreme political council, a high court of justice (*Parlement*), a financial office, the chancellery. Likewise, provincial administration could no longer be left in the hands of a few prelates and hereditary vassals who were usually more concerned with their own interests than those of the King. Henceforward, what was needed was career men, salaried, transferable, subject to recall; and, to help them, a cohort of lesser officials, plus a number of travelling inspectors to supervise their work and maintain contact with central departments.

Even at this stage, the framework of French administration was still less highly developed than that of the English, less complex than that of the Pope, less systematic than that of Sicily, although it was partly modelled on them. Although French administration soon attained an efficiency which was to grow with time, this was not due to its structure, but to its personnel. On the whole, French administrators were better versed in theology, in law, and in accountancy than their English colleagues. They were inevitably more devoted to the dynasty than were the employees of an elected Pope, or of a Sicilian king constantly threatened by rebellion and the ups-and-downs of political strife. The highest officials, in France, belonged mostly to the lesser aristocracy, and were eager to seek their fortunes as civil employees of a king who was disinclined for warlike adventure. Under them, new men were making their way; their only claim to distinction stemmed from their studies and their only source of power derived from the fact that they represented and reflected the king's majesty.

Like so many officials of modern times, the employees of Philip le Bel often behaved as petty, fussy, over-bearing, and sometimes bribable meddlers. It was not uncommon for the king to reproach them for exceeding their briefs, as when, for example, they challenged feudal immunities or municipal privileges that were perfectly legitimate, or when they ruled in favour of anyone who appealed to the King against his immediate lord. We shall never know for sure in which cases the King sincerely desired to spare his subjects, or in which cases he was imputing to his employees the blame for extortions from which he himself was in fact receiving the profits, or in which instances he was resenting the fact that his representatives were keeping for themselves the proceeds of graft. His employees, however, continued to work for him, boring the 'feudal system' as termites bore wood. The age of plume and sword was slowly moving towards the age of pen and ink-well.

IV. WAR AND ITS COST

If we consider the expansion of the royal domain under Philip Augustus and his successors, we are struck by the fact that armed force played, practically no role in it. There were pressures, confiscations and political marriages, but there was no large-scale battle after Bouvines (or rather, one only; the defeat inflicted on Philip IV by the Flemings in 1302).

The gradual annexation of Languedoc is a typical example. In 1208, when Innocent III set in motion the Crusade against the Albigensians and the great feudal lords of the French South, under blanket charges of heresy, the French king confined himself to giving permission to the most restless among his vassals to participate in it. He did not intervene even when their leader, Simon de Montfort, made himself the lord of the conquered fiefs; he did, however accept his homage (1216). Subsequently, the king took advantage of the weakness of Amaury, Simon's son and successor, to get a foothold in Languedoc without striking a blow (1226). Then, instead of attacking Raymond VII of Toulouse, the legitimate — and excommunicated — Count, the King helped him to obtain absolution, but required him to surrender some fiefs to the crown and mortgaged the remainder by marrying off Raymond's only daughter to his own brother

(1229). When the latter died without issue in 1271, the King seized the last remnant — sixty-three years after the beginning of a war which resulted in his ultimately gathering in all the fruits without having run the gauntlet of either its hatreds or its dangers.

Cavalry is frozen in its tradition

A slow process, one might well say. But war, as practised still in the 13th century, reduced the advantages of the suzerain over the vassal to a minimum. The art of fortification was the only aspect of warfare which had made spectacular advances from the 10th century onwards. Walls had become stronger and stronger, there were more and more battlements, buttresses, keeps and machicolations. In the hands of a mere handful of determined defenders, a well-built castle could make an indefinite stand against a whole army, unless the garrison was starved out or betrayed. The invincible Richard Lionheart met his death hard by the walls of the castle of an insignificant French vassal.

On the battle field, personal courage counted for more than the number of fighting men or the skill of their leaders. This ideal, an essential part of the code of chivalry, was not belied in actual performance. Though recent research has brought to light some applications of an elementary art of war, these applications seem to have been the exception rather than the rule. Strategy usually remained very simple; the knights of the opposing armies hurled themselves upon each other in a frontal attack, sometimes all together and sometimes in successive waves, and sought to cut down the foe in single-handed combat. Tactics were subordinated to logistics, the art of moving and feeding troops. Except where the distances involved were short, it was difficult to transport and supply more than 3 or 4,000 knights. Whatever the chroniclers say, the pay rolls show that during the 14th century the king of England never managed to field 10,000 knights on any one occasion.

The king lost no face if, like St Louis, he sought peace. If, however, he decided to give battle, he had to risk his own neck, just like the humblest of his vassals and gamble both his life and his kingdom.

At Muret, in 1213, Peter II of Aragon dismissed as 'cowardly' a suggestion that he should entrench around Simon de Montfort's 'crusaders' besieged in the town and wait for hunger to do his work for him. His only concession to deceit was one which the knight's code of chivalry permitted to a sovereign; he donned the armour of one of his followers, so as not to be a chosen target. At the height of the battle, however, he did not resist the temptation to reveal himself and he was promptly surrounded and killed. Simon de Montfort had fewer than a thousand knights, Peter and his allies had double that number, to say nothing of their infantry which took no active part in the battle. Yet the death of the king was enough to seal the fate of the Cathar cause, of the Languedocian nobility, and of all Aragonese hopes for expansion north of the Pyrenees. Admittedly, Peter I had the reputation of being a hot-head, but his grandson, Peter II, and

Charles of Anjou, both of them cool realists, nevertheless gave serious consideration to the idea of deciding the struggle for the possession of Sicily by a duel.

Infantry is not suitable for kings

To make use of all his available manpower, and to spare his own person, a king ought to have banked not on the cavalry but on the infantry. The Italian Communes had proved its effectiveness as early as the 12th century. At Legnano, the steady resistance of foot-soldiers armed with long pikes and massed around the *Carroccio* (a chariot drawn by oxen and bearing the standard of the Commune) was the decisive factor of the victory of the Lombard League against the crack cavalry of the Emperor. Still more deadly, whenever bourgeois forces met the German knights, were the arrows loosed by crossbowmen (Fig. 61). Their effect was so murderous that a Council in 1179 tried to ban the arbalest or crossbow as an inhuman weapon — in vain, of course. In the 13th century, the heavy arbalests in the army of the German Knights of the Sword were instrumental in breaking the resistance of the Estonian pagans. Frederick II, Alfonso X, and to a lesser extent other Western sovereigns, adopted both pike and arbalest as auxiliary weapons, but the heart and soul of a feudal king remained with the cavalry.

Again and again, the lessons were repeated at the beginning of the 14th century. There was the victory of the Flemish infantry at the Battle of the Golden Spurs, then a triumph of the Catalan infantry over the Frankish barons of Greece; Scots infantry prevailed over the English invaders at Bannockburn; Swiss infantry crushed the Austrian knights at Morgarten. Eventually, the English learned from the Welsh how to use a simpler but faster type of bow, which was much less powerful and accurate than the crossbow — the longbow — but was more easily handled and reloaded more promptly. They displayed it first in the Hundred Years' War, overwhelmed the outnumbered and outshot Genoese auxiliary crossbowmen, and the French cavalry, Europe's best, was crushed at a blow at Crécy in 1346 (Pl. 31).

Still, the reluctance of kings to change their tactics was not entirely due to prejudice. The Italian Communes usually fought in a limited space and in regions fertile enough to provide food for a numerous army. Their infantry fought without pay. A somewhat similar situation loomed in France only for a few years when the royal domain was still small and the Communes already inured to war. Then there was a brief honeymoon for the king and the bourgeoisie; Philip Augustus was free with concessions to towns which supplied troops to the royal army (infantry, light cavalry, transport waggons) and these troops helped him to plug loopholes in the ranks of the heavy cavalry supplied by his noble vassals. But the speed with which the royal domain expanded in the 13th century gave rise to mounting logistical problems. It was too costly and unpractical to move over long distances troops who were not first-class soldiers and who had to be demobilised within weeks, for urban troops as well as feudal contingents served without pay, but for a strictly limited period.

Therefore the successors of Philip Augustus encouraged towns and vassals to redeem their military obligations in cash. These funds were used to recruit a small but professional army, composed of knights chosen from among landless nobles. Thus as royal authority grew, the obligation to shed one's blood for one's native land disappeared; a paradoxical development, when one comes to think of it.

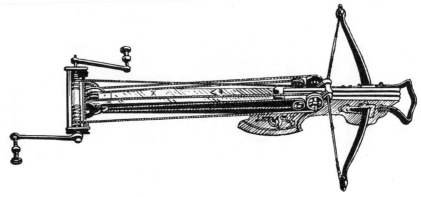

Fig. 61. Portable arbalest (crossbow), type used in fourteenth and fifteenth centuries.

Peace budgets and war budgets

Paying, feeding and equipping a few thousand knights, deploying them as and where necessity demanded, does not at first sight seem much of a task for the sovereign of the richest kingdom in Europe, the more so as he could use the monies paid by towns and vassals for that very purpose by way of redemption of military obligations. And yet the financial resources of the king of France were so modest that his budget was quickly unbalanced. (We may properly use the term 'budget', since the English word derives from an Old French word meaning 'little purse').

With a domain restricted to Ile-de-France and a feudal and urban army serving at its own charges, Philip Augustus had brought to a brilliant conclusion the financial year 1202–03: revenue, approximately 197,000 pounds; expenditure, approximately 95,000 pounds. St Louis, with a much larger kingdom, in spite of a much heavier fiscal pressure (especially in regard to towns, some of which he drove to bankruptcy) barely succeeded in making both ends meet by preserving peace most of the time. It took him three years to prepare the crusade of 1248, five years and more to pay for it (the bills of exchange drawn by him on lenders in Genoa and Piacenza were still unpaid in 1253), and twelve years passed before he could undertake a second crusade.

Yet he had hardly any standing army and no navy at all; the ships for the crusades were chartered from the Italian towns.

Philip 'the Fair', embroiled in wars at opposite ends of his kingdom — in Flanders and Aquitaine — also aspired to the maintenance of a navy of his own. In 1295, he assembled more than 700 ships (according to chroniclers), some of them chartered abroad but others built in his new arsenal, and spent more than a million pounds in the course of an undistinguished naval campaign against England. By 1299, the annual balance sheet of the French treasury was closed with a deficit as follows: income, 1,571,977 Parisis pounds; expenditure, 1,642,649 pounds. Though a precise comparison with the balance-sheet of 1202 is impossible for various reasons (the value of the pound changed, there were other public funds unaccounted for, certain sums were carried over from one year to the next), it is no less true that the contrast between the two periods is startling. Fortunate indeed were those kings who succeeded in maintaining peace.

Feudal monarchies, unlike the financially subtle Communes, had not experimented with floating or funded public loans. They had neither the power nor the ruthlessness of bleeding the subject white as many ancient and Oriental despotisms had done. Still there was no lack of expedients in procuring the indispensable money. The quickest way was to manufacture it, taking advantage of royal prerogative to reduce the metal content of the coinage without changing its face value. This remedy was unpopular and delusive: what little the King gained from paying off old debts with 'bad money' he lost again when he collected his revenue in the same debased coinage. Despite the efforts of the Masters of the Mint to keep these alterations secret, the public got wind of them and adjusted prices accordingly, with surprising exactitude.

Actually, in a period of economic expansion, inflation was not without advantages for economic growth. It introduced into circulation a bulk of new means of payment, thus temporarily creating an abundance of currency available for investment. This form of reasoning, however, may at best be intelligible to modern economists. Mediaeval French traders merely saw that instability of currency threw their monetary agreements into chaos; the clergy, the nobility, and others who depended on fixed rents, saw that the purchasing power of their cash revenue decreased. The King took advantage of this at times to indulge in blackmail: he threatened an issue of 'bad money' to face an emergency, then gave it up in return for a special sum to be paid by those whose interests were bound up with the preservation of sound money.

Taxes are the cement of the national structure

Some other methods of extortion increased the popularity of the monarch. When the King charged with embezzlement one of his employees who had robbed the subjects (usually with the sovereign's implied consent) and confiscated the ill-gotten gains, there was no lack of people to applaud him, espe-

Fig. 62. Measure for the collection of tithes. Chateau at Dinan (Brittany).

cially if the individual concerned happened to be a foreigner. The applause was so much the heartier if the villains were Jews or 'Lombards' (Italians from the north and Tuscany); then the routine was to arrest them as usurers, threaten them with expulsion, only to re-instate them on condition they wrote off the king's debts and paid him damages in addition, or made him a loan. Similar operations were often conducted against these foreign or infidel sinners, and they were invariably successful. Still, it was necessary to be careful not to kill the goose that laid the golden eggs.

That is what happened with the Templars. After the loss of the Holy Land, the Knights of the Temple no longer possessed the original justification for their existence. They had not been prudent enough to find another by transferring to another crusading ground (like the German Knights) or by intensifying their help to the sick (like the Hospitallers). Not without cause, people accused them of all manner of vice: pride, cruelty, homosexuality, avarice. . . . Despite all that has been said of them, the Templars were never professional bankers or 'usurers', but they had custody of the king's money, and made loans to him as need arose, drawing for it on the revenues of their vast landed estates. In 1307, Philip 'the Fair' had them arrested, tried and condemned wholesale by a trial which seemed irregular even in an age accustomed to the methods of the Inquisition. A weak Pope, Clement V, finally ratified the condemnation, albeit against his inclination. The Grand Master and several of the Knights were burned alive, the Order was suppressed and its goods and assets passed to the Hospitallers; but not before the King had obtained cancellation of his debts to the Temple and an award of a large sum as re-imbursement of real or imaginary credits. Other kings took advantage of the Papal condemnation to act in a similar manner in their own States. They did, however, have the decency not to send the accused to the stake.

All these measures were but palliatives. The monarchy, when it took over the reins of national life, ought to have resurrected a regular income tax system, the fundamental basis of both Roman and modern finance (Figs. 62 and 63). But the 13th century was not ripe for such radical reform. The King could merely ask his subjects for 'help' in times of crisis. Philip 'the Fair' acted in such a way as to keep a 'crisis' going, almost without interruption, and his successors improved even more on these methods.

Almost every year, towns and nobles of the kingdom were invited to redeem in terms of cash the 'help' they owed in terms of military service. The sums payable varied according to agreements drawn up each time, after long bargaining, by the sovereign and specific taxpayers. Redemption by a lord ought to have included the dues of his serfs, but the kings endeavoured to reach the latter directly offering them their liberty against payment, in the same way as the Italian Communes had already done. The collective enfranchisement of peasants, begun under St Louis, reached its peak in 1315, when a decree by Louis X set free all serfs in the royal domain 'since according to natural law all men should be free.' To make the royal intention clear, however, the decree added that should anyone choose 'to remain in the humiliation of servitude', he would have none the less to pay a special tax 'to assist our present war.' Another special tax, which was not very productive but highly unpopular, was levied on commercial transactions and known as the 'maletôte', 'ill-begotten'. Only a few towns of the direct domain, where taxes pressed most heavily, paid it.

Theoretically, ecclesiastical revenues were not taxable. In practice, the Pope allowed the sovereign to use certain revenues from the Church provided that this appropriation was invested with an appearance of being useful to the Church — however vaguely. In the fifty-eight years between the death of St Louis and that of Charles IV (1270–1228), the clergy yielded the ecclesiastical tithe to the King forty-nine times, not counting other smaller contributions. In spite of this, the impatience of Philip le Bel when Papal authorisation was slow in arriving led him into open conflict with Boniface VIII. The latter in his reply made the mistake of drawing attention to an antagonism about which he could well have kept silent: 'That laymen are ill-disposed towards the clergy,' he wrote, 'is something which both past and present clearly prove.' After a short pause, hostilities began again with increased fury and ended in the dramatic episode at Anagni which we have already described. As in the time of the Investiture Struggle (but with greater subtlety and learning), a host of propagandists worked to strengthen the case on both sides. The French clergy, on the whole, supported the King, and helped him to wrest from the second successor to Boniface, Clement V (1305–1314) an almost complete surrender. Thus a Pope bowed before a lay sovereign, and Canossa and the two centuries which followed it were undone — an event all the more humiliating since Boniface had demanded nothing that his immediate predecessors had not been in the habit of asking for, and getting.

National unity, it is often said, is cemented on the battlefield and disintegrated by excessive taxation. This is true when a people fights for its own freedom and pays for its own enslavement. But in the 13th and 14th centuries, matters do not run in this groove; the king's wars do not concern the people very closely; only a handful of men, almost all mercenaries, are directly employed in these wars. Taxes, on the contrary, are not the outcome of unilateral and arbitrary action, but a facet of the feudal contract. The king asks for a maximum, the nobles offer a minimum, and they compromise mid-way between the two. No doubt their negotiations are not always harmonious, but negotiations there are, and the discussion of opposing interests eventually brings to light the existence of a common ground.

Under St Louis, this kind of negotiation has barely begun. The King's financial requirements are modest, and he obtains what he needs almost without discussion, from subjects who love, respect and fear him. Philip 'the Fair', whose needs are greater and whose prestige is lower, keeps a weather eye on the aspirations and antipathies of the people. When about to commit himself up to the hilt against the Pope, he makes sure by means of popular consultation (1302–1303) that he has nobles, clergy and bourgeoisie behind him. Under his three sons and successors (1314–1328) consultation becomes more frequent, more complex, indeed almost a regular feature — like new taxes. Even the serfs, whom no-one ever consults, are being enticed with offers of freedom.

From this last point of view — freedom for serfs, even though this be merely a way of squeezing money out of them — France is ahead of other European monarchies. But as far as the development of parliamentary and representative institutions is concerned, it is beaten to the post by other kingdoms at which we should now look.

Fig. 63. Tithe Barn at Provins (Champagne) thirteenth century.

V. THE CORPORATE KINGDOM AND REPRESENTATIVE INSTITUTIONS

Every monarchy based on the feudal contract is by definition limited. The king has the right to ask advice from the vassals and the duty to heed it. As long as nothing more than ordinary administration is involved, he finds it sufficient merely to consult the *Curia Regis*, usually composed of men from the court and dignitaries of the region. It is only in special circumstances — an important military expedition, a problem of succession, the trial of a high-ranking prisoner, promulgating new laws, or asking for special levies — that the king calls a general assembly. In this case, vassals are theoretically obliged to hasten from all parts of the kingdom, at their own expense, in order to deliberate with the sovereign and take their share of responsibility for putting mutual decisions into effect.

> The assembly itself goes back still further in both Germanic and Romance countries. At the end of the 9th century, in a Wessex still unfeudalized, King Alfred 'the Great' describes the comings and goings of important personages attending the meetings of the 'Council of Wise Men' (*Witenagemot*), 'some by a long, bad and difficult road, others by a long, good and direct road, others by a short but narrow and dirty road, still others by a short, smooth and good road.' In the Venice of 971, still Byzantine, the Doge has a written record made of the verbal proceedings of a parliament in which 'a great part of the people, that is upper classes, middle-classes and lower classes, are consulting together' and undertaking not to supply arms to the Moslems. We have already seen that a general assembly (*Althing*) has been meeting in Iceland since 930 without any need of a feudal sovereign to summon it. It is presided over by the *lögsögumadhr*, who well deserves this post by the fact that he has learned by heart all the laws which are in force and has to recite them from beginning to end once a year.

Although feudal theory certainly did not create the assembly, it did place emphasis on collaboration between assembly and sovereign. In order to define it, law experts will at a later stage borrow from the Justinian Code this noble maxim: 'Let that which concerns everyone be approved by everyone.' These words can be read at the top of the invitations which will be sent out by Edward I of England to barons, knights and bourgeois of his kingdom when he summons them to the Plenary Parlement of 1295, a milestone in European constitutional history.

From feudal assembly to representative assembly

In the age of localism, however, one could not yet say that the affairs of the king concerned everyone. If Hugh Capet, in a fit of megalomania, had taken it into his head to summon together the nobles and ecclesiastics of the entire kingdom, most of them would not have deigned a reply; distances were too great, and the king was too weak for the effective direction of any venture of common interest.

> The Emperor himself rarely made any call upon the general assembly. He could only be sure of the presence of a few faithful supporters, who were willing to travel with him, and of the few people who happened to be in

the vicinity of the meeting place at the propitious moment: a place which moreover, was variable, since the Emperor had no fixed capital. In Germany, those who attended the sessions were above all the great rural vassals; in Italy, from the 10th century on, there were even a few spokesmen from the main towns. Moreover, those present could commit only themselves and their direct dependents. Absences could be interpreted equally well as tacit agreement, indifference or opposition. Lesser States alone had in some cases assemblies which were sufficiently numerous and well attended to ensure that opinions aired in them constituted at least an elementary opinion-poll of the different classes and regional groups, even though they did not present a real cross-section of public opinion.

What was still lacking to transform these ocassional essemblies of the 10th and 11th centuries into regular and efficient instruments of constitutional government? Better means of communication were needed; sovereigns and their subjects had to be convinced of the advantages of closer collaboration: the many absentees should find some way of being represented by the few who were present. Between the end of the 11th century and the beginning of the 14th, granted, progress was general and continuous as far as communications were concerned, but it was erratic and unpredictable in respect of collaboration, and more than unspectacular in the field of representation.

Yet this idea of representation was new and had a great future. The democracies of antiquity were attached to an absolute ideal (everyone shall participate directly in the management of public affairs) and had not anticipated any compromise (the mass of the people may exercise its rights indirectly through the intermediary of elected representatives). This is why the Graeco-Roman city-states degenerated into demagogies, oligarchies or tyrannies as soon as the numbers of citizens grew to such a degree that direct consultation was impossible or chaotic. The communal democracies of the Middle Ages developed along the same lines. Not least among the claims to glory of monarchical states was the fact that they achieved, however unconsciously, the first halting steps towards a system of indirect and representative democracy.

Diverse origins, different solutions

For all that they were to lead to new results mediaeval representative institutions were nevertheless built up from pre-existing materials of dissimilar origin.

The feudal system made its contribution not only through the advisory powers of vassals but also through its chain of dependencies. Indeed, the vassal in the king's command, while not the elected representative of his own vassals, was nevertheless held responsible for their behaviour and was obliged in his turn to take their opinions into account.

Local administrations and groups — urban communes, village communities, 'universities' and *patriae* (homeland unions) of valleys and districts, courts and tribunals of the county, dioceses and monastic orders — all were useful fields of experiment. In their own particular assemblies, which were more frequent and more intimate than general assemblies, men of diverse social classes acquired the art of self-government, learned how to agree on common policy and how to negotiate with the king and his officers through the intermediary of delegates. Some of the groups involved are as small and compact as a craft gild or a specific monastery; some are very large and ill-defined like the *états*, estates or orders of the aristocracy, the clergy, the bourgeoisie, the free peasants, which are emerging in many States as organized bodies. They all become more articulate, find among themselves matters of common interest, and are willing to strive for their privileges or 'liberties' through collective petitions to the King, discussion with his officials, and, if need be, the threat of rebellion.

This motley experience was finally brought into focus through abstract concepts emanating from private Roman law and adapted to mediaeval public law by men who were schooled in canon, 'Romance' and customary jurisprudence. Most important were the corporate personality or 'mystical body' of the kingdom, and representation in the strict sense of the word, that is, the use of procurators or proxies entrusted with full powers to act in the name of a whole community.

Like the members of the human body, members of the mystical body politic were of unequal importance and dignity. According to John of Salisbury, the English prelate and philosopher who died at Chartres in 1180, the King corresponds to the head, the clergy to the heart and soul, the nobility to the arms, the peasants to the feet. Not everyone thinks exactly alike on this point — a layman, for instance, may not award to the clergy such an exalted position — but nobody would dream of putting the head and the feet on the same level and paying equal attention to every member of society. At the top of the scale are the most important people, whom it is expedient to summon in person to every assembly; at the bottom, the lowly and the poor, whose opinions one can safely do without; in the middle are those who cannot be totally ignored but do not have to be individually consulted.

It is for the latter group and for that group alone — people of some importance but not at the very top — that the representative system will be devised. This innovation is not meant to fling wide the doors to an egalitarian and proportional democracy, but it leaves them discreetly ajar in favour of a few groups among the in-between classes.

The chosen groups will vary according to countries. The free peasants will only succeed in sending delegates to the parliaments of a few mountain regions or little urbanised areas, such as the Tyrol and Friuli. The clergy will often choose not to get entangled with laymen, whom they regard as their inferiors, and will aspire to direct negotiation with the king in special assemblies. Town delegates will play a very important role in

Spain and Portugal, but no role at all in Scandinavia. The lesser noblemen will have their own representatives in England, and in Aragon, but in Catalonia as in France, they will be overshadowed by the vassals with whom they rub shoulders in the same group. The familiar story of 1789 brings to our mind the three *états* or estates (clergy, nobility, 'tiers état' of the bourgeoisie) which will clash on the threshold of the French Revolution. But in the 13th century, these 'Estates General' of the kingdom were not yet in existence, and the assemblies which preceded them in numerous regions of France were not regularly divided into three sections.

The English experiment

England was not first in the field in creating representative institutions; but on the other hand, those which she did create showed themselves to be the most capable in surviving crises and improving with time.

Up to the latter years of the 13th century, the English 'parliament' was usually composed only of great vassals or barons who were summoned individually. Sometimes, however, the King also invited to the session a few representatives of the lower nobility and the merchant class. More often he would summon the latter (when he needed them) to separate meetings, in each of the towns or regions to which they belonged. But in 1265, the leader of the rebel barons invited to a parliament, beside the barons, two knights from every shire and two members of the bourgeoisie from each borough (free town). The same pattern was adopted by King Edward I for the Plenary Parliament of 1295 and from that time this mixed assembly (half-individual, half-representative) became accepted practice. Legal and political matters of prime importance continued, nevertheless, to be discussed normally with the barons alone. From the knights and the bourgeois all that the king asked was consent for the levy of new taxes, and a respectful hearing for any plans of action already decided on in their absence, so that the representatives of the lesser nobility and of the towns might convey their purport to their respective peers. In actual fact, the lesser nobility and the citizens of free boroughs constituted less than one tenth of the English population; and this feeble minority was entitled to two delegates per shire or town, no matter what the population of that circumscription.

The importance of representative institutions, therefore, in their early days was more symbolic than real. An English writer, of whose name and dates we are not certain (possibly one William Ayreminne, at the beginning of the 14th century) will even go as far as to assert that 'the king may summon a parliament without bishops, *earls* or barons' because the 'proxies of the clergy, the knights from the *shire*, and the citizens and burghers represent the entire English community; one cannot say as much of the barons, for of them each one represents only himself in parliament.' Obviously, the writer does not take into account the actual situation in England but is merely giving expression to an idea current at the time, an especially meaningful idea in the oldest of the national monarchies. The conviction that all Englishmen belonged to a community, with customs and interests binding together the whole kingdom, had found a convenient platform in representative institutions. Such was the outcome of an evolution which began in military defeats, continued amidst disturbances, yet ultimately bore fruit in harmony between king and subjects.

Here, briefly, are the stages through which this development passed. With *Magna Carta* King John had been forced to promise that he would impose no unusual taxes without the consent of the 'common council' of the kingdom, then consisting of the greater lay and ecclesiastic vassals who were summoned by personal letters of invitation. Under the name of Parliaments (from *parler*, to speak), these assemblies gave consent over a number of years to the constant requests for money by Henry III, but took every available opportunity to resist his political ambitions in foreign countries and his favouritism towards foreigners. They had good reason for this, yet their protests had a nationalistic undertone which would have been inconceivable only a few years before, when one third of France consisted of English fiefs.

It was, however, a French immigrant, Simon de Montfort, son of the homonymous conqueror of the Albigensians and brother-in-law to Henry III, who led a revolt of the barons in 1258. The King was rescued from bankruptcy, but placed under tutelage: under the 'Provisions of Oxford' a committee, appointed partly by the rebels and partly by the King, took over the administration of the kingdom. At the same time, it seems, it became the practice to summon Parliament regularly three times a year to discuss affairs of State and hear petitions. In the end, quarrels among the barons and interventions by the Pope and St Louis in support of royal authority led to a fresh coup d'état. The King was defeated and captured, and virtually all his powers were transferred to a new Parliament, to whose meetings Simon de Montfort, finding himself threatened by barons who resented his leadership, invited representatives of the knights and the bourgeois. For a few months in 1265, England experienced a regime foreshadowing, however vaguely, the constitutional and representative monarchies of modern times.

The experiment was far ahead of its time. Before the year was out, Simon de Montfort met his death in a battle against Crown Prince Edward. But the lesson was not to be wasted. After his accession, Edward I (1272–1307) voluntarily summoned both parliaments of barons and plenary parliaments, for discussions which became more frequent as time went on. Such a policy, adopted — let us stress the point — by a strong king, gave England a government which although much less open to commoners than that of the Communes, did at least introduce as much of a balance of powers as one could hope for in a mediaeval monarchy. The King has recovered his supreme authority and wields it firmly; to put it in the words used at an earlier moment by Bracton, the greatest English jurist of the 13th century, 'the king is under no man, even if he is under God and the law.' The Parliament of barons, for its part, gives approval to new laws 'after deliberation and conference on the subject'. Finally, what Bracton had called, in advance of events, 'the common engagement (*sponsio*) of the republic' is supplied by the plenary parliament.

The kingdom, a republic; does not this formula conjure up a memory of that Roman Empire which right to its last days had retained the name and outward appearance of a republic? But 14th century England did not stop short at appearances. While keeping in his hands the reins of the kingdom, the King, head of the body politic, will no longer be able to ignore the wishes and demands of the other members of the 'mystical body' of the English nation.

In the rest of Europe

In one form or another, the notions so forcefully expressed by the English jurists have become commonplace in legal theory throughout Europe. They spell out yearnings which are spreading in almost all countries and underlie most of the constitutional upheavals of the 13th century, whether violent or peaceful. Only in England, however, do theory and practice coincide. Elsewhere the kings are either too weak or too powerful, their subjects too much at variance one with another or too engrossed in the interests of their own particular class (or region), to work together in the building of vigorous and durable representative institutions.

In Hungary, for example, the 'Golden Bull' of 1222 (often compared, quite wrongly, with Magna Carta), entrusts what had been a sturdy patriarchal monarchy to a numerous, unruly aristocracy whose main concern is to get themselves exempted from the payment of taxes. In Castille, the Cortes are much older in tradition than the English Parliament and would seem destined for a more brilliant future; but they meet less frequently, almost invariably in separate session for each part of the State (Castille proper, León, and Estremadura), and they do not succeed in reconciling the demands of the towns with those of the nobles or clergy. In France the disharmony is even more marked; so much so that the King will not summon the Estates-General before the 14th century, and even then, he will often find it more convenient to deal with the Estates of each region, splitting the opposition so as to be better able to reign.

In the kingdom of Sicily, the despotic authority of Frederick I and his successors tames the parliaments to such an extent that they hardly give a clue to the real feelings of their members. There is opposition, of course, but it takes the illegal form of plots and desertions the moment an enemy army appears. In Germany, conditions are even less favourable to an effective parliament; no-one, not even a Frederick II, can work the miracle of creating representative institutions capable of instilling new life into the dismembered body of the Empire. That does not mean that there is no feeling of nationalism in Germany or Italy; but it is hampered by the 'universal' structure of the State and it therefore expresses itself as best it can in literature, law, and in the very way in which people think and live.

VI.   IMPONDERABLE ELEMENTS OF NATIONALISM AND 'INERT' LAYERS OF SOCIETY

To say that nations and nationalism, as we understand them today, did not exist in the Middle Ages is mere truism. On the other hand, to abandon for this reason any search into the conscious or unconscious forms of national spirit and feeling would be tantamount to shutting one's eyes to one of the most interesting aspects of 13th century European life.

Devotion to king and dynasty, pride in clan and parish, common bonds of language, literature and customs, common antagonism towards oppressor and neighbour — these are all facets of patriotism sparkling with new light on the backcloth of the 13th century. No doubt the Popes and Emperors of the early Middle Ages had enlisted faithful supporters; the Investiture Dispute had inflamed passions on both sides; but a Fredrick II and his opponents, too, a Gregory X, an Innocent IV, will have more complex personalities with which to beguile their friends and exasperate their enemies. Very likely the haunting words 'sweet France', so often recurring in the *Song of Roland*, got there only as an echo of classical literary formulae; nevertheless we hear from a chronicler that as early as 1066, Roland's poem, sung by a minstrel who went with the expeditionary force, spurred the French adventurers of William of Normandy on to the conquest of England. We have seen what a strange charm the epic remembrance of an old defeat has had on the great conquering peoples in Europe.

The patriotism of a doomed nation: in Wales

A conquered nation, for its part, may derive enduring courage from remembering its former glory, be it real or imaginary. A Welsh chaplain, Geoffrey of Monmouth (who died in 1154), eagerly collects all legends which have grown around the very small nucleus of historical fact concerning the Britons and King Arthur, and he enlarges on them with the aid of his fervid imagination. In his *Historia Regum Britanniae* the Celts are the heroes and the Anglo-Saxons are traitors and tyrants. It makes no difference that serious historians almost at once denounce his web of fiction; English literature itself promptly adopts these fables and embellishes them in a variety of ways, and other literatures, too, quickly follow suit. Arthur outshines Beowulf; Lancelot, beloved of all women, puts strait-laced Roland in the shade. By the 13th century, Arthur will usually be included in an imaginary constellation of the 'big nine' (Pl. 28), one of whom, Hector, is perhaps still more legendary than he, while the other seven have rather more worthy claims on history: Alexander the Great, Julius Caesar, Joshua, David, Judas Maccabaeus, Charlemagne and Godefroy de Bouillon.

A more scrupulous writer than Geoffrey of Monmouth, Gerald de Barri (Giraldus Cambrensis, died in 1220), composed some interesting little works on Wales and Ireland: 'having described plainly the character, customs and habits of the British nation and collected and expounded anything which might usefully add to its credit and glory,' he also sets out 'certain details in which it seems to have strayed from the path of virtue.' The Welsh, his compatriots, are rough, extravagant and undisciplined, 'constant only in inconstancy'. But, on the other hand, they have undaunted courage, remarkable intelligence, incomparable musical talent, and a language dignified by close relationship to the classical languages (*pump*, five, he rightly points out, is the equivalent of the Greek *pente*). The Welsh do not fight, as do the English, for reasons of ambition or for love of money — they fight for the liberties of the region of which they are the 'natural inhabitants.' Whatever their present troubles, when the last Judgement dawns no nation, no tongue other than the Welsh tongue, shall speak before the Supreme Judge for this little corner of earth.'

Patriotism in the bosom of universality: Italy and Germany

In Italy, where literacy is widespread enough to lend great power to the written word, literature is asserting itself as a decisive factor in national unity. Virgil and other poets of the Augustan age had implanted in Italy the dangerously arrogant belief that she was destined from all time to rule the world, and the pleasant — but inaccurate — notion that she was endowed with singular agricultural wealth. Dante and the other poets of the age of Communes will reproach her for having allowed world empire to slip through her hands, but they will fashion for her a new literary language comparing favourably with the Latin of their ancestors. They make her boundaries coincide with those which Augustus had marked out for Italy when she was the heart of the Empire. 'The Alps which bar Germany at the Tyrol,' 'the Carnaro which fences Italy in and laps at her edges': here in Dante's words, are the frontiers which were to be those of Italy between the two World Wars.

There are in existence other stimulants to national awareness — geography, language, historical traditions, religious ties, political and commercial bonds — but they exert a less powerful influence than literature. Italy is a natural region, but the same may be said of the Iberian Peninsula or the Balkan Peninsula which have ultimately produced more than one nation. The languages of Italy have a common base, but Sardinian and the Gallo-Italian dialects of Northern Italy are incomprehensible to anyone knowing only the Tuscan of Dante. There is a 'kingdom' of Italy, but it is linked with Germany, truncated south of Rome; the area defined and extolled by Virgil and Dante never was a single independent state except for a few decades under the Romans, and for a few more under the Ostrogoths. The Pope and a large part of his entourage are usually Italians, but not always; moreover, in 1309, the entire Pontifical Court will move to France and become almost French. Although Guelphs and Ghibellines alike desire victory for their own party in the whole of Italy, woe to anyone who interferes with the independence of any of the States of which it is composed! At times Italian merchants from rival towns unite in order to face a foreign world (the fairs at Champagne, for instance); but they take the first favourable opportunity of torpedoing each other. Not that their expressions of agreement are altogether hypocritical; for is it not possible to be at one and the same time both a believer and a sinner?

As for Germany, her patriotic poetry came to full flower in the 13th century, as if the waning of the Empire had set her writers free from their universalist reverie. Like the members of the French and English assemblies summoned by Philip 'the Fair' and Edward I, the German poets are critical of popes who meddle too intimately in the internal affairs of their countries, of Jewish and Italian moneylenders, and of foreigners in general. Admittedly, they also find fault with their compatriots; a greedy aristocracy, a clergy tainted by simony, corrupt judges, over-ambitious peasants. But let us listen as they extol the German people as a whole: ' 'Twixt Elbe and Rhine, and beyond that into Hungary, there dwell the finest people known to the world. . . German men are well set up, their women veritable angels!' So exclaims Walther von der Vogelweide, the greatest of the *Minnesingers* (love poets); and this, after all, is no more than what his contemporary, Aegidius of Corbeil (1140–1224?), claims for the country on the other side of the fence: France is 'the only land which makes men human'. More wisely, in another poem, Walter sings the praises of the universal brotherhood of men: 'Lord, many men call Thee Father, but do not accept me as brother.... We are all made from the same substance.... Christian, Jew and pagan alike serve Him by whom all living wonders are sustained!'

Long is the list of patriotic claims and counterclaims; equally long would be a list of cases where every vestige of nationalism is submerged in universal ambitions, in local disputes, in class solidarity and prejudice. Richard Coeur-de-Lion and Saladin understand one another better than can lords and serfs in many a village. These are contradictions which are not peculiar to the Middle Ages. Let us merely establish that there is an awakening of national feeling without trying to gauge the unfathomable elements of which it is made up.

Indeed, there is much more to be gained by delving beneath those layers of society which are politically active to examine the inert strata underneath. Even in our times, and in advanced countries at that, a very large number of people simply submit to the will of others, or put a brake on it merely by their passive resistance, often unaware that they are doing so. Tossed from pillar to post, being swept along by history rather than shaping its ends, these elements are nevertheless of utmost importance, as fundamental at times as geographical features, climate or soil. Thanks to them, the nation gets fed and perpetuates itself, and either rises to the efforts demanded of it or, if they do not play their part, strives in vain. There is no need to penetrate into their innermost thoughts to be able to guess and understand to what extent the wretchedness of inarticulate masses contributed to the defeat of the Roman Empire, or their weakness to the dissolution of the Carolingian Empire, or their revival to reconstruction and revival of Europe in the late Middle Ages.

What are the peasants thinking?

Not that we are by any means indifferent to the state of mind of the silent majority of the population; what do original texts have to tell us?

Peasants are almost never in evidence in 13th century political chronicles. Even their sporadic revolts, which up to that time had occasionally gone together with the ups and downs of economic growth and the awakening of urban society, seem to have ceased. Progress continued, however, and, so far as we can tell from a mass of impersonal, ill-explored documents of all kind — economic, legal, linguistic, archaeological — it became faster in the course of the century. That it never matched the progress of townspeople can hardly surprise us; it is harder to increase dramatically the harvest yield than to step up commercial movement and industrial production. Nevertheless it is clear enough that for the agricultural masses, as for the bourgeoisie, the 13th century was a time of relative plenty, the best, perhaps, which Europe experienced prior to the 18th century.

The agents of progress are the same as in the preceding period, but it is in the 13th century that they have the greatest impact. New agricultural techniques, relaxation of the restrictions of liberty, the combined pull of opportunities in towns and of inflation, which force the lords to convert the labour dues of the peasants into fixed payments and then cause the real value of these payments to fall — all these are body-blows at the established order. This is perhaps the main reason why the peasants no longer rebel; time is working for them, and the peasants are of all people the most willing to let time bring things to maturity.

By contrast, the decline of the lesser rural nobility in some instances borders on destitution. The lord of a manor near Siena is reduced to asking for a subsidy from the Sienese Commune to buy a pair of sandals. Some Provençal gentlemen, who are burdened with over-large families and have failed to try their chance in business, are seen driving their donkeys loaded with manure for sale in the town market. At the same period, prosperous peasants move to Florence and elbow their way into the bourgeoisie, much to the disgust of Dante, who feels that they are contaminating the 'purity' of the old citizen stock. There is a similar immigration into Paris, and the same contempt for it. Rutebeuf, an impoverished poet, comforts himself by proclaiming that the Devil himself would not countenance such villiens in Hell: their smell is too nasty!

Far from the larger cities, in the depths of the country, the contrast between aristocrats who are coming down in the world and peasants who are taking a step up is perhaps less dramatic, but it is just as real. An Austrian poet, Seifried Helbling, bewails the fact that peasants live like knights, marry into the nobility, and use their money freely, much too freely, to buy their way in. One of his fellow citizens warns the nobles against oppressing the villeins, for these are more than capable of destroying the finest castle: a statement that the Swiss mountaineers will later take it upon themselves to confirm, to the detriment of the Dukes of Austria and their vassals. In his *Meier Helmbrecht* a Bavarian novelist warns the peasants against their own excessive ambitions. He tells the story of a rich farmer's son, who, with encouragement from his mother, disguises himself as a knight and becomes one of the many bandits with which the region is infested; one fine day he will be arrested, his eyes gouged out, and he will be sent back to his village, where he will ultimately be massacred by his former friends. Lastly, Neidhart von Reuenthal, poet and knight, boasts of his amorous successes with fair country maids and delights in arousing the jealousy of young herdsmen.

For all its bantering and supercilious overtones, this literature, engendered in the heart of Europe, is much more representative of the true state of affairs in rural areas than is the coarse satire of the French 'fabliaux' or the flood of pastoral poetry in the various Romance languages, or the musical play, *Jeu de Robin et Marion*, by Adam de la Halle (Fig. 64). All this, however, is scarcely enough to compensate us for the silence of the real actors, the peasants.

Fig. 64. Puppet theatre, fourteenth century. Jeu de Robin et Marion: lyrical drama by Adam de la Halle (thirteenth century); The Bodleian, Oxford.

What are women thinking?

We are not much better informed regarding a good half of the mediaeval population — the women. Although it is clear that in a material sense conditions for them have improved, we are kept in ignorance of their state of mind, interpreted or rather disguised by the literary output of men. We do have the passionate letters of Héloïse (whom Abelard, however, exhorts to silence in his replies!), and the pleasing but unoriginal poems of Marie 'de France' (perhaps the Mother Abbess of Shaftesbury, half-sister of Henry of Anjou, alias Henry II of England); there are also the poems of an 'accomplished maid' from Tuscany, of whom all we know is that her father wished to marry her off by force; some poems of the Countess de Die; some medical literature ascribed, perhaps

wrongly, to women doctors of the School of Salerno; a few memorable pronouncements of notable women, quoted by chroniclers, hagiographers or
story-tellers. . . not much, in all conscience, for a sex often regarded as chatter-
boxes!

We have to wait until the 14th century for two lady writers, very different in
temperament, to win a place of honour in literature. One of them, Catherine
Benincasa, daughter of a dyer in Siena, is a mystic destined to be canonised;
but withal she is ever ready to plunge passionately into political life in the
cause of the Church and of peace. The other, Christine de Pisan, is the daughter
of a Venetian astrologer at the French court, a disconsolate widow and a
devoted mother, and she is indefatigable in seeking out and extolling instances
of feminine talent and courage.

As for 13th century women, at the mercy of masculine pens, let us acknowledge that they do not always cut much of a figure. 'In Heaven', writes Jacques
de Vitry, 'there was but one woman between Adam and God — but she had
no rest until she got her husband banished from the Garden of Eden and Christ
condemned to the agony of the Cross.' One may shrug one's shoulders and
retort like Chaucer's 'Wife of Bath' that 'a priest has nought good to say of a
woman, unless he speaks of a Saint.' Still we should not attach too much
importance to the favourable influence which the growing devotion to the
Blessed Virgin exerted over the lot of woman; for the *Corpus Juris Canonici*
says categorically that 'woman was not created in the image of God. . . and that
is why it is clear that wives are bound to be subject to their husbands, virtually
their servants.'

Neither should we take too literally the knight's cult of ideal womanhood.
'Courtly love', as this cult came later to be called, was a conventional mannerism
limited to a very small circle of men, each of whom dedicated himself to the
service of one particular lady, while acting as he pleased with all other women,
including his own wife. 'Being married,' states the first rule of the text-book on
courtly love compiled by André,
Chaplain to the King of France,
'is no excuse for not falling in
love.' A superfluous piece of advice in an age when marriages
were arranged by parents, often
when both the bride and the
bridegroom were still children!

*Fig. 65. A lady training a falcon. Brocade
from Lucca, fourteenth century; Museum
of Fine Arts, Boston.*

It is easy to laugh at the guiles of many wives, or wonder at the almost in-human virtue of an exceptional Griseldis, as Boccaccio and Chaucer (both of them at a somewhat later period) do. One must also consider that women, often married off at twelve or thirteen, in many cases to a lad of fourteen or to a man of sixty, were subject to a marital authority which despite some relaxa-tion over the centuries still retained the powerful support of the law, of religion and of custom, and they were far too frequently exposed to the dangers of childbirth, a very great hazard at that time. Were they much more unhappy than women of the present day?

Even as equality between the sexes and material comfort are no guarantee of success in a modern marriage, so, we believe, were the inequalities and tribulations of mediaeval life not necessarily an impediment to conjugal hap-piness. As women of the Middle Ages saw it, life was hard for men too. Their own subjection, which they endured in common with all other women, was not a personal injustice but a misfortune inherent in the very nature of things. Besides, while nobody disputed a husband's right to beat his wife, there is no lack of proof that the wife occasionally replied in kind.

A wife's existence was not limited to household chores, to the church or her children. There was dancing for people of all classes, songs to suit all tastes, stories for the few who could read and the many more who wanted to listen. One of their favourite games, blind-man's buff, would seem childish to us if we overlooked the fact that these young-marrieds were sometimes no more than twelve years old. Women were often more skilled than men at the elegant sport of falcony (Fig. 67); John of Salisbury explains this by saying: 'the worst people are always more inclined to look for prey.' Although fashion changed less fast than in our day, ribbons, make-up and pomades were relatively cheap and there was a great sale for them.

Outside the convent walls, there were few professions open to women; milking, spinning, brewing were within their province. To these may be added cases where the widow of a weaver would continue her deceased husband's work, or a merchant's wife take care of his business while he was away on his travels, or the daughter of the manor manage the estate while waiting for a suitable husband to be found for her. At the top of this pyramid, queens such as Blanche and Berengaria, grand-daughters of Aliénor of Aquitaine ruled respectively over the kingdoms of France and Castille 'like men' during the minority of the legitimate sovereign and they certainly had someone to live up to. It is true that Aliénore had been foolish enough in her youth to forsake a king who loved her (Louis VI, of France) to wed another (Henry II of England) who, besides being younger than she, was unfaithful, choleric and domineering. In 1189, how-ever, at the age of 67 and a widow, with ten pregnancies behind her and long years in prison, she displayed indomitable energy in coming to the aid of her son, Richard Coeur de Lion. Her political talent, which had gone to waste for so long, now came in full light.

In the Holy Land, where kings and barons were continuously being summoned to war, it sometimes happened that their wives took care of things more than they did themselves. Is this perhaps one of the reasons why the country of the Crusaders acquired in the minds of the conservative circles back in Europe the black reputation of a kingdom ruled by women and by lasciviousness? It is probable, nonetheless, that even in the Holy Land, the greatest desire of women, as the 'Wife of Bath' so aptly says, 'was not to reign over nations, but to rule their own husbands'.

VII.   THE NONCONFORMISTS: HERETICS AND JEWS

In one way or another, nearly all the inhabitants of Catholic Europe derived some benefit from the economic, intellectual and political awakening of the 12th and 13th centuries. Even those almost unorganised peoples around the Baltic who lost their independence, gained some advantage from association with a more mature civilisation than their own. Only the nonconformists, heretics or Jews experienced the disappearance of the relative security they had enjoyed up to then, despite sporadic bursts of ill-feeling on the part of the people and intermittent persecutions under the law. There was no practical gain which compensated, or could compensate, for the threat of violent death to which they were henceforth constantly exposed.

This change was tragically highlighted in a letter written by the 'Pillars of the World' (as the proud chiefs of the Jewish community in Mainz called themselves) in reply to a circular from the French communities, dated 1096. Stricken with fear at the sight of the new spectacle of hundreds of knights embracing the cross, French Jews had ordered a period of fasting, with the hope of appeasing Divine wrath, and they implored their co-religionists in the Rhenish towns to do the same. As a gesture of solidarity, the Pillars of the World complied with their wishes, but made the point that it could not happen in Mainz, since 'no sword hung over their heads'. Their confidence could not have been more misplaced: the Jews of Mainz were among the first victims of the First Crusade.

The turn of heretics would not be long in coming; not as a side show of expeditions launched with other objects as their primary aim, but as a result of special crusades dedicated wholly to their destruction. The Crusade against the Albigensians, those against the Yugoslav Bogomils, the Crusade waged from 1306–7 against the Adventists of Fra Dolcino in the Alps — every one of these Crusades was more merciless than any undertaken against the Moslems. And while enthusiasm for war in the Holy Land gradually waned, then died out in the course of the 13th century, hostility towards nonconformists relentlessly increased throughout Catholic Europe. Much later, when oversea Crusades had become a thing of the past, it was at home that the West put the torch to the stakes of the *autos da fé*.

The religious problem: toleration or repression?

On the surface, the disasters falling upon those who do not conform would seem to be by-products of triumphant religion. As theological thinking became more thorough and more precise, and as the masses moved on from an almost passive observance of ritual to direct spiritual experience and action, inevitably the presence of scabby sheep in the Christian fold would stand out as a shameful blemish. Nevertheless, one might ask: was violence necessary to remove it? Once more, we come face to face with the questions we asked about the Crusades. Saint Bernard of Clairvaux, a pious but stern man, who promoted the Second Crusade and was an implacable enemy of Abelard, definitely opposed this kind of violence: 'The Church', he wrote,' can overcome the Jews by convincing them and converting them day by day better than by putting them all to the sword.' As for heretics, 'it is not by force of arms that we must crush them, but by argument...... by education and persuasion.'

In the 13th century, the policy of persuasion found other eloquent partisans. St Francis, bearing no arms at all, joined the Crusade of 1219 so that he could preach the Gospel to the Moslems of Egypt, unsuccessfully, it is true. Raymond Lull, shining light of the Franciscan Order, endeavoured to promote mutual understanding by encouraging the study of languages spoken by the Infidels (Fig. 70). After a long and brave apostolate in North Africa, he was martyred at Bougie in 1315. Other Franciscans, however, were more fortunate. In Europe they led thousands of heretics peacefully back to the fold. In Asia they set up new dioceses, as a result of which the eastern boundary of the Catholic Church advanced step by step from Syria to China.

St Dominic of Guzmán also joined the Crusade against the Albigenses as an unarmed preacher. In a moment of stress, however, he gave way to a few words which appeared to favour violence: 'During many years, I have sought in vain to convince you by gentleness, by preaching, by tears, by prayer; but as one of my country's proverbs says, where blessings achieve nothing, blows will succeed. We will summon princes and prelates against you. . . .' His famous disciple, Thomas Aquinas, while disapproving of forced conversions, expressed himself harshly against the Jews and approved extreme measures against heretics as a means to protect the great mass of the faithful from danger of infection. Could he have expressed himself otherwise without running the risk of conflict with his superiors? As early as 1233, Dominicans and Franciscans had been placed in charge of that 'prophylactic' institution — the Inquisition.

In truth, the danger was not an imaginary one. Heretics were skilful and tireless in their propaganda. As for the Jews, who did not actually seek to proselytize, their faith had nevertheless attracted notable churchmen like Bodo in the Carolingian age, or Wecelin in the 10th century, or Andrew of Bari in the 11th. Later, in the 13th century, it was considered necessary to put to death anyone who publicly embraced Judaism. To become a convert, one had to hide or go into exile.

Public opinion was divided. Intolerance gained ground in the 13th century, but there also was an undercurrent disposed to respect good men of every creed. The tolerant expressions of Walther von der Vogelweide which we have quoted, Dante's reluctance to admit that there could be no salvation outside the Church, the praise of Buddha set down by Marco Polo, may be just extraordinary opinions of extraordinary men. But the fable of the 'three rings' has a flavour of popular wisdom about it. First told at the beginning of the 13th century by the Dominican preacher Stephen of Bourbon, it was subsequently passed on by word of mouth and through other writers till it reached Boccacio, who fashioned it into a masterpiece. It tells the story of the father of three sons, equally dear to him, who has only one precious ring to bequeath them. He has two identical copies made, and on his deathbed gives to each of his sons, secretly, 'the ring.' This is how it is with the three religions, Christian, Jewish and Moslem: 'The Father who gave it knows which is the best; as for the sons. . . . each thinks he holds the true one.'

Fig. 66. English caricature of Jews; from a Tallage Roll *of 1233, London, Public Record Office.*

Many Italian towns leave the nonconformists to live their lives in peace, at least while there is no interference by foreign agents and agitators. This is the case with the Cathar community of Concorezzo, near Milan, and the heretical groups in Verona, Brescia, Mantua, and with most of the Jewish communities scattered throughout the peninsula. About 1300, at Erice in Sicily, the *Universitas judeorum* meets peacefully in the synagogue, and even, on occasions, in the Church of St Julian, ordinarily the seat of the *Universitas terrae*, the Christian Commune. The Jews of Erice, who are craftsmen, members of the liberal professions, or agriculturists (but seldom usurers) associate freely with Catholics and appear to enjoy equal rights.

   In the Iberian peninsula, where nonconformists are especially numerous, the atmosphere is somewhat more strained, but there also there are often men and groups of different religions living amicably together. In England, where the climate is less favourable to the Jews (Fig. 66), one can quote the case of Canterbury, in 1187, where Jews and Christians pray and struggle together against the soldiers and the excommunications of a tyrannical archbishop. During the 13th century, there was in that town only one instance of violence against the Jews, and it resulted in no deaths. For heretics, provided they are discreet, conditions are still better; throughout the Middle Ages, England will be remarkable for her comparatively indulgent attitude to them.

Economic interests, political solidarities

Is religious zeal really the main cause of intolerance? Certainly, religion provides a reason or pretext for violence, silencing those who might wish to protect nonconformists. Old calumnies, repeated with malice or in good faith, add fuel to the fire. The multifarious charges which had been levelled at pagans and Manichaeans in the early centuries of Christianity flare up anew against every kind of heretic: they worship the Devil, they want to destroy the established order, they meet together in order to fornicate. To strike at the Jews, whose right to existence — an inferior existence, to be sure — had never been denied by the Church, the terrible weapon is refurbished which the pagans had used to persecute Christians: it is now the turn of the Jews to be accused of ritual homicide. After centuries of oblivion, this morbid charge reappears at Norwich in 1144, then elsewhere, with ever more gruesome details. The Jews kidnap, torture and kill Christian children, to use their blood for Passover rites; they also steal and desecrate the Sacred Host! For once, Frederick II and Innocent II, these implacable enemies, are in agreement to repudiate publicly the absurd invention, but to no avail. It is already too late to prevent the purported victims of the Jews from performing miracles; the populace is grateful for the miracles, the custodians of the relics obtain a most profitable source of income.

Thus we come to touch upon the economic interests which do not singly account for religious issues, but are closely interwoven with them. An unimpeachable witness, Innocent III, accuses Simon of Montfort, the scourge of the Albigensians, of 'shedding the blood of just men. . . in order to advance his own interests and not the cause of religion.' Canon William of Newburgh calls the Jews a 'perfidious people' but denounces the instigators of a number of pogroms perpetrated in England, 1189–1190, as 'reckless and greedy men. . . whose consciences are devoid of Christian scruples.' In Germany, landless noblemen and pennyless bourgeois take the lead in attacking Jews and heretics. In the richer provinces of Italy, there is a reverse situation; the possessions of Jews and heretics do not give rise to envy, but the denunciation of wealth and the glorification of poverty on the part of certain radical sects do inspire fear.

At all events, when one comes to look closely, the most basic cause of intolerance is probably one of which people are least conscious — incipient nationalism. It is less strong with the intellectuals, but it asserts itself both at the top of the social hierarchy and at the bottom of the scale.

In the eyes of the masses, the worst sin of the nonconformists is that they are different, unassimilable and bound up in some mysterious way with malignant forces from outside — invasions, extortions, epidemics, poor harvests. Characteristically, an Inquisitor points out as probable heretics all those who 'do not kneel down and join their hands like the others when they pray.' They are people who should be kept at arm's length, excluded from political and professional associations and relegated to the odious and unpleasant jobs. If they counter-attack, they lay themselves open to vengeance from an infuriated mob. If they shut themselves completely away inside their mountain villages or town ghettos, they incur even more suspicion. If they abandon their beliefs, they are made to denounce and defame their former co-religionists as proof of their sincerity.

In the view of the authorities, the non-conformists are guilty of every fault ascribed to them by the masses, plus that of being stubborn rebels to whom the normal provisions of the law cannot be applied. This does not alter the fact that it is sometimes expedient to protect them in order to exploit them. This, of course, is a dangerous game when it comes to heretics, for these people have no right even to existence; governments who wish to make use of their talents must pretend that they are good Christians and treat them as such. As for Jews, civil and religious law concedes them a right to live, as witnesses of the Truth revealed in Holy Scripture, but condemns them to bondage as the people responsible for the Crucifixion. Kings, princes and prelates take advantage of the situation to make use of the Jews in some way as both a sponge and a filter. The filter serves to trap all the resentments and complaints of the people, and it can be discarded when it has fulfilled its purpose. The sponge absorbs the wealth of the nation and squeezes it back into the royal coffers.

A Jew making his way up may move on from a pawnbroker's shop to the direction of public finances, may build himself an elegant mansion, sit at the table of the King — and even win his friendship, if the King happens to be generous and truly broadminded. But for all this, he will continue to be a 'serf of the Royal Treasury' and a 'slave of the Church'. The latter, according to St Thomas Aquinas, 'may claim all that a Jew owns', and the King has the same right. In England, William 'the Conqueror' imported Jews into the country to help him in the exploitation of his new subjects (and to be squeezed in their turn from time to time). In 1255, exhausted by two hundred years of this regime, all of the Jews of England are 'put in pawn' to Richard of Cornwall for the paltry sum of 5,000 marks; they are hardly worth more. In 1290, they will be expelled, with only the permission to take along their movable belongings. In France, three decrees of expulsion (1182, 1254 and 1306) strip the Jews of their possessions, but are not fully carried out. No matter; even where exile is averted, the degradation of the Jews is inevitable so long as governments and nations force them to abandon trade and the crafts and to specialize in the despised and accursed occupation of usury. It is of little avail that some writers, such as Gilles le Muisit, remark that many Jewish lenders charge lower rates than their Christian colleagues. The only chance of regaining some public esteem would be through employment in honourable trades, and such a chance is offered only to a few Jews in a few liberal or cynical countries, Italy above all.

Systematic persecution

The Popes constantly opposed violence against the Jews and the putting to death of repentant heretics. Great credit is due to them on that account. Still they did sanction systematic persecution, partly under pressure of public opinion, which almost forced them into it, and partly because they themselves were princes desirous of enhancing their authority and stamping out exceptions to the rule. Their decisive acts are dated 1184 and 1215.

In 1184, Pope Lucius III, in agreement with Frederick Barbarossa, anathematized the Cathars, the Waldensians and other heretics, entrusting the secular authority with the task of punishing them. (He does not, however, specify the kind of punishment he has in mind; an ironic twist of fate ordains that the first to send unrepentant heretics to the stake shall be that Peter II of Aragon who will himself meet death when fighting on the side of the Albigensians!) In 1215, Innocent III, with the backing of an oecumenical council, lays down a number of restrictions to be to be imposed on Jews, one of them being that they must wear a distinguishing mark on their clothing 'so that they cannot plead any error in identification should there be fornication.' (It is curious to note that this idea stems from Moslem law which for similar reasons demanded that both Jews and Christians should wear distinguishing marks).

The decree of 1184 is the first of a veritable avalanche of drastic measures against heretics, and a flood of commissions of enquiry endowed with full powers. For half a century, pontifical commissioners will operate without the guidance of any precise directive and often without discrimination or pity; heretics, real or imaginary, will hit back in the fury of despair; moderation in any shape or form will disappear in the the the turmoil. Somewhere about 1233, two pontifical legates, Conrad von Marburg in Germany, and Robert le Bougre in Northern France, will carry out what they believe to be their mission with such ferocity that the former will be done to death by an outraged crowd and the latter recalled by the Pope and sentenced to life imprisonment. Subsequently, Gregory IX, displaying his juridical skill, will incorporate all the commissions into one single institution, more efficient, and less arbitrary: the Inquisition (a word derived from the Latin and meaning 'enquiry'.)

Looked at one by one, the methods of the Inquisitors which are most distasteful to modern juridical feeling all possess a precedent in Roman law or mediaeval custom; recourse to anonymous denunciation, torture, solitary confinement, secret trial, no lawyer for the defence, no cross-examination of witnesses, assumption of guilt in the case of any accused who absconds from trial or cannot prove his innocence. Taken as a whole, they constitute a machine capable of annihilating anyone to whom the slightest suspicion attaches. If, in spite of this, there are acquittals and conviction itself does not inevitably mean the stake, it is because mediaeval Christianity has not lost its habit of leniency and also because Church and State have not broken all resistance to their will. Between 1308 and 1323, Inquisitor Bernard Gui will extract 613 confessions, but he will only hand over to the 'secular arm' some 45 heretics. Not a large number of victims, it has been said. But even so, among them there will have been men of outstanding talent and courage. Besides, is not the mere knowledge that one single indiscretion can mean trial, torture, confiscation of possessions or imprisonment enough to do incalculable harm to liberty of thought?

As regards the decree of 1215, it had disastrous social consequences, although it was not directly responsible for any deaths. For the distinguishing mark which the Jews have to wear is nothing short of a catastrophe for them; they will try to escape it by every means in their power. As long as they could not be recognized at a glance, they could go about peacefully outside their own quarter, make friends with Christians, forget the burden of their bondage and enjoy the right to life. Now, branded like cattle, they are lower than the lowest of serfs, and liable to all manner of outrage; the yellow sign is taking their ghetto with them everywhere. They may as well shut themselves up in real ghettos for good and hope for some feeble protection from their walls. On Saturdays, in the synagogue, 'every Jew is a king.' (Pl. 28).

The ghetto: prison and touchstone

The culture of the ghetto will save the Jews from losing their identity, which is the fate reserved for the greater part of conquered nations: but it will result in a withering of their creative power. The humble flowers of their vernacular poetry will fade, in Germany after Süsskind von Trimberg, a Jewish minstrel of the beginning of the 13th century, and in Italy after Immanuel Romano, Dante's contemporary and his imitator. Biblical exegesis, already brought to its peak by Rashi of Troyes (1040–1105) is still earnestly pursued, it is true, but without real originality. Hovering about Talmudic studies is the threat of decrees condemning the Talmud itself to the flames. Jewish doctors still find patients outside the ghetto, but there are only two thinkers who exert any marked influence on 13th century Christian philosophy, and both of these have flourished and died at an earlier time outside Catholic Europe; Salomon ibn Gabirol of Malaga (1021–1069) who, moreover, is generally taken for a Moslem, and Moses Maimonides of Cordova (1135–1204). Maimonides, moreover, is too steeped in Greek philosophy for the liking of many of his co-religionists who suspect him of heresy. Intolerance begets intolerance: the battle against nonconformists flares up in the very bosom of the Jewish communities, and there will be fanatics who are ready to invoke the aid of Christian authorities in proscribing the heretical books of their fellow Jews.

Yet in the depth of their misery, these people who persist in living as if Moses had never died, as if Christ had never been born, are a disturbing presence in the midst of the Catholic nations of Europe. To reassure them, it is not enough that accredited prophecies declare that the conversion of the Jews will occur immediately before the end of the world. There are those who chafe with desire to convert them more quickly, by the method which schools and parliaments have made popular: public debate. Discussions of this kind are arranged between Christian and Jewish theologians, here and there, during the 13th century. But the Jewish advocate, hemmed in by a hostile crowd, looks too much like a bull in the arena for his inevitable defeat to dispel the feeling of uneasiness.

Dante, in his despair at the corruption in the Christian society, takes his co-religionists to task in these terms: 'Be men, not mad sheep — so that the Jew in your midst should not scoff at you.' Indeed, this is the function of nonconformist: to serve as a touchstone and a warning. In vain do illuminated books and cathedral stained glasses depict blindfolded Synagogues alongside Churches gazing on the future (Fig. 67). So long as there are synagogues, it will be impossible to deny that the terrestrial and cosmic order of medieval Christian thought, which has no room for the Jews, leaves something to be desired.

Fig. 67. The Church and the Synagogue, Mosan art; Stavelot Abbey (Belgium) Brussels, Royal Museum of Art and History.

Chapter 3

FROM MICROCOSM TO MACROCOSM

I. A UNIVERSE STRAINING TOWARDS GOD

'CONSIDER the seed from which you are sprung! — You were not born to live like brutes — but to pursue virtue and knowledge.' 'Our peace lies in His will! — God's will is the sea into which everything flows — that He creates or that nature makes.' Whose are these two voices which speak in such different strains in the *Divine Comedy?*

The first is that of Ulysses. In the fiery glow of his everlasting torment (he was a hero, but a deceiver), Ulysses evokes the last thrilling moment of his mortal life, when he caught a glimpse of the mountain of Purgatory and Earthly Paradise before being swallowed by the sea and Hell. The second voice is that of Piccarda Donati. In the transparent light of heaven's lowest circle (she had intended to become a nun, but people had forced her to break her vows), Piccarda explains how any seat in Paradise offers perfect bliss in the contemplation of God.

Thus, Piccarda's shaky faith has achieved what Ulysses' daring reason could not possibly attain. Still, reason, too, is an impulse which comes from God. The words which Dante places on the lips of Ulysses express in poetical terms an old concept of Aristotle, which was itself based on those of Plato, and had been adapted to Christian philosophy by Aquinas: the human race has been created with the 'potentiality' or acquiring wisdom and virtue. He who endeavours to translate this potentiality into 'actuality' is therefore acting in accordance with the purpose of God, in whom all possibilities are perfectly fulfilled. So long as reason is guided by faith, 'nothing is difficult unless one loses heart', said Adalard of Bath around 1100.

The great philosophical syntheses of the 13th century

Much water has passed beneath the bridges since the days when St Peter Damian (died in 1072) called dialectics — that is, the art of reasoning — a mere 'handmaiden of theology', or when conservative men were shocked by such statements as Adalard of Bath's: 'However far human knowledge can go, we must follow it up; we must not appeal to God except where it stops.' Certainly, revealed Truth still constitutes a horizon beyond which philosophers may not go; but the horizon grows wider and wider as the power of reason increases.

The 13th century is the age of the great syntheses. They absorb the methods and terminology of the chief Greek thinkers and their Moslem and Jewish commentators, but they do not stop there; from that platform they spur men to climb higher and see further.

Three men, all of them teachers at the University of Paris, dominate the philosophic thought of the period: Siger of Brabant (died about 1284), St Bonaventure of Bagnorea (died 1274) and, surpassing them both, St Thomas Aquinas (1225–1274). Dante will endeavour posthumously to reconcile them in the harmony of Heaven, making them sing each other's praise. Actually, their views and their careers were thoroughly different.

Fig. 68. Portait of Dante, by Giotto, his contemporary; before restoration.

Their ideas defy summary description. Concerning Siger, it may be enough to point out that he was accused of spreading the most radical doctrines of Averroes, the Arab commentator of Aristotle. That meant denying the Creation, the immortality of the individual soul, and the existence of free will. When charged with heresy, Siger tried to justify the study of such horrors by calling it a mere exercise in the history of philosophy, without any danger to faith. Whatever his real opinions, posterity traced to him (and to Averroes before him) the theory of the double truth: the truth of faith, which must be accepted without question, and that of reason, which cannot always be reconciled with that of faith. This is an assumption which might well have led to a total repudiation of reason, but instead was destined to furnish arguments for integral rationalism, for scepticism and for agnosticism.

The philosophical world of St Bonaventure, discreetly open to the influence of Aristotle but firmly rooted into the neoplatonic tradition of Augustine, is considerably more serene. We are on the threshold of a moderate Franciscan mysticism; as a matter of fact, Bonaventure was appointed general of the Franciscan order and strove to reconcile the radical and the conservative factions in it. His *Itinerary of the Mind towards God* suggests three stages in a spiritual pilgrimage: first, discovery of the imprint of the Creator in the tangible world; then, contemplation of His reflection in the human soul; ultimately, loss of self in direct contemplation and ecstasy.

While Bonaventure wrote especially for the nobler minds, for monks and Saints, Thomas Aquinas addresses himself to society as a whole. His desire is to convince the layman, and even to put forward arguments capable of influencing Infidels. A formidable worker, he succeeds in incorporating in the monumental synthesis of his *Summae,* almost the whole of Aristotle as well as the greater part of his Moslem and Jewish commentators; he also works into it the astronomical system of Ptolemy, discarding that which is incompatible with Christian tenets; but the final interpretation of the great problems is his own. His system covers every branch of knowledge, from metaphysics to politics, and finds in reason subsidiary proof for practically every article of faith. This is why Thomas Aquinas, like Abelard before him, will create the impression that he is a dangerous rationalist. In 1277, the Archbishop of Paris will condemn several of his theses, associating them with 'Averroism'; the Archbishop of Canterbury will immediately echo this censure and England will remain a centre of opposition even after the canonisation of Thomas in 1323.

Paradoxically, the controversy will ultimately end in favour of Thomas only when Aristotle, Ptolemy and the other secular sources of his philosophical rationalism have lost their last disciples: in 1879, a Pontifical Encyclical accords to the system of Thomas the prestige of special approval, without repudiating, however, other Catholic systems of philosophy.

If one considers the increasingly uncompromising attitude of orthodoxy towards nonconformists, one will be surprised perhaps that three authorised spokesmen of the Church could dare to propound such differing opinions. But the Middle Ages are not the Counter-Reformation. The Council of Trent has not yet forged its armour for the protection of doctrine; the immutable series of questions and answers which will be the Catechism has not yet been formulated. It is still permissible to have doubts on a number of fundamental issues which will later be defined in the form of dogmas.

At the beginning of the 13th century, only the Nicene Creed (352) and a few other articles of faith going back to the early centuries of Christianity are in force, and have been for so long that the violent controversies which raged when they were adopted have almost been forgotten. But when in 1215 the Lateran Council declares the new dogma of Transubstantiation (the transformation in the Eucharist of bread and wine into the body and blood of Christ) many consciences are disturbed by what seems to be in contradiction to the Aristotelian science of the age. Fifty

Fig. 69. Castelnuovo di Magra, near La Spezia, where Dante is said to have composed part of the Divine Comedy.

years later, a Czech priest, who felt unable to accept this doctrine, saw the Host turn red in the chalice. The Holy See lost no time in giving all possible publicity to this miracle, instituting the Feast of Corpus Christi and ordering the new cathedral at Orvieto to be consecrated to it.

Reality and allegory

In general, faith is still sufficiently adaptable in the 13th century for the great majority of Catholic thinkers to feel no more bound by its dogmas than the confirmed liberal or marxist today feels fettered by the basic principles of liberalism or marxism, or the modern scientist mind by a mathematical postulate. Conflict between faith and reason cannot always be avoided but in most cases it is successfully solved by an allegorical interpretation of the sacred writings.

This kind of interpretation appeals to European mediaeval mentality in more ways than one. For had the Fathers of the Church not already taught that references in the Bible to natural phenomena were reflections of the scientific opinions of its time and need not always be taken at face value? St Augustine in particular, developing an idea which Galileo would later take up — in vain! — suggested that 'if we happen across a passage in Holy Scripture which lends itself to various interpretations, we must not . . . . . . bind ourselves so firmly to any one of them that if one day the truth is more thoroughly investigated, our interpretation may collapse, and we with it.'

The early mediaeval writers, as we have seen, seized upon allegory with the typical enthusiasm of ages poorly equipped with exact information

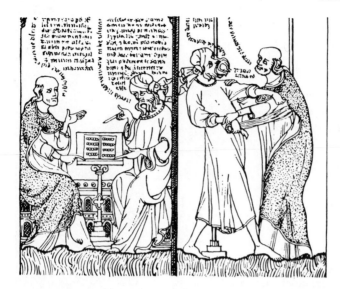

Fig. 70. Raymond Lull learning Arabic with his Moorish slave, who blasphemes and quarrels with him; from a miniature of Raymond Lull's contemporary biography, Generallandes Archiv, Karlsruhe.

and clear ideas. Every event and every phenomenon seemed to them to defy all explanation except as a symbol or omen of some aspect or other of God's will. Hence their taste for the fanciful dross which Latin encyclopaedists incorporated into the pure metal of Greek knowledge; hence the stunning popularity of a fascinating, yet childish booklet, the *Physiologus*, a miscellany of 'moralized natural science' for the use of the Christians of Alexandria in the 2nd century. It is from the *Physiologus* and the countless mediaeval 'bestiaries', its descendants, that the literary zoology of our ancestors derived a few of its oddest specimens: from the phoenix, symbol of the death and resurrection of Christ, to the ant-lion, born of an ant and a lion, who cannot allay its hunger either with meat or with grain and is doomed to perish, like all men who aspire to serve God and the Devil at the same time.

In writings of the 13th century, realism and allegory, penetrating observations and absurd fables elbow each other for room. (Fig. 70 and 71). The same phenomenon will occur even in more scientific times than were the late Middle Ages; like the phoenix, symbolism never dies and legends hallowed by tradition die but slowly. Besides, as long as Arabia remained unexplored and inaccessible, who could have stated categorically, against all the concordant evidence from ancient and mediaeval naturalists, that the Arabian phoenix did not really exist? Is the real giraffe much less odd than the mythical ant-lion? The two most ambitious literary works of the period, the *Roman de la Rose* — two authors, 24,000 lines, and generations of eager readers — and the *Divina Commedia*, present this superimposition of the most complex allegory over the strictest realism, reflecting a whole way of thinking, of seeing the world differently from ours. To elucidate these mediaeval attitudes without a detailed study of the ideologies that engendered them, we must reduce them to their simplest terms.

Besides, it is in their most simplified form that the speculations of intellectuals left their mark on the cultured public. For the ignorant, even the *Physiologus* was very difficult.

Man at the centre of creation

It is frequently said that European civilisation in the late Middle Ages was fashioned by faith in God. We should add, at least, 'and by faith in Man, created in the image of God.' After he had paid his humble homage to the infinite power and wisdom of the Creator, mediaeval man took pride in the fact that he had been chosen, despite his unworthiness, to be the physical and moral centre of all creation.

Fig. 71. Allegorical representation of Raymond Lull leading the Army of Truth, marching against Error and Ignorance (in the chariot are the banners of philosophy wisdom, virtue etc).

In their desire to extract from the chaotic experience of daily life harmonious and symmetric theories, pagan scientists had constructed an intelligent universe, mathematically and geometrically ordered, in which the function of the Gods and Fate was not clearly defined, but in which Man was the measure of all things and the highest step in the ladder of animate and inanimate objects. Jewish prophets, more aware of the moral than of the physical order, saw Man as the earthly masterpiece of God, an incomplete and intractable masterpiece to be sure but supreme among creatures and capable of rising to unlimited heights because of the Spirit which breathed in him and of his knowledge of good and evil, stolen from the Tree of Life. Finally, the Gospels had announced that the Son of God became flesh and died to perfect the masterpiece and make amends for original sin.

Is it any wonder then, if men in the 13th century, contemplating as they were the whole panorama of pagan, Jewish and Christian wisdom, sought for the ultimate explanation of natural phenomena not in possible external causes but in the depths of their own beings, their consciences, the mirror of divine will?

It is in the doctrine of microcosm that the theory of man at the centre of Creation finds its most literal expression: man was to be a small-scale model or microcosm, of the universe or macrocosm. This was not really a new idea, for it is connected with the early atomistic theories of the Greeks: nor is it exclusively a western idea, for it may go back to Egyptian beliefs and it attracted Moslem mystics and Jewish cabalists. In a slightly different form it is also encountered in China. In the mediaeval West, this doctrine did have a few adherents among the Fathers of the Church, but did not become prominent until the 12th century, as a result of a short treatise in cosmology by Bernard of Tours (*De Mundi universitate sive Megacosmus et Microcosmus*) and of the medico-mystical dreameries of St Hildegard of Bingen. From then on nearly all philosophers were to take it as an evident truth or at least a logical assumption.

Human microcosm and universal macrocosm being organised along more or less similar lines, they can explain each other and qualify each other by analogy and by mutual influence. There is a whole web of influence and similarity between the seven 'planets' (including the sun and the moon but not the earth, of course), the seven metals, the seven orifices of the human face, the seven 'moods' (from the lunatic to the venereal, the jovial, the saturnine). The four humours circulating in the human body (blood, phlegm, bile and atrabile) correspond to the four constituent elements of all matter in the universe (air, fire, water, earth). The spirit, the fifth indestructible essence of man, corresponds to quintessence, the incorruptible basis of all other things.

In turn, the four humours and the four elements are themselves the product of various combinations of the four basic principles (heat, cold, humidity, dryness). The instability of these principles in the heavens is mirrored in the four seasons on earth and in the nature and destiny of Man. Quintessence itself does not vary; he who succeeds in mastering it can use it to transmute matter and extend the resistance of the vital spirit in man. As a result, astrology and alchemy are clues of psychology and medicine.

Moreover, since the laws of the microcosm are equally valid for the macrocosm, the motive forces of the universe can be compared with the motivations of man. Man strains towards God more or less enthusiastically and more or less constantly according to the qualities and defects of his soul: other bodies act and move with more or less efficiency, more or less continuity, according to the qualities and defects of their matter. Consequently, ethics and metaphysics are clues of mathematical and natural science.

The 'moralized' universe

In a world thus 'moralized' there is no place for chance or indifference. Objects and phenomena are good or bad, depending on whether they strain towards the ends specifically assigned to them by God or fail to respond to His will. They are noble or base in proportion to their innate power (potentiality) accomplish acts which bring them closer to the Creator, or acts useful to man, the chosen protagonist of Creation.

The circular movement of the planets is better and nobler than the irregular movement of men, because it is continuous and uniform and bathed in divine light. The inertia of the earth's centre, where everything sinks towards Satan, himself a motionless prisoner in everlasting darkness, is bad and base. Evil, however, is not so much a force or an active substance as a deficiency, the absence of good. In reality, all sources of energy add up to one source only; love gushing forth from God towards creatures, and being returned by creatures to God.

This harmonious, unitary and symmetrical vision of a coherent universe organised in singleness of purpose explains why 13th century philosophers are at the same time powerful logicians and careless observers. True science, in their opinion, does not consist in quantitative measurement of specific phenomena, but in qualitative assessment of the trend, the useful function of everything. Their great scientific question is not 'how and how much?' but 'for what purpose?'

In our times, more thorough observation has revealed indifferent sources of energy quite unsuspected in the Middle Ages and has led us to abandon the quest as to the 'why' of nature. It would be impossible today to attempt a return to the lost paradise of a universe wholly straining towards God, wholly organised around man. One may well wonder, too, if it really was such a paradise: our anguish as we survey an inexplicable world is perhaps less cruel than that suffered by those who, having glimpsed the Divine plan, were always afraid lest they violated its decrees. Today we are better equipped for life, but more lonely when facing death.

II. LIBERAL AND MECHANICAL ARTS

Like the 'feudal system', scholasticism (that is, philosophy combined with
theology and science, as taught in the mediaeval schools) is mentioned in scorn
oftener than in praise. In spite of recent attempts by 'neo-scholastics' to give
it a new look, it is still associated in most minds with the sarcasms of Galileo
and Moliere and the quixotic fights of the die-hards in behalf of Aristotle and
Aquinas agaist experimental methods and modern science. But the stale scholasticism of the 17th century is not a fair image of its mediaeval progenitor. In the
13th century, 'modern science' was that of Aquinas, as opposed to die-hard neo-
platonism or literal reading of the dogma; and though experiment proper
played second fiddle to logic, there was a wealth of recorded observation,
whether inherited from the Greeks or supplied by the scholastics themselves.

Nevertheless, it cannot be denied that the tight system of St Thomas because
of its very cogency tended to become petrified during the succeeding centuries.
Nothing is harder than rejecting a perfectly consistent, rational picture. Once
it had reached the narrow plateau where practical scientific learning encountered the intuitions of theology, scholastic philosophy could climb no higher.
The *Summa* had the answer for almost every question, it countered almost every
objection, it had a logical explanation for almost every natural phenomenon,
without impairing the supreme truth of faith. Why then, that being so, should
one endure the torture of closer analysis and risk, like Averroes, the possibility
of finding oneself faced with the problem of the double truth? 'Mankind, be satisfied with the *quia*' says Dante: there is a limit beyond which reason cannot go.

The philosophers of light and 'experimental science'

Without going beyond this limit, however, it was possible to argue ad infinitum
on the respective merits of the old School and the new and to support some
aspects of platonism in St Augustine against the discreet aristotelism of St
Thomas. The Augustinian theory of divine illumination as the source of all
human knowledge never lost its appeal. St Bonaventure made it the starting
point for his own pathway to God through a progression of divine illuminations.
The theories of the Oxford School of philosophers were linked with it too, but
from a different angle, for their goal was not so much divine wisdom as divine
power.

For the Oxford philosophers, in fact, light is 'the prime corporeal force',
which generates motion and material things; to put it in modern words, it is
the primary source of energy. Hence they do not strive to demonstrate truths
of faith by the use of reason, but rather to explain luminous phenomena by
direct observation and by a few practical experiences. Let us ungrudgingly
acknowledge the importance of this method, the method which Roger Bacon
in his *Opus Maius* (between 1266 and 1268) will describe as 'experimental
science.' However, let us not be carried away by the label before we have seen

what is underneath it. What were the aims of the Oxford School? What were its actual achievements?

Its first exponent, Robert Grosseteste, Chancellor of the University (died in 1253), re-examines the optical theories of the Greeks and the Arabs, emphasizes the analogy between the propagation of light and that of sound, and makes a study of reflection and refraction. His research into the rainbow enables him to formulate a new quantitative law of refraction, 'proved by experiments' (his 'law', however, is inaccurate). His famous disciple, Roger Bacon, progresses further along the same alley, extending his research to the anatomy of the eye, to various types of concave mirrors, to flat and convex lenses. Finally, two learned men less directly connected with Oxford — Witelo, born in Silesia about 1230, and Dietrich of Freiburg, a Saxon, who died about 1311 — carried out fresh theoretical and experimental work on the rainbow and other branches of optics. From one experiment to another there is undeniable progress. But it is modest progress in a limited sphere.

The ambitions of the Oxford School are much greater than its achievements. 'It is possible to build machines which will allow us to sail without oarsmen,' declares Bacon, 'carts without animals to pull them.... machines for flying.... machines which can move in the dephs of the seas and rivers, even on their bottoms.... bridges with no piers or supports.... and other unheard of apparatus. These machines were put to work in Antiquity and... in our days, too, except perhaps for the flying-machine.'

At this point, however, Bacon is leaving the threshold of science to enter the castle of dreams. The ancient inventors of whom he is thinking are neither Greek scholars nor Roman engineers, but, rather, the Alexander the Great of the literature of chivalry, that Alexander whom miniatures of the time depict as mounted upon his chariot and carried through the atmosphere by four spirited griffins. As for his inventors 'of our days' Bacon does claim acquaintance with an 'expert' who has 'thought of a way' to make a flying-machine. So be it, but is thinking without testing enough to become an 'expert'?

> Even in the optical field, 'experimental science' stops too soon. Grosseteste suggests the use of lenses for increasing the size of both small and distant objects and bringing them nearer. Bacon suggests convex lenses for the correction of long-sightedness, but neither of them hits on the idea of making a very simple 'machine' — spectacles. It will take some obscure Italian craftsmen to invent these, perhaps, it is true, with the help of some monk or other who has read *Opus Maius*. In 1300, the corporation of glassmakers of Venice, wishing to exploit the new invention commercially, enacts a special regulation concerning 'wheels for the eyes' ... and these wheels, in their turn, will help philosophers to prolong their reading life.

Science, magic, technique: the alchemists

Science, it has been claimed, was born of a marriage of mathematics and magic. Without the drive of irrational impulses, illusion, imagination, it would be hard for scholarship to climb out of the old rut. There is no reason, therefore, to be shocked when Bacon maintains that it is possible, thanks to astrology, to sound out 'experimentally' the sentiments and intentions of indicted people waiting for trial. (Actually his unshakable faith in astrology will be the cause of his being sentenced to imprisonment by his ecclesiastical superiors.) Yet to be of help to what we call science today, magic has to emerge from the castle of dreams; it must not be afraid to get its hands dirty in testing and re-testing through an infinite series of experiments. From this standpoint, it is not the philosophers of light who are to carry off the laurels, but the alchemists.

> Spurred on by a greedy desire to manufacture gold, most alchemists had a dubious reputation even in their own times. We must not, however, confuse impostors, who naturally were plentiful in a field such as this, with respectable men of learning. These, too, were planning to transform 'imperfect' metals into 'perfect' gold, but material profit was not their ultimate aim. What they longed for, above all, was a means of rising from worldly, unstable and corruptible matter to the eternal perfection of God. Their leading idea, stemming from Greek and Arab science but adjusted to Christian philosophy, was that all earthly substances are impure mixtures of sulphur and mercury, these two in turn being corrupt forms of 'philosophic' sulphur and mercury. By means of manifold manipulations designed to modify the four principles in the four elements (that is, by heating, cooling, drying or wetting processes) the alchemists hoped to isolate the fifth element (the quintessence, or philosophers' stone) and thus to eliminate the impurities in matter.
>
> Their first victory will be the creation of 'Fire-water', that is, alcohol at 60° (the earliest description of the process of distillation, in western sources, goes back to the beginning of the 12th century); their second achievement will be the preparation of 'water of life', eau-de-vie or alcohol at 95°. Gold, however, is more elusive. When a leading mediaeval naturalist and philosopher, Albert 'the Great', the teacher of Aquinas, places some samples of 'alchemic gold' in the furnace for testing, he has to stand helplessly by as it disintegrates into ashes. Yet there is no doubt in his mind as to the fact that metals can be converted into other metals; the only problem is to find the right way.

The philosophers of light happened to take a few steps on the way that opened out into modern optical science; the alchemists missed the narrower way that ultimately led to nuclear fission. But in their fumbling they developed new methods of chemical analysis, made a great variety of laboratory instruments, distilled a number of vegetable oils, produced nitric acid and sulphuric acid. . . While for them these discoveries were of no immediate use, other branches of knowledge profited thereby. Mediaeval science was still simple enough to have no rigid specialization and no watertight compartments; Arnold of Villanova, alchemist, astrologer, philosopher and physician at the court of Aragon (died about 1313) was in the habit of recommending 'water of life', eau-de-vie, to his patients. And he was not far wrong, for while it did not constitute the elixir of

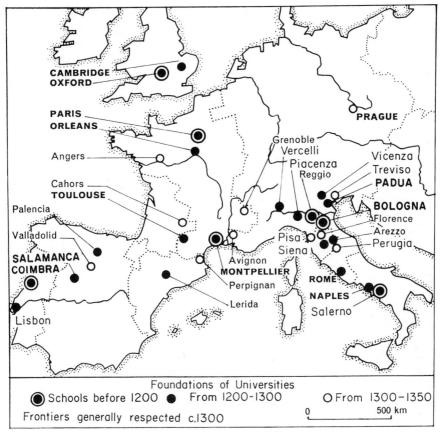

Map 23. *Universities in the Middle Ages*

life and the fountain of youth the alchemists had hoped for, brandy was none-theless a good disinfectant and a powerful narcotic.

The connection between science and technology was much looser than that existing between the different branches of science. It was not, however, entirely missing. The 'hermetic' or secret language in which alchemists sought to couch their formulae did not prevent their experiments from influencing the practical development of distillation, the techniques of metallurgy, or the manufacture of explosives. In reverse, the empirical knowledge of sailors using the magnetized needle was utilized by Pierre de Maricourt in 1269 in his remarkable treatise on magnetism. The theoretical algebra of Leonardo Fibonacci of Pisa, about 1200, was based on the everyday arithmetic of his father, a commercial employee of the Pisan colony at Bougie in North Africa.

Artists sometimes bridged with their imagination the gulf separating the mechanics of philosophers, based on divine love and the innate potentiality of elements, from the mechanics of craftsmen, based on everyday practice.

Dante compared the harmonious dances of the blessed with the precise movement of a mechanical clock with escapements (an invention of his time). The
illustrator of a Provençal philosophical manuscript depicted two angels who,
motivated by the love of God, are turning the First Movable Heaven by means
of a great handle on a pivot, another mediaeval invention (Pl. VII). Nevertheless, what has been called the gap between 'the thinkers and the tinkers'
remained.

The aristocracy of studies

The 13th century possessed the basic human elements that were to combine
at a later period and produce the scientific revolutions of modern times: the
manual and mental ingenuity of practical inventors, the inquisitive spirit of
theoretical philosophers, and to give both a favourable surrounding, the pressure
of a growing economy. Religious and political restraints existed, but they were
less tight and efficient than in the early modern age, the springboard of the
scientific revolution. What prevented the men of the 13th century from taking
full advantage of opportunities was above all a lack of communication, and
this lack stemmed from the persisting prejudices of the 'liberal arts' against
the 'mechanical arts' — a legacy of antiquity which had become more firmly
entrenched in feudal society.

In Dante's time, as in the days of Aristotle, the 'liberal arts' were the only
studies considered worthy enough to prepare a citizen for a full intellectual,
moral and social life. Varro, Cicero's learned friend, had listed nine such arts:
grammar, rhetoric, logic, music, arithmetic, geometry, astronomy, medicine
and architecture. But the last two subjects, considered less dignified because
they involved a certain degree of manual work, were eliminated in the Imperial
age; Martianus Capella and, at the beginning of the barbarian age, Cassiodorus
would acknowledge only seven liberal arts.

In our own times, too, the liberal arts play a fundamental part in education,
but they do not crowd out all other disciplines and skills. In the Middle Ages,
however, when schools re-emerged from the barbarian doldrums, only those
seven disciplines which had been listed by Capella and Cassiodorus (and which
did not dirty one's hands) found an honourable place in the course of studies.
It is true that a mystic philosopher of the early 12th century, Hugh of St
Victor, put in a good word for the other seven specialities, which together made
up the 'adulterine' science of mechanics: making of clothes, arms and fortification (which, oddly enough, carried in its trail architecture at large), navigation,
agriculture, hunting, medicine, theatrical arts. There also were a few writers
who pointed out that every pure or liberal art had its counterpart in an applied
or 'fabrile' technique. Nevertheless, universities crystallized the *curriculum*
solely around the liberal arts; 'mechanical' skills had to be learned in the shops
of master craftsmen or in technical schools of a lower grade.

Even so, the standard university programme was extensive and imaginative.
It began with the three literary arts of the *trivium* ('trivial', that is, elementary):

basic Latin conversation and composition (grammar); stylistics as applied to the writing of formal letters, documents, and sometimes poems in Latin (rhetorics); methodical reasoning, debate, and, by extension, initiation into philosophy (logics or dialectics). Then came the four scientific arts of the *quadrivium:* arithmetic, geometry, astronomy, 'music' or rather musicology (the mathematical theory of interval and frequency, which also led up to general reflections on the harmony of the spheres). Finally, the student was ready to tackle the queen of all learning: theology. Should he prefer, however, to devote himself to the study of God's justice in its pale, earthly form, he could work to perfect his knowledge of canon and civil law. Or else — but here religious justification was tenuous and one got perilously close to the 'mechanical' arts — the student could drop his gaze from the health of the soul to that of the body and take up medicine.

None of the other special subjects which we would today describe as definitely intellectual contrived to win a place in university teaching: not the art of the architect, although it was hallowed in church building and indispensable in setting up castles; not the eloquence of the orator or the competence of the notary, despite the fame of the special schools of the *ars dictaminis* and the *ars notaria;* not the science of the alchemist even though it dangled the glistening secret formula of wealth and long life. This discrimination implied also a social ostracism; even Hugh of St Victor, the defender of the 'mechanical arts', recommended them for 'plebeians' only.

In the more exclusive circles, discrimination was extended even to such 'liberal arts' as have a practical, concrete side. In the University of Paris, the prestige attaching to philosophical and theological study tends to atrophy all other subjects. The *quadrivium* is sacrificed to the *trivium* and, in the latter, rhetoric is subordinated to dialectics; medicine is neglected; the study of canon law does not include that of civil law.

Admittedly, the case of Paris is exceptional. Many universities in England and in Mediterranean countries have the highest regard for the *quadrivium* and give a prominent place to their faculties of medicine and law. In the 12th century, Italy was already shocking a German observer, Otto of Freising, by actually putting into highest public office 'workers in the mechanical arts, who in other nations would be rejected like the plague from honourable and liberal studies.' But even in Italy, a very distinct line of demarcation between theoretical subjects and technical learning slows down the free exchange of ideas and methods, lowers the standard of instruction given to the majority of people (those who merely go to lower schools or learn a trade), and encourages the minority, those who are simply and solely scholars, to carry on their reasoning in a vacuum.

However, one should not be too hard upon these scholars. When one reflects that in 1284 the Paris faculty of Arts (Pl. 14.) had only one hundred and twenty professors and perhaps fewer than 2,000 students, one might well stand amazed that such a restricted group could produce such a variety of profound

ideas. No doubt their imaginative scholarship was enhanced by the fact that no
utilitarian activity distracted them from pure thought. At any rate, how can we
make a fair assessment of the practical value of mediaeval studies if we take into
account only disciplines based on theory and aiming at heaven? Rather should
we turn our attention to a marginal case, that of medicine, which was at the
same time liberal art and quasi-mechanical practice.

III.   PHYSICIANS, ASTROLOGERS, MIRACLE-MEN

In the early Middle Ages, medicine, like every other science, had taken refuge
in the monasteries and had kept itself going by a modest amount of reading;
yet it was the first science to come out of monasteries and the first to reconsider
empirical methods.

   As far back as the 10th century, learned monks in France and Lotharingia
were talking enviously about the doctors at Salerno, who for the most part were
laymen 'lacking literary culture but equipped with great experience and a
natural talent.' Salerno, a seaport and the capital of a 'Lombard' principality,
was exposed to the influence of Islam and Byzantium. In addition, it was close
to the famous abbey at Monte Cassino, founded by St Benedict, and endowed
with one of the finest libraries of the period. In the 11th century, Abbot Desiderius (the future Pope Victor III), proudly described the miracles performed by
the founder-saint: having appeared in a dream to the Duke of Bavaria, Benedict
had operated on him for a stone and placed the stone between his hands without

*Fig. 72. Disc showing
medicaments and the
time when they are to
be administered.* Codex
Paneth, MS. *written in
Bologna; Medical Lib-
rary, Yale University.*

waking him up! Nevertheless, when Desiderius fell ill, he went to Salerno to be treated.

At the beginning of the 12th century, the medicine of the soul was declared incompatible with that of the body. The Church forbad monks to become professional doctors, a ban renewed in 1219 and extended at the same time to include the legal profession and cover the secular clergy. Hospital service, on the other hand, remained almost completely in the hands of monks and nuns; originally designed for the poor and for travellers (whether sick or healthy), hospitals multiplied and became specialized. And, of course, the clergy were not forbidden to write treatises on medicine or to treat other members of their calling.

From Salerno to Bologna

Having become entirely a lay concern during the 11th and 12th centuries, the Salerno school of medicine was able to combine theory and practice. Its output of writings was considerable. Garioponto or Guarimpoto, the first mediaeval author whom we can identify (before 1050) adopts Claudius Galen's views as his own and draws inspiration from Hippocrates: the patient must be put to bed, he says, and nature allowed to take its course. Before long, the scientific stock in trade of the Salerno school is enriched by more recent authorities — Byzantine, Jewish, Arabic — not forgetting the inevitable Aristotle. Nevertheless, the best works produced at Salerno bear the unmistakable imprint of fresh and direct experience. They range from the gynaecological treatise ascribed to a certain Trotula, to the *Anatomy of the Pig,* by one Cafo, from the *Manual of Surgery* by Roger to the anonymous poetic pot-pourri *Regimen Sanitatis Salernitanum* from which maxims are still being quoted today.

Theory and practice are nicely balanced in the curriculum laid down by Frederick II about 1240, for all those who want to practise medicine in the kingdom of Sicily; three years of logic, five years of medicine (including surgery and anatomy), one year's probation with a licensed doctor. Licenses had been required ever since Norman times; but Frederick was the first to decree that royal officials had no right to confer it except with the approval of professors from Salerno. He was also first to insist on the public dissection of one human corpse at least once every five years.

In the 13th century, however, the prestige of the old Salerno school was eclipsed by that of newer universities — Montpellier, Padua and, above all, Bologna, where the empiricism of the school of medicine dovetailed the pragmatism of the faculty of law. Whereas at Salerno it had been thought sufficient to learn anatomy from books and dissected animals, students at Bologna were required to witness the dissection of a human corpse at least once a year. In medicine as in law, teachers drew from their own professional experience to enrich their lectures at the university; like the lawyers, who built up collections of their *Responsa* (legal opinions concerning actual cases), the physicians began to publish their *Consilia* or clinical consultations. On a loftier plane, there were

Fig. 73. Leper House at Perigueux (Dordogne) twelfth century.

treatises inserting medical theory into the scholastic framework: Peter of Abano who taught both in Paris and in Padua, compiled a *Conciliator. . . praecipue medicorum*, where conflicting authorities were listed, discussed and reconciled with the method first used by Gratian in canon law and Peter Lombard in philosophy. At a lower level, and often outside the universities, there were manuals of popular medicine: just as Vacarius had summarized all civil law in his *Book of the Poor*, so Peter of Lisbon ('Peter Hispanus', who in 1276 became Pope John XXI) summed up the treatment for every malady in his *Treasure of the Poor*.

Was it really a treasure? Its nucleus consisted of the Graeco-Roman and Arab-Jewish legacies, themselves a mixture of real jewels and fake stones: anatomy was correct in outline, but marred by total misunderstanding of the circulatory system; physiology was characterized by a wealth of instructive insight, but dominated by the theory of the 'four humours'; pathology was more successful in describing and distinguishing symptoms of illnesses than in identifying their causes and remedies; pharmacology was remarkably skilled in the preparation of well tested herbs, but clumsy and often whimsical in the use of chemical compounds. The doctors of Salerno and Bologna deserved great praise for recovering and interpreting this vast legacy, but did not go far in weeding out what was obviously wrong. Thus, for instance, Mondino dei Liuzzi of Bologna in his famous treatise on anatomy (1316) confirmed and supported with his own observations everything that Galen had reported correctly, but would not, or could not amend such errors of Galen as his dissections ought to have bared. Things were still worse in the case of illustrations; those which accompanied a manual presented by Guido of Vigevano in 1345 to his royal patient, Philip VI of France, are no more than rough sketches, far too clumsy and elementary to guide the hand of a beginner, and certainly useless for an experienced practitioner.

And yet these doctors, who were so shy of challenging the theories of the Ancients, proved their excellence and independence in the practice of surgery and external medicine. Anaesthesia, sutures, daring operations of all kinds gave occasion to experiments and observations which are described with outstanding lucidity in the manuals of great 13th century surgeons. Hugh Borgognoni, a doctor at Lucca, a professor at Bologna, and a crusader in Egypt (1160–1252), during his long life sparks off a revolt against Galen: instead of making wounds suppurate by means of greasy ointments, as prescribed by the most revered Graeco-Roman authority, one should, he said, disinfect them with wine. Guglielmo of Saliceto, professor at Bologna in 1269, is up in arms at the misuse of cauterization as practised by the Arabs and re-introduces the use of the scalpel. One may dispute the validity of the grounds for this or that mediaeval innovation, but not deny the fact that medical science is on the march.

Progress in internal medicine and public health is less spectacular, which is understandable. Though most towns maintain physicians and midwives to give free assistance to the poor, and make provisions for public bath-houses and a supply of pure drinking water, sewage is generally inferior and refrigeration non-existent. Fresh air and food in the country do not make up for an unbalanced diet and the lack of medical care; on the whole, the life expectation of the peasant seems to have been much shorter than that of town dwellers. Above all, mediaeval doctors, like the Greeks and Arabs before them, are forced to grope their way without microscopes, without thorough chemical analyses, without an accurate conception of general biology. That certain illnesses are contagious, they know, but effective (and indeed drastic) isolation measures are taken only against leprosy (Fig. 73).

In the 12th century, leprosy was the most widespread epidemic disease in Europe. It slowly diminished ever since, but it is difficult to distinguish the effect which prevention and treatment had and that of collective im-

Fig. 74. The Infirm-ary at Ourscamp Abbey (Oise) thir-teenth century.

munization (Fig. 74). Even today, the identification of the leprosy microbe has not led to a definite cure, and one of the substances which we still use to fight it, Chaulmoogra oil, was already used in the Middle Ages.

The influence of the stars

The doctors did their best, but people did not rely exclusively on them. A poem by Pietro d'Eboli, courtier to the King of Sicily and probable author of a short work on the thermal springs at Pozzuoli, is adorned with a miniature representing William II on his deathbed (1189) with a doctor and an astrologer in attendance (Fig. 75). The doctor has not come from Salerno, as might have been expected in such a case, but is either an Arab or a Jew ('Achim Medicus'). On his head he wears a turban and he is holding the humble vessel used for making analyses (analysis was by sight and smell in the Middle Ages whereas it is effected chemically in our day and age — but the liquid is ever the same). The astrologer, for his part, is also turbanned: he is holding an astrolabe and in front of him is a gigantic star, which, although not a comet, bodes nothing good. As a matter of fact, in the subsequent scene, the miniature shows the king lying dead, surrounded by mourners, and an empty chapel (for what is the use of praying any more for his cure ? — and it is too early yet to recommend his soul to God).

Fig. 75. King William II of Sicily, treated first by a physician and then by an astrologer; Pietro d'Eboli, Liber ad honorem Augusti, *Town and University Library, Berne.*

The presence of the astrologer must not be regarded as a phenomenon of popular superstition, but, on the contrary, as a proof that the patient was being cared for in accordance with the most advanced methods of the age. In the anthropocentric world of the Middle Ages, let us repeat, the idea that the stars could move about heedless of man would have seemed as unreasonable as the hypothesis of a God creating the world haphazardly with no definite plan. The only doubts were encompassed in the old, unsolvable dilemma of predestination and free will. The omniscience and omnipotence of God being granted, to what degree could man extrictate himself from the influence of the stars? Dante sums up the most widely held opinion, by explaining that the heavens set man in motion, but his will is free. Men have 'a hard fight in their early battles against the sky,' but they can ultimately overcome all obstacle.

It was therefore heresy to maintain that the influence of the stars was insuperable; for just such an assertion Cecco of Ascoli, professor of astrology at Bologna and bitter critic of Dante, was burned alive in 1327. Yet nothing would have been more presumptuous or more discreditable than to deny the role which the stars played in the destinies of the human soul and body.

In the 13th century, the astrologer occupied a position rather like that of the modern psychoanalyst. To be assured of his private services at all times one had to be very wealthy; but people of relatively modest means could ask him for a horoscope, which would be rapidly worked out on the astrolabe (for the sun and the stars) and on the *equatorium* (for the planets); even those who were not in the habit of consulting him knew something about the professional jargon and the principles of astrology. Was the faulty forecast of one or other of them damaging to the prestige of astrology in general? Not a bit of it — no more than today one wrong diagnosis on the part of any individual doctor reflects discredit on the whole profession. There was an easy explanation for apparent inconsistencies, such as twins with different destinies; the stars, although shining at the same place in the same day for all men, combine their influences in a thousand ways: the free will of each man may resist them and even overcompensate their impact, or collaborate mildly, or submit abjectly, so that one and the same firmament lends itself to contradictory deductions and forecasts. On the other hand, what a great number of predictions came ominously true! Let us recall just one, illustrated in the famous Bayeux tapestry; Halley's comet, pale and sinister, appeared in 1066 to foretell the dramatic events of that year — the battle of Hastings and the fall of the Anglo-Saxon monarchy.

Although his science is on the wrong track, the astrologer is every inch a scientist. Therefore he does not oppose the physician, but instead tries to guide him by suggesting to him the propitious moment for dealing with the 'damp, dry, hot or cold' condition of the patient, so that the ordinary remedies of medicine may be administered under the best possible heavenly conjunction. Like the good doctor, the good astrologer is amenable to a change in his prescriptions, according to the effects they produce, or appear to produce, during the course of the illness.

Hope in the miracle

Religion, in its intransigent or superstitious forms, could be a more redoubtable foe of the physician. When the Church abandoned the practice of medicine to laymen, she did not do so merely for the reasons she alleged (preventing ecclesiastics from seeking personal gain or staining their hands with blood) but also from a conscious or unconscious feeling that in many cases sickness may be a divine punishment against which no weapon is permissible apart from repentance and prayer.

Here is an example of this way of thinking, taken at random from the illustrations of the *Cantigas* of Alphonso X of Castille; a woman has the urge to steal flour from the pilgrims who have asked her for hospitality, but by mistake (or rather by divine punishment) she plunges a knife into her throat. Doctors try in vain to extract the knife. Overcome by remorse, the woman prays to the Blessed Virgin and turns to her confessor, who pulls out the knife without the slightest difficulty. Nothing but a legend, of course. Still, how many other sinful women will have turned to their confessors rather than to the doctor? How many other cures will have been the work of miraculous healers? There is hardly a monk in odour of sanctity who does not get called to the bedside of a critically sick patient, a parish priest who is not asked by someone to exorcise a possessive devil, a sanctuary which fails to draw a crowd of sick people full of hope. The sickness which we call scrofula, but which in the Middle Ages men knew as 'the King's Disease', could be cured by touching a king, even if this touch were only a brush from his sacred cloak. Let us add that magic formulae circulated by word of mouth, charms went from hand to hand, old wives' remedies from family to family; these were usually the only drugs accessible to the poor, and they were not without a certain psychosomatic value.

Finally, what is left for true medical science? A slender beam shining as best it can in the castle of the nobles and the houses of the upper bourgeoisie, barely filtering through to the hospitals, and leaving the great majority of mankind in the shadows.

IV.   THE EXPLORATION OF THE EARTH

Shall we try to do full justice to the power of observation and the inventive skill of the Middle Ages? Then let us leave the world of theory and come down to the root level of manual and mental techniques. This is where are worked out the innumerable inventions which enable farmers, merchants and craftsmen to better their way of life from generation to generation. Thanks to these humble inventions, Catholic Europe will have succeeded in creating a social order which Aristotle had declared impossible and unnatural — a world without slaves. More than that: in the Italy of the Communes, in many French provinces, in Flanders and in other advanced countries, we even get a glimpse of a world without serfs bound to the soil.

Certainly, today as in the Middle Ages, it is easier to take in the beauty of a cathedral than that of the wheeled plough of the Norman peasant or the pedalled loom of the Brabant weaver, easier to appreciate the symmetry of a poem than that of the register of a Genoese lawyer or an English clerk. But when conquests in the practical field went beyond the everyday horizon, when nautical maps and great voyages were involved, then imaginations were fired, in the Middle Ages as today.

The age of approximation and day-dreams

There was no dearth of travellers even during the early Middle Ages; pilgrims went to Rome, Compostela and Jerusalem, ambassadors journeyed to Constantinople and Cordova, and there were adventurers, soldiers, merchants. But they were not accurate observers, nor did they report what they saw very accurately. While Cosmas 'Indicopleustes' ('navigator to the Indies') does tell of something new and interesting in connection with Eastern Asia, his primary object is to counter the unholy idea that the Earth might be round. Is it not compared in the Bible to a 'tabernacle,' in other words, a rectangle canopied by the sky and shaded by a mountain behind which the sun hides at night?

Later on, bold voyages by the Irish and the Frisians, and then more daring ventures by the Scandinavians in the North Sea towards America and in Russia, might well have supplied a wealth of geographical knowledge which not even the Greeks possessed. But what little information about these journeys trickles through to educated circles is too inaccurate and too interwoven with legends to constitute any real gain. While a picture of Vinland (America?) pierces momentarily through the mists, only to be thrust back into them almost immediately, an imaginary St Brendan's Isle, the isle of the Earthly Paradise, gets established in the Atlantic Ocean with such a wealth of detail that not before the 19th century will every trace of it disappear from all nautical maps. Finland borders on to Amazon country, and this is inhabited by sorcerers, who 'sell wind to sailors.' Scandinavia is usually an island.

Anyhow, what does accuracy matter, when geographical maps are no more than simple diagrams innocent of proportion or real shape? We are in an age of allegory and hallowed symbols; granted that the continents are three in number, surrounded by the Ocean and separated by the Mediterranean and the Red Sea (or the Nile), 'cartographers' are quite content to diagrammatize them by a capital T inscribed in a capital O.

It is true that the geography of the centuries before the 13th is not invariably confined to this world of approximation. From Bede onwards, the best thinkers are not encumbered overmuch with the literal sense of the Scriptures and compare the earth, in its position at the centre of the Universe, to the yolk of an egg, which is tantamount to saying that the earth is spherical. A comparatively small sphere, it was noted; Boethius, one of the most widely-read writers throughout the Middle Ages, states that 'in proportion to the Universe, the earth is no more than a dot'. Such people as the Norwegian explorer Ohthere, who sailed the White Sea and the Baltic in the 9th century, and the Anglo-Saxon King Alfred who had his report included in a manuscript on world history, were undoubtedly motivated by scientific curiosity, however elementary. And if we single out the few attempts there were to depict the inhabited lands realistically, instead of reducing them to diagrams, then even cartography cuts a better figure. In the Anglo-Saxon 'Cotton Map' (10th century? or 12th century?) the three continents, though grossly misshapen, are not mere geometrical abstractions; one even observes an effort to make room for the Nordic countries joined to the Catholic community of Europe a short while before.

When we compare the Cotton Map with the Hereford Map (about 1280) or the Ebsdorf Map (1284), we find it hard to believe that in the interval the Crusades have taken place, Western trade has penetrated far into Asia, and Ptolemy's *Almagest* has appeared in Latin translation. For the new maps are scarcely better than the Cotton Map, though they are made easier on the eye by elaborate representations of fantastic animals and men-monsters seated on the ground with their heads in the shade of their one gigantic foot. Far superior to these attempts at representing the whole world is a map of Great Britain, drawn by the chronicler-illustrator Matthew Paris about 1250; but it also shows a fanciful sense of proportion. 'If this page were large enough,' says the author casually, 'the whole island ought to be more elongated'. Yet the same Matthew Paris, having seen an elephant (a gift from St Louis to Henry III), was the first Englishman who tried to draw it realistically, putting a man beside the elephant, so that the reader 'could get an idea of the enormous size of the beast.'

Geography is born mature

What, then, is missing in the scholars and artists of the age of Matthew Paris? Probably not the technical dexterity or the information necessary to draw better maps, but rather the conviction that statistical or 'photographic' accuracy may be better than a suggestive symbol or a colourful adjective.

In 1204, as his eyes light on Constantinople, to him an unknown, hostile metropolis enclosed in forbidding walls, the crusader-historian Villehardouin exclaims: 'There was no man so bold that his flesh would not creep!' This is a striking picture; yet no sooner is he entered therein as conqueror and looter than he finds nothing except vague and commonplace expressions to describe it. Granted, Villehardouin belongs to that class of rough soldiers whom a Moslem gentleman of Syria, Usamah, will call 'animals gifted with courage in battle and naught else.' The fact remains that at this time all Westerners —

except a few scholars and the merchants, who do not yet write travel books —
are most narrow in outlook. Even inside their own world, they decry all differences in custom between their manor, town or province and the others; confronted with the great foreign civilizations of Byzantium and Islam, they pass
judgement and condemn before making any effort to understand. Anything
which is strange to them they take as an offense rather than a curiosity and
perhaps something that might be worth learning. At the same time they hope in
hidden treasures, mountains of gold and crystal in some remote corner; Joinville,
the companion of St Louis, sees spices fallen from the trees of Paradise afloat
on the Nile.

This explains the success of the most sensational hoax since the Donation of
Constantine: the letter of 'Priest John' to the Emperor of Constantinople.
Prester John — who does not know it? — was the wise king-priest of the
'three Indies', the overlord of seventy kings, above all the master of immense
wealth. A zealous Christian, he was burning with desire to distribute his riches
to his European co-religionists and join them in a pincer attack to destroy the
Moslems. Sometimes confused with the Nestorian (non-Catholic Christian)
khan of a Turkish tribe in Central Asia, and sometimes with the Negus of
Ethiopia, this peerless and inaccessible monarch will for centuries symbolize
all that Europe hopes from unknown lands.

Yet while most Europeans tarry in dreamland, the practical experience of
sailors and merchants is preparing a new geography. It will spring out suddenly, fully mature. Thanks to the compass and the astrolabe, Mediterranean
navigators will build from scratch a series of maps whose accuracy will not be
surpassed until the end of the 19th century. The first reference to them appears
in 1270, earlier than the clumsy Hereford and Ebsdorf maps: St Louis having
been easily convinced by his brother that Tunis lies on the route to Jerusalem,
suspects that his Genoese admiral and sailors are treacherously leading him
astray when they steer for Sardinia; the admiral shows that it is the shortest
route for Tunis by pointing it out on a nautical map. The oldest extant maps
of this kind date from then or twenty years later and all come from Genoa;
on them, the Mediterranean and the Black Sea are correctly drawn in full detail, with the coast of Northern Europe still sketched in lightly. But towards
1325, Angelino dell'Orto, also from Genoa, represents the coastlines of Great
Britain and Denmark quite faithfully. Shortly after, the gifted cartographers
of Majorca (most of them of Jewish origin) will add a new feature: a detailed
map of the area of the gold-bearing rivers of Senegal, that El Dorado which
was far more authentic than the country of Prester John.

Alongside the nautical maps, we should not overlook the *portolani*,
which were books of sailing directions with descriptions of ports and
coast lines. There is nothing of the kind for the interior, but in England
we finally come across a really good road map (Gough Map), which may
have been used by royal officials on their trips. Then there are the instructions of Francesco di Balduccio Pegolotti as to the way to get from the

Sea of Azov to Peking, first by bullock cart, then by horse carriage, by boat, by camel cart, on the back of a donkey, and finally on horseback again. On this route, and on others opened across Central Asia, China and India by the new Mongolian order (and also by the mighty power of the Sultan of Delhi), we have already encountered Western merchants in search of spices and missionaries in search of souls. It remains for us to emphasise the great contribution which their voyages made to our knowledge of the Earth.

The zest for China

In the late Middle Ages, much as in the Age of the Enlightenment, China was the object of a veritable infatuation for the few Europeans who learned to know her. These same Westerners who had set their faces against any attempt to study and understand a Near-East which they already knew in part, showed a very real urge to know everything, and to explain everything, about a Far-East which they hardly knew at all. This constituted a real contribution to science.

At the outset, however, things did not augur well for them. The Mongols, who in 1220 were still confused in people's minds with the followers of Prester John, soon revealed their real intentions; massacres perpetrated in Russia, in Poland, in Hungary, and lightning conquests, demands to submit or be crushed when they arrived — these were their methods. The story is told of how Frederick II, when he received an ultimatum of this nature, sarcastically applied for the post of falconer to the Great Khan. Three years later, the defeat of the Duke of Silesia and the Teuton knights at Legnica and that of the King of Hungary on the banks of the Sajo, rendered the danger so obvious that Frederick, by now alarmed but still flippant, asked the other Western kings to help him to 'despatch the Tartars back to the Tartarus.'

For his part, the new Pope, Innocent IV, called for a Crusade against the Mongols, but did not omit to send out at the same time brother Giovanni da Pian del Carpine and a few missionaries to sound out the plans of the Great Khan and to see whether there were not some way of converting him to Christianity. The missionaries bore with them a pontifical letter accusing the Khan of having "lost all sense of human brotherhood' and threatening him with divine vengeance, The Great Khan's reply was another ultimatum.

Fortunately, as the Mongols became more civilized and less aggressive, there came a change in the tone of these exchanges. In the space of about one hundred years, their Empire was split into four States, more or less orderly and benevolent(China, Turkestan, Persia and Golden Horde or Kipchak), though all four were destined to founder in anarchy later on. The metamorphosis was too rapid for Europe to be able to take full advantage of it, but it did allow, for a certain period at least, of religious, military and commercial understanding.

An alliance against the Sultan of Egypt, common foe both of the Il-Khan (provincial khan) of Persia and the barons of the Holy Land, might have meant the salvation of the hard-pressed kingdom of Jerusalem. Such an alliance was suggested in veiled terms by Innocent IV, and proposed quite openly by the Armenian Kings of Cilicia, and it was discussed at length by emissaries of the French and English kings. But it had a beginning of execution only between 1299 and 1301, when the king of Jerusalem had taken shelter in Cyprus and Mongolian Persia was in full decline. Kings and diplomats do not always think fast.

Franciscan and Dominican missionaries, however, did not fritter away their time. Avoiding theological disputes of the kind which had rendered collaboration with the Greek Church impossible, they established contact with the Nestorians and other dissenting Christian sects scattered throughout Asia. They knew how to skim over the special tenets of Christianity in order to exploit to the full the vague monotheism of a Great Khan who used to compare the various religions to the fingers on his hand, all equally fit so long as they were honestly used. Even though the missionaries did not succeed in promoting large-scale conversions, they gained enough proselytes to guarantee an increase of churches and convents in the wide Orient. Their missions became prosperous, thanks to financial contributions and moral support from Mongolian governments, to which were added offerings made by merchants from the West.

The churches and convents were doomed to disappear before the end of the 14th century, but the 'human brotherhood' advocated by Innocent IV and practised there still shines through in the missionaries' tales of their travels. The most unbiassed of these reports is perhaps the earliest, that of Giovanni da Pian del Carpine, who still considered the Mongols as a scourge from Heaven, yet described their customs with an accuracy and moderation not equalled by those who came after him. The most scholarly account is that of William of Rubruk, that monk from French Flanders who was the first to point out the linguistic relationship between Turkish, Cuman and Uigur, between Hungarian and Bashkir, between Crimean Gothic (no longer extant today) and German. He also pointed out the mutual affinities of the Slav languages and the characteristics distinguishing one from another the Chinese, Tibetan, Tangut and Uigur scripts. The most moving pages come to us from Giovanni da Montecorvino and they describe the slow progress of his apostolate; the most vivid story is probably that of Odorico da Pordenone, and the most striking prophecy that which Jordan de Séverac attributes to the Hindus; 'The day will come when Europeans will conquer the world.' Taken as a whole, we have in all this a mine of information, as a result of which the India and China of the period are better known to us than many a country in Europe itself.

The most remarkable of all these reports is still the *Million* by Marco Polo, Venetian trader, and, if he has not bragged more than he had ground for, confidential man to Kublai Khan. It is also the most instructive, despite its faults. Fascinated by his imperial protector, the author embraces the ideas of the conquerors, giving no place at all to the feelings of the conquered, the Chinese; it is true that he may have been distorted by the mediocre writer to whom he dictated his memoirs, a man addicted to stressing the wonderful and the colossal. It will take another merchant, Pegolotti, to show us the other side of the picture: Chinese silk, when it reaches Europe, goes somewhat threadbare during the voyage, and is worth only half as much as silks from Turkestan; no European cloth, except linen of the finest quality, is worth the cost of transport to Peking. All this is true, but Europe is getting ready to export marvels of her own to the Land of Marvels, whether these be Venetian glassware or the latest inventions of her mechanical skill: clocks, and mechanical fountains. Chinese silk is relatively cheap, and so plentiful that the weavers of Lucca, with an eye to speedier production, will achieve a minor technological revolution before 1273; they will employ water-power to work their silk-twisting machines.

Fig. 76. The Mongol Emperor Hulagu Khan; from a miniature in the British Museum.

Travellers who mind their business

The Western khans of Persia and South Russia (Golden Horde) gave wider facilities to Europeans than did China, but the less exotic atmosphere of their territories did not stimulate the imagination of writers to the same degree. A Latin-Persian-Cuman dictionary, probably compiled by a Genoese merchant in 1303, is perhaps the only important literary text and the result of a penetration which is amply revealed in non-literary sources. There were numerous and flourishing Genoese trading colonies, Genoese fleets in the Caspian Sea and the Persian Gulf, a Genoese astronomer at the observatory of Hulagu Khan (Fig. 76) at Maragha, mixed marriages, and Genoese children of the upper bourgeoisie baptised with Mongolian names such as Hulagu and Abagha......
A trader from Pisa, it appears, supplied the Persian minister Rashid al-Din with the summary of a history of Europe which he required for a historical

encyclopaedia, which also included a brief history of China. Both are dull, uninteresting accounts, and make us regret that such an extraordinary encounter of peoples did not produce an equally exceptional historian.

Perhaps the most extraordinary adventure of the 13th century was one which had a tragic end. In 1291, two brothers from Genoa, Ugolino and Vadino Vivaldi set course for Gibraltar and westwards, to the 'divers parts of the world'; only their closest business associates knew that they planned to reach the 'Indies by crossing the Ocean, so that they might bring there useful goods.' The Indies by the route taken by Vasco da Gama two hundred years later, or by the route of Christopher Columbus? There is room for argument here, for the documents give no precise details and we shall never know for sure. The Vivaldi brothers minded their business and left no tips to possible competitors. Their galleys were last sighted in the Atlantic, off Morocco, whence they disappeared without trace.

Their loss was not in vain, if it is true, as seems the case, that Dante combined the legend of St Brandan's Isle, refuge of the Blessed in mid-ocean, with the mysterious reality of the Vivaldi voyage, and out of it his imagination created the ultimate adventure of Ulysses. Thus, in Dante's eyes, as in our own, it is in world exploration that secular science in the Middle Ages made its supreme effort.

V. ANOTHER TRACK FOR SCIENCE

We have still to deal with the other road taken by science, that which St Francis of Assisi extolls, in his *Admonitions*, in the following terms: 'Even supposing that you have sufficient perspicacity and science to know everything, suppose that you are familar with every language, the course of the stars and all else, what is there in all this to boast of? One single demon knows more about any of them than all mortal men together. Yet there is one thing of which the Devil is incapable and which constitutes the glory of man; loyalty to God.' Or again, in his conversation with Brother Mazzeo as related in the *Fioretti:* 'Do you wish to know why men follow me? It is because the eyes of the Most High...... have perceived among sinners no one who is meaner, more inadequate or more sinful than I; they lighted on me to carry out the marvellous work which God has undertaken... Thus it was that he sought to mortify all the beauty and grandeur and all the strength and science of this world.'

The man who spoke these words was the one Christian whom the faithful felt they could compare with Jesus without being accused of blasphemy. Far be it from us to attempt his portrait in a stroke or two. But no description of the moral climate of the 13th century could neglect the Franciscan movement. In the face of a self-assured secular society, and against the philosophic and theocratic tendencies prevailing within the Church herself, the triumphs of the Franciscan movement are witness of the unbroken power of the original ideal, the mystical thirst after God. Its defeats, or perhaps one should say its compromises, show to what degree pure ideal must be adapted to meet the demands of everyday life.

The life of the Gospel

In a revealed religion, any reform has to be presented as a restoration of the old order. But the Franciscan reform movement is so sweeping that it becomes, in consequence, revolutionary. It is not content merely to graft a new branch on to the old tree of St Benedict (like the earlier reforms by the Cistercians and Premonstratensians which ran in the same direction) it aims at Christian reconstruction of the whole of society.

Its basic organisation is an original mixture of severity, compromise and indulgence. *Severity* for the 'Friars Minor,' apostles in the truest sense of the word, who preach 'the life of the Gospel.' They must have need of nothing, for God gives them everything — wisdom, sustenance, courage, serenity and perfect joy. Therefore they will have no 'superiors' but only *ministri* or servants (not abbots or priors), no discipline except mutual brotherly admonition, no possessions except what is absolutely necessary to clothe oneself and to carry out some manual task or other, no book beyond the Psalter or (in the case of priests) the text of the Divine Office. *Compromise* is for the 'Brothers of Penitence' (what later will be called the Third Order) who want to live the evangelic life without abandoning their family, or job, or the habits and occupations of the lay world. For them no ascetic self-mortification is required; it will be enough if they dress simply and keep a modest table, help the poor and the sick, and renounce fighting weapons, disputes in court, and every kind of violence. Finally, *Indulgence* is for those who cannot manage to observe even this minimum of discipline and commit sin, but, having sinned, turn humbly to God.

Women, as much as men, also have their ascetic order (the 'Second Order') and their lay sisterhood. Indeed, animals and even inanimate things, also have a share in Christian brotherhood. In the exquisite *Canticle of the Creatures*, Francis will invite all creatures to praise the Lord, and in all of them, even in Death itself, he will find equal beauty. If one creature is better than another, it is because it is unaware of this.

> Altogether an original formula, as we have said, but not an unprecedented one. We can watch it grow in the earlier period, especially among those heretical or nearly heretical movements which had developed while the official Church seemed too absorbed in practical problems and the Orders of the Cistercians and Premonstratensians seemed to be relaxing their primitive tension.
>
> The Franciscan distinction between the Minors and the Brothers of Penitence bears some resemblance to the Cathar distinction between 'Perfect' apostles, who are held to the most rigorous asceticism but consecrated and sustained by a special sacrament (the *consolamentum*), and 'Believers', that is, ordinary laymen who endeavour to live in the world

according to Cathar principles and will receive the *consolamentum* and perfection on their deathbed or shortly before death. The Franciscans, however, find consolation and perfect joy not in being called 'perfect' but in realizing their own innumerable imperfections. And while the Cathars call the world a work of the Devil and the Roman Church the Devil's instrument, St Francis admires God's work on the earth and reveres the Church as the giver of Eucharist and other divine tokens of grace.

Somewhat closer to the Franciscan ideas is the slightly hazy mysticism of a Calabrian abbot, Joachim da Fiore (died in 1202). He forecasts the coming of a Third Kingdom after that of the Father (or of Law) and that of the Son (or of Grace): the Kingdom of the Holy Ghost (or of Liberty). In that kingdom, all faithful will march together towards perfection, under the leadership of a monastic Order which will include ecclesiastic and lay members alike and will supersede the formal hierarchy of the Church. A former Cistercian and hence a distant disciple of St Bernard, Joachim agrees with him in feeling that 'truth is hidden from the wise and revealed to children; dialectics. . . is the mother of useless talk, of rivalries and of blasphemy'. But he lacks St Francis' gift of speaking to simple minds. For all his dreams of massive social redemption, he will remain a solitary ascetic, like that other Calabrian, St Nilus, whom a biographer had compared to the unicorn, 'that animal who lives in freedom according to his own inclination'.

Very close to St. Francis are the Waldensians, the Poor Lombards, the *Humiliati*, all sects which were preaching to the crowds a gospel of humility, setting divine illumination far above knowledge and recommending poverty as the basic principle of the perfect life. The *Humiliati*, in particular, are pledged to earn their livelihood like the most wretched of commoners, chiefly by weaving coarse cloth. Their organization anticipates that of the Franciscans: for men as for women, a conventual order and a lay brotherhood. All these lovers of poverty do not challenge orthodox beliefs, and there is nothing startling about their way of life to an age quite used to other mystic oddities. But their propaganda against corrupt clergy and corrupting wealth, although in no sense inciting to violence, did threaten to precipitate once more that crisis of discipline which the Pope considered to have ended with his victories over the Simoniacs. Loose talk, even if it does not mean to be rebellious, may easily become intemperant.

In 1179, Alexander III inadvertently provoked the Waldensians to revolt by forbidding them to preach without the bishop's authorization. Five years later, Lucius III unleashed the great drive against nonconformism and classed as heretics almost all radical advocates of poverty. Innocent III, while agreeing in principle, saw the danger of losing too many souls through intransigence, and tried to recover those who seemed recoverable by means of moderate concessions. In 1201, he brought back into the fold a great part of the Lombard *Humiliati* by allowing them to preach in public every Sunday without interference from the bishop, on condition that they did not discuss articles of faith.

A former Waldensian even obtained his approval for an order of 'Poor Catholics' in Aragon. Time is short and mass defection is at the gates: in 1205, Viterbo, the second town of Latium, has entrusted to heretics the government of the Commune (Fig. 77). In these extremities, a man like St. Francis may appear as the saviour.

The rule is put to test

In 1210, Francis of Assisi submits a first rough draft of his Rule for the approval of Innocent III. The Pope is prepared to compromise, and the Saint is decided on obedience — and here we are dealing with the two greatest men produced by the Church in the 13th century. Yet it will need thirteen years more and the mediation of Cardinal Ugolino (the future Gregory IX) before the Pope — another Pope — approves the final Rule of 1223.

This incorporates the basic principles of the original plan, but rounds off its corners. What was intended as a peaceful revolution is watered down as a moderate reform. Absolute equality among members of the Order has gone. So has the definition of alms as 'the inheritance of the poor and the justice due to him.' Also gone are the formal obligation to work, the absolute ban against violent resistance to evil and the virtual prohibition of owning books. Francis, steadfast in obedience, but changed from apostle of joy to a solitary ascetic, will die on October 2nd 1226, on his lips the words of the Psalm 'Me expectant iusti.' On his macerated body his followers will see the stigmata and one may well believe that this portent originated in the belief which the Saint expressed: that he was abandoned and betrayed like his Master.

Was this belief justified? It was, if we consider the gap between the 'life of the Gospel,' open to all, and the stark reality of an Order enclosed in formal discipline; if we reflect that followers of this man, who had set above learning an almost chivalrous 'loyalty' to Lady Poverty, were to gain fame and wealth by teaching theology in the universities; if we think over the paradoxical fact that in 1233, those who preached non-resistance to evil had to become judges of heretics in the courts of the Inquisition. But is it not the fate of truly great men to suffer a lonely end? ... After Christ, St Francis. At his level, no disciples could have endured for long.

Hemmed in, yet sustained by the new discipline, the Franciscans will serve the Church by preaching, teaching, tending the sick, doing missionary work, and even playing a part in pontifical diplomacy and administration, with a moral prestige that no other monastic Order of the period could have attained. None, that is, except perhaps the Order of St Dominic, founded at the same period on the double pattern of the Augustinian Rule and the Franciscan example and, from 1216, reconciled with the practical demands of the Roman Church. Not a difficult reconciliation in this case, for from the beginning the aims of St Dominic were more in line with monastic tradition.

'Discipline engenders affluence: affluence, unless it is carefully watched, destroys discipline; the collapse of discipline brings in its train the destruction of affluence.' Such, according to the Cistercian monk Caesarius of Heisterbach, is the fatal cycle through which all Orders would pass, one after another. There is no way to avoid corruption — except to become a hermit or to found a new Order.

During the hundred years following the death of St Francis the problem of poverty was the root-cause of the conflicts which tore his Order apart. Amidst the many varying opinions, two tendencies come uppermost, each reflecting only one of the two aspects of the Franciscan ideal; imitation of Christ, and apostolate of the people. The *Lassi* ('relaxed'or, as will be said later, the Conventuals) relinquish the idea of perfection in the life of the Gospel in order to increase their influence and spread their word further afield; they bow to circumstances by sacrificing the principle of simplicity of heart, they become learned themselves so that they may also preach to the learned. Those who favour poverty, the *uso povero*, or 'Spirituals' (*Spirituali*), stress that Christ and the Apostles possessed absolutely nothing and they reject and abhor worldly possessions. Outside this sphere of controversy, there remain only the contemplatives, who live in isolation with God, and the cynics who, with no qualms whatever, accept whatever the world has to offer.

The expectation of the Holy Ghost and the angelic Pope

Between the Spirituals and the Relaxed, the Popes could not be long in choosing their side. Much as they might respect the integrity of the former, the obedient activism of the latter was far more suited to the religious and political aims of the Church.

At first, it is true, the partisans of the strict rule had won some victories. St. Claire had still managed to prevent Gregory IX from releasing her, as a frail woman, from her vow of absolute poverty. The Rule of 1223 still directed the Friars to regard themselves as stewards, not owners, of their humble dwellings and modest churches. Dwellings and churches, however, soon became less humble. In 1245, Innocent IV legitimized the acquisition of all manner of property, stating that ownership would be vested in the Pope, the Franciscans to retain the indefinite use. This was an ingenious solution, but it appeared as inadequate for the administrative institutions of the *Lassi* as it seemed suspect to the rigid consciences of the *Spirituali*. The latter, with the personal support of the minister-general of the Order, protested in vain. Later in 1279, the *Spirituali* obtained some degree of assistance from Nicholas III in combating the flood of honours, privileges and gifts which deluged the Order, and again in 1312 from Clement V. However, this assistance was only transitory and partial. Their 'final ruin' was accomplished in the year 1322 to 1323, when two decretals of John XXII declared the doctrine of the absolute poverty of Christ

and the apostles to be heretical and transferred to the Franciscans direct ownership of all the Order's possessions.

Disappointed by the Holy See, kept out of positions of authority and at times
persecuted by their immediate superiors, many Spirituals sought vindication in
the apocalyptic prophecies of Joachim da Fiore. Even moderate elements
among them recognised in St Francis the Angel of the Apocalypse 'bearing the
imprint of the Living God' (the stigmata); in those Franciscans who were
faithful to the strict Rule they saw the predestined monastic order preparing
humanity for the coming of the Holy Ghost; in the material and moral crisis
of the Papacy, and in the defeats suffered by Christians in the Holy Land, they
saw a sign of the imminent end of the world. The fanatics among them had no
hesitation in fixing the date according to Joachim's calculations: precisely in
1260. In that year, crowds of flagellants travelled the roads of urban and
merchant Italy, scourging themselves: a visible warning to some, an object of
scorn and criminal frenzy to others.

The year ended without a catastrophe, though not without tension. Expecta-
tions were then turned upon another object: the coming of an 'angelic Pope'
who would carry on the work of St Francis by purifying the Church before the
impending Last Judgement. And come he did, in 1294, this angelic Pope, in
the person of Celestine V, an aged hermit from the mountains of the Abruzzi,
founder of a confraternity very like the Spirituals, and revered as a saintly
man. A crowd delirious with hope assisted at his consecration in the beautiful
church (perhaps too beautiful for a hermit) of St. Maria di Collemaggio at
Aquila. St Celestine revealed his artless piety by distributing privileges to all
and sundry; his humanity, by authorizing a group of Spirituals to form themselves into a separate order and to live according to their consciences. But
he felt crushed beneath the weight of the worldly demands of the Pontificate,
and abdicated even before a year was out, the only Pope ever to have carried
to extremity the traditional formula of those who became Popes: 'Sovereign
Pontiff, unworthy though I be . . . . . .'

Boniface VIII, who succeeded him, was diametrically opposite in temperament, for he was more monarch than shepherd. Without delay, he cancelled the
concession to the Spirituals, and protected himself against a possible change of
mind of Celestine by having him shut up in a castle, where, before long, the old
man died. Political and religious adversaries of Boniface accused him of having
assassinated the angelic Pope, disputed the validity of Celestine's abdication and
the ensuing election, and demanded that a council should be summoned to pass
judgement on the 'unlawful' Pope. But Boniface triumphed over them militarily,
and scattered them in the 'crusade' of Palestrina. The most famous of the conspirators, brother Jacopone da Todi, a Franciscan poet who extolled poverty
and despised science, was cast into prison.

It availed nothing that the Spirituals compared the Church of Boniface to
the prostitute of Babylon. At that time, as before the Gregorian reform,

Fig. 77. Viterbo; rose window of the Church of San Giovanni in Zoccoli, thirteenth century.

the mass of the faithful accepted the fact that individual clerics might be unworthy, provided that the clergy as a whole continued to administer the Sacraments and offer intercession to God for their souls. When Boniface announced special indulgence for those who would go to Rome on the Jubilee year 1300, the crowd of pilgrims was so great that the flow of people over the St Angelo bridge had to be controlled by making those who used it in either direction keep to the right — the earliest known example of traffic regulation. Yet this tumultuous success was full of dangers, for it distracted the Pope's attention from the loud protests which were nevertheless rising from every part of Europe against the Roman Church, from the quiet disaffection of the many who despaired of it and sought God in direct mystical experience, and even from the spirit of doubt, which was beginning to re-appear after centuries of unquestioned faith. The humiliation inflicted on Boniface VIII by Philip 'the Fair' in 1303 seemed to some a punishment he had well deserved, but it did not represent the purification of the Church for which so many people had been hoping. While in Italy and southern Europe persecutions failed to extinguish the Spiritual faction, the cult of poverty and the thirst for mystical religion gained ground in northern Europe, here through the Beguines and Beghards of Belgium and the neighbouring countries, there with Johannes Eckhart, the German Dominican, and his followers. 'Let God waken within you, in the fiery kernel of your soul', said Eckhart.

An answer outside the Church?

The *Respublica Christiana*, founded by Charlemagne and maintained in some way by a long series of emperors and popes, was definitely falling to pieces.

Those were the years when young Dante was going through the hard trial of
public office in his Commune (from 1295 to 1301); then, in 1302, he was sentenced to perpetual exile, even death if he dared come back to Florence. His
dangerous utopia was a world of independent states, kept at peace with justice
by the arbitration of an emperor and a pope who would not interfere with one
another.

A true son of his age, Dante had taken his full share of the boisterous
pleasures offered by a great Italian city, fought in its army against the nearest
town, studied all branches of art and science (not in formal university training
but in a local school and abroad with a renowned teacher), written love rhymes
and prose, sinned, repented, and sinned again. Too great not to see that the
world was changing, yet too conservative to like the change, he spent the best
part of his later years rebuilding in his imagination — not for his own time, but
for eternity — the harmonious universe which was collapsing before his eyes.
A very symmetrical, internally consistent universe: nine divisions to each of the
three reigns of afterlife, and again and again and again the same numbers,
reappearing through the ninety-nine cantos (plus an introductory canto to make
a hundred) of his stunning poem in third rhyme, where everything must be read
on three levels of interpretation (literal, allegorical, mystical). Into his *Comedy*,
Dante poured all he knew and felt, which was altogether more, and better said,
than any other man in the Middle Ages could singly achieve. We shall not
presume that a historian can capture all this in a few lines; let us return to
Dante's collapsing universe.

Was it at all possible, since one could hardly hope for an angelic Pope, that
salvation might come in the shape of an emperor or some other lay prince who
would take the reform of the Church in his own hands and restore peace and
justice on earth? Dante believed this to be so; but in his lifetime, the
one emperor who came to Italy, Henry VII of Luxemburg (1307–1313), met
with no success. The Empire was too far gone to achieve what Frederick II
had been unable to do more than fifty years before, with Sicily already in his
hands.

The Pope was no less defeated than the Emperor. In 1305, the second successor of Boniface VIII — Clement V, French-born and friend of Philip 'the
Fair' — flatly refused to leave the security of his native country for the treacherous foreign city that was Rome. Thus began the sequence of Avignon Popes,
the voluntary exile which later generations would call 'the Babylonian captivity'.
Undoubtedly, the Popes of 'Babylon' were not bereaved of faith or zeal, nor
were they without administrative talent; as far as that goes, some of them had
perhaps too much of it. Yet prestige lost in Rome, on the ground hallowed by
the blood of the Apostles and set apart by virtue of centuries of universal
domination and devotion, could not easily be recovered in a small corner of
France. In the 13th century already, many of the faithful thought that the Pope
was too involved with the secular interests of a restricted territory, even if it
included Rome. In the 14th century, the dissatisfaction of regional churches,

of lay princes and of adolescent nations broke through, not only in abandoned Italy, but even in France.

It fell to Lewis of Bavaria, elected 'King of the Romans' by the majority of German electors (1314), to make the last move in the game of Universal Empire versus Universal Papacy. Excommunicated by the Avignon Pope, John XXII, Lewis had himself crowned in Rome by a noble layman, who claimed to represent the Roman people who had first created the Empire. He was supported by some of the greatest minds of the time, such as the two political philosophers Marsil of Padua and Jean de Jandun, the philosopher and theologian William of Ockham, the Franciscan minister-general Michael of Cesena (who had rebelled against John's policy concerning poverty). But he had too few soldiers, and still less money or credit. In Italy, he did not even succeed in mobilizing all those Ghibelline governments which had temporarily espoused the cause of Henry VII (to no avail). In Germany, resentment against the Pope, more than respect for the aspirant to the Empire, provoked the prince-electors and the Diet to declare that the imperial power and dignity proceeded directly from God. Hence a 'King of the Romans' properly elected by the people had no need whatsoever to be confirmed in office by the Pope (1336).

This declaration (*Licet Juris*) was to be the springboard for the constitution of the Empire promulgated by Charles IV in 1356 (the *Golden Bull*). Its practical effect, however, was to state formally that the electoral body, as well as the residual authority of the Emperor, was centred in Germany, as had been the case for a long time. Italy went its way; the idea of the imperial sovereignty of the Roman people was taken up again in 1347, not for the benefit of a foreign monarch, but in behalf of a Roman petty bourgeois, Cola di Rienzo. He styled himself 'tribune of democracy and liberator of the Holy Roman Republic'; not the successor of Augustus and still less that of Charlemagne, but the would-be heir of Gracchus. His megalomaniac dreams were shattered, but the ideal survived.

Something was new in the air of Europe; not yet a proper awareness of a new community of nations, but a definite feeling that the old names and institutions no longer applied. Divided into States of different character, yet alike in culture and in the way of life, the peoples were unknowingly European, in the same way as Moliere's 'bourgeois gentilhomme' made prose without realizing it. Their frantic quest for a new equilibrium, however, was entangled in a profound crisis, to which we shall devote the closing pages of the present book.

TOWARDS A NEW EQUILIBRIUM

I. SATURATION, CONTRACTION, CRISIS

'FROM famine, pestilence and war, deliver us Oh Lord!' Repeated year in, year out in every Western and Eastern church, but rendered less urgent in the euphoric age of expansion and prosperity, this invocation recovered real poignancy in the 14th century.

The food problem, which for the poor had never quite been solved, was first in becoming acute again, with the great famine of 1315–1317. Even the most fertile provinces of Europe did not go unscathed; a town as rich and as close to the sea as Ypres could not collect enough food to prevent 3000 people dying of starvation in six months, about one fifth of its population. The plague, almost forgotten since the great epidemic of 747–750, re-appeared exactly six hundred years later. It carried off at least one third of the European population, the proportion being higher in the towns. War, it is true, had never quite disappeared. But in the 14th century, during the Turkish campaigns against the Byzantine Empire, in the struggle between the Teuton Knights and the Lithuanians, in the long duel between England and France, it rose to unusual ferocity and extent (Pl. 31).

Demographic recession

These calamities were not self-contained disasters, like those which had occurred from time to time even during the age of expansion. Each was the first of a series of catastrophes which renewed, prolonged and aggravated each other. War quickly flared up at other places in Southern Italy, in the Iberian countries, all round the Baltic, within that urban and feudal chaos which still passed by the name of Empire, and between social classes and parties inside the great kingdoms of the West. As it involved much larger armies than of old, war took manpower from work, scorched great stretches of land and kept capital out of productive investment. The plague recurred at almost regular intervals (1348 -1350, 1360–1363, 1371–1374, 1381–1384) while a resurgence of malaria created wide empty spaces around Siena, Pisa, Narbonne, Aigues-Mortes, and the Scandinavian settlements in Greenland succumbed to cold and hunger.

The slow agony of this remote appendix of Europe, dramatically reflected in the gradual shrinking of the skeletons buried in the cemetery at Herjolfsnes in Greenland, is obviously an extreme case. But we also come across an increasing number of abandoned villages in the colonization areas of Germany, where a few years before expansion still was in full swing. In the Iberian peninsula, where the progress of the *Reconquista* keeps creating no-man's land strips along the moving frontier, the military and religious Orders of Calatrava, Alcantara, Aviz, and others, to which kings are now entrusting the task of re-populating conquered areas, can do no more than transform them into cattle ranches. Even in the best cultivated countries, the most fertile, agriculture is losing ground. In England, though the number of farmers has diminished, the price of agricultural commodities has fallen to such a degree that the lords are endeavouring to get rid of tenants, and the tenants or freeholders earn too little to pay taxes and rents or to buy what they need in the urban markets.

Towns are doubly affected, by their own losses and by those of the rural areas on whose prosperity they depend. Though they are capable of withstanding local or temporary crises, they are powerless against severe slumps or prolonged difficulties. At first they try to react by drawing on the reservoir of the rural population for the unskilled workers of today, who normally are expected to become the apprentices of tomorrow and the well-to-do bourgeois of a later day. Soon, however, the depleted reservoir will have nothing to offer except destitute vagrants and outlaws. Business endeavours to keep going by diverting to luxury production (or, at the opposite extremity, to production of the cheapest goods) most of its former output of avarage goods for average consumers. In the long run, however, this cannot make up for the general decline of the demand. Then the 'open horizons' will become narrower, the old bourgeoisie will lose heart and entrench itself wherever it still can stand. Immigration and apprenticeship will be restricted, no new towns will be founded, none of the existing ones will enlarge its walls, it will even be impossible to fill up with houses such suburban areas as have been walled during the last years while the going was good.

How about figures? We have too few of them, and some might even seem to contradict what we have just said. In the 14th century, just as in the 4th, general distress does not preclude some partial recoveries and a few isolated successes. In the statistics and narrative sources of the 15th century, Rouen is portrayed as a town in full vigour. However, while it had enlarged its walls three times between 1150 and 1350, it will build no new walls during the seven succeeding centuries, and in the time of Louis XV it will not yet have filled up the whole surface enclosed in the walls before 1350. Florence will witness a decline in population from 100,000 in the time of Dante, to some 50,000 after the Black Death of 1348–1350; it will not rise above 75,000 during the time of the Medici bank and that of Michael Angelo. Zurich, a medium-sized mediaeval town with no special history, will decline (after the Black Death) from 12,375 inhabitants in 1350 to 4,713 in 1468.

Concerning the population of entire regions we have no reliable assessments except in the case of England; 3,700,000 inhabitants before the Black Death, 2,200,000 or thereabouts in 1377, and 3,200,000 around 1550. In France, according to inevitably hazardous calculations, the number of households counted during the census of 1789 would seem to have been no more than 10 per cent greater than the number existing in 1328. In Catalonia, where all statistical evidence is later than the Black Death, there was a slight recovery between 1359 and 1369 (from 86,895 to 95,258 households) but this did not last (77,973 in 1379 and less than 60,000 in 1497).

A whole hemisphere in crisis

The Middle Ages ends in a crisis, just as it has begun. One again, a whole hemisphere is involved. Dare we say, this time, 'the whole world,' since the 14th century saw the collapse of the Empire of Maya in Central America and of the pre-Inca states in South America?

In the Byzantine Empire, Egypt, Persia, Turkestan, Mongolia and China, abandoned and crumbling villages are to be found everywhere. War of one kind or another is spreading and grows fiercer from end to end of what had been the Mongolian Empire, in Asia Minor, in Syria, in North Africa. The Plague, which always originates in the Far East, first ploughs a furrow across Asia before attacking Europe; nor do Egypt and Western Africa escape it. As for famine, how can we, in countries where the masses never have enough to eat, make a distinction between especially terrible manifestations of famine and the constantly recurring periods of want which may be called almost normal? Let us point out, however, that India, that ant-heap where any irregularity in the monsoon spells death for millions of people, seems to have experienced in the 14th century the most terrible drought in its history. There are references to whole years without rain and bad harvest every year for twelve years on end; even kings, it is said, at times went short of food.

Information on climate, though less scanty for the 14th century than for the 4th, is woefully inadequate and ill-explored. Still, what little we know would seem to indicate at that period both the crest of a 'pulsation' (that is, of a slow fluctuation stretching over several centuries) and a number of short-run deviations which sharpen the effect of the basic trend. Admittedly, climatic changes never affect the whole earth in the same way; but within each climatic zone, they generally have a uniform impact. We have seen that in India, the 14th century brings drought in its train; we are told that it is the same in the Maya countries. Further north, on the other hand, winters are becoming wetter and colder everywhere.

Without tarrying in continents about which too little is known, let us concentrate on Europe. The Viking's sea route via Iceland to Greenland is becoming unnavigable because of icebergs. The Baltic Sea is completely frozen over in 1296, 1306 and 1323. About the same time, the Frisian and Dutch coasts suffer disastrous flooding, and in Western Germany the rivers overflow their banks. Glaciers in the Alps expand. It is no longer possible, as it was a century earlier, to get grain to ripen in the greater part of Norway. Grapes can no longer be grown in England.

Unusually severe winters and abundant precipitations may not have had such serious consequences in southern Europe, but they probably throw out of balance an agricultural system designed for a warm, dry climate. At any rate, in southern Europe the problem is complicated by deforestation, the inevitable result of four centuries of demographic and economic expansion. Clearing, grazing, fires, all of this has conspired against the modest resources of forests in the Mediterranean regions. Seriously impaired by intensive exploitation in the Graeco-Roman age, then partially restored in the early Middle Ages, these resources soon proved inadequate to meet the requirements of the late mediaeval Commercial Revolution. Since iron and steel were as yet very sparingly used because of their high cost, wood was the main industrial material; it was virtually the only fuel.

As far back as the time of the Crusades, the Moslem navy was handicapped by the lack of timber. In the 13th century, the Apennines were losing their forests; Genoa, before undertaking the construction of a fleet of ships for St Louis, demanded that he supply the wood. In the 15th century, Venice, in spite of her proximity to the richer resources of the Alps, will be hard put to it to keep her yards supplied. If it seems somewhat far-fetched to see in this lack of timber the chief cause of the decline of Islam, or Venice (for is it not true that a rich and powerful nation can buy or seize whatever it needs wherever it finds it?), the effects of deforestation on agriculture are more obvious. Without a protecting mantle of forests, running water becomes a problem as soon as rainfall or snow exceeds the normal level, On the heights, good soil is swept away in landslides. In the hollows, water collects and forms mosquito-breeding marshes.

Even in the North, the problem of deforestation is not unknown in the densely populated and fairly industrialised centres of the Low Countries and England; so much so, that by the 13th century, the outcropping coal seams at Lille and Newcastle begin to be tapped, despite the inconveniences of this strange fuel — dirt and smell. Elsewhere in the North wood is still plentiful, but it constitutes the wealth of a backward economy, where agriculture reigns supreme (or almost) and the scanty population has not succeeded in taming the primordial forest; an economy at the mercy of climatic upheavals and turns in demographic trends.

Exhaustion of an under-developed economy

We must stress that the Europe of 1300, despite the immense progress achieved during the course of the preceding four hundred years, was still what today we should call an under-developed continent. It is pretty certain that the average expectation of life, which was 25 years in Roman times according to jurists and tomb inscriptions, had risen to about 35 years in the England of the 13th century. But this figure barely matches that of China in 1946, and does not much exceed that for Egypt in 1948 (31 years). Reaching adult age was a privilege reserved for the few. In the 14th century, when the figure again fell to below 25, these few were reduced to a point below the danger limit.

> It is true that in normal times, the high birthrate amply compensated for a high deathrate. In the 13th century, the English village of Taunton saw its population more than doubled, and the agrarian economy of Lincoln-shire had to support a population almost as great as that of an indust-rialised Lincolnshire in the 19th century. Could it be then that the decrease in population after 1300 had brought economic relief? The low price of corn at the end of the 14th century has been quoted as proof of the return of plenty after some generations of enforced malthusianism.
>
> That may be so, but this supposed age of plenty will also prove an age of popular revolts, all of them repressed in blood, in Flanders as well as in the Balkans, in Majorca as in Lübeck and London. Each of the revolts has its own specific cause, but their simultaneous outbreak calls for some kind of general explanation. What then, can there be in common between the *Tuchins* of the countryside of Languedoc and the *Ciompi* of the work-shops of Florence, unless it be a sudden arrest of social progress, crystal-lizing that difference which an Austrian poet prosaically sums up as fol-lows: 'The rich have their coffers full, the poor have empty stomachs.'?

Men have been the fuel of the Commercial Revolution. The small demographic surpluses of the 10th century have sparked it up, the response they have provoked has made it possible for greater and greater surpluses to keep going. While this chain reaction has continued — commercialization, industrialization, techno-logical improvement, expansion into new fields and new lands — the rhythm of production and the standard of living have risen apace. When the population has stopped growing, the whole movement was bound to stop or, at least, to slow down.

In the 13th century already, a lessening of impetus can be perceived here and there. We have noted, in the North, the withering away of cultures which had waited too long before opening out: Balts, Slavs of the Elbe, and, up to a point, Scandinavians and Celts. In the South, by contrast, the regions which stand in danger are those which had developed first and spent their best energy too early: Southern Italy, Southern France, Southern Spain, not to mention the Byzantine Empire. Individual towns such as Pisa, Ratisbon, Tournai and Sigtuna, have been outstripped by more active rivals. Yet that still does not mean that the Commercial Revolution had stopped dead; in a society on the move, it is only natural that weak, weary or unlucky competitors are left behind.

In the 14th century, it is the giants who suffer the worst set-backs. At Ypres and in the other major Flemish centres, cloth production has been declining since 1320. It is the same in Florence, where in 1378 unemployed workers will vainly try to force contractors to bring up again to a minimum of 25,000 pieces of cloth a production which fifty years earlier had exceeded 70,000. This difference alone cancels out the whole of England's contribution: 43,000 pieces of cloth exported on an average in the years 1392–1395, years of peak production in the one wool-making sector which is expanding in this period of general contraction.

What about trade? In 1293, the collectors of taxes on trade in the port of Genoa were forecasting receipts totalling almost four million pounds; in 1334, they will be hardly hoping for two million; in the second half of the century, this figure will very seldom be exceeded. The rapid depreciation of the pound transforms this apparent stabilization into a continuous downward trend. Yet Genoa, with Venice, remained one of the two greatest ports in Europe. At Marseilles, where the general crisis was heightened by local difficulties, the tax returns indicate a still more dramatic decline. As for northern ports, the impression of stability, or even recovery, which certain statistics may give, is due to the fact that in their case we have no figures which are earlier than 1350.

What about banking? After the great failures of the banks of Siena, dating back to the end of the 13th century, there comes the turn of the Florentine banks. Financial crashes of the Peruzzi, the Acciaiuoli and the Bardi ,'the pillars of Christianity,' as they used to be called (1343–1346), will leave nothing but small companies still going; we shall have to wait for the 15th century to find, in the Medici bank, a concern anything like as vast as any one of the three companies which had foundered a century earlier. There are banks elsewhere in Italy, granted, but their scope is small and will remain so up till the 16th century.

What about expansion beyond the frontiers? One after another, China, Central Asia and Persia are closing the gates to merchants from the West. The Byzantine Empire is in its death throes; the Turks, who will finally collect its dilapidated estate, make Western traders pay dearly for the privilege of buying and selling with them. Egypt, herself engulfed in the general decline, raises her prices, increases customs dues, and browbeats foreigners. The great book of Catholic advances in Europe, which had arrived at its two last chapters back in the 13th century, stops abruptly: Granada stays Moslem, Lithuania remains pagan.

II.   EUROPE GETS OVER THE CRISIS

Nevertheless, the Middle Ages will end much better than they had begun. True, the demographic, economic and social difficulties aggravate, complicate all the other problems of the tense period that may be called, according to one's point of view, either 'the twilight of the Middle Ages' or 'the dawn of the Renaissance'. But this is not the thing that matters most. More important is the fact that Europe will get over the crisis. There shall not be, after 1350, another barbaric age such as there had been a thousand years before.

Perhaps we should rather say that a kind of barbaric age did fall upon Russia, with the Mongol invasion, as early as the 13th century; the Turks had the same effect on Byzantium and the Arabian Levant, and the Eskimos in far-away Greenland. Only the Eskimos, however, are really primitive. The Mongols and the Turks, savage conquerors though they are, still are skilled organizers, capable of assimilating ideas and techniques quite promptly. What is more, their victory in the East keeps them off the West. One could say that the role of the Greeks and the Latins has been reversed since the first barbarian age, when Byzantium was a firm bulwark whereas the submerged West was a safety valve for the civilized East.

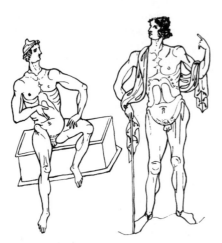

Fig. 78. Study of the human figure, thirteenth century. From the Album of Villard de Honnecourt.

Fig. 79. Reclining Eros, bas relief of the Cathedral at Auxerre, fourteenth century, inspired by an antique.

This time, Catholic Europe has no enemies to fear apart from her own children. Church and Empire, entangled in their problems, fail their adherents. France and England plunge into the Hundred Years War. Kings, princes, urban tyrants and popular agitators, carried away by their ambition, exploit and oppress their subjects. The great collective enterprises, the syntheses of the preceding centuries, are disintegrating: all efforts to resurrect the Crusades fall through, the system of Aquinas is under attack, and although cathedrals are still being built, the accumulation of superfluous ornament cannot conceal the aging of the Gothic style. Melancholy or bitter satire are replacing optimism. Poets insist that all, all is vanity. . . . For the first time, a Petrarch will condemn wholesale both his own time and the earlier Christian centuries: not an age enlightened, despite its faults, by the Redemption, but a barbarian age, a dismal anti-climax after the glory that were Greece and Rome (Fig. 78 and 79).

What does it matter, since men hold fast! There is no trace, in the last years of the Middle Ages, of that gloomy resignation, that disintegration of the individual which had marked the early Middle Ages. Although there are prophets of doom and flagellants, most of those who deplore the corruption of the world are not thinking of giving it up, but seek their personal salvation in

Fig. 80. Fourteenth century view of Florence; from a painting from the Loggia of Bigallo, at Florence (detail).

private devotion, in mysticism, or, more simply, in a blameless life. Even if revolts of the masses do fail, if democratic institutions in the towns degenerate, if representative assemblies in the kingdoms seldom prevail, those resistances constitute such limits for despotism as the late antiquity and the early Middle Ages had never known. Nothing is more striking than a comparison between the inhuman fiscal pressure of the last of the Roman Emperors, or the exactions without counterpart in services of the barbarian conquerors, and the increasing but bearable levies of the late mediaeval French and English kings, or the taxation system of several Italian communes, which is scaled in proportion to wealth.

Collective art (if there is such a thing) may be on the wane, but artistic individualism, which had been taking shape for some time, is coming fully to the fore. In the 14th century, anonymity in painters and sculptors becomes the exception rather than the rule; portraits no longer are idealized representations but become photographic likenesses; religious music, once the reign of choral song, is turning to instrumental polyphony and centred around a few powerful personalities, such as Guillaume de Machault. In Italy, it is the early Renaissance already. In France, a professor, whose fame has curiously been linked to an anecdote of which he may not be the author — Jean Buridan, whose donkey, it is said, could not make up his mind whether to move towards a pail of water or an equally distant stack of hay and died of thirst and hunger — gets a first glimpse of the principle of inertia, the basis of modern mechanics.

The first age of individualism? One hesitates to use this description to single out the period which follows the century of St Francis and Dante. Surely the Middle Ages did not lack outstanding personalities. But the crises which accompanied its ending, by sharpening individual tempers rather than destroying them, prepared mankind for the great shock which was to hurl it from its comfortable place at the centre of the Creation to an unspectacular position on a swirling planet — a planet which itself is not the centre of the Universe.

SELECT BIBLIOGRAPHY

PERIODICALS

Beside their variable fare of articles, periodicals supply the best means of gaining bibliographic information and keeping it up to date. In English, the following seems most helpful on that score: *American Historical Review* (1895 ff.); *Church History* (1932 ff.); *Economic History Review* (1927 ff.); *English Historical Review* (1886 ff.); *History* (1912 ff.); *Past and Present* (1952 ff.); and, above all, *Speculum* (1926 ff.), embracing all aspects of mediaeval civilization. Among periodicals of the latter kind, the following include contributions in English: *Journal of World History* (1953 ff.); *Moyen Age* (1888 ff.); *Studi Medievali* (1904 ff.)

Some important serials also are partly in English, notably the quinquennial Reports of the International Congresses of Historical Sciences (Paris, 1950; Rome, 1955; Stockholm, 1960; Vienna, 1965); the annual volumes of the *Settimane di Studio del Centro Italiano sull'Alto Medioevo* (Spoleto, 1953 ff.); and those of the *Recueil de la Société Jean Bodin* (Brussels, 1937 ff.)

GENERAL WORKS

The Cambridge Medieval History (6 vols, 1911–36) is still the largest general survey in English, with the usual assets and liabilities of the Cambridge series: a distinguished international team of writers, full bibliographies, emphasis on political facts and great men, uneven quality and coverage, loose organization. But it is old, and the abridgment by C. W. PREVITÉ-ORTON, *Shorter Cambridge Medieval History* (1952) is still more old-fashioned. Much more modern, although not immune to some of the shortcomings of the series, is the *Cambridge Economic History of Europe* (3 vols, for the Middle Ages, 1941–63).

A shorter co-operative survey, more recent or recently revised (but not altogether as valuable), is the Methuen's *History of Medieval and Modern Europe* (4 vols for the Middle Ages, respectively by M. DEANESLEY, 1956; Z. N. BROOKE, repr. 1951; C. W. PREVITÉ-ORTON, repr. 1951; W. T. WAUGH, rev. 1960).

World War II interrupted C. K. OGDEN and H. E. BARNES's *History of Civilization*, a most ambitious collection which was to translate France's largest joint venture, H. BERR's *L'Evolution de l'Humanité* (Paris, 1920 ff.; New York and London, 1924 ff.) and to add other essays. Of other joint ventures now being planned, little has appeared in print as yet, but we shall list individual titles and, more sparingly, a few shorter books included in collections aimed chiefly at undergraduates, but useful as introductions for the general reader, such as the *Berkshire Studies in European History*, Cornell University's *The Development of Western Civilization*, and Hutchinson's *University Library*, as well as Heath's *Problems in European Civilization* (collected excerpts of modern historians) and Holt and Rinehart's *Source Problems in World Civilization* (collected excerpts from mediaeval writers).

One-volume surveys for college use, too numerous to be listed, include successful achievements (within the limitations of their purpose), such as those of R. H. C. DAVIS, R. HOYT, J. LA MONTE, C. STEPHENSON (rev. by B. LYON), J. STRAYER and D. C. MUNRO. More stimulating, if lop-sided, is H. PIRENNE, *History of Europe* (New York, 1939). R. L. REYNOLDS, *Europe Emerges* (Madison, Wis., 1961) has interesting perspectives. *The Legacy of the Middle Ages* (ed. by C. G. CRUMP and E. F. JACOB) is a valuable if uneven round-up of mediaeval civilization, by several authors. A similar emphasis is to be expected of the mediaeval volume (by G. WIET, V. ELISSEEFF and P. WOLFF) of the UNESCO *History of the Scientific and Cultural Development of Mankind*, soon to appear.

Those who would rather learn directly from primary sources can be guided by C. P. FARRAR and A. P. EVANS, *Bibliography of English Translations from Medieval Sources* (New York, 1946). Among source books that have appeared later, we may note H. S. BETTENSON, *Documents of the Christian Church* (London and New York, 1947); D. C. DOUGLAS *et al.*, *English Historical Documents* (London, 1953 ff.); E. HOLT, *A Documentary History of Art* (Garden City, New York, 1957); C. W. JONES, *Mediaeval Literature in Translation* (New York, 1950); R. S. LOPEZ and I. W. RAYMOND, *Medieval Trade in the Mediterranean World* (New York, 1955); J. B. ROSS and M. M. McLAUGHLIN, *The Portable Medieval Reader* (New York, 1949).

SPECIAL PERIODS AND TOPICS

Any list of books of a restricted, yet fairly broad scope is bound to be unsatisfactory, more so when it excludes untranslated foreign works, and articles (which sometimes are more enlightening and crisp than longer essays). Except for a few unimpeachable choices (which we have starred), any title may appear too old or too untested, too heavy or too light, too generalizing or too specialized, too questionable or too obvious, too abstract or too unimaginative. We have endeavored to suggest one book (and only one) for each important topic, but it would be easy to fill a longer list with titles we have omitted with regret. No biography has been included; the *Encyclopaedia Britannica* usually supplies the titles of major biographical works.

R. ALTAMIRA, *A History of Spanish Civilization* (London, 1930)

F. B. ARTZ, *The Mind of the Middle Ages* (rev., New York, 1959)

E. AUERBACH, *Introduction to Romance Languages and Literature* (New York, 1961)

R. H. BAINTON, *The Medieval Church* (Princeton, 1962)

G. BARRACLOUGH, *The Origins of Modern Germany* (Oxford, 1946)

*M. BLOCH, *Feudal Society* (London and Chicago, 1960)

J. BRONDSTED, *The Vikings* (London, 1960)

C. BROOKE, *Europe in the Central Middle Ages, 962–1154* (London and New York, 1964)

J. B. BRYCE, *The Holy Roman Empire* (various editions)

H. CAM, *England before Elizabeth* (London, 1950)

C. M. CIPOLLA, *Money, Prices and Civilization in the Medieval World, 5th to 17th Century* (Princeton, N. J., 1956)

M. V. CLARKE, *The Medieval City State* (London, 1926)

N. COHN, *The Pursuit of the Millennium* (Fairlawn, N. J., 1957)

G. G. COULTON, *The Medieval Scene* (Cambridge, 1930)

A. C. CROMBIE, *Medieval and Early Modern Science* (Garden City, N. Y. 1959)

*E. R. CURTIUS, *European Literature and the Latin Middle Ages* (New York and London, 1953)

*C. DAWSON, *The Making of Europe* (London, 1932)

H. DELEHAYE, *The Legends of the Saints* (London, 1907)

A. P. D'ENTRÈVES, *The Medieval Contribution to Political Thought* (Oxford, 1939)

F. DE SANCTIS, *History of Italian Literature* (New York, 1931)

W. C. DICKINSON, *Scotland from Earliest Times to 1603* (Edinburgh, 1961)

B. W. DIFFIE, *Prelude to Empire: Portugal Overseas before Henry the Navigator* (Lincoln, Nebraska, 1960)

F. DVORNIK, *The Making of Central and Eastern Europe* (London, 1949)

E. G. EAST, *An Historical Geography of Europe* (London, 1935)

R. FAWTIER, *The Capetian Kings of France* (London, 1960)

*H. FICHTENAU, *The Carolingian Empire* (Oxford, 1957)

F. L. GANSHOF, *Feudalism* (London, 1952)

E. GILSON, *History of Christian Philosophy of the Middle Ages* (New York, 1955)

A. HARMAN, *Mediaeval and Early Resaissance Music* (Fairlawn, N. J., 1958)

*C. H. HASKINS, *The Renaissance of the Twelfth Century* (Cambridge, Mass., 1927)

A. HAUSER, *The Social History of Art* (London, 1951)

A. HAVIGHURST, *The Pirenne Thesis* (Boston, 1958)

D. HAY, *Europe: the Emergence of an Idea* (Edinburgh, 1957)

H. HEATON, *Economic History of Europe* (rev., New York, 1948)

F. HEER, *The Medieval World: Europe 1100–1350* (London, 1962)

W. T. H. JACKSON, *The Literature of the Middle Ages* (New York, 1960)

G. H. T. KIMBLE, *Geography in the Middle Ages* (London, 1935)

D. KNOWLES, *Great Historical Enterprises and Problems in Monastic History* (London, 1964)

P. LAVEDAN, *French Architecture* (London, 1956)

G. LEFF, *Medieval Thought: St Augustin to Ockham* (London, 1958)

S. LILLEY, *Men, Machines, and History* (London, 1948)

R. S. LOPEZ, *The Tenth Century: How Dark the Dark Ages?* (New York, 1959)

*F. LOT, *The End of the Ancient World and the Beginnings of the Middle Ages* (London, 1931)

*G. LUZZATTO, *An Economic History of Italy (to 1500)* (London and New York, 1961)

*C. H. McILWAIN, *The Growth of Political Thought in the West* (New York, 1932)

R. B. MERRIMAN, *The Rise of the Spanish Empire: The Middle Ages* (New York, 1918)

C. R. MOREY, *Mediaeval Art* (New York, 1942)

A. P. NEWTON, ed., *Travel and Travellers of the Middle Ages* (New York, 1926)

C. W. OMAN, *The Art of War in the Middle Ages* (rev., Ithaca, N. Y., 1953)

Oxford History of England (in progress)

S. PACKARD, *Europe and the Church under Innocent III* (New York, 1927)

S. PAINTER, *French Chivalry* (Baltimore, 1940)

C. PETIT-DUTAILLIS, *The Feudal Monarchy in France and England* (London, 1936)

*H. PIRENNE, *Early Democracies in the Low Countries* (rev., New York, 1963)

T. F. T. PLUCKNETT, *A Concise History of the Common Law* (London, 1948)

*E. POWER, *Medieval People* (rev., New York, 1963)

H. RASHDALL, *Universities of Europe in the Middle Ages* (rev., Oxford, 1936)

G. O. SAYLES, *The Medieval Foundations of England* (London, 1948)

K. SETTON, ed., *A History of the Crusades* (Philadelphia, 1955 ff.)

R. C. SMAIL, *Crusading Warfare* (Cambridge, 1956)

*R. W. SOUTHERN, *The Making of the Middle Ages, 918–1272* (London and New Haven, Conn., 1953)

H. O. TAYLOR, *The Medieval Mind* (New York and London, 1925)

G. TELLENBACH, *Church, State and Christian Society at the Time of the Investiture Contest* (Oxford, 1940)

A. S. TURBERVILLE, *Mediaeval Heresy and the Inquisition* (London, 1923)

G. TURVILLE-PETRE, *The Heroic Age of Scandinavia* (London, 1951)

P. VILLARI, *Mediaeval Italy from Charlemagne to Henry VII* (London, 1910)

P. VINOGRADOFF, *Roman Law in Medieval Europe* (Oxford, 1929)

H. WADDELL, *The Wandering Scholars* (London, 1927)

W. G. WAITE et al., *The Art of Music, a Short History of Musical Styles and Ideas* (New York, 1960)

D. P. WALEY, *The Papal State in the Thirteenth Century* (London, 1961)

J. M. WALLACE-HADRILL and J. McMANNERS, ed., *France: Government and Society* (London, 1957)

L. WHITE, *Medieval Technology and Social Change* (Oxford, 1962)

APPENDIX

THE following regnal lists show the succession of temporal, and some spiritual, rulers of West European States in the period from the reign of Constantine to the year 1300. Lists of rulers of some States whose history is not dealt with in this volume are included selectively because the State concerned borders on territory whose history is the subject of this book, or there has been significant contact between it and some Western political unit.

KINGS OF ARAGON

Ramiro I	1035–1063	Jaime II	1291–1327
Sancho I	1063–1094	Alfonso IV, the Fair	1327–1336
Pedro I	1094–1104	Pedro IV	1336–1387
Alfonso I. the Battler	1104–1134	Juan I	1387–1395
Ramiro II	1134–1137	Martin I	1395–1410
Petronilla (Queen)	1137–1162	Ferdinand I	1410–1416
Alfonso II	1162–1196	Alfonso V, the	
Pedro II	1196–1213	Magnanimous	1416–1458
Jaime I, the Conqueror	1213–1276	Juan II	1458–1479
Pedro III	1276–1285	Ferdinand II, the Catholic	1479–1516
Alfonso III, the Magnificent	1285–1291	(from 1474 Ferdinand V of Castile)	

RULERS OF BOHEMIA

Princes

Wenceslas I (Saint), the Good	*c.* 922–*c.* 929	Vladislav II (as King, I)	1140–1173
Boleslav I, the Cruel	*c.* 929–967	Sobeslav II	1173–1189
Boleslav II	967–999	Conrad Otho I	1189–1191
Boleslav III	999–1002	Wenceslas II	1191–1192
Vladivoj I	1002–1003		
Jaromir I	1003–1012	*Kings*	
Ulrich I	1012–1037	Premysl Ottokar I	1198–1230
Bretislav I	1037–1055	Wenceslas I	1230–1253
Spytihinev II	1055–1061	Premysl Ottokar II	1253–1278
Vratislav II (King)	1061–1092	Wenceslas II	1278–1305
Bretislav II	1092–1110	Wenceslas III	1305–1306
Borivoj II	1110–1120	Rudolf I of Hapsburg	1306–1307
Vladislav I	1120–1125	Henry of Carinthia	1307–1310
Sobeslav I	1125–1140	John	1310–1346

CALIPHS

Following is a list of Caliphs from the death of Mohammed until the extinction of the genuine caliphate at Bagdad in 1258. Those marked O were of the Omeyyad House. Thereafter the remainder were Abbasids. Those marked B were dominated by Buweiyid princes and ministers. Those marked S were virtually vassals of the Seljuk Turks.

Abu Bekr		632–634	Al Mutawakil		847–861
Omar I		634–644	Al Muntasir		861–862
Othman		644–656	Al Mustain		862–866
Ali		656–661	Al Motazz		866–869
Hasan		661	Al Muhtadi		869–870
Moawiya I	O	661–680	Al Motamid		870–892
Yezid I	O	680–683	Al Motadid		892–902
Moawiya II	O	683–684	Al Muktafi		902–907
Merwan I	O	684–685	Al Muktadir		907–932
Abd-el-Melik	O	685–705	Al Kahir		932–934
Welid I	O	705–715	Ar-Radi		934–940
Suleiman	O	715–717	Al Muttaki		941–944
Omar II	O	717–720	Al Mustakfi		944–946
Yezid II	O	720–724	Al Muti	B	946–974
Hisham	O	724–743	Al Tai	B	974–991
Welid II	O	743–744	Al Kadir	B	991–1031
Yezid III	O	744	Al Kaim	B	1031–1075
Ibrahim	O	744	Al Muktadi	S	1075–1094
Merwan II	O	744–750	Al Mustazhir	S	1094–1118
Abul Abbas (as Saffah)		750–754	Al Mustarshid	S	1118–1135
Al Mansur		754–775	Ar Rashid	S	1135–1136
Al Mehdi		775–785	Al Muktafi	S	1136–1161
Al Hadi		785	Al Mustanjid	S	1161–1170
Haroun Al Rashid		786–809	Al Mustadi	S	1170–1180
Al Amin } Al Mamun }		809–813	An-Nasir	S	1180–1225
			Zahir	S	1225–1235
Al Mamun alone		813–833	Al Mustansir	S	1235–1242
Al Motassim		833–842	Al Mustasim		1242–1258
Al Wathik		842–847			

ARCHIBISHOPS OF CANTERBURY

The following is a list since the foundation of the see

Augustine	597–605	Theodore	668–690
Laurentius	605–619	Berhtwald	693–731
Mellitus	619–624	Taetwine	731–734
Justus	624–627	Nothelm	734–740
Honorius	627–653	Cuthbert	740–758
Deusdedit	655–664	Breogwine	759–762

Jaenberht	763–790	Robert of Jumièges	1051–1052
Æthelheard	790–803	Stigand	1052–1070
Wulfred	803–829	Lanfranc	1070–1089
Fleogild	829–830	Anselm	1093–1109
Ceolnoth	830–870	Ralph de Turbine	1114–1122
Æthelred	870–889	William de Corbeuil	1123–1136
Plegemund	891–923	Theobald	1139–1161
Æthelm	923–925	Thomas Becket	1162–1170
Wulfelm	928–941	Richard	1174–1184
Odo	941–958	Baldwin	1185–1190
Ælsine	958–959	Reginald Fitz-Jocelin	1191
Dunstan	959–988	Hubert Walter	1193–1205
Æthelgar	988–989	Stephen Langton	1207–1228
Sigeric	990–994	Richard Wethershed	1229–1231
Ælfric	995–1005	Edmund Rich (of Abingdon)	1233–1240
Ælfeah or Alphege	1006–1012	Boniface of Savoy	1240–1270
Lyfing	1013–1020	Robert Kilwardby	1273–1278
Æthelnoth	1020–1038	John Peckham	1279–1292
Eadsige	1038–1050	Robert Winchelsea	1293–1313

KINGS OF CASTILLE AND LEON (from 1033)

Though Ferdinand I ranks as the first King of Castille proper, this monarchy traced its history back to the Christian remnant which continued to resist at the height of Mohammedan power in Spain. This early history, however, is obscure, and many of the kings mentioned are known merely as names.

Castille and Leon, although often ruled by the same sovereign, were not finally united until 1230, under (Saint) Ferdinand III.

Sovereign	Leon	Castille	Sovereign	Leon	Castille
Ferdinand I, the Great	1037–1065	1039–1065	Alfonso IX, the Slobberer	1188–1230	
Sancho II		1065–1072	Enrique I		1214–1217
Alfonso VI	1065–1109	1072–1109	Ferdinand III, the Saint	1230–1252	1217–1252
Urraca	1109–1126	1109–1126			
Alfonso VII	1126–1157	1126–1157	*Kings of Castille and Leon*		
Sancho III		1157–1158	Alfonso X, the Wise		1252–1284
Ferdinand II	1157–1188		Sancho IV, the Fierce		1284–1296
Alfonso VIII, the Good		1158–1214	Ferdinand IV		1296–1312

SOVEREIGNS OF DENMARK

Gorm the Old	*d.c.* 940	Knut the Great	1018–1035
Harald Bluetooth	936–986	Hardicanute	1035–1042
Svein Forkbeard	*c.* 986–1014	Magnus the Good	
Harald II	1014–1018	(of Norway)	1042–1047

Svein II Astridsson	1047–1074
Harald III (Hein)	1074–1080
Knut IV the Good (Saint)	1080–1086
Olaf Hunger	1086–1095
Eric the Evergood	1095–1103
Nils	1103–1134
Eric Emune	1134–1137
Eric Lam	1137–1147
Svein III	1147–1157

Knut V (for three days)	1157
Valdemar I the Great	1157–1182
Knut VI	1182–1202
Valdemar II the Victorious	1202–1241
Eric Plough-penny	1241–1250
Abel	1250–1252
Christopher I	1252–1259
Eric Klipping	1259–1286
Eric VI	1286–1319

KINGS OF EAST ANGLIA

Uffa	*fl.* 575
Redwald	593–617
Eorpwald	617–628
State of anarchy	628–631
Sigeberht	631–634
Egric	634–635
Anna	635–654
Ethelhere	654–655
Ethelwald	655–664
Ealdwulf	664–713
Elfwald	713–749
Beorna	749–?

Ethelberht	?–794
Kings of Mercia (*q.v.*)	794–823
Athelstan of Wessex	?829–?839
Ethelweard	?839–?854
Oswald	?854–?856
Edmund (Saint)	?856–870

Danish Kings

Guthrum I (Guttorm)	878–890
Eohric (Eric)	890–902
Guthrum II	902–917

KINGS OF ENGLAND

Egbert (of Wessex)	802–839
Ethelwulf	839–858
Ethelbald	858–860
Ethelbert	860–865
Ethelred I	865–870
Alfred the Great	870–899
Edward the Elder	899–925
Athelstan	925–939
Edmund I	939–946 assassinated
Edred	946–955
Edwy	955–959

Edgar	959–975
Edward the Younger	975–978 assassinated
Ethelred II (the Unready)	979–1016
Edmund II (Ironside)	1016

Princes

Canute the Great	1016–1035
Harthacanute	1035
Harold I	1035
Harold I (alone)	1035–1040

Harthacanute (again)	1040–1042	Stephen	1135–1154
Edward the Confessor	1042–1066	Henry II	1154–1189
Harold II	1066	Richard I	1189–1199
William I (the Conqueror)	1066–1087	John	1199–1216
William II (Rufus)	1087–1100	Henry III	1216–1272
Henry I	1100–1145	Edward I	1272–1307

FRANKISH MONARCHY

MEROVINGIAN KINGS OF THE SALIC
   FRANKS

Merovech	alive in 451	Charles the Bold	840–877
Childeric of Tournai	463–480	Louis the Stammering	877–879
Clovis	481–511	Louis III	879–882
Childebert I	511–558	Carlman	879–884
Clotaire of Soissons	558–561	Charles the Fat	882–887
Caribert	561–567	[Odo]	888–898
		Charles the Simple	898–923
Kings of Neustria		Robert	922–923
Chilperic I	567–584	Raoul of Boulogne	923–936
Clotaire II	584–628	Louis the Exile	936–954
Dagobert I	628–638	Lothaire	954–986
Clovis II	638–658	Louis V	978–987
Clotaire III	658–670		
Thierry III	670–691		
Clovis III	691–695	*Capetian Kings of France*	
Childebert III	695–711	Hugh Capet	987–996
Dagobert III	711–715	Robert	996–1031
Chilperic II	715–720	Henry I	1031–1060
Clotaire IV	717–719	Philip I	1060–1108
Thierry IV	722–741	Louis VI	1108–1137
Childeric III	741–752	Louis VII	1137–1180
		Philip II, Augustus	1180–1223
CAROLINGIAN DYNASTY		Louis VIII	1223–1226
Charlemagne	771–814	Louis IX, the Saint	1226–1270
Louis the Pious	814–840	Philip III	1270–1285

'GERMAN' EMPERORS

Charles I (Charlemagne)	800–814	Charles II (the Bald)	875–881
Louis I (the Pious)	814–840	Charles III (the Fat)	882–887
Lothar I	840–855	Guido (in Italy)	887–894
Louis II (in Italy)	855–875	Lambert (in Italy)	894–896

Arnulf	896–899	*Hohenstaufen*	
Louis the Child	899–901	Conrad III	1138–1152
Louis III of Provence		Frederick I (Barbarossa)	1152–1190
(in Italy)	901–911	Henry VI	1190–1197
Conrad I	911–915	Philip as rivals	1197–1208
Berengar (in Italy)	915–918		
Saxons			
Henry I (the Fowler)	918–936	Otto IV, alone	1208–1212
Otto I. King of the E Franks	936–962	Frederick II	1212–1250
H. R. Emperor	963–973	Henry Raspe	1246–1247
Otto II	973–983	William of Holland	1247–1256
Otto III	983–1002	Conrad IV	1250–1254
Henry II (the Saint)	1002–1024	Interregnum	1254–1257
Salians			
Conrad II (the Salic)	1024–1037	Richard of Cornwall	1257–1272
Henry III (the Black)	1037–1056	Alfonso of Castille	1257–1272
Henry IV	1056–1106	Rudolf I of Hapsburg	1273–1291
Rudolf of Swabia	1077–1081	Adolf of Nassau	1292–1298
Hermann of Luxemburg	1081–1093	Albert I of Hapsburg	1298–1308
Conrad of Franconia	1093–1106		
Henry V	1106–1125		
Lothar II	1125–1138		

KINGS OF MERCIA

Creoda	*d. c.* 593	Offa	757–796
Pybba	*c.* 593–*c.* 606	Ecgfrith	796
Cearl	*c.* 606–*c.* 626	Coenwulf	796–821
Penda	626–655	Ceolwulf I	821–823
Peada	655–656	Beornwulf	823–825
Oswy (of Bernicia)	656–659	Ludeca	825–827
Wulfhere	659–675	Wiglaf	827–829
Ethelred	675–704	Egbert (of Wessex)	829–830
Cenred	704–709	Wiglaf (restored)	830–839
Ceolred	709–716	Beorhtwulf	839–852
Ethelbald	716–757	Burgred	852–874
Beornred	757	Ceolwulf II	874

KINGS OF NORTHUMBRIA

Bernicia			
Ida	547–559	Edwin (of Deira)	617–632
His elder sons	559–586	Eanfrith	632–633
Ethelric	586–593	Oswald	633–642
Ethelfrith	593–617	Oswy	642–670

Deira

Aelle	560–588	Alhred	765–774
Ethelric (of Bernicia)	588–? 593	Ethelred I	774–779
Ethelfrith (of Bernicia)	? 593–617	Elfwald I	779–788
Edwin	617–632	Osred II	788–790
Osric	632–633	Ethelred I (restored)	790–796
Oswald (of Bernicia)	633–642	Osbald	796
Oswine	642–651	Eardwulf II	796–808
Ethelwald	651–655	Elfwald II	808
Oswy (of Bernicia)	655–670	Eardwulf II (restored)	808–810

All Northumbria

Ecgfrith	670–685	Eanred	810–840
Alfrith	685–704	Ethelred II	840–844
Eardwulf I	704–705	Raedwulf	844
Osred I	705–716	Ethelred II (restored)	844–848
Cenred	716–718	Osberht	848–866
Osric	718–729	Elle	866–867
Ceolwulf	729–737	Egbert I	867–872
Eadberht	737–758	Ricsige	873–876
Oswulf	758	Egbert II	*fl.* 876
Ethelwald Moll	759–765	Eadwulf	? –913

KINGS OF NORWAY

Halfdan the Black	*c.* 839–*c.* 860	Eystein I	1103–1122
Harald I Fairhair	*c.* 860–933	Sigurd I, the Pilgrim	1103–1130
Erik Bloodaxe	930–935	Magnus IV, the Blind	1130–1135
Haakon I the Good	935–961	Harald Gille	1130–1136
Harald II Greyskin	961–970	Sigurd II, Mund	1136–1155
((Jarl) Haakon of Lade	970–995	Inge	1136–1161
Olaf I Tryggyason	995–1000	Eystein II	1142–1157
(Jarls) Erik and Svein	1000–1015	Haakon, II, the Broad-	
Olaf II, Saint	1015–1030	shouldered	1161–1162
Svein Knutsson	1030–1035	Magnus V	1162–1184
Magnus I, the Good	1035–1047	Sverre	1184–1202
Harald III, the Stern	1048–1066	Haakon III	1202–1204
Olaf III, the Quiet	1067–1093	Anarchy	1204–1217
Magnus II	1067–1069	Haakon IV, the Old	1217–1263
Magnus III, Barelegs	1093–1103	Magnus VI	1263–1280
Haakon	1093–1095	Erik	1280–1299
Olaf IV	1103–1116	Haakon V	1299–1319

PAPACY

39. St. Anastasius I, 399–401
40. St. Innocent I. 401–17
41. St. Zosimus, 417–18

42. St. Boniface I, 418–22
    Eulalius, antipope, 418–19
43. St. Celestine I, 422–32

	613–641	
	638–641	
	641	
	641	
	641–668	
	659–668	
	659–681	
	659–681	
gonatus	668–685	
metus	685–695	
	695–698	
r	698–705	
metus	705–711	
	706–711	
es	711–713	
mius	713–716	
	716–717	

CONSTANTINE VII, Porphyrogenetus	913–919
ROMANUS I, Lecapenus	919–944
Constantine VII	919–944
Christopher Lecapenus	921–931
Stephen Lecapenus	924–945
Constantine Lecapenus	924–945
CONSTANTINE VII, Porphyrogenetus	944–959
Romanus II	c. 950–959
ROMANUS II	959–963
Basil II	960–963
Constantine VIII	961–1025
BASIL II, Bulgaroctonus	963
NICEPHORUS II, Phocas	963–969
Basil II	963–976
JOHN I, Tzimisces	969–976
BASIL II, Bulgaroctonus	976–1025

n	717–740	
	720–740	
pronymus	740–775	
	750–775	
	775–780	
	776–780	
	780–797	
	797–802	
	802–811	
	811	
abe	811–813	
ian	813–820	

CONSTANTINE VIII	1025–1028
ROMANUS III, Argyrus	1028–1034
MICHAEL IV, the Paphlagonian	1034–1041
MICHAEL V, the Caulker	1041–1042
ZOE and THEODORA, Porphyrogenetae	1042
CONSTANTINE IX, Monomachus	1042–1055
THEODORA, Porphyrogeneta	1055–1056
MICHAEL VI, Stratioticus	1056–1057
ISAAC I, Comnenus	1057–1059

Ducas Dynasty

CONSTANTINE X, Ducas	1059–1067
Michael VII	c. 1060–1067
MICHAEL VII, Parapinaces	1067–1068
ROMANUS IV, Diogenes	1068–1071
Michael VII	1068–1071

morian	820–829	
	821–829	
	829–842	
Drunkard	842–867	
	866–867	

MICHAEL VII, Parapinaces	1071–1078
NICEPHORUS III, Botaniates	1078–1081

Comnenian Dynasty

ALEXIUS I, Comnenus	1081–1118
Constantine, Ducas	1081–1090
John II	1092–1118

asty		
donian	867–886	
	869–880	
	870–886	
	871–912	
	886–912	
	911–913	
	912–913	

44. St. Sixtus III, 432–40
45. St. Leo I, 440–61
46. St. Hilarius, 461–8
47. St. Simplicius, 468–83
48. St. Felix III, 483–92
49. St. Gelasius I, 492–6
50. Anastasius II, 496–8
51. St. Symmachus 498–514
   Laurentius, antipope, 498–*c.* 505
52. St. Hormisdas, 514–23
53. St. John I, 523–6
54. St. Felix IV, 526–30
55. Boniface II, 530–2
   Dioscorus, antipope, autumn 530
56. John II, 533–5
57. St. Agapetus I, 535–6
58. St. Silverius, 536–7
59. Vigilius, 537–55
60. Pelagius I, 555–61
61. John III, 561–74
62. Benedict I, 574–9
63. Pelagius II, 579–90
64. St. Gregory I, 590–604
65. St. Sabinian, 604–6
66. Boniface III, 607 (Feb.–Nov.)
67. St. Boniface IV, 608–15
68. St. Deusdedit (or Adeodatus I), 615–18
69. Boniface V. 619–25
70. Honorius I, 625–38
71. Severinius, 638–40
72. John IV, 640–2
73. Theodore I, 642–9.
74. St. Martin I, 649–55 (*d.* in exile)
75. St. Eugenius I, 654–7
76. St. Vitalian, 657–72
77. Adeodatus II, 672–6
78. Donus, 676–8
79. St. Agatho, 678–81
80. St. Leo II, 681–3
81. St. Benedict II, 683–5
82. John V, 685–6
83. Conon, 686–7
   Theodore and *Paschal, rival antipopes*, 687 (Sept.)
84. St. Sergius I, 687–701
85. John VI, 701–5

86. John VII, 705–7
87. Sisinnius, 708 (Jan.–Feb.)
88. Constantine, 708–15
89. St. Gregory II, 715–31
90. St. Gregory III, 731–41
91. St. Zacharias, 741–52
92. Stephen II, 752–7
93. St. Paul I, 757–67
   Constantine, antipope, 767–8
   Philip, antipope, 768 (July)
94. Stephen III, 768–72
95. Adrian I, 772–95
96. St. Leo III, 795–816
97. Stephen IV, 816–17
98. St. Paschal I, 817–24
99. Eugenius II, 824–7
100. Valentinus, 827 (Aug.–Sept.)
101. Gregory IV, 827–44
   John, antipope, 844 (Jan.)
102. Sergius II, 844–7
103. St. Leo IV, 847–55
104. Benedict III, 855–8
   Anastasius, antipope, 855
105. St. Nicholas I, 858–67
106. Adrian II, 867–72
107. John VIII, 872–82
   (wrongly called Martin II)
108. Marinus I, 882–4
109. St. Adrian III, 884–5
110. Stephen V, 885–91
111. Formosus, 891–6
112. Boniface VI, 896 (Apr.)
113. Stephen VI, 896–7
114. Romanus, 897 (Aug.–Nov.)
115. Theodore II, 897 (Nov.–Dec.)
116. John IX, 898–900
117. Benedict IV, 900–3
118. Leo V, 903 (July–Sept.)
   Christoper, antipope, 903–4
119. Sergius III, 904–11
120. Anastasius III, 911–13
121. Lando, 913–14
122. John X, 914–28
123. Leo VI, 928 (May–Dec.)
124. Stephen VII, 928–31
125. John XI, 931–5
126. Leo VII, 936–9
127. Stephen VIII, 939–42

128. Marinus II (wrongly called Martin III), 942–6
129. Agapetus II, 946–55
130. John XII, 955–964 (deposed Dec. 963)
131. Leo VIII, 963–965 } Rivals, one or other of whom may be regarded as an antipope
131. A. Benedict V, 964–5 or 966 }
132. John XIII, 965–72
133. Benedict VI, 973–4
 Boniface VII, antipope, 974 (June–July), expelled
134. Benedict VII, 974–83
135. John XIV, 983–4 (expelled)
 Boniface VII, antipope, returned, 984–5
136. John XV, 985–96
137. Gregory V, 996–9
 John XVI, antipope, 997–8
138. Sylvester II, 999–1003
139. John XVII, 1003 (June–Dec.)
140. John XVIII, 1004–09
141. Sergius IV, 1009–12
142. Benedict VIII, 1012–24
 Gregory, antipope, 1012 (May–Dec.)
143. John XIX, 1024–32
144. Benedict IX, 1032–44
145. Sylvester III, 1045 (Jan.–Mar.)
146. Benedict IX, 1045 (Apr.–May), resigned
147. Gregory VI, 1045–6
148. Clement II, 1046–7
149. Benedict IX (restored), 1047–8
150. Damasus II, 1048 (July–Aug.)
151. St. Leo IX, 1049–54
152. Victor II, 1055–7
153. Stephen IX, 1057–8
 Benedict X, antipope, 1058–9
154. Nicholas II, 1059–61
155. Alexander II, 1061–73
 Honorius II, antipope, 1061–72
156. St. Gregory VII, 1073–85
 Clement III, antipope, 1080, 1084–1100
157. Bl. Victor III, 1086–7

158. Bl. Urban II, 1088–99
159. Paschal II, 1099–1118
 Theodoric, antipope, 1100
 Albert, antipope, 1102 (Feb.–Mar.)
 Sylvester IV, antipope, 1105–11
160. Gelasius II, 1118–19
 Gregory VIII, antipope, 1118–21
161. Calixtus II, 1119–24
162. Honorius II, 1124–30
 Celestine II, antipope, 1124 (Dec.)
163. Innocent II, 1130–43
 Anacletus II, antipope, 1130–8
 Victor IV, antipope, 1138 (Mar.–May)
164. Celestine II, 1143–4
165. Lucius II, 1144–5
166. Bl. Eugenius III, 1145–53
167. Anastasius IV, 1153–4
168. Adrian IV, 1154–9
169. Alexander III, 1159–81
 Victor IV, antipope, 1159–64
 Paschal III, antipope, 1164–8
 Calixtus III, antipope, 1168–78
 Innocent III, antipope, 1179–80
170. Lucius III, 1181–5
171. Urban III, 1185–7
172. Gregory VIII, 1187 (Oct.–Dec.)
173. Clement III, 1187–91
174. Celestine III, 1191–8
175. Innocent III, 1198–1216
176. Honorius III, 1216–27
177. Gregory IX, 1227–41
178. Celestine IV, 1241 (Oct.–Nov.)
179. Innocent IV, 1243–54
180. Alexander IV, 1254–61
181. Urban IV, 1261–4
182. Clement IV, 1265–8
183. St. Gregory X, 1271–6
184. St. Innocent V, 1276 (Jan.–June)
185. Adrian V, 1276 (July–Aug.)
186. John XXI, 1276–7
187. Nicholas III, 1277–80
188. Martin IV, 1281–5
189. Honorius IV, 1285–7
190. Nicholas IV, 1288–92
191. St. Celestine V, 1294–(July–Dec.)
192. Boniface VIII, 1294–1303

KINGS OF POLAND

Mieszko	96
Boleslaw the Brave	992
Mieszko II	1025–
Casimir I the Restorer	1040–
Boleslaw II the Bold	1058–
Wladislaw Herman	1079–
Boleslaw III the Wry-Mouthed	1102–

Partitional Period of Rival Duchies,

	1138–1
Wladislaw	1138–1
Boleslaw the Curly	1146–1

ROMAN EMPIRE

Honorius	393–
Constantine III	407–
Constantius III	4
John	423–4
Valentinian III	425–4
Maximus	4
Avitus	455–4
Majorian	457–4
Severus	461–46
Anthemius	467–47
Olybrius	47
Glycerius	47
Julius Nepos	473–48
Romulus	475–47

NOTE: Romulus surnamed Augustulus is wrongly known as the last Roman Emperor in the West; he was never recognized in the East and Julius Nepos survived him.

EASTERN ROMAN EMPERORS
from the foundation of Constantinople, 330 A. D.

(Usurpers in italics. The *Basileus Autocrator's* name is given always in capitals. Constantine II and Constans I are not included. as they never exercised effective power in the East.)

Constantine III
Heracleonas
CONSTANTINE III
HERACLEONAS
CONSTANS II
Constantine IV
Heraclius
Tiberius
CONSTANTINE IV
JUSTINIAN II, Rh
Leontius
Tiberius III, Ap
JUSTINIAN II, Rh
Tiberius
PHILIPPICUS, Ba
ANASTASIUS II, A
THEODOSIUS III

Isaurian Dynast
LEO III, the Isa
Constantine V
CONSTANTINE V,
Leo IV
LEO IV, the Cha
Constantine VI
CONSTANTINE V
IRENE
NICEPHORUS I
STAURACIUS
MICHAEL I, Rha
LEO V, the Arm

Amorian Dynas
MICHAEL II, the
Theophilus
THEOPHILUS
MICHAEL III, th
Basil I

Macedonian D
BASIL I. the Ma
Constantine
Leo VI
Alexander
LEO VI, the W
Constantine V
ALEXANDER

JOHN II, Calojohannes	1118–1143	*Robert*	1221–1228
Alexius	1119–1142	*Baldwin II*	1228–1237
MANUEL I	1143–1180	*John of Brienne*	1228–1237
Alexius II	1172–1180	*Baldwin II (alone)*	1237–1261
ALEXIUS II	1180–1183		
Andronicus I	1182–1183		
ANDRONICUS I	1183–1185		

Angelus Dynasty

Lascarid Dynasty (Nicaean Empire, 1204–1261)

ISAAC II, Angelus	1185–1195	THEODORE I, Lascaris	1204–1222
ALEXIUS III	1195–1203	JOHN III, Ducas Vatatzes	1222–1254
ALEXIUS IV	1203–1204	THEODORE II, Lascaris	
Isaac II	1203–1204	Vatatzes	1254–1258
ALEXIUS V, Murtuphlus	1204	JOHN IV, Ducas Vatatzes	1258

Latin Emperors

Palaeologan Dynasty

Baldwin I	1204–1205	MICHAEL VIII, Palaeologus	1258–1282
Henry	1206–1216	Andronicus II	1272–1282
Peter of Courtenay	1216–1217	ANDRONICUS II	1282–1328

SCOTLAND

Constantine I	789–820	Cullean	967–971
Kenneth I (McAlpine)	832–860	Kenneth II	971–995
Donald	860–863	Cuilean	967–971
Constantine II	863–877	Kenneth II	971–995
Eocha	881–889	Constantine IV	995–997
Donald I	889–900	Kenneth III	997–1005
Constantine III	900–942	Malcolm II	1005–1034
Malcolm I	942–954	Duncan	1034–1040
Indulf	954–962	Macbeth	1040–1057
Dubh	962–967	Lulach	1057–1058

KINGS OF SWEDEN

Olaf and Emund	*c.* 850–*c.* 882	Inge II Halstansson	*c.* 1118–1130
Eric Emundsson	*c.* 882–*c.* 905	Sverker	*c.* 1132–1155
Bjorn Ericsson and Ring	*c.* 905–*c.* 950	Eric IX (Saint)	1150–1160
Eric the Victorious	*c.* 950–*c.* 993	Charles VII	1160–1167
Period of confusion	*c.* 993–999	Knut Ericsson	1167–1196
Olaf Scatt-King	999–1022	Sverker Carlsson	1196–1205 (?)
Anund Jacob	1022–1050	*Period of confusion: rival*	
Emund the Old	1050–1060	*kings*	1205–1250
Stenkil	1060–1066	Valdemar	1250–1275
Period of confusion	1066–1080	Magnus I Ladulas	1275–1290
Halstan	*c.* 1080–*c.* 1093	Birger	1290–1318
Inge the Good	*c.* 1090–*c.* 1118		

PRINCES OF WALES

Maelgwn Gwynedd	?–550
Rhun ap Maelgwn	547–584
Cadvan	584–617
Cadwaladr ap Cadwallon	617–634
Idwal ap Cadwaladr	634–661
Rhodri Molwynog	661–728
Cynan and Hywel	728–755
Mervyn Frych	825–844
Rhodri the Great	844–877
Anarawd, Cadell, and Mervyn	877–943
Idwal Foel	915–943
Hywel Dda, the Good	909–950
Ieuan and Iago	948–979
Hywel ap Ieuaf	979–984
Cadwallon II	984–986
Meredith ap Owen	986–999
Idwal (II) ap Meyric ap Idwal Foel	992–997
Aedan (usurper)	998
Llewelyn ap Seisyll	1018–1023
Gruffydd ap Llewelyn ap Seisull	1039–1063

Bleddyn Rhywallon, Meredith ap Owain	1067–1073
Trahaiarn ap Caradoc ⎫ Meilir ⎬ Caradoc ⎭	1073–1079
Gruffydd ap Cynan ⎫ Rhys ap Tewdwr ⎪ Cadwgan ap Bleddyn ⎬ Iorwerth ab Bleddyn ⎭	1079–1137
Owain Gwynedd	1137–1169
Howel ab Owain Gwynedd ⎫ Daffydd ap Owain Gwynedd ⎭	1169–1194
Llewelyn (II) ap Iorwerth, the Great	1194–1240
Dafydd ap Llewelyn	1240–1246
Llewelyn (III) ap Gruffydd ('Llewelyn y Llyw Olaf')	1246–1282

From 1301 the Prince of Wales has always been the eldest son of the English sovereign.

KINGS OF WESSEX

Cynric	*fl.* 552–*d.* 560
Ceawlin	560–592
Ceol	591–597
Coelwulf	597–611
Cynegils	611–643
Cenwalh	643–645
Penda (of Mercia)	645–648
Cenwalh (restored)	648–672
(Queen) Seaxburg	672–674
Escwine	674–676

Centwine	676–685
Caedwalla	685–688
Ine	688–726
Ethelheard	726–740
Cuthred	740–756
Sigeberht	756–757
Cynewulf	757–786
Beorhtric	786–802
Egbert, KING OF ENGLAND	802–839

INDEXES

44. St. Sixtus III, 432–40
45. St. Leo I, 440–61
46. St. Hilarius, 461–8
47. St. Simplicius, 468–83
48. St. Felix III, 483–92
49. St. Gelasius I, 492–6
50. Anastasius II, 496–8
51. St. Symmachus 498–514
    Laurentius, antipope, 498–*c.* 505
52. St. Hormisdas, 514–23
53. St. John I, 523–6
54. St. Felix IV, 526–30
55. Boniface II, 530–2
    Dioscorus, antipope, autumn 530
56. John II, 533–5
57. St. Agapetus I, 535–6
58. St. Silverius, 536–7
59. Vigilius, 537–55
60. Pelagius I, 555–61
61. John III, 561–74
62. Benedict I, 574–9
63. Pelagius II, 579–90
64. St. Gregory I, 590–604
65. St. Sabinian, 604–6
66. Boniface III, 607 (Feb.–Nov.)
67. St. Boniface IV, 608–15
68. St. Deusdedit (or Adeodatus I),
    615–18
69. Boniface V. 619–25
70. Honorius I, 625–38
71. Severinius, 638–40
72. John IV, 640–2
73. Theodore I, 642–9.
74. St. Martin I, 649–55 (*d.* in exile)
75. St. Eugenius I, 654–7
76. St. Vitalian, 657–72
77. Adeodatus II, 672–6
78. Donus, 676–8
79. St. Agatho, 678–81
80. St. Leo II, 681–3
81. St. Benedict II, 683–5
82. John V, 685–6
83. Conon, 686–7
    Theodore and *Paschal, rival
        antipopes*, 687 (Sept.)
84. St. Sergius I, 687–701
85. John VI, 701–5

86. John VII, 705–7
87. Sisinnius, 708 (Jan.–Feb.)
88. Constantine, 708–15
89. St. Gregory II, 715–31
90. St. Gregory III, 731–41
91. St. Zacharias, 741–52
92. Stephen II, 752–7
93. St. Paul I, 757–67
    Constantine, antipope, 767–8
    Philip, antipope, 768 (July)
94. Stephen III, 768–72
95. Adrian I, 772–95
96. St. Leo III, 795–816
97. Stephen IV, 816–17
98. St. Paschal I, 817–24
99. Eugenius II, 824–7
100. Valentinus, 827 (Aug.–Sept.)
101. Gregory IV, 827–44
    John, antipope, 844 (Jan.)
102. Sergius II, 844–7
103. St. Leo IV, 847–55
104. Benedict III, 855–8
    Anastasius, antipope, 855
105. St. Nicholas I, 858–67
106. Adrian II, 867–72
107. John VIII, 872–82
    (wrongly called Martin II)
108. Marinus I, 882–4
109. St. Adrian III, 884–5
110. Stephen V, 885–91
111. Formosus, 891–6
112. Boniface VI, 896 (Apr.)
113. Stephen VI, 896–7
114. Romanus, 897 (Aug.–Nov.)
115. Theodore II, 897 (Nov.–Dec.)
116. John IX, 898–900
117. Benedict IV, 900–3
118. Leo V, 903 (July–Sept.)
    Christoper, antipope, 903–4
119. Sergius III, 904–11
120. Anastasius III, 911–13
121. Lando, 913–14
122. John X, 914–28
123. Leo VI, 928 (May–Dec.)
124. Stephen VII, 928–31
125. John XI, 931–5
126. Leo VII, 936–9
127. Stephen VIII, 939–42

128. Marinus II (wrongly called
     Martin III), 942–6
129. Agapetus II, 946–55
130. John XII, 955–964 (deposed Dec.
     963)
131. Leo VIII,   } Rivals, one or other
     963–965   } of whom may be
131. A. Benedict   } regarded as an anti-
     V, 964–5 or   } pope
     966
132. John XIII, 965–72
133. Benedict VI, 973–4
     Boniface VII, antipope, 974 (June–
     July), expelled
134. Benedict VII, 974–83
135. John XIV, 983–4 (expelled)
     Boniface VII, antipope, returned,
     984–5
136. John XV, 985–96
137. Gregory V, 996–9
     John XVI, antipope, 997–8
138. Sylvester II, 999–1003
139. John XVII, 1003 (June–Dec.)
140. John XVIII, 1004–09
141. Sergius IV, 1009–12
142. Benedict VIII, 1012–24
     Gregory, antipope, 1012 (May–
     Dec.)
143. John XIX, 1024–32
144. Benedict IX, 1032–44
145. Sylvester III, 1045 (Jan.–Mar.)
146. Benedict IX, 1045 (Apr.–May),
     resigned
147. Gregory VI, 1045–6
148. Clement II, 1046–7
149. Benedict IX (restored), 1047–8
150. Damasus II, 1048 (July–Aug.)
151. St. Leo IX, 1049–54
152. Victor II, 1055–7
153. Stephen IX, 1057–8
     Benedict X, antipope, 1058–9
154. Nicholas II, 1059–61
155. Alexander II, 1061–73
     Honorius II, antipope, 1061–72
156. St. Gregory VII, 1073–85
     Clement III, antipope, 1080, 1084–
     1100
157. Bl. Victor III, 1086–7

158. Bl. Urban II, 1088–99
159. Paschal II, 1099–1118
     Theodoric, antipope, 1100
     Albert, antipope, 1102 (Feb.–Mar.)
     Sylvester IV, antipope, 1105–11
160. Gelasius II, 1118–19
     Gregory VIII, antipope, 1118–21
161. Calixtus II, 1119–24
162. Honorius II, 1124–30
     Celestine II, antipope, 1124 (Dec.)
163. Innocent II, 1130–43
     Anacletus II, antipope, 1130–8
     Victor IV, antipope, 1138 (Mar.–
     May)
164. Celestine II, 1143–4
165. Lucius II, 1144–5
166. Bl. Eugenius III, 1145–53
167. Anastasius IV, 1153–4
168. Adrian IV, 1154–9
169. Alexander III, 1159–81
     Victor IV, antipope, 1159–64
     Paschal III, antipope, 1164–8
     Calixtus III, antipope, 1168–78
     Innocent III, antipope, 1179–80
170. Lucius III, 1181–5
171. Urban III, 1185–7
172. Gregory VIII, 1187 (Oct.–Dec.)
173. Clement III, 1187–91
174. Celestine III, 1191–8
175. Innocent III, 1198–1216
176. Honorius III, 1216–27
177. Gregory IX, 1227–41
178. Celestine IV, 1241 (Oct.–Nov.)
179. Innocent IV, 1243–54
180. Alexander IV, 1254–61
181. Urban IV, 1261–4
182. Clement IV, 1265–8
183. St. Gregory X, 1271–6
184. St. Innocent V, 1276 (Jan.–June)
185. Adrian V, 1276 (July–Aug.)
186. John XXI, 1276–7
187. Nicholas III, 1277–80
188. Martin IV, 1281–5
189. Honorius IV, 1285–7
190. Nicholas IV, 1288–92
191. St. Celestine V, 1294–(July–Dec.)
192. Boniface VIII, 1294–1303

KINGS OF POLAND

Mieszko	962–992	Mieszko the Old	1173–1177
Boleslaw the Brave	992–1025	Casimir II the Just	1177–1194
Mieszko II	1025–1034	Mieszko the Old (again)	1194–1202
Casimir I the Restorer	1040–1058	Wladislaw Longshanks	1202–1206
Boleslaw II the Bold	1058–1079	Leszek the White	1206–1227
Wladislaw Herman	1079–1102	Henry the Bearded	1231–1238
Boleslaw III the Wry-		Henry the Pious	1238–1241
Mouthed	1102–1138	Boleslaw the Modest	1243–1279
		Leszek the Black	1279–1288
Partitional Period of Rival Duchies,		Henry Probus	1289–1290
	1138–1305	Przemyslaw	1295–1296
Wladislaw	1138–1159	Waclaw	1300–1305
Boleslaw the Curly	1146–1173		

ROMAN EMPIRE

Honorius	393–423	*Constantinian Dynasty*	
Constantine III	407–411	CONSTANTINE I, the Great	*d.* 337
Constantius III	421	CONSTANTIUS	337–361
John	423–425	JULIAN, the Apostate	361–363
Valentinian III	425–455	JOVIAN	363–364
Maximus	455	VALENS	364–378
Avitus	455–456		
Majorian	457–461	*Theodosian Dynasty*	
Severus	461–465	THEODOSIUS I, the Great	379–395
Anthemius	467–472	ARCADIUS	395–408
Olybrius	472	THEODOSIUS II	408–450
Glycerius	473	MARCIAN	450–457
Julius Nepos	473–480		
Romulus	475–476	*Leonine Dynasty*	
		LEO I	457–474
		LEO II	474
		ZENO	474–491
		Basilicus	475–476
		ANASTASIUS I	491–518

NOTE: Romulus surnamed Augustulus is wrongly known as the last Roman Emperor in the West; he was never recognized in the East and Julius Nepos survived him.

Justinian Dynasty	
JUSTIN I	518–527
JUSTINIAN I	527–565
JUSTIN II	565–578
TIBERIUS II	578–582
MAURICE	582–602
Theodosius, Co-Emperor	590–602
PHOGAS	602–610

EASTERN ROMAN EMPERORS
from the foundation of Constantinople,
330 A. D.

(Usurpers in italics. The *Basileus Autocrator's* name is given always in capitals. Constantine II and Constans I are not included. as they never exercised effective power in the East.)

Heraclian Dynasty	
HERACLIUS I	610–641

Constantine III	613–641
Heracleonas	638–641
CONSTANTINE III	641
HERACLEONAS	641
CONSTANS II	641–668
Constantine IV	659–668
Heraclius	659–681
Tiberius	659–681
CONSTANTINE IV, Pogonatus	668–685
JUSTINIAN II, Rhinotmetus	685–695
Leontius	695–698
Tiberius III, Apsimar	698–705
JUSTINIAN II, Rhinotmetus	705–711
Tiberius	706–711
PHILIPPICUS, Bardanes	711–713
ANASTASIUS II, Artemius	713–716
THEODOSIUS III	716–717

Isaurian Dynasty

LEO III, the Isaurian	717–740
Constantine V	720–740
CONSTANTINE V, Copronymus	740–775
Leo IV	750–775
LEO IV, the Chazar	775–780
Constantine VI	776–780
CONSTANTINE VI	780–797
IRENE	797–802
NICEPHORUS I	802–811
STAURACIUS	811
MICHAEL I, Rhangabe	811–813
LEO V, the Armenian	813–820

Amorian Dynasty

MICHAEL II, the Amorian	820–829
Theophilus	821–829
THEOPHILUS	829–842
MICHAEL III, the Drunkard	842–867
Basil I	866–867

Macedonian Dynasty

BASIL I. the Macedonian	867–886
Constantine	869–880
Leo VI	870–886
Alexander	871–912
LEO VI, the Wise	886–912
Constantine VII	911–913
ALEXANDER	912–913

CONSTANTINE VII, Porphyrogenetus	913–919
ROMANUS I, Lecapenus	919–944
Constantine VII	919–944
Christopher Lecapenus	921–931
Stephen Lecapenus	924–945
Constantine Lecapenus	924–945
CONSTANTINE VII, Porphyrogenetus	944–959
Romanus II	c. 950–959
ROMANUS II	959–963
Basil II	960–963
Constantine VIII	961–1025
BASIL II, Bulgaroctonus	963
NICEPHORUS II, Phocas	963–969
Basil II	963–976
JOHN I, Tzimisces	969–976
BASIL II, Bulgaroctonus	976–1025

CONSTANTINE VIII	1025–1028
ROMANUS III, Argyrus	1028–1034
MICHAEL IV, the Paphlagonian	1034–1041
MICHAEL V, the Caulker	1041–1042
ZOE and THEODORA, Porphyrogenetae	1042
CONSTANTINE IX, Monomachus	1042–1055
THEODORA, Porphyrogeneta	1055–1056
MICHAEL VI, Stratioticus	1056–1057
ISAAC I, Comnenus	1057–1059

Ducas Dynasty

CONSTANTINE X, Ducas	1059–1067
Michael VII	c. 1060–1067
MICHAEL VII, Parapinaces	1067–1068
ROMANUS IV, Diogenes	1068–1071
Michael VII	1068–1071

MICHAEL VII, Parapinaces	1071–1078
NICEPHORUS III, Botaniates	1078–1081

Comnenian Dynasty

ALEXIUS I, Comnenus	1081–1118
Constantine, Ducas	1081–1090
John II	1092–1118

JOHN II, Calojohannes	1118–1143	*Robert*	1221–1228
Alexius	1119–1142	*Baldwin II*	1228–1237
MANUEL I	1143–1180	*John of Brienne*	1228–1237
Alexius II	1172–1180	*Baldwin II (alone)*	1237–1261
ALEXIUS II	1180–1183		
Andronicus I	1182–1183		
ANDRONICUS I	1183–1185		

Lascarid Dynasty (Nicaean Empire, 1204–1261)

Angelus Dynasty

ISAAC II, Angelus	1185–1195	THEODORE I, Lascaris	1204–1222
ALEXIUS III	1195–1203	JOHN III, Ducas Vatatzes	1222–1254
ALEXIUS IV	1203–1204	THEODORE II, Lascaris Vatatzes	1254–1258
Isaac II	1203–1204	JOHN IV, Ducas Vatatzes	1258
ALEXIUS V, Murtuphlus	1204		

Palaeologan Dynasty

Latin Emperors

Baldwin I	1204–1205	MICHAEL VIII, Palaeologus	1258–1282
Henry	1206–1216	Andronicus II	1272–1282
Peter of Courtenay	1216–1217	ANDRONICUS II	1282–1328

SCOTLAND

Constantine I	789–820	Cullean	967–971
Kenneth I (McAlpine)	832–860	Kenneth II	971–995
Donald	860–863	Cuilean	967–971
Constantine II	863–877	Kenneth II	971–995
Eocha	881–889	Constantine IV	995–997
Donald I	889–900	Kenneth III	997–1005
Constantine III	900–942	Malcolm II	1005–1034
Malcolm I	942–954	Duncan	1034–1040
Indulf	954–962	Macbeth	1040–1057
Dubh	962–967	Lulach	1057–1058

KINGS OF SWEDEN

Olaf and Emund	c. 850–c. 882	Inge II Halstansson	c. 1118–1130
Eric Emundsson	c. 882–c. 905	Sverker	c. 1132–1155
Bjorn Ericsson and Ring	c. 905–c. 950	Eric IX (Saint)	1150–1160
Eric the Victorious	c. 950–c. 993	Charles VII	1160–1167
Period of confusion	c. 993–999	Knut Ericsson	1167–1196
Olaf Scatt-King	999–1022	Sverker Carlsson	1196–1205 (?)
Anund Jacob	1022–1050	*Period of confusion: rival kings*	1205–1250
Emund the Old	1050–1060	Valdemar	1250–1275
Stenkil	1060–1066	Magnus I Ladulas	1275–1290
Period of confusion	1066–1080	Birger	1290–1318
Halstan	c. 1080–c. 1093		
Inge the Good	c. 1090–c. 1118		

PRINCES OF WALES

Maelgwn Gwynedd	?–550
Rhun ap Maelgwn	547–584
Cadvan	584–617
Cadwaladr ap Cadwallon	617–634
Idwal ap Cadwaladr	634–661
Rhodri Molwynog	661–728
Cynan and Hywel	728–755
Mervyn Frych	825–844
Rhodri the Great	844–877
Anarawd, Cadell, and Mervyn	877–943
Idwal Foel	915–943
Hywel Dda, the Good	909–950
Ieuan and Iago	948–979
Hywel ap Ieuaf	979–984
Cadwallon II	984–986
Meredith ap Owen	986–999
Idwal (II) ap Meyric ap Idwal Foel	992–997
Aedan (usurper)	998
Llewelyn ap Seisyll	1018–1023
Gruffydd ap Llewelyn ap Seisull	1039–1063

Bleddyn Rhywallon, Meredith ap Owain	1067–1073
Trahaiarn ap Caradoc, Meilir, Caradoc	1073–1079
Gruffydd ap Cynan, Rhys ap Tewdwr, Cadwgan ap Bleddyn, Iorwerth ab Bleddyn	1079–1137
Owain Gwynedd	1137–1169
Howel ab Owain Gwynedd, Daffydd ap Owain Gwynedd	1169–1194
Llewelyn (II) ap Iorwerth, the Great	1194–1240
Dafydd ap Llewelyn	1240–1246
Llewelyn (III) ap Gruffydd ('Llewelyn y Llyw Olaf')	1246–1282

From 1301 the Prince of Wales has always been the eldest son of the English sovereign.

KINGS OF WESSEX

Cynric	*fl.* 552–*d.* 560
Ceawlin	560–592
Ceol	591–597
Coelwulf	597–611
Cynegils	611–643
Cenwalh	643–645
Penda (of Mercia)	645–648
Cenwalh (restored)	648–672
(Queen) Seaxburg	672–674
Escwine	674–676

Centwine	676–685
Caedwalla	685–688
Ine	688–726
Ethelheard	726–740
Cuthred	740–756
Sigeberht	756–757
Cynewulf	757–786
Beorhtric	786–802
Egbert, KING OF ENGLAND	802–839

INDEXES

INDEX OF PERSONS AND PEOPLES

INDEX OF PLACES

INDEX OF SUBJECTS